EDEN ESTATES
187 LEWISHAM WAY
Tuesday

Pass **ECDL4**
Modules 1-7

Using Microsoft Office 2003

F.R. Heathcote
P.M. Heathcote
O.H.U. Heathcote
R.P. Richards

Published by

PAYNE-GALLWAY
PUBLISHERS LTD

An imprint of Harcourt Education Limited
Halley Court, Jordan Hill, Oxford OX2 8EJ

www.payne-gallway.co.uk

Acknowledgements

We are grateful to the following organisations for granting us permission to reproduce articles, screenshots and photographs:

Intel Corporation

Sun Microsystems

RSPB

WWF-UK for the following photograph:

Image No: 37167

Indian Tiger, Thailand © WWF-Canon / Martin Harvey

Every effort has been made to contact copyright owners of material published in this book. We would be glad to hear from unacknowledged sources at the earliest opportunity.

Cover design by Direction Advertising and Design Ltd

First Edition 2004. Reprinted 2004 (twice), 2005.

10 9 8 7 6 5 4 3

A catalogue entry for this book is available from the British Library.

10-digit ISBN: 1 904467 05 9
13-digit ISBN: 978 1 904467 05 2

Printed in Malta by Gutenberg Press

Disclaimer

Preface

Who is this book for?

This book is suitable for anyone studying for ECDL Version 4.0, either at school, adult class or at home. It is suitable for complete beginners or those with some prior experience, and takes the learner step-by-step from the very basics to the point where they will feel confident using a number of different software packages, using the Internet and organising their work efficiently.

The approach

The approach is very much one of "learning by doing". Each module is divided into a number of chapters which correspond to one lesson. The student is guided step-by-step through a practical task at the computer, with numerous screenshots to show exactly what should be on their screen at each stage. Each individual in a class can proceed at their own pace, with little or no help from a teacher. At the end of most chapters there are exercises which provide invaluable practice. By the time a student has completed a module, every aspect of the ECDL syllabus will have been covered.

Each module is self-contained with its own Table of Contents and Index, so that any particular topic can easily be looked up for revision purposes. Individual modules can also be purchased separately (see inside back cover for details).

Software used

The instructions and screenshots are based on a PC running Microsoft Windows XP and Microsoft Office 2003 with Internet Explorer and Outlook Express. However, it will be relatively easy to adapt the instructions for use with earlier versions.

Extra resources

Answers to practice exercises and other useful supporting material can be found on the publisher's web site www.payne-gallway.co.uk/ecdl.

About ECDL

The European Computer Driving Licence (ECDL) is the European-wide qualification enabling people to demonstrate their competence in computer skills. Candidates must study and pass the test for each of the seven modules listed below before they are awarded an ECDL certificate. The ECDL tests must be undertaken at an accredited test centre. For more details of ECDL tests and test centres, visit the ECDL web site www.ecdl.com.

Module 1: Concepts of Information Technology

Module 2: Using the Computer and Managing Files

Module 3: Word Processing

Module 4: Spreadsheets

Module 5: Database

Module 6: Presentation

Module 7: Information and Communication

Table of Contents Modules 1–7

Module 1

Concepts of Information Technology

This module will give you an understanding of some of the main concepts of IT at a general level. You will learn about:

- types of computers and the component parts of a computer
- types of software and the uses of software applications in everyday life
- how computer networks are used, including the use of the Internet, e-mail and e-commerce
- health and safety issues relevant to the use of computers
- security issues arising from the use of computers
- legislation such as the Data Protection Act and legal issues regarding copyright

Module 1 Table of Contents

General Concepts

CHAPTER 1.1

A world of computers

In this module you'll be learning about what a computer is and about some of the thousands of ways in which computers are used today. Amazingly, the history of commercial computing goes back only to around 1960, when the first computers were used by a very few large organisations to perform repetitive tasks such as processing the company payroll. These computers were massive, occupying whole floors in office blocks, and yet had only a fraction of the computing power of a modern pocket calculator. The computer that controlled the first manned spaceship to the moon in 1969 had less calculating capability than a mobile phone in 2003!

The term **Information Technology** (IT) has been coined to refer to the use of computers, and machines like fax machines and telephones which contain tiny computers, to process and transfer information. Computers are now commonly used to communicate information, as well as performing tasks like word processing or calculations. You may often hear the term **ICT** or **Information and Communication Technology** used instead of IT.

Hardware and software

In order to work, a computer needs two things – hardware and software.

Hardware is the physical part of a computer – the bits you can see and touch. The casings for computers and their associated pieces of hardware such as monitors and printers are usually made of tough plastic. The hardware inside the casings is made up of electronic switches and integrated circuits (commonly known as 'chips') mounted on boards (**printed circuit boards** or **PCBs**).

Software is the list of instructions that are coded in a special way so the computer can understand them. These computer **programs** tell the computer exactly what to do. There are many different types of program – for example:

- **applications software** such as a word processor or an e-mail package.
- **operating system software** such as Windows which works away in the background and lets you decide which applications software to run.

Many common household devices such as washing machines, microwave ovens, video recorders and digital alarm clocks contain computer hardware and specialised software to make them perform the tasks they are designed to do.

Types of computer

Different types of computers are used for different applications.

Mainframe computers are large, fast and expensive. They are used by very big organisations such as electricity companies, banks or multinational companies. Hundreds or thousands of users may be connected to and using a mainframe at the same time.

Each user has a **computer terminal** that is connected to the mainframe. Some types of terminal cannot be used for anything unless they are connected to the mainframe – these are known as **dumb terminals**. All the computer's calculations take place in the mainframe. Alternatively, an ordinary PC may be connected to a mainframe and this can do useful work even if it is not connected at any particular time. A PC used in this way is sometimes known as an **intelligent terminal**.

The terminals connected to a mainframe computer may be in different parts of the country, or even overseas.

A **network** computer (normally referred to as a network **server**) has a number of personal computers connected to it to create a computer network. The server is typically used to store information for use by all the users on the network.

Personal computers

A **personal computer** or **PC** has become an almost indispensable piece of equipment for office workers from the managing director down to the humblest clerical worker.

The most popular type of PC is the **desktop model**. The main **system unit** is designed to sit on top of the user's desk. **Tower models** are also popular as the system unit can be sited on the floor, so taking up less desk space.

The picture below shows the main parts of a desktop PC:

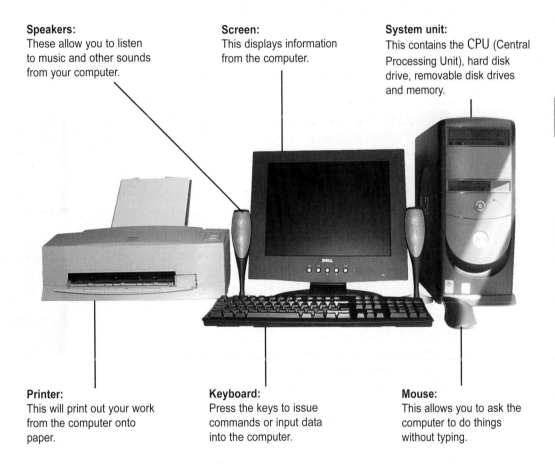

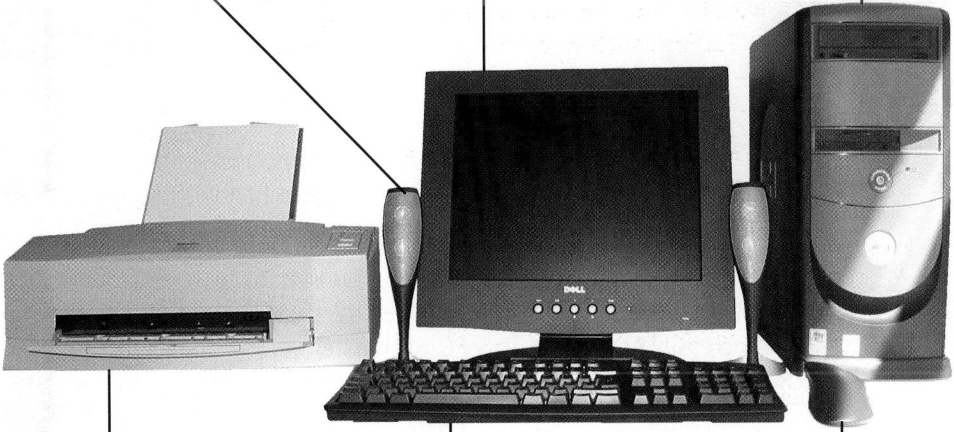

Speakers:
These allow you to listen to music and other sounds from your computer.

This displays information from the computer.

This contains the CPU (Central Processing Unit), hard disk drive, removable disk drives and memory.
Printer:
This will print out your work from the computer onto paper.

Press the keys to issue commands or input data into the computer.

This allows you to ask the computer to do things without typing.

Tip:
Hardware devices such as the screen, keyboard, mouse etc. connected to the main system unit are often referred to as **peripherals**.

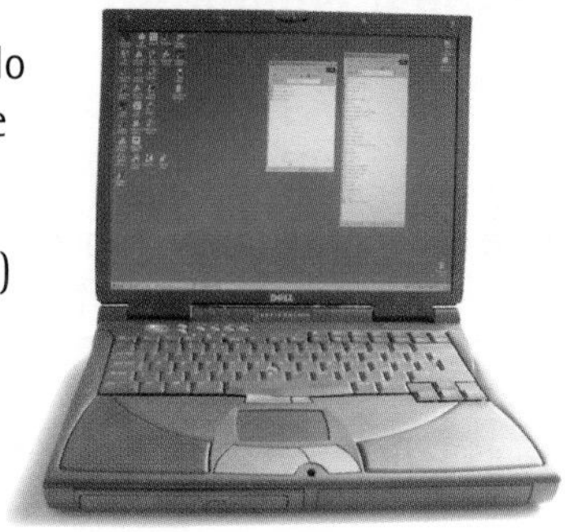

Portable computers were introduced so that users could easily transport their PC to different locations and even do some work en route, perhaps on a train journey. There are two main types:

Notebook computers (sometimes called laptop computers) are portable computers that have an integral keyboard and monitor and a rechargeable battery.

Palmtops are really small and, as their name suggests, can fit in the palm of your hand. They are becoming more and more powerful as the technology improves. Some palmtops allow the user to draw on the screen with a special pen – the drawings are then converted into text and diagrams.

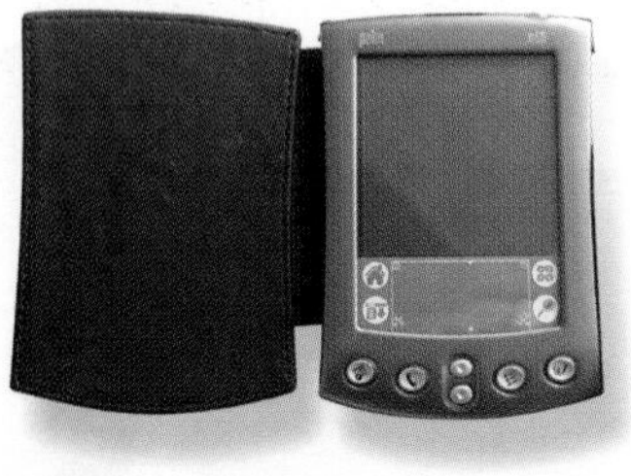

A **PDA** or Personal Digital Assistant is a handheld computer which can also be used as a mobile phone. The PDA began as an electronic organiser, after the success of the paper-based Filofax in the mid-1980s. The handheld device looks very much like a calculator. Recent models include spellcheckers, small games and notepad functions, and some models with larger screens now have handwriting-recognition software.

PDAs tend to fall into two categories; keyboard- and pen-based devices. Both types of devices have similar features. They sometimes have a headset if being used as a telephone. They have cut-down versions of PC applications and can be easily connected to a PC to transfer data.

	Capacity	Speed	Cost	Typical users
Mainframe	Very large disk storage. Very large main memory	Very fast in order to process vast amounts of data	Extremely expensive	Large companies (often multinational), Health Authorities etc.
Network server	Large disk storage (now measured in Gigabytes (Gb). Large main memory (RAM)	Fast - measured in GHz	Expensive due to components and software for networking functions, backup etc.	Smaller companies, schools, hospitals etc.
PC	Probably smaller disk storage and main memory (RAM) than a server (especially if networked)	Fast - measured in GHz	Becoming cheaper all the time.	Employees wthin all sizes of organisation, home users etc.
Laptop	Similar to a PC	Similar to a PC	Often more expensive than for a comparably powered PC due to miniaturisation of components	Mostly business users, commuters etc.
PDA	Much smaller disk storage capacity and main memory than a PC	Slower than a PC	Relatively expensive compared to a PC	Mostly business users, commuters etc.

Hardware

CHAPTER 1.2

Central Processing Unit

Within the system unit the main brain of the computer is the **Central Processing Unit** (CPU). This is where all processing and calculations take place. It consists of two different parts:

- The processor
- Memory

The processor

The processor consists of two main components - the **control unit** and the **arithmetic/logic unit** (ALU). The control unit fetches instructions from the computer's memory, decodes them and synchronises all the computer's operations.

The **arithmetic/logic unit** (ALU) is where all of the work is carried out. The ALU can perform two sorts of operations on data. **Arithmetic** operations include addition, subtraction, multiplication and division. **Logical** operations consist of comparing one data item with another to determine whether the first data item is smaller than, equal to or greater than the second data item.

Physically the processor is a small silicon **chip**, which consists of complex electronic circuits. This chip, together with other chips that do different jobs, are mounted on **printed circuit boards** (PCBs).

Computer memory

A computer has a 'memory' which stores information. There are two kinds of memory: **Random Access Memory** (RAM) and **Read-Only Memory** (ROM).

RAM (sometimes known as **immediate access memory**) is divided into millions of addressable storage units called **bytes**.

Each byte consists of 8 bits or binary digits. A bit can be set either ON or OFF, depending on whether an electric current is switched on or off, representing a 0 or a 1. All numbers, text, sounds, graphics etc are held as different patterns of 0s and 1s in the computer.

One byte can hold one character, or it can be used to hold a code representing, for example, a tiny part of a picture, a sound, or part of a computer program instruction. The total number of bytes in main memory is referred to as the computer's memory size.

Computer memory sizes are measured using the following units:

Measurement	Power of 2	Size (bytes)	Symbol
1 Kilobyte	2^{10}	1,024 (just over 1 thousand)	Kb
1 Megabyte	2^{20}	1,048,576 (just over 1 million)	Mb
1 Gigabyte	2^{30}	1,073,741,824 (just over 1 billion)	Gb
1 Terabyte	2^{40}	1,099,511,627,776 (just over 1 trillion)	Tb

So for example this paragraph contains approximately 180 characters or bytes. The text in this module is stored as a **file** which contains approximately 60,000 characters (approximately 59 kb). Files are organised into **directories** or **folders**. Files and folders are given names so that they can easily be found on the computer.

The amount of memory that comes with a standard PC has increased exponentially over the past 20 years. In about 1980, BBC microcomputers with 32K of memory were bought in their thousands for home and school use. In 1981, Bill Gates of Microsoft made his famous remark "640K ought to be enough for anybody". By 2003, a PC with 256Mb or 512Mb of memory was standard, costing less than £1,000 including bundled software.

Instructions and data being processed are held in **RAM**. If you are writing a letter using MS Word, for example, both Word and your letter will be held in RAM while you are working on it. If you accidentally switch off the machine, or there is a power cut while you are working, you will lose the letter if you have not saved it and when you restart the computer, you will have to load Word again. (i.e. the MS Word software will be copied from your hard disk into RAM). When you finish your letter, save it and close Word, RAM is freed up for the next task.

RAM has these two major characteristics:

- Each location in RAM has its own unique address. It can be randomly accessed – the computer can be instructed to fetch the data it needs from any given address in memory.
- RAM is **volatile** – its contents are lost when the power is switched off.

A PC will also only have a very small amount of **ROM**. Unlike RAM, its contents can never be changed, and all the instructions held in ROM have to be burned into the memory chip before it leaves the factory. The contents of ROM are not lost when the computer is switched off. The tiny program which starts running as soon as you switch the computer on is held in ROM. This program tells the computer to start loading the operating system (e.g. Windows) from disk.

ROM has these two major characteristics:

- ROM cannot be written to or used to hold ordinary user application programs such as word processing software.
- ROM is **non-volatile** – its contents are NOT lost when the power is switched off.

Tip:

Many household machines contain ROM chips - for example your washing machine, dishwasher or video recorder. You can, for example, select which washing program to use, but you cannot change how many minutes the cycle takes or use the washing machine to cook your dinner instead!

Computer performance

Two main factors impact on a computer's performance: **processor speed** and **amount of RAM**.

Processor speed is measured in **kilohertz** or **gigahertz**. (1GHz is equal to one million KHz.)

Each year, as technology advances, processor speed increases. Twenty years ago a computer with a processor speed of a few hundred kilohertz (KHz) would have been considered very powerful. Now a processor speed of 1.8GHz is not unusual – that is about 10,000 times faster!

The other factor in determining the performance of a computer is the amount of memory (or **RAM**) it has. Modern software takes up a huge amount of memory.

When you install software such as Microsoft Word on your computer, it is stored on the hard disk inside the system unit, which may have a capacity of anything between say, 10Gb and 160Gb. When you open Word to write a letter, for example, the software program (Word) has to be copied into RAM (which may have a capacity of say, 256 or 512Mb) before the computer can execute the program instructions which enable you to type your letter.

If a computer does not have enough memory to hold all of Microsoft Word in memory (RAM) at once, it will swap bits of the program in and out of memory from disk as they are required. This takes time.

The same happens when you have several programs running at once. They all take up memory space, and your computer may run more slowly because instructions and data are being copied from disk to memory as needed.

Thus, the **number of applications** running at any one time also affects the performance of a computer.

Input devices

All the data that is fed *into* a computer is called **input**. The items of hardware used to input data are called **input devices**. These are some of the most common input devices:

Keyboard

The most common way to enter data into a PC is by **keyboard**. Computer keyboards have their keys arranged in a similar way to those on a typewriter. This way of arranging keys is called QWERTY because of the order in which the keys appear in the first row of letters. Extra keys carry out specific jobs depending on the software being used.

Some keyboards, especially on laptop computers, incorporate a **tracker ball** that performs the function of a mouse.

Mouse

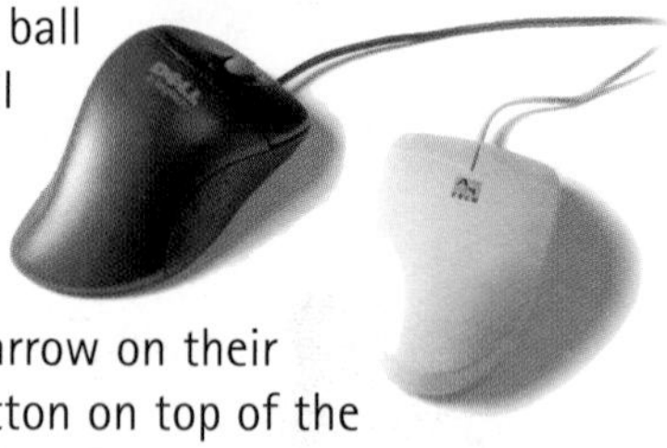

A **mouse** is a small hand-held input device which has a ball fitted underneath. When the mouse is moved, the signal created by the movement of the ball is transmitted to the computer. This controls a pointer on the screen which moves in a direction corresponding to the direction of the mouse. Once the user has pointed the arrow on their screen at something it can be selected by clicking a button on top of the mouse. There are usually two or three buttons on a mouse. The left-hand button is normally used to make selections.

Tracker balls are also types of pointing device. They are often used instead of a mouse on portable computers. The user rotates a ball to move the cursor over the screen.

Touch pads can also replace the mouse, they too are often found on the keyboards of portable computers. The user moves their finger over the surface of the pad to move the cursor.

Microphone

If your computer has a sound card it should have the ability to receive sound input from a **microphone** through the sound card microphone port. This may be useful for recording voice or sounds on your computer.

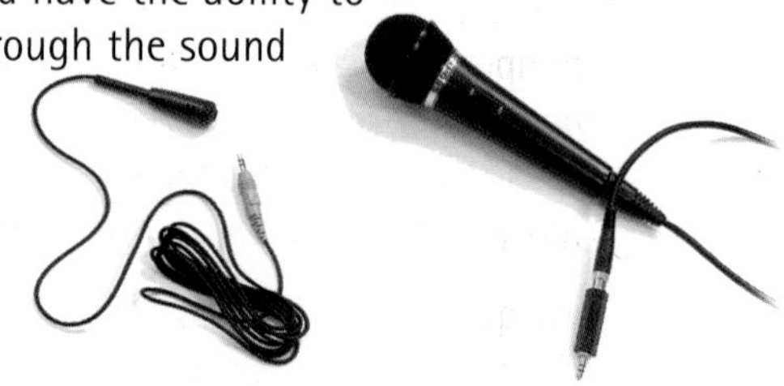

Light pen

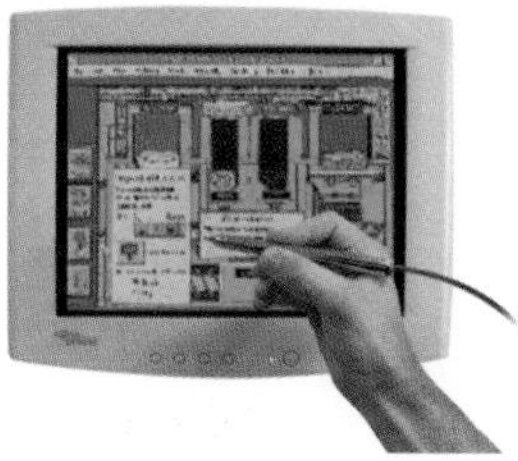

A light pen is a small pen-shaped wand which contains light sensors. The light pen is used to choose objects or commands on the screen either by pressing it against the screen or by pressing a small switch on its side. This sends a signal to the computer, which then works out the exact location of the light pen on the screen.

Scanner

Scanners are used to input text, diagrams and pictures to the computer. They can be hand-held but usually they are 'flat bed' devices which sit on the desk. Printed text can be scanned using OCR (Optical Character Recognition) software so that it can be word-processed. Images can be scanned and loaded into graphics software where they can be altered or enhanced.

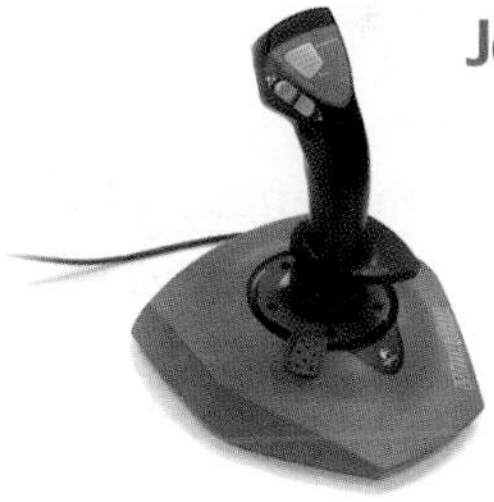

Joystick

A joystick is often used to play games on a PC. It controls the way things move on the screen and can control movement from side-to-side, up and down and diagonally. A joystick normally has at least one button that can be used in a game, for example to make a character jump or fire a missile.

Digital camera

A major benefit of using a digital camera is that you can transfer photos directly to your PC without sending a film off to be developed. A cable supplied with the camera can connect it to a port on the back of your PC.

Using a digital camera is very similar to using a traditional camera. They both use the basic components such as a lens, flash, shutter and viewfinder. Most digital models now incorporate an LCD screen so that you can get a good view of your subject as you take the photo, and you can then review the picture afterwards.

The quality and number of digital pictures that can be taken will depend on the amount of memory in the camera.

Output devices

The information that a computer produces is called output. The items of hardware that receive this output are called output devices. The most common output devices are shown below:

Screen

A screen (or monitor) displays the output information from a computer. The size of a monitor is measured in inches diagonally across the screen; 15, 17, 19 and 21 inch monitors are the most common sizes. The picture on a monitor is made up of thousands of tiny coloured dots called pixels.

The quality and detail of the picture on a monitor depends on the resolution which is measured in pixels going across and down the screen. The more pixels the screen has, the higher the resolution and the better the picture. Resolutions typically range from 800 x 600 to 1,600 x 1,200. Another factor which affects the quality of the image is its refresh rate. This is measured in hertz (Hz) and indicates how many times per second the image on the screen is updated. To avoid flickering images which can lead to eyestrain and headaches, the refresh rate of a monitor should be at least 72Hz.

The most common monitors work in the same way as televisions where electrical signals are converted into an image on the screen by a Cathode Ray Tube (CRT).

New flat-screen monitors take up much less desk space than CRTs. These Liquid Crystal Display (LCD) screens are similar to those provided on portable computers.

Printer

A good printer can help you produce professional-looking printed output from your PC. There are three main categories of printer, each of them suitable for different types of job.

Many PCs are supplied with an inkjet printer. These print pictures or characters by forcing small dots of ink through tiny holes. The ink is stored in replaceable cartridges, normally separate for colour and black ink. These printers can also print on envelopes, labels, acetates and other specialist paper.

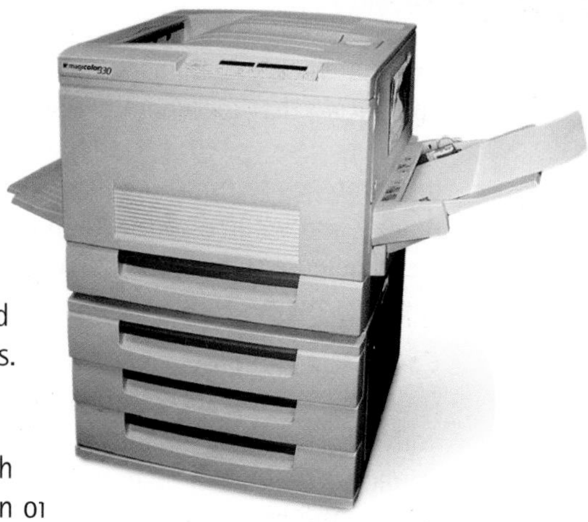

Laser printers produce very high quality printed output very quickly. They are suitable for large volume printouts. Colour laser printers are expensive but black and white laser printers cost only a few hundred pounds and are standard in many large and small businesses. The main running expense is the cost of replacement toner (powdered ink) cartridges every few thousand pages.

Dot matrix printers have steel pins which strike an inked ribbon to create a pattern of tiny dots which form a character. How good the print is depends on how many pins the machine has 24 pins will produce better quality print than 9 pins.

This type of printer is not normally supplied with a PC for home use, as the quality is not as good as an inkjet or laser printer. As they work by striking the paper, they are called **impact** printers and are often used by businesses to print on multi-part stationery for producing documents such as invoices. A top copy goes to the customer, a second 'carbon copy' may be used as a delivery note and a third copy may be kept in the office. Laser printers and inkjet printers cannot print two or more copies of a document simultaneously in this way.

Plotter

A **plotter** is another device for producing hard-copy from a computer. It uses several coloured pens to draw the computer output on paper. Plotters can produce very accurate drawings and are often used in Computer-Aided Design (CAD) applications to produce engineering or architectural drawings.

Speakers

External speakers are supplied with multimedia PCs. These are computers that incorporate a sound card, CD-ROM and speakers. The system can then combine text, sound and graphics to run programs such as games. The quality and volume of the sound produced can be adjusted either within software or on the speakers themselves.

Computers can produce output in the form of sound by using a speech synthesiser. This converts electrical signals into sound waves. Sound software can be used to mix musical sounds and create new sounds. Some of the sounds can replicate human speech – this is called speech synthesis which is used by some telephone enquiry systems.

Input/Output devices

Some devices can be classed as input or output devices.

Touchscreen

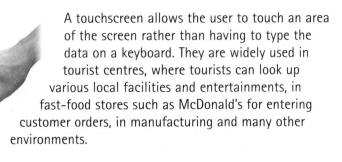

A touchscreen allows the user to touch an area of the screen rather than having to type the data on a keyboard. They are widely used in tourist centres, where tourists can look up various local facilities and entertainments, in fast-food stores such as McDonald's for entering customer orders, in manufacturing and many other environments.

Storage devices

Disk storage

To save your work when the computer is turned off, you need to save it onto a disk. There are three main types of disk: floppy disk, hard disk and CD-ROM.

A **floppy disk** is not floppy at all (although the actual disk is made of flexible plastic). It has a hard protective casing and a storage capacity of 1.44 Mb. You can insert a floppy disk into a computer yourself, store your work on it and then remove it. You could take the disk and insert it into another PC and carry on with your work. Before a floppy disk can be used it must be **formatted**. This means that the disk is checked for errors and set up to accept data. Nowadays the vast majority of floppy disks in the shops are pre-formatted.

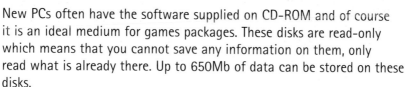

A **hard disk** is housed permanently inside your computer. These disks have a much larger storage capacity than a floppy disk, and transfer data to and from computer memory much more quickly.

The capacity of hard disks is measured in megabytes (Mb) or gigabytes (Gb). Most modern PCs have a hard disk with a capacity of at least 10Gb.

PCs are often fitted with a **CD-ROM** (Compact Disk Read Only Memory) drive and speakers. CD-ROMs are removable and can hold large amounts of programs or data. Data is often in the form of text, pictures, music and animations.

New PCs often have the software supplied on CD-ROM and of course it is an ideal medium for games packages. These disks are read-only which means that you cannot save any information on them, only read what is already there. Up to 650Mb of data can be stored on these disks.

CD-RW (read-write) disks save data which can then be erased and overwritten with new data.

DVD drives are also now being supplied as removable storage, allowing you to watch films on your PC. A DVD-ROM can hold up to 135 minutes of high-quality video and CD-quality sound.

Other removable storage

Some PCs are fitted with **Zip** drives. Zip disks are also removable storage media that can be written to as many times as you wish. Newer disks can hold up to 250Mb of data.

A Zip drive is often an option on a PC, together with a CD-ROM or DVD drive and a floppy drive. Alternatively, you can purchase an external disk drive for any of these. While they are faster than floppy disks, they are still much slower than hard disks.

Jaz drives are the big brother of Zip drives; they use similar technology but the disks have a larger capacity of up to 1Gb.

Magnetic tape or **DAT** (Digital Audio tape) is used almost exclusively for backups and for archiving old data that needs to be kept but which will probably never be used. Large amounts of data can be stored very cheaply and compactly using this medium, which is also known as a **data cartridge**. Tapes are much slower to access than a floppy disk, Zip/Jaz disk or CD-ROM.

The table below gives a comparison between the different types of removable PC storage.

Device	Capacity	Price of Drive (approx)	Price of Media (approx)
Floppy Disk	1.44Mb	£25	£0.50
CD	650Mb	£150	£1.00
Jaz	2Gb	£270	£80.00
Zip	250Mb	£150	£10.00
DVD	17Gb	£450	£25.00
DAT	60Gb	£500	£100

Tip:

These prices are changing all the time - only use this table for the sake of comparison.

Exercises

1. A friend tells you that his son's new PC has 100Gb of RAM. Is this plausible? Look up some advertisements for PCs to find a typical figure for RAM and hard disk capacity.
2. Describe **two** differences between RAM and ROM; give a typical use for each.
3. All computers from mainframes to palmtops have certain elements in common, such as a central processing unit (CPU), input, output and storage devices.
   (a) Describe briefly a typical user of each of a **mainframe computer** and a **palmtop**.
   (b) What unit is the speed of the CPU measured in?
   (c) Name the **two** main parts of the CPU and describe the function of each.
4. Explain the terms **Information Technology**, **hardware** and **software**.
5. Describe the functions of each of the following devices and state whether they are input or output devices:
   (a) Touchpad
   (b) Plotter
   (c) Joystick
   (d) Scanner
6. Suppose you have typed a page of text using a word processor. The text contains about 2,000 characters including spaces. Approximately how much RAM will this text occupy?
7. What type of printer would you recommend for each of the following users? Justify your answers.
   (a) An author working at home on her latest novel.
   (b) A small garage printing purchase orders for spare parts. Three copies of each purchase order is required.
   (c) A student who needs to print out his geography project in colour at home.
8. A graphic artist needs to send artwork that he has created on his computer to his client. The graphics files are 50Mb. Name and justify a suitable medium for storing and posting the files.
9. Describe two typical uses of each of the following devices attached to a PC:
   (a) Touch screen
   (b) Speakers
   (c) DVD drive

CHAPTER 1.3

Software

Types of software

Computer software programs tell the computer what to do. They are divided into two general areas: systems software and applications software. All software is continually being updated, for example Microsoft Windows 95, 98, 2000 or XP. New programs generally provide more flexibility and features for the user. It is usually possible to upgrade from one version to the next.

Updates to improve the reliability and security of software are often supplied free of charge by the manufacturer. For example Windows Service Pack updates and Office Service Pack (or Release) updates can be downloaded from the Microsoft web site (www.microsoft.com) to keep your PC up-to-date with the latest versions.

It is useful to be aware which software you are working with, since for example you will not be able to open a document created in Word 2002 on a PC with Word 97.

Operating system software

An **operating system** is a series of programs that organise and control a computer. The computer will not work without it. Most PCs use an operating system called **Microsoft Windows**. There have been several versions of Windows and there are bound to be more versions in the future. The main functions of an operating system are:

- To provide a user interface so that the user can communicate with the computer.
- To communicate with all the hardware devices such as keyboard, screen and printer. When the user gives an instruction to print, for example, the operating system checks that the printer is switched on and ready.
- To organise the storage and retrieval of data from disk. The operating system has to keep track of where every file is stored on disk so that it can be retrieved quickly.
- To manage the smooth running of all the programs currently in RAM. The operating system will allocate processing time to each program in turn. For example, while you are thinking what to type into Word, the computer may be busy receiving an e-mail message or saving a spreadsheet you have just been working on.

Graphical User Interface

Windows has a Graphical User Interface (GUI). This means that instead of users having to type complicated text commands, they can use the mouse to point at icons and menus on the screen.

Tip:
A GUI is sometimes called a WIMP interface (Windows, Icons, Mouse and Pointer).

Tip:
Examples of other operating systems include MS-DOS, OS/2, Unix and Linux.

Applications software

Application packages are available for specific tasks. It is up to you to decide which you want on your computer. The most commonly used applications on a PC are Word Processing, Spreadsheets, Databases and Internet/e-mail software.

Word processing software deals mainly with words. You can type all kinds of documents such as letters, CVs, reports etc. When you have finished a document you can print it and save it on a disk. One of the most popular word processing packages is Microsoft Word.

Spreadsheet software deals mainly with numbers. It is very useful for calculations involving money. One of the most popular spreadsheet packages is Microsoft Excel. Most spreadsheet packages are fairly similar in use.

Database software is used to store information about people or items. It allows you to sort the information and find a particular record very quickly. Microsoft Access is one of the most popular database packages.

Internet browser software such as Internet Explorer and Netscape Navigator allows you to surf the World Wide Web. Internet Explorer is supplied as part of Windows and is therefore one of the most popular web browsers.

E-mail software allows you to send messages to other people who have a mailbox e.g. family and friends. Many people use this to keep in touch with family who live abroad. Outlook Express is supplied as part of Windows, and you will probably find this installed on your PC. There are alternatives such as Eudora and Netscape Messenger.

Presentation software helps the user to create visual slide show presentations on a personal computer. These can display text, graphics, limited sound and some animation. The slides can also be printed onto acetates for use in an OHP presentation. Microsoft PowerPoint is often used to produce this type of presentation.

Desktop Publishing such as Microsoft Publisher is used to produce many different types of documents from simple party invitations to more complex applications such as professional-looking newspapers and magazines. Professional users in the publishing industry often use more powerful packages such as QuarkXPress or Pagemaker.

Accounting software helps businesses take control of all bookkeeping and accounting tasks such as calculating VAT returns, producing invoices, tracking cash flow and managing payment and receipts. Sage software is one of the most widely used accounting packages.

Systems development

Computer-based systems are developed by specialist teams of system analysts and programmers. A **systems analyst** analyses the feasibility of a computer system for business, and supervises the design, specification and implementation of the system. A **programmer** writes and tests the computer programs that make up the system. The programmer will be trained to write the programs in a programming language – some you may have heard of include Java, Visual Basic or C++.

The development of large computer-based systems can involve dozens of people working for several months or even years. This means that formal methods and procedures must be applied to ensure that the project is delivered on time and meets the specification. These stages are normally defined, with each stage being completed before the next one begins. The whole process is often known as the **systems life cycle**.

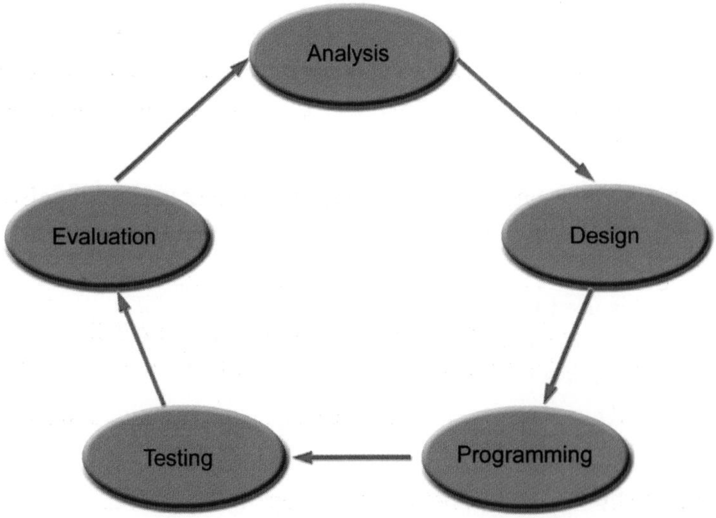

Analysis

When a user has identified a problem or a need for a new computer system, a systems analyst will start by analysing the requirements. For example, what is the expected capacity of the new system? How will information be input into the system? What processing is required? What output is required?

Design

Work now starts on designing the overall system, followed by the detailed design of each subsection. This will include screen layouts, user interfaces, methods of input, defining the format of all the data that needs to be stored, the processing required, and the output in the form of hard copy or on-screen reports.

Programming

The actual programming may be passed out to a team of programmers who will each work on a module of the final package.

Testing

Each module is first tested individually then as part of the whole suite of programs. Special data is prepared for the testing including 'normal' data and erroneous data to make sure that the program will not 'crash', whatever the user enters.

Evaluation

The new system must be evaluated once it has been put into operation to ensure that it is performing as expected.

Sooner or later there will be a perceived need for a new system and the whole process will start all over again.

Exercises

1. (a) Name the two main types of software found on a PC.

   (b) Why are there often several different versions of software packages, each with their own version number? Name an example of some software that has at least two versions.

   (c) Give two reasons why a user may decide to upgrade the software that he is using to the latest version.

2. (a) Explain what is meant by a Graphical User Interface (GUI).

   (b) Give two reasons why a computer user may find a GUI interface easier to use than an alternative where commands have to be typed in.

3. Describe briefly four of the standard development stages in applications software development.

4. Describe briefly the main functions of the operating system.

CHAPTER 1.4

Information Networks

Local area networks

Although a PC will function perfectly well as a 'standalone' machine, there are many advantages to an organisation of connecting all the computers together into a **network**.

A **local area network** or **LAN** links together via cabling, computers on the same site e.g. within one building. This enables the users connected to the network to share information and to share resources such as printers that are connected to the network. If you are studying on a course at college, you will probably be connected to a LAN.

In a **client/server** network, a powerful computer called a **server** controls the network and stores data which can be used by other computers on the network. The other computers are referred to as **clients**.

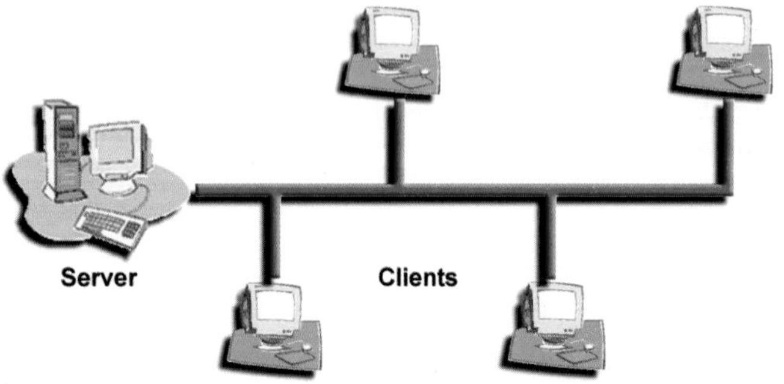

Advantages of networks

- Workstations can share devices like printers. This is cheaper than buying a printer for every workstation.
- Users can save their work centrally on the network server. They can then retrieve their work from any workstation on the network.
- Users can communicate with each other and transfer data between workstations very easily.
- One copy of each application program can be loaded onto the file server and shared by all users. When a new version comes out it only has to be loaded onto the server instead of onto every workstation.

Disadvantages of networks

- Special security measures are needed to stop users from using programs and data that they shouldn't have access to.
- Networks are complicated to set up and must be maintained by skilled ICT technicians.
- If the file server develops a serious fault all the users are affected.
- If a virus enters the network all the users may be affected.

Wide area networks

A wide area network or WAN connects computers in different geographical locations all over the world. They are connected using the telephone system. Large multinational companies depend on this type of network to communicate between different parts of their organisations in different countries.

The Internet is an example of a worldwide computer network (WAN) made up of smaller networks.

The telephone network in computing

A modem is required for communication between computers over telephone lines. This device converts the data from one computer (digital data which is a pattern of 0s and 1s) into a form that the telephone system can deal with (analogue data) and another modem at the other end will convert the data back into a form that the other computer can understand. The speed at which data is transmitted (the transfer rate) is measured in bits per second (bps).

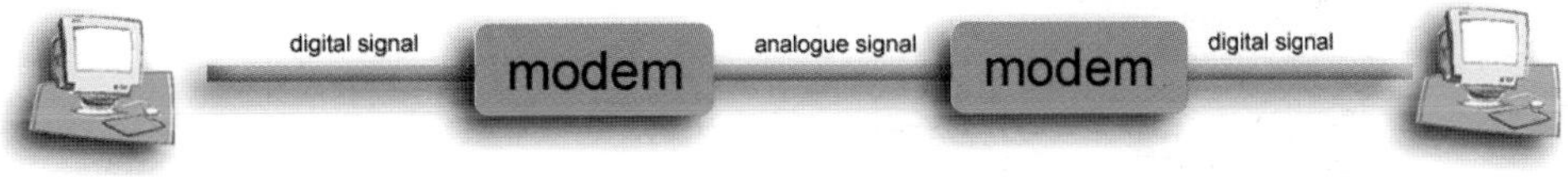

PSTN

Short for Public Switched Telephone Network, this is the international telephone system that we are all familiar with for regular telephone calls. It is also referred to as the Plain Old Telephone Service (POTS).

ISDN

The amount of data that can be sent over a line depends partly on the bandwidth, which is the range of frequencies that the line can carry. The greater the bandwidth, the greater the rate at which data can be sent, as several messages can be transmitted simultaneously. A network that is capable of sending voice, video and computer data is called an Integrated Services Digital Network (ISDN), and this requires a high bandwidth.

ADSL

Asymmetric Digital Subscriber Line (ADSL) is a newer technology which enables existing copper wire telephone lines to be used to transmit computer data at extremely fast rates. The subscriber needs an ADSL modem and two ADSL devices. A 'splitter' (which is a filter), one at the user end and one at the exchange end, separates the telephony signal from the ADSL signal. This means that telephone calls can be made at the same time that data is being sent or received (i.e. a customer can surf the Internet and still make telephone calls).

The Internet

The Internet is a huge number of computers – including yours – connected together all over the world. Using the Internet you can look up information on any subject you can imagine, or send and receive messages through e-mail.

Many people use the Internet to 'surf' the **World Wide Web** – the fastest-growing area of the Internet, made up of millions of web sites.

Every web site consists of one or more documents called pages. A home page is the first page of a web site and serves as an introduction to the whole site. Every page on the web has its own address, called a **Uniform Resource Locator** or **URL**.

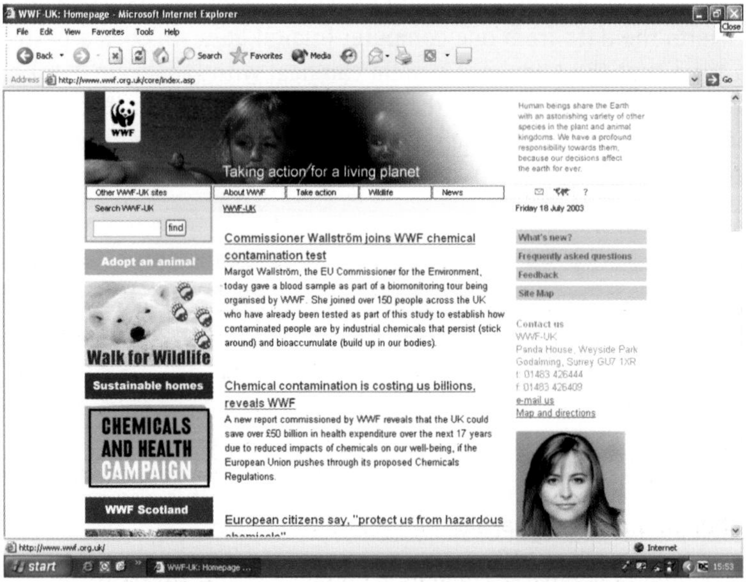

To connect to the Internet you will need a PC with at least a 486 processor and Windows 95 upwards. You will also need a modem installed and connected to a phone outlet. You will then need to choose an **Internet Service Provider** or **ISP** to connect you to the Internet. Many ISPs do not charge for their services (apart from the phone bill) or offer unlimited access for a flat fee. Their software does all the installation for you. There are lots of free trial CDs on offer in high-street shops and magazines.

E-commerce

The growth of the Internet over the past ten years has been phenomenal. In 1989, Tim Berners-Lee introduced the world wide web to his colleagues at CERN. In 1993, there were 130 servers on the web. A year later there were 500. By the beginning of 2003, there were over 35 million.

Virtually every organisation of any size – and a large proportion of small companies – now have their own web sites, and find them as indispensable as the telephone. Everything from travel tickets to office supplies can be purchased over the Internet, often more cheaply than from a High Street store. Online banking is quick, efficient and often cheaper.

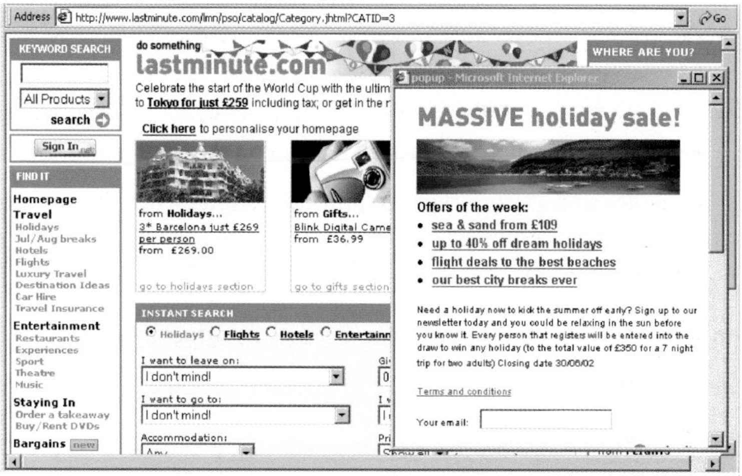

Purchasing over the Internet

When you purchase goods over the Internet, you have to enter your name and address. Usually you will also have to enter a credit card number for payment of the goods. The organisation that owns the web site must have a 'secure site' which means that any credit card number that you enter is encrypted, or 'scrambled' in some way, so that it cannot be intercepted. No transaction can be 100% safe but handing your credit card to a waiter in a restaurant is just as risky, if not more so. A consumer who purchases goods over the Internet has the right to return unsatisfactory goods.

Internet shopping has many advantages for the shopper:

- The shopping facility is available 24 hours a day, 7 days a week
- You don't have to leave home to shop
- You can surf the Internet to find the best deal before making a purchase.

However there are some disadvantages:

- You cannot see, touch or try on goods before purchasing
- You may miss the human contact and advice available in a store
- There may be some risk involved in giving a credit card number over the Internet.

Alternative methods of payment

If you are trading online, but don't wish to use a credit card or send cheques through the post there are alternative payment methods. For example NOCHEX (www.nochex.co.uk) allows you to send or receive money from anyone with an e-mail address and a UK debit card. Having opened your NOCHEX account you simply transfer money into it from your bank account or from other NOCHEX users. Similarly you can withdraw money from your bank account to send to retailers. PayPal (www.paypal.com) offer similar facilities.

E-mail

One of the reasons that many people choose to connect to the Internet is e-mail. It has become one of the most popular forms of communication.

Here are some of its advantages over regular mail:

- An e-mail message arrives almost instantaneously anywhere in the world
- It is very quick and easy to reply to an e-mail, simply by clicking the Reply button and writing a message
- The same message can be sent to several people at once
- Long documents or photographs can be sent as attachments
- A message can easily be forwarded to another person

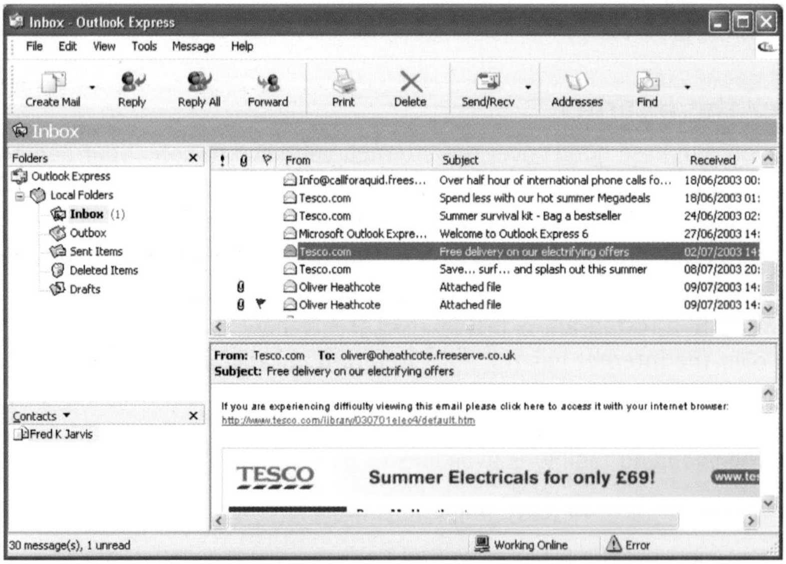

Software such as Outlook or Outlook Express (above) is needed to send and receive e-mails. The hardware needed is a computer, telephone line and a modem.

Intranets and Extranets

An **intranet** is similar to the Internet but is internal to an organisation, owned and used only by people in the organisation. It allows employees to share information, fix up appointments with each other, circulate important documents internally and many other functions. Remember that in a large organisation not everybody will be working on the same site or even at the same time.

An **extranet** is an intranet that is partially accessible to authorised users. An intranet is accessible only to people who are members of the same company or organisation, an extranet provides various levels of access to users outside of the local network.

You must have a valid username and password to access an extranet and your identity determines which parts of the extranet you can view.

Exercises

1. Explain what is meant by a **client-server network**.
2. (a) Distinguish between a wide area network (WAN) and a local area network (LAN).

   (b) Describe briefly three advantages of connecting PCs into a network rather than using standalone computers.
3. What hardware is needed to connect to the Internet?
4. Name two advantages of ADSL over PSTN for connecting to the Internet.
5. What is the function of a modem?
6. Give 3 advantages and 3 disadvantages of shopping over the Internet compared with shopping in a High Street store.
7. Explain the terms Intranet and Extranet. Why might an organisation choose to have an Intranet?
8. Describe four facilities provided by an e-mail package such as Outlook Express.
9. Describe four advantages of e-mail over ordinary mail.
10. (a) What type of software do you need to surf the world wide web?

    (b) Describe briefly three advantages to a company of having its own web site.

CHAPTER 1.5 Computers at Work

Computers or people?

Computers are an indispensable part of our daily lives. There are many reasons why this is so:

- Computers can calculate millions of times faster than humans
- Computers never get tired or need a rest
- Computers can do jobs that it would be dangerous for a human to do
- Computers can store large amounts of information in a very small space
- Computers can find information quickly
- Computers never lose or misplace information

However, no computer has come up with a play or book worth reading, conjured up a new recipe for something worth eating, or given comfort, sympathy or understanding to someone in distress. Computers can aid people in these tasks, but they can never replace them.

In this chapter we'll look at some of the ways in which computers are used in organisations such as businesses, industry, hospitals and schools. We'll start by looking at some large-scale applications.

Business

Business Administration Systems

Computers are used in businesses for keeping customer records, recording orders, printing invoices, keeping accounts, calculating payroll and managing stock, to name just a few applications.

Airline booking systems

Using a network of computers, airlines are able to instantly record a booking on any flight. Using a computerised booking system it is impossible to sell the same seat twice, even though thousands of people all over the world may be booking flights with a particular airline at any one time.

Online banking

Most banks now offer some form of online banking. Advantages to the customer include access to their account details at any time without the need to travel to a high street branch. Many people are still concerned about the level of security of these systems and the lack of personal contact if problems arise. The main advantage to the banks is a reduction in the cost of running and staffing branches which can lead to job losses.

Insurance claims processing

The Insurance industry, like many other organisations, has to maintain huge databases of customers and their insurance policies. When a customer makes a claim, the computer can quickly find the customer's record and determine the conditions under which payment will be made and, if so, how much. In addition, the computer can be used to automatically send renewal notices to customers when the policy is about to run out.

Government

Many government-run organisations rely heavily on computers to process millions of records every month. Some of these are listed below.

Census

Every few years the government takes a **census** to determine how many people live in the UK, as well as various statistics on age, ethnic origin and income. These census records are held on computer and can be analysed to ensure that the right number of schools, hospitals and other facilities are made available in different areas of the country.

Electronic voting

A voting register of all adults eligible to vote is regularly updated and held on computer. Electronic voting, either at a polling booth or from home via a computer or telephone, has been trialled in local elections and is likely to become widespread.

Vehicle registration

The DVLC computers at Swansea keep a record of every licensed vehicle in the UK, including the make of car, registration number and registered owner.

Revenue collection

The Inland Revenue keeps records of every tax payer, and processes their income tax returns. It is now possible to fill in an income tax return online rather than using a paper form.

Healthcare

Patient records systems

Doctors' surgeries are computerised with more patient record systems being introduced. Appointment booking systems are computerised and doctors automatically print out prescriptions from their PCs.

Ambulance control systems

Many ambulance services are computerised. The objectives of such a system include

- Call-taking, accepting and verifying incident details
- Determining which ambulance to send
- Communicating details of an incident to the chosen ambulance
- Positioning suitably equipped and staffed vehicles in locations where they are most likely to be needed, so minimising response times to calls

Diagnostic tools and instruments

Computerised diagnostic tools include equipment to take scans or analyse blood, urine and tissue samples. Specialised equipment is also used to monitor vital signs such as heart rate and temperature. Computerised devices such as pacemakers and prostheses (artificial limbs) have enabled tens of thousands of people to live longer and fuller lives.

Specialist surgical equipment

Computers are now used to assist surgeons carrying out surgical operations. Special equipment can provide three-dimensional vision and eliminate hand tremor by scaling down the range of motion.

Education

Student registration and timetabling systems

Computers are widely used in schools and colleges to keep student records. In some schools, students register their presence each day by swiping a magnetic card through a machine.

School timetabling systems are commonly used to work out the timetable for each individual class or pupil.

Computer-based training (CBT)

Software packages which enable students to learn any subject at their computer screens are widely available. They are used not only in schools but also in organisations to teach anything from a foreign language to how to advise a customer on the correct mortgage.

Homework using the Internet

The Internet is an excellent resource to help students complete homework. Some schools and colleges use e-mail to set and collect homework.

Distance learning

ICT is spreading rapidly in education from Primary schools right through to Universities. With ICT firmly on the National Curriculum, students now gain invaluable experience of ICT in the classroom before they embark on a career.

Spending on ICT facilities in educational establishments has increased dramatically over the last decade, and a majority of schools and colleges have dedicated ICT staff and management. Most schools and colleges operate their computers on a network basis so students can access their files and materials from any terminal in their institution. Some can gain access remotely, e.g. from home, which is especially useful to those who cannot attend school for whatever reason.

Teleworking

This term means replacing the journey to work that many people make each day with the use of telecommunications and computers. When teleworking first became acceptable business practice, it was often programmers who had no daily face-to-face contact with other people who became teleworkers. Now, more and more organisations, particularly large ones, are allowing employees to spend time out of the office working from home, for some or all of their weekly hours. The number of teleworkers in Europe is expected to grow from 10 million in 2000 to more than 28.8 million in 2005, according to researcher IDC.

The benefits to employees of teleworking include:

- reduced cost of travelling
- long commuting journeys avoided
- opportunity to work in the comfort of their own home environment
- increased productivity
- greater ability to focus on one task
- flexible schedules
- reduced company space requirements
- easier childcare arrangements

The drawbacks include:

- lack of personal contact with fellow workers
- lack of teamwork and participation with shared projects
- home distractions may interfere with work
- lack of benefits given to other employees who attend the office, e.g. medical plans, pensions and bonuses

Ergonomics

As people spend more and more time using computers it is essential to create an **ergonomic** working environment. Ergonomics refers to design and functionality and encompasses a range of factors:

- **Lighting**. The room should be well lit. Computers should neither face windows nor back onto a window so that the users have to sit with the sun in their eyes. Adjustable blinds should be provided.
- **Ventilation**. The room should have opening windows to allow free circulation of air and to prevent overheating.
- **Furniture**. Chairs should be of adjustable height, with a backrest which tilts to support the user at work and at rest, and should swivel on a five-point base. It should be at the correct height relative to a keyboard on the desk.
- **Accessories**. Document holders, mouse mats, paper trays, foot rests etc. should be provided where appropriate.
- **Hardware**. The screen should tilt and swivel and be flicker-free. Ideally it should be situated so that it avoids reflecting light. A removable monitor filter can be useful to prevent glare. The keyboard should be separately attached.

All computer users should be encouraged to take frequent breaks away from the computer.

Health issues

Computers can be held responsible for many health problems, from eyestrain to wrist injuries and back problems.

- **Repetitive Strain Injury** (RSI). This is the collective name for a variety of disorders affecting the neck, shoulders and upper limbs. It can result in numbness or tingling in the arms and hands, aching and stiffness in the arms, neck and shoulders, and an inability to lift or grip objects. The Health and Safety Executive say that more than 100,000 workers suffer from RSI.
- **Eyestrain**. Computer users are prone to eyestrain from spending long hours in front of a screen. Many computer users prefer a dim light to achieve better screen contrast, but this makes it difficult to read documents on the desk. A small spotlight focused on the desktop can be helpful. There is no evidence that computer use causes permanent damage to the eyes but glare, improper lighting, improperly corrected vision (through not wearing the correct prescription glasses), poor work practices and poorly designed workstations all contribute to temporary eyestrain. Users should be allowed regular breaks away from the screen.
- **Back problems**. Poor seating and bad posture whilst sitting at a computer screen can cause back problems.

Safety precautions

All cables should be safely secured and power points not overloaded. Working surfaces should be clean and tidy.

The environment

There are a number of measures that computer users can take to help the environment:

- recycle printer toner cartridges
- recycle printer paper
- use systems that use less power while inactive
- CD-ROM materials, electronic documents and on-screen help all reduce the need for printed materials

Exercises

1. Describe briefly five situations when you may use or encounter computers other than your own PC, in everyday life.
2. Describe briefly three large-scale uses of computers by government, describing in each case what data is held and how it may be used.
3. Give three advantages and three disadvantages of computer-based training in a school or company.
4. Describe briefly three health hazards associated with working long hours at a computer. In each case, describe one method of minimising the hazard.
5. (a) Describe briefly three ways in which users can minimise the detrimental effects of computers on the environment.

   (b) Describe three ways in which computers could be said to be contributing positively towards preserving the environment.
6. What is meant by **teleworking**? Name two advantages to:

   (a) the employer

   (b) the employee

CHAPTER 1.6

Legal Issues and Security

Copyright

Computer software is copyright material – that means it is protected in the UK by the Copyright, Designs and Patents Act 1988. It is owned by the software producer and it is illegal to make unauthorised copies.

When you buy software it is often supplied in a sealed package (e.g. CD ROM case) on which the terms and conditions of sale are printed. This is called the software licence and when the user opens the package they are agreeing to abide by the licence terms (this is often referred to as the End User Licence Agreement). The CD or package will have a unique Product ID number which you may need to type in when installing the software. Once installed, you can see the Product ID number by clicking on the Help menu and selecting an option such as, for example, About Microsoft Word.

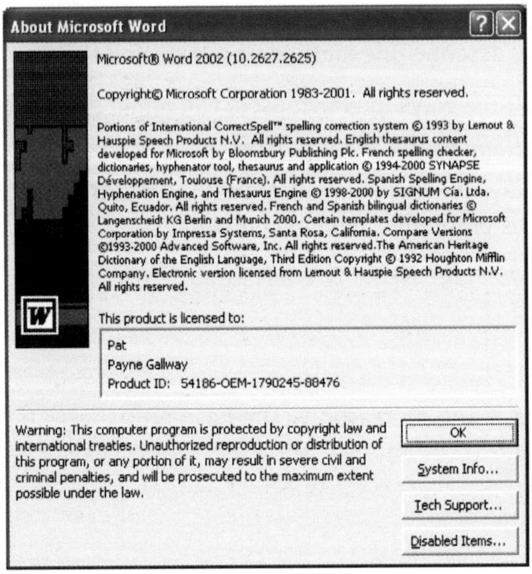

Software licences usually permit the user to use one copy on any single computer. It is considered to be in use if it is loaded into either the computer's temporary memory (RAM) or onto the hard disk drive. With network licences the software is often loaded onto the file server and the licence specifies how many users on the network can access it at any one time.

It is illegal to make copies of the software, except for backup purposes, so you are breaking the law if you copy some software from a friend onto removable media such as floppy disk, CD or Zip disk to use on your own computer.

Some software is classed as **shareware**. This can be downloaded from the Internet for evaluation. If you like the program you pay a fee and register with the manufacturer. Most programs of this type allow you to use them a limited number of times and then cease to load correctly when the evaluation period expires.

Freeware programs can be downloaded from the Internet and used for no cost.

Files downloaded from the Internet containing text, graphics, audio or video clips may also be copyright. It is illegal to use such material in your own publications without the consent of the author or creator.

Personal privacy

The **right to privacy** is a fundamental human right and one that we take for granted. Most of us, for instance, would not want our medical records freely circulated, and many people are sensitive about revealing their age, religious beliefs, family circumstances or academic qualifications. In the UK even the use of name and address files for mail shots is often felt to be an invasion of privacy.

With the advent of large computerised databases it became quite feasible for sensitive personal information to be stored without the individual's knowledge and accessed by, say, a prospective employer, credit card company or insurance company to assess somebody's suitability for employment, credit or insurance.

Case study: James Wiggins – a true story

In the US, James Russell Wiggins applied for and got a $70,000 post with a company in Washington. A routine pre-employment background check, however, revealed that he had been convicted of possessing cocaine, and he was fired the next day, not only because he had a criminal record but because he had concealed this fact when applying for the job. Wiggins was shocked – he had never had a criminal record, and it turned out that the credit bureau hired to make the investigation had retrieved the record for a James Ray Wiggins by mistake, even though they had different birthdates, addresses, middle names and social security numbers. Even after this was discovered, however, Wiggins didn't get his job back.

If the pre-employment check had been made before Wiggins was offered the job, he would not have been offered it and no reason would have been given. The information would have remained on his file, virtually ensuring that he would never get a decent job – without ever knowing the reason why.

The Data Protection Act

The **Data Protection Act** 1998 came into force on 1 March 2000. It sets rules for processing information about people and applies to paper records as well as those held on computers. It is intended to protect the privacy of individuals.

The Data Protection Principles

Anyone holding personal data must comply with the eight enforceable principles of good practice. They say that data must be:

- Fairly and lawfully processed
- Obtained only for specific purposes
- Adequate, relevant and not excessive
- Accurate and up-to-date
- Not kept longer than necessary
- Processed in accordance with the data subject's rights
- Not transferred to other countries without adequate protection
- Secure and safe from others who don't have rights to it e.g. other employees and hackers

Any organisation holding personal data about people (for example employees or customers) must register with the Data Protection Registrar. They have to state what data is being held, the sources and purposes of the data and the types of organisations to whom the data may be disclosed.

As an individual you are entitled, on making a written request to a data user, to be supplied with a copy of any personal data held about yourself. The data user may charge a fee of up to £10 for each register entry for supplying this information but in some cases it is supplied free.

Usually the request must be responded to within 40 days. If not, you are entitled to complain to the Registrar or apply to the courts for correction or deletion of the data.

With some exceptions, data cannot be held about you without your consent.

For more information on Data Protection visit the following web site: www.dataprotection.gov.uk

Data security

One of the legal requirements of the Data Protection Act is that data about individuals must be kept secure. This means that it must be properly protected from unauthorised view or loss. Moreover, the data held on a computer system can be one of the most valuable assets of a company. Security controls must be put in place to protect it from damage and unauthorised access.

To deal with security risks, most organisations have an information security policy. A typical security policy will cover:

- Administrative controls such as careful screening of prospective employees and disciplinary procedures in the event of security breaches
- Backup procedures
- Control of access to data by means of smart cards, ID badges, sign-in/sign-out registers
- Protection against fire and flood
- Access controls to computer systems and data by means of user IDs, passwords and access rights
- Procedures for reporting security incidents
- Training to make staff members aware of their responsibilities

Backup procedures

Backing up data involves copying it to a removable storage device such as magnetic tape, CD-ROM, Zip drive etc. A backup of all data is typically made on a daily basis, or more frequently, depending on the nature and importance of the data. The backup media must be clearly labelled and should be stored in a fire-proof safe, or better still on a different site, so that should a disaster or emergency occur, the backup media will be safe.

Access controls

Most networks require a user to log on with a **user-id** and **password** before they can gain access to the computer system. The user-id is normally assigned to you, and is open to view. The password is secret and does not appear on the screen when you type it in – the letters may be replaced by asterisks as you type. You can change your password whenever you like.

If you are authorised to access particularly sensitive data which only certain people are allowed to view, you may need to enter a second password. For example, on a company database the Accounts clerks may be able to view customer records but they may not be allowed access to personal data about colleagues. These **access rights** are used to protect the privacy of individuals and the security of confidential data.

In order to be completely secure there are some basic rules you should follow when using a password:

- Never write the password down – commit it to memory
- Never tell your password to another person
- Do not use an obvious word or name as a password – a combination of at least 6 letters and numbers is best
- Change your password regularly

Theft

The theft of a laptop computer, PDA or mobile phone can have disastrous consequences for the owner if they have not backed up their data. Confidential files, lists of phone numbers which could be misused, contact details or months of work can be lost if they are not properly protected and backed up.

Computer viruses

Viruses are generally developed with a definite intention to cause damage to computer files or, at the very least, cause inconvenience and annoyance to computer users. Precautions to avoid your PC being infected with a virus include the following:

- **Virus checkers** need to be installed on all computer systems so that they automatically check for any infected data when the computer is started up. Manual checkers can also be used to check for viruses on floppy disks.
- You should not share or lend floppy disks that could introduce viruses into your system.
- Care should be taken when downloading files from the Internet. The proliferation of viruses over recent years is due in part to e-mail communication. Never open an unrecognised e-mail message or an e-mail attachment from someone that you don't recognise – it could well introduce a virus to your system.

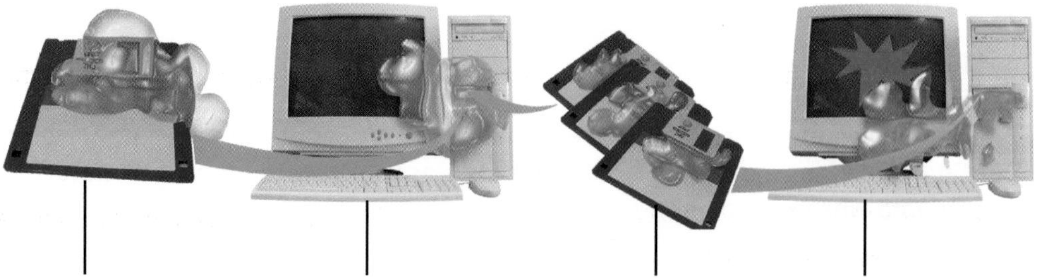

ORIGINATION
A programmer writes a program - the virus - to cause mischief or destruction. The virus is capable of reproducing itself.

TRANSMISSION
Often, the virus is attached to a normal program. It then copies itself to other software on the hard disk.

REPRODUCTION
When another floppy disk is inserted into the computer's disk drive, the virus copies itself on to the floppy disk.

INFECTION
Depending on what the original programmer wrote in the virus program, a virus may dsiplay messages, use up all the computer's memory, destroy data files or cause serious damage.

As approximately 300 new viruses are unleashed each month it is a good idea to install a virus checker that provides an online update service. You will automatically receive a message to update which can be done online.

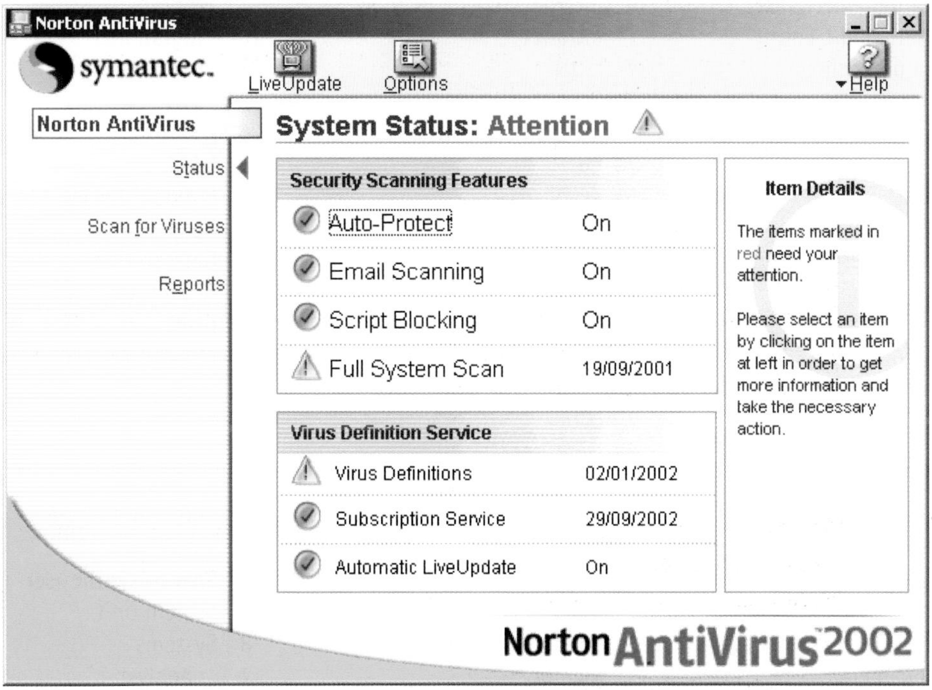

The virus checker software should be capable of not only detecting the virus, but also of removing it from the infected file (this called **disinfecting** the file).

Exercises

1. What is meant by the terms shareware and freeware? Can you use such software without paying, on your computer?
2. Before using a photograph that you have downloaded from the Internet in a publication of your own, what should you do?
3. (a) What is the name of the Act that protects the privacy of personal data held on a computer?

   (b) List four provisions of this Act.
4. What rights do you have as an individual, regarding the holding of personal data about yourself on a computer?
5. (a) What is a computer virus?

   (b) Name three measures you can take to minimise the possibility of your computer being infected with a virus.

Module 2

Using the Computer and Managing Files

In this module you will learn to become competent in using the common functions of a personal computer and its operating system. You will learn how to:

- adjust main settings
- use the built-in help features and deal with a non-responding application
- operate effectively within the desktop environment and work with desktop icons and windows
- manage and organise files and directories/folders
- duplicate, move and delete files and directories/folders, and compress and extract files
- use virus-scanning software
- use simple editing tools and print management facilities available within the operating system

Module 2 Table of Contents

The Desktop

CHAPTER 2.1

First steps

This module will give you invaluable skills in using your computer's operating system – in this case, MS Windows. The version of Windows used here is Windows XP, but you will find that other versions of Windows work in much the same way. The things you will learn in this module will help you to organise all the work you do using applications such as word processing and spreadsheets.

It will also help you to 'trouble shoot' and know what to do when something unexpected happens. Hopefully it will take a lot of the bafflement and frustration out of using your computer!

Switching on

- Check that the floppy disk drive is empty.
- Press the power switch on the front of the system unit. Also remember to switch on the screen and the printer.
- If you are working on a network you will probably be asked to enter a user ID and password. Do that now. For security reasons, the password will not be displayed on the screen.

Wait for the screen to stop changing. It should end up with some small symbols (called icons) and a coloured background – this is called your desktop.

Depending on how your computer has been set up you may see a different background and you may not see the Office toolbar – this provides shortcuts to some programs.

Let's look more closely at the desktop.

Icons

Desktop icons come in a variety of different forms. Here are some of the common ones:

- A directory/folder icon. You can double-click a folder icon to open the folder. Then you can select a file from the folder. (We will be looking at files and folders in the next chapter.)

- A file icon. Double-click a file icon to open the file in the appropriate application – in this case, Word.

- An application icon. You can double-click on an application icon to open the application.

- The recycle bin (wastebasket). When you delete a file from your hard drive, it goes into the recycle bin. You can retrieve it from there if you change your mind about deleting it.

- Printer icon. You will learn more about printing later in this module.

You will have a completely different selection of icons on your desktop, and maybe a different background as well. Later on in Chapter 2.5 you will learn how to select a different background for your desktop.

Task bar

The Task bar at the bottom of the screen shows application programs that are currently open. It also has icons on it which you can click to return to the desktop if it is not currently visible, launch Internet Explorer and view the current date and time.

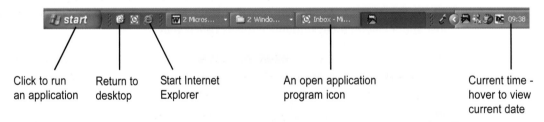

- Hover the mouse over any icon on the Task bar. A Tool tip appears telling you its function.

Using the mouse

This is the left button, and is the one most often used. When you are asked to click the mouse button, press this button once.
This is the right button, and is used to bring up a pop-up menu in Windows, so called because the menu pops up from nowhere.

Depending on where the mouse pointer is on the screen, or what the computer is doing, a different icon appears. Here are some examples:

This is the general pointer and means the computer is ready for you to do something.

The hour-glass shows the computer is busy, maybe loading a program, and you should wait until the normal pointer appears before you do anything

When the pointer changes to a two-headed arrow you can re-size a window.

Mouse clicks

There are basically three different ways of clicking a mouse button that you will be using. You will also need to drag to select or move text or objects.

- Single-click. When you are told to 'click', this means Click the left button once. Clicking once selects an item. Try clicking on one of the desktop icons. It changes colour but nothing else happens.
- Double-click. Generally speaking, clicking selects an item, and double-clicking activates it - but there are plenty of exceptions to this rule. Try double-clicking the My Computer icon, for example, to open the My Computer window. You can leave this window open on the desktop for now.
- Right-click. When you are told to right-click, click the right-hand button once. This opens a pop-up menu showing various things that can be done. Try this by right-clicking on the desktop. Click away from the pop-up menu to close it again.
- Drag. Click on an item and hold down the left mouse button while you drag the mouse. The selected item will move.

Try moving a desktop icon by dragging it.

Tip:

If the icon won't move, right-click the Desktop and select Arrange icons By. Make sure Auto Arrange is not selected.

The Start button

The Start button at the bottom left of the screen is used to select an application to run or a task that you want to do – including shutting down your computer!

We'll open a games application now.

- Click the Start button.
- On the menu that appears, click Programs.
- On the submenu, select Games. On the next menu, select Solitaire.

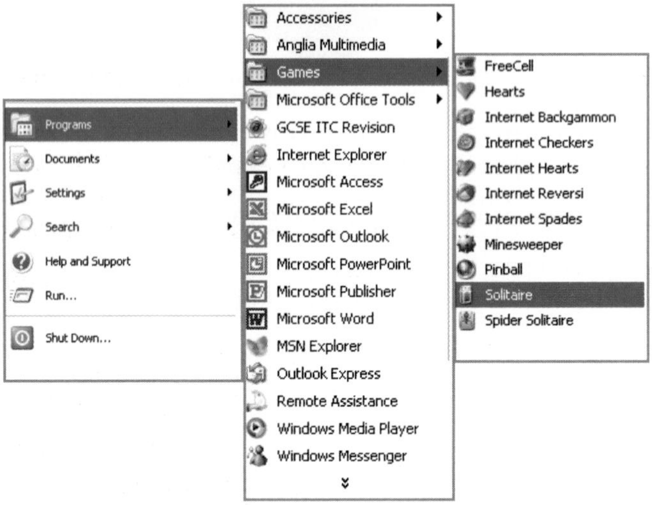

Tip:
If your start menu looks different, right-click the Start button and click Properties. Click the Start Menu tab and select the Classic Start menu option.

The Solitaire window opens.

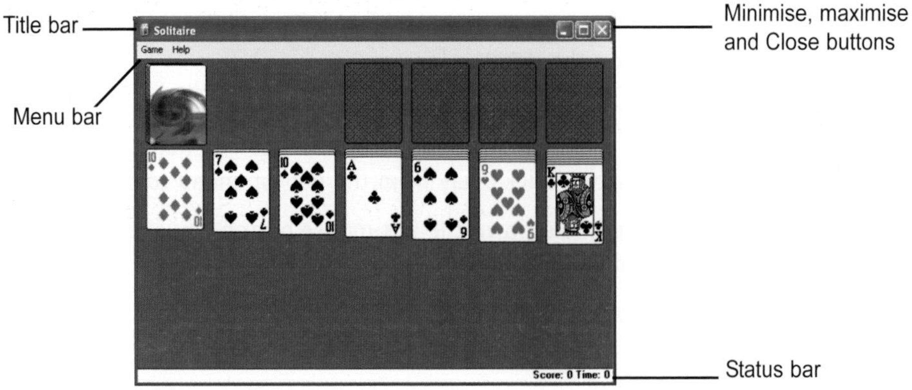

Ooh! I can put that Ace up!

The parts of a window

If you can tear yourself away from the game, or can't figure out how to play, we'll look now at the parts of a window.

You should have two windows open on the desktop – the My Computer window and the Solitaire window. You'll notice that each of them has the following parts in common:

- A Title bar showing the name of the program. Click in the title bar of each window in turn to bring it to the foreground.
- A Menu bar that has labels that when clicked produce dropdown menus with options to choose from.
- A Status bar which provides information about the current state of what you are viewing in the window.

- A Minimise button. Click this button once in the Solitaire window. The window disappears, but the application is still open. Look in the Task bar and you will see an icon named Solitaire. Click it to restore the window to the desktop.

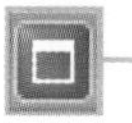

- A Maximise button. Click this once in the Solitaire window. The window now occupies the full screen.

- Notice that the Maximise button has now changed to a Restore Down button. Click this once now to restore the window to its original size.

- A Close button. You would click this once to close the window. Don't do this now. If you do close one of the two open windows, open it up again!
- Horizontal and vertical scroll bars that can be moved to allow you to see all parts of the window.

Moving and resizing a window

Either click the icons on the task bar or click the Title bar of a window to switch between open windows. You can move a window around on the screen by dragging its Title bar.

To change the size of a window, move the cursor over one of the window borders so that it changes to a double-headed arrow. Then drag one way or the other to make the window bigger or smaller.

- Try making the My Computer window smaller so that scroll bars appear.

You can drag a scroll bar to see parts of the window that are hidden from view.

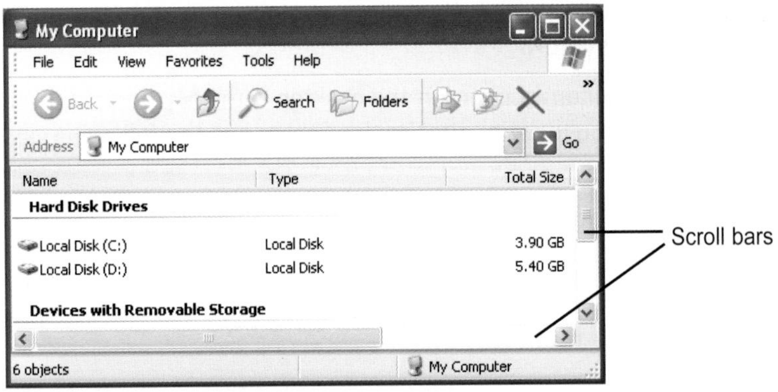

Notice that this window also has a Toolbar with buttons which you can click.

Try arranging the windows on the desktop so that they don't overlap. A quick way to do this is to right-click in the Task bar and from the pop-up menu, select Tile Windows Horizontally or Tile Windows Vertically.

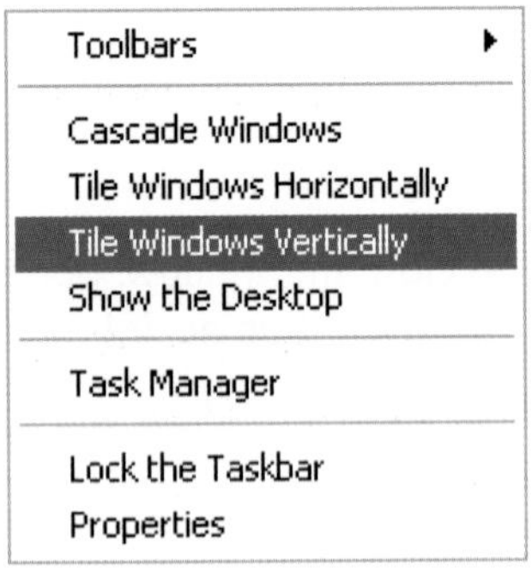

- Close both the open windows when you have finished practising.

Switching off your computer

Before you switch off your computer you must close any programs that are open. You should then close your computer down in the recommended way. If you don't do this and just switch off, your computer will not restart normally next time.

- When you have closed all your programs you should see only the Windows desktop on the screen.
- In the bottom left-hand corner of your screen, click Start.
- Click Shut Down.
- In the box that appears check that the Shut down option is displayed and click OK.

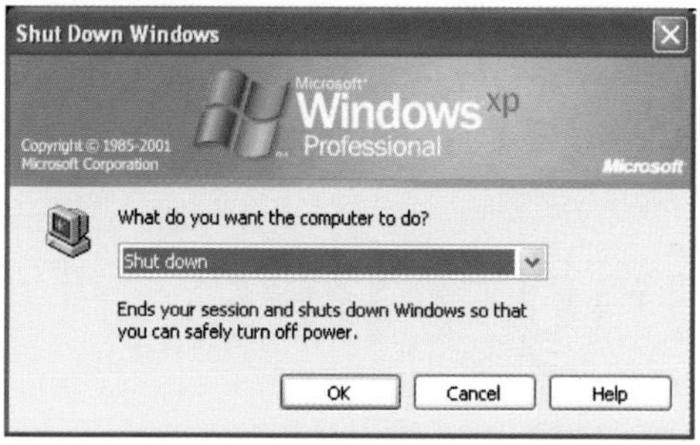

- Wait for the screen to go black, or for a message to say that it is safe to turn off your computer and then switch off the computer.

Tip:
With Windows 2000 or later versions, the PC switches itself off.

Restarting your computer

Instead of closing down your computer you can choose to restart it. You may want to do this if you have loaded some new software and the instructions tell you to restart Windows.

- When you reach the dialogue box shown above, click the down-arrow and select Restart from the dropdown list.

Exercises

1. Switch on your computer and look at the Windows desktop. Write down the answers to the following questions on a sheet of paper.
   (a) Do you have to enter a Windows username and password?
   (b) What are icons?
   (c) Write down the names of all the icons you can see.
   (d) What is the recycle bin icon used for?
   (e) Where would you find the current date and time on your Windows desktop?
   (f) What does it mean when you see an hour-glass on the screen?
   (g) Describe how you would open the Solitaire game.
2. Open the My Computer window and the Solitaire game and answer the following questions:
   (a) Describe the purpose of the window Minimise and Maximise buttons.
   (b) Describe how you would resize a window.
   (c) Draw a rough sketch of a screen with two windows tiled vertically.
3. Why shouldn't you just switch off your computer without closing down correctly?
4. How would you restart your computer?
5. Give one example of when you might need to restart your computer.

CHAPTER 2.2 Creating and Printing Files

In this chapter we'll open some of the applications that you will learn about in other modules, and save some sample files of different types in a folder.

A text editing application

First we will create a short document and save it.

- From the Start menu select Programs, Accessories, Wordpad.

Tip:

This is a short way used in this book of saying 'Click Start. From the submenu select Programs. From the next submenu select Accessories. From the next submenu select Wordpad.'

Wordpad is a simple text editor that is supplied free with Windows.

- Type a short sentence – you can be more imaginative if you like!

  This is a test document created in Wordpad.

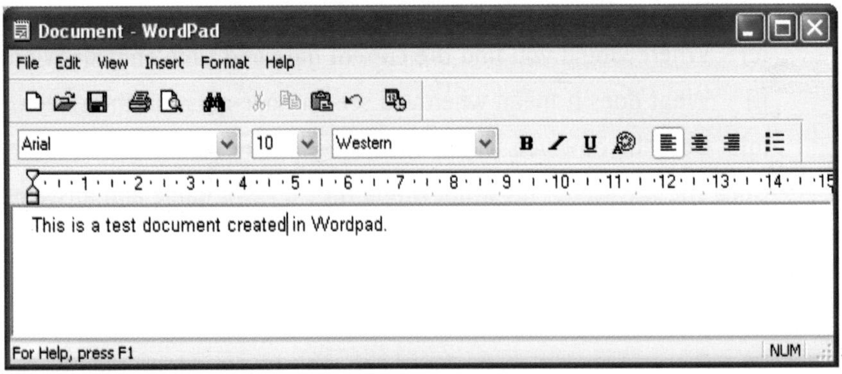

- From the File menu, select Save.

A window will open, probably showing the default My Documents folder in the Save in: box. If it shows something different, you can either ask for help from your teacher or just save it in the folder shown. Later, you will learn how to move it.

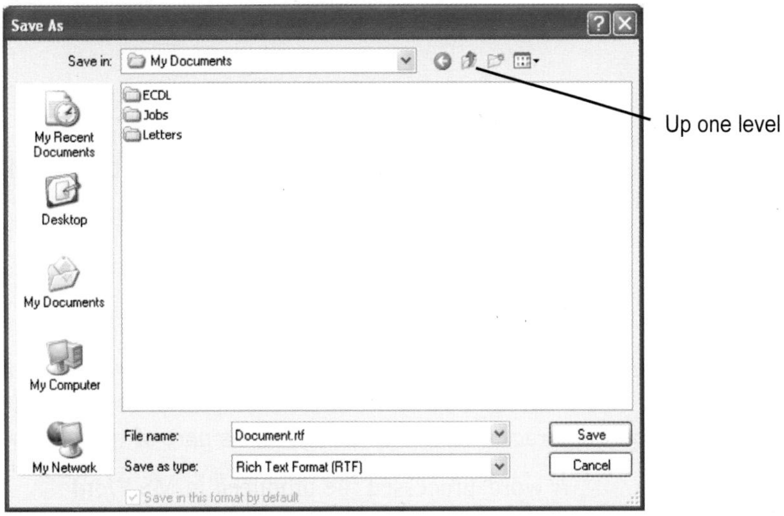

- In the File name box type the name Wordpad-Test.

Notice that by default, it will be saved as a type of file called Rich Text Format. A full stop followed by the three letters RTF will be added to the end of your file name. These letters are known as the file extension.

- Click Save. The window will close automatically.
- Close Wordpad by clicking the Close icon or by selecting File, Exit.

Opening an existing file

Now practise re-opening Wordpad and opening the new file you created.

- Open Microsoft Wordpad.
- Select File, Open.

The Open dialogue box will be displayed.

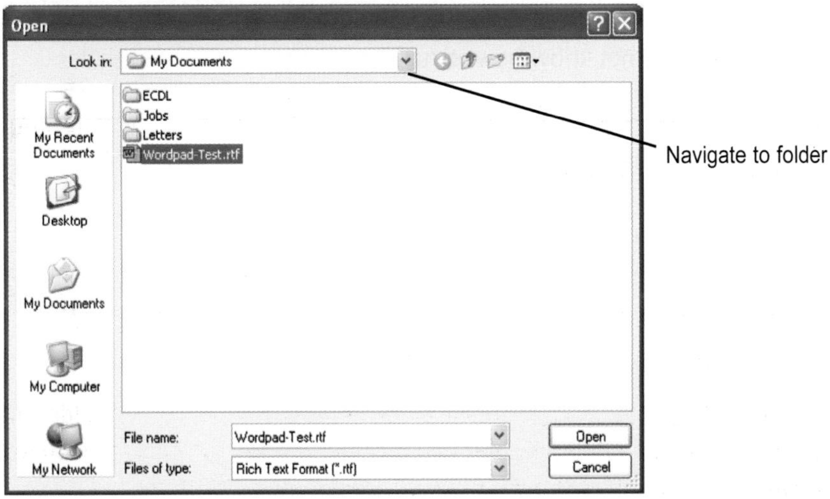

- Navigate to the correct file(s), select the files(s).
- Click Open.

Tip:

If you wanted to open more than one file, you can hold down the Shift key while you select each file.

File types

Windows recognises many different file types. The file type depends on which application the file was created in. Here are some examples of common file types, each identified by the three-character extension which forms part of the file name.

.doc	A word-processed file produced in MS Word
.xls	A spreadsheet produced in MS Excel
.mdb	A database created in MS Access
.ppt	A presentation file created in MS PowerPoint
.bmp	A bitmapped graphic created in a graphics package
.jpg, .gif, .tif	Different types of graphics file
.mp3, .mid, .wav	An audio file
.avi, .mpeg, .mov	A video file
.txt	A plain text file
.zip	A compressed file
.htm	A web page file
.tmp	A temporary file

Tip:

In Chapter 2.3 you will learn how to rename a file. However, you have to be careful not to change the extension because the software will not recognise the file type and will not know how to handle your file.

Creating Word documents

Next we'll create three very short documents using Word. We need some files of different types so that we can practise moving them, copying them, renaming them and so on in the next chapter!

- Open Word. You can do this by clicking the Word icon in the Office toolbar, if you have one. Alternatively, click the Start button and select Programs, Microsoft Word.
- Type a short invitation to your friend Sharon.

> Dear Sharon
>
> We're having a party on Friday 13th. Hope you can come!

- From the File menu select Save. Save the document in the same folder as before, naming it Sharon.
- Now edit the letter by changing the name Sharon to Robert.
- This time, you don't want to select Save from the File menu because that would simply overwrite the contents of the original file, leaving you with a letter to Robert with the file name Sharon. Instead, select Save As.
- Type the new file name Robert.
- Edit the letter once more, to send an invitation to Kim.
- Save this file as Kim.

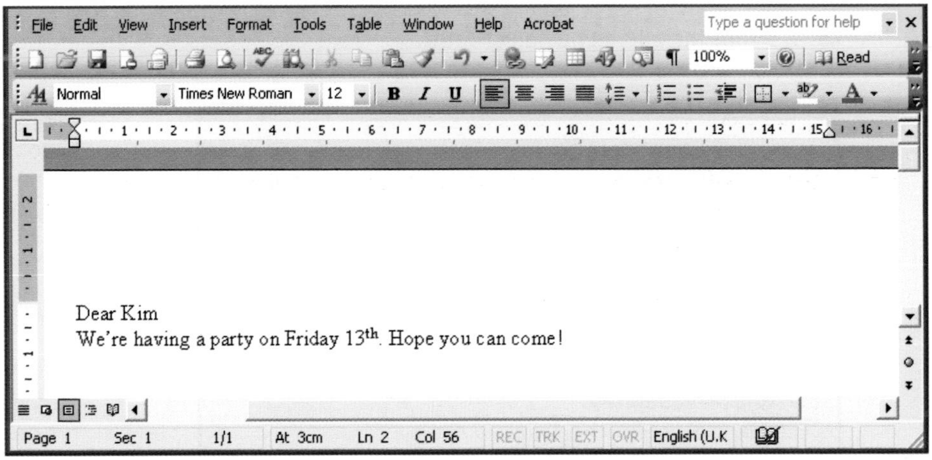

Creating some spreadsheet files

Now we'll create some spreadsheet files.

- Open Microsoft Excel. This program is used to hold numerical information and you'll learn all about it in Module 4. For now, we'll just enter a single number in cell A1.
- In cell A1 enter the number 1. Press Enter.
- Save the spreadsheet as SS1.
- Create 3 more spreadsheets, naming them SS2, SS3 and SS4. You can do this in the same way as you created the three Word documents.

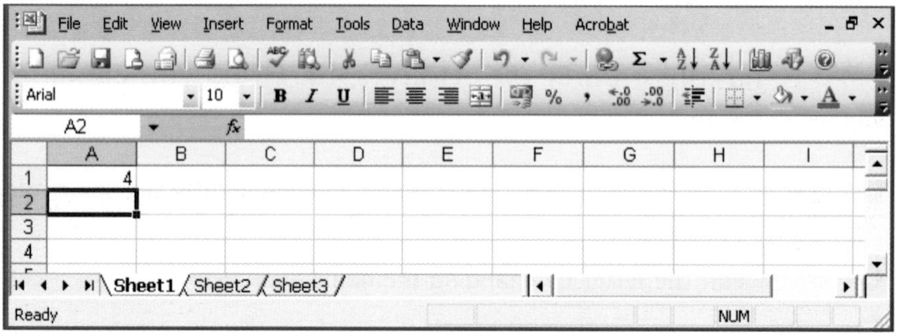

- Close Excel by clicking the Close icon or by selecting File, Exit.

Printing a file

If you have not closed down Microsoft Word, you should see the name of the last document that you saved in the Task bar.

- Click the file name in the Task bar and the document will open.
- From the File menu select Print.

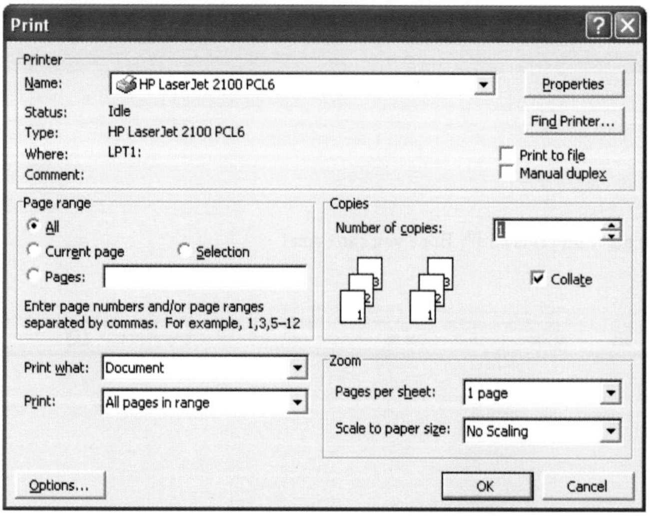

The print dialogue box allows you to choose many options including which printer you want to use (if you are working on a network), which page you want to print (for longer documents) and how many copies you would like.

- Check that there is some paper in the printer.
- Make sure that only one copy is selected and click OK.

Your letter will print out.

The desktop print manager

When you send a document to the printer to be printed, a printer icon appears in the System Tray at the right-hand end of the Task bar.

You can right-click on this icon to view the print job's progress. The following window will be displayed:

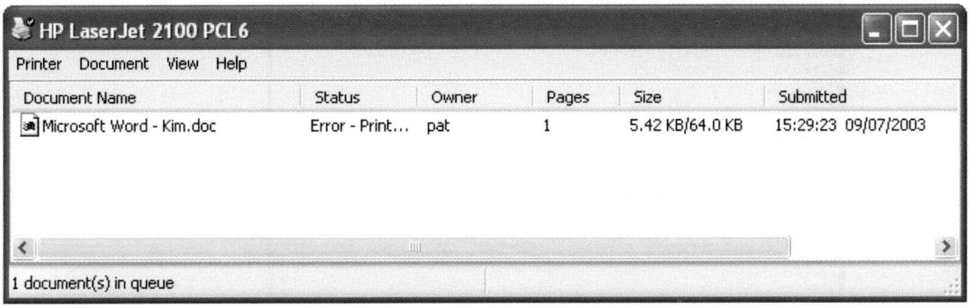

Pausing, restarting or deleting a print job

In the screenshot for the print job, the status is given as Error. (In this case it was because the printer was not switched on.)

You can pause, restart or cancel a print job by clicking the file name. A pop-up menu appears:

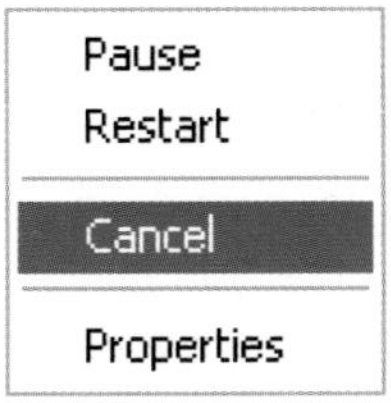

Shutting down a non-responding application

From time to time, just when you think things are going really well and that you are getting to grips with using a PC, everything suddenly grinds to a halt and it refuses to respond. Your application has 'crashed'!

If your screen locks up so that you cannot use the keyboard or mouse, you can try to find out which program is causing the problem.

- Press Ctrl-Alt-Del on the keyboard (all at the same time). In the window that appears click Task Manager.

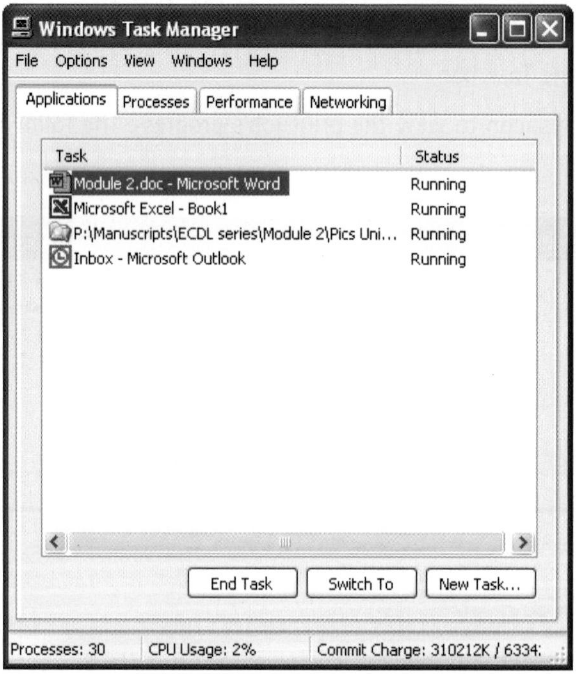

All the applications currently running in your computer will be listed. One of them will probably show a status of Not Responding. This will be the offending program.

- Click the name of the program and click End Task to close it.

This should close down the faulty program and allow you to carry on working. If it doesn't, follow the Shut Down procedure – this will close your PC down safely.

Unfortunately, either way you will lose anything you have been working on in the application – for example, all the changes to a document since you last saved it. The only lesson to be learned is to save your work every few minutes. Everything that you have saved to a floppy disk or hard disk is safe.

Tip:

A quick way to save a document you are currently working on is to press Ctrl-S (Ctrl and S together) on the keyboard. Alternatively, click the Save icon.

- Close Microsoft Word.

Exercises

1. Open a new WordPad document.
2. Enter the following text:

   Different file types include the following:

3. Move to a blank line by pressing Enter and type in the names of as many common file types as possible. Leave a couple of spaces between each one.
4. Save this document as File types.rtf in your My Documents folder.
5. Open a new Microsoft Word document.
6. In the document describe how you would access the desktop print manager and explain what it does.
7. Save this document as Print Manager.doc in your My Documents folder.
8. Click on your document File types.rtf in the Task bar and print it out.
9. Return to Print Manager.doc and print that too.
10. Add some more text to the document Print Manager.doc. This should explain how to close a non-responding application.
11. Save the document with the name Useful tips.doc and print out a copy.
12. Close the file Filetypes.rtf and close WordPad.
13. Close Print Manager.doc and Useful tips.doc and close Word.

CHAPTER

2.3 Folders and Files

Disk drives on your computer

You probably have several disk drives on your computer. Windows assigns a letter to each of them. The floppy drive is usually A:, the hard drive C:, the zip drive (if you have one) is probably D:, the CD drive E: and so on. On a network the hard drive is usually divided or 'partitioned' into several 'logical drives' called, for example, F:, G:, H: etc.

You can see what drives your computer has, and how much free space there is on each disk.

- Go to the Desktop. You can do this by clicking the Desktop icon next to the Start button at the bottom left of the screen, or by right-clicking in the Task bar and selecting Show the Desktop.
- Double-click the My Computer icon. You should see a window similar to the one below:

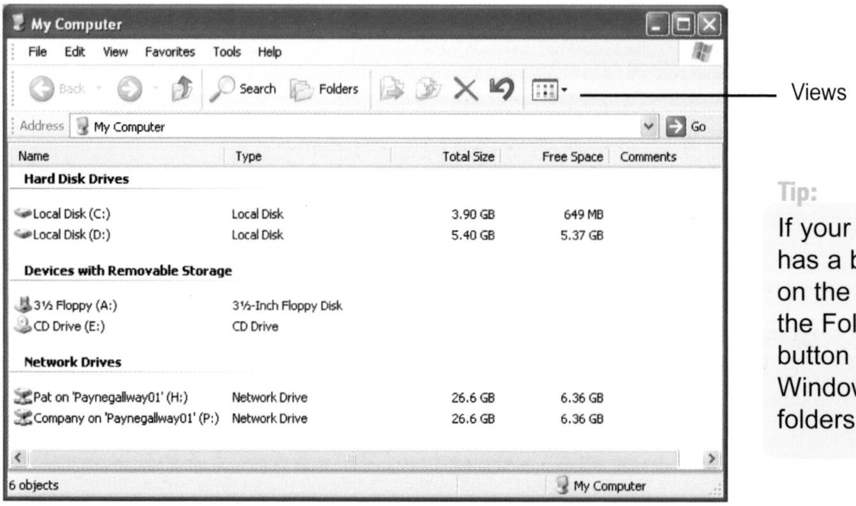

Tip:
If your window has a blue pane on the left, click the Folders button to display Windows classic folders.

The screenshot shows two hard disk drives, C: and D:. Actually there is only one physical drive, but for convenience it has been divided into two partitions. The same has been done on the network drive. What drives do you have on your computer?

Your screen may still look different. You can change the appearance of the window by clicking the Views button, and selecting one of the other options.

Directories/folders

All the documents you create on your PC are referred to as files. These files have to be given names (you can use up to 255 characters) and it is a good idea to use meaningful file names so that you can easily find a particular file later on.

As you use your computer more and more you will have lots of files stored on your hard drive (C:). You will need to keep your work organised so that you can go to it quickly.

Files are organised by saving them into folders that are also given names. These folders can contain subfolders. One very important folder that is set up automatically for you is My Documents. This is where Windows expects you to create your own subfolders to store your work.

Tip:

You will see the My Documents icon on the desktop.

Here is an example of a folder structure within My Documents:

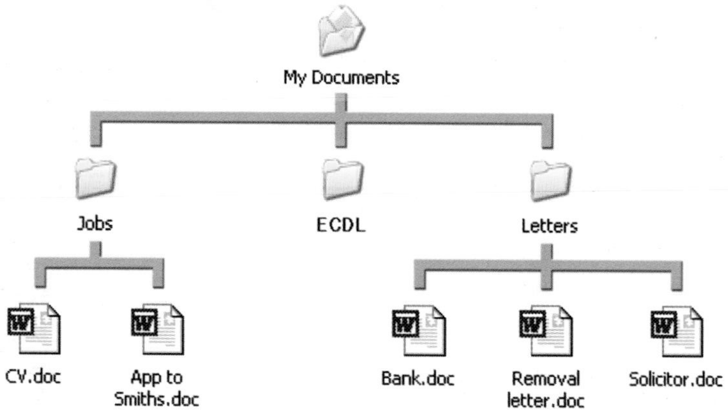

The location of files is specified by their pathname. For example in the diagram above, the pathname to the word-processed file Removal letter would be as follows:

C:\My Documents\Letters\Removal letter.doc

- Double-click the C: drive icon.

You will now see a window displaying the folders on the C: drive. (Your window will have different folders.)

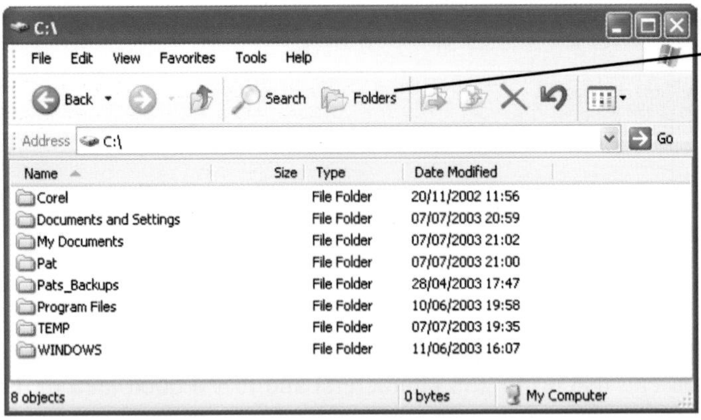

- Click the Folders button if it is not already selected. This shows you a more detailed view.

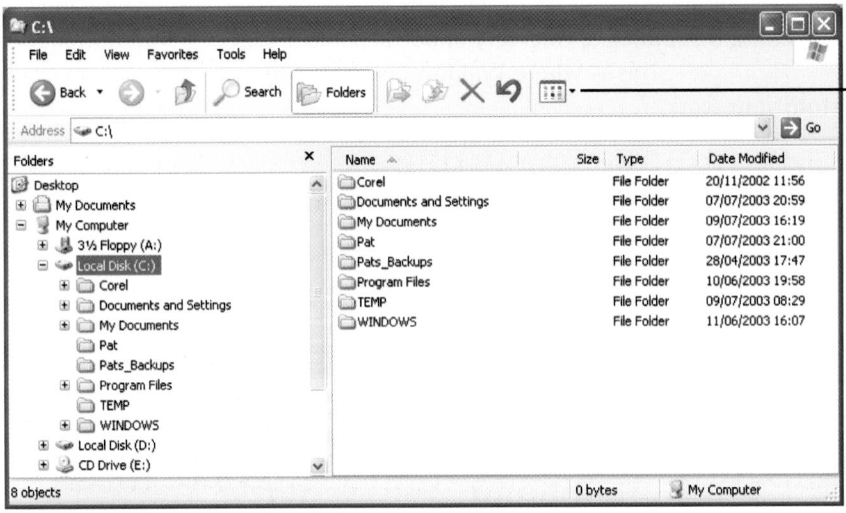

Tip:
The view shown above is the Details view. Click the Views button to change to this view if your screen looks different.

Creating a new folder

We will set up the folders and subfolders shown on the previous page.

- Double-click on My Documents. The folder opens.
- From the File menu, select New. Then select Folder.
- Type the name Jobs as the New Folder name.

- Click the Back button to go back to the My Documents folder.
- Create the other two folders ECDL and Letters in the same way.
- Click the ECDL folder and create the two subfolders Module1 and Module2.

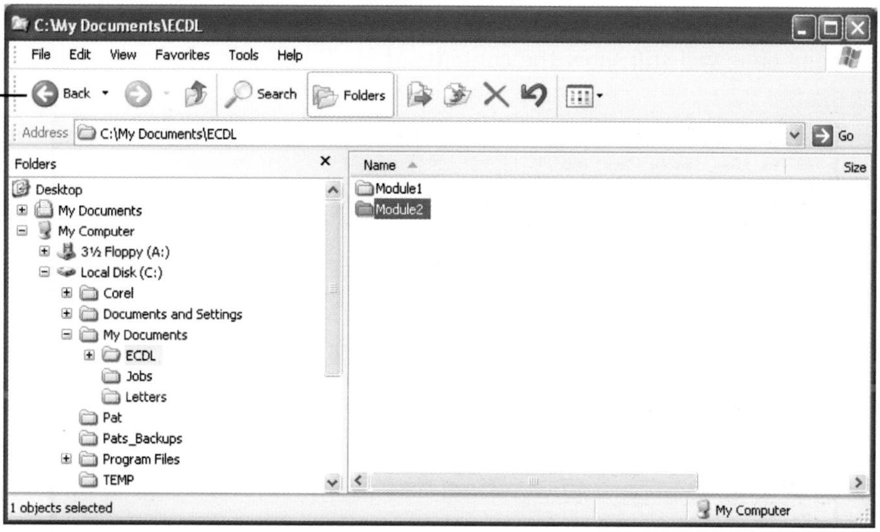

Tip:
Right-clicking on a folder and selecting Properties will tell you the total size of the folder and the number of subfolders and files it contains.

Navigating to a file or folder

- In the left-hand pane, click My Documents. Now you should see all the subfolders you created, and all the files you saved in My Documents.

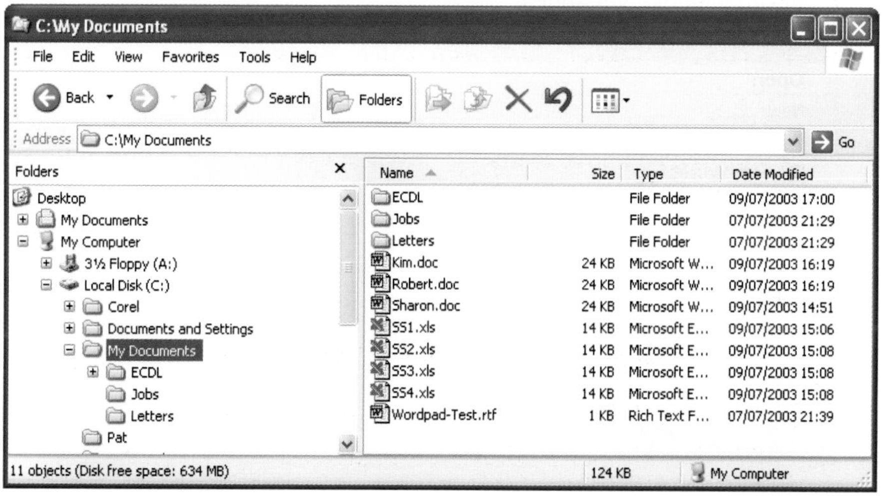

Notice that you can now see the hierarchy of folders and files: when you clicked My Documents, the little + sign beside it in the left-hand window changed to a – sign. The + sign indicates that there are subfolders within this folder, which can be viewed by clicking to expand the structure.

This needs practice. For example, if you click the + sign beside the ECDL folder, you will see it expanded in the left-hand window, but it is not the selected folder so the right-hand pane will still show the contents of My Documents, the selected folder.

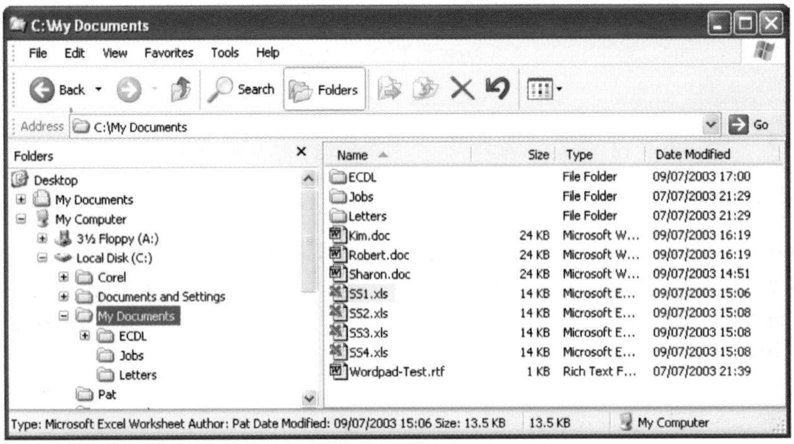

- Practise clicking the + and – signs beside various folders, and selecting folders and subfolders, until you are clear about how the system works. Leave your screen looking like the one above for the next task.

Renaming a file

You can rename any file or folder.

- Right-click on Kim.doc. Then select Rename.

A pop-up window will appear:

- Change the file name to Tom.doc by typing the new name over the old one and pressing Enter. If you do not enter .doc correctly, you will be warned that changing the extension may make the file unusable. Be sure to get it right!

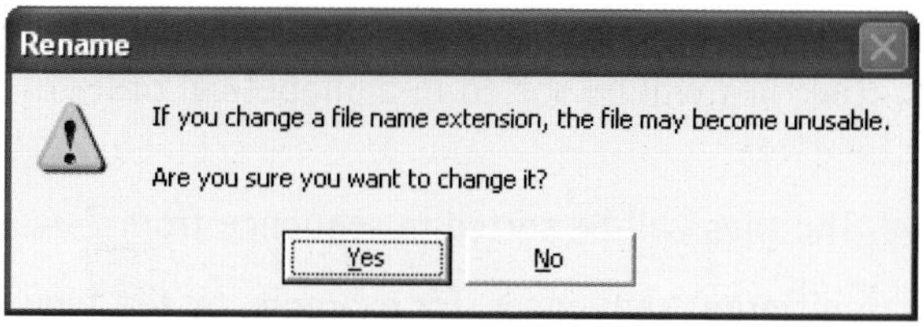

Changing file status

- Right-click on Robert.doc. Then select Properties.

The Properties window appears and you can change the file status to Read-only if you don't want to accidentally change the file. Sometimes you may find that a file has accidentally been set to Read-only, and you can reset it to Read/Write (i.e. not Read-only) in this window.

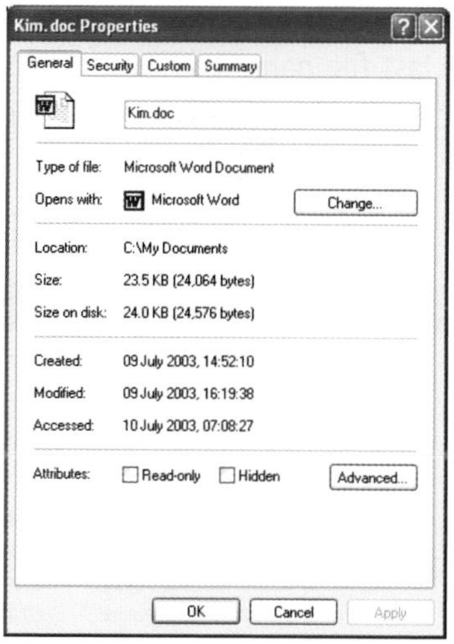

Tip:

When a file is set to Read-only, you won't be able to save any changes you make to it if you try and edit it. A message will be displayed:

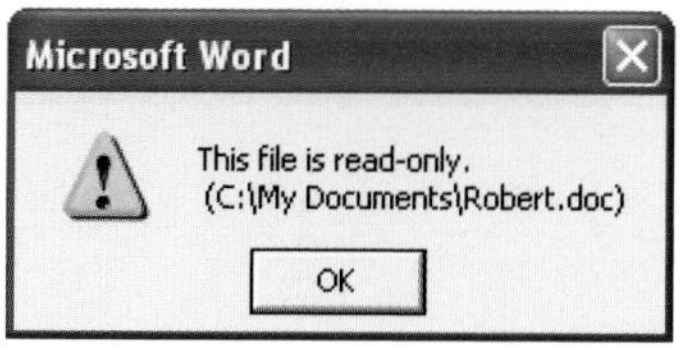

Sorting files

You can change the order in which files are displayed in the right-hand window by clicking in the bar on Name, Size, Type or Date Modified to sort the files and folders in any of these sequences.

- Click once on Name. The files will be sorted in alphabetical order of name, from A-Z.
- Click again on Name. The files will be sorted in sequence from Z-A.
- Try sorting the files in different sequences, for example, by file type. Leave the files sorted in ascending order of name.

Selecting files and folders

Sometimes you need to reorganise your files, perhaps moving them into different folders. Other times you may want to copy one or more files into a different folder or onto a floppy disk for backup.

Instead of moving them one at a time, you can select all the files you want to move and then move them in one operation.

- To select several adjacent files or folders, click the first file name. Then hold down the Shift key while you click the last file name you want to select.
- To select non-adjacent files, hold down the Ctrl key while you select each one.
- Select all the .doc files.

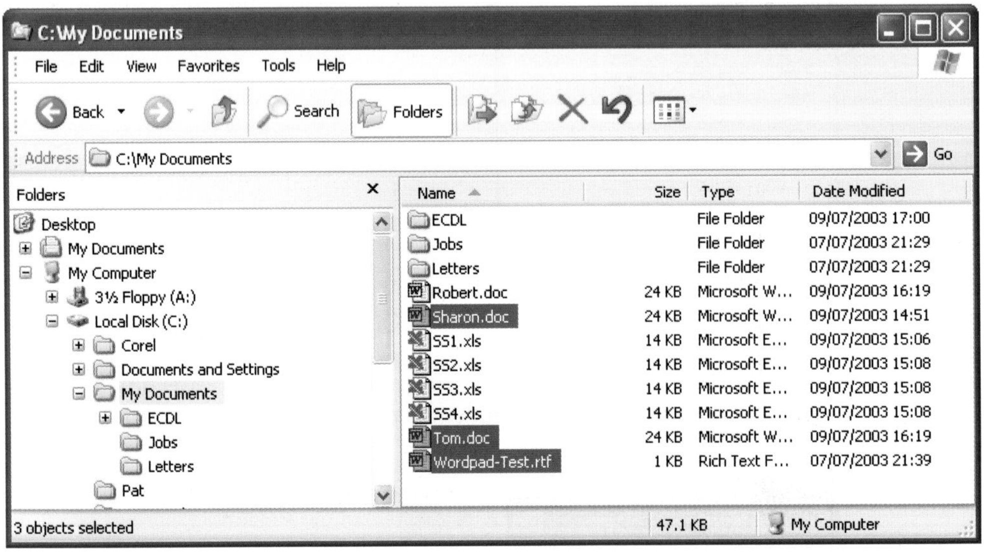

Copying and moving files and folders

You can copy a file to another folder or disk drive by first copying it to the Clipboard, and then pasting it to the desired location.

The Clipboard is a temporary storage area which will hold the latest file or folder that you cut or copy. The next time you cut or copy something, the previous contents will be overwritten.

We will copy all the Word documents to the Letters folder.

- With the .doc files selected, click Edit, Copy. This copies all these files to the Clipboard.
- In the left-hand window, click on the folder name Letters.
- Select Edit, Paste. The files will be copied to the Letters folder.

Now there are two copies of each of these files – in My Documents and in Letters.

Note that folders can be copied in the same way. When you copy a folder, all its contents are copied too. You can copy to another drive such as the A: drive in exactly the same way.

Making backup copies

Copying files for backup purposes is an essential skill for everyone using a computer! Sooner or later some disaster will occur such as your hard disk crashing, your laptop being stolen, or your file being infected with a virus. That's when you will be glad you have a recent copy of your work on a floppy disk safely tucked away in your desk drawer at home.

Deleting files and folders

You can delete the documents from their original location.

- Click on My Documents.
- Select the .doc files again.

- Press the Delete key on the keyboard. Alternatively, you can press the Delete button.

You will see a message:

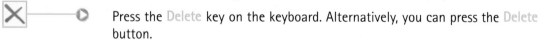

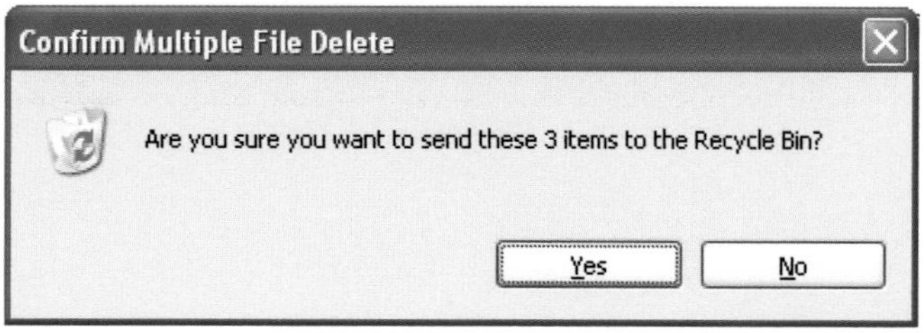
Confirm Multiple File Delete
Are you sure you want to send these 3 items to the Recycle Bin?
Yes
No

- If you are sure you have selected the correct items, click Yes.

Tip:

You could use Edit, Cut instead of Edit, Copy when moving files. But you may find it's safer to copy them and then delete the ones you don't want!

The Recycle Bin

So what is this Recycle Bin? It all sounds very environmentally friendly!

When you delete a file or folder, it is not completely deleted – it is moved to a storage area called the Recycle Bin. This is very useful because it means that if you deleted the wrong file by mistake, you can retrieve it from the bin!

If you realise your mistake immediately, the easiest way to get your files back is to press the Undo button.

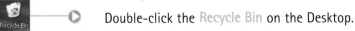

Suppose you just want to restore the file Tom.doc.

- Go to the Desktop by clicking the Desktop icon next to the Start button in the Task bar. Alternatively, you can right-click in the Task bar and select Show the Desktop.

- Double-click the Recycle Bin on the Desktop.

A window opens showing the contents of the Recycle Bin.

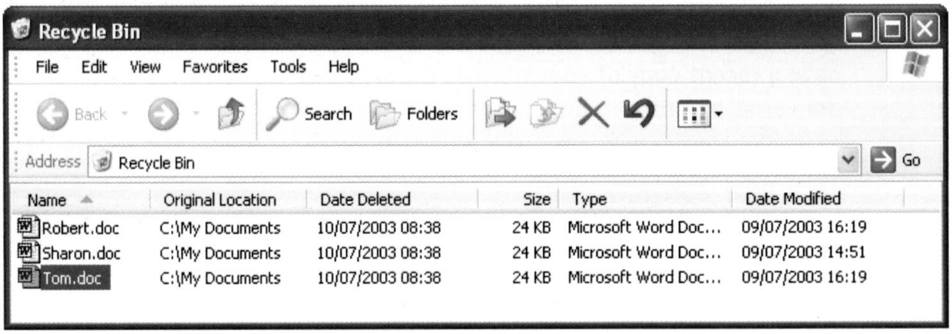

- Right-click Tom.doc and from the pop-up menu, select Restore.

Your file will be restored to the My Documents folder.

You can restore deleted folders in the same way.

Emptying the Recycle Bin

The contents of the Recycle Bin take up space on your hard disk and it is a good idea to empty it now and then.

- On the Desktop, right-click the Recycle Bin and select Empty Recycle Bin. You will be asked to confirm your request. Remember there is no getting those files back now!

Drag and Drop

Another way of copying or moving files is to select them and then drag them into the new location.

Be aware of the following rule:

- Dragging a file or folder to a new location on the same drive moves the file or folder.
- Dragging a file or folder to a different drive copies the folder.

If you want to use drag and drop to copy a file to a new location on the same drive, hold down Ctrl while you drag.

We'll use the Drag and Drop technique to move the spreadsheet files to the folder Module2, which is a subfolder of ECDL.

- Restore the C: window to the desktop. It may be minimised in the Task bar.
- Click the + sign next to the ECDL folder name so that its two subfolders are visible.
- Click SS1, then hold down Shift and click SS4 to select the four spreadsheets.

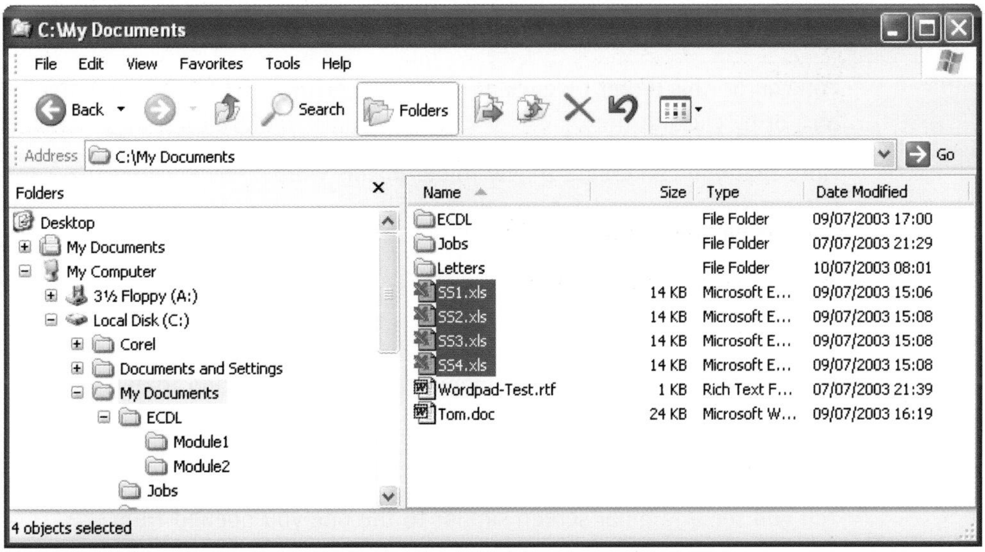

- Hold down the left mouse button while you drag the files and drop them onto Module2.

Navigating within an application

Very often you need to find a file, save a file in a particular folder, create a new folder or delete a file from within an application such as Word.

For example, suppose you want to open the file Kim.doc in Word.

- Open Word. From the File menu select Open.

The following screen appears:

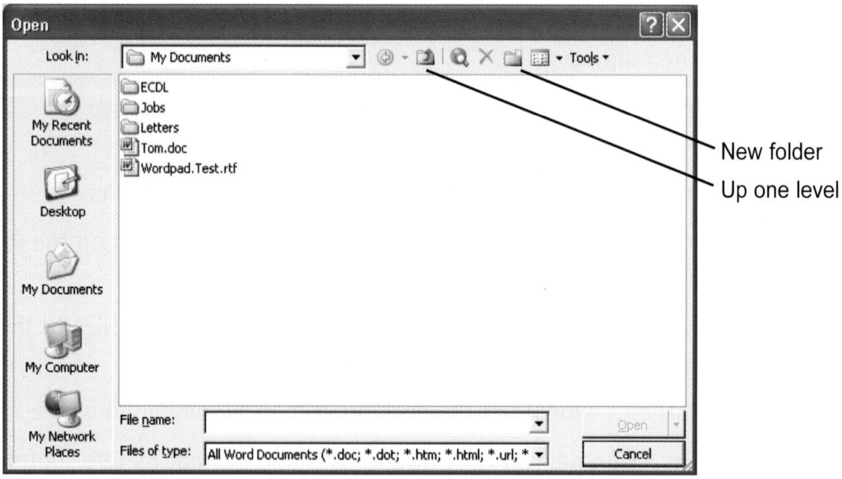

Now suppose you can't remember where the file is saved and you decide to look in Module2. You double-click on ECDL to display its subfolders. Then double-click Module2 – no documents! This folder only contains spreadsheets.

You need to navigate backup through the folder structure, and across to Letters.

You can do this either by clicking the down-arrow next to the file name in the Look in: box, or by clicking the Up one level button until you are back at My Documents.

Note that you can create a new folder in this window by clicking the New Folder button. You can also delete a selected file using either the Delete key or the Delete button in this window.

Windows Explorer

Another way of looking at and manipulating your files and folders is by using Windows Explorer.

- Right-click the Start button and select Explore.

You will see a familiar screen similar to the one you opened from My Computer.

Exercises

In this exercise you are asked to create a folder structure which will help organise the computerised files of a double-glazing sales office.

1. Create a folder named Sales on your disk. Create two subfolders within the Sales folder. Name these folders Quotes and Appointments.
2. Create two word processing files and save them in the Sales folder. Name these files Windows.doc and Conservatories.doc.
3. Create the following subfolder structure within the Appointments subfolder as represented by the diagram below

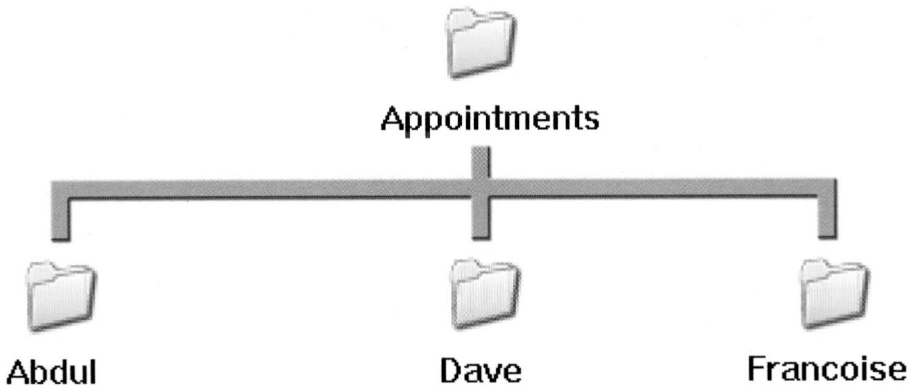

4. Copy the files Windows.doc and Conservatories .doc to the Quotes folder.
5. Re-name the folder Francoise to Francis.

CHAPTER

2.4 Working with Files

Compressing files

If you want to send a file as an attachment to an e-mail, zipping or compressing the file will make it much faster to send and receive. Some ISPs cannot receive large files. As a general rule if the size of the file you are sending is more than half a megabyte (500Kb) then you should compress it.

Most newer PCs have a program called WinZip installed which allows you to 'zip up' files.

Tip:

You can download a trial version of WinZip from www.winzip.com.

- Using My Computer find a large file.
- Right-click on the file and choose Send to. Then select Compressed (Zipped) folder.

In the screenshot below cat.jpg has been compressed, and a new folder cat.zip appears.

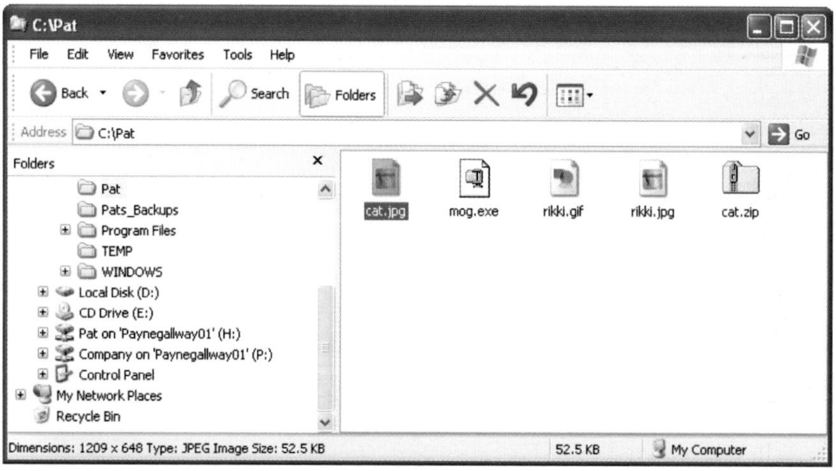

At the bottom of the screen it will tell you how big the current file is. Compare the zipped file with the unzipped file – is it a lot smaller?

Extracting a compressed file

To unzip the file, right-click it and select Extract All. An Extraction Wizard will appear, and you can follow the steps to extract the file.

Searching for files

If you lose a file you can use the Search facility in My Computer to find it again. We will look for Sharon.doc.

- Open My Computer if it is not already open. Navigate to C: and click the Search button.

You will see the following window:

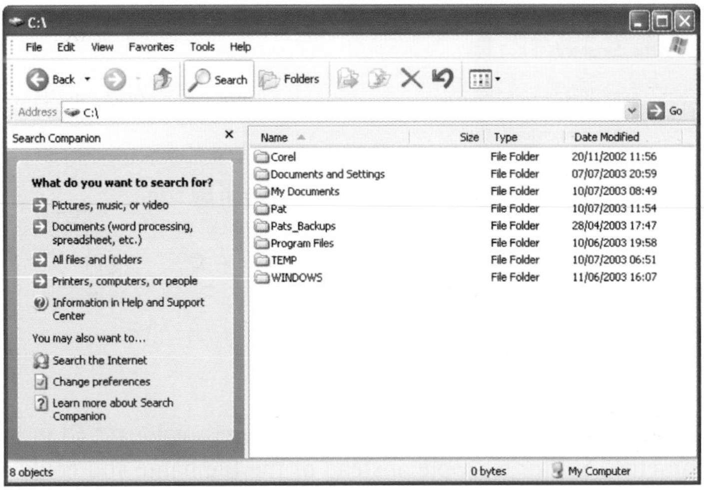

- In the box on the left-click on Documents.

If you know that you created or modified the document within the last week, say, you can click on the appropriate box.

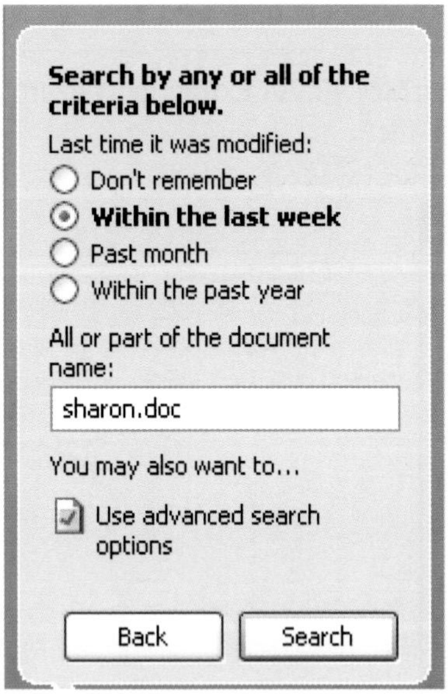

You can click on Use advanced search options to search by a range of other criteria such as size.

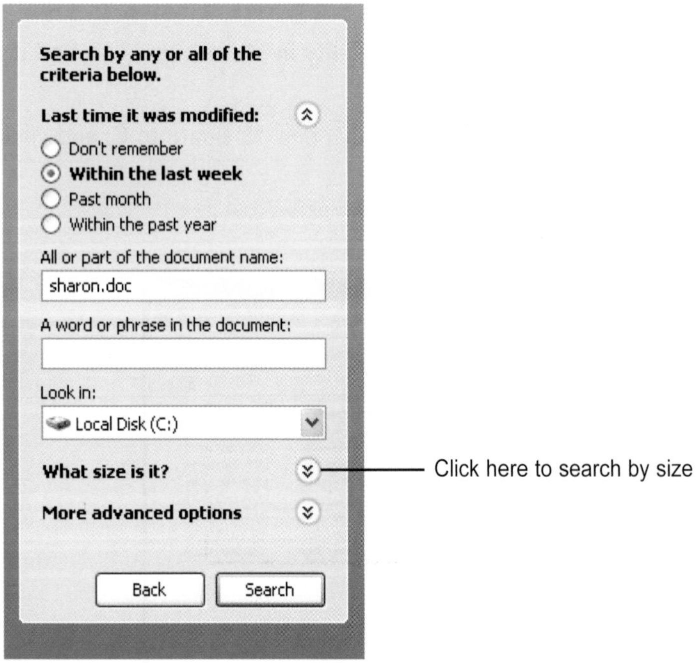

If you can't remember the whole file name, you can use a wildcard (*) in place of any number of characters. So, for example, instead of the file name you could enter *.* to find all files, *.doc to find all files with a .doc extension, or sh*.doc to find all documents starting with the letters sh.

You can also search by content, by entering a word or phrase in the document in the search box, or by size.

- Click Search.

The computer will find the file you are looking for.

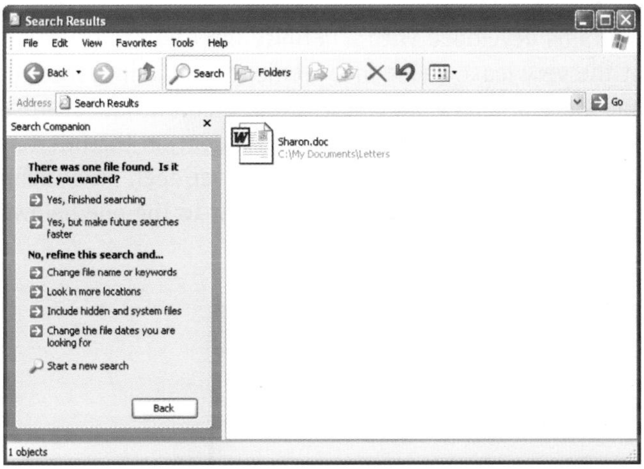

You can open the file in Word simply by double-clicking on it now.

Notice that at the bottom of the screen is a count of the number of files found. You could use this to count all the files of a particular type, by entering say, *.doc in the Search box and then searching a named folder.

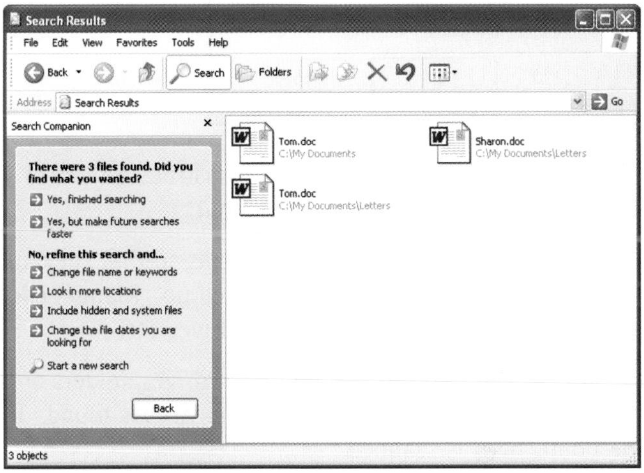

Viewing a list of recently used files

If you want to open or search for a recently used file, there is another way you can do this.

- From the Start menu select My Recent Documents or just Documents, depending on your computer's setup. A list of recent documents will be displayed and you can open any of them by clicking on the file name.

Viruses

We'll end this chapter with a short warning about viruses, and advice on how to avoid them.

Viruses are small programs developed with a definite intention to cause damage to computer files or, at the very least, cause inconvenience and annoyance to computer users. You should not share or lend floppy disks that could introduce viruses into your system and care should be taken when downloading files from the Internet. Viruses are often sent as attachments to e-mails, so you should never open an attachment that you don't recognise. You will generally see a message similar to the one below when you attempt to open an e-mail attachment.

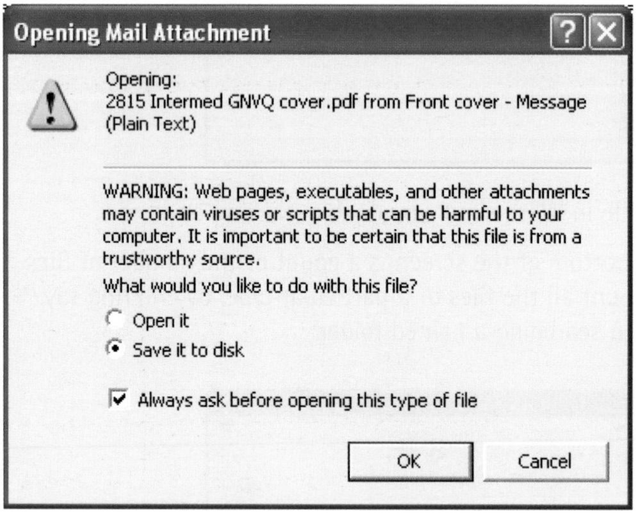

You should take precautions to avoid the potentially disastrous effects of viruses - like some or all of the files on your computer being wiped out.

Virus checkers should be installed on all computer systems so that they automatically check for any infected data when the computer is started up. Manual checkers can also be used to check for viruses on floppy disks, hard drives etc.

Typical anti-virus software enables you to specify which drives, folders or files you wish to scan and disinfects the file (i.e. removes the virus) if a virus is found. In this example drive A: (the floppy disk) is scanned.

- From the Start menu select the VirusScan software.
- Browse through your files and folders and select which drive, folder or file you wish to scan.

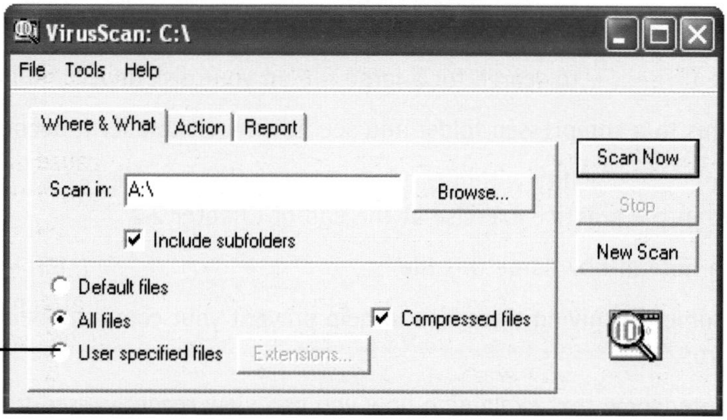

If you select this option you can choose files with a particular file extension

- Click Scan Now.

The software will check all the files on drive A: and report any problems in the bottom section of the window.

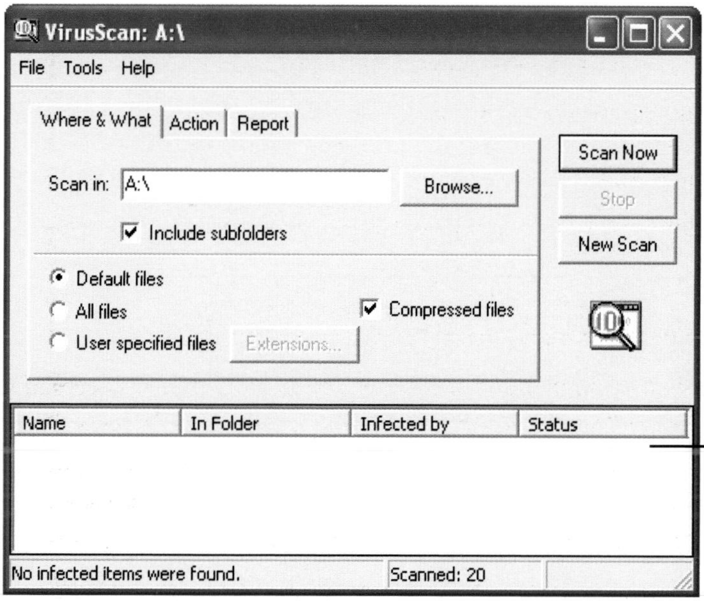

In this case no infected files were found

As new viruses are being discovered all the time the anti-virus software companies issue frequent updates. It is a good idea to install a package that provides an online update service which will send you a message to remind you to update which can then be done online.

Exercises

1. Use My Computer to search for a large file on your disk drive.
2. Send this to a compressed folder and see how much smaller it becomes.
3. Use the Search facility within My Computer to find the file Useful tips.doc you created in the practice exercise at the end of Chapter 2.2.
4. Make a note of how large this file is.
5. Enter some text giving three tips to help prevent your computer being infected by a virus.
6. Next enter some text explaining how you can view recently-used files.
7. Edit the document so that each section of text has an appropriate heading.
8. Save and print this file.
9. Use My Computer to check the size of this file after the extra text was added.

Managing the Desktop

CHAPTER 2.5

Creating and removing a desktop icon

You can create a shortcut on the desktop for any program so that you can open it quickly, instead of using the Start menu.

- From the Start menu select All Programs and find the Solitaire program as you did earlier.
- This time right-click the word Solitaire and move the mouse pointer over Send to.
- Click Desktop (create shortcut) from the menu.

A shortcut icon will appear on the desktop.

- Drag the icon into the position you want.
- Try opening the Solitaire program using your new shortcut icon. You can then close it again!
- Remove the shortcut by right-clicking it and selecting Delete. This removes the icon, not the program.

Tip:
You can also create a shortcut icon by pointing to the file name, holding the right mouse button down and dragging onto the desktop.

Creating a printer icon

It can be useful to have the default printer icon on your desktop so that you can check the print status of any job.

- From the Start menu select Settings, Printers and Faxes.

- Drag the default printer icon (the one with the tick mark against its name) onto the desktop.

Creating and using a file icon

If you are in the middle of writing a book, say, or a project which is likely to take a few weeks, it is useful to have the file icon on the desktop. You can then open the document in the correct software (e.g. Word or Excel) simply by clicking on the icon.

We'll try this with a document you created in Word.

- Use My Computer to navigate to a document, e.g. Sharon.doc. Drag the file name onto the desktop.

- Now double-click the icon. The document opens!

Basic system information

It is useful to be able to view basic information about the computer system you are using.

- From the Start menu, select Control Panel and then double-click System.
- Click the General tab.

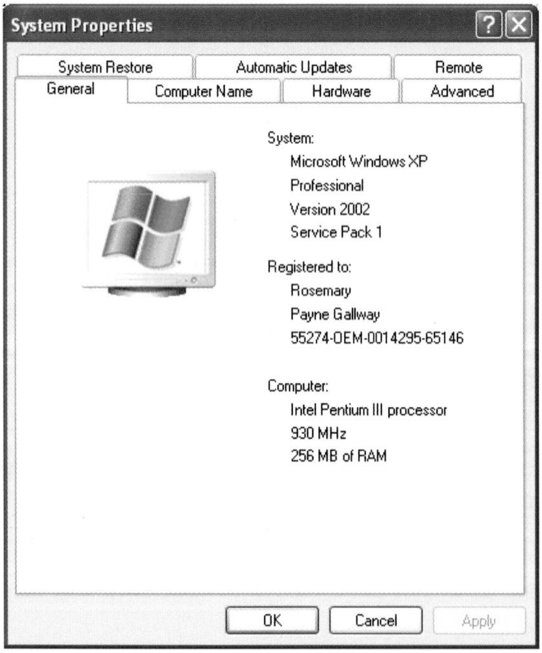

This tells you which operating system and version number you are using, e.g. Windows XP Professional version 2002, Service Pack 1. It also tells you which processor type is installed and its speed, e.g. Intel Pentium III (930MHz). Finally it tells you how much Random Access Memory is installed in the system, e.g. 256Mb of RAM.

This kind of information can be useful if you are reporting a fault on your computer, or want to check whether your computer has the recommended minimum amount of RAM to run a new software package.

Changing the background

If you don't like the desktop background you can easily change it.

- Right-click the mouse on the desktop picture.
- In the menu that appears left-click the Properties option.
- In the Display Options box that appears click on the Background tab.
- Scroll down the list and click on a background. You will see a preview of what it looks like.
- When you find one you like, click OK.

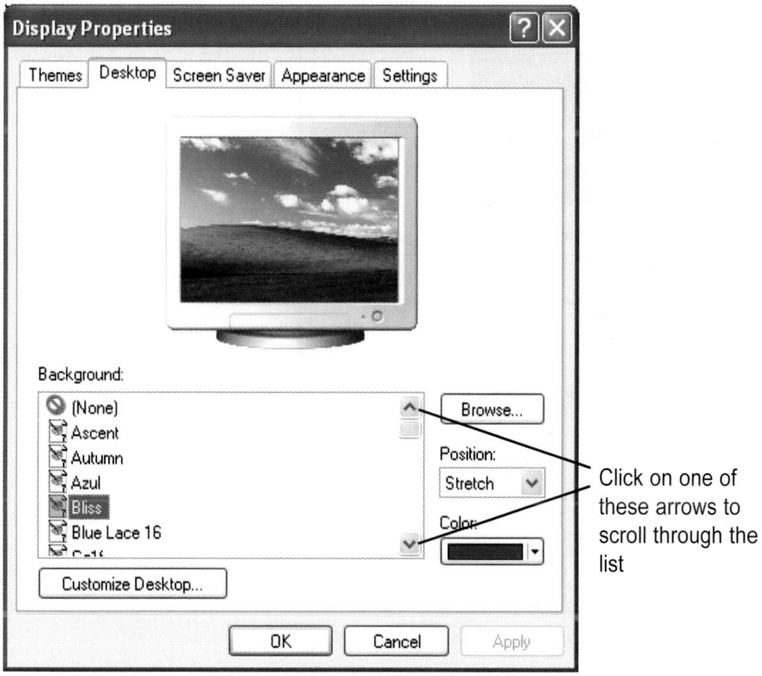

Tip:

To scroll up and down a list of items click on one of the arrows on the scroll bar.

Setting up a screen saver

A screen saver is a moving picture or pattern that appears on your screen when you have not used the mouse or keyboard for a specified period of time. As well as being interesting and entertaining these can help protect the screen from burn-out in particular spots.

- From the Start menu select Control Panel and then double-click Display.
- Click the Screen Saver tab.

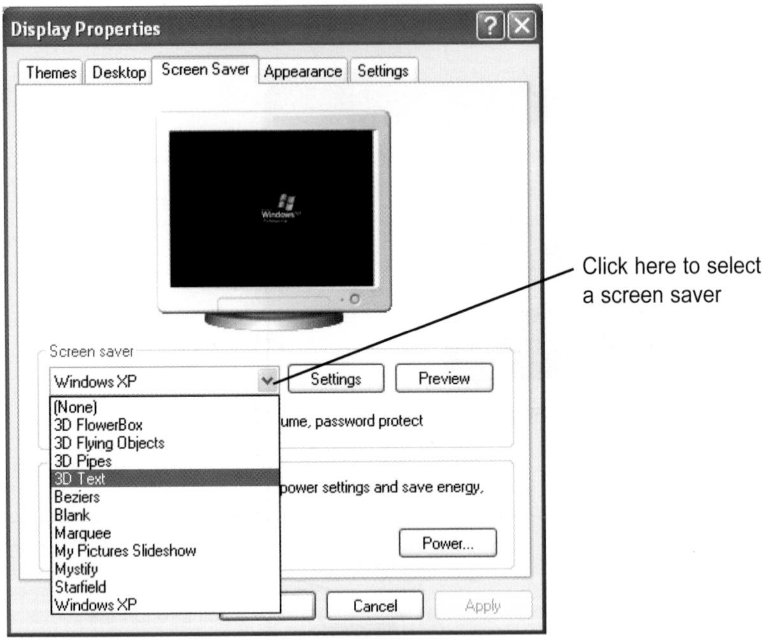

- Click the down-arrow to view a list of screen savers. Click the Preview button to see what the option you choose will look like.
- When you have decided on one, click Apply and OK.

Changing the screen resolution

Screen resolution is the setting that determines the amount of information that appears on your screen, measured in pixels. Low resolution, such as 640 x 480, makes items on the screen appear large and 'blocky'. High resolution, such as 1280 x 1024 makes individual items such as text and graphics appear small but clearly defined.

- From the Start menu select Control Panel and click on Display.
- Click the Settings tab.
- Drag the bar to change the resolution.

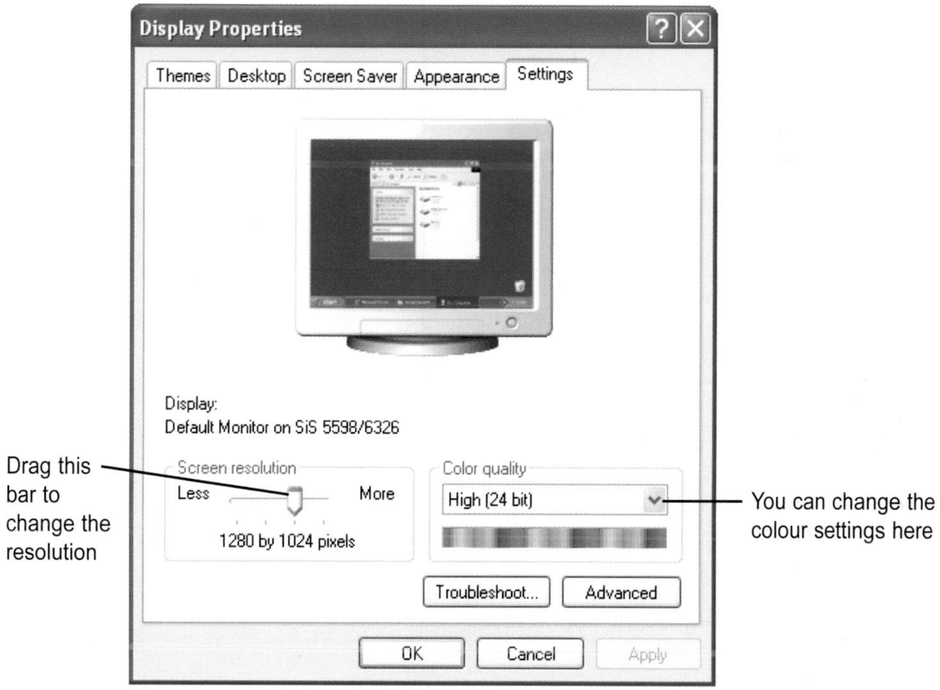

- Click the Apply button.

The screen will momentarily go black and then the dialogue box will be redisplayed.

- Click OK.

Other display settings

Using the Display Properties dialogue box Themes tab you can set up themes which comprise a background plus a set of sounds, icons and other elements to help you personalise your computer. If you click the Appearance tab you can change the appearance of fonts, windows and dialogue boxes.

Changing the computer's date and time

You shouldn't need to change the date and time as it should have been set up correctly for the correct time zone by the manufacturer. However if you do need to it's quite straightforward:

- From the Start menu, select Control Panel and then double-click Date and Time. Make any changes in this dialogue box and click OK.

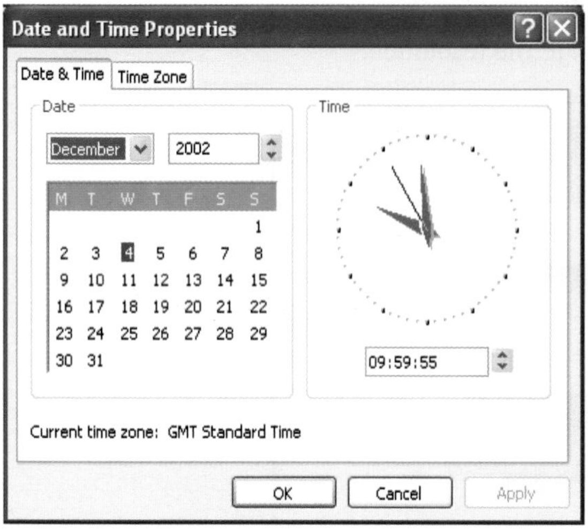

Change the volume settings

- From the Start menu, select Control Panel and then double-click Sounds and Audio Devices.
- Drag the bar to adjust the sound level.

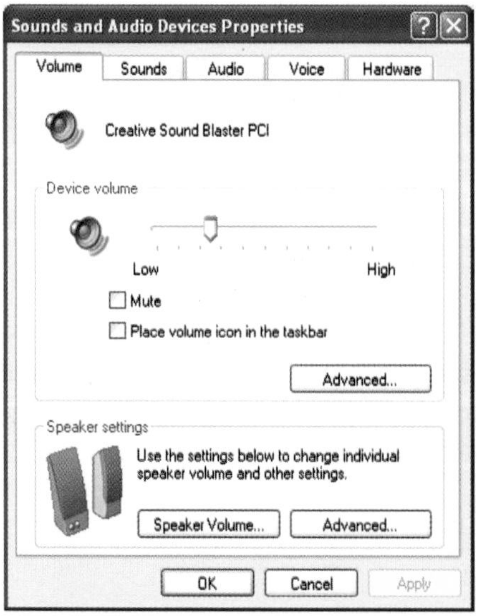

Change keyboard language

Your computer will have a language set as default, probably English (United Kingdom).

If you need to enter text in a different language you can add different keyboard layouts.

- From the Start menu select Control Panel, Regional and Language options.

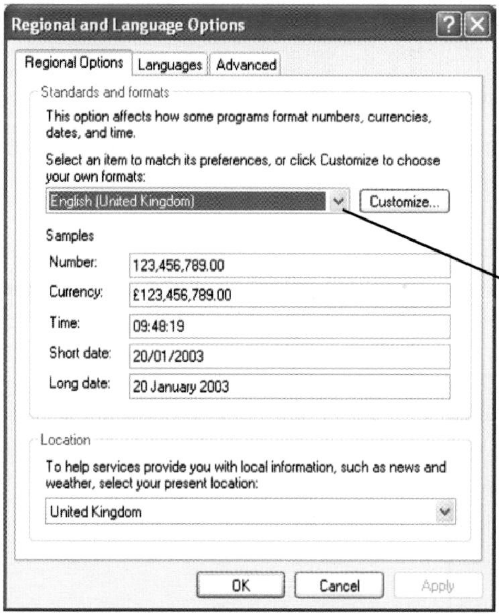

Change regional setting here e.g. English (US)

- Click the Languages tab.

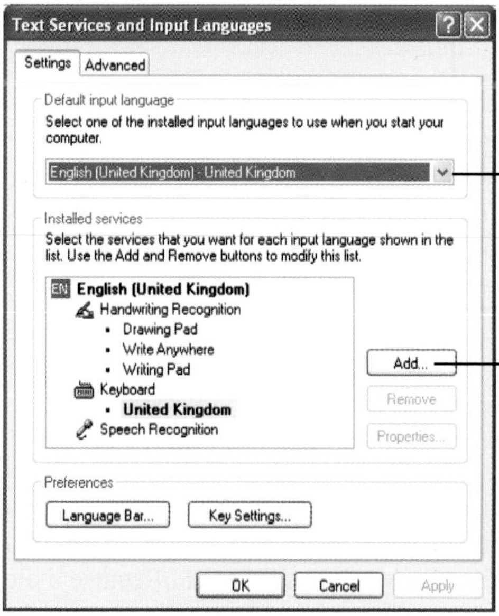

Select the language you wish to use

Click here to add another keyboard layout

Formatting a floppy disk or a zip disk

Most floppy disks and zip disks are pre-formatted when you buy them. However if you need to format one this is the procedure:

- Insert the disk into the floppy drive.
- From the Start menu select My Computer.
- Click the disk you want to format.
- From the File menu select Format.
- Click the Quick Format option and then click Start.

You will receive a message warning you that all the data on the disk will be erased and asking you if you want to continue.

- Click OK.

The formatting will begin and you will receive a message when it is complete.

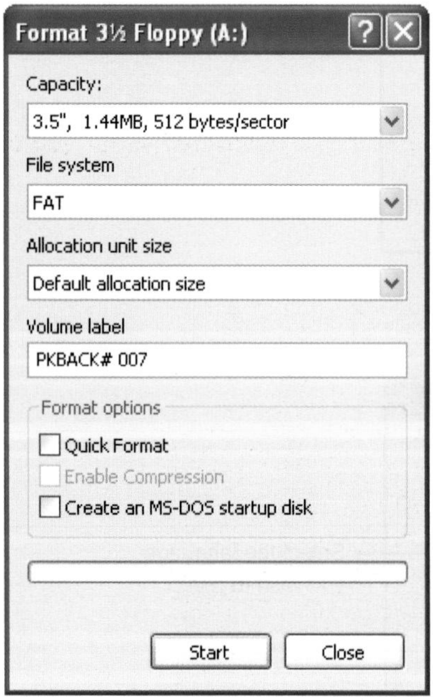

Installing/uninstalling a software application

Most application programs supplied on CD-ROM auto-run when the CD is inserted into the drive and on-screen instructions explain how to proceed. To remove an application program file, it must be uninstalled correctly. Some applications place an uninstall routine in the Start menu. Otherwise you should use the Add/Remove dialogue box in the control panel.

- From the Start menu select Settings, Control Panel, Add or Remove Programs.

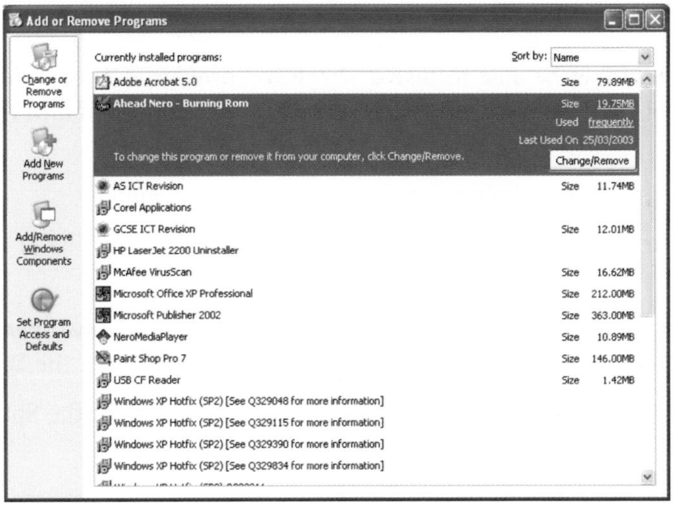

- Click on Change or Remove Programs to uninstall an application.
- Click on Add New Programs to install a new application.

The Windows Help and Support Centre

If you have problems with any of the tasks we have covered so far you can always visit the Windows Help and Support Centre.

- On the Start menu click Help and Support.

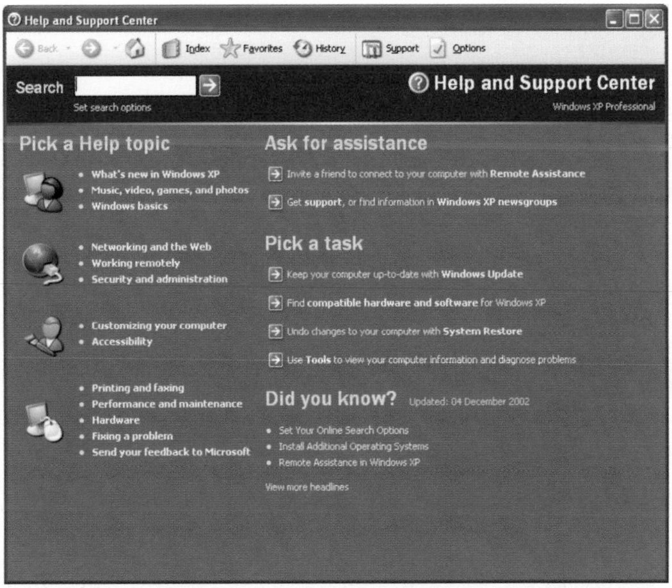

- You can either click on a Help topic or type a keyword into the Search box.

Each individual application that you run on your computer (e.g. a game, word processor, spreadsheet etc.) will have its own Help system too.

Print screen facility

Sometimes it is useful to be able to take a screenshot of what is on your screen and paste it into a document – just as the screenshots have been pasted into this document.

You can either capture the whole screen, or just the current window.

- Press the key labelled Prt Scr next to the F12 key on the top line of keys on the keyboard.

This copies a picture of the whole screen to the Clipboard. If you now open a new or existing Word document, you can paste it in by selecting Paste from the Edit menu.

To capture just the current window, press the Alt key (to the left of the Space bar) at the same time as pressing Prt Scr.

Tip:

You can see what has been copied to the Clipboard by selecting Edit, Office Clipboard in Word. This opens the Clipboard on the right-hand side of the screen. Click any item to paste.

Changing the default printer

The default printer is used when you click Print on the File menu of many Windows-based programs. To change the default printer:

- From the Start menu select Printers and Faxes.
- Right-click the printer you want to use as the default printer, and then click Set as Default Printer.

A check mark appears next to the printer icon in Printers and Faxes.

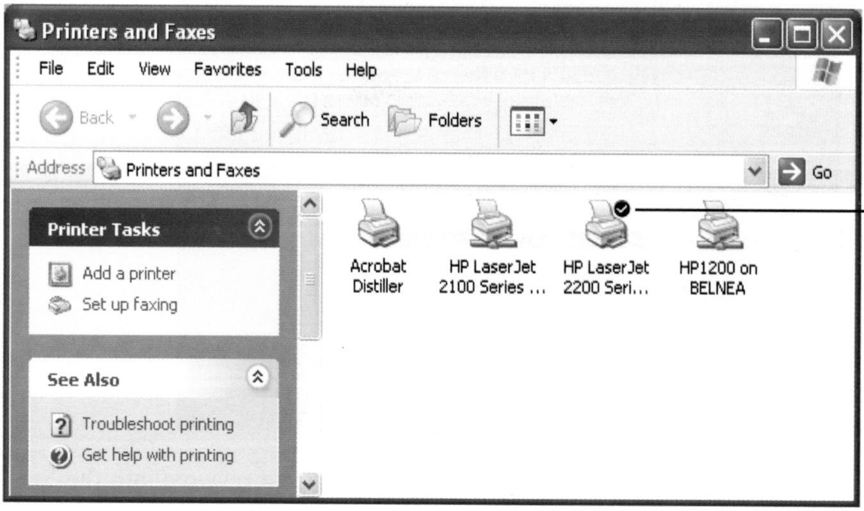

This check mark indicates the default printer

Installing a new printer

Most printers are now Plug and Play. This means that you can attach a new device to your computer and begin using it right away, without having to configure it or install additional software. If you are using an older printer it may be non-Plug and Play. In this case you should use the Add Printer wizard supplied with Windows XP.

- From the Start menu select Printers and Faxes.
- In the Printers and Faxes dialogue box, click Add a printer under Printer Tasks.

The Add Printer Wizard will be displayed.

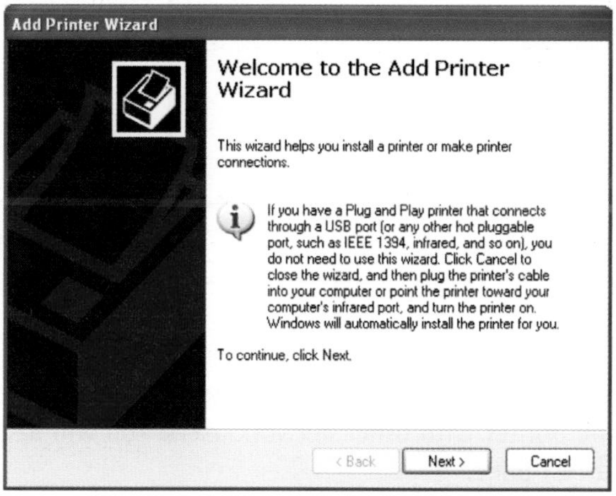

- Click on the Next button.
- On the following screen select whether you are installing a network printer or a local printer (i.e. directly connected to your PC).
- Click Next.
- Follow through the remaining stages of the wizard: you will be asked which printer port you want to use.

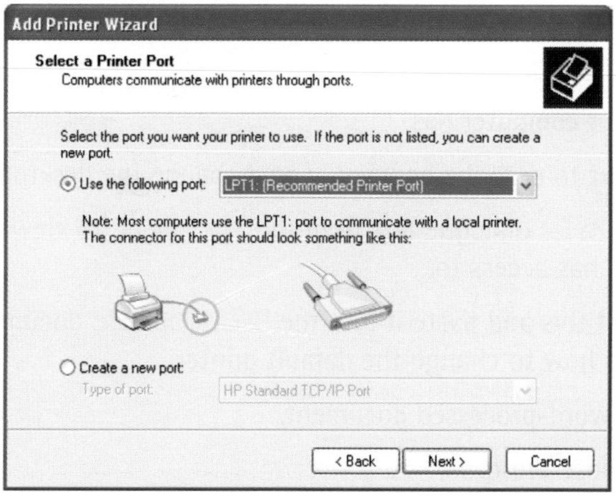

- Select a port and click Next.

You will then be asked for manufacturer and model of the printer:

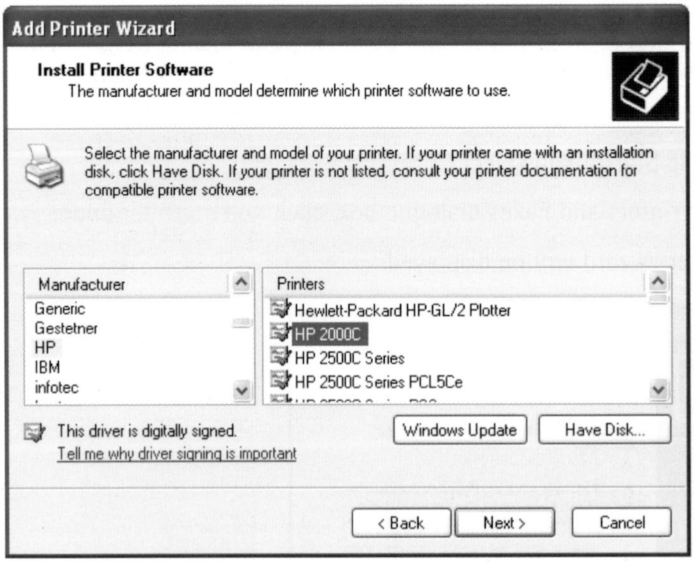

- Make your selection and click Next.
- On the next two screens assign a name to the printer and select whether or not you want to share the printer with other network users. You will also be given the option to print a test page.
- Click Finish on the final screen to complete the installation.

Exercises

1. Open My Computer and navigate to the file Useful tips.doc.
2. Create a shortcut to this document on the desktop.
3. Open the document using the shortcut icon.
4. Use My Computer to view the Basic System information about your computer.
5. In the Useful tips.doc document make a note of the type of processor and amount of RAM your computer has.
6. Now enter some text to describe how you would change the desktop background.
7. Open the Printer & Faxes dialogue box from the Start menu to view the printers that your computer has access to.
8. Take a screenshot of this and paste it into the Useful tips.doc document together with some notes on how to change the default printer.
9. Save and print the word-processed document.
10. Close the file and close Word.

Module 3

Word Processing

This module covers the basics of word processing. You will learn how to accomplish everyday tasks associated with creating, formatting and finishing small documents. You will learn how to:

- copy and move text within or between documents
- create standard tables
- use pictures and images within a document
- use mail merge tools
- print documents

Module 3 Table of Contents

CHAPTER 3.1

First Steps

For this module you will be using Microsoft Word, one of many word processing packages. Word 2003 has been used in this book but you should not have any problems following the instructions if you are using a different version of Word.

For some of the exercises you will need to use files that can be downloaded from our web site. To do this:

- Log on to the Payne-Gallway web site **www.payne-gallway.co.uk/ecdl**.
- Follow the instructions to download files when you need them. Save them in a convenient folder.

You're ready to start!

Loading Word

- Load **Microsoft Word**. You can do this in one of two ways:
- *Either* double-click the **Word** icon

- *Or* click **Start** at the bottom left of the screen. Click on **Programs**, then click

The opening screen

Your opening screen will look something like this:

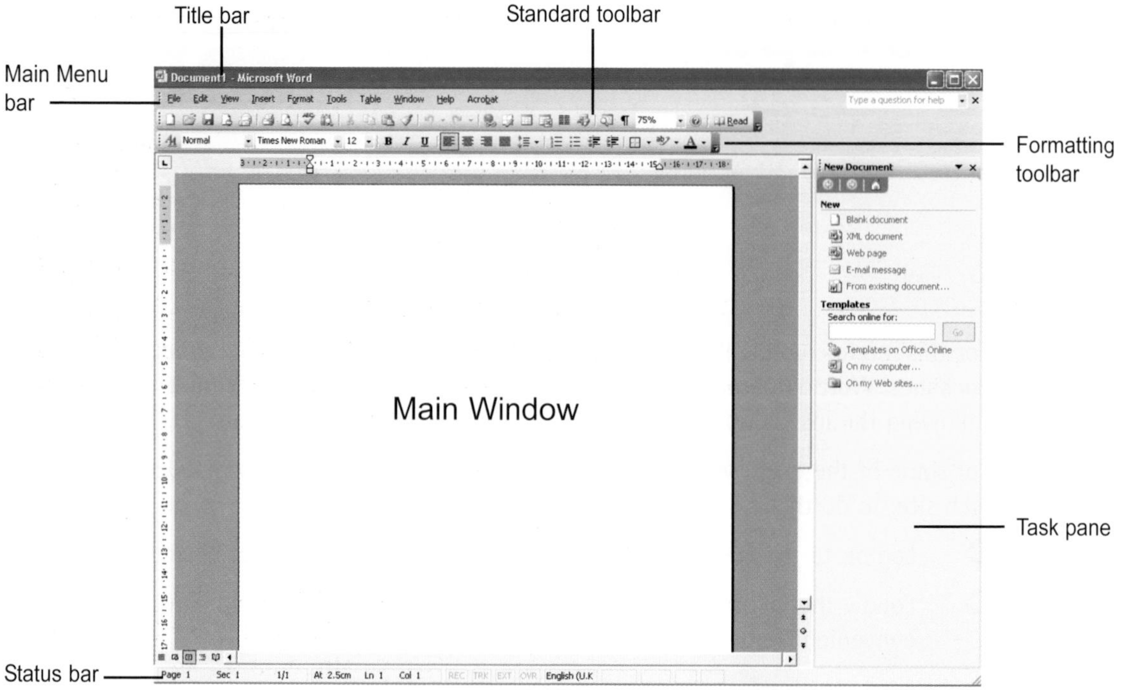

- The **Title bar** shows the name of your document, which might be, for example, a story or letter. If you have not given it a name yet, it will say **Document1** or perhaps **Document2** if this is your second document since you started **Microsoft Word** in this chapter.
- The **Main Menu bar** has options for you to choose from. You'll be using it when you need to edit, print or save your document.
- The **Standard toolbar** has a number of buttons with pictures called **icons** which are sometimes clicked instead of choosing from the main menu.
- The **Formatting toolbar** has icons which let you change the way your text looks – for example, making the letters bigger or smaller, bold or italic.
- The **Main Window** is the area of the screen in which you type.
- The **Status bar** shows what page you are on and how many pages there are in the document.
- The **Task pane** opens and closes automatically depending on what you are doing. You can close the Task pane at any time by clicking the **Close** icon (X) in its top right-hand corner.

The keyboard

Your keyboard will look like this:

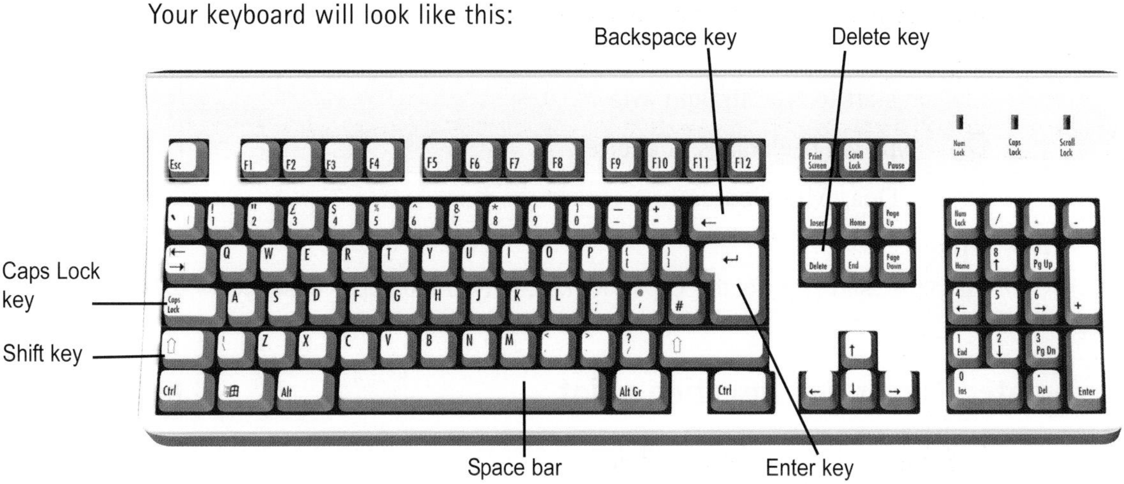

Some of the keys have been labelled on the diagram:

🛈 The **Shift** key. As long as you hold this down, all the letters you type will be in capitals.

🛈 The **Caps Lock** key. If you want a whole sentence to be in capitals, you can use the **Caps Lock** key. Just press it once and release it. All the letters you type after that will be capitals. Press **Caps Lock** again when you want to stop typing capitals.

🛈 The **Backspace** key. This deletes the letter to the left of where the cursor is flashing. If you are typing something and press a wrong letter, pressing **Backspace** will delete it and you can then type the right letter. Very useful!

🛈 The **Delete** key. This deletes the letter to the right of where the cursor is flashing. It is not as useful as the **Backspace** key for correcting mistakes that you make as you are going along, but you will find it comes in useful.

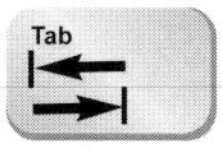

🛈 The **Tab** key – Use this to advance the cursor to the next tab stop.

🛈 The **Enter** key – Use this when you want to go to a new line.

Tip:

There are two **Enter** keys on the keyboard - one marked with a bent arrow and the other marked '**Enter**'. They both do exactly the same thing. People who are typing lists of numbers find it easier to use the key near the numbers, while those using the main part of the keyboard to type text would probably prefer the one near the letters.

Creating a new document

When you start Word, a new document automatically appears on the screen. You can see in the Title bar that it is called **Document1**.

You can start to type straight away.

- Type the beginnings of a letter:

  Dear Mrs Coates

Tip:
Use the **Shift** key, not the **Caps Lock** key, to type the upper case letters **D**, **M** and **C**.

The pointer, cursor and insertion point

As you move the mouse around, the pointer moves around the screen. The pointer looks different depending on where it is on the screen.

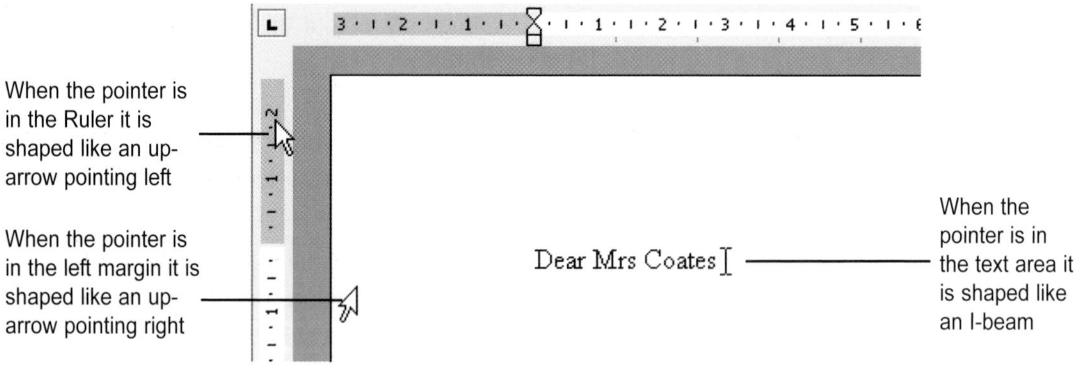

When the pointer is in the Ruler it is shaped like an up-arrow pointing left
When the pointer is in the left margin it is shaped like an up-arrow pointing right
Dear Mrs Coates
When the pointer is in the text area it is shaped like an I-beam

If you click in different places in and around your text, the flashing vertical line (called the **cursor**) appears in different places. It marks the **insertion point** – that is, the point at which text will be inserted when you start to type.

- Position the pointer at the end of the line. Take care that the pointer is the **I-beam** shape – not an arrow shape – before clicking.
- Press **Enter** twice. (Pressing **Enter** takes you to a new line, so pressing it twice will leave one blank line between paragraphs.)
- Type the following sentences. (Do not press **Enter** at the end of each line.) You should leave one space after a comma (but not before) and one or two spaces after a full-stop. Decide which you prefer and then stick to it!

> I am writing to invite you on a trip to Tanzania to see some of the current conservation work being sponsored by the Global Environment Association. You will be able to see first-hand the areas your money is reaching and the difference it can make.

You will notice that Word starts a new line automatically when it reaches the end of a line. You should only press **Enter** when you want to start a new paragraph.

Editing text

Now you can practise inserting and deleting text.

There are two 'editing modes' known as **Insert** and **Overtype**. The mode is controlled by pressing the **Insert** key on the keyboard. (It is just to the right of the **Backspace** key.) Try pressing this key once, and you will see that the letters **OVR** appear in the Status bar at the bottom of the screen. When you press the **Insert** key again, the letters **OVR** are greyed out, because the **Insert** key acts as a toggle.

In **Overtype** mode, when you click in your text to edit it, anything that you type will replace what is already there. In **Insert** mode, anything that you type is inserted into the text.

- Make sure that you are in **Insert** mode (the words **OVR** at the bottom of the screen should be greyed out. If they are not, press the **Insert** key once.)
- Place the cursor just after the **a** of **on a trip**, click to create an insertion point and type **n interesting**. The text should now read

  I am writing to invite you on an interesting trip …

You can alter text by highlighting it and then typing the new text. A single word can be highlighted by double-clicking it. To highlight longer pieces of text, click and hold the left mouse button while you drag across the text.

- Double-click **interesting** to select it. It should appear white on a black background.
- Type the word **exciting**. This will replace the selected word.

Tip:
When text is selected you don't have to delete it before typing over it.

- Place the cursor just after the **t** of **current** and click to create an insertion point. Press the **Backspace** key several times to delete the word **current**. Insert the word **currently** after **work**.
- Now click at the end of the sentence you have typed, and press **Enter** twice.
- Finish off the letter by typing

> With best regards
>
> Brian Harding
> Fundraising Executive

Your letter should now look like this:

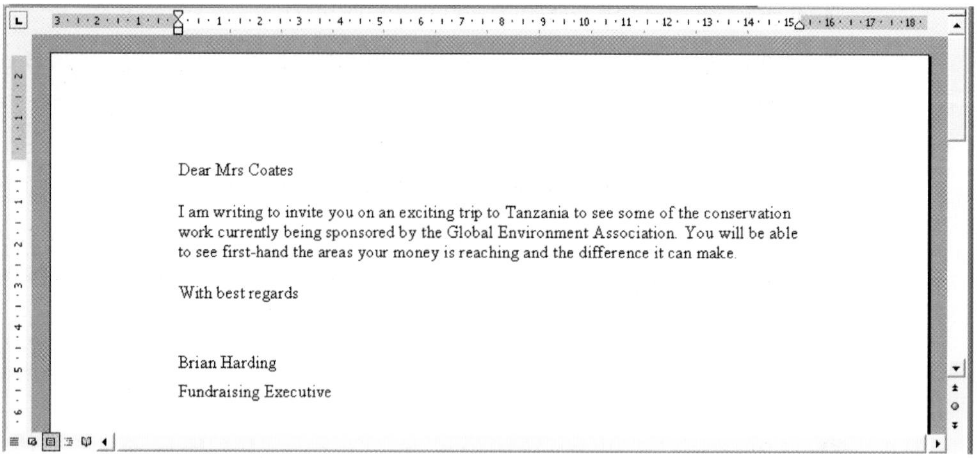

Dear Mrs Coates

I am writing to invite you on an exciting trip to Tanzania to see some of the conservation work currently being sponsored by the Global Environment Association. You will be able to see first-hand the areas your money is reaching and the difference it can make.

With best regards

Brian Harding

Fundraising Executive

Saving your work

If you want to keep your work, so that you are able to add to it or change it at any time, you must keep it safe in a **file** on a disk. (This is called **saving a file.**)

You can save files on the **hard disk** inside the computer, or on a **floppy disk** that you can insert into the floppy disk drive and take out when you have finished saving.

- Click **File, Save** on the Main Menu bar.

You'll see a screen rather like the one below. You will have different folders and subfolders from the ones shown.

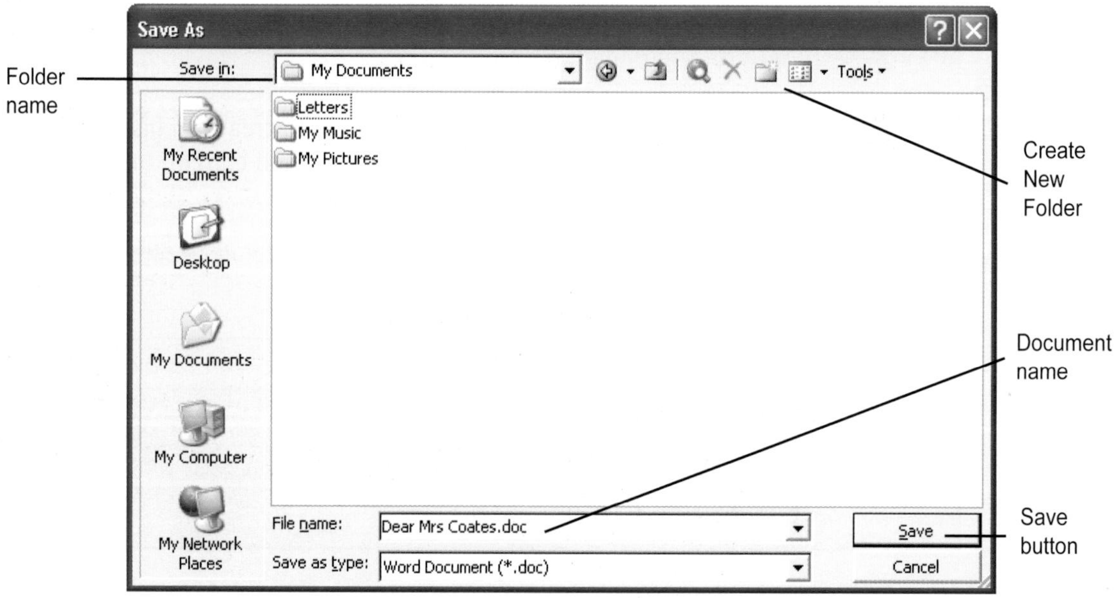

Word guesses a name for your file, which will be the first word or first few words you typed. The name appears in the **File name** box. The file name will be highlighted to show that it is selected ready for you to change it if you want to.

- Type a new file name. Choose a name that will remind you of what the file contains, like **TanzaniaLetter**.

Microsoft Word will add a full stop and the three letters **doc** to the name you choose. This shows that it is a document created using **Microsoft Word**.

You will be given the choice of which folder you wish to save your document in.

In the figure opposite, **Letters** is a subfolder of **My Documents**. If you want to create a subfolder in your own **My Documents** folder, click the **Create New Folder** button and then give your folder a suitable name.

To save in the **Letters** folder shown in the figure above:

- Double-click **Letters** to put it in the **Save in:** box.
- Leave the **Save as type:** box as **Word Document (*.doc)**. Before you click the **Save** button, read the next paragraph. Clicking **Save** saves your document and automatically closes the dialogue box.

Saving as another file type

By default your letter will be saved as a Word document, shown by the so-called **extension**, in this case **.doc**, at the end of the file name. If you click the down-arrow in the **Save as type:** box, you will see that you have the option of saving the file as another type.

- If you wanted to put this document on a web site, you would save it with the extension **.htm**.
- To save a document in **Rich Text Format**, select the extension **.rtf**. This is a useful format if you wish to transfer text between different word processing packages or versions without losing formatting information.
- To save the document as a text file with no formatting, which can be imported into another type of package, save it with the extension **.txt**.
- To save a document as a template (such as the customised fax template discussed in Chapter 3.4) save with the extension **.dot**.
- Scroll down to see other options. For example, you can save the document so that it can be read in an earlier version of Word.

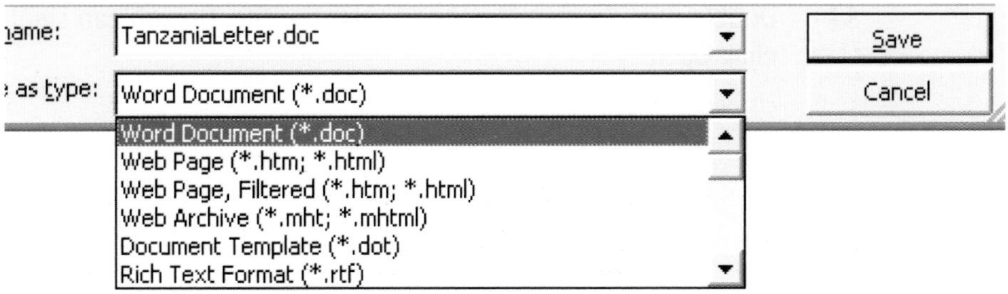

- You can also save a document with a software specific file extension (e.g. **.wps** for Works 2000), or in a format that can be read by a previous version of Word (e.g. Word 6.0).

- Now click **Save**. Close your document by selecting **File**, **Close** from the **Main Menu bar**.

Opening an existing document

You can open your document again any time to edit or print it.

- From the main menu select **File**.

You will see at the bottom of the menu a list of the most recently used documents.

- Click the file name **TanzaniaLetter**. Your document opens ready for you to work on.

- Now close the file again so that you can practise opening it a different way.

- From the menu select **File**, **Open**. You will see a window similar to the one below:

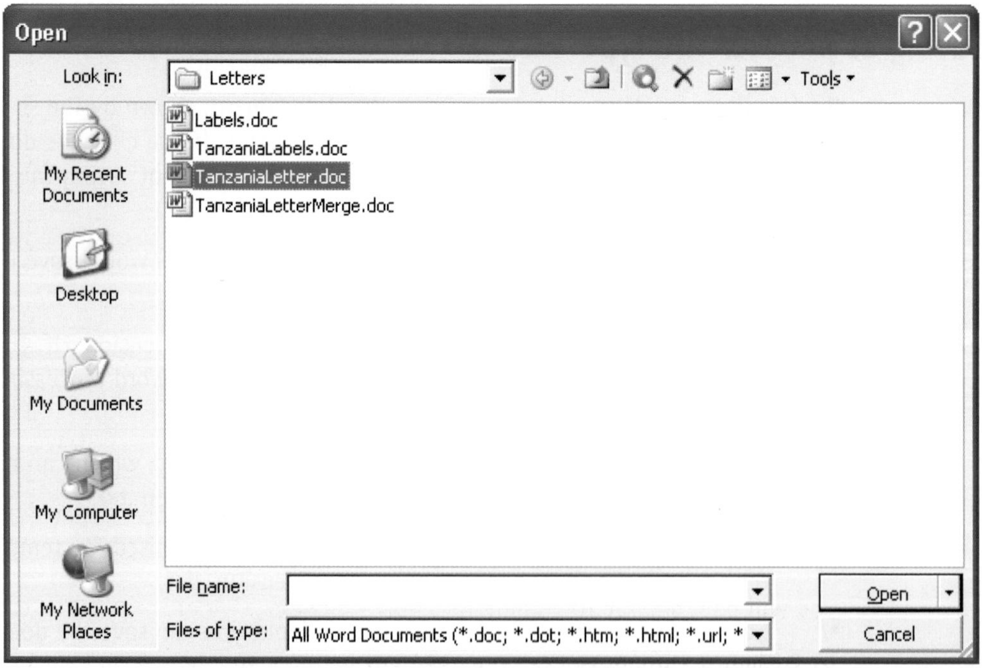

- Double-click **TanzaniaLetter** to open the file. Or, you can single-click it and then click **Open**.

Changing defaults and preferences

By default (i.e. unless you tell it otherwise) Word saves your documents in a folder called **My Documents** on the **C:** drive. You can change this default as well as many other preferences.

- From the main menu select **Tools, Options**.

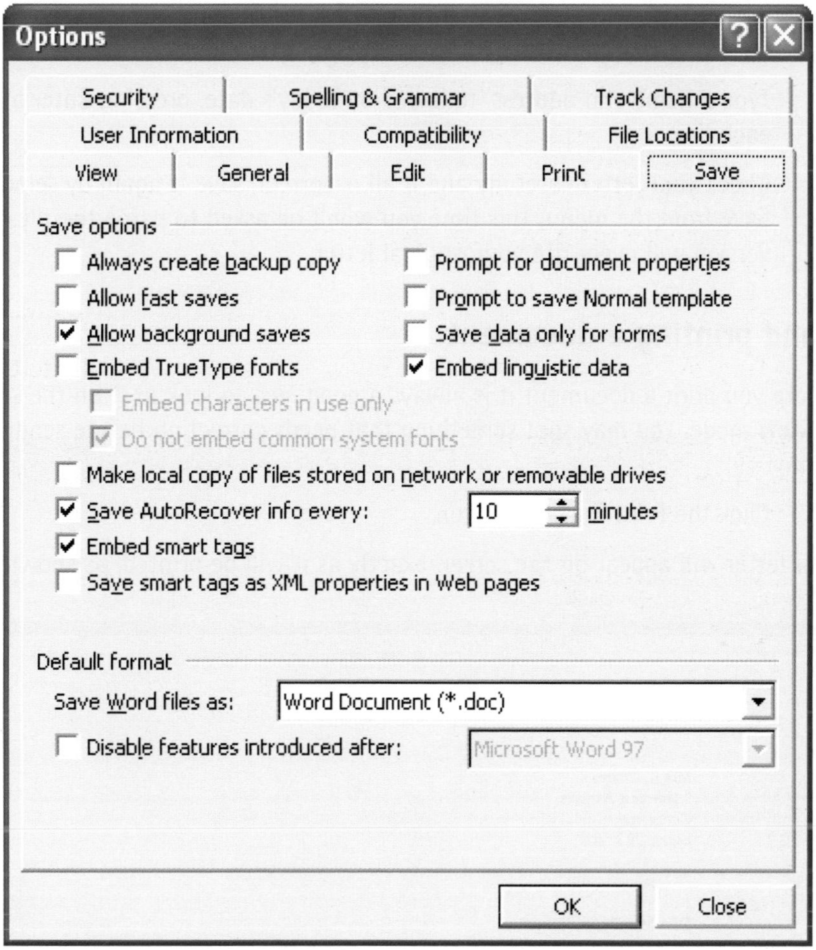

- Click the **File Locations** tab.

You will now be able to change the default directory for opening and saving files.

By clicking on the **Save** tab in the Options window, you can change various defaults such as how frequently your document is automatically saved.

Clicking on the **User information tab** will open a window which allows you to change the name of the author of documents you write. This name appears in a 'tip' as you hover over a file name in Windows Explorer or when opening a file.

Inserting a paragraph

You can insert the recipient's address and a date at the head of the letter. You can assume that the letter would be printed on headed stationery, so you need to leave some space at the top of the letter for this.

- Make sure the insertion point is at the top of the letter.
- Press **Enter** several times to give yourself some blank lines, and then press the **up-arrow** key to put the cursor on the new blank line.
- Type a name and address, followed by today's date, pressing **Enter** at the end of each line.
- Check your letter carefully and if all is correct, save it again by selecting **File**, **Save** from the menu. This time you won't be asked to name the file. The new version will overwrite your original letter.

Previewing and printing a document

Before you print a document it is always a good idea to look at it on the screen in **Print Preview** mode. You may spot something that needs correcting before sending it to the printer.

- Click the **Print Preview** button.

Your letter will appear on the screen exactly as it will be printed, as shown below:

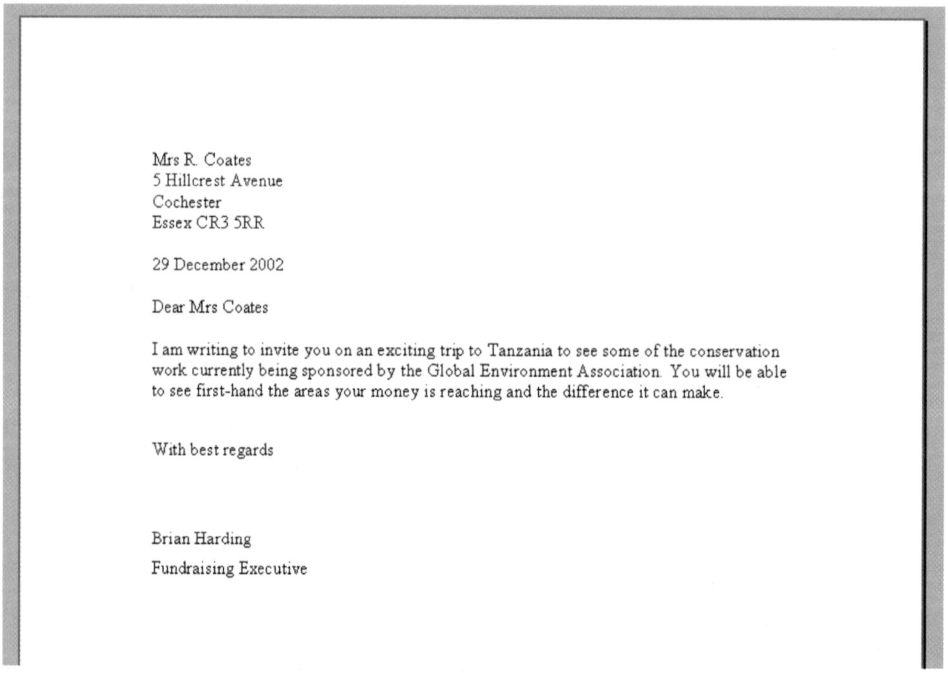

Mrs R. Coates
5 Hillcrest Avenue
Cochester
Essex CR3 5RR

29 December 2002

Dear Mrs Coates

I am writing to invite you on an exciting trip to Tanzania to see some of the conservation work currently being sponsored by the Global Environment Association. You will be able to see first-hand the areas your money is reaching and the difference it can make.

With best regards

Brian Harding

Fundraising Executive

If you need to make any further corrections, press **Esc** or click the **Close** button on the **Print Preview** menu bar to return to **Print Layout** view.

- When you have made any corrections, look at the document again in **Print Preview** mode, and then select **File**, **Print** from the menu bar. You will see the following window appear:

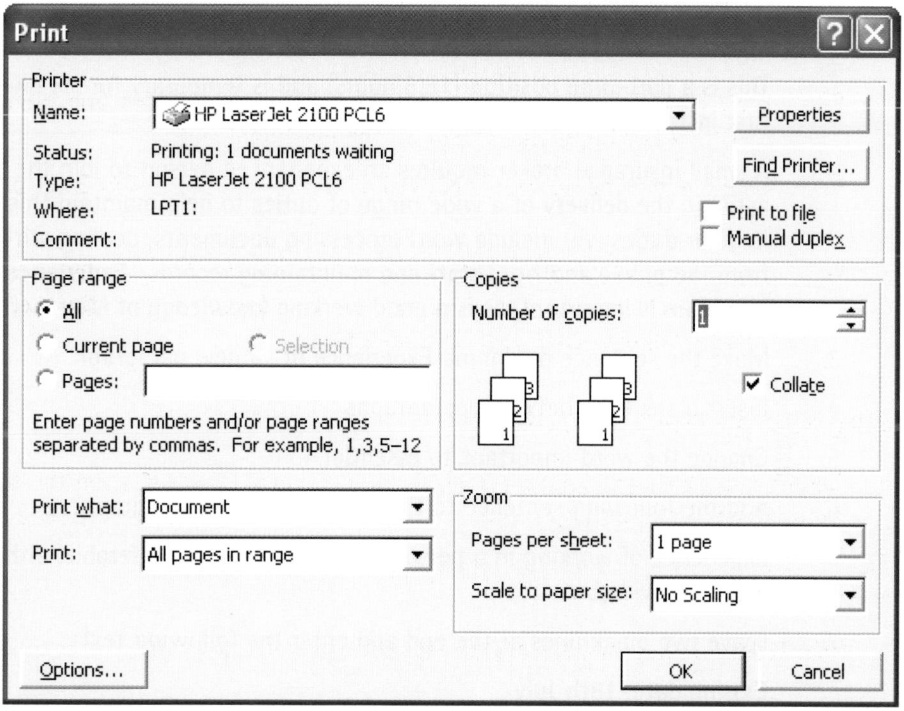

In this window you can select print options such as: print entire document, specified pages, specified number of copies, print a document to file, switch collation on or off.

You can also select which printer to send the output to. If you have no printer available, you can click the **Print to File** checkbox to send a Print File to, say, a floppy disk from where it can be printed later, perhaps on another computer attached to a printer.

- Make sure that your computer is connected to a printer, that the printer is turned on and that paper is loaded.
- Click **OK** to print the document.
- If all is well, select **File**, **Close** from the menu bar to close the document.

Closing Microsoft Word

There are several ways of closing **Word**.

- Click the **X** in the top right-hand corner.
- Click the **Word** icon in the top left-hand corner and from the dropdown menu select **Close**.
- From the **File** menu select **Exit**.

Exercise

You are preparing an advertisement for the local newspaper.

1. In a new Microsoft Word document enter a title **Clerical Assistant.**
2. Leave a blank line and then enter the following information:

   This is a part-time position (18.5 hours) and is temporary for six months in the first instance.

   A small insurance broker requires an experienced person to join the team and assist in the delivery of a wide range of duties to help maintain this busy office. Regular duties will include word processing documents; dealing with queries from the public and from staff and maintaining records. Experience of working in a team is important, as is a good working knowledge of Microsoft Office.
3. Make the sentence beginning **Experience of..** a new paragraph.
4. Insert blank lines between paragraphs.
5. Change the word **important** to **essential.**
6. Add the following sentence to the end of the third paragraph:

   Experience of working in a personnel environment is preferable, although training will be provided.
7. Leave two blank lines at the end and enter the following text:

   Closing date: 18th July

   Contact: Jane Hall on 01578 23455.
8. Delete the words **in the first instance** in the first paragraph.
9. Save the document as **Job advert.**

> Clerical Assistant
>
> This is a part-time position (18.5 hours) and is temporary for six months.
>
> A small insurance broker requires an experienced person to join the team and assist in the delivery of a wide range of duties to help maintain this busy office. Regular duties will include word processing documents; dealing with queries from the public and from staff and maintaining records.
>
> Experience of working in a team is essential, as is a good working knowledge of Microsoft Office. Experience of working in a personnel environment is preferable, although training will be provided.
>
> Closing date: 18th July
> Contact: Jane Hall on 01578 23455

Formatting

CHAPTER 3.2

In this chapter you will learn to improve the appearance of a document by formatting it.

The document that you will format may be downloaded from the web site **www.payne-gallway.co.uk/ecdl**. (See Page 3-3 for instructions how to do this.) It is called **Itinerary.doc**. You should save the document in a suitable folder.

Alternatively, you can type it yourself. The text is given below. You are to imagine that you work for an Environmental organisation called the Global Environment Association (GEA). You are preparing an itinerary for a visit to Tanzania of a group of Association members.

Itinerary
Day 1
Depart London Heathrow on British Airways flight
Day 2
Arrive at Dar es Salaam Airport. Our representative will meet and transfer the group to the hotel. The morning will be at leisure to rest after the overnight flight. After lunch our representative will meet and escort you to the GEA offices. The Country Representative, Dr Henry Ngowi, will give a presentation and brief you on the GEA projects in Tanzania.
Day 3
After breakfast your guide will meet you for the transfer to Mikumi Kiboga Camp.
Dinner and Overnight – Mikumi Kiboga Camp
Day 4
You will be met and escorted for an early morning game drive through the Mikumi Park.
Return to your accommodation for breakfast.
Following breakfast your guide will escort you on the transfer to Udzungwa Mountain National Park. Followed by an accompanied late afternoon walk in the forest
Day 5
The day includes trekking and sightseeing in the area.
After breakfast your guide will escort the group on a leisurely walk to Sanje Falls, with a chance to take a refreshing swim in the falls. A picnic lunch will be provided.

Saving with another name

- Open **Word** if it is not already open.
- If you have saved the downloaded document **Itinerary.doc** in your own folder, click **File**, **Open** and open the document now.
- If you have not downloaded and saved the document, you can either do so now, or type it in as shown on the previous page.

When you click the **Save** icon or use the **Save** command from the **File** menu, your document will automatically be saved using the same file name as the one that you have previously used when saving it. If you want to keep the original copy safe and save a second version of the file, you should use the **File**, **Save As**. command, which allows you to save the document using a different name to the same or a new folder.

- From the menu bar select **File**, **Save As** to save the document as **NewItinerary.doc**.

Fonts

Font is an alternative word for **typeface**. Both words describe the actual shape of the letters that appear on the screen when you are typing. Fonts have different names like **Times New Roman**, **Arial**, and **Comic Sans MS**.

Types of font

There are two basic types of font, called **Serif** and **Sans Serif**. A serif is the little tail at the top and bottom of each letter.

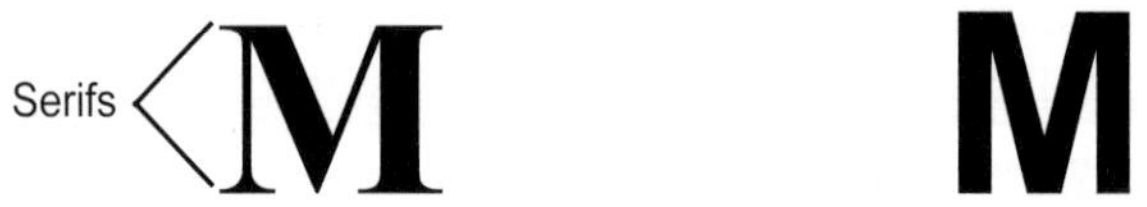

This is written in a Serif font called Times New Roman

This is written in a Sans Serif font called Arial

Taken from the French for '**without Serif**', **Sans Serif** fonts are very clear and are used in places where text needs to be clear and easy to read, such as road signs and textbooks.

Serif fonts are more often used for large amounts of text that will be read quickly, such as in newspapers or books. The serifs 'lead your eye' from one word to the next.

You should not use too many different fonts on a page – it can end up looking a mess.

Font sizes

Font sizes are measured in **points**. 6 point is about the smallest font you can read without the aid of a magnifying glass.

This is 6 point Times New Roman

This is 12 point Times New Roman

This is 24 point Times New Roman

Applying an existing style to a word, line or paragraph

Look at the formatting toolbar. The name and size of the default font are shown in the Style box - this is the font that **Microsoft Word** will choose for you automatically, before you change it to whatever you wish.

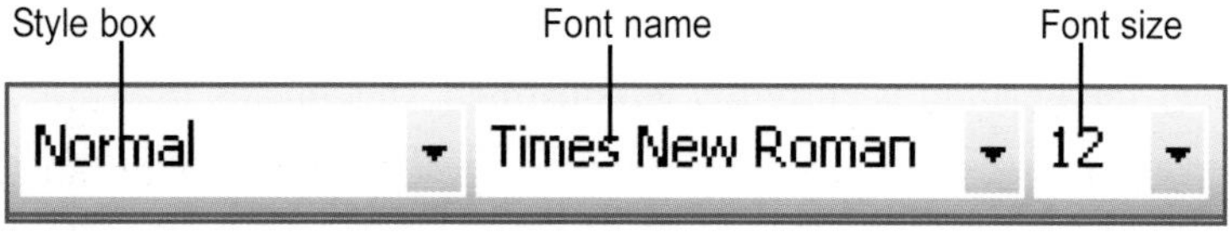

You can use the Style box to apply different built-in styles to different parts of a document.

- Click the word **Itinerary**.
- Click the down-arrow in the **Style** box.
- Click the **Heading 1** style. The style of the heading will change.
- Now select the second line, **Day 1**. Click the down-arrow in the **Style** box and select the **Heading 2** style.
- Select the next paragraph and change the style to **Normal**.

Changing font and font size

We will start by changing the font and size of the heading. To change the character formatting of a single word, it is not necessary to select the whole word. It is sufficient to click anywhere in the word.

- Click in the title **Itinerary**.
- On the Formatting toolbar, click the down-arrow beside the Font box and change the font to **Arial** if it is not already in this font.
- Click the down-arrow beside the **Font Size** box and select Font Size **24**.

Text alignment and emboldening

You can centre the heading and make it bold, using buttons on the Formatting toolbar.

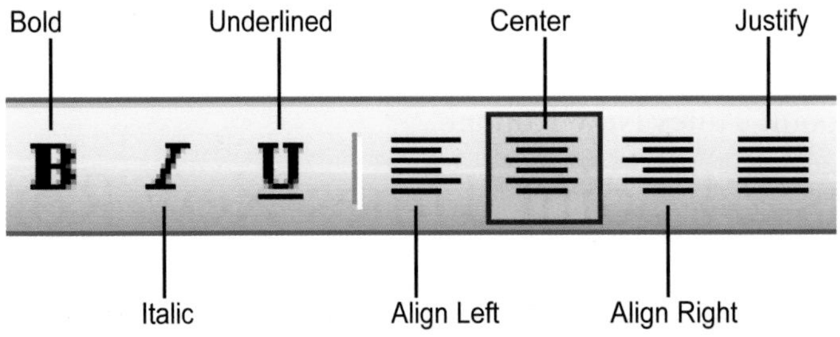

- With the cursor still somewhere in the heading, click the **Center** button. It will look pressed in when **selected** – as in the picture above.
- Click the **Bold** button to make the heading bold. Now make it underlined and italic as well.

The text under the heading is currently **left-justified**. This means that it is all lined up against the left-hand margin, and the text does not make a straight edge against the right-hand margin. You can make it do so by **justifying** the text.

- Select all the text except the title by dragging the mouse across it with the left button held down.
- Click the **Justify** button.

You can experiment with the other alignment buttons to see what the text looks like when it is centred or right-aligned.

The Undo and Redo commands

You can use the **Undo** button to undo the last action. Clicking **Undo** 3 times, for example, will undo the last 3 actions.

Click the **Redo** button to redo the last action that you undid.

Return to justified text when you are satisfied you know what each of these buttons does.

Tip:
If you are unsure as to what any toolbar button does, simply move the pointer over it and a tip will appear informing you of its function.

Setting text colours

To change the colour of text, you must first select the text and then click the **Font Color** button.

- Select the title **Itinerary** and click the down-arrow next to the **Font Color** button.
- Select the red colour.
- Click in the left margin beside **Day 1** to select the line.
- With the heading selected, click the **Font Color** button and select blue from the colour palette which appears.

Now you can make the other headings for Day 2, Day 3 etc the same blue. To do this we will practise using the **Repeat** command.

- Select the heading **Day 2**.
- From the **Edit** menu select **Repeat Font Color**.
- Do this again for each of the other **Day** headings.

Applying case changes and other formats

You can apply formatting or case changes (e.g. make all letters uppercase) to any selected text using the **Format** command from the menu bar.

Suppose you wanted to change the case of the words **Day 1**.

- Select the text **Day 1**.
- From the **Format** menu select **Change Case**.

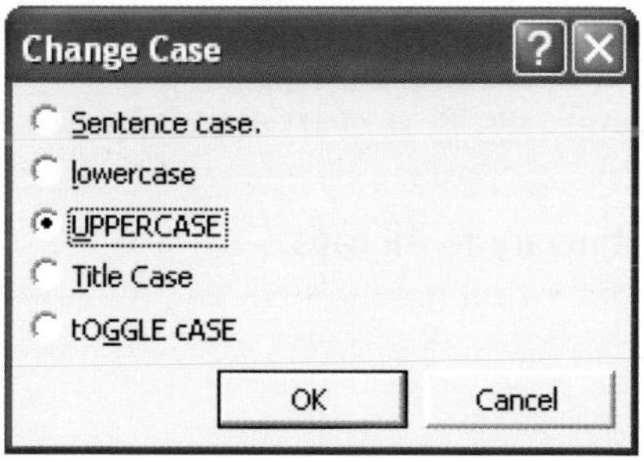

- In the Change Case dialogue box, click the case you want to apply to the text. Try selecting the option **UPPERCASE** and click **OK**.
- It looked better in Sentence case, so click the **Undo** button.

Now suppose you want to give the heading **Itinerary** a double underline.

- Select the word **Itinerary**.

- From the **Format** menu select **Font**.

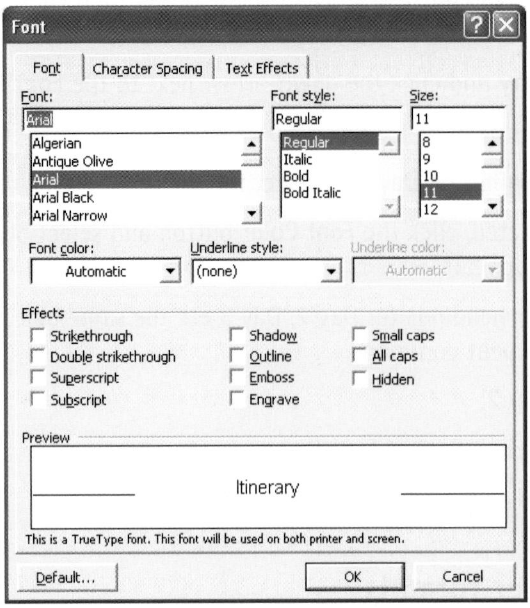

- In the **Underline Style** box choose a double underline. Click **OK**.
- You can either leave this format or Undo it by clicking the **Undo** button.

Note:

There are options in this window for applying all kinds of formatting such as **bold**, **italic**, **underline**, **superscript**, **subscript**, **small caps**, **all caps** to text. Try out these effects so that you know what they all do.

Text ^{superscript} **Text** $_{\text{subscript}}$

THIS IS TEXT IN SMALL CAPS... and THIS IS TEXT IN ALL CAPS

- Change the case of the heading **Itinerary** to **All caps**.

Changing line spacing

The document looks rather cramped and needs to be spaced out. One way of spacing out the text would be to insert a blank line between paragraphs.

- Insert a blank line under the title **Itinerary** by clicking at the end of the line and pressing **Enter**.

You can double-space all the text. This is very useful when you are creating a draft of a document which will be checked and edited by someone else, as it allows space for corrections to be made by hand on the printed document. We'll try it now.

- Select all the text under the title.
- From the **Format** menu, select **Paragraph**. The following window appears:

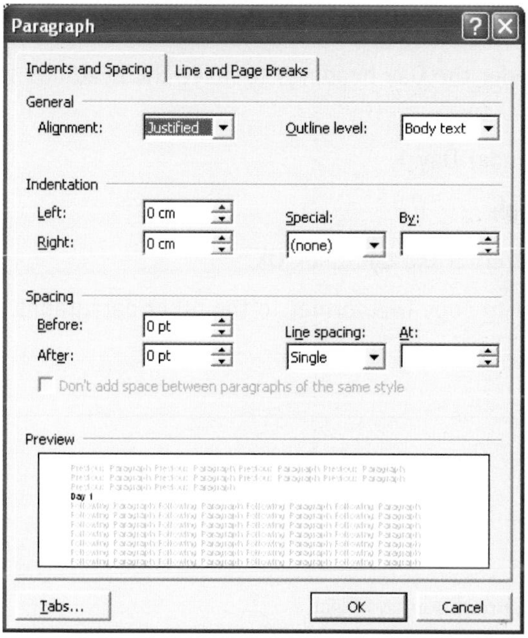

- In the **Line Spacing** box, select **Double**. Click **OK**.
- Examine the effect on the text. It is not quite what we want here, so click the **Undo** button to restore it to how it was.

We will try an alternative, which is to put some space before each of the 'Day' headings.

- Select the heading **Day 1**. Then select **Format**, **Paragraph** again.
- In **Spacing**, **Before** click the up-arrow to select **6 pt** and click **OK**.
- Make this heading **Bold** and **Italic**.

Copying a format

You can now copy this format to other paragraphs using the **Format Painter**. To use this tool once, you select the text whose format you wish to copy, and then you select the text you want to copy the format onto. Try it like this:

- With **Day 1** selected, click the **Format Painter** button once.
- Select the heading **Day 2**. Both the character formatting (Italic) and paragraph format (6pt spacing) is copied to **Day 2**.

To copy the same format to several different bits of text, you must first select the text whose format you wish to copy, then double-click the format painter. Then you can select as many bits of text as you like. Try it now:

- With either **Day 1** or **Day 2** selected, double-click the **Format Painter** button.
- Select **Day 3**, **Day 4** and **Day 5** in turn to change the formatting of these lines. Then click the **Format Painter** button again to turn it off.

Indenting paragraphs

We can indent all the text under the Day headings to make the headings stand out more.

- Select the paragraph under **Day 1**.
- Select **Format, Paragraph**.
- Under **Indentation, Left** enter **0.5 cm**. Click **OK**.
- Use the **Format Painter** to copy this format to the other paragraphs.

Your text should now look like this:

> # ITINERARY
>
> *Day 1*
>
> Depart London Heathrow on British Airways flight
>
> *Day 2*
>
> Arrive at Dar es Salaam Airport. Our representative will meet and transfer the group to the hotel. The morning will be at leisure to rest after the overnight flight. After lunch our representative will meet and escort you to the GEA offices. The Country Representative, Dr David Moshi, will give a presentation and brief you on the GEA projects in Tanzania.
>
> *Day 3*
>
> After breakfast your guide will meet you for the transfer to Mikumi Kiboga Camp.
> Dinner and Overnight – Mikumi Kiboga Camp
>
> *Day 4*
>
> You will be met and escorted for an early morning game drive through the Mikumi Park.
> Return to your accommodation for breakfast.
> Following breakfast your guide will escort you on the transfer to Udzungwa Mountain National Park. Followed by an accompanied late afternoon walk in the forest.
>
> *Day 5*
>
> The day includes trekking and sightseeing in the area.
> After breakfast your guide will escort the group on a leisurely walk to Sanje Falls, with a chance to take a refreshing swim in the falls. A picnic lunch will be provided.

- Save and close your document.
- If you are finished for now, exit **Word**.

Exercise

In this exercise you will format the job advertisement you created in the exercise at the end of Chapter 3.1.

1. Open the file **Job advert.doc**. Save the file as **Job advert1.doc**.
2. Format the heading **Clerical Assistant** to size 18, Times New Roman, bold.
3. Now format the heading dark blue and double-underlined.
4. Delete the blank lines between paragraphs.
5. Insert spacing of 6pt before the first four paragraphs.
6. Insert the following text in on a line beneath the main heading:

   Ipswich £12k-£13.5k pro rata
7. Format this text Times New Roman, bold, size 12, dark blue and right-aligned.
8. Format the word **essential** in the third paragraph italic and bold.
9. Insert a superscript number **1** after the word **hours** in the first sentence.
10. Insert the following text on a new line at the end of the advert.

    [1]hours per week
11. Finally indent all paragraphs by 1cm on the left and 2cm on the right.
12. Save your work. It should look something like this:

Clerical Assistant

Ipswich £12k-£13.5k pro rata

This is a part-time position (18.5 hours[1]) and is temporary for six months.

A small insurance broker requires an experienced person to join the team and assist in the delivery of a wide range of duties to help maintain this busy office. Regular duties will include word processing documents; dealing with queries from the public and from staff and maintaining records.

Experience of working in a team is ***essential***, as is a good working knowledge of Microsoft Office. Experience of working in a personnel environment is preferable, although training will be provided.

Closing date: 18th July
Contact: Jane Hall on 01578 23455
[1]hours per week

CHAPTER 3.3 Basic Operations

In this chapter you will be learning how to perform basic operations such as selecting, copying and pasting text. You will also learn how to display or hide toolbars, and how to select print options.

- Load **Word**. A new blank document should appear on your screen. If you already have Word running, you can click the **New Blank Document** button to start a new document.

Type the first five lines of the first verse from **Old MacDonald**. Remember to press **Enter** at the end of each line.

> Old MacDonald
>
> Old MacDonald had a farm, E-I-E-I-O
> And on his farm he had a cow, E-I-E-I-O
> With a "moo-moo" here and a "moo-moo" there
> Here a "moo" there a "moo"
> Everywhere a "moo-moo"

Tip:
Use the double-quote marks above the 2 on the keyboard. "Straight quotes" will be replaced with "smart quotes" (i.e. opening and closing quotes) if the options are set to do this under **Tools**, **AutoCorrect Options**, **AutoFormat**.

Selecting text

There are many different ways of selecting text. It is well worth getting to know them. You have already practised selecting text by holding down the left mouse button and dragging across the text. This method applies to any amount of text, from a single character to a whole document, but some quicker ways are described as follows.

When selected, black text shows up white on a black background.

To select a word:

Double-click anywhere in the word.

To select one or more lines:

Click in the left margin beside the line to select a line. Drag down the left margin to select several lines.

To select a sentence:

Hold down **Crtl** and then click anywhere in the sentence.

To select a paragraph:

Triple-click anywhere in the paragraph.

To select an entire document:

From the **Edit** menu choose **Select All**. Or, you can use the shortcut key combination **Ctrl-A**.

To select a large block of text:

Click the mouse at the beginning of the text you want to select. Then scroll to the end of the text and hold down **Shift** while you click again.

To select non-adjacent text:

Select the first bit of text, then hold down **Ctrl** while you select another piece of text.

> **Tip:**
> If you want to apply a format such as **Bold** to a word, you do not have to select it first. Just click anywhere in the word and then click the **Bold** button.

You can try out some of these techniques on the text you have just typed:

- Select all the text and change the font to **Comic Sans MS, Bold,** size **13.5**.
- Select the heading and make it size **18**.
- Select both the occurrences of **E-I-E-I-O**. Then make this text blue.

Copying text

The last line of the verse is a repetition of the first line.

You are going to use the **Copy** and **Paste** buttons to save yourself the trouble of having to write out the same line again.

- Select the line **Old MacDonald had a farm, E-I-E-I-O** by clicking in the left-hand margin next to the line.

- Click the **Copy** button on the **Standard toolbar**.
- Press **Enter** after the last line.
- Click at the beginning of the new blank line.

- Click the **Paste** button.

The line will be copied into the text.

Tip:
You will see an icon which looks like the **Paste** button appearing under your text. This is called a **smart tag**. It allows you to change the formatting of the text you have copied.

- Now type in the first five lines of the next two verses, leaving a blank line between each verse.
- Use the **Format Painter** to copy the formatting - make each E-I-E-I-O blue.

Old MacDonald had a farm, E-I-E-I-O
And on his farm he had a horse, E-I-E-I-O
With a "neigh, neigh" here and a "neigh, neigh" there
Here a "neigh" there a "neigh"
Everywhere a "neigh, neigh"

Old MacDonald had a farm, E-I-E-I-O
And on his farm he had a pig, E-I-E-I-O
With a (snort) here and a (snort) there
Here a (snort) there a (snort)
Everywhere a (snort)

Cutting and pasting

Suppose we've made a mistake and Old MacDonald had a pig *before* he had a horse!

We can move the third verse back to become the second verse using the **Cut** button.

- Select the verse you have just typed (about the pig) by clicking in the margin to its left and dragging down.
- Click on the **Cut** button on the Standard toolbar. The selected text will disappear, but it is not lost completely: It is being stored for you.
- Now click immediately before the first line in the second verse (about the horse) and click the **Paste** button. The verse is now pasted from the clipboard into the text exactly where you want it.
- Press **Enter** after your pasted verse if you need to insert another blank line.

Cutting and pasting is very useful when you are writing your own text and want to move things around.

You have been using buttons from the Standard toolbar to **Cut**, **Copy** and **Paste**. However, if you prefer, you can use these other ways:

1. Click **Edit**, followed by **Cut**, **Copy** or **Paste** from the **Main Menu** bar.
2. Use the keyboard: for **Cut**, press **Ctrl-X**, for copy, press **Ctrl-C**, for **Paste**, press **Ctrl-V** (i.e. Keep **Ctrl** pressed down while you press the letter on the keyboard).

- Now use the **Copy** and **Paste** buttons again to duplicate the parts of the rhyme that repeat (i.e. lines 3-5 from each verse and the last line). The completed rhyme should look something like this:

> **Old MacDonald**
>
> Old MacDonald had a farm, E-I-E-I-O
> And on his farm he had a cow, E-I-E-I-O
> With a "moo-moo" here and a "moo-moo" there
> Here a "moo" there a "moo"
> Everywhere a "moo-moo"
> Old MacDonald had a farm, E-I-E-I-O
>
> Old MacDonald had a farm, E-I-E-I-O
> And on his farm he had a pig, E-I-E-I-O
> With a (snort) here and a (snort) there
> Here a (snort) there a (snort)
> Everywhere a (snort)
> With a "moo-moo" here and a "moo-moo" there
> Here a "moo" there a "moo"
> Everywhere a "moo-moo"
> Old MacDonald had a farm, E-I-E-I-O
>
> Old MacDonald had a farm, E-I-E-I-O
> And on his farm he had a horse, E-I-E-I-O
> With a "neigh, neigh" here and a "neigh, neigh" there
> Here a "neigh" there a "neigh"
> Everywhere a "neigh, neigh"
> With a (snort) here and a (snort) there
> Here a (snort) there a (snort)
> Everywhere a (snort)
> With a "moo-moo" here and a "moo-moo" there
> Here a "moo" there a "moo"
> Everywhere a "moo-moo"
> Old MacDonald had a farm, E-I-E-I-O

Finding and replacing text

Suppose that after completing your lyrics, you decide that you would prefer the pig in the rhyme to **grunt** rather than **snort**.

As you can see this word appears many times and you need a quick way of changing each occurrence.

- Click at the start of the first line.

- From the Main Menu bar, select **Edit** then **Replace** (or press **Ctrl-H** on the keyboard).

You will see a dialogue box and you can type the word or phrase you want to replace, and the word or phrase to replace it with.

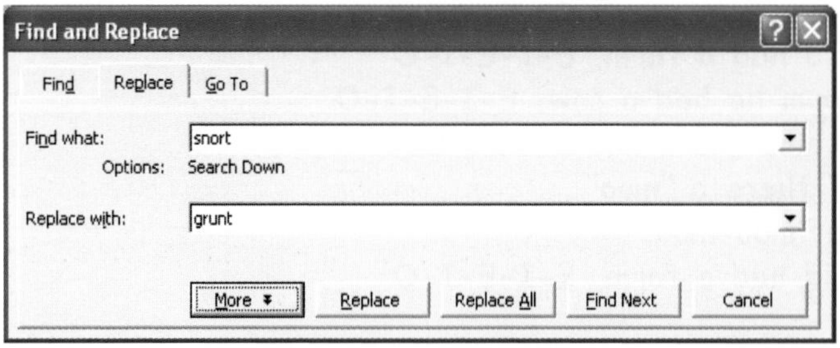

You can get the computer to replace all occurrences, or search for them one at a time so that you can decide whether or not to replace each one. In this case you want them all replaced.

- Click the button marked **Replace All**. Word tells you how many words have been replaced.

- Save your document as **Old Macdonald.doc**.

Note that if you simply want to find a specific word or phrase you should select **Edit**, **Find** from the Main Menu bar.

Displaying and hiding built-in toolbars

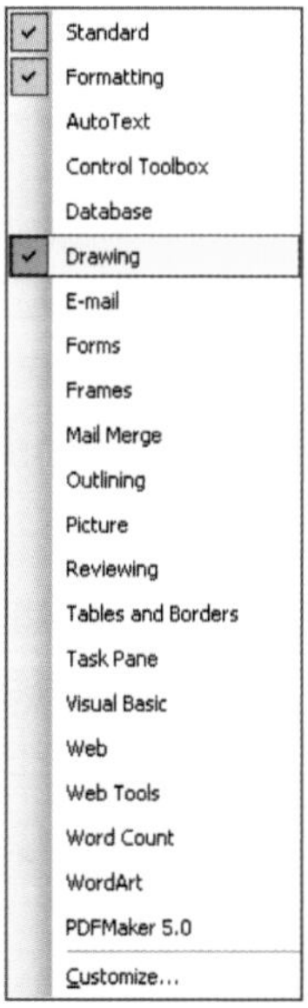

When you open **Word**, the Standard toolbar and the Formatting toolbar should be displayed by default. There are many other toolbars which you may need from time to time. And if for some reason the Standard toolbar or Formatting toolbar is not displayed, you need to know how to get them back!

- From the **View** menu on the menu bar, select **Toolbars**.

A list of toolbars appears.

Notice that the toolbars that are ticked are the ones that are visible on your screen. If you click them to deselect them, they will no longer be displayed.

- If the Drawing toolbar is not ticked, select it now.

The Drawing toolbar usually appears at the bottom of the screen.

This toolbar is used to draw lines, shapes and text boxes. We will draw a line between each verse.

Drawing a horizontal line

- Select the **Line** tool from the Drawing toolbar.
- Keep your finger on the **Shift** key while you draw a line between the first and second verse. You can drag it to position it correctly.

Tip:
Keeping your finger on **Shift** while you draw a line ensures that it will be horizontal.

- With the line still selected, click the **Line Style** button, and set a different line style.
- Now comes the clever bit! Press both **Shift** and **Ctrl** and keep them pressed down while you drag the line down to between the second and third verses. Then drag again to the end of the third verse.

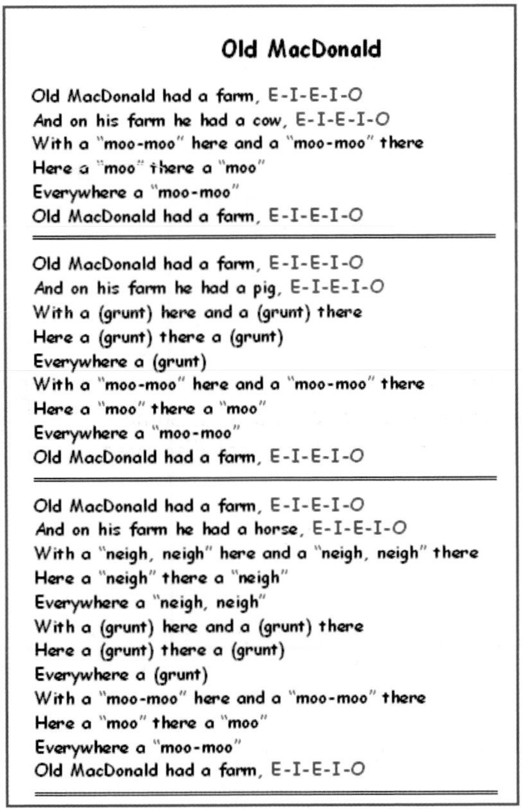

Old MacDonald

Old MacDonald had a farm, E-I-E-I-O
And on his farm he had a cow, E-I-E-I-O
With a "moo-moo" here and a "moo-moo" there
Here a "moo" there a "moo"
Everywhere a "moo-moo"
Old MacDonald had a farm, E-I-E-I-O

Old MacDonald had a farm, E-I-E-I-O
And on his farm he had a pig, E-I-E-I-O
With a (grunt) here and a (grunt) there
Here a (grunt) there a (grunt)
Everywhere a (grunt)
With a "moo-moo" here and a "moo-moo" there
Here a "moo" there a "moo"
Everywhere a "moo-moo"
Old MacDonald had a farm, E-I-E-I-O

Old MacDonald had a farm, E-I-E-I-O
And on his farm he had a horse, E-I-E-I-O
With a "neigh, neigh" here and a "neigh, neigh" there
Here a "neigh" there a "neigh"
Everywhere a "neigh, neigh"
With a (grunt) here and a (grunt) there
Here a (grunt) there a (grunt)
Everywhere a (grunt)
With a "moo-moo" here and a "moo-moo" there
Here a "moo" there a "moo"
Everywhere a "moo-moo"
Old MacDonald had a farm, E-I-E-I-O

You should have three identical lines. Keeping a finger on **Ctrl** copies, rather than moves, an object. Keeping a finger on **Shift** means that the object can only move vertically while you drag down, which ensures that all the lines will be perfectly lined up.

Spell-checking

You should always spell-check a document before you print it. When you type a document, any words that Word does not recognise are underlined with a red squiggle.

It will also underline in red repeated words, so if for example you write '**I went to the the cinema**', the second occurrence of '**the**' will be underlined in red.

Parts of the text that Word thinks are not grammatical will be underlined in green, though you may disagree. You will also see a green wavy line if you leave two spaces rather than one between words.

Word cannot know when you have simply typed the wrong word, like "widow" instead of "window" or "their" instead of "there", so you still need to check your own spelling carefully even if nothing is underlined in red.

To try out the spell-checker, put some errors in Old Macdonald.

- Delete the **h** in **everywhere** in the first verse. Replace every other occurrence of **everywhere** with this misspelt word.
- Replace the first occurrence of **there** with **their**.

- Now position the pointer at the start of the document and click the **Spelling and Grammar** button.

A window opens offering you suggestions for the first misspelling:

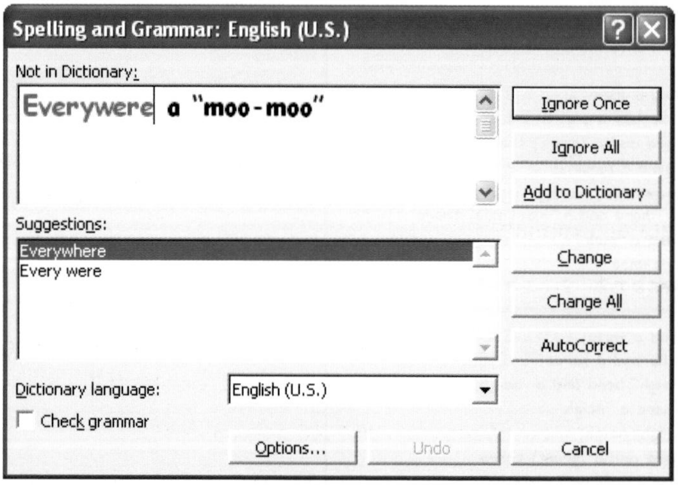

- You can accept the first suggestion, which looks correct, and change every occurrence. Click **Change All**.

Word does not find the misspelling of **there**. You will have to correct that one yourself.

- Put one more misspelling in so that you can try out the shortcut menu. Change **Old** to **Oold**.
- As soon as you click away from the word it will be underlined in red. Right-click the word and the shortcut menu appears.

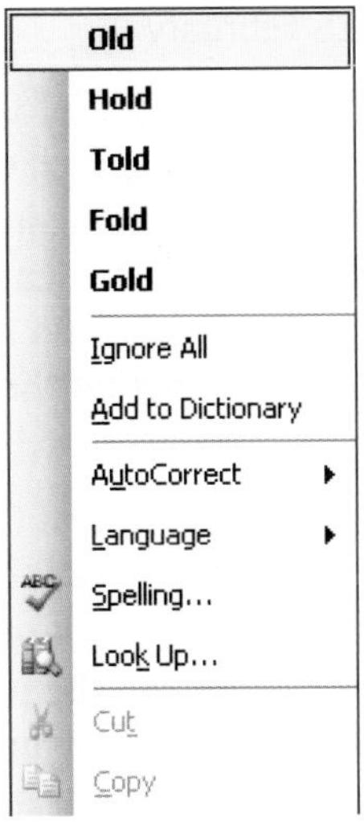

- Click the correct spelling and the word will be corrected.

If Word does not recognise a word that you know is correctly spelt, you can add it to the dictionary. For example, the word 'misspelt' is not recognised, but it is correctly spelt so you could click **Add to Dictionary**. Alternatively, if you have a word or an abbreviation that you want to use frequently in your current document, but you do not want to add it to the dictionary, you can click **Ignore All**. The word will only be ignored in the current document.

- Save your document.

Proofreading your document

Before you print a document you should proofread it carefully. Check the spelling and grammar and then check for errors of layout and presentation, including appropriate margins, font sizes and formats.

Previewing your document

When you have carefully checked your document you should preview it before printing it. This will show you what the page will look like when it is printed.

- Click the **Print Preview** button on the Standard toolbar.
- Click the **Close Preview** button to return to Print Layout view and make any corrections that are needed before you print.
- Close your document, saving again if you have made any changes.
- Close **Word**.

Exercise

You have been asked to produce a match report for a school football match.

1. Enter the following text into a new word processing document. Use Arial, size 11 font.

   Year 7 Football Barksfield v Holdbrook, Thursday 25 February

   There was plenty of action in both halves during the first period of the game, with both goalies having plenty to do. The finest save of the match came from the brilliant Jamie Dereham in the Barksfield goal. As a shot came in from the edge of the area, flying into the bottom corner of the net, Jamie leapt up to deftly punch it away. Unfortunately a Holdbrook forward picked up the rebound and before Jamie was back on his feet the opposition had netted their first. The score remained the same until half time.

   In the second half Barksfield rallied well with both Doug Glere and Chris Holmes creating some good runs and direct passes to feet. The visitors won a corner which was fired onto the head of a Holdbrook player, but the shot was superbly cleared off the line by Alex Beardshaw. Holdbrook maintained the pressure and won another corner. This time Barksfield were not so lucky and a superb goal was scored directly from the corner flag. This was a closely fought game between two well-matched sides. Full time score: Barksfield 0 Holdbrook 2.

2. Run the spell-checker and correct any typing errors.
3. Make the heading Arial, size 14 and bold.
4. Cut the complete sentence **This was a closely fought...** in the last paragraph and paste it at the beginning of the first paragraph.
5. The visiting team is called **Holdbroom**, not **Holdbrook**. Use the Find and Replace feature to replace all occurrences of the word **Holdbrook** with **Holdbroom.**
6. This may be used as an article in the school newsletter. As such it will require a horizontal line beneath the article. Display the Drawing toolbar and draw a short thick line, centred beneath the text.
7. Proof read the document before you save it.
8. Check the document in Print Preview before printing it.

Working with Many Documents

CHAPTER 3.4

In this chapter you will be doing some more work on the travel itinerary that you started in Chapter 3.2.

Imagine that you want to write some more information about the places that the tourists will visit. However, you want to check your facts first by sending a fax to someone in Tanzania to cast an eye over.

Using a template

Word has many different **templates** which are used for different types of document such as a letter, fax, memo, formal report or web page. In fact, every time you open a new document you are using a template, probably without realising it.

- Load **Word**. From the **File** menu select **New**.

The Task pane appears on the right of the screen, if it is not already visible.

- In Office 2003, click on **On my computer** under **Templates**. In Office XP, in the **New from Template** list at the bottom of the Task pane, select **General Templates**.

The following screen will be displayed:

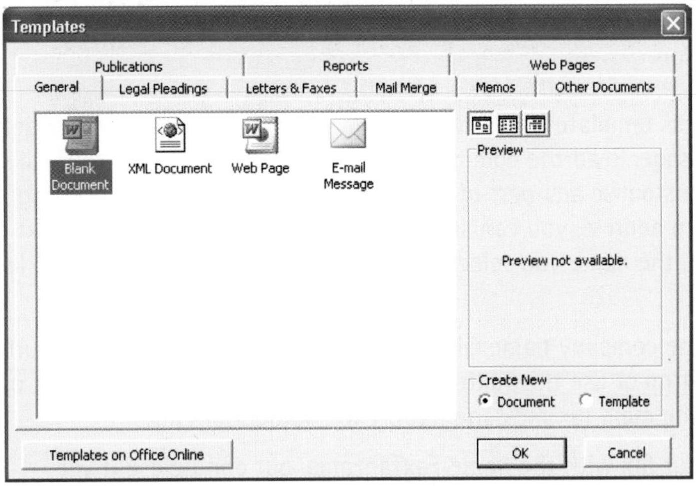

Normally you would select **Blank Document**. This is the default template that Word uses when you simply click the **New Blank Document** icon.

This time, however, we are going to select a template that will be suitable for writing a fax.

- Click the **Letters & Faxes** tab. You will see that there are several different templates for you to choose from.
- Select the **Professional Fax** template, and click **OK**.

You will see the following document appear:

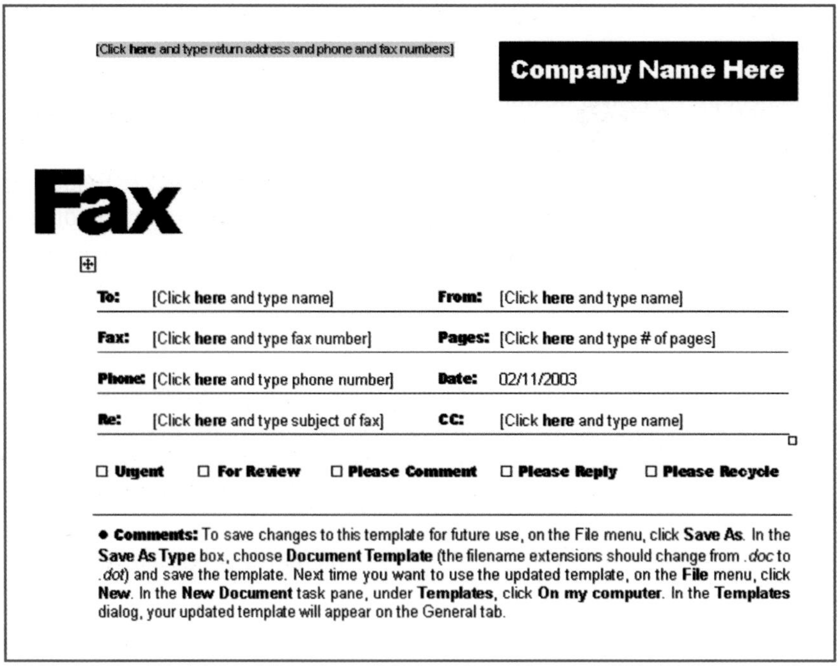
[Click here and type return address and phone and fax numbers]

Company Name Here

Fax

To:	[Click **here** and type name]	**From:**	[Click **here** and type name]
Fax:	[Click **here** and type fax number]	**Pages:**	[Click **here** and type # of pages]
Phone:	[Click **here** and type phone number]	**Date:**	02/11/2003
Re:	[Click **here** and type subject of fax]	**CC:**	[Click **here** and type name]

☐ **Urgent** ☐ **For Review** ☐ **Please Comment** ☐ **Please Reply** ☐ **Please Recycle**

• **Comments:** To save changes to this template for future use, on the File menu, click **Save As**. In the **Save As Type** box, choose **Document Template** (the filename extensions should change from *.doc* to *.dot*) and save the template. Next time you want to use the updated template, on the **File** menu, click **New**. In the **New Document** task pane, under **Templates**, click **On my computer**. In the **Templates** dialog, your updated template will appear on the General tab.

Tip:

cc stands for **carbon copy**. Only use this if you are sending a copy of the fax to a second person.

You can use this template to insert your own company name and other details including message. Read the comments at the bottom of the fax. You will see that if you want to customise any part of this template, for example by inserting a company logo and return address, you can save your customised template. The next time you want to use it, the name you select (e.g. **GEAFaxForm**) will appear in the list of templates.

- Fill in the company name **Global Environment Association** and return address (make it up or use the address shown on Page 3-36). Fill in all the other items above the main fax message. Type **1** for Number of Pages.
- Save your fax with the name **FaxTanzania**, but don't close it yet.

- Highlight the bulleted paragraph beginning **Comments:** and in its place type the text:

> Henry:
> Could you please check these paragraphs and make sure I have got all the facts right?

- Under this text type the following paragraphs:

> Dar es Salaam is the largest city in Tanzania with an estimated 3.0 million people. It is the gateway to Zanzibar, a 75-minute ferry ride away and a starting point to the Northern and Southern safari circuit.
>
> Mikumi National Park covers an area of 3230 sq km and is the third largest park in Tanzania. It is one of the most popular parks in Tanzania and is an important centre for education, where students go to study ecology and conservation. It contains a wide range of wildlife.

Using styles

There are several different styles of text in this document.

- Click on the line which contains the name and address. In the formatting toolbar you will see the name of the style that is being used displayed in the **Style** box.

The Style name is **Return Address**, and the font is **Arial**, **8pt**, **left-justified**.

- Click in other parts of the Fax document and note the different style names. You should find **Company Name**, **Document Label**, **Message Header**, **Emphasis** and **Body Text**.

When you deleted the **Comment** in the body of the fax and typed your own message, it may have appeared in the **Emphasis** style, which was the style of the word **Comment**.

You can change this style to **Body Text** as follows:

- Select the message text by dragging down the left margin.
- Click the down-arrow in the **Style** box to display a list of all available styles.
- Click **Body Text** and press **Enter**.

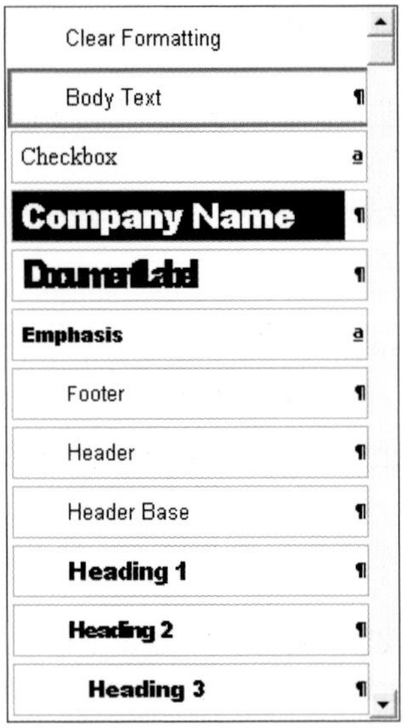

- Now press **Enter** at the end of the message to go to a new line. This time, we will apply a new style before typing anything.
- Click the down-arrow in the **Style** box to display a list of all available styles.
- Click **Emphasis** and press **Enter**.
- Type **Yours, Brian**.

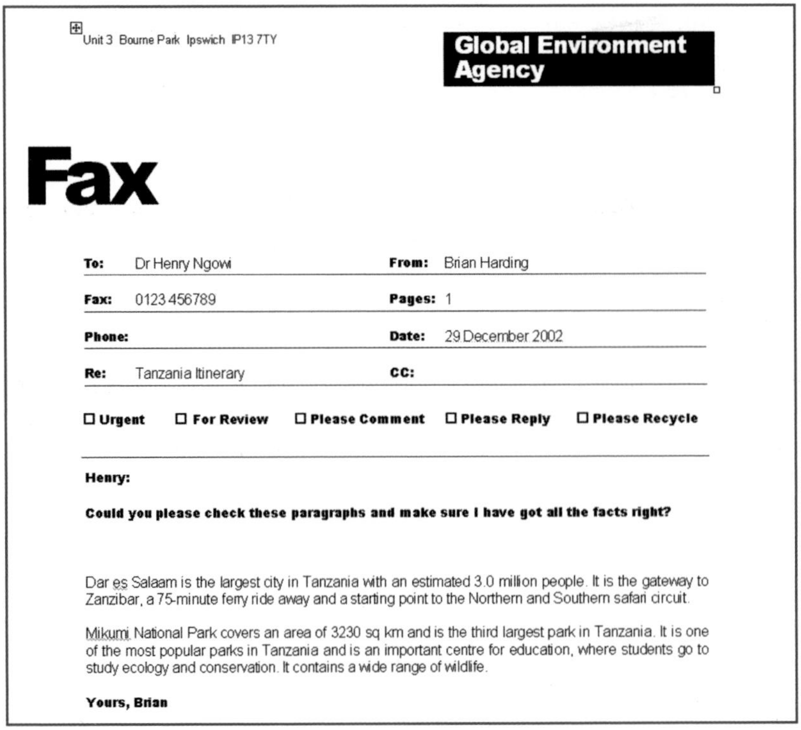
Unit 3 Bourne Park Ipswich IP13 7TY

Global Environment Agency

Fax

To:	Dr Henry Ngowi	**From:**	Brian Harding
Fax:	0123 456789	**Pages:**	1
Phone:		**Date:**	29 December 2002
Re:	Tanzania Itinerary	**CC:**	

☐ Urgent ☐ For Review ☐ Please Comment ☐ Please Reply ☐ Please Recycle

Henry:

Could you please check these paragraphs and make sure I have got all the facts right?

Dar es Salaam is the largest city in Tanzania with an estimated 3.0 million people. It is the gateway to Zanzibar, a 75-minute ferry ride away and a starting point to the Northern and Southern safari circuit.

Mikumi National Park covers an area of 3230 sq km and is the third largest park in Tanzania. It is one of the most popular parks in Tanzania and is an important centre for education, where students go to study ecology and conservation. It contains a wide range of wildlife.

Yours, Brian

- Save this document (**FaxTanzania.doc**) and close it.

Copying text between documents

Now suppose that the content of the fax message has been confirmed by Henry and you are ready to insert it into your travel itinerary.

You are going to copy the text from the document **FaxTanzania.doc** into the itinerary document.

- Open the document **NewItinerary.doc** that you created in Chapter 3.2.
- Open **FaxTanzania.doc** by clicking its icon in the Task bar.
- Select the paragraph about Dar-es-Salaam and copy it to the clipboard by pressing **Ctrl-C**.
- Click the icon for **NewItinerary.doc** to open it.
- At the end of the paragraph under **Day 2**, (just before **Day 3**), press **Enter** to insert a new paragraph.
- Press **Ctrl-V** to insert the text that you just copied.

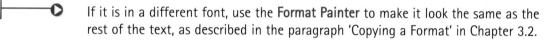

- If it is in a different font, use the **Format Painter** to make it look the same as the rest of the text, as described in the paragraph 'Copying a Format' in Chapter 3.2.
- Indent the new paragraph 0.5cm as described at the end of Chapter 3.2.

- Similarly, insert the paragraph about Mikumi National Park under Day 3. This time, format it by selecting **Match Destination Formatting** from the **smart tag** which appeared when you pasted the paragraph.
- Delete any extra blank lines at the end of the new paragraphs by clicking on the blank line and pressing **Backspace**.

Deleting text

To delete text, first select it and then select **Cut** from the **Edit** menu. Alternatively, click the **Delete** key on the keyboard or click the **Cut** button.

Moving text between open documents

To move text between open documents, you can first delete it from the original document by one of the methods described above. Then click in the second document where you want the text to appear, and select Paste from the **Edit** menu, click the **Paste** button or press **Ctrl-V**.

Inserting special symbols

We will put an aeroplane symbol before and after the sentence 'Depart London Heathrow on British Airways flight'.

- Click at the start of the sentence.
- From the **Insert** menu select **Symbol**.
- In the **Symbol** window select the font **Wingdings**.

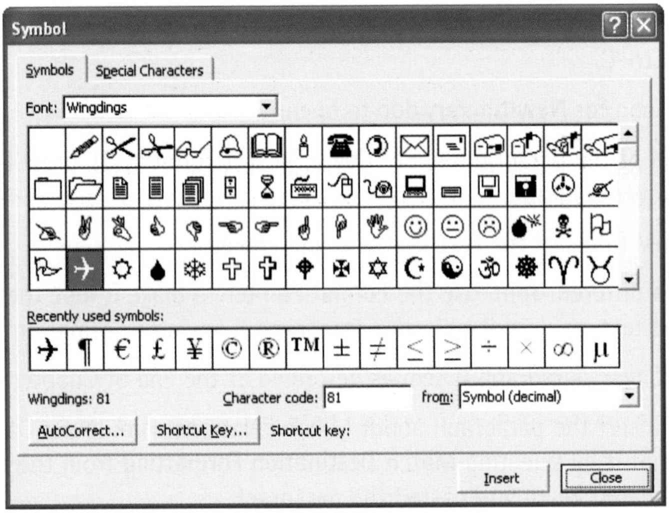

- Find the aeroplane symbol and click **Insert** and then **Close**.
- Now insert a second aeroplane symbol at the end of the sentence.

You can also insert special characters such as ©,®, etc into a document. To do this click the **Special Characters** tab in the Symbol window shown above. The following screen appears:

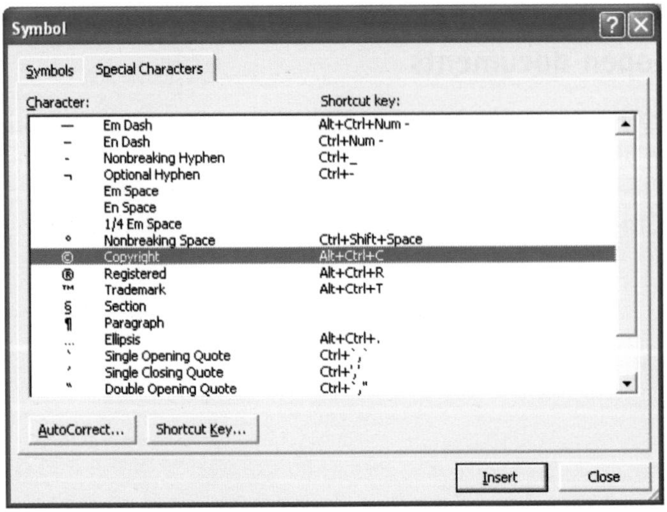

You don't need any of these characters in this document. Your itinerary should look like this:

> **ITINERARY**
>
> *Day 1*
>
> ✈ Depart London Heathrow on British Airways flight ✈
>
> *Day 2*
>
> Arrive at Dar es Salaam Airport. Our representative will meet and transfer the group to the hotel. The morning will be at leisure to rest after the overnight flight. After lunch our representative will meet and escort you to the GEA offices. The Country Representative, Dr David Moshi, will give a presentation and brief you on the GEA projects in Tanzania.
>
> Dar es Salaam is the largest city in Tanzania with an estimated 3.0 million people. It is the gateway to Zanzibar, a 75-minute ferry ride away and a starting point to the Northern and Southern safari circuit.
>
> *Day 3*
>
> After breakfast your guide will meet you for the transfer to Mikumi Kiboga Camp.
> Dinner and Overnight – Mikumi Kiboga Camp
>
> Mikumi National Park covers an area of 3230 sq km and is the third largest park in Tanzania. It is one of the most popular parks in Tanzania and is an important centre for education, where students go to study ecology and conservation. It contains a wide range of wildlife.
>
> *Day 4*
>
> You will be met and escorted for an early morning game drive through the Mikumi Park.
> Return to your accommodation for breakfast.
> Following breakfast your guide will escort you on the transfer to Udzungwa Mountain National Park. Followed by an accompanied late afternoon walk in the forest.
>
> *Day 5*
>
> The day includes trekking and sightseeing in the area.
> After breakfast your guide will escort the group on a leisurely walk to Sanje Falls, with a chance to take a refreshing swim in the falls. A picnic lunch will be provided.

➲ Save your work, close all your documents and exit Word!

Exercise

As home-watch coordinator you need to prepare a letter to send to homes in your local area about a special crime awareness initiative.

1. Open the **Elegant Letter** template provided with Microsoft Word and use it to create the following letter. Save the file as **letter.doc**.

JOHN RUDDICK
HOME WATCH CO-ORDINATOR
26 THE GARDENS, DARKSHAM, HANTS TY5 4RF

May 3rd 2003

Mr & Mrs K Hills
The White House
Belevedere Road
Darksham
Hants TY5 23RF

Dear Mr & Mrs Hills

As we enter the holiday season the local police have asked Home Watch co-ordinators to remind local people about the increased risks of burglary. If you are planning a break away this summer please ensure that your home is left secure. A house that presents itself as unoccupied and insecure is far more likely to be targeted than one that is properly secured.

Make it look as though your house is occupied and do not advertise your absence.

Install automated / programmable light switches.

Have a neighbour pop round to clear your letter box or doorstep regularly.

Encourage a neighbour to park on your drive.

Do not advertise that you are going away.

Do cancel all regular deliveries.

Do not announce your departure to a shop-full of people.

Do not have your address showing on your luggage for the outward journey.

Help us to fight local crime and enjoy that holiday!

Yours sincerely

John Ruddick
Home Watch Coordinator
☎ 01543 672345

2. Right-align the date and left-align the closing text as shown.
3. Double-line space the list of security measures and insert the telephone symbol as shown.
4. Click on each section of text and count the number of different styles used.
5. Save the document.
6. Copy and paste the list of security measures into a new document and save as **poster.doc**. You will use this at the end of the next chapter.

Tabs, Borders and Lists

CHAPTER 3.5

Introduction to tabs

In this chapter you will be learning how to make neat lists – such as price lists, lists of travel times, numbered steps in assembling flat-pack furniture, or any other list you can think of.

When you want items to line up neatly in columns, you need to use the **Tab** key. Pressing the **Tab** key will advance the cursor to the next preset Tab stop. In the list below, the first column is left-aligned, the second is centre-aligned, the third is aligned on the decimal point and the last column is right-aligned. This is achieved by setting different tab stops, which appear as marks on the ruler underneath the Formatting toolbar.

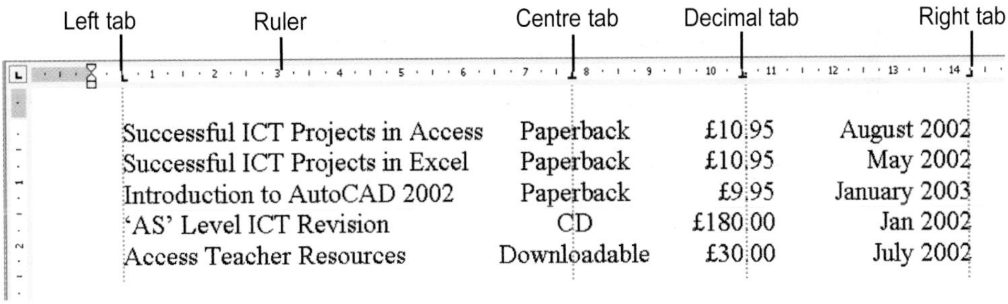

Before you set any tab stops, Microsoft Word has **default tab positions** which appear as faint marks below the ruler.

- Open a new document and look at the ruler line at the top of the screen. The default tab positions are probably set at intervals of 0.5 inches or 1.27cm.

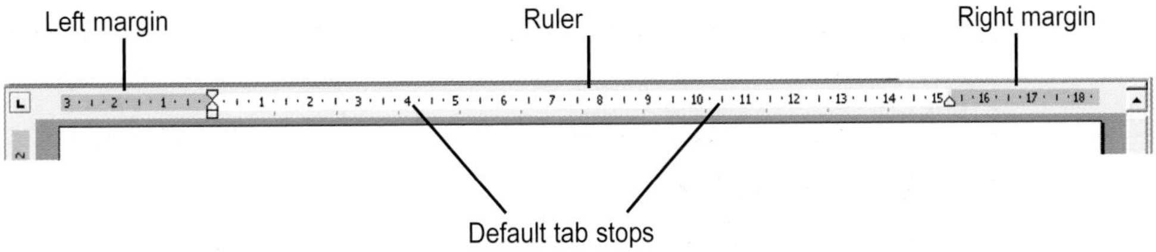

You are going to produce a price list for a company selling stationery items, similar to the one at the bottom of this page.

Setting default tab stops

We will start by changing the default tab positions.

- Select **Format** from the Main Menu bar. Then click on **Tabs**. A dialogue box like this should appear.

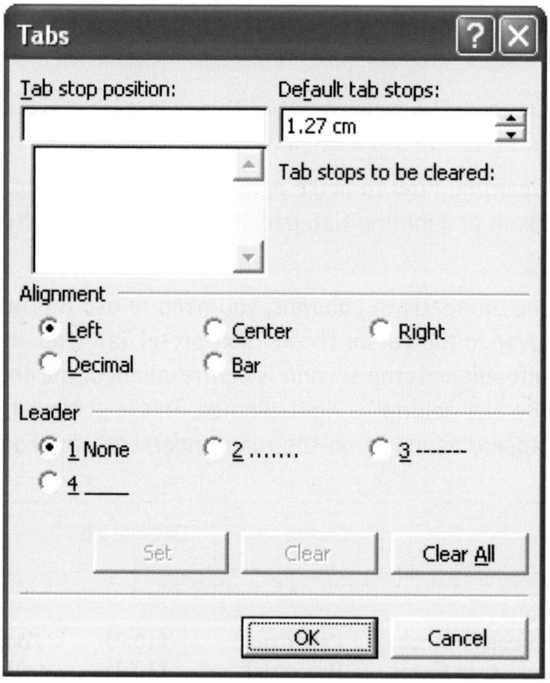

- Click the up-arrow on the right-hand side of the **Default tab stops** box until it is set at **3cm**. Then click **OK**.

Typing the price list

Type the following list, pressing **Tab** between each entry. You will need to press **Tab** twice after the word **Description**.

ECONOMY SQUARE-CUT FOLDERS

Product Code	Description	Qty	Price per pack
ESF151	Coloured folders	100	£12.99
ESF152	Buff Folders	50	£4.49
ESF003	Assorted coloured folders	100	£11.99
ESF004	Assorted coloured folders	10	£6.99

You may see a red wavy line under the word **coloured**. This is because Microsoft Word, being an American product, thinks this word is spelt wrongly.

- Right-click the word **Coloured**. A pop-up window appears. You can select either **Ignore All**, or **Add to Dictionary**. You will probably have to do this twice, for the capitalised and non-capitalised words.

Tip:
If you are working on a network, you may not be able to add words to the dictionary.

Displaying non-printing characters

Although the list looks quite neat, it would be better if the quantities were right-aligned, and the prices lined up on the decimal point.

Many of the characters that Word stores in your document are 'non-printing' and do not normally show on the screen. These characters include **Tab**, **Enter** and even spaces between words.

Sometimes it is useful to be able to see these characters and you can display them by clicking the **Show/Hide** icon.

- Click the **Show/Hide** icon on the Standard toolbar.

Your document now appears like this:

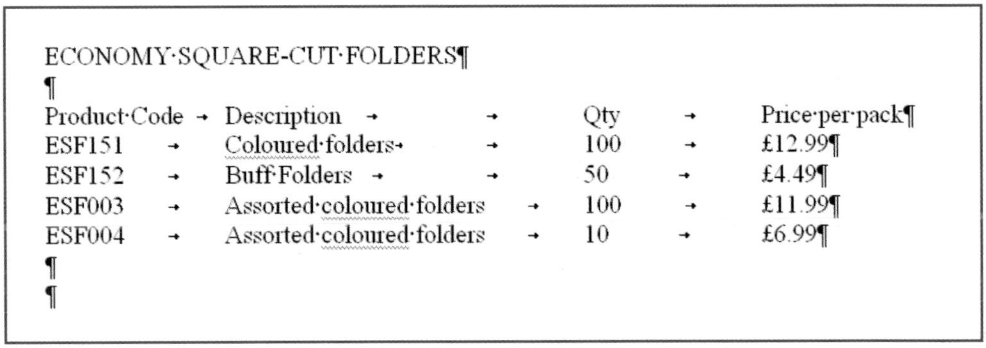

ECONOMY·SQUARE-CUT·FOLDERS¶
¶
Product·Code → Description → → Qty → Price·per·pack¶
ESF151 → Coloured·folders→ → 100 → £12.99¶
ESF152 → Buff·Folders → → 50 → £4.49¶
ESF003 → Assorted·coloured·folders → 100 → £11.99¶
ESF004 → Assorted·coloured·folders → 10 → £6.99¶
¶
¶

Note:
The different symbols which appear are for a **Space**, **Enter** and **Tab**. Wherever the **Enter** key has been pressed to create a new paragraph, a sign like a backwards P appears, as on the **Show/Hide** icon.

You can see that you have two **Tab** characters in some places, for example between **Description** and **Qty**.

- Click **Show/Hide** again to hide the non-printing characters.

Setting custom tabs

We will set our own tab positions.

- Select the list and the column headings you have just typed, starting at **Product Code**.
- Select **Format** from the Main Menu bar. Then click on **Tabs**.
- In the **Tab Stop Position** box, type **3** and then click **Set**.

The next tab position needs to be right-aligned at approximately 9.5cm.

- In the **Tab Stop Position** box, type **9.5**. Under **Alignment**, click **Right**. Then click **Set**.
- In the **Tab Stop Position** box, type **14.5**. Under **Alignment**, click **Decimal**. Then click **Set**.

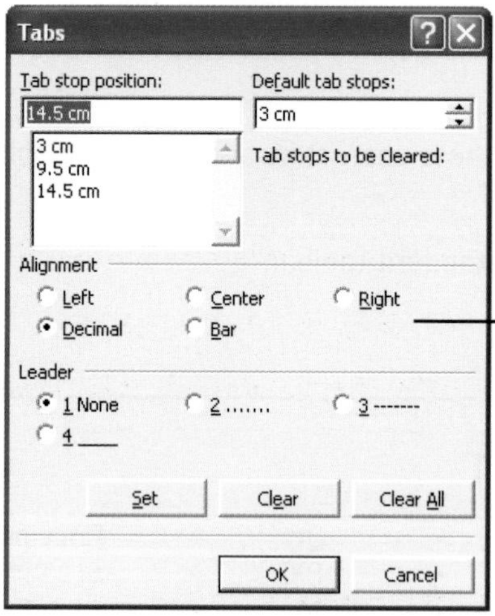

Here you can select a left, centre, right or decimal tab

- Click **OK**.

Oh dear! What has gone wrong? The problem is that when you set custom tabs, the default tabs disappear. Remember that you pressed **Tab** twice after **Description**. Now we only have one tab stop where previously there were two.

ECONOMY SQUARE-CUT FOLDERS

Product Code	Description		Qty
	Price per pack		
ESF151	Coloured folders		100
	£12.99		
ESF152	Buff folders		50
	£4.49		
ESF003	Assorted coloured folders	100	£11.99
ESF004	Assorted coloured folders	10	£6.99

Luckily this is easy to fix. You need to delete the extra **Tab** characters.

- Click **Show/Hide** again to display the hidden **Tab** characters.
- Click just before the word **Qty** and press **Backspace**.
- Click just before **100** on the next line and press **Backspace**.
- Delete the other superfluous tab on the next line.
- Hide the **Tab** characters again.

Now everything is looking pretty good except that the prices are too far to the right.

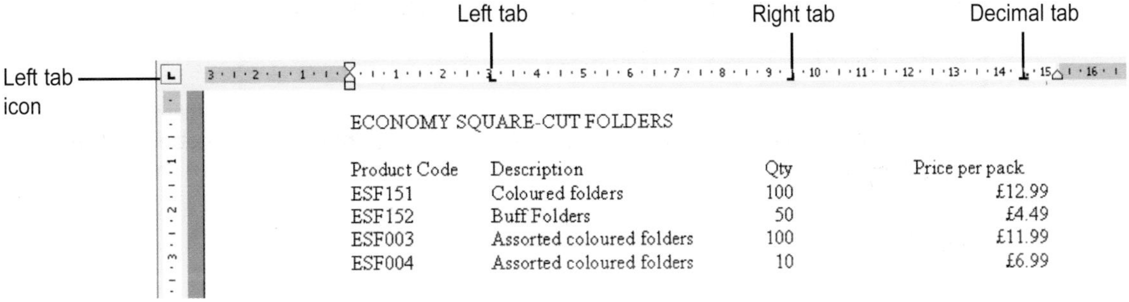

Adjusting tab stops on the ruler

You can change the position of a tab stop by dragging it left or right on the ruler.

- Highlight the four lines of the list, excluding the column headers.
- Look at the ruler line and at the far right at position 14.5, note the **Decimal tab icon**.
- Drag the **Decimal tab icon** to 13.5 on the ruler.

Setting and removing left, centre, right and decimal tabs

At the left of the ruler you will see the tab alignment button.

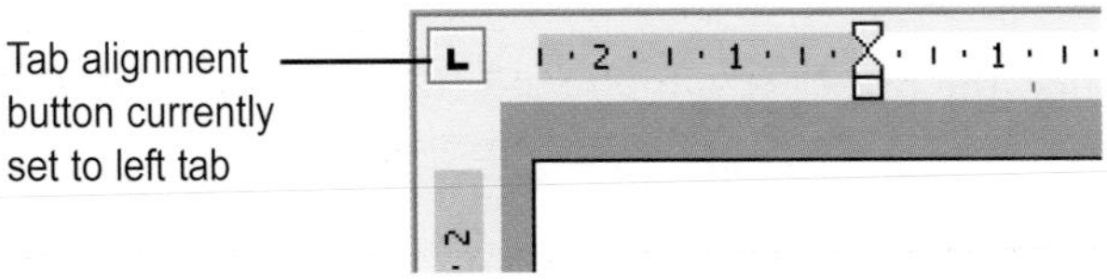

To set a left, centre, right or decimal tab, you click this button repeatedly until the tab type that you want is shown. Then click in the ruler line at the position where you want the tab stop.

Left tab | Centre tab | Right tab | Decimal tab

You can delete an unwanted tab stop by dragging it up or down off the ruler.

Adding a border

We can add a border to the list.

- Select the whole list and the headings.
- From the menu select **Format, Borders and Shading**.
- Under **Setting**, click the **Box** icon. The other options should be as shown below.

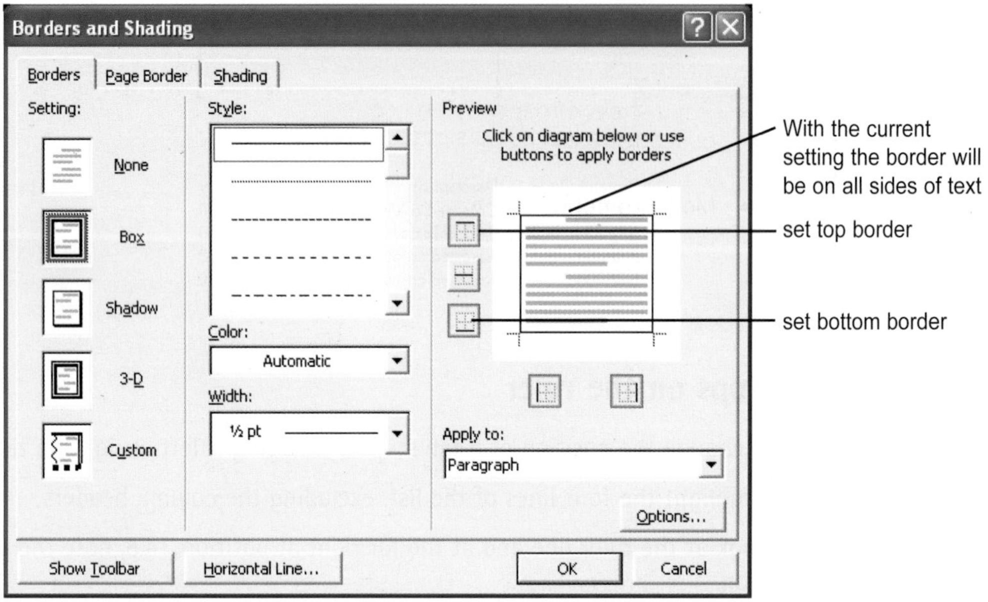

- Currently the **Box** border is selected, and the picture on the right-hand side of the window shows that a border will be placed all around the text.

Note that to put a border at the top and/or bottom of the list instead of all around it, you would click the icons as shown in the screenshot above and then click **OK**.

- Click **OK**.

A box will appear around the price list.

- You can make your headings bold and increase the font size of the main heading.

ECONOMY SQUARE-CUT FOLDERS

Product Code	**Description**	**Qty**	**Price per pack**
ESF151	Coloured folders	100	£12.99
ESF152	Buff folders	50	£4.49
ESF003	Assorted coloured folders	100	£11.99
ESF004	Assorted coloured folders	10	£6.99

- Save your list as **Price List.doc**.

Creating a bulleted list

You are going to create a poster to help with a typical office problem – working the coffee machine.

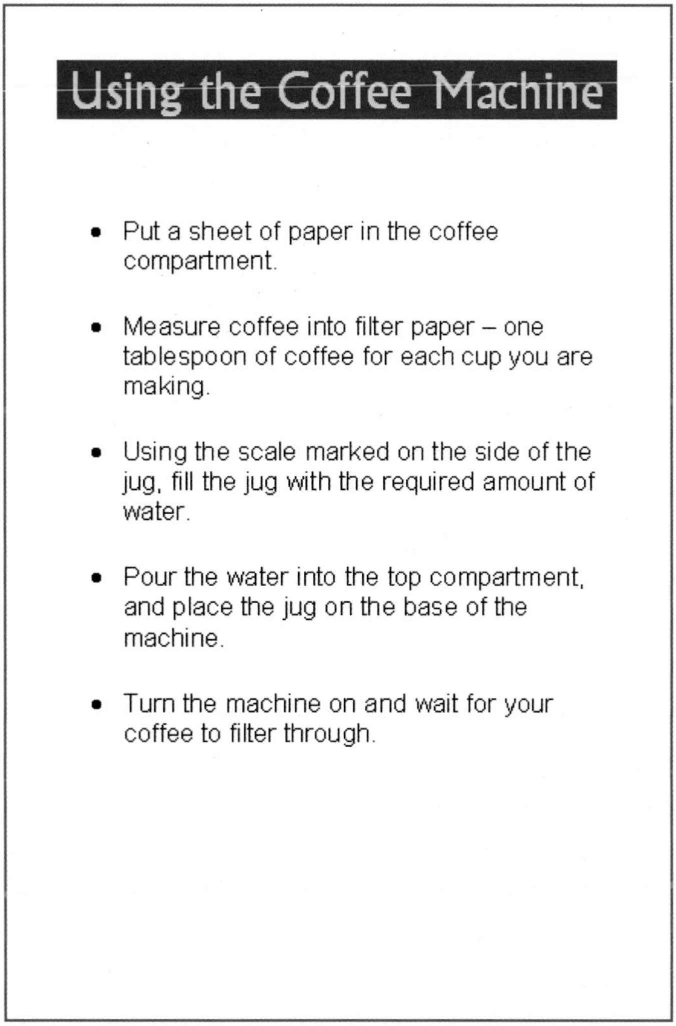

Using the Coffee Machine

- Put a sheet of paper in the coffee compartment.
- Measure coffee into filter paper – one tablespoon of coffee for each cup you are making.
- Using the scale marked on the side of the jug, fill the jug with the required amount of water.
- Pour the water into the top compartment, and place the jug on the base of the machine.
- Turn the machine on and wait for your coffee to filter through.

Modifying the document setup

When you open a new document the page size, orientation (portrait or landscape) and margins are set to default values. You can change any of these attributes.

- Open a new document.
- From the **File** menu select **Page Setup**.

The Page Setup window will appear:

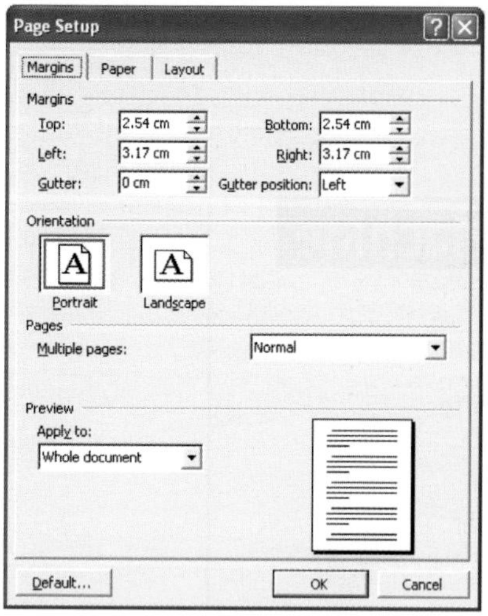

- Click the **Paper** tab.
- Change the **Paper size** to **A5** and then click the **Margins** tab.
- Change the top, bottom, left and right margins to **2cm**. Leave the gutter size as it is, and leave the orientation as **Portrait** rather than **Landscape**. Click **OK**.
- Select a suitable font for the title. The one shown on the previous page is **Albertus Medium**, size **26**.
- Type the heading and make sure that it is **Centred**.
- Press **Enter** twice after the heading and change to a different font. The one shown above is **Arial**, size **14**.

Tip:
Use **Landscape** orientation when you want the page to be wider than it is long.

Making bullets

- Click the **Bullets** button on the Formatting toolbar.
- Type the instructions listed in the figure on the previous page. Each time you press **Enter**, a bullet will automatically appear on the next line.
- After typing the last item in the list, press **Enter** once more.
- Turn off the bullets by clicking the **Bullets** button again.

Tip:
You can add bullets after typing a list, rather than before.
Just select the items you want to bullet, and then click the **Bullets** button.

Customising bullets

You can alter the appearance of bullets.

- Select the list.
- From the **Format** menu select **Bullets and Numbering**.

The following window will appear:

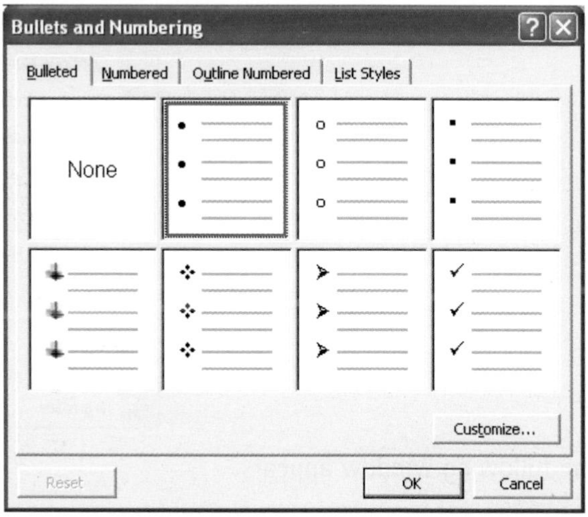

- Select a different type of bullet, and click **OK**.

To remove bullets, select the bulleted list and then click the **Bullets** button. This button acts as a 'toggle'.

Tip:
Further customising options are available if you click the **Customize** button in this window

A numbered list

Instead of using bullets, sometimes you may want to number your steps.

- Select the list.

- Click the **Numbering** icon on the Formatting toolbar.

Your list will appear with numbers instead of bullets. Note that you can customise numbers in the same way as you customised the bullets. Sometimes you may want a list that uses Roman numerals, or one that has some unnumbered text in the middle of the list. Then you will have to select **Format, Bullets and Numbering** and use the **Customize** options to get the numbering correct.

- Click the **Numbering** icon again to remove the numbers.

Leave the list as a bulleted list for the purposes of this exercise.

Spacing paragraphs

Every time you press **Enter**, you create a new paragraph. So, in your list, **Word** treats each separate bullet point as a separate paragraph. You can put extra space between each bullet point so that the list fills the page more neatly.

- If the list is not already selected, select it now.
- Right-click the list to display a shortcut menu.

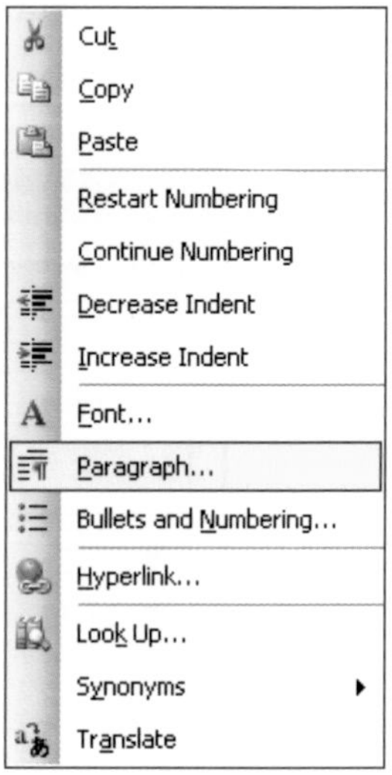

- Select **Paragraph**. The following window appears:

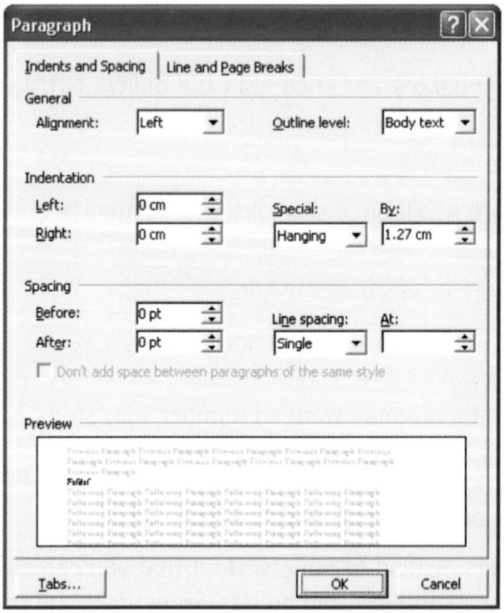

- In the **Spacing Before** box, click the up-arrow until **12** is displayed. Click **OK**.
- If that is not enough spacing to comfortably fill your page, try again. You could try increasing the **Spacing Before** to size **18**, or alternatively you could insert some **Spacing After** each paragraph using the Spacing After box.
- Experiment until you are happy with the layout.

Indenting paragraphs

Notice that in the paragraph dialogue box shown in the figure opposite, under **Indentation** in the box labelled **Special**, **Hanging** appears. What is a hanging indent? It is an indent that is the opposite of a first line left indent. In other words, the first line is not indented but all the subsequent lines in the paragraph are. So in this list, the bullets are not indented but the text is indented by 1.27cm.

If you wanted to change the amount of space between the bullet and the text, you could do it here.

If you are writing a letter or story, you might want to set a **first line** indent, to indent the first line of each paragraph. You would do this by selecting **First line** in the **Special** box.

You can set left and right indents by selecting appropriate options in this dialogue box.

Inserting a soft carriage return

Sometimes you want to have a second paragraph under a bullet point, that does not have its own bullet. You can insert a soft carriage return (line break) by holding down **Shift** and pressing **Enter**.

- Try pressing **Shift** and **Enter** at the end of the first paragraph and inserting the words:

The filter papers are in the drawer under the counter.

- Click the **Show/Hide** icon to see what hidden character has been inserted. Click it again to hide the hidden characters.

Placing a border around the page

You can put a border round the whole page.

- On the **Format** menu, select **Borders and Shading**.

- Click the **Page Border** tab. Click the **Box** icon and then click **OK**.

Shading the title

We will make the heading yellow on a blue background.

- Select the title by clicking in the left margin next to it.

- Click on the arrow next to the **Font Color** button on the Drawing toolbar, and select a colour for your title.
- Now, keeping the heading selected, select **Format** from the Main Menu bar. Then click on **Borders and Shading**.
- Make sure the **Shading** tab is selected.

A dialogue box like the one below will appear:

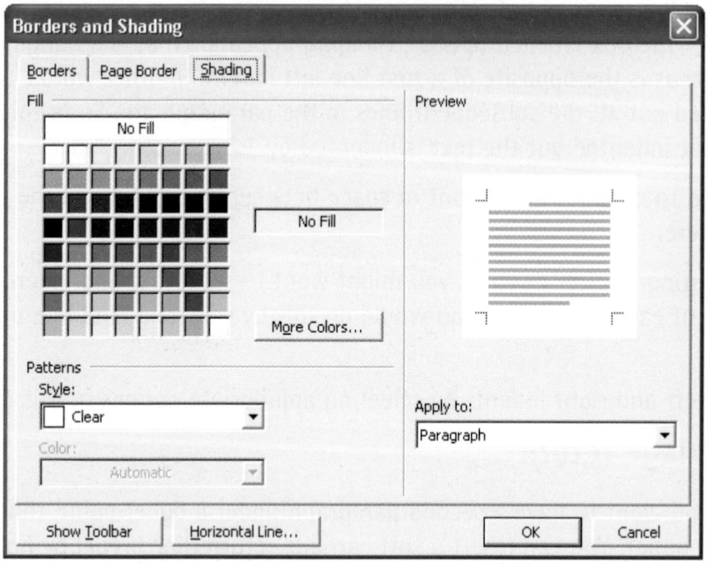

- Choose a shade to go behind your heading, and click **OK**.
- When you are happy with your poster, save and print it.

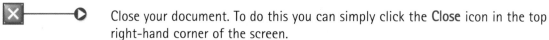

- Close your document. To do this you can simply click the **Close** icon in the top right-hand corner of the screen.

Automatic hyphenation

If a word is too long to fit on the end of a line, Microsoft Word moves the word to the beginning of the next line instead of hyphenating it. You can turn on automatic hyphenation from the **Tools** menu by selecting **Language**, **Hyphenation** and then selecting **Automatically hyphenate document**.

You can turn automatic hyphenation off using the same dialogue box. Hyphenation is useful to eliminate gaps in justified text or to maintain even line lengths in very narrow columns of text.

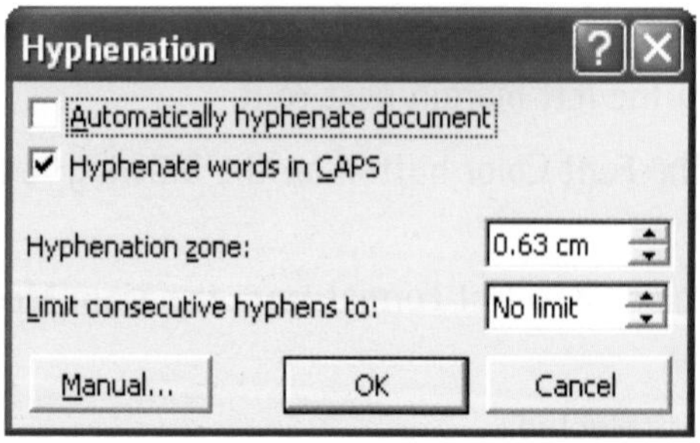

Exercise

This exercise develops the poster that you began at the end of the previous chapter.

1. Open the file **poster.doc.**
2. Insert a heading **Going on holiday?** in Comic sans MS, size 24, bold.
3. Colour the text and shade the title in colours of your choice.
4. Change the font of the list items to Comic Sans MS, size 16, single line-spaced.
5. Add bullets to the list of security measures. Choose special coloured symbols for the bullets.
6. Insert paragraph spacing of 18pt before each bullet point.
7. Leave a blank line beneath the list and change the font size to 14. Enter the following text:

   For more advice contact Darksham Police station on 01543 587435 or one of your local Home Watch co-ordinators:
8. Leave a blank line and set up custom tab stops at 3.5cm and 11cm. Select leader dots for the second tab stop. Enter the following details:

   Stanley Smith 01543 723433

   Samir Dall 01543 423788

   John Ruddick 01543 672345
9. Insert a decorative border around the page.
10. Save your work.

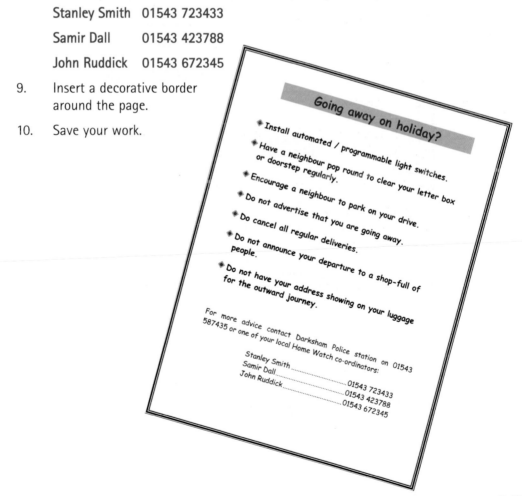

CHAPTER

3.6 Using Tables

In this chapter, you will learn how to insert a table into a document and type out a timetable or itinerary like the one shown below:

Programme for Winter Sports Holiday

	Monday	**Tuesday**	**Wednesday**	**Thursday**	**Friday**	**Saturday**
10-12	Snowboarding	Snowboarding	Beginners Skiing	Snowboarding	Snowboarding	Beginners Skiing
12-2	LUNCH BREAK					
2-4	Beginners Skiing	Tobogganing	Experienced Skiing	Skidoo	Tobogganing	Experienced Skiing
4-6	Experienced Skiing	Skidoo	Ice Skating	Skidoo	Tobogganing	Snowboarding
6-8	DINNER					
8-late	Apres-Ski	Karaoke	Late-night Skiing	Apres-Ski	Ice Skating	Leaving Party

- Begin by opening a new document.
- Type the heading – Programme for Winter Sports Holiday.
- Make the heading Arial, size 20, Bold and Centred.
- Press Enter twice and change the font back to Times New Roman, size 10, left aligned and not bold.

Inserting a table

- From the Main Menu bar, select **Table**, **Insert**, **Table**.

You will see a dialogue box like the one below.

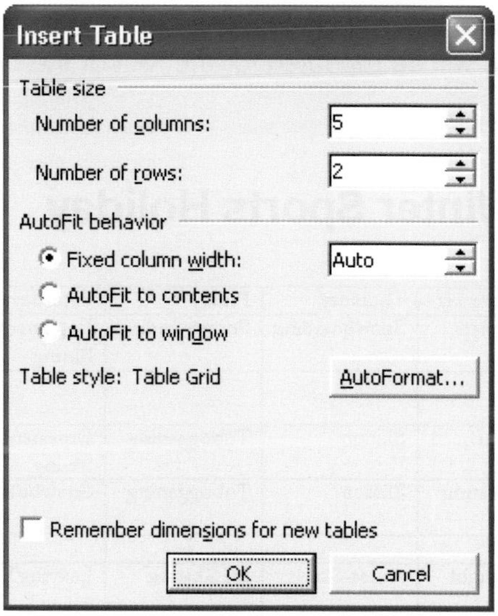

- Type **7** as the number of columns (or use the arrows).
- Press the **Tab** key to move to the next box and enter **7**.
- Leave the **Column width** as **Auto** and click the **OK** button.

A table will be inserted into your document like this:

Programme for Winter Sports Holiday

- The cursor should be flashing in the first **cell**, which is in the top left-hand corner of the table.
- The first cell is going to remain blank. Press **Tab** to move one cell to the right.
- Type **Monday** and then tab to the next cell.
- Type **Tuesday**, **Wednesday**, etc in the cells across the top row.

- Press **Tab** to go to the first cell of the second row.
- Now fill in the rest of the programme so that it looks like the one below.

Tip:

Once you have typed the first few letters of **Monday**, Word guesses what you are typing and displays **Monday** as a tool tip. You can now just press **Enter** to complete the rest of the word. This will be repeated for the rest of the days that you enter.

Programme for Winter Sports Holiday

	Monday	Tuesday	Wednesday	Thursday	Friday	Saturday
10-12	Snowboarding	Snowboarding	Beginners Skiing	Snowboarding	Snowboarding	Beginners Skiing
12-2	LUNCH BREAK					
2-4	Beginners Skiing	Tobogganing	Experienced Skiing	Skidoo	Tobogganing	Experienced Skiing
4-6	Experienced Skiing	Skidoo	Ice Skating	Skidoo	Tobogganing	Snowboarding
6-8	DINNER					
8-late	Apres-Ski	Karaoke	Late-night Skiing	Apres-Ski	Ice Skating	Leaving Party

Selecting cells

When you want to change the format of one or more cells, for example to change the font or shading, you first have to select the cells to change. Here are some of the ways of selecting cells:

- To select the **entire table**, click the cursor in any of the cells in the table. Then from the Main Menu bar select **Table**, **Select**, **Table**. Or, drag across all the cells in the table.
- To select a **row**, click next to the row in the left margin. Or, drag across all the cells in the row.
- To select a **column**, move the pointer above the column till it turns into a down-arrow, then click. Or, drag across all the cells in the column.
- To select a **cell**, from the Main Menu bar select **Table**, **Select**, **Cell**. Or, triple-click in the cell.

Tip:

You can use the **Table**, **Select** menu to select a table, column, row or cell. You may have noticed a small four-pointed arrow in a box over the top left-hand corner of your table. By clicking on it you can select the whole table. This is quicker and more convenient than using the menu.

Modifying row height

The programme looks rather cramped. It would look better if it was more spread out.

- With the cursor in any of the cells of the table, select **Table** from the Main Menu bar. Then click **Select, Table**. The whole table will be highlighted.
- Select **Table** again from the Main Menu bar. Then click **Table Properties.**

A dialogue box will appear.

- Click on the **Row** tab and make entries to match those entered below. The height of each row should be **At least 1cm**.

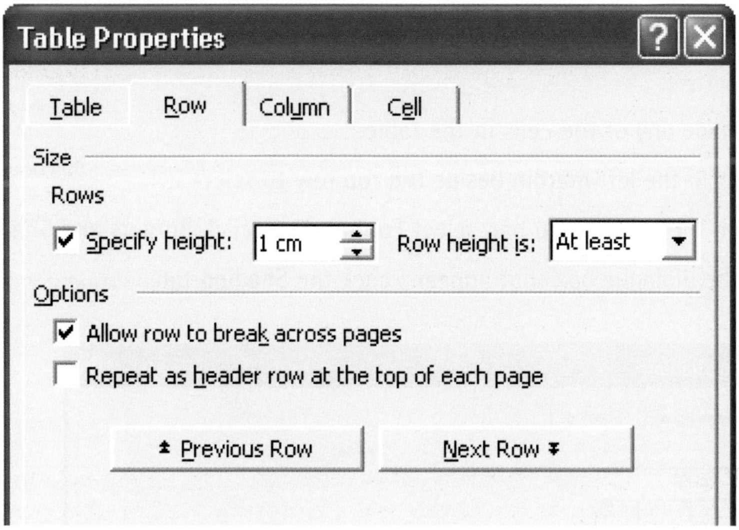

- Click the **Table** tab. In the Alignment section, click the button for **Center** alignment and then click **OK**. This will centre the table between the left and right margins of the page.

Merging cells in a table

If you look at your programme, you will see that the breaks for lunch and dinner occur at the same time every day. You are able to spread the words **Lunch Break** and **Dinner** across several cells to make your table look more balanced.

- Drag across the row of cells for the **Lunch Break** period.
- From the Main Menu bar, select **Table**. Then select **Merge Cells.**
- Click the **Center** and **Bold** buttons on the Formatting toolbar. You can probably make the font bigger too – say size **18**.
- Repeat this process for the **Dinner** period of your table.

Formatting text in cells

- Click in the first cell of the table and drag across and down until you are in the bottom right corner of the table to select the cells.

- Click the **Center** button on the Formatting toolbar.
- Click in the left margin beside the top row to select it. Click the **Bold** button on the Formatting toolbar.

You can try out this way of selecting a column – position the cursor just over the top line of the column until it changes to a downward-pointing arrow. Then click.

- Select all the cells in the first column and make them **Bold**.

Shading

You can shade any of the cells in the table.

- Click in the left margin beside the top row to select it.
- From the Main Menu bar, select **Format**. Then click **Borders and Shading**.
- In the dialogue box that appears, click the **Shading** tab.

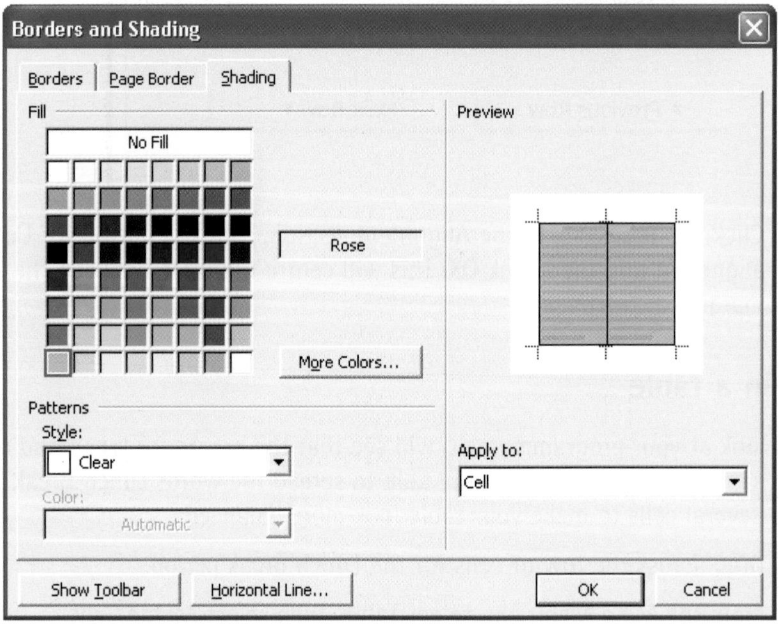

- Click a colour for the shading and then click **OK**.

	Monday	Tuesday	Wednesday	Thursday	Friday	Saturday
10-12	Snowboarding	Snowboarding	Beginners Skiing	Snowboarding	Snowboarding	Beginners Skiing
12-2	LUNCH BREAK					
2-4	Beginners Skiing	Tobogganing	Experienced Skiing	Skidoo	Tobogganing	Experienced Skiing
4-6	Experienced Skiing	Skidoo	Ice Skating	Skidoo	Tobogganing	Snowboarding
6-8	DINNER					
8-late	Apres-Ski	Karaoke	Late-night Skiing	Apres-Ski	Ice Skating	Leaving Party

Changing cell borders

You can set the borders of any cell, or the whole table, to a specified width and style.

- Click anywhere in the table.
- From the Main Menu bar, select **Format**. Then click **Borders and Shading**.
- In the dialogue box that appears, click the **Borders** tab.

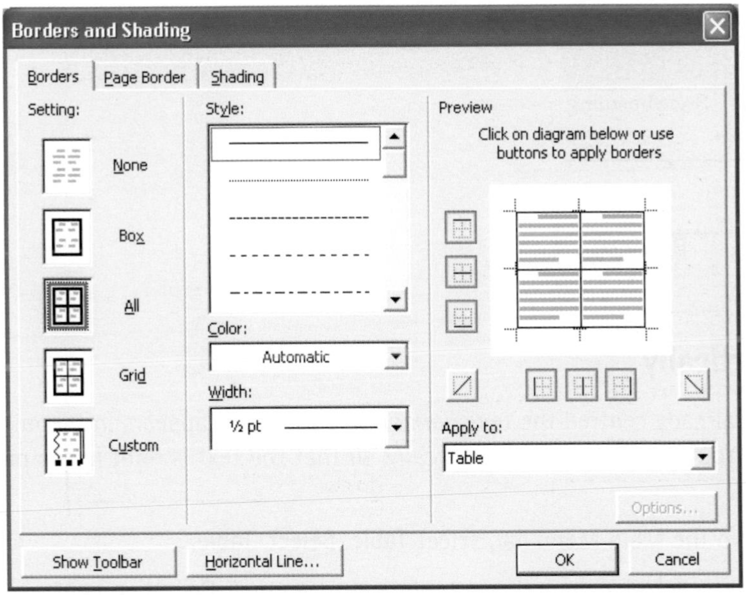

- Make sure **Setting** is set to **All**. Scroll down the styles in the Style box to select a different style or leave the style as it is. Change the width to **1pt**. Notice that this border style will **Apply to** the **Table**.
- Click **OK**.

Tip:
Notice that you can change the colour of the borders in this dialogue box by clicking the down-arrow in the **Color:** box and selecting a colour.

Inserting and deleting rows and columns

Suppose you wanted to insert an extra row above the row for **2-4**.

- Click anywhere in the row for **2-4**, then from the Main Menu bar select **Table**, **Insert**, **Rows Above**.
- Delete the row again by selecting **Table**, **Delete**, **Rows**.
- If you want to insert an extra row at the end of a table, click in the very last cell (in the bottom right of the table) and press the **Tab** key. You can delete this row again if you wish.

Columns are inserted and deleted in exactly the same way, by selecting **Column** instead of **Row** from the **Table**, **Insert** or **Delete** menu.

Changing column widths

To change the width of a column, put the pointer over one of the boundary lines separating the cells. When the pointer changes to a double-headed arrow, you can drag the boundary line either way to make the column wider or narrower.

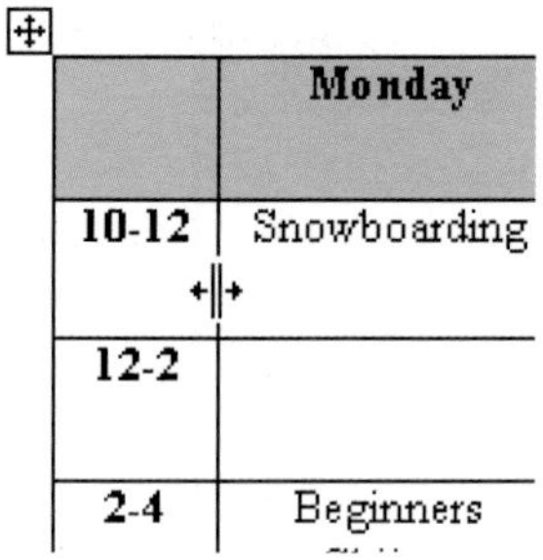

Centring text vertically

You have already centred the text *horizontally* so that it appears in the middle of the columns. You can also centre it *vertically*, so that the text is right in the middle of the cell.

- From the Main Menu bar, select **Table**, **Select**, **Table**.
- Right-click anywhere in the table and hover over **Cell Alignment**.
- Of the nine options given, choose the middle one - **Align Centre**.

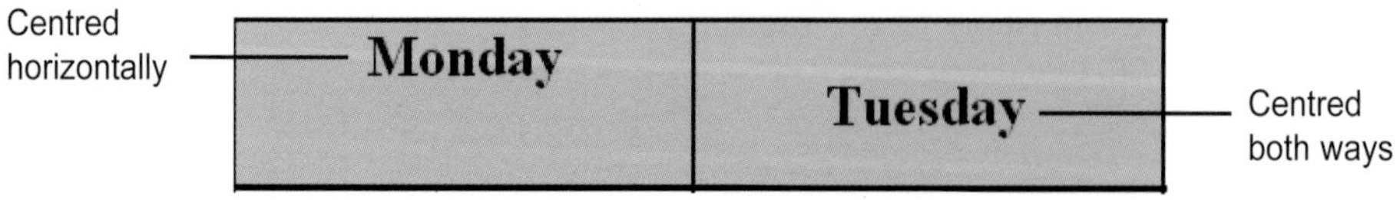

- Save your table with a suitable name and view it in Print Preview mode before printing it.

Exercise

You have been asked to produce a programme of events for the annual agricultural show.

1. In a new Word document create a table of 3 columns and 12 rows.
2. Enter the following information:

Barksfield Show 2003		
Day 1 – Wed 28 May		
Time	**Event**	**Venue**
9.00am	**Judging – Dairy goats**	**President's ring**
	Judging – Flower arranging	**Main marquee**
10.00am	**Horse shoeing competition**	**Heavy horse ring**
	Sheep shearing	**Sheep rings**
12.30pm	**Birds of Prey**	**President's ring**
	Sheepdogs	**Sheep rings**
3.00pm	**Judging – Commercial pigs**	**Ring 9**
	Judging – Rare cattle	**Cattle rings**
	Vintage tractors	**President's ring**

3. Make the heading in the first cell Arial size 20, bold and dark green.
4. Merge and centre the cells in the top row.
5. Make the remaining text in the table Arial, size 14. Adjust the column widths to fit.
6. Insert a blank row above each of rows 4, 6, 8 and 10.
7. Insert line spacing of 3pt above each of and 3pt below in all cells.
8. Centre the table on the page.
9. Embolden, merge and shade cells as shown in the finished programme below.

Barksfield Show 2003		
Day 1 – Wed 28 May		
Time	**Event**	**Venue**
9.00am	Judging – Dairy goats	President's ring
	Judging – Flower arranging	Main marquee
10.00am	Horse shoeing competition	Heavy horse ring
	Sheep shearing	Sheep rings
12.30pm	Birds of Prey	President's ring
	Sheepdogs	Sheep rings
3.00pm	Judging – Commercial pigs	Ring 9
	Judging – Rare cattle	Cattle rings
	Vintage tractors	President's ring

10. Save the document as **Programme.doc**

CHAPTER 3.7

Headers, Footers and Graphics

In this chapter we will create a report with a header and footer. We will also import a graphic to insert in the report.

Headers and footers are used to display text that is to appear on every page of a document. A header appears at the top of a page and a footer at the bottom. Either may contain information such as the page number, date, author, file name etc.

For this exercise, there is no need to type an enormous amount of text to illustrate the use of headers and footers. We will just type a heading and one or two sentences on each of two pages.

- Open a new blank document.
- Type the following text, using **Heading 1** style for the headings and **Normal** style for the text.

Tip:
Either select the style from the **Style** box before you start typing, or select the text after typing it and apply the style by selecting it from the **Style** box.

> **Letter from the Chairman**
>
> This year marks our fortieth anniversary – a milestone of which we can be proud. The GEA has come a long way since 1962, and the journey has been both challenging and fruitful.
>
> **Our work**
>
> All GEA's work has a global impact. Although we are best known for our work to protect endangered species, this is merely a part of what we do.

Inserting a header and footer

We will insert a header that contains a date, and a footer that contains the file name on the left and the page number in the middle.

- From the **View** menu select **Header and Footer**.

A Header and Footer toolbar appears automatically.

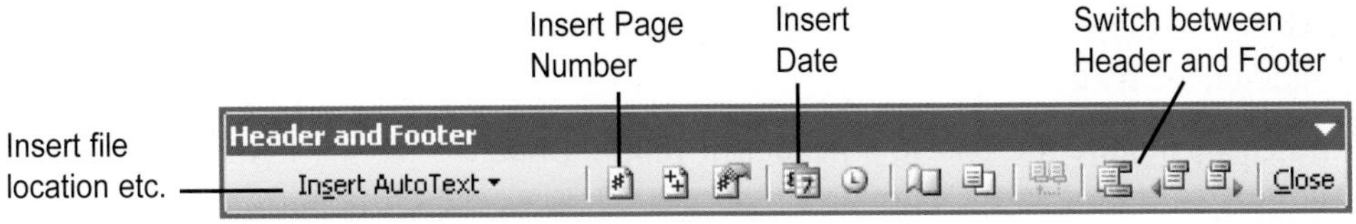

The cursor will be positioned in the Header ready for you to enter something, and the text in the rest of the document will be greyed out.

- Click the **Insert Date** button on the Header and Footer toolbar. Today's date will be automatically inserted. It may appear in the American format of **mm/dd/yyyy**, and the easiest way of getting the correct format is to delete it and type the date in yourself!
- Click the **Switch between Header and Footer** button.
- In the Footer, press the **Tab** key. Click the **Insert Page Number** button and a **1** appears.
- Now press the **Space** bar, type **of** and press the **Space** bar again. Then find and click the **Insert Number of Pages** button.
- Press **Tab** again and type **Chairman's Report**.

Tip:
There are three set Tab positions in the Header and Footer, for the left, centre and right-hand side. Pressing **Tab** once moves the cursor to the centre of the footer.

Your footer should look like this:

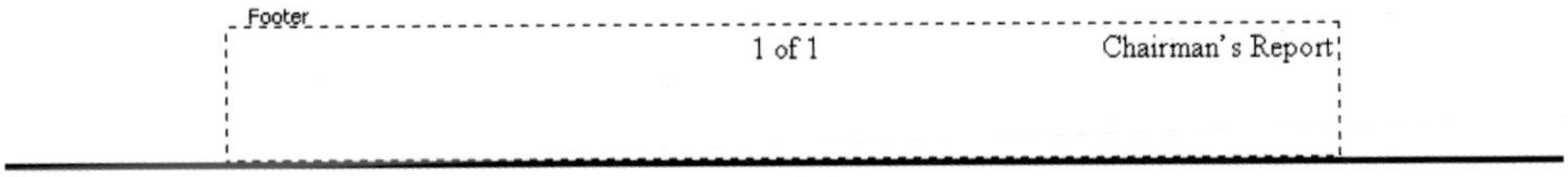

Note that you can enter other items such as the file name and path (i.e the file location) in the header or footer – if you select **Insert Autotext** you will see the following list which you can select from:

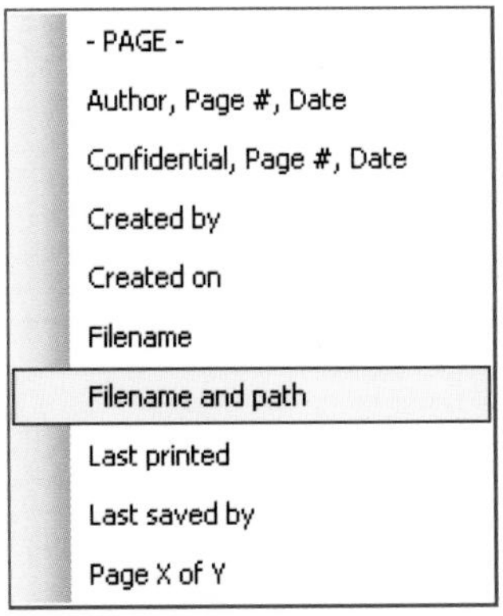

Tip:
If you just want a page number and nothing else, use **Insert**, **Page Number** instead of inserting a footer.

- Click the **Close** button on the Header and Footer toolbar so that you can see the document text.

You can easily modify the text in a header or footer. Double-click the footer and then edit the text so that it **says Chairman's report 2003**. Click the **Close** button in the Header and Footer toolbar. To edit text in the header, double-click the Header.

- Save the document as **Chairman's Report**.

Inserting a page break

- Now insert a page break before the second paragraph by clicking just before the second heading and holding down **Ctrl** while you press **Enter**.

You can also insert a page break by selecting **Insert**, **Break** from the menu bar, then specifying **Page Break**.

Notice that the footer now says **1 of 2** because you have created a second page.

Using the Zoom tool

You will probably not be able to see the whole page on the screen. You can 'zoom out' using the **Zoom** tool to display the whole page.

- Click the down-arrow beside the **Zoom** tool and select **75%**.

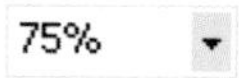

If you still cannot see the whole page, try typing **65%** into the box and pressing **Enter**.

Note:
You can also zoom in to take a closer look at part of a page. This can be useful when you are working with graphics ... or if your eyesight is poor.

Changing the page display mode

It can be useful to view your text in a different layout, especially now it is on two pages.

- Click **Normal** from the **View** menu. Now your document will appear like this:

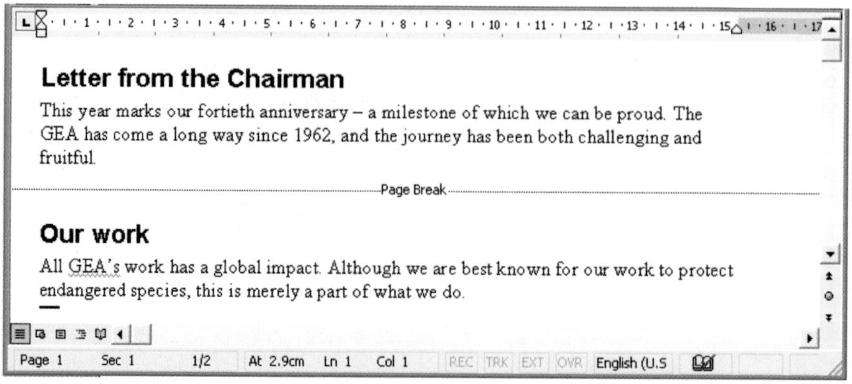

Saving a document for the Web

You can also select **Web Layout** view, to see what the page would look like if it was posted on a web site.

- Click **Web Layout** from the **View** menu.

You can save a document in a format suitable for saving to the Web.

- From the File menu select **Save As**.
- In the **Save As Type** box, click the down-arrow and select **Web Page (*.htm; *.html)**

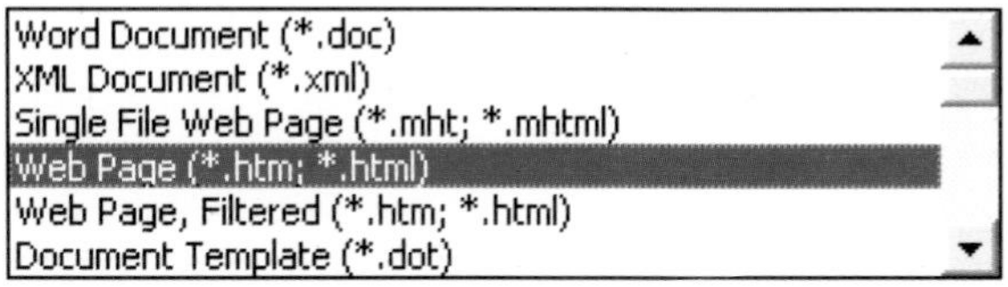

- Click **Cancel** for now because we are not going to post this page to a web site.
- Return to **Print Layout** view by selecting it from the **View** menu.
- Save your document as **ChairmansReport.doc**.

Importing graphics

We will import a graphics file to put in the report. The graphics file is called **fishcage.jpg** and can be downloaded into your computer from our web site **www.payne-gallway.co.uk**. To do this, click **Resources** on the Home page and select **Student**. From then on it will be self-explanatory.

First of all, add a bit more text to the end of your document.

- Type the following text, using style **Heading 3** for the heading and **Normal** for the rest of the text:

Marine Conservation

The goal of our marine programme is to improve nature conservation, resource management and pollution prevention. We work with people whose livelihoods depend on the seas to secure the long-term health of marine ecosystems.

- Make sure you have pressed **Enter** at the end of the text so that the cursor is on a new line. Press **Enter** again to leave a blank line.

- From the **Insert** menu select **Picture, From File.**
- Find the picture **fishcage.jpg** which you downloaded.

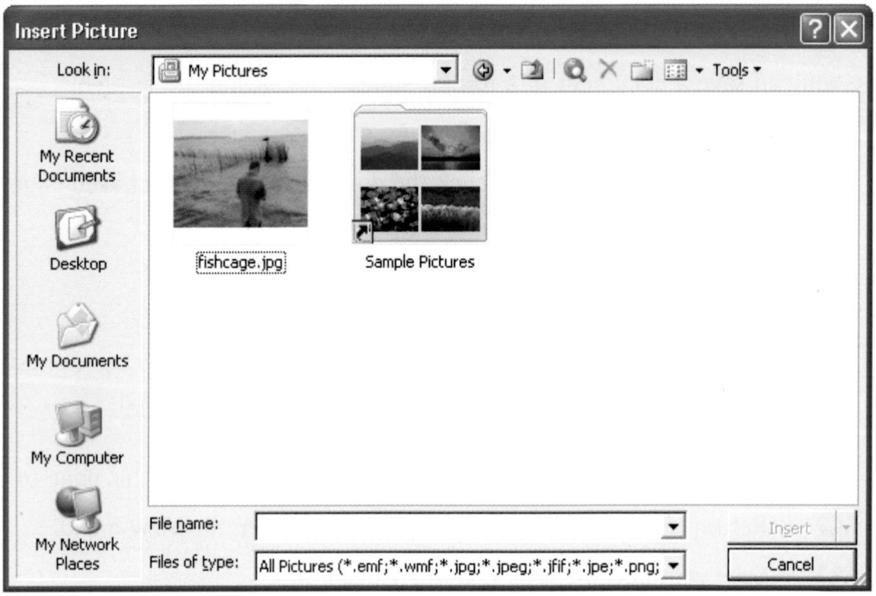

- Click **Insert.**

The graphic will now appear underneath the text.

- Click the graphic to select it. Black handles will appear around it.

Re-sizing an image

Once a graphic is selected you can drag any of the corner handles to make it bigger or smaller. If you drag one of the handles in the middle of a side you will change the proportions of the picture and it will appear distorted.

- Drag the bottom right-hand handle (which is hard to see against the background of the sea) upwards and inwards to make the picture about half the size. The pointer changes to a diagonal double-headed arrow when you click and hold over a corner handle.
- Centre the picture while it is still selected by clicking the **Centre** button on the Formatting toolbar.

Moving an image

When a selected graphic has black handles around it, it is embedded in the text and cannot be moved about except by positioning it to the left, right or centre as you can with text.

If you want to move it, you must change the **wrapping style**.

- With the graphic selected, select **Format Picture** from the menu bar.

Tip:
You can also use a shortcut: Right-click the picture and select **Format Picture**.

- The Format Picture window appears. Click the tab labelled **Layout**.

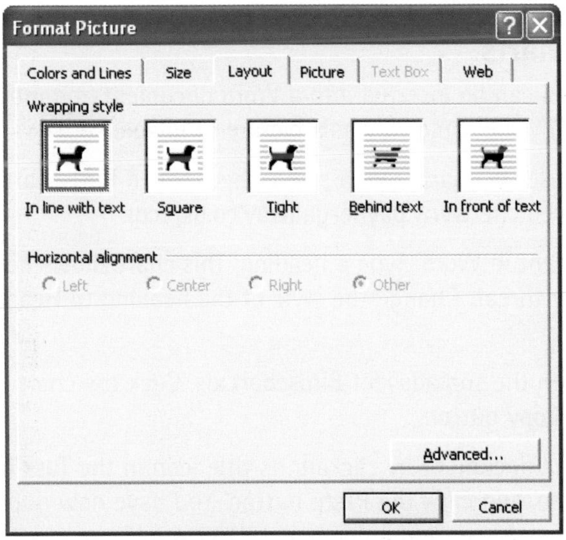

- Click the **Tight** layout and click **OK**.

The image should now have white handles around it and you can drag it up into the text.

- Position the graphic to the right of the text. Size it if necessary.

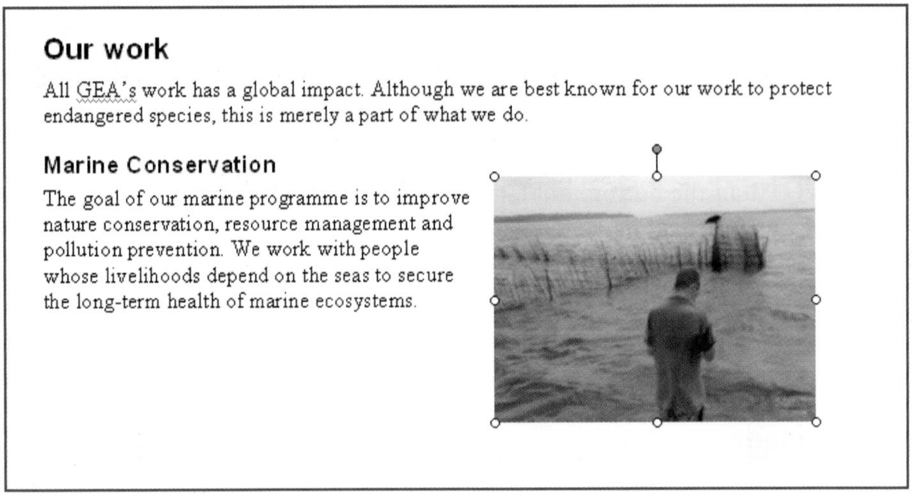

Our work

All GEA's work has a global impact. Although we are best known for our work to protect endangered species, this is merely a part of what we do.

Marine Conservation

The goal of our marine programme is to improve nature conservation, resource management and pollution prevention. We work with people whose livelihoods depend on the seas to secure the long-term health of marine ecosystems.

Copying or deleting an image

Once the image is selected, you can delete it simply by pressing the **Delete** key. You can also cut or copy it onto the clipboard and then paste it to another part of your document, or into another document.

- Try copying the graphic to the first page of the document by clicking the **Copy** button while the graphic is selected. Move to the first page and click the **Paste** button.
- Undo the Paste, as you do not need two copies of the image.
- Save and close the document.

Inserting and manipulating charts

Charts created in **MS Excel** can be inserted into a Word document and moved, resized, copied, or deleted in exactly the same way as a picture or image.

In this exercise you will insert a chart from a spreadsheet called Birdschart.xls. You can download this from the web site **www.payne-gallway.co.uk/ecdl**.

- Open a new document in Word. Type a heading, **This chart shows how English songbirds are under threat**. Change the style of the heading to **Heading 1** style. Press **Enter**.
- Open Excel and open the spreadsheet **Birdschart.xls**. Click the chart to select it and then click the **Copy** button.
- Return to your Word document by clicking its title icon in the **Task bar** at the bottom of the screen, and click the **Paste** button. You have now duplicated the chart between a spreadsheet and a document. (you would use exactly the same technique to copy a chart, picture or image to another open document).
- With the chart still selected, drag a corner handle until it fits neatly under the report heading.

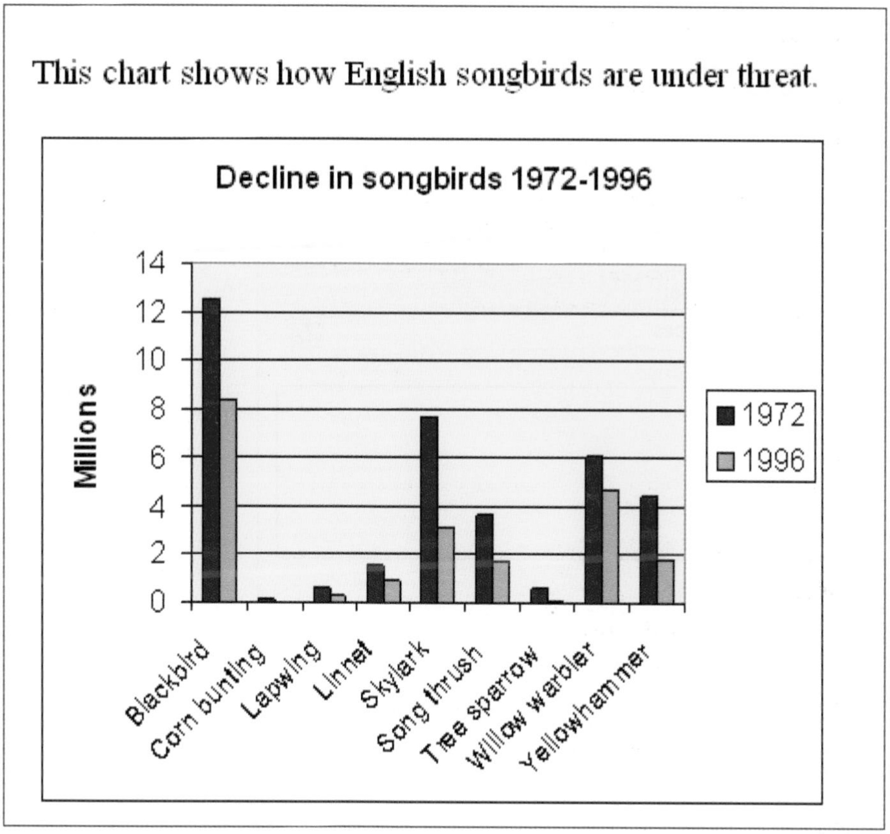

Note that when the chart is selected, it has black handles. To move it, you must change the wrapping style exactly as you did when moving an image. When it has white handles you will be able to drag it wherever you want it.

To delete that chart, you would simply select it and press the **Delete** key.

Inserting and manipulating a Clip Art picture in a document

Occasionally you may want to brighten up a document by inserting some Clip Art. MS Office has a collection of Clip Art pictures which you can use in your documents, and you can also purchase Clip Art collections on CD or borrow them from the local library.

You can try inserting a picture of a bird underneath the chart.

- Double-click underneath the chart to create an insertion point.
- From the **Insert** menu select **Picture, Clip Art**.
- A **Clip Art** pane appears and you can type a word into the Search box to say what you are looking for.

- Try typing **Bird**. Then click a picture that is not too awful, and it will be inserted into your document.

When you click the Clip Art picture it will be selected, and is surrounded by black handles.

Note:

- To resize the picture, drag a corner handle.
- To move the picture, use the same procedure as for an image, already described on Page 3-67.
- To copy the picture to another location in the same document, click to select it, then click the **Copy** button. Click where you want to copy it to and click the **Paste** button.
- To copy the picture (or an image or chart) into another document, or into your spreadsheet, click to select it, then click the **Copy** button. Restore the spreadsheet by clicking its Title icon in the Task bar, click where you want the picture to appear and click the **Paste** button.
- To delete a picture, image or chart, select it and press the **Delete** key.

Using the Help system

If you want to perform a particular function and are uncertain how to do it, you can always try the online Help system.

The **Office Assistant** takes the form of a paperclip, cat, dog or a number of other options.

- If the Office Assistant is not already visible on your screen, click **Help** on the menu bar and select **Show the Office Assistant**.

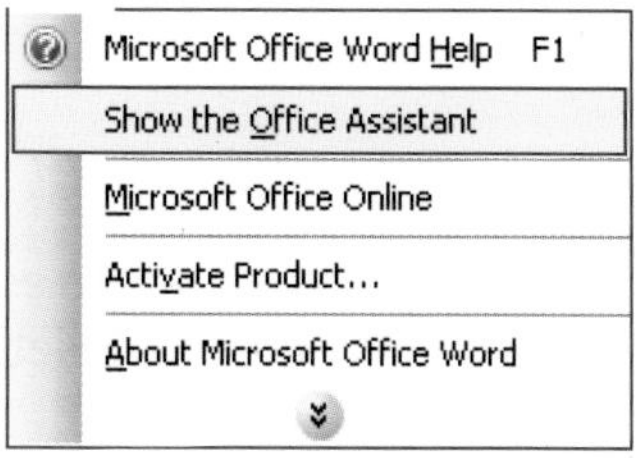

As an example, suppose you need to insert a page break and cannot remember how to do this. The Office Assistant can tell you how to do this.

- Click the Office Assistant cartoon.

Tip:
To change the appearance of the Office Assistant, right-click it and select **Choose Assistant.**

- Type in **Start a new page.**

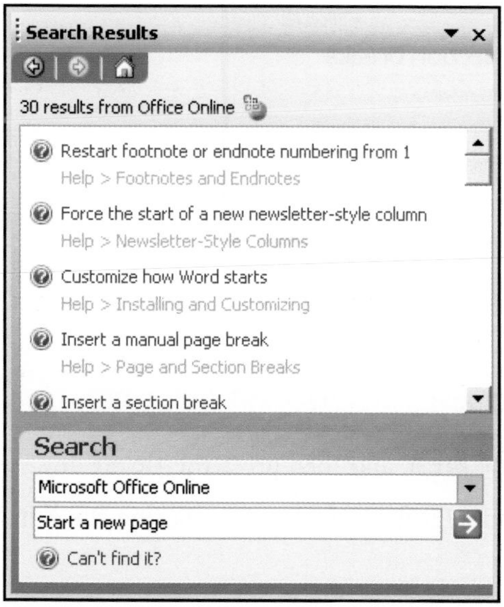

- From the new list, select **Insert a manual page break.**

Instructions are displayed:

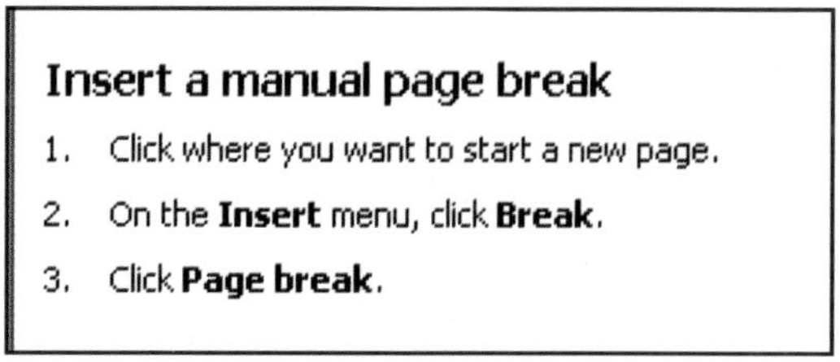

Insert a manual page break

1. Click where you want to start a new page.
2. On the **Insert** menu, click **Break**.
3. Click **Page break**.

Deleting a page break

- Now see if you can use the Help system to find out how to delete a manual page break. Try clicking the Office Assistant and typing into the box **Delete a page break.**

It may come up with a selection which includes **Troubleshoot page breaks.** If so, select this. It will recommend that you switch to Normal view, select the page break and then press **Delete.**

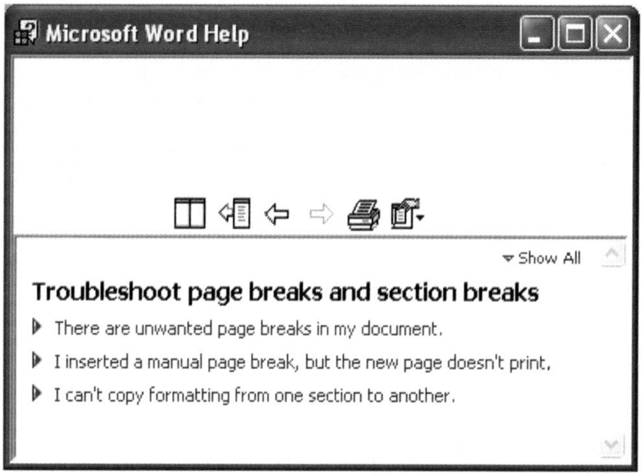

- On the main menu, click **View, Normal.**

Tip:
Note that the image does not appear in Normal view!

- Click on the line saying **Page Break** and then press the **Delete** key.
- You can close the **Help** window if it is still open by clicking the **X** in its top right-hand corner.
- Return to **Print Layout** view.

- Save your document and click the **Print Preview** button to view it in Print Preview mode.

Exercise

In this exercise you will develop the programme for the local agricultural show (that you began at the end of the end of the last chapter) into a multi-page document.

1. Open the file **Programme.doc**.
2. Insert a page break before the table. On this first page enter a large heading **Barksfield Show 2003 Programme of events**. Enter a sub-heading in a smaller font **Organised by Barksfield Town Council**.
3. Insert an appropriate piece of Clip Art onto this front cover.
4. Add a decorative border to this page.
5. Copy the table (now on page 2) and paste it onto pages 3 and 4 of the document.
6. Edit the contents of the table on the two new pages to show events taking place on days 2 and 3 of the show.
7. Insert a footer (on all pages except page 1) that displays the page number in the centre and the text **Barksfield Show 2003** on the right.
8. Save the document as **Complete Programme.doc** and print.

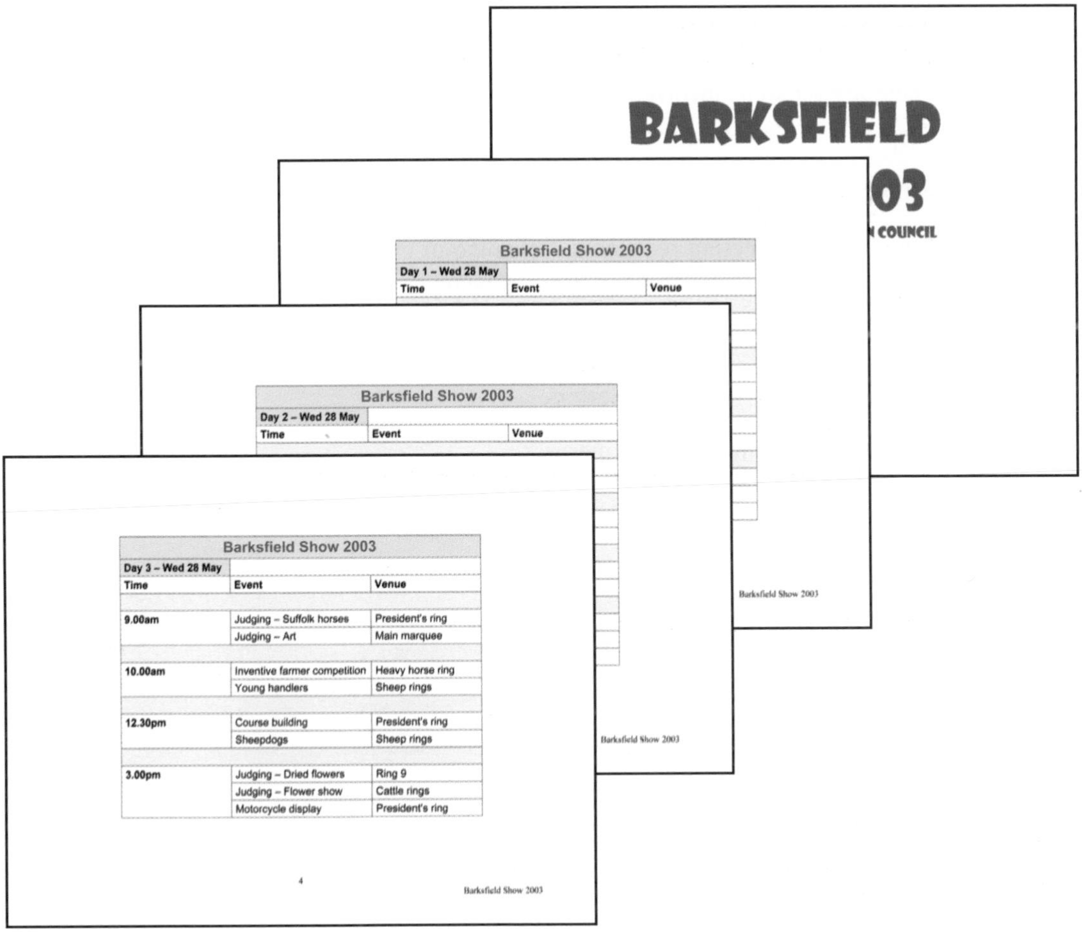

CHAPTER

3.8 Mail Merge

The mail merge facility is very useful when you want to send the same letter to a number of different people. You can personalise each letter by inserting the correct name, address and other details from a database or other data file.

In this chapter you will edit the letter that you created in Chapter 3.1 and prepare a personalised version to send out to several recipients, and also create address labels for the envelopes.

Creating the letters

There are six steps involved in setting up a mail merge:

Step 1: Selecting the type of document you are working on.

Step 2: Setting up and displaying your document.

Step 3: Selecting recipients – opening or creating the list of names and addresses to whom the document is being sent.

Step 4: Writing your letter.

Step 5: Previewing the letters.

Step 6: Completing the merge.

Step 1: Selecting the type of document you are working on.

- Open the letter you created in Chapter 3.1 – it should be saved as **TanzaniaLetter.doc**.
- From the Main Menu bar, select **Tools, Letters and Mailings, Mail Merge** (**Mail Merge Wizard** in Office XP). The Mail Merge Task pane should appear on the right of the screen.

- Make sure you have selected **Letters** as the document type you are working with.
- Now click on **Next: Starting document** at the bottom of the Task pane. This will take you on to Step 2.

Step 2: Select starting document – setting up your letter

- You already have the letter open that you want to work on. So select **Use the current document**.

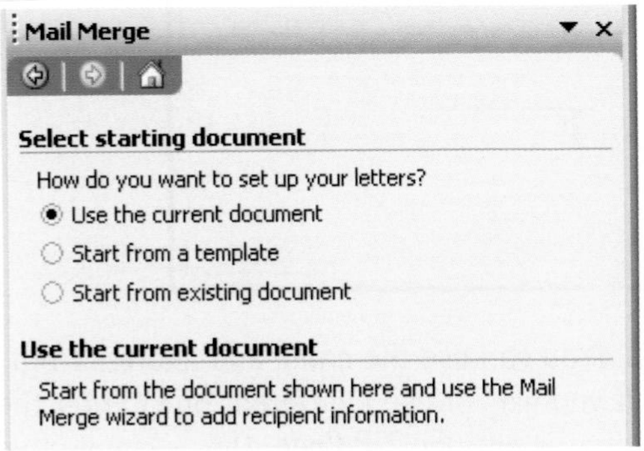

- Click on **Next: Select recipients** to move on to Step 3.

Step 3: Selecting recipients

You now have the choice of using an existing data file such as a database table or a spreadsheet, or creating a new list. If you select **Use an existing list**, you will be able to browse through the files on your computer until you find the file you want to use. The data will appear in a **Mail Merge Recipients** box exactly as described near the end of Step 3.

- You don't currently have any lists or contacts, so you need to create your own. Select the **Type a new list** option and click on **Create** in the section that appears. A dialogue box like the one below should appear.

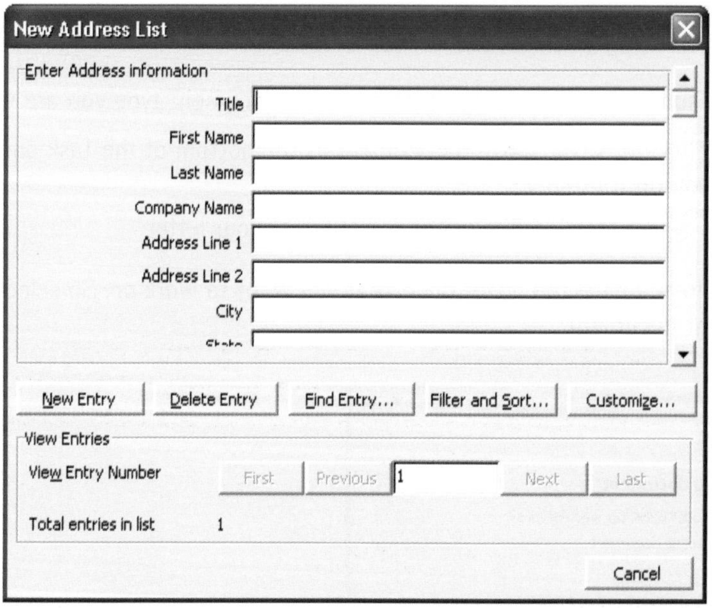

- Enter a name and address. (You can use the name and address from the letter that you have on-screen if you like, or use a different one.) Enter the post code of the address in the box that is entitled **ZIP Code**. This is simply the American equivalent of our post code.

Tip:
You can press the **Tab** key to move from one box to the next.

You will have left a lot of the boxes in the dialogue box blank – for example **Company name** and **State**. You can delete these unneeded boxes from your records.

- Click the **Customize** button in the dialogue box. A further dialogue box will appear.
- Click on the first field name that you don't need – **Company Name**. With this selected, click on the **Delete** button, then click **Yes** to confirm. Repeat this for the other field names that you don't need for your address list. Click **OK**.
- Now you are back in the **New Address List** box. Click on **New Entry** and the boxes will clear. Don't worry about your first entry – it is automatically saved for you. You can now enter the name and address of a second person to whom you want to send the letter.
- Fill in the details for your second person and click **New Entry**. Repeat this until you have entered 5 or 6 addresses for your list and then click **Close**. Another dialogue box will appear:

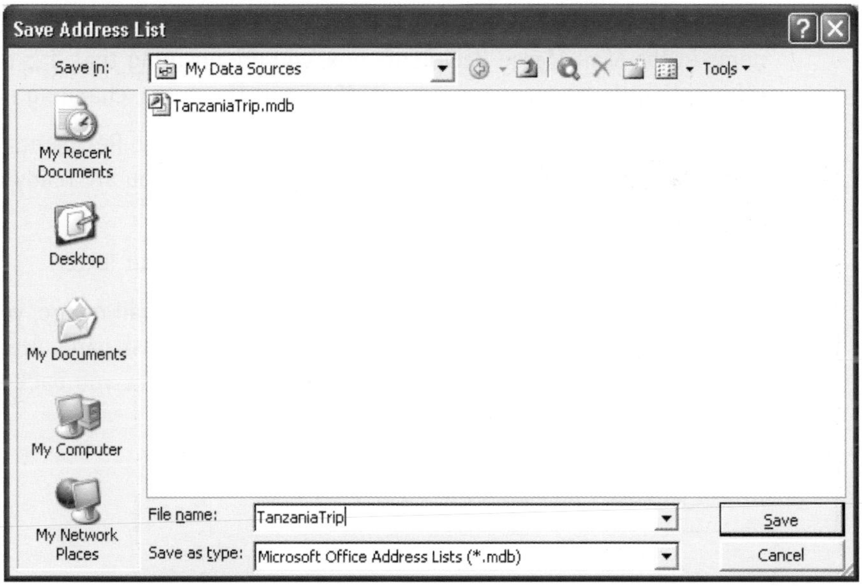

Your address list will automatically be saved as an **.mdb** database file in the **My Data Sources** area of your computer.

- Save your address list as **TanzaniaTrip.mdb**.

When you have saved your address list, a further box will appear – the **Mail Merge Recipients** box. This allows you to view your completed list of names and addresses and make any amendments – for example you may want to arrange them in a particular order, or perhaps change one of the addresses.

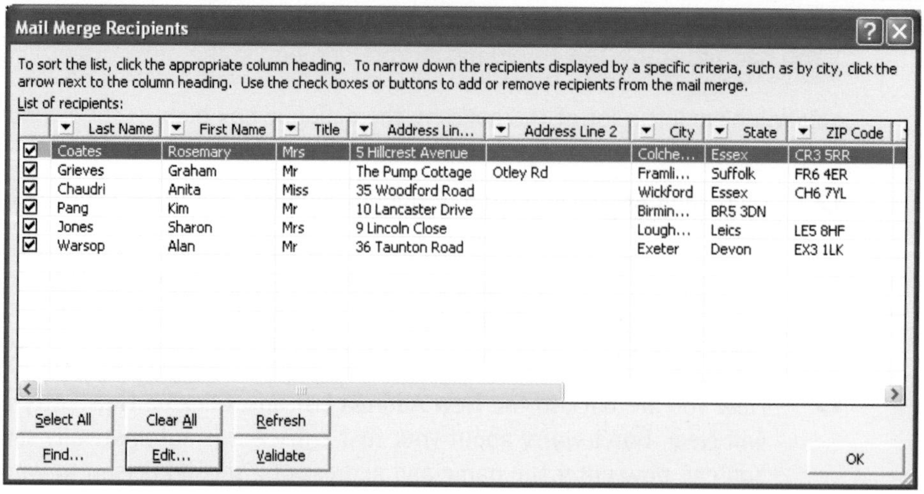

Suppose in the example above you wanted to change **Grieves** to **Greaves**.

- Select the whole entry by clicking anywhere along the line that contains his information. Then click on the **Edit** button.
- The box that appears is the same as the original **New Address List** box, except it is now full of the information you stored in it. By selecting Graham Grieves's name in the Mail Merge Recipients box, you are ensuring that it is his information that appears on-screen. Now edit the name, changing it to **Greaves**.
- Click on **Close** and you are taken back to the Mail Merge Recipients box, in which the amended name appears. Now click **OK** and you are ready to move on to Step 4 of your mail merge.
- At the bottom of the Task pane, click on **Next: Write your letter**.

If at any point you wish to return to a previous step of your mail merge, you can do so by clicking the back arrow in the top left of the mail merge Task pane. Alternatively, click on **Previous** at the bottom of the Task pane and it will take you back to the last step that you completed.

Step 4: Write your letter

You have already written your letter. However, you do want to add recipient information, in the form of the names and addresses you saved in the previous step. Also, you want to add a greeting line so that all of your letters don't say **Dear Mrs Coates** like the original letter.

- In your original letter, highlight the name and address you entered beginning **Mrs R. Coates** and ending with the postcode.
- Now click on **Address Block** in the Task pane. A dialogue box will appear:

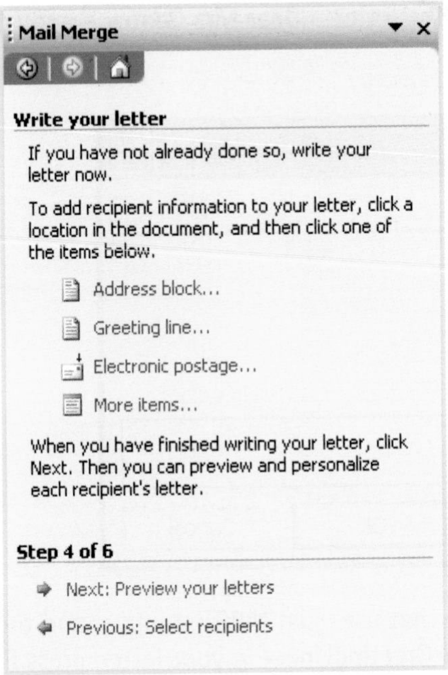

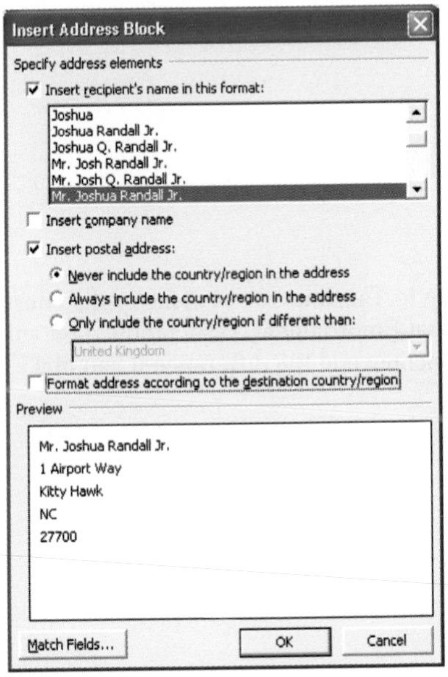

- Choose a suitable format for the recipient's name and set the other options as above. Click **OK**.
- With the insertion point positioned after **««AddressBlock»»**, press **Enter** to create a blank line.

You can carry out many of these tasks using the **Mail Merge** toolbar, which does appear automatically above your main page when carrying out a mail merge. However, it is much easier if you follow the steps through using the **Mail Merge Wizard**, as we have been doing in this chapter.

- Now highlight the first line of the letter – **Dear Mrs Coates** – and click on **Greeting line** in the Task pane.

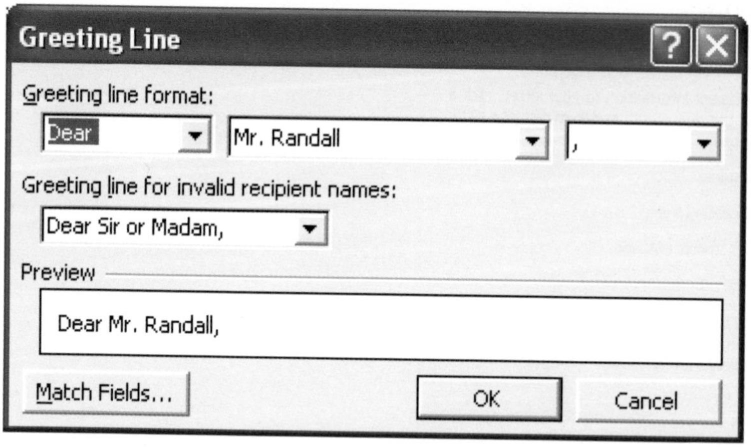

- Select the Greeting line format that uses just the first name, and then click **OK**. With the insertion point after **««GreetingLine»»** in your letter, press **Enter**.

The screen should now be looking something like this:

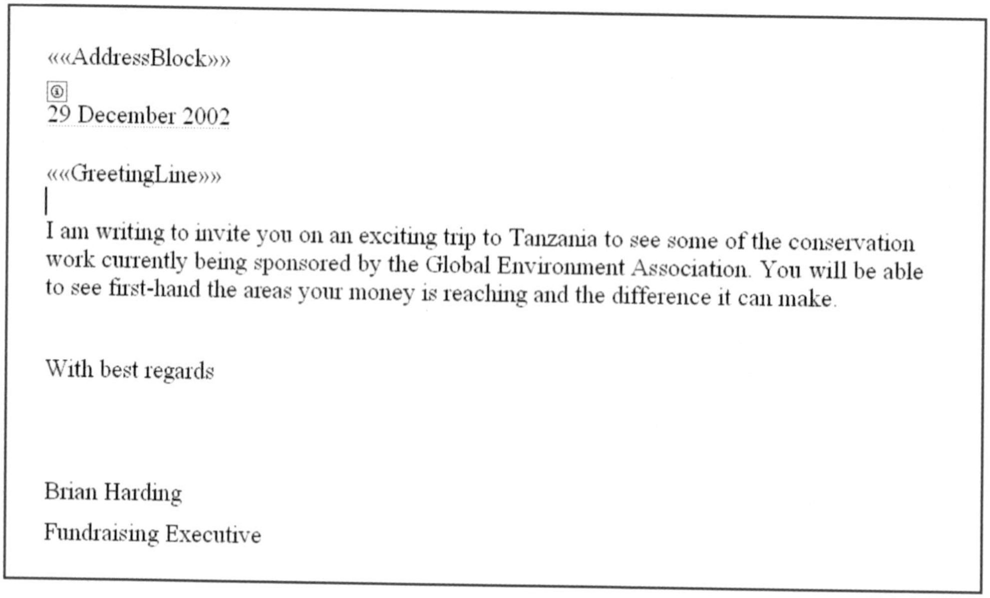
««AddressBlock»»

29 December 2002

««GreetingLine»»

I am writing to invite you on an exciting trip to Tanzania to see some of the conservation work currently being sponsored by the Global Environment Association. You will be able to see first-hand the areas your money is reaching and the difference it can make.

With best regards

Brian Harding

Fundraising Executive

With your letter completed, you are now able to preview and personalise each recipient's letter.

- Click **Next: Preview your letters** at the bottom of the Task pane.

Step 5: Previewing your letters

- You should see the preview of the first of your letters, with the address block and the greeting line inserted as you selected. Click on the arrow button to the right of **Recipient: 1** to preview the other letters.

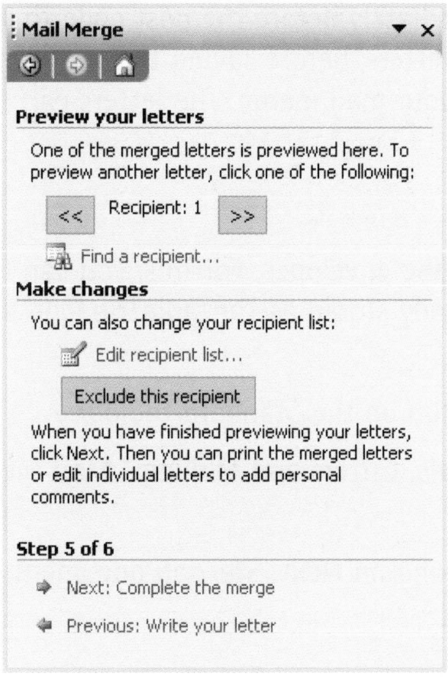

In the address block for each letter, the post code appears on the same line as the city. You may want to change this to ensure that the post code appears on a line of its own - you will be doing this during the final step of the merge.

- Click **Next: Complete the merge** to move on to the last step of your merge.

Step 6: Completing the merge

You are now ready to complete the merge and produce your letters. However, first you must edit your individual letters to ensure that the post codes are properly positioned in the text.

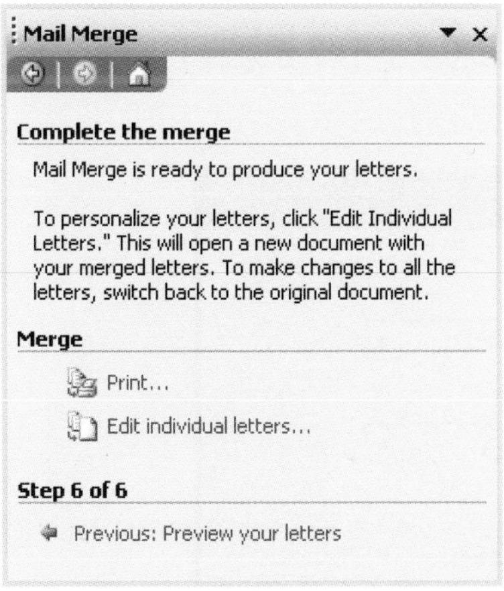

- Click on **Edit individual letters.**
- In the **Merge to New Document** dialogue box select **All** and click **OK.**
- A new document automatically opens containing all your letters. This document will be called **Letters1**, and you can now scroll down through each letter individually.

- In your first letter, press **Enter** immediately before the post code to send it to a new line. Repeat this for the other letters, before saving the file and finally printing. You have now completed your mail merge. The letters can be printed.

Creating mailing labels

You can now create the labels to stick on the envelopes. For this, you can use the same name and address data that you have already stored as **TanzaniaTrip.mdb** and choose to create labels instead of Form letters.

- Click the **New Blank Document** button on the Standard toolbar.
- From the Main Menu bar, select **Tools, Letters and Mailings, Mail Merge**. The Mail Merge Task pane again appears.
- Select the **Labels** option before clicking on **Next: Starting document**.

- With **Change document layout** selected, click on **Label options** to choose the size of your labels.

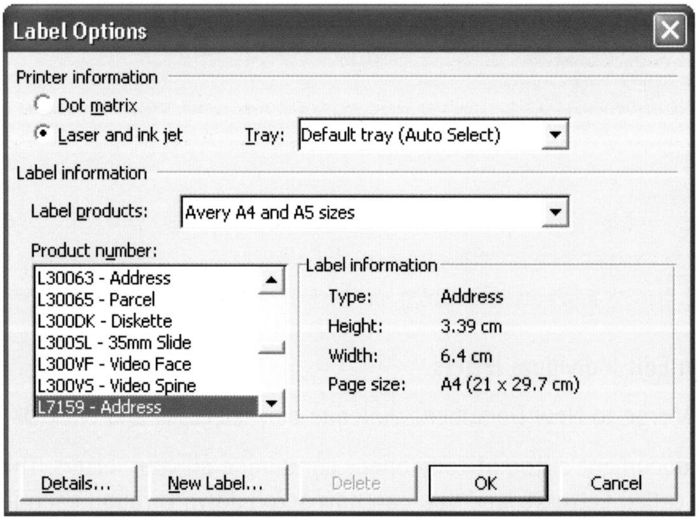

Tip:
If you want a specific type of label that does not appear as an option in the dialogue box, you can create your own custom labels by clicking on **New Label** and entering your own specifications.

- Select your own size of label from the options shown and click **OK**. A grid of label outlines will appear in your document.
- Click on **Next: Select recipients** at the bottom of the Task pane.
- You want to use the same list of data that you used previously in setting up your mail merge. With **Use an existing list** selected, click on **Browse**.

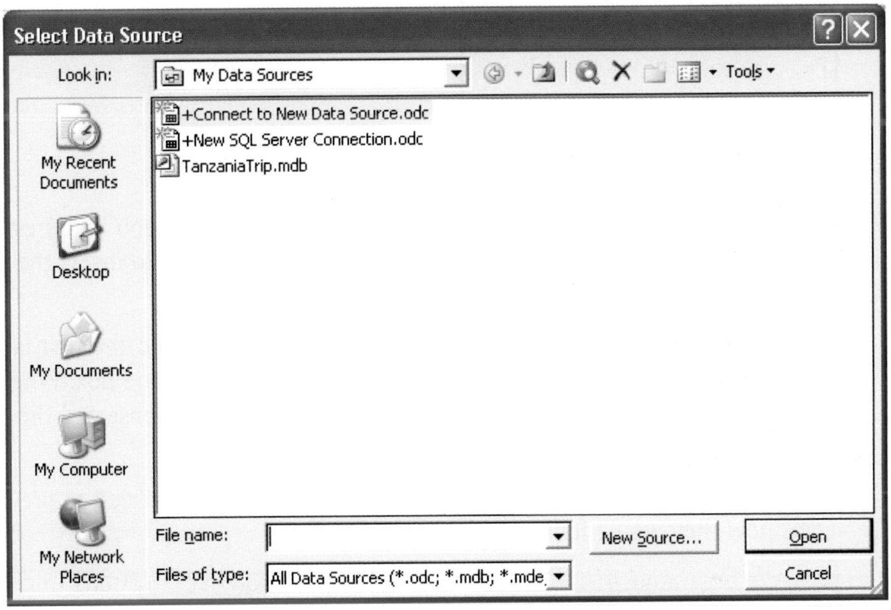

- In the dialogue box, select the file **TanzaniaTrip.mdb** that you created earlier in the chapter and click **Open**. The Mail Merge Recipients box will open showing the information you saved earlier – simply click **OK**.
- With the insertion point in the first box in your grid, you are ready to begin putting your data onto the labels. Click on **Next: Arrange your labels** at the bottom of the Task pane.

When performing the actual mail merge, you inserted an **Address block** into your letter. However, you then had to edit the address block because it automatically positioned the post code on the same line as the city. This time you are going to insert the data fields manually.

- Click on the **More items** option.

The dialogue box below will appear:

The **Insert Merge Fields** box presents you with the fields that you had previously saved in your database when performing the mail merge. You want to insert the name and address fields into your labels.

- With **Title** selected, click on **Insert** to insert the field into the first label. Select and insert every other field up to **ZIP code** in the dialogue box. When you have inserted ZIP Code, click on **Close** (which once you have inserted the first field replaces the **Cancel** button in the figure above).

Your fields currently have no spacing between them, so if you tried to preview your labels now they would look like the one below.

- Insert a space between **«Title»** and **«First_Name»** by placing the insertion point directly after **«Title»** and pressing the Space bar. Repeat this to insert a space between **«First_Name»** and **«Last_Name»**.
- Insert a line break after **«Last_Name»** by placing the insertion point directly after it and pressing **Enter**. Repeat this to insert line breaks at the end of every other field in your label apart from the last line of the address, the post code.
- Once you have arranged your data fields into the right format, click on the **Update all labels** button to ensure that all of your labels have the same format.

- Now you are ready to preview your labels – click on **Next: Preview your labels** at the bottom of the Task pane. They should look like this, although you may only see one label at this stage.

Mr Alan Warsop 36 Taunton Road Exeter Devon EX3 1LK	Mrs Sharon Jones 9 Lincoln Close Loughborough Leics LE5 8HF	Mr Kim Pang 10 Lancaster Drive Birmingham BR5 3DN
Miss Anita Chaudri 35 Woodford Road Wickford Essex CH6 7YL	Mr Graham Greaves The Pump Cottage Otley Rd Framlingham Suffolk FR6 4ER	Mrs Rosemary Coates 5 Hillcrest Avenue Colchester Essex CR3 5RR

- Click on **Next: Complete the merge** to go to the final stage of creating your labels.
- In the final Task pane, click on **Edit individual labels**. In the **Merge to new document** dialogue box that appears, make sure **All** is selected before clicking **OK**. This creates a new document containing your actual labels with the names and addresses on, probably called **Labels2.doc**. You are now able to make any changes you think need making before saving the labels.
- Save your labels as **TanzaniaLabels.doc**. If you want to print labels, you should make sure that you have the correct label stationery loaded in the printer.
- You can save the document which contains the label format as **Labels.doc**.
- Close both documents.

Exercise

In this exercise you will create a list of names and addresses to receive the letter created at the end of Chapter 3.4. You will use the letter produced at the end of that chapter to perform a mail merge.

1. Open the file **letter.doc**.
2. Delete the addressee details.
3. Use this letter as your starting document in the mail merge.
4. Enter a new list of six contacts that are to receive the letter.
5. Produce the merged letters.
6. Create mailing labels for the envelopes.
7. Save and close your work.

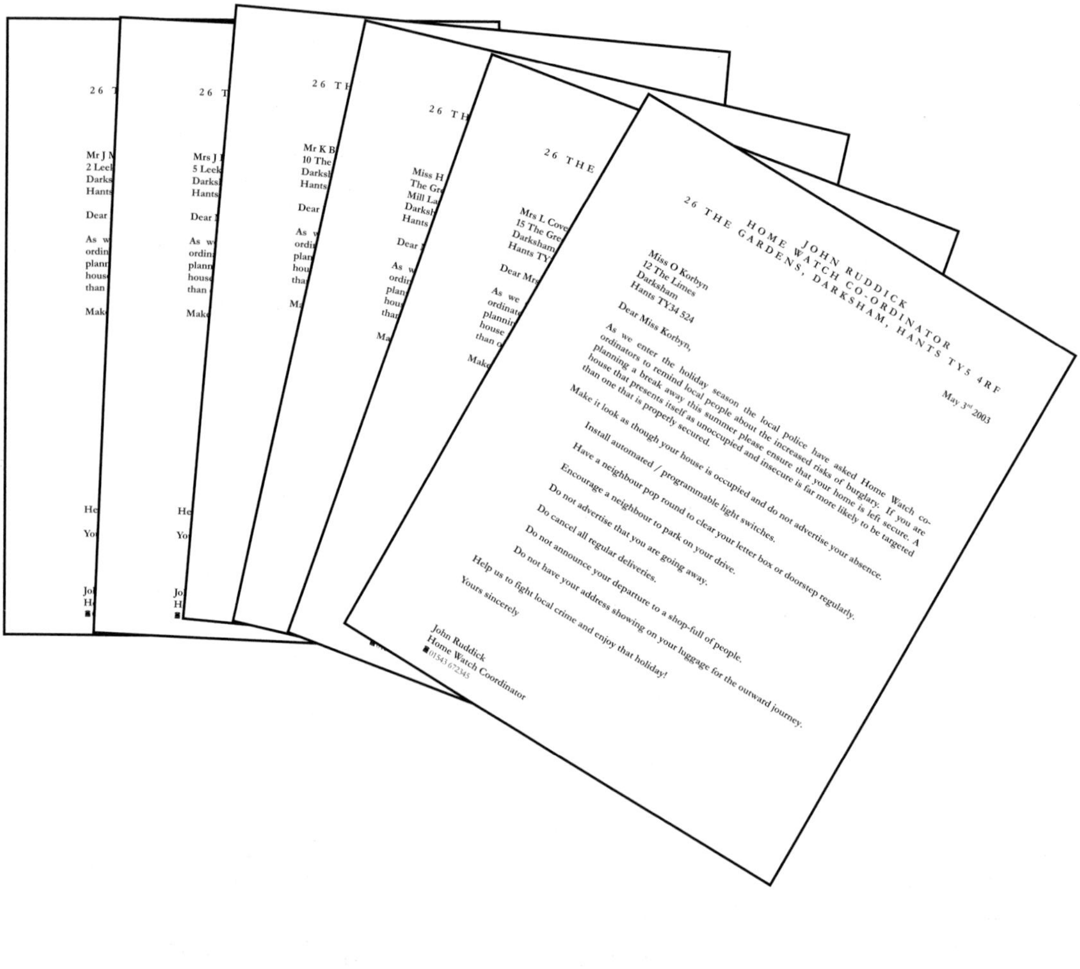

Module 4

Spreadsheets

In this module you will learn the basic concepts of spreadsheets and how to use a spreadsheet application on a computer. You will learn how to:

- create a spreadsheet
- format a spreadsheet
- edit a spreadsheet
- generate and apply standard formulae and functions
- create graphs and charts
- format graphs and charts

Module 4 Table of Contents

What is a Spreadsheet?

CHAPTER 4.1

Getting Started

A spreadsheet is a very useful piece of computer software mainly used for working with numbers. Spreadsheets are used in thousands of different applications which involve doing calculations or drawing charts.

Spreadsheets are often used for planning budgets and working with financial data. Different figures can be entered and the effect of the changes will be calculated automatically.

Microsoft Excel is one of many different spreadsheet packages. In Excel, spreadsheets are referred to as workbooks. Just to make it even more confusing, a workbook can contain several worksheets.

In this chapter you will learn how to move around a worksheet and enter text and numbers.

- Load Microsoft Excel. You can do this in one of two ways:
- *Either* double-click the Excel icon on your windows desktop
- *Or* click Start at the bottom left of the screen, then click Programs, then click

Your screen will look like this:

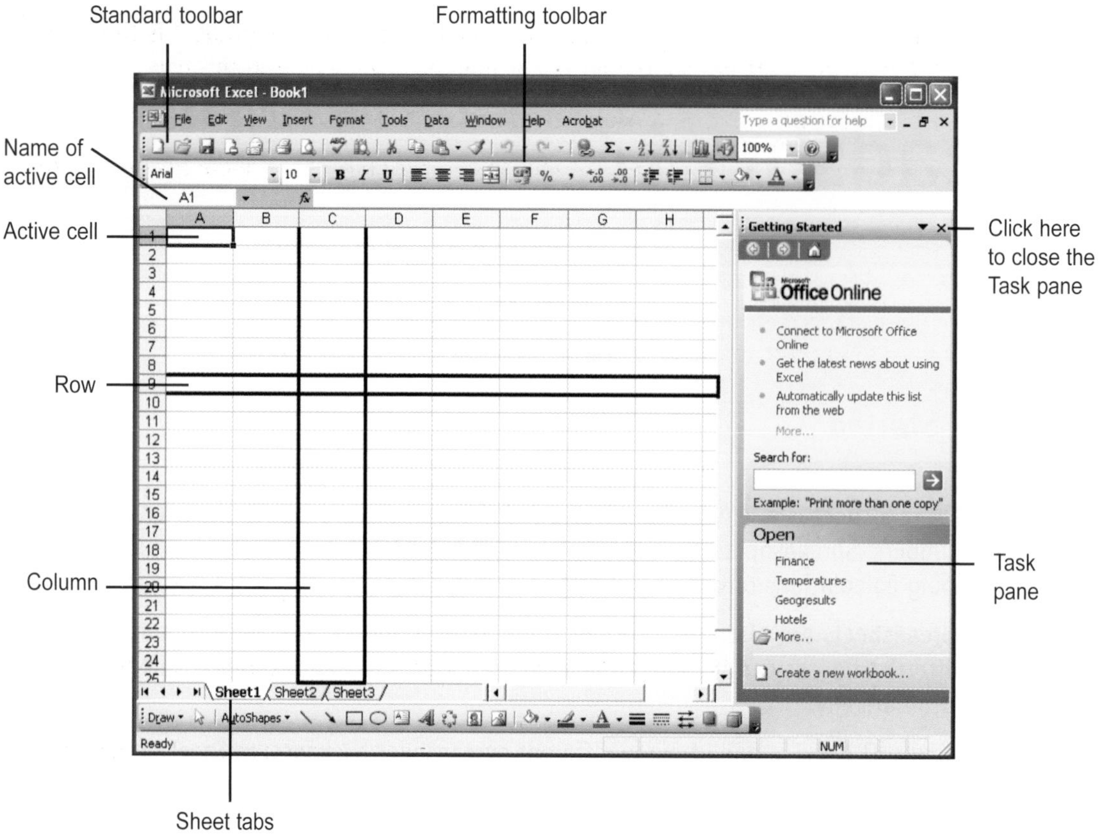

- A worksheet contains 256 columns and 16,384 rows – you can only see a few of these on the screen.
- The columns are labelled A, B, C and so on. The rows are labelled 1, 2, 3 etc.
- The worksheet is divided into cells in which you can type a number, a label or a formula. The address of the cell in the top left-hand corner is A1, because it is in column A and row 1.
- A workbook contains several blank worksheets named Sheet1, Sheet2, Sheet3 etc. These names are on the sheet tabs shown above.

Note:

The Task pane was new in Excel 2002. It lists the workbooks you recently opened and other options. Close it now by clicking the **Close** icon at the top of the Task pane.

Moving around the worksheet

When you open a new workbook, cell **A1** is highlighted, showing that it is the **active cell**. When you start typing, the letters or numbers will appear in this cell.

You can move around the spreadsheet to make a cell active by:

- Moving the pointer using the mouse and clicking the left mouse button in the cell you want.
- Using one of the arrow keys to go up, down, left or right.
- Using the **Page Up** or **Page Down** keys.
- Pressing the **Tab** key.

Experiment!

- Try moving around the spreadsheet using the arrow keys and **Page Up**, **Page Down** keys.
- Try holding down the **Ctrl** key while you use any of the arrow keys. What happens?
- What is the name (i.e. address or cell reference) of the very last cell in the worksheet?
- With the active cell somewhere in the middle of the worksheet, try pressing **Ctrl-Home**. Where does this take you?

The Zoom tool

You can easily change the size of the spreadsheet on your screen.

- Make sure you can see the **Zoom** tool on the **Standard** toolbar.

- Enter a higher percentage to make the sheet bigger, or a smaller percentage to make the sheet smaller and view more of the page on the screen.

Toolbars

You will learn about what individual toolbars and buttons do as they become relevant whilst you are creating your spreadsheet. Below are a few tips that apply to all toolbars, which will be useful if you cannot find a particular toolbar or think that you are missing a button or two! You may find that you already know most of this – it will be pretty much the same as you have experienced in other Microsoft applications such as Word or PowerPoint.

Hiding and displaying toolbars

You can select which toolbars are displayed on your screen. If you find that you can't find a particular button it might be worth checking that you have the right toolbar ticked.

- Select View, Toolbars and select the toolbar you want from the list that appears.

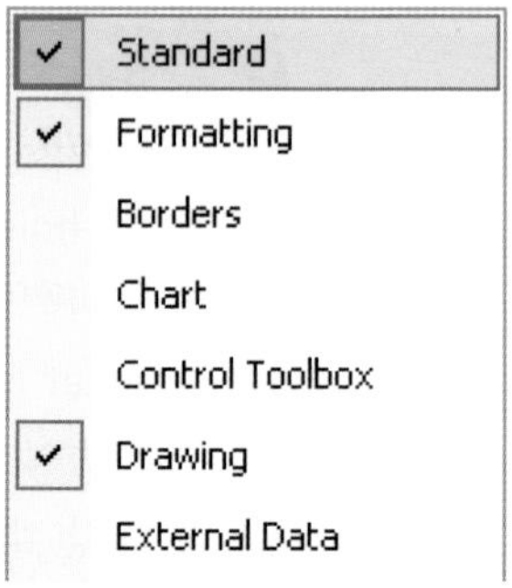

Tip:
To hide a toolbar, simply click on it in the list again so that the tick disappears.

Customising Toolbars

As well as choosing which toolbars you want displayed, you can also choose which buttons are displayed on each toolbar.

To remove a button from view:

- Hold down the Alt key, then click and drag the button off the toolbar.

To replace a button:

- On the toolbar that the button you want belongs to, click the Toolbar Options arrow at the end of the toolbar.

- Click Add or Remove Buttons, select the name of the toolbar (e.g. Formatting or Standard), then click to select and deselect buttons.
- Click away from the menu when you have finished editing the buttons.

Changing defaults and preferences

By default (i.e. unless you tell it otherwise) Excel saves your documents in a folder called My Documents on the C: drive. You can change this default as well as many other preferences.

- From the main menu select Tools, Options.

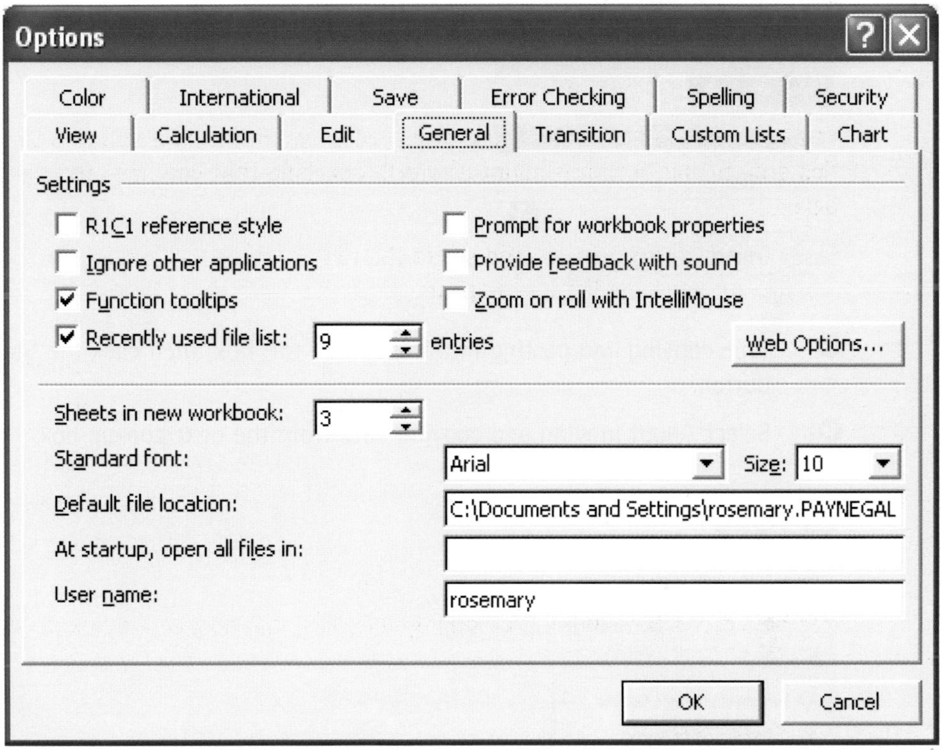

- Click the General tab.

You will now be able to change the default directory for opening and saving files. You can also change the user name, the standard font and how many sheets a new workbook should have.

By clicking on the Save tab in the Options window, you can change various defaults such as how frequently your document is automatically saved.

Using the Help functions

If at any time you aren't sure how to do something in Excel, you can search the Help files for instructions on your chosen subject. For example, let's search for help on copying and pasting.

- Select Help, Microsoft Excel Help from the menu.

You will see the Excel Help window appear.

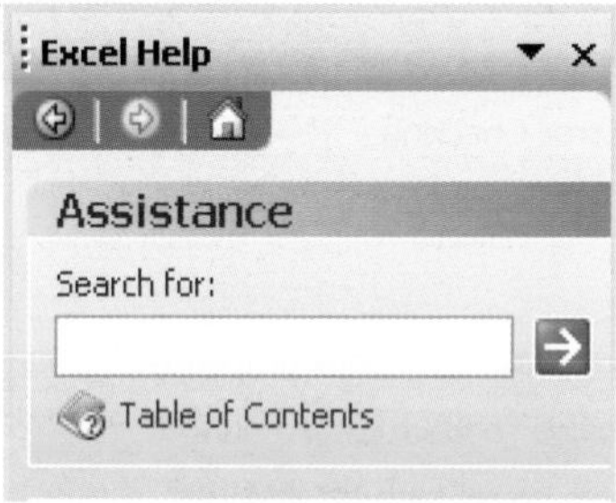

- Type copying and pasting into the Search for: box, then click the Start searching button.
- Select About moving and copying data from the next pop-up box.

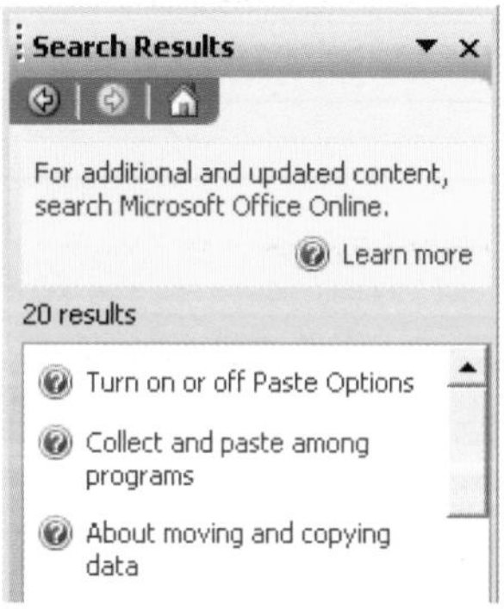

A Help window appears giving information on this topic.

- Click the Close icon to close the Help window.

Entering data

Suppose that you have to produce a list of all the employees in an office along with the number of days holiday they have taken so far this year.

The list will look like this:

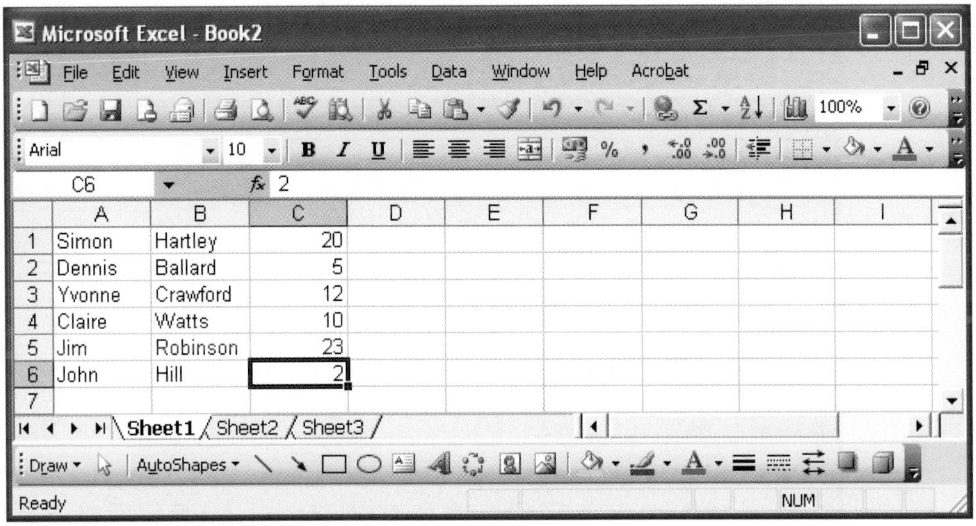

- Click in cell **A1**.
- Type the name **Simon**.
- Press the right arrow key.
- Type the surname **Hartley**. Press the right arrow key again and type the number **20** in cell **C1**.
- Press **Enter**. Excel guesses that you are typing a list and goes to cell **A2**. (If it does not, click in cell **A2** or use the arrow keys to go there).
- Copy the rest of the list. If you make any mistakes, don't worry because you can correct them in a minute.

Tip:

If you start to type another name beginning with, say **S** in cell **A7**, Excel will guess that you are going to type **Simon** again and enter the letters for you. If you were going to type **Simon**, you can just tab out of the cell or press **Enter**. If you were going to type **Stuart** or some other name beginning with **S**, just carry on typing. Try it out.

Editing data

One name has been spelt wrongly. It should be spelt Clare, not Claire. There are several ways of putting it right.

First way

- Click in the cell containing the name Claire. You will see that the name appears in the Formula bar, as shown below:

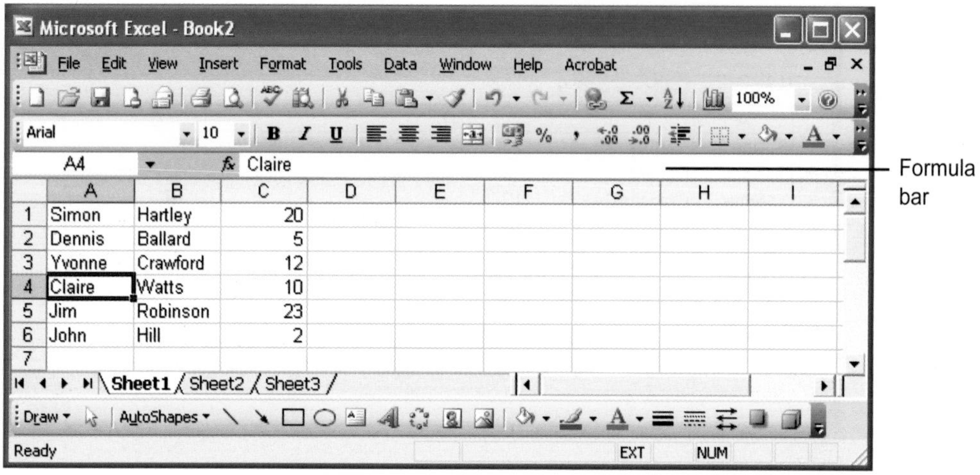

Click in the Formula bar. Use the arrow keys to move the insertion point between i and r, and then press the Backspace key. You will see that the change is made in the cell A3 at the same time as you edit the name in the Formula bar.

- Press Enter to register the change.

Second way

Another way to edit a cell is simply to type over the text in the cell. Suppose Simon's surname is actually Hemmings, not Hartley.

- Click in the cell containing the surname Hartley.
- Type Hemmings.
- Press Enter.

Deleting the contents of a cell

To delete the contents of a cell, click in the cell and then press the Delete key.

- Delete the surname Robinson.

Inserting and deleting rows and columns

We can delete the whole of row 5 so that no gap is left between Clare's and John's records.

- Right-click the row header for row 5 (see the figure below).
- Left-click Delete from the shortcut menu which appears.

The entry for John moves up to row 5.

Tip:
Delete columns in a similar way: right-click the column header and select Delete from the shortcut menu.

The numbers 1,2,3... down the side of the worksheet are called the row headers. Right-click 5 to select row 5 and display the shortcut menu.

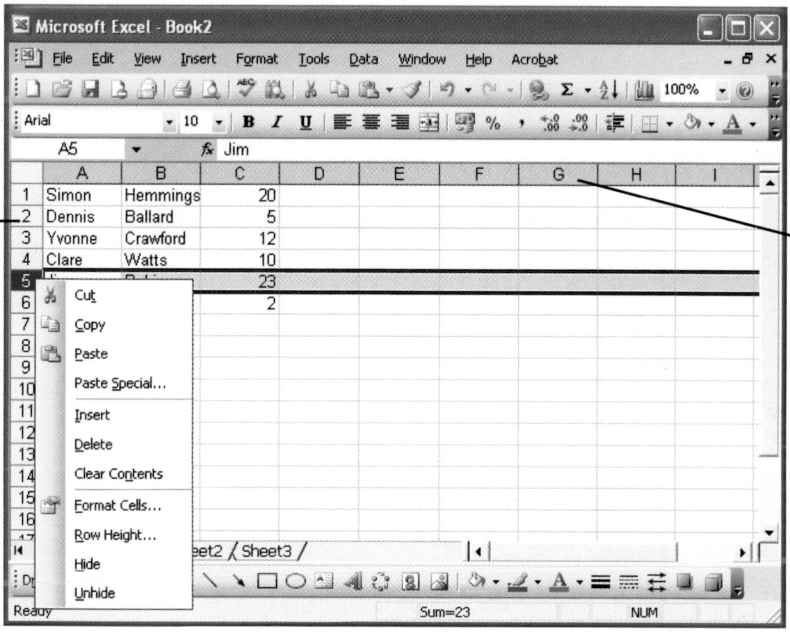

Column header

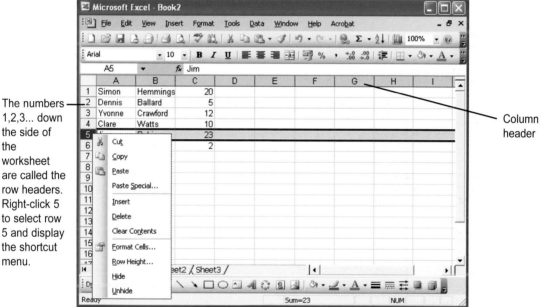

Now suppose we want to put a heading at the top of the worksheet, above the names. We need to insert a new row.

- Right-click the header for row 1.
- Select Insert from the shortcut menu.
- Click the left mouse button in cell A1.
- Type Holiday Days Taken in cell A1 in the new row. Press Enter.
- Insert another blank line below the heading in the same way.

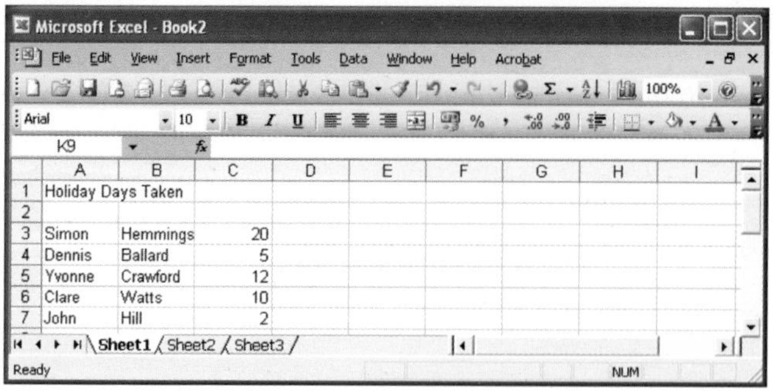

Tip:
Insert columns in a similar way: right-click the column header immediately to the right of where you want to insert the new column. Select **Insert** from the shortcut menu.

Saving your work

- Click **File**, **Save** from the main menu.

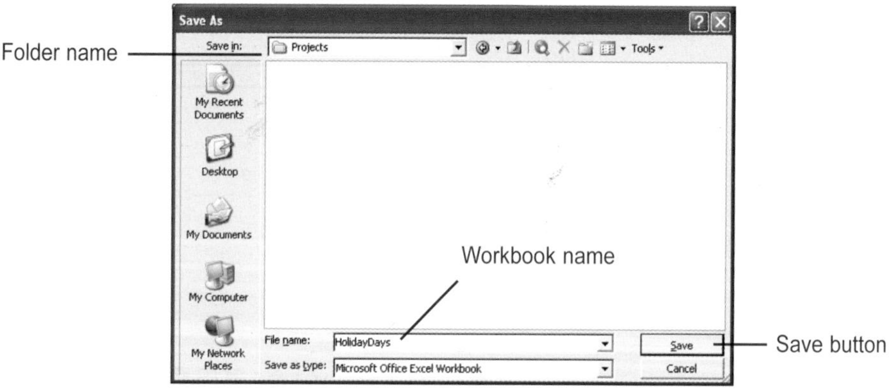

Excel gives your workbook a default name such as **Book1.xls** or **Book2.xls** The name appears in the **File name** box.

Tip:
If you don't see **Save** on the **File** menu, click the double arrow at the bottom of the menu to see more options.

- Make sure the right folder is displayed in the **Save in** box, then enter the name **HolidayDays** in the **File name** box.
- Click the **Save** button to save the workbook.
- Close the workbook by selecting **File**, **Close** from the menu.

- Close **Excel** by clicking the **Close** icon in the top right of the window.

Tip:
You can close a workbook by clicking the **Close** icon in the top right of the window.

Exercise

Suppose you want to prepare a costing for a children's birthday party. There are several options open to you – holding the party at home or taking them out on a trip somewhere. If the party is held at home you can safely accommodate 20 children. Create a spreadsheet to calculate these costs. You will develop this further at the end of Chapter 4.2.

1. In a new Microsoft Excel worksheet enter a main title **Party Budget – at home.**
2. Enter the first column heading **Item.**
3. Enter the other column headings as follows:

   Cost **Total Cost**

   Where: **Cost** is the unit cost for that item

   Total Cost is the total price for that item for all the children attending

   Enter the data shown below:

Item	Cost	Total Cost
Catering	3	
Magician	60	
Party bag	1	
Balloons	10	
Cake	15	

4. Edit the last two column headings as follows:

   Cost(£) **Total Cost(£)**

5. Insert a blank line after the main title and one after the column headings.
6. Insert a new column between **Item** and **Cost** to show the number of items as follows:

Number
20
1
20
1
1

7. Save your file as **Birthday1** and close Excel.

CHAPTER 4.2 Formulae

The really useful part of spreadsheets is formulae. Using a formula Excel will perform calculations for you automatically.

To see how formulae work in Excel, we'll start by doing a page of 'sums'. We'll be using the following mathematical symbols:

+ add

- subtract

* multiply

/ divide

() brackets are used whenever necessary

The first task is to set out the page just how you want it.

Project: Create a worksheet to do calculations

	A	B	C	D	E	F	G
1	ADD		SUBTRACT		DIVIDE		MULTIPLY
2	100		100		230		57.3
3	400		56		14.5		12.5
4							

- Open up Excel; a new blank workbook should automatically be created.
- Type the text ADD, SUBTRACT, DIVIDE, MULTIPLY in cells A1, C1, E1 and G1 as shown above.
- Type all the numbers as shown in the correct cells.

Tip:
If a new workbook doesn't appear when you open Excel, just click the New button on the Standard toolbar.

Selecting cells

In order to format the text in certain cells by making it bold or changing the font, the cells first have to be selected. Try the following ways to select a range of cells:

- Click in the intersection of the row and column headers to select every cell in the worksheet. All the selected cells appear highlighted.

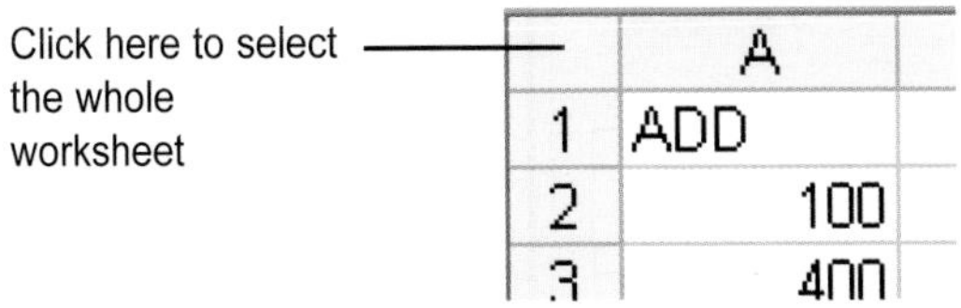

- Click in column header A to select column A. The new selection replaces the previous one.
- Click in row header 1 to select row 1.
- Drag the mouse across cells A1 to G1 to select those cells.
- To select just cells A1, C1, E1 and G1, click in cell A1 and then hold down the Ctrl key while you click each of the other cells.

Tip:
To select a range of adjacent rows or columns, drag the mouse across the row or column headers. To select a range of non-adjacent rows or columns, hold down the Ctrl key while you click the row or column headers.

Formatting cell contents

You can format text and numbers in a worksheet by selecting the appropriate cells and then using buttons on the Formatting toolbar.

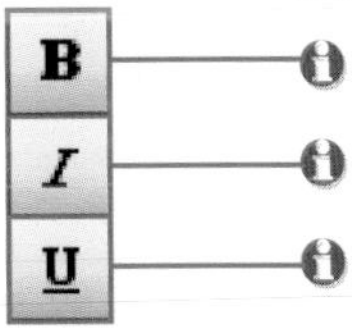

- Embolden cell contents using the Bold button.
- Italicise cell contents using the Italic button.
- Underline cell contents using the Underline button.

Try making the headings bold.

- Make sure cells A1 to G1 are selected.
- Press the Bold button on the Formatting toolbar.

Additional formatting options such as double underline, superscript, subscript and colour are available from the Format Cells dialogue box. Have a look at the options available.

- Select Format, Cells and click on the Font tab.

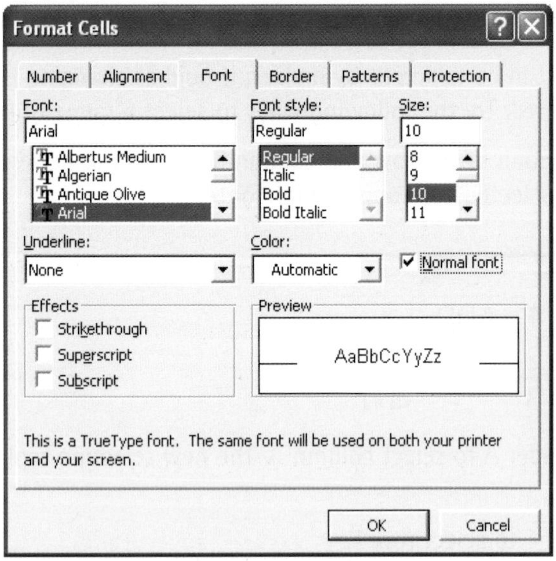

- Click Cancel to close this dialogue box.

Inserting a border

Cells A4, C4, E4 and G4 need a thick top and bottom border.

- Click in cell A4. Hold down Ctrl while you click each of the other cells to select them.
- From the main menu select Format, Cells.
- This time click the Border tab.

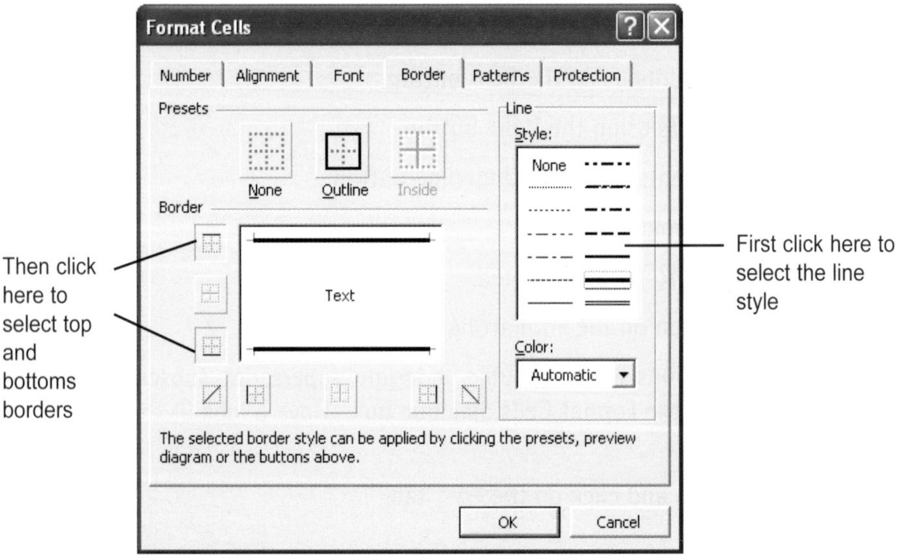

- Select the line style by clicking a thick line in the Style box.

- Click the Border boxes as shown above to specify top and bottom boxes.
- Click OK.
- Click away from the cells and you will see that all the cells you selected now have a top and bottom border.

	A	B	C	D	E	F	G	H
1	**ADD**		**SUBTRACT**		**DIVIDE**		**MULTIPLY**	
2	100		100		230		57.3	
3	400		56		14.5		12.5	
4								
5								

- Before you do any more work, save the workbook, naming it Sums.

Tip:
You don't need to click File, Save – you can just click the Save icon.

Entering formulae

Formulae are entered using cell references.

- Click in cell A4.
- Type an equals sign (=) to tell Excel that you are about to enter a formula.
- Type a2+a3 so that the formula appears as shown below:

IF ▾ ✗ ✓ fx =a2+a3

	A	B	C	D
1	**ADD**		**SUBTRACT**	
2	100		100	
3	400		56	
4	=a2+a3			
5				

- Press Enter. The answer appears!
- In cell C4, type =c2-c3 and press Enter.
- In cell E4, type =e2/e3 and press Enter.
- In cell G4, type =g2*g3 and press Enter.

Tip:
Don't forget to type the equals (=) sign!

Now your worksheet should look like this:

	A	B	C	D	E	F	G	H
1	**ADD**		**SUBTRACT**		**DIVIDE**		**MULTIPLY**	
2	100		100		230		57.3	
3	400		56		14.5		12.5	
4	500		44		15.86207		716.25	
5								

Automatic recalculation

The great thing about a spreadsheet is that once you have entered the formula, you can change the contents of the other cells and the answers will still be right.

- Change cell A2 to 75. What is the answer now?
- Delete the contents of cells C2 and C3 by selecting them and then pressing the Delete key. What is the answer in cell C4?

Standard error values

If you try and make Excel do a formula it can't, an error value will appear instead of an answer.

For example, let's try and divide a number by zero:

- Replace the contents of the cell E3 with 0 and click Enter. Now Excel will try and divide 230 by 0 – the answer when you divide anything by zero is infinity, which isn't a number. What answer does Excel give?

	A	B	C	D	E	F	G	H
1	**ADD**		**SUBTRACT**		**DIVIDE**		**MULTIPLY**	
2	75				230		57.3	
3	400				0		12.5	
4	475		0		#DIV/0!		716.25	
5								

Whenever Excel returns #DIV/0! as the answer to a formula, it is because it is trying to divide something by zero.

Tip:
You can undo your last action by clicking the Undo button. Redo an action by clicking the Redo button. If the last action cannot be redone, the Redo button will be 'greyed out'.

- Delete the contents of cell G2 by selecting it and pressing the Delete key. Enter a space in the cell by pressing the Space bar then press Enter. The cell is empty, but an error message has appeared in cell G4.

Tip:
A Space is a text (non-numeric) character even though it is invisible!

- If you ask Excel to do a calculation on a non-numeric value, it will give the error message #VALUE!.

	A	B	C	D	E	F	G	H
1	ADD		SUBTRACT		DIVIDE		MULTIPLY	
2	75				230			
3	400				0		12.5	
4	475		0		#DIV/0!		#VALUE!	
5								

Tip:
Some other standard error values include:

#####	This indicates that the cell contents cannot be displayed because the column is too narrow.
#Name?	This is displayed if Excel does not recognise text in a formula.
#NUM!	This is returned if invalid numeric values are used in a formula.

Entering formulae by pointing

Instead of typing in a formula such as =a2+a3 you can use the mouse to point to the cells in the formula.

- Restore the worksheet to how it looks at the top of Page 4-18. Delete all the formulae in row 4.
- In cell A4, type = and then click the mouse in cell A2.
- Type + and then click the mouse in cell A3.
- Press Enter. Try entering the other formulae in the same way.
- When you have finished experimenting, save your workbook.

Formatting numbers

Notice that data starting with a letter is automatically **left-justified** in a cell. **Numeric** data on the other hand is automatically **right-justified**.

Numbers can be formatted in several ways. For example it is sometimes neater to have a comma to indicate thousands: 1,532,000 is easier to read and grasp than 1532000.

We'll format the cells in this spreadsheet to do this.

- Click in cell **A2** and drag across to cell **G3**. Right-click in the selection and select **Format Cells** from the list.
- Click the **Number** tab in the **Format Cells** dialogue box. Select **Number** from the left-hand list, and click the checkbox for **Use 1000 Separator (,)**.

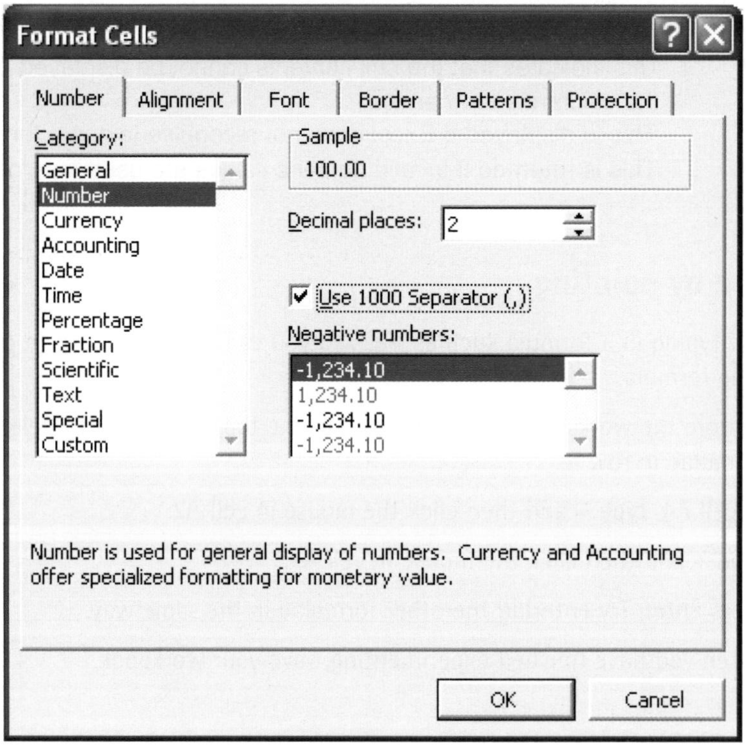

- Click **OK**. Try entering a value greater than **1000** to see how it is displayed.
- Save and close the **Sums** workbook.

Tip:
This is the dialogue box you would use to format numbers as currency or percentage – you will do this later.

Exercise

In Exercise 4.1 you entered the costs for a children's birthday party. You will now perform some calculations on the data and format the spreadsheet.

1. Open the file **Birthday1.xls**. Your spreadsheet should look like this:

	A	B	C	D	E
1	Party Budget - at home				
2					
3	Item	Number	Cost(£)	Total Cost(£)	
4					
5	Catering	20	3		
6	Magician	1	60		
7	Party bag	20	1		
8	Balloons	1	10		
9	Cake	1	15		

2. Make the main title in row **1** and the column headings in row **3** bold.
3. Format cells **C5** to **C9** and cells **D5** to **D11** to 2 decimal places.
4. In cell **D10** create a thick top and bottom border.
5. In cell **D5** enter a formula to calculate the total cost for catering: **B5 x C5**
6. Insert similar formulae to calculate the total cost for the other items.
7. Enter a label **Total** in cell **C10**. Make it bold.
8. In cell **D10** insert a formula to find the Grand Total:

   D5 + D6 + D7 + D8 + D9
9. In cell **C11** enter a label **Per child**. Make it bold.
10. In cell **D11** enter a formula to divide the grand total by 20:

    D10 / 20

    Your spreadsheet should now look like this:

	A	B	C	D	E
1	**Party Budget - at home**				
2					
3	**Item**	**Number**	**Cost(£)**	**Total Cost(£)**	
4					
5	Catering	20	3.00	60.00	
6	Magician	1	60.00	60.00	
7	Party bag	20	1.00	20.00	
8	Balloons	1	10.00	10.00	
9	Cake	1	15.00	15.00	
10			**Total**	165.00	
11			**Per child**	8.25	

11. Save the file as **Birthday2.xls**.

CHAPTER 4.3 Columns of Data

In this chapter we'll look at changing the way the numbers are displayed in the spreadsheet, and make Excel automatically create column totals.

Project: Create a spreadsheet to hold data on baby statistics

We will create a spreadsheet to hold data about the weights and lengths of newly born babies on a maternity ward.

- Open a new Excel workbook.
- Type the title BABY STATISTICS in cell A1. It will overflow the cell, but that's OK. Press Enter.
- Select cell A1 again and make it bold by clicking the Bold button.
- Now add the title SOMERVILLE WARD in cell D1. Make it Bold.

Changing column widths

You can change the width of column A so that the title Baby Statistics fits into cell A1.

- Position the pointer so that it is on the line between column headers A and B. The pointer will change to a double-headed arrow.

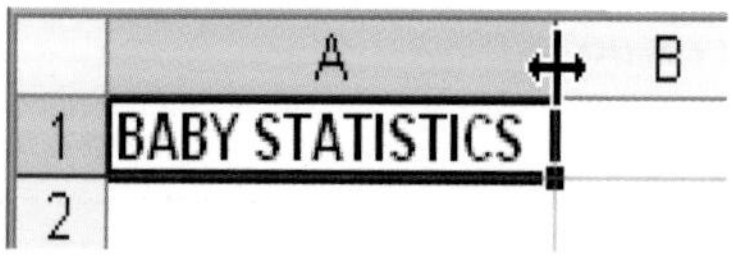

- Press the left mouse button and hold it down while you drag to the right. The column will widen. Make it wide enough to contain the whole title.
- Now type the rest of the column headings as shown in the next figure.

Now try a second way of widening a column.

- Position the pointer between the column headers of columns D and E containing the words Somerville Ward.
- Double-click the left mouse button. The column automatically widens to fit the heading.

Tip:
This is called autosizing the cell width.

- Save your workbook, calling it Stats.

Formatting decimals

- Now fill in the rest of the headings, months and numbers.

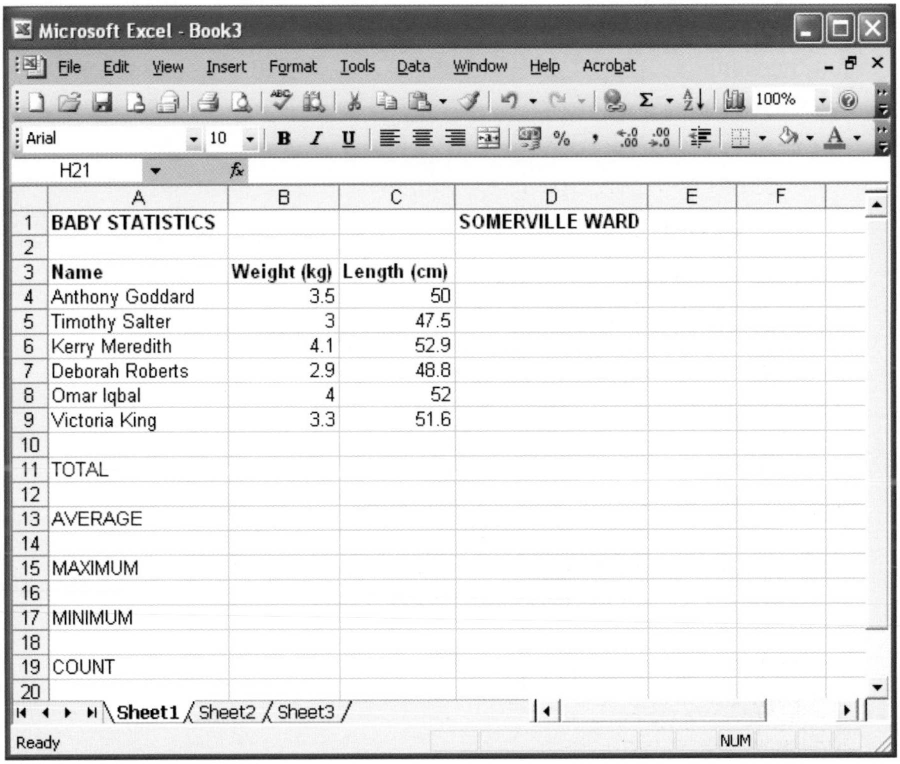

The measurements would look much better if they were all shown to 2 decimal places. At the moment, if a measurement is entered as 3.0, Excel automatically shortens this to 3.

- Select cells B4 to C19 by dragging across them.

- Click the Increase Decimal button on the Formatting toolbar.

All the measurements should now be shown to 2 decimal places, as shown in the next figure.

	A	B	C	D	E	F
1	**BABY STATISTICS**			**SOMERVILLE WARD**		
2						
3	**Name**	**Weight (kg)**	**Length (cm)**			
4	Anthony Goddard	3.50	50.00			
5	Timothy Salter	3.00	47.50			
6	Kerry Meredith	4.10	52.90			
7	Deborah Roberts	2.90	48.80			
8	Omar Iqbal	4.00	52.00			
9	Victoria King	3.30	51.60			
10						
11	TOTAL					
12						
13	AVERAGE					
14						
15	MAXIMUM					
16						
17	MINIMUM					
18						
19	COUNT					

Adding a column of numbers

We want to add up each of the baby's weights to get the total weight of all the babies on the ward.

- Click in cell B11 to make it the active cell.

- Click the AutoSum button on the Standard toolbar.

Excel guesses which cells you want to sum. Your screen will look like the one below:

COUNT =SUM(B4:B10)

	A	B	C	D	E
1	**BABY STATISTICS**			**SOMERVILLE WARD**	
2					
3	**Name**	**Weight (kg)**	**Length (cm)**		
4	Anthony Goddard	3.50	50.00		
5	Timothy Salter	3.00	47.50		
6	Kerry Meredith	4.10	52.90		
7	Deborah Roberts	2.90	48.80		
8	Omar Iqbal	4.00	52.00		
9	Victoria King	3.30	51.60		
10					
11	TOTAL	=SUM(B4:B10)			
12		SUM(**number1**, [number2], ...)			
13	AVERAGE				
14					
15	MAXIMUM				
16					
17	MINIMUM				
18					
19	COUNT				

Tip:

It is a good idea to include cell B10 in the Sum formula. If you later need to add an extra row, you can insert it above Row 10 and the Sum formula will still be correct.

- Press Enter. The answer appears.
- Find the total Length of all the babies on the ward.

Save your workbook.

In the next chapter we'll look at the other functions such as Average, Minimum and Maximum.

Renaming a worksheet

You can change the names of the worksheets to something more meaningful than Sheet1 and Sheet2.

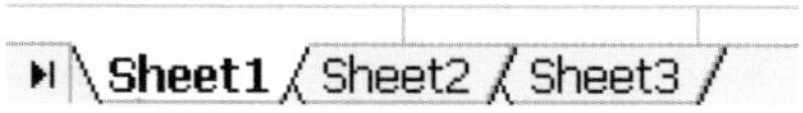

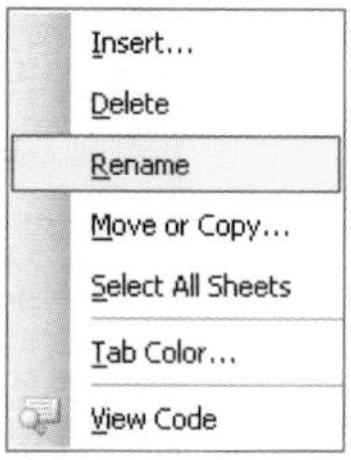

- Right-click on the Sheet1 sheet tab.
- Select Rename from the shortcut menu that appears. The text on the sheet tab is now selected.

Tip:
You can also rename a sheet by double-clicking the sheet tab then typing a new name.

- Now type Birth Stats. The text will appear on the sheet tab. Just click away from the sheet tab when you have finished typing.
- Repeat this for Sheet2, renaming it Daily Weights.

Inserting and deleting sheets

- To delete Sheet3, right-click the sheet tab then select Delete from the shortcut menu that appears.
- To insert a new sheet between Birth Stats and Daily Weights, right-click the Daily Weights sheet and select Insert from the shortcut menu.

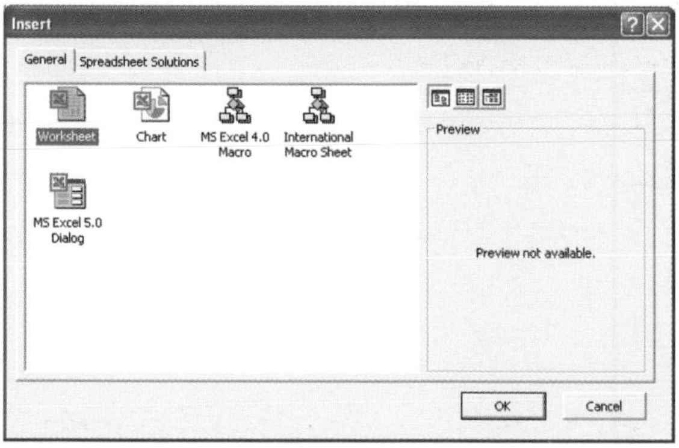

- Make sure Worksheet is selected then click OK.

Copying a worksheet

You can copy a worksheet within a spreadsheet or between open spreadsheets.

- Open a new workbook by clicking the New icon on the Standard toolbar.
- In the Stats spreadsheet, right-click the Birth Stats worksheet and select Move or Copy from the menu.

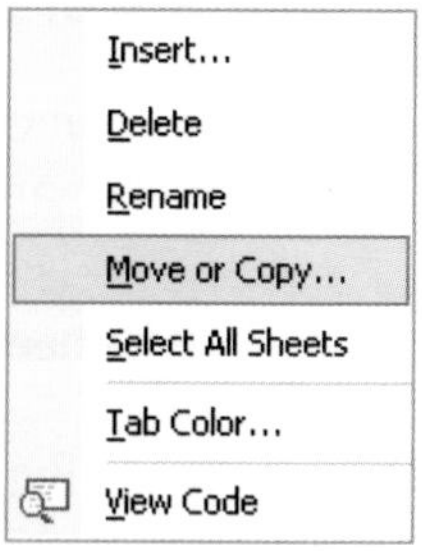

You are now asked where you want to copy or move it to.

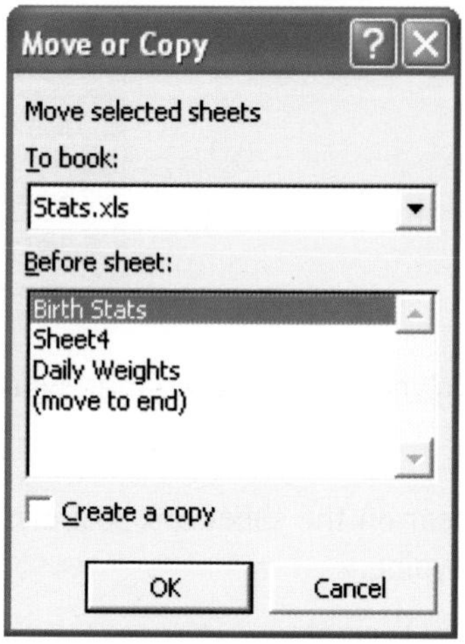

- In the first dropdown list, select the new workbook you have just opened, it will be called something like Book3.
- Select where exactly you want the sheet to be put in the second list box. We want to make a copy rather than move it, so click on the Create a copy checkbox.

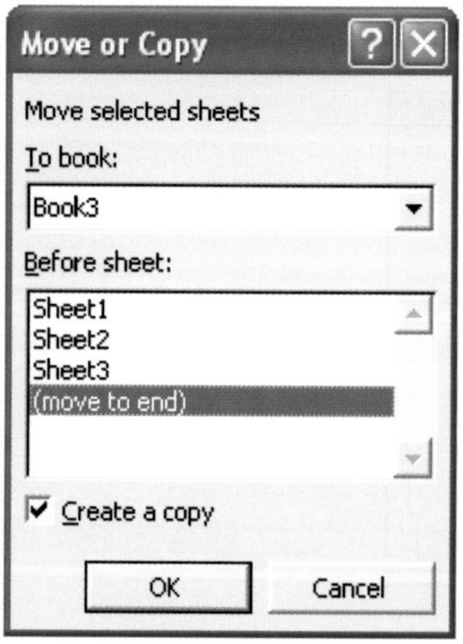

- Click OK. The worksheet should now be copied to the new workbook.

Note that if you wanted to move a worksheet to another workbook you would use the same method, but without clicking the Create a copy checkbox.

- You can now close the workbook you have just opened (Book3). There is no need to save it.

Moving worksheets

- You can easily move worksheets by first selecting a sheet then clicking and dragging it to the new position.

- Save the Stats workbook. You will need it again in the next chapter so you don't need to close it.

Exercise

This exercise continues with the spreadsheet you created at the end of Chapter 4.2. Now you enter data relating to the costs of holding the party at a Theme Park. In this case only 10 children can be accommodated because of transport limitations.

1. Open the spreadsheet Birthday2.xls.
2. Widen the columns so that everything fits in neatly.
3. Right-justify the contents of cells B3 to D3.
4. Remove the formula in cell D10 and replace it with a formula using the Autosum button. Edit the formula in cell D11 to divide by 10 (as there will now only be 10 children).
5. Rename the worksheet Home.
6. Make a copy of worksheet Home.
7. Rename this copy Trip.
8. Move the worksheet Trip before Sheet2.
9. Edit the data on the Trip worksheet so that it looks like this:

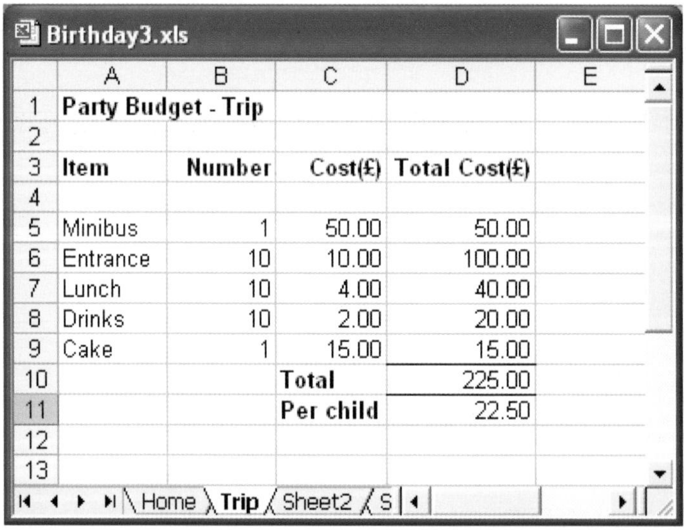

	A	B	C	D	E
1	**Party Budget - Trip**				
2					
3	**Item**	**Number**	**Cost(£)**	**Total Cost(£)**	
4					
5	Minibus	1	50.00	50.00	
6	Entrance	10	10.00	100.00	
7	Lunch	10	4.00	40.00	
8	Drinks	10	2.00	20.00	
9	Cake	1	15.00	15.00	
10			**Total**	225.00	
11			**Per child**	22.50	
12					
13					

10. Save the spreadsheet as Birthday3.xls.

Functions

CHAPTER 4.4

In this chapter you will continue to work on the **Stats** spreadsheet that you started in the last chapter. You'll learn how to use some of Excel's built-in functions to calculate the **average**, **maximum** and **minimum** baby weights and lengths.

A function is a formula used in a calculation. Excel provides over 200 functions to help with business, scientific and engineering applications. Don't worry, you only need 3 or 4 at this stage!

- Load the spreadsheet **Stats** that you created in the last unit, if it is not already open.

It should look something like the one below. The **Formula bar** and the **active cell** have been labelled in the screenshot.

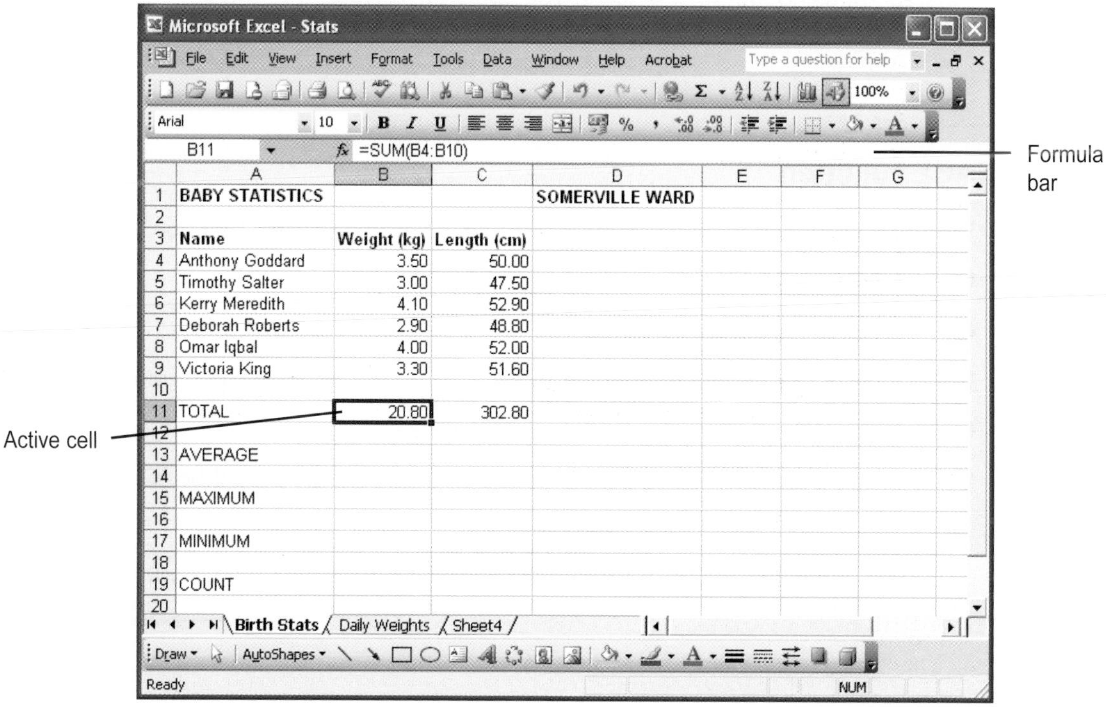

Microsoft Excel - Stats
B11
=SUM(B4:B10)
BABY STATISTICS
SOMERVILLE WARD
Name
Weight (kg)
Length (cm)
Anthony Goddard 3.50 50.00
Timothy Salter 3.00 47.50
Kerry Meredith 4.10 52.90
Deborah Roberts 2.90 48.80
Omar Iqbal 4.00 52.00
Victoria King 3.30 51.60
TOTAL 20.80 302.80
AVERAGE
MAXIMUM
MINIMUM
COUNT
Birth Stats
Daily Weights
Sheet4
Formula bar
Active cell

The SUM function

You have already used one of Excel's built-in functions – the SUM function.

Look at the Formula bar in the screenshot on the previous page. It tells you what formula has been used to get the answer 20.80 in the active cell, B11.

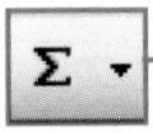

You entered the SUM function by clicking the AutoSum button. Adding up a row or column of numbers is such a common task in spreadsheet work that this special shortcut button is provided.

You can also enter a function by typing it into the cell. We'll try that now.

- Click in cell B11.
- Press the Delete key to delete the formula currently in the cell.
- Type =sum(in the cell (including the open bracket).
- Now click in cell B4 and hold the left mouse button down while you drag down to cell B10. Notice that Excel is automatically filling in the formula as you do this in both the cell and the Formula bar.
- Type) to finish the formula.
- Press Enter. Click in cell B11 again and the formula =SUM(B4:B10) appears in the Formula bar as shown in the figure on the previous page.

You'll find out why we included the blank cell B10 in the formula in a minute.

Note:
Instead of using the SUM function you could have typed a formula =B4+B5+B6+B7+B8+B9+B10. It would NOT be correct to type = SUM (B4+B5+B6+B7+B8+B9+B10).

The AVERAGE function

The AVERAGE function works in much the same way as the SUM function.

- Click in cell B13.
- Type =average(.
- Click in cell B4 and drag down to cell B10. Type) to finish the formula.
- Press Enter. The answer, 3.47, appears in the cell.
- In cell C13 find the average length of all the babies (it should be 50.47).

Tip:
You can use either upper or lower case letters for the function name, or even a mixture of both.

MAX and MIN functions

To find the maximum measurements, you need the MAX function.

- Click in cell B15.
- Type =max(in the cell (including the opening bracket).
- Click in cell B4 and drag down to cell B10. Type) to finish the formula.

Tip:
In the latest version of Excel, you don't need to type the closing bracket. Excel will add it for you when you press Enter.

- Press Enter. The answer, 4.10, appears in the cell.
- Now do the same for the maximum length.
- Use the MIN function to find the minimums.

Your spreadsheet will look like this:

	A	B	C	D	E	F	G
1	**BABY STATISTICS**			**SOMERVILLE WARD**			
2							
3	**Name**	**Weight (kg)**	**Length (cm)**				
4	Anthony Goddard	3.50	50.00				
5	Timothy Salter	3.00	47.50				
6	Kerry Meredith	4.10	52.90				
7	Deborah Roberts	2.90	48.80				
8	Omar Iqbal	4.00	52.00				
9	Victoria King	3.30	51.60				
10							
11	TOTAL	20.80	302.80				
12							
13	AVERAGE	3.47	50.47				
14							
15	MAXIMUM	4.10	52.90				
16							
17	MINIMUM	2.90	47.50				
18							
19	COUNT						
20							

Birth Stats / Daily Weights / Sheet4

The COUNT function

To count the number of babies, you need the COUNT function.

- Click in cell B19.
- Type =count(. Click in cell B4 then drag down to cell B10. Press Enter.

Excel automatically adds the closing bracket for you. The answer 6.00 should appear in the cell. Notice that although we included 7 rows in the COUNT formula, Excel has only counted those rows where a value has been added.

- Repeat this for the Length column.

Highlight cells **B19** and **C19** then click the **Decrease Decimal** button twice. You can only have whole numbers of babies so we don't need any decimal points!

Adding another record

Suppose another baby is born on the ward and its measurements have to be recorded on the spreadsheet.

- Right-click the row header for row **10**. The shortcut menu will appear.

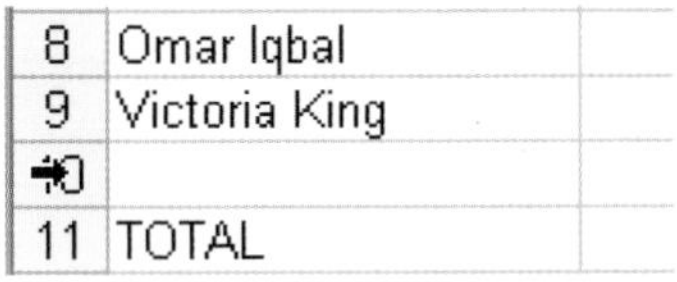

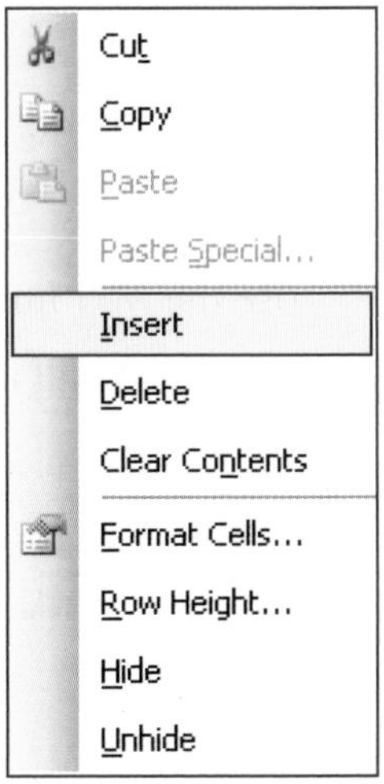

- Select **Insert** from the menu to insert a new row.

Tip:
When you added the column of numbers you included row 10. When you insert a new row above row 10 the Sum formula is still correct!

- In the new row, enter the data for **Jacob Walton**, who weighs **3.7kg** and is **51cm** long.
- Click in cell **B12** and look at the formula in the Formula bar.

The formula has automatically adjusted to include the new row – which saves us having to change it!

Now we'll double-underline the title **Baby Statistics**.

Select cell **A1** then click in the selection with the right mouse button.

- Select **Format Cells** from the shortcut menu.
- Click the **Font** tab. Now choose **Double** from the list in the **Underline** box.

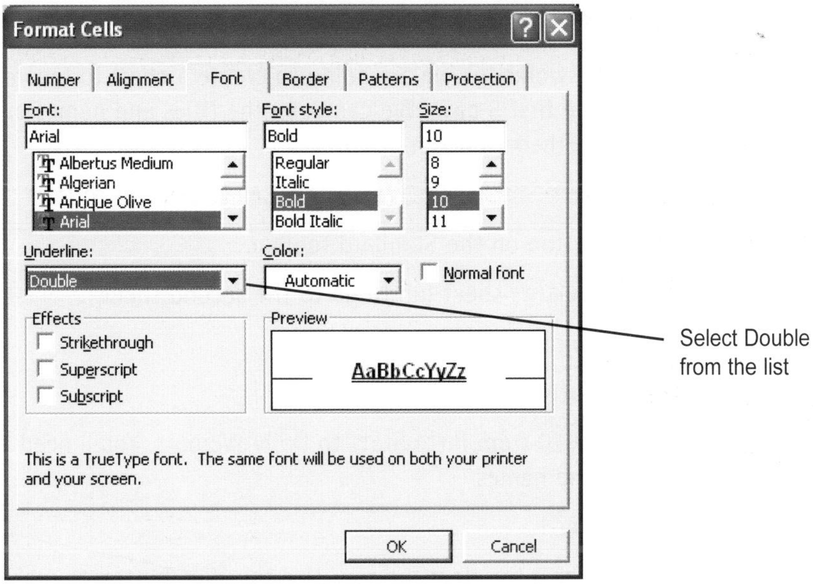

Click OK. The spreadsheet will now look like this:

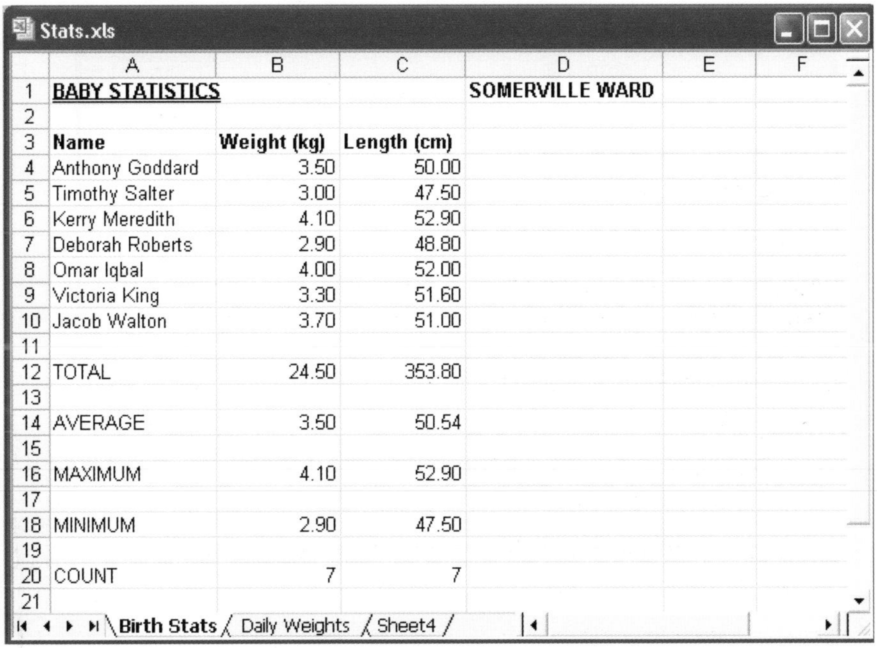
Stats.xls

	A	B	C	D	E	F
1	BABY STATISTICS			SOMERVILLE WARD		
2						
3	Name	Weight (kg)	Length (cm)			
4	Anthony Goddard	3.50	50.00			
5	Timothy Salter	3.00	47.50			
6	Kerry Meredith	4.10	52.90			
7	Deborah Roberts	2.90	48.80			
8	Omar Iqbal	4.00	52.00			
9	Victoria King	3.30	51.60			
10	Jacob Walton	3.70	51.00			
11						
12	TOTAL	24.50	353.80			
13						
14	AVERAGE	3.50	50.54			
15						
16	MAXIMUM	4.10	52.90			
17						
18	MINIMUM	2.90	47.50			
19						
20	COUNT	7	7			
21						

If your spreadsheet looks different from this – check the formulae.

If you had not included Row 10 in your formulae originally, the formulae would not have adjusted when you entered a new row. That's because the new row would be outside the range specified in the formulae.

Save your spreadsheet.

Copying data between sheets

On another sheet in the workbook we are going to create a chart to record the weights of all the babies over the first 5 days. We can copy the titles and names of all the babies to save us typing them in again.

- Make sure the Birth Stats sheet is selected. Select cells A1 to D1.

- Click the Copy button on the Standard toolbar.
- Click the Daily Weights sheet tab to go to the second sheet.
- Click in cell A1 to make it the active cell.

- Click the Paste button.
- Copy cells A3 to A10 from Birth Stats to Daily Weights. You'll need to widen column A to fit the names.
- In cell B3 type Day 1.
- Click in row header 3 to select the row. Use the Bold button to make all the cells bold. (You may have to click it twice).

Now your worksheet should look similar to the one below:

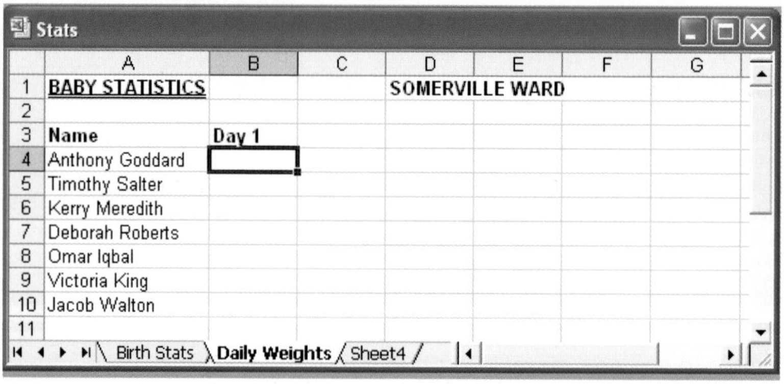

Tip:

Copy a single cell or a range of cells within a worksheet and between open workbooks in the same way.
To move a single cell or a range of cells within a worksheet, between worksheets or open workbooks use the Cut button instead of Copy.

Filling a series

Instead of typing all the other days, Day 2, Day 3 etc in cells C3 to F3, you can let Excel do it for you.

- Click cell B3.
- Click and drag the small black handle in the bottom right-hand corner of the cell. This is called the Fill handle. Drag it to cell F3.

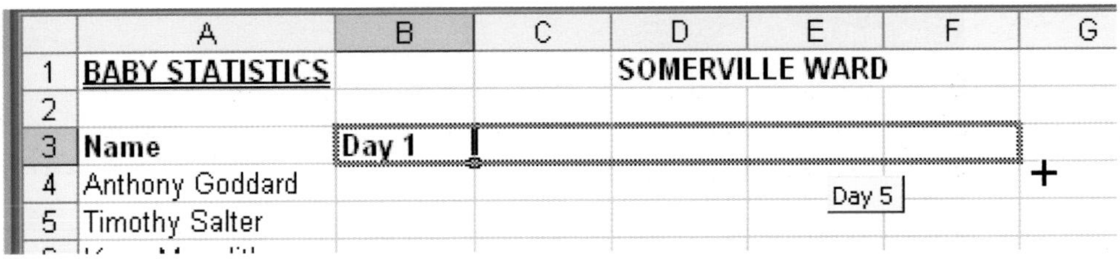

Now your headings should look like this:

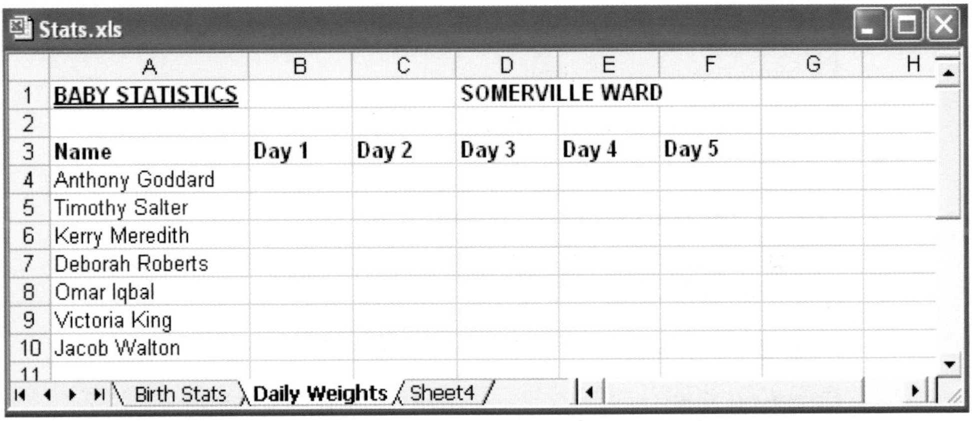

- Save your workbook.

Tip:
If the first cell is not numeric or part of a series, dragging the Fill handle will copy the data rather than increment.

Hiding and unhiding rows

Hiding rows and columns is useful if you don't want certain data to appear on a printout, or simply to make data in a large spreadsheet easier to view on-screen.

Hiding rows

We'll hide the Total row (row 12) in the Stats spreadsheet.

- Click on the Birth Stats tab to make it the active sheet.
- Click anywhere in row 12.
- Select Format, Row, Hide from the menu.

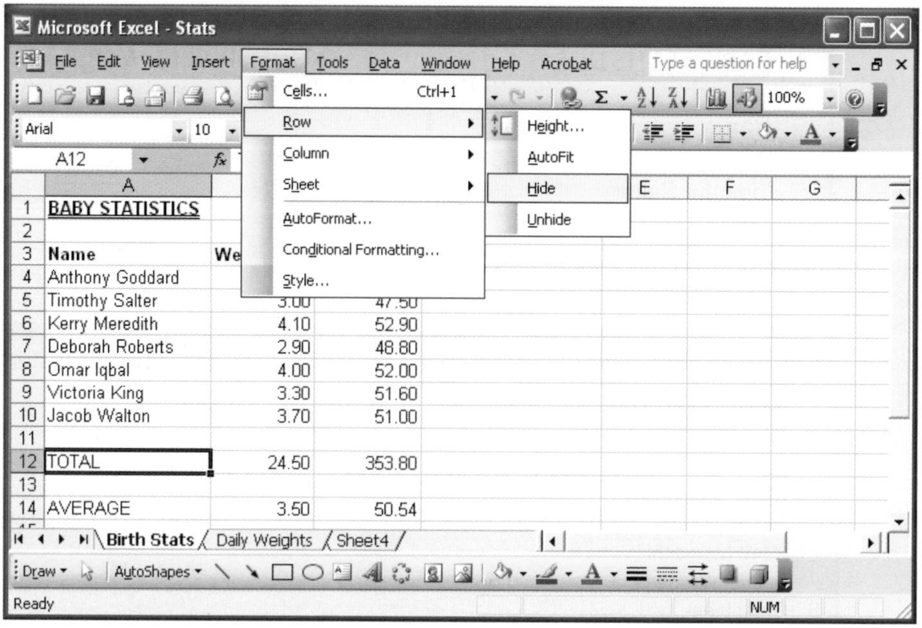

Row 12 is now hidden – notice that there is no row 12 row header.

Unhiding rows

- Select two cells in rows 11 and 13 (see next figure).

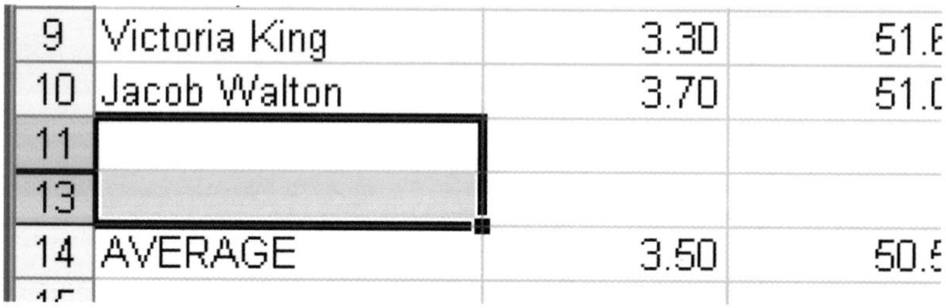
Victoria King 3.30
Jacob Walton 3.70
AVERAGE 3.50

- Select **Format**, **Row**, **Unhide** from the menu. row 12 should now be visible.

Hiding and unhiding columns

- Hide column C by clicking anywhere in it, then selecting **Format**, **Column**, **Hide** from the menu.
- Unhide column C by selecting cells in columns B and D, then selecting **Format**, **Column**, **Unhide** from the menu.

Freezing row and column titles

In a big spreadsheet, it is useful to have the row and column titles frozen so that no matter where you scroll in the spreadsheet you can see them.

First we'll make the Stats spreadsheet a bit bigger.

- Make Daily Weights the active sheet.
- Click in cell F3. Use the Fill Handle to extend the headings to Day 50.
- Click in cell A11 and type Baby 1. Use the fill handle to enter babies 2 to 50.
- To freeze the row and column titles, you have to place the cursor in the nearest cell to A1 that you don't want frozen. That sounds like a bit of a mouthful! Basically, we need Column A frozen, and row 3 frozen. For this we need to make cell B4 the active cell.
- Select Window, Freeze Panes from the menu. Black lines will appear next to the frozen panes.

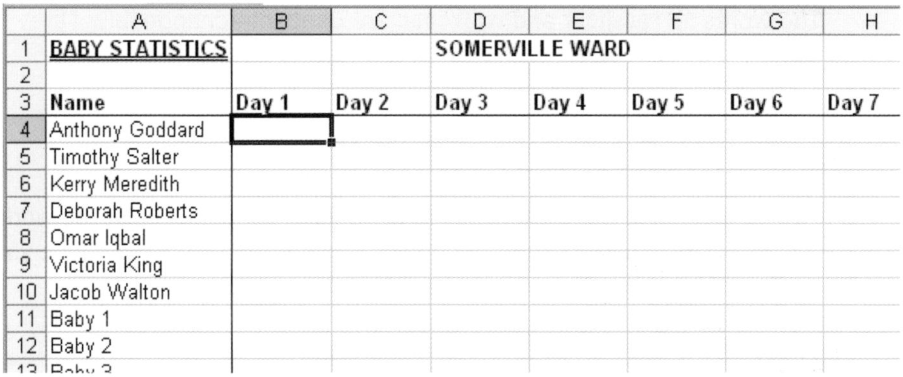

A B C D E F G H
BABY STATISTICS
SOMERVILLE WARD
Name
Day 1 Day 2 Day 3 Day 4 Day 5 Day 6 Day 7
Anthony Goddard
Timothy Salter
Kerry Meredith
Deborah Roberts
Omar Iqbal
Victoria King
Jacob Walton
Baby 1
Baby 2

- Scroll across to Day 50 – the baby names should still be visible. This would be invaluable for anyone entering data, else they would have to scroll left to see which baby was in each row before entering the data.
- Now try scrolling down to Baby 50 to see the effect of the frozen column headings.

Tip:
To freeze just a column, or several columns, select the column to the right of where you want the split to appear and then select Window, Freeze Panes.
To freeze just a row, or several rows, select the row below where you want the split to appear and then select Window, Freeze Panes.

Unfreezing panes

- Select Window, Unfreeze Panes from the menu. It doesn't matter which cell is the active cell for this.

The black lines will disappear.

Opening several workbooks (spreadsheets)

This is very straightforward. You can open a second spreadsheet in just the same way you did the first.

With the Stats spreadsheet open, either

- Click the New icon on the Standard toolbar to open a new spreadsheet, or
- Click Open on the Standard toolbar to open a previously created spreadsheet.
- To flick between workbooks, *either* select Window from the menu then the sheet you want *or*
- Use the buttons at the bottom of your screen.

Tip:
The words spreadsheet and workbook are used interchangeably – they mean the same thing.

Saving under another name

- To save an existing workbook under a different name, open the workbook then select File, Save As from the menu. You will then be asked where you want to save it and what name you want to save it under.

Saving as a different file type

By default, Excel will save your workbooks as .xls files, but you can choose from many other file types.

Tip:
A spreadsheet that is to be posted on a web site should be saved as a *.htm or *.html file.
To save a spreadsheet as a text file that can be imported into other operating systems, choose the .txt file type.
To save a spreadsheet as a template, choose the .xlt file type.
You can also save a spreadsheet in an earlier Excel format (e.g. Excel 2.1, 3.0 or 4.0) or in a different software format (e.g. .wk4 for Lotus 1-2-3 or .dbf for dBase)

- To save a file as a different file type, select File, Save As from the menu.

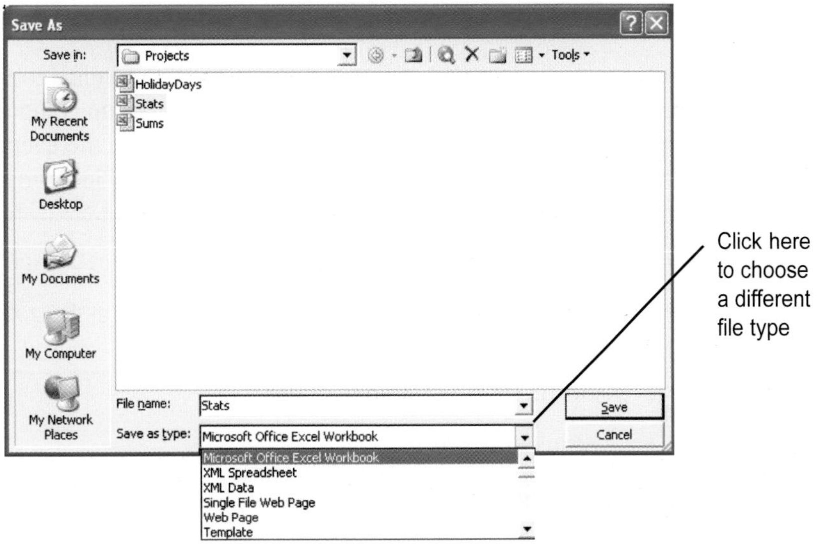

- Type a name for the file in the **File name** box, and choose a folder location for the file.
- Click the down-arrow in the **Save as type** box to view all the different file types. Select the one you want, then click **Save**.
- Close the **Stats** workbook.

Exercise

A local community council has organised a Quiz Night to raise funds. Ten teams have entered and the organisers want a spreadsheet running on a laptop computer to enter the scores and quickly calculate the winners of particular rounds, the overall champions and winners of the wooden spoon award. Teams can nominate a Joker round for which they are awarded double points.

1. Enter the following data into a new worksheet and save it as Quiz.xls.

	A	B	C	D	E	F	G	H	I	J	K
1	**Quiz Night**										
2					Round						
3		1	2	3	4	5	6				
4		History	TV	Music	General knowledge	Geography	Film	Joker round	Total points	Joker points	Grand Total
5											
6	Team 1	18	10	15	10	19	16	1			
7	Team 2	15	8	13	8	17	14	2			
8	Team 3	8	10	9	12	9	11	2			
9	Team 4	17	15	14	17	19	18	4			
10	Team 5	12	15	10	13	10	18	4			
11	Team 6	7	9	9	9	10	11	4			
12	Team 7	12	14	13	15	13	16	6			
13	Team 8	19	17	14	18	13	15	1			
14	Team 9	12	13	16	17	12	19	6			
15	Team 10	10	11	15	12	11	12	4			
16											
17	Average score									Champions	
18										Wooden spoon	

2. In cell I6 insert a formula that uses the SUM function to add up the points that Team 1 has scored over the 6 rounds (excluding extra Joker points).
3. Fill this formula down to cell I15.
4. In cell J6 insert a formula that enters the number of extra points for Team 1's Joker round (i.e. contents of cell B6).
5. Enter a similar formula into cells J7 to J15.
6. In cell K6 enter a formula to add up the total points and the Joker points.
7. In cell K17 insert a formula that uses the MAX function to find the highest Grand Total.
8. In cell K18 insert a formula that uses the MIN function to find the lowest Grand Total.
9. In cell B17 insert a formula that uses the AVERAGE function to find the average score for each round. Were any rounds particularly difficult?
10. Save and Close your work.

Charts

CHAPTER 4.5

Charts are a very good way of presenting information in a way that is easy to grasp immediately.

In this chapter we'll look at how the number of songbirds in the UK has declined over the past 3 decades.

This alarming decline is partly due to modern farming methods. Many hedgerows, meadows and marshes have disappeared, so birds have nowhere to live. Chemicals sprayed on fields kill insects that birds need for food.

Project: Draw charts relating to the number of songbirds in England

Decline in songbird numbers between 1972 and 1996

(Numbers given in millions)

	1972	1996
Skylark	7.72	3.09
Willow warbler	6.06	4.67
Linnet	1.56	0.925
Song thrush	3.62	1.74
Lapwing	0.588	0.341
Yellowhammer	4.4	1.76
Blackbird	12.54	8.4
Tree sparrow	0.65	0.0845
Corn bunting	0.144	0.03

Source: British Trust for Ornithology

- Open a new workbook.

- Type the headings and the names of the birds in the survey as shown below:

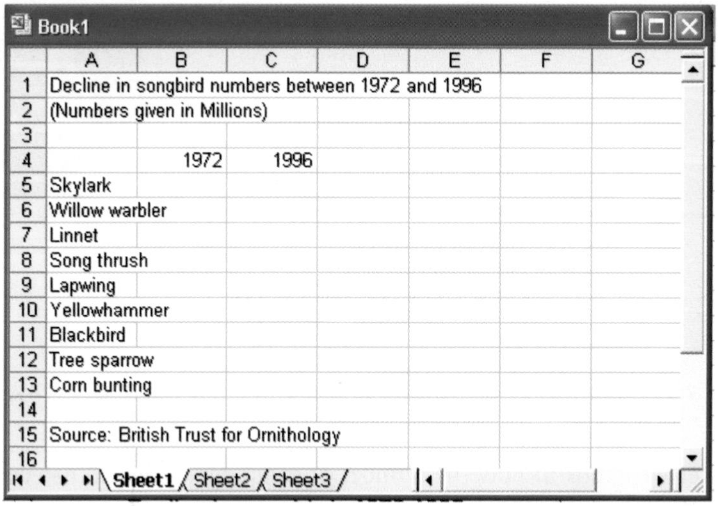

	A	B	C	D	E	F	G
1	Decline in songbird numbers between 1972 and 1996						
2	(Numbers given in Millions)						
3							
4		1972	1996				
5	Skylark						
6	Willow warbler						
7	Linnet						
8	Song thrush						
9	Lapwing						
10	Yellowhammer						
11	Blackbird						
12	Tree sparrow						
13	Corn bunting						
14							
15	Source: British Trust for Ornithology						
16							

- Position the pointer between the column headers A and B. Drag to the right to widen column A.
- Click in row header 1, and hold down the Ctrl key while you click in row headers 4 and 15. This selects all three rows.

- Click the Bold button on the Formatting toolbar to make these rows bold.
- Click in cell A15 and click the Italic button to make it italic.
- Enter the data given on the previous page.

When you have done that, your spreadsheet will look like this:

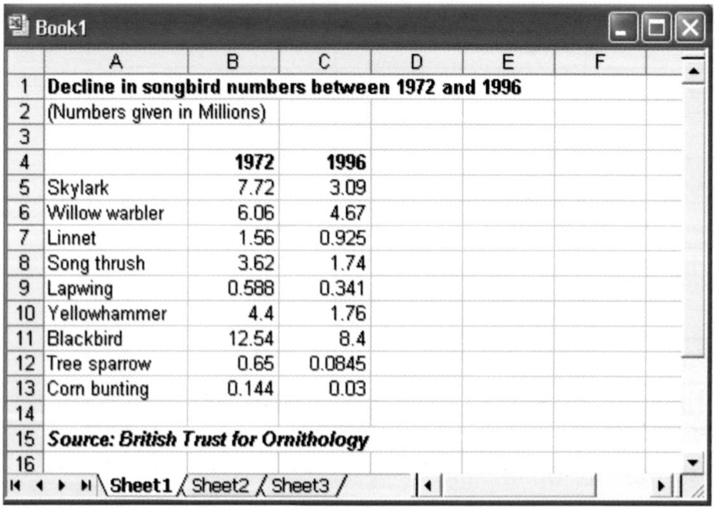

	A	B	C	D	E	F
1	**Decline in songbird numbers between 1972 and 1996**					
2	(Numbers given in Millions)					
3						
4		**1972**	**1996**			
5	Skylark	7.72	3.09			
6	Willow warbler	6.06	4.67			
7	Linnet	1.56	0.925			
8	Song thrush	3.62	1.74			
9	Lapwing	0.588	0.341			
10	Yellowhammer	4.4	1.76			
11	Blackbird	12.54	8.4			
12	Tree sparrow	0.65	0.0845			
13	Corn bunting	0.144	0.03			
14						
15	***Source: British Trust for Ornithology***					
16						

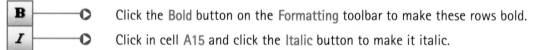

- Save your workbook, naming it Birds.

Sorting data

It would be neater if the birds were sorted in alphabetical order.

- First we need to select the data we want to sort. Click to select cell A5 and drag to cell C13.
- Select Data, Sort from the menu.
- We want to sort by the bird names, which is Column A. Fill in the boxes as shown below:

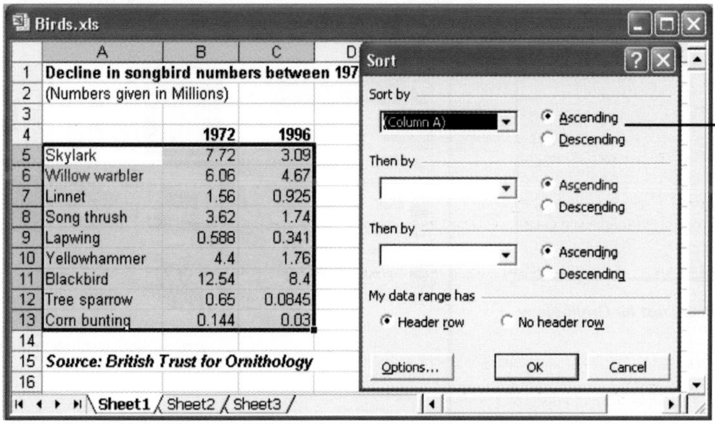

Choose to sort in ascending or descending order

- Click OK. The names should now be sorted.

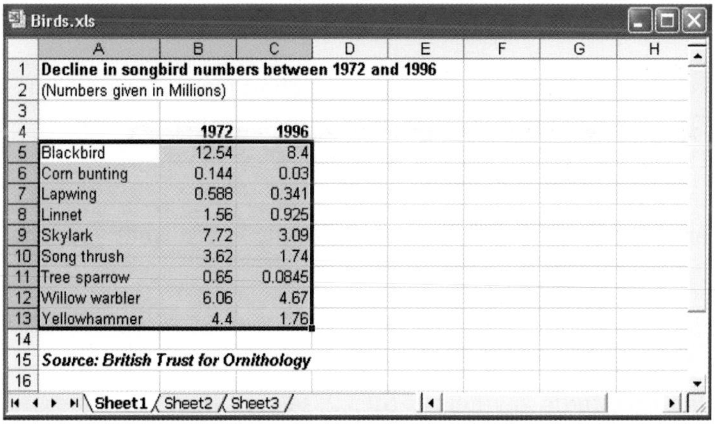

Tip:

You can also sort in descending alphabetical order by selecting the Descending option in the Sort dialogue box.
Columns or rows of numbers can be sorted in ascending or descending order in the same way.

Drawing a bar chart

Now we can draw a bar chart to show this data.

- Click in **A4** and drag diagonally through to **C13** to select the cells to be charted.

- Click the **Chart Wizard** button on the **Standard** toolbar.

You will see a dialogue box like the one in the next figure.

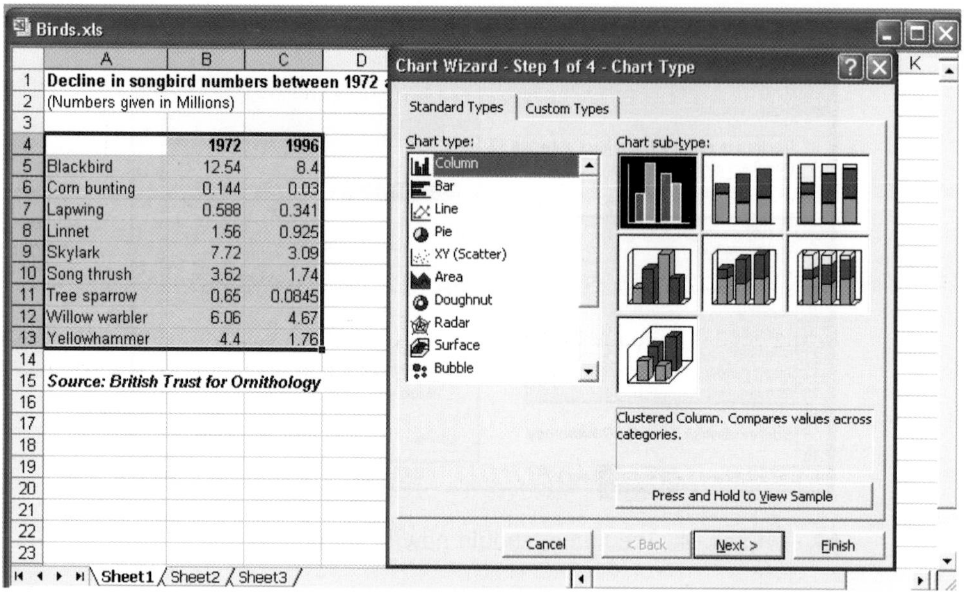

Tip:
For a Bar chart, choose the second standard chart type. This presents the data in horizontal bars instead of vertical columns.

- Leave the first **Chart sub-type** selected.
- Click and hold **Press and Hold to View Sample** to see what your chart will look like.
- You could click **Finish** now for a quick chart, but we will go through steps 2, 3 and 4 to add a title to the chart. Click **Next**.
- We don't need to do anything in **Step 2**, so click **Next** again.

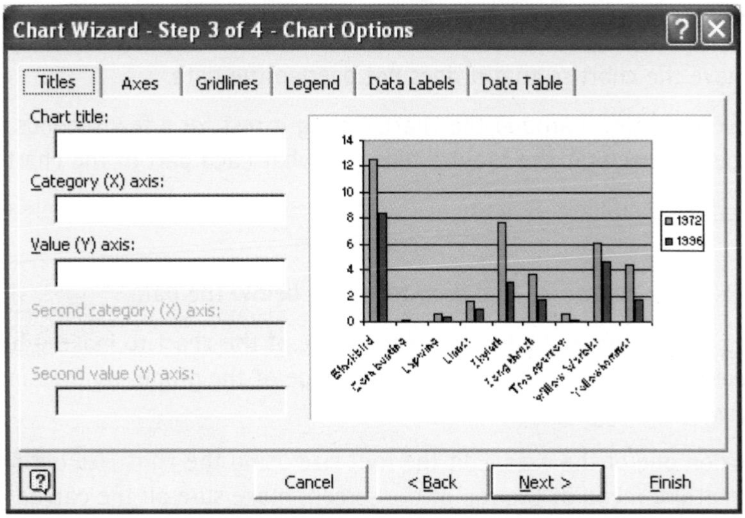

- In the **Chart title** box, type **Decline in songbirds 1972-1996** and then click **Next**.

In the **Step 4** dialogue box you can specify where you want the chart to appear. It can either be placed on its own in a new chart sheet, or it can be placed in the current sheet, **Sheet1**.

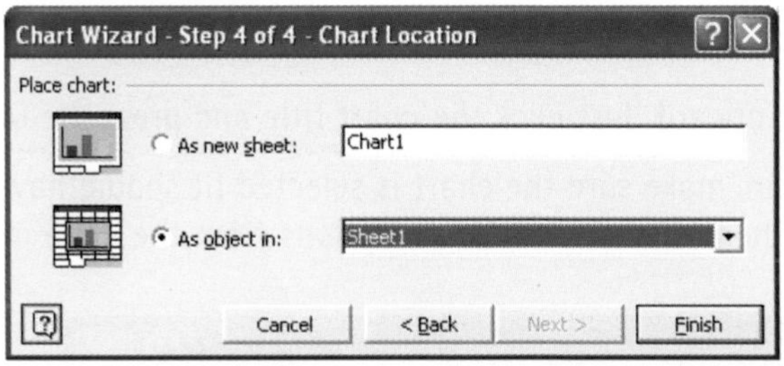

- Leave the default, **As Object in Sheet1**. Click **Finish**.

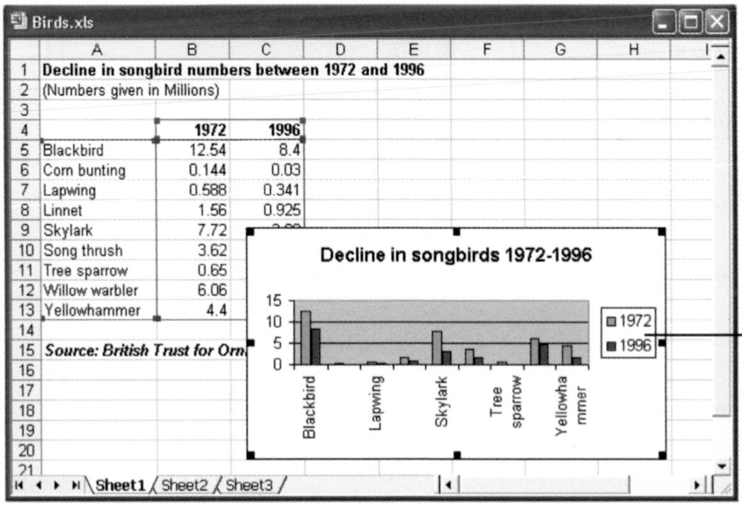

This is called the **legend**. It shows what the bars in the graph refer to

Moving and sizing a chart

You can move the chart so that it does not overlap the data.

- Move the pointer around the chart, letting it rest for a few seconds in different places. Notice that the **tool tip** tells you what each part of the chart is called.
- See if you can identify parts of the chart called **chart area**, **plot area**, **category axis**, **value axis**, **series "1972"**, **series "1996"**.
- Click in the **chart area** and drag the chart below the data.
- Drag the bottom right-hand corner handle of the chart to make it bigger. To make it bigger without distorting the shape of the graph, try pressing the **Shift** key whilst dragging the handle.
- Click on one of the axes. Edit the font size using the **Font Size** option on the **Formatting** menu at the top of the screen; make sure all the category names appear on the axis.

Tip:
If you right-click the chart title, legend or either axis, a shortcut menu will appear. Using the **Format** option you can change options such as the **Font**.

Deleting the title

- This is very straightforward. Just click the chart title and press the **Delete** key.
- To add the title again, make sure the chart is selected (it should have small black handles around it) then select **Chart**, **Chart Options** from the main menu.

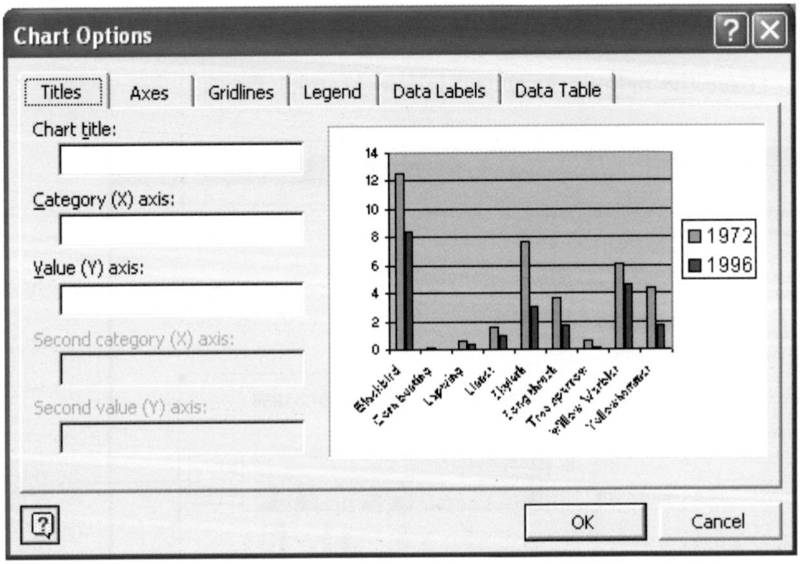

The Chart Options window appears. Notice that you can make changes to many parts of the chart using this window.

- Make sure the Title tab is selected, then enter the same title as before, Decline in songbirds 1972-1996. Click OK.

Adding axis titles

It would be nice to have a data label on the Y axis, to make it clear that the figures are in millions.

- Open the Chart Options window by selecting Chart, Chart Options from the menu.
- Under the Title tab, enter Millions in the Value (Y) axis: box. Click OK.
- You can delete the axis title by clicking to select it, then pressing the Delete key.

Tip:
If you can't see the Chart option on the menu, it's probably because you don't have the chart selected. Click anywhere in the chart to select it.

Changing the background colour

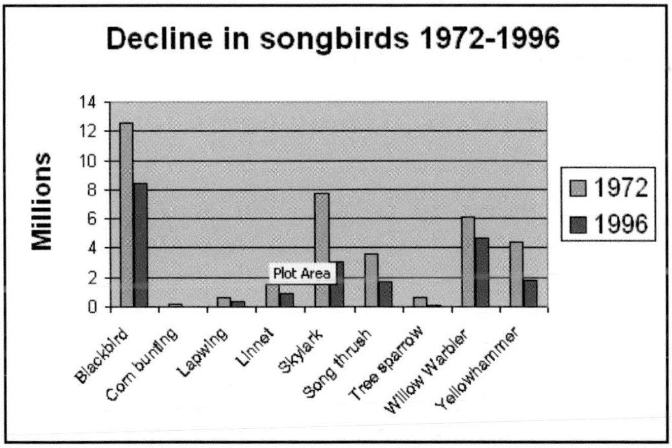

- Place the cursor over the Plot Area. If you're not sure which is the Plot Area, just leave the mouse pointer there for a few seconds and the tool tip should tell you.
- Click the right mouse button. A shortcut menu appears.
- Select Format Plot Area from the menu.

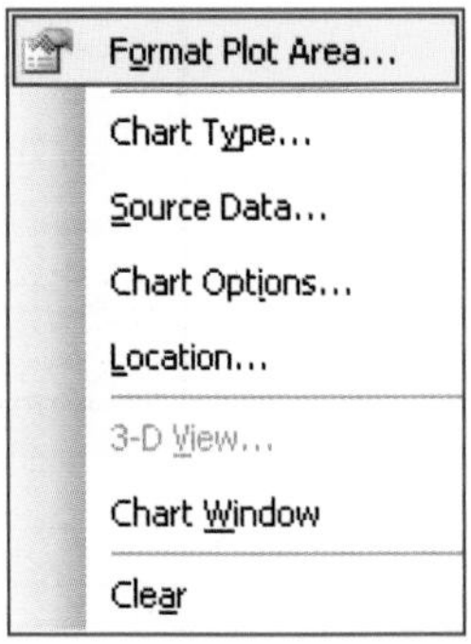

Here you can change both the border style and colour, and the background colour (the background is the part that is currently grey).

- Have a play with the settings, and try a different background colour. Click OK.

Changing the colour of the bars

You have to change the colour of the 1972 series separately from the 1996 series. We'll start by changing the 1972 series.

Tip:
You can always click Undo if you don't like the changes!

- Place the mouse over any bar in the 1972 series. After a few seconds the tool tip should say Series "1972" followed by the bird name and number of the particular bar you are on.

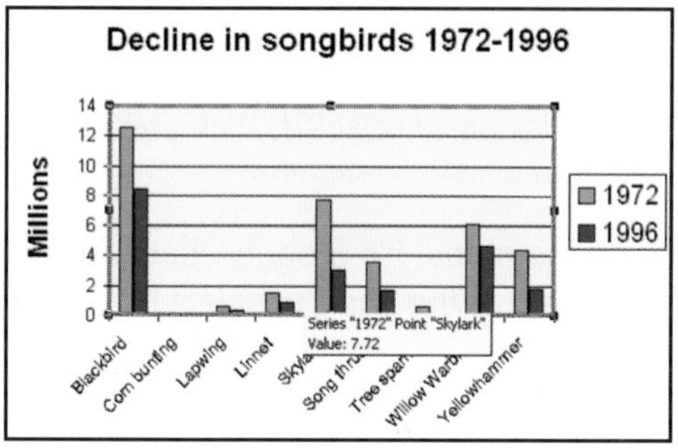

- Click the right mouse button. The shortcut menu appears.

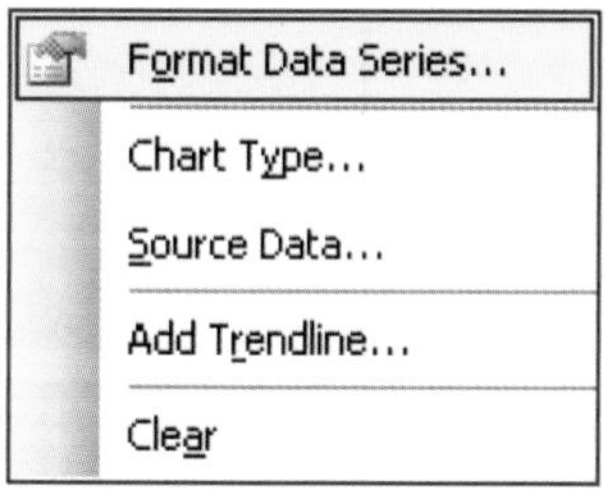

- Click Format Data Series on the menu.

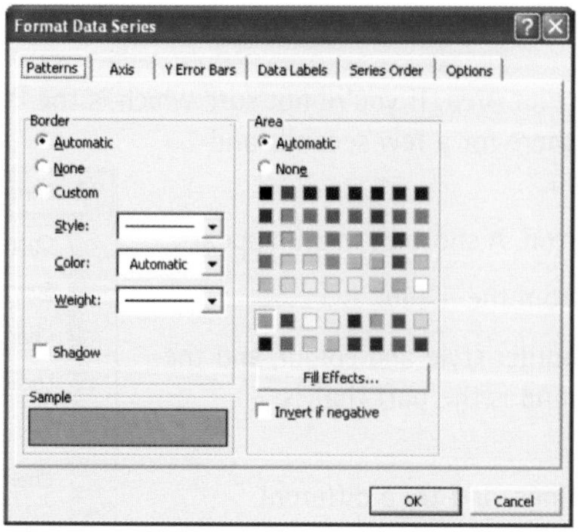

The **Format Data Series** window appears. Here you can change the border around each bar and the fill colour of the bars.

- Choose a new fill colour by clicking a colour in the right-hand box, under **Area**. Click **OK**.
- Now repeat this for the 1996 series. Follow exactly the same method, but just make sure that you right-click on the 1996 series to start.

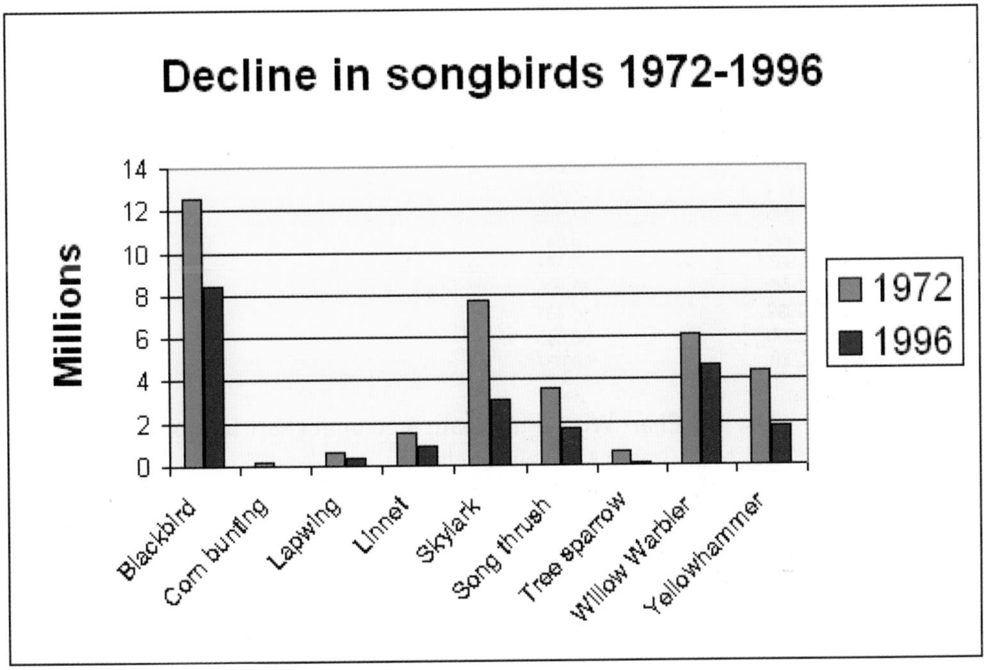

- When you are happy with the way the chart looks, save your spreadsheet.

Exercise

The National Statistical Office publishes annual estimates of the UK population. In this exercise you are asked to produce and format a column chart to show these estimates for a ten year period.

1. Enter the following data into a new worksheet and save it as Population.xls. Use the Fill Series feature to enter the Years.

	A	B
1	**UK Population Estimates**	
2		
3	**Year**	**Number (thousands)**
4	1992	57,556
5	1993	57,672
6	1994	57,797
7	1995	57,928
8	1996	58,043
9	1997	58,167
10	1998	58,305
11	1999	58,481
12	2000	58,643
13	2001	58,837

2. Use the Chart Wizard to create a column chart to represent this data. Use cells A4 to A13 as the X-axis labels.

Tip:
In Step 2 of the Chart Wizard, click the Series tab and you can enter a range for the X axis labels.

3. Enter a main chart title UK Population Estimates.
4. Label the X and Y axes appropriately and delete the legend.
5. Insert the chart alongside the spreadsheet data.
6. Change the colour of the text (i.e. headings, labels etc.) to blue and change the colour of the columns to yellow.

Your chart should look something like this:

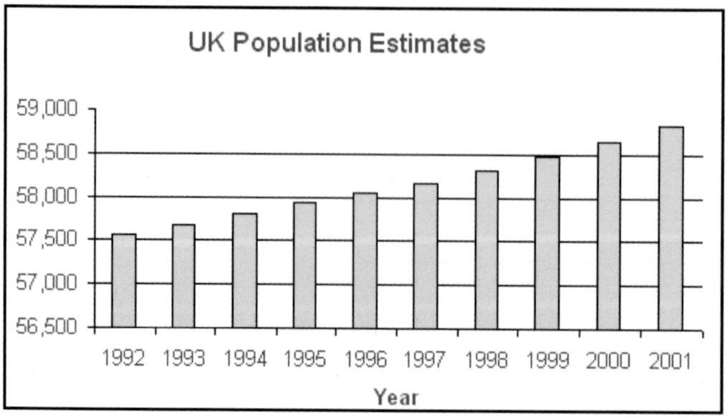

7. Save and close your work.

Pie Charts

CHAPTER 4.6

Creating a pie chart

We'll use another sheet in the same workbook to enter some data from the RSPB 2003 Garden Bird Watch Survey (www.rspb.org.uk/birdwatch). We will then use this data to create a pie chart.

- Make sure the Birds workbook is open.
- Click on the tab for Sheet2.
- Enter the following data.

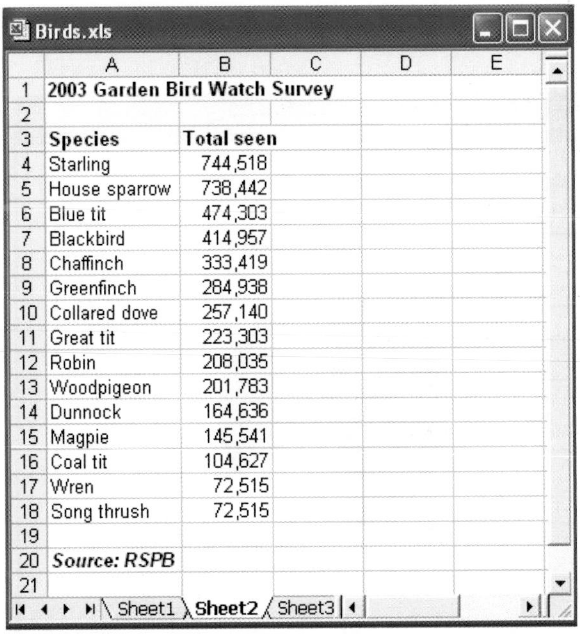

	A	B	C	D	E
1	**2003 Garden Bird Watch Survey**				
2					
3	**Species**	**Total seen**			
4	Starling	744,518			
5	House sparrow	738,442			
6	Blue tit	474,303			
7	Blackbird	414,957			
8	Chaffinch	333,419			
9	Greenfinch	284,938			
10	Collared dove	257,140			
11	Great tit	223,303			
12	Robin	208,035			
13	Woodpigeon	201,783			
14	Dunnock	164,636			
15	Magpie	145,541			
16	Coal tit	104,627			
17	Wren	72,515			
18	Song thrush	72,515			
19					
20	***Source: RSPB***				
21					

- Drag across cells A4 to B18 to select them.

- Click the Chart Wizard button on the Standard toolbar.

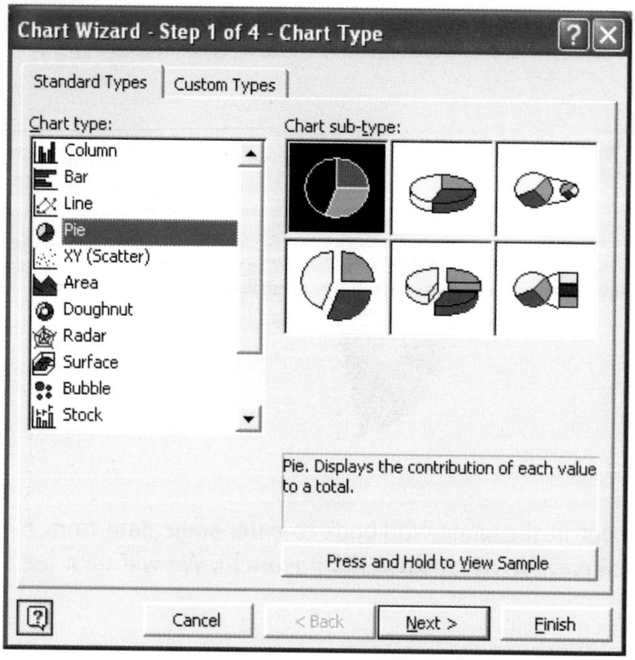

- In the dialogue box, select **Pie** from the **Chart** type list box. Leave the first option selected for the **Chart sub-type**. Click **Next**.
- Click **Next** in the **Step 2** dialogue box.
- Make sure the **Titles** tab is selected. Type the title **Garden Birds 2003**.

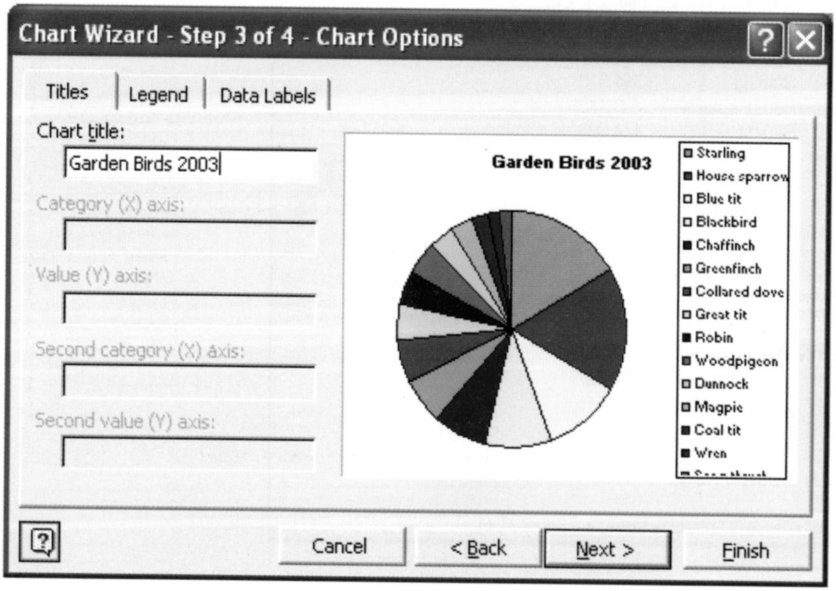

- Click the **Legend** tab just to see what the options are.
- You can experiment to see where you want to put the legend. In the screenshot below, **Right** has been selected.

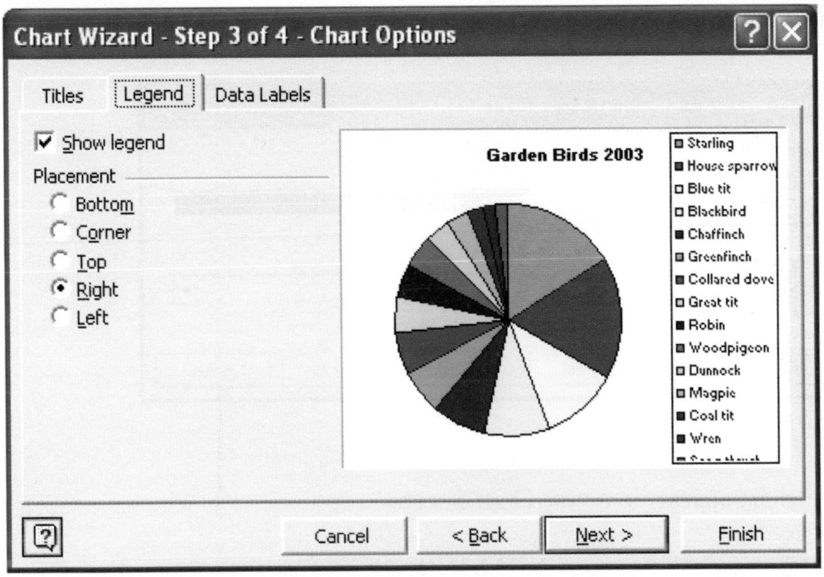

Click the **Data Labels** tab.

At the moment **Data Labels** is set to **None**.

Click **Percentage** and **Category Name**.

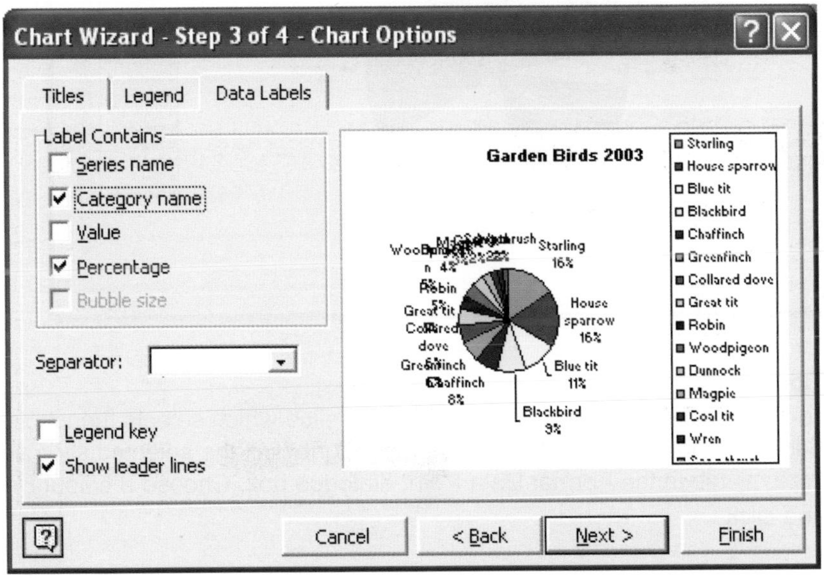

Tip:
Don't worry if the labels are muddled – we'll fix this later.

Click **Next**.

- This time we will place the chart in a separate Chart sheet. Click As new sheet.

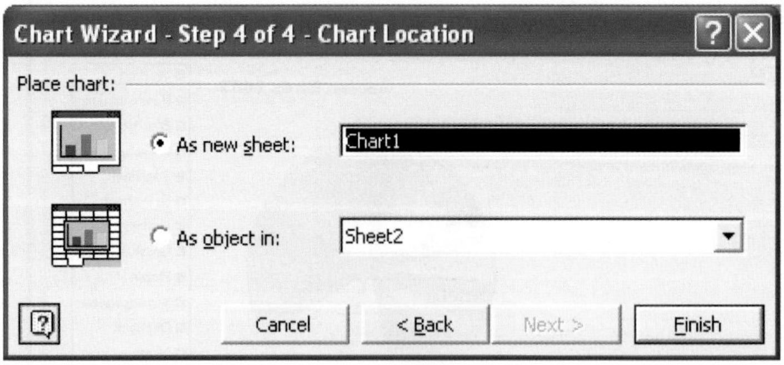

- Click Finish.

The chart appears in a new Chart Sheet.

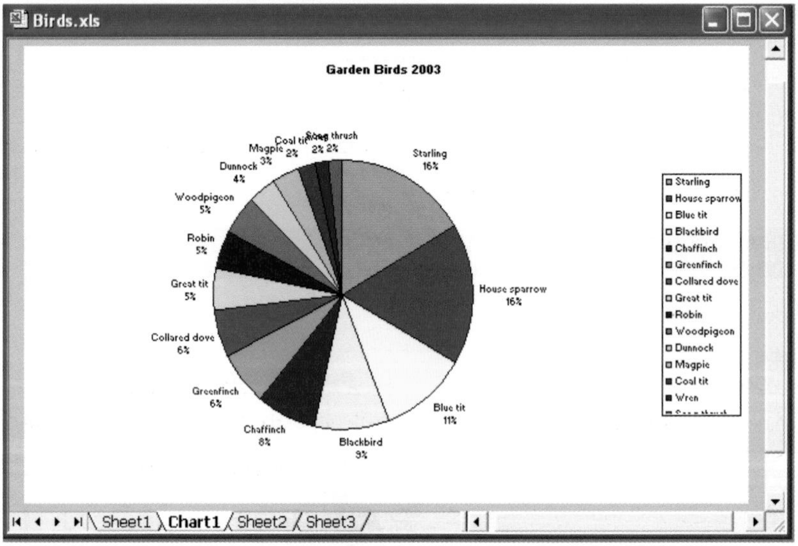

Tip:
To change the pie slice colours, click on a slice which selects the whole chart. Click on it again to select just that slice. Right-click the selected slice and click the Patterns tab in the Format Data Point dialogue box. Choose a colour or fill effect and click OK.

Formatting the data labels

We need to make the labels a bit bigger – they're too small to read!

- Right-click any of the data labels.
- A shortcut menu appears. Click Format Data Labels.

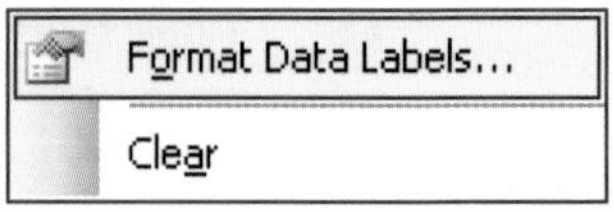

The Format Data Labels dialogue box appears.

- Click the Font tab in the dialogue box.

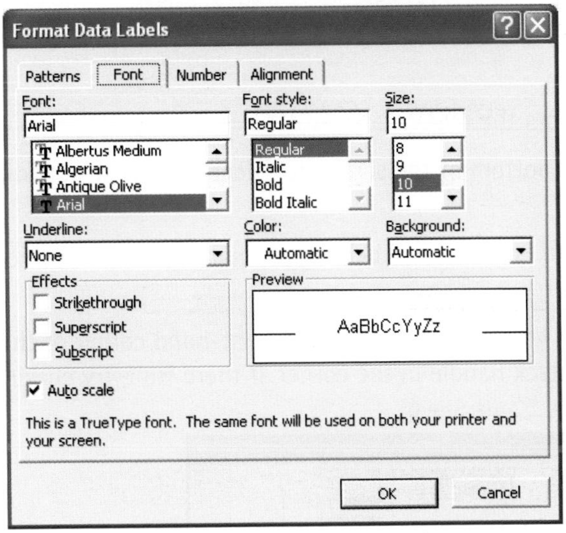

- Change the font size to 12. Click OK.
- If any labels are overlapping, click them and drag them away from each other.
- Format the legend so the text is 12 point.
- Format the Chart Title to 18 point.
- Change the title to Garden Bird Numbers 2003.

Tip:
To change the text of the Chart Title, click it to select it and then click in the text where you want to insert or delete text. To delete the title, click to select it and press the Delete key.

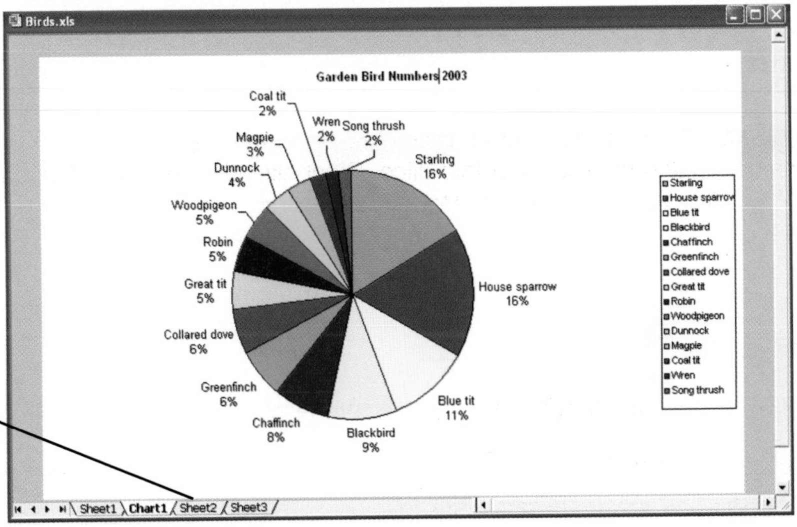

Click here to return to Sheet2, where you typed the data.

- Save your workbook.

Copying and pasting charts

We'll copy and paste the pie chart onto a new sheet.

- Click once on the **Chart Area** of the pie chart (this is the white background) to select it.
- Select **Edit**, **Copy** from the menu.
- Click **Sheet3** at the bottom of the screen to select it. Now select **Edit**, **Paste** from the menu.

The pie chart is pasted into **Sheet3**. It's much bigger than we want it so now we'll resize it.

- Scroll down so that you can see the bottom right-hand corner of the chart. There should be a small black handle in the corner. If there isn't, try clicking the chart to select it.

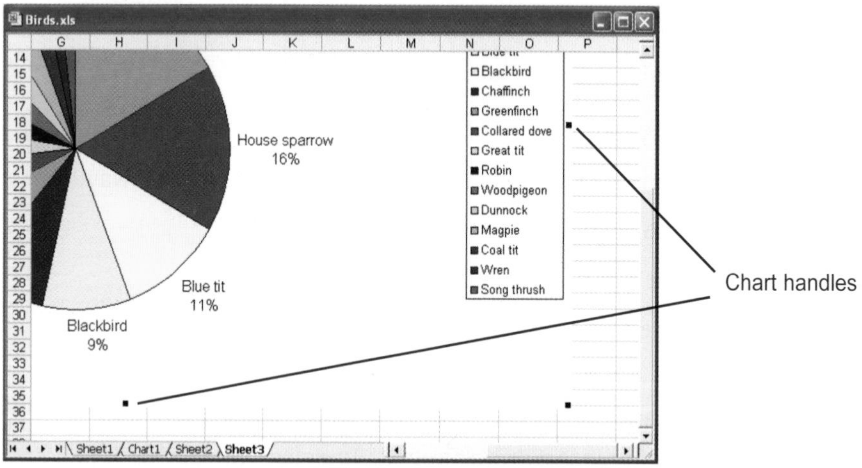

- Click and drag the handle towards the top left corner whilst holding down the **Shift** key, until it is a similar size to the one below.

Tip:
Holding down the **Shift** key will resize the chart in proportion to its original shape.

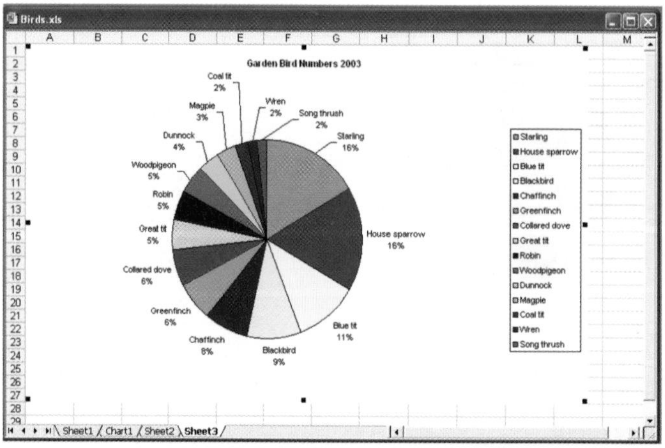

Copying a chart into a different spreadsheet

You can copy a chart into another open spreadsheet in the same way. Suppose you wanted to use the chart for comparison purposes in a new spreadsheet that will record bird numbers in 2004.

- Open a new workbook by clicking the New icon. Save this new file as Birds2004.
- Click on the original Birds workbook in the Task bar to display it.

- Click once on the Chart Area of the pie chart (this is the white background) to select it.
- Select Edit, Copy from the menu.
- Click on the Birds2004 workbook in the Task bar to display it.
- Select Edit, Paste from the menu and resize the chart appropriately.
- Save and close this new workbook.

Changing the chart type

It's easy to change the chart type, for example from a pie chart to a bar or line chart even after you have created it.

- With the Birds workbook displayed make sure Sheet3 is selected. Right-click on the Chart Area. The shortcut menu appears.

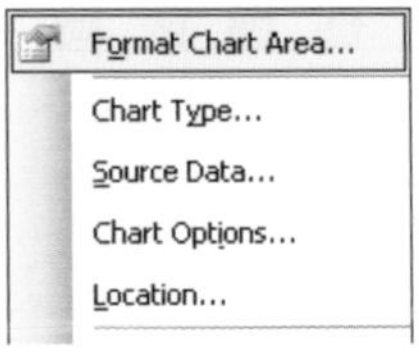

- Select Chart Type from the menu.

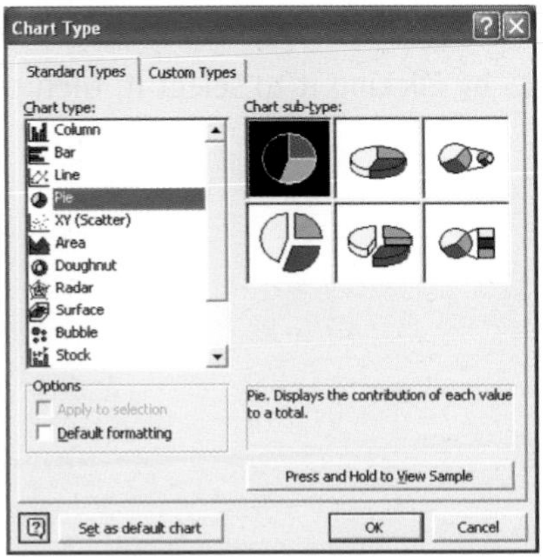

- Here all you need to do is choose another chart type. Try a Line chart. Click OK.

A line chart can be formatted in a similar way to a bar chart or a pie chart. For example try changing the colour of one of the lines.

- Right-click the line and select Format Data Series from the shortcut menu.
- Click the Patterns tab, select a different colour and click OK.

It doesn't actually make any sense to make this chart a line chart. Line charts should only be used when the order of the categories along the x-axis has a meaning. In this example, the birds are placed on the x-axis in a random way.

- Change the chart type to a column chart.
- Delete the labels above each column by right-clicking on a column and selecting Format Data Series from the shortcut menu. Refer to the section above where you inserted the labels into the pie chart if you need to.

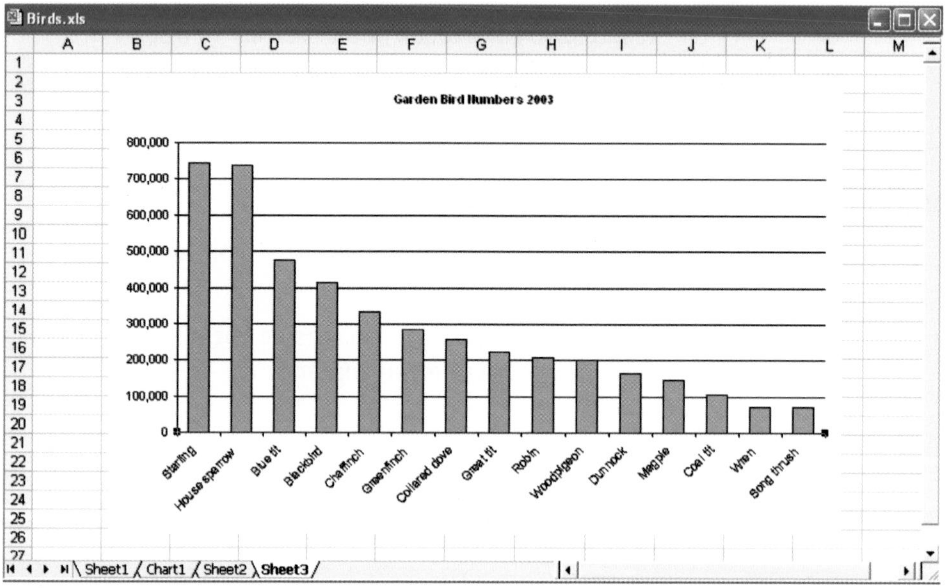

Deleting a chart

- Now delete the bar chart on Sheet3 by clicking it to select it, then pressing the Delete key.

- Save your workbook.

Exercise

At the end of the last chapter you created a column chart to show UK population estimates for a ten year period. Statistics are also produced that break these figures down into age groups. You are now asked to create a pie chart to show the age distribution of the UK population.

1. Enter the following data into a new worksheet and save it as Population2.xls.

	A	B	C
1	**UK population by age group**		
2			
3	**Age**	**Percentage**	
4	0–4	5.9	
5	5–15	14.2	
6	16–44	40.1	
7	45–64M/59F	21.3	
8	65M/60F–74	10.9	
9	75 and over	7.5	

2. Use the Chart Wizard to create a pie chart to represent this data.
3. Insert a main chart title UK population by age group.
4. Display the legend.
5. Add data labels as percentages.
6. Display the chart in a separate worksheet.

   Your pie chart should look like this:

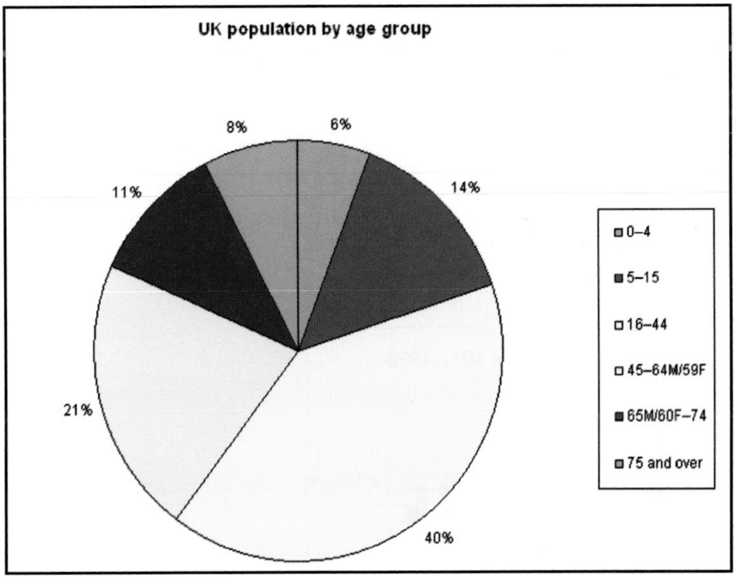

7. Save and close your work.

CHAPTER 4.7 Printing

Now we're going to try printing various parts from the **Birds** workbook.

- Make sure the **Birds** workbook is open.
- Click **Sheet1** to select it.

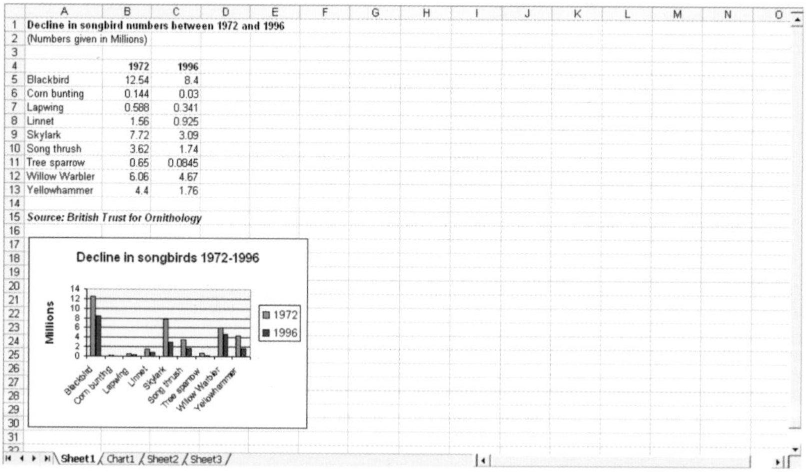

Printing a chart

Firstly we'll see what the chart would look like printed on its own.

- Make sure the chart is selected. (It will have handles around it. Click the **Chart Area** to select it if it is not already selected).

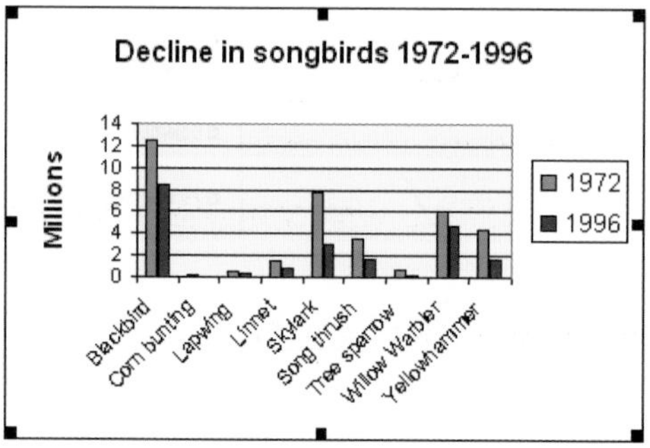

Click the **Print Preview** button.

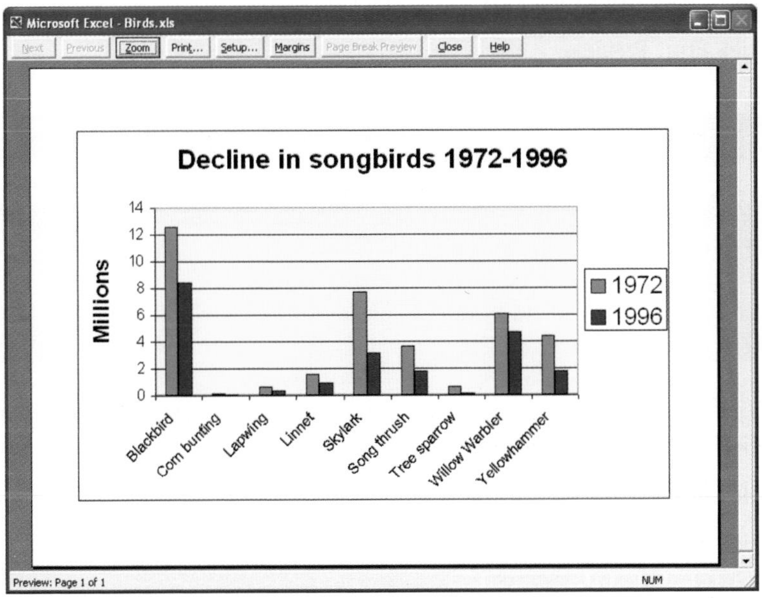

This is how your chart will look when it is printed.

- Now click the **Print** button at the top of the screen.

You will see the **Print** dialogue box.

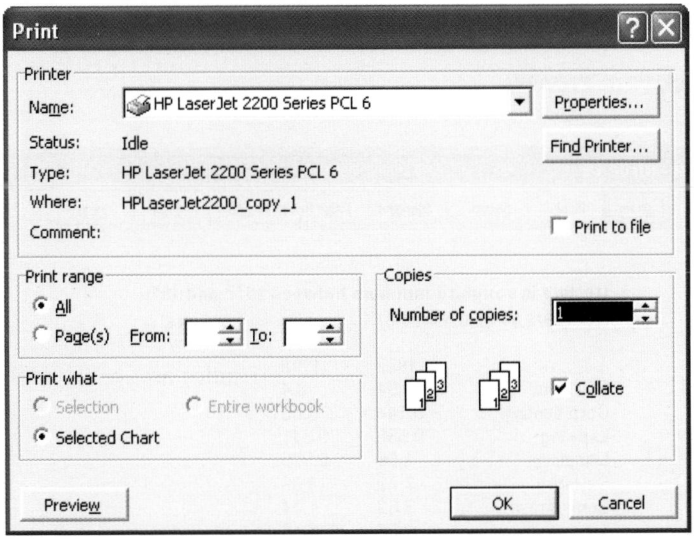

Here you can change various options such as the number of copies and which printer to print on.

- When you are happy with the options, click **OK** to print.

Printing an entire worksheet

- Click away from the chart to deselect it.

- Click Print Preview.

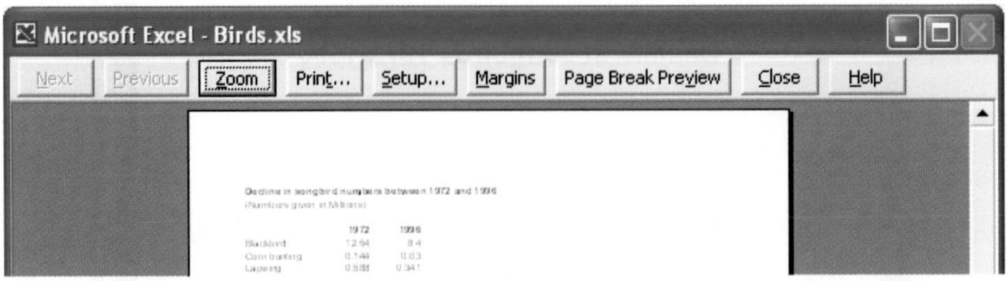

- When you move the pointer over the page, it changes to a magnifying glass. Click it to zoom in on the page.
- Click Print at the top of the screen.
- Click OK to print.

Printing a cell range

You can specify the cell range that you want to print. We'll use this method to print only the figures on Sheet1, without the chart.

- Click cell A1 and drag across to cell F15 – these are the cells we want to print.
- Select File, Print Area, Set Print Area.
- Now click Print Preview.

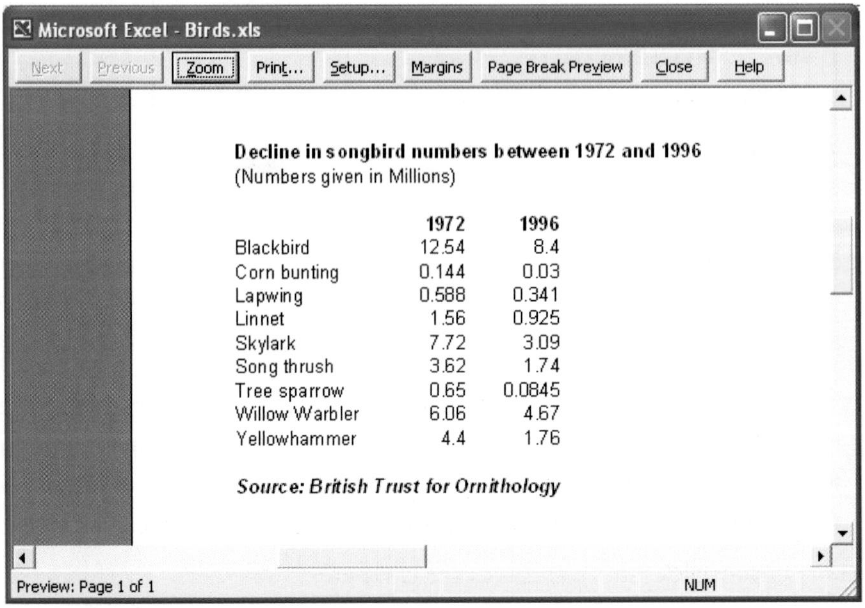

Only the selected cells appear in the print preview.

- Click Print, then OK to print.

- If you wanted to print the whole sheet again, you could either select the print range to include the chart, or you can select File, Print, Print Area, Clear Print Area.

Printing an entire workbook

You can print all the sheets in a workbook.

- Clear the print area that you set earlier by selecting File, Print Area, Clear Print Area.
- Make sure the chart isn't selected, then click Print Preview.

Here only the current sheet is shown. You can specify to print the entire workbook in the Print dialogue box.

- Click the Print button.

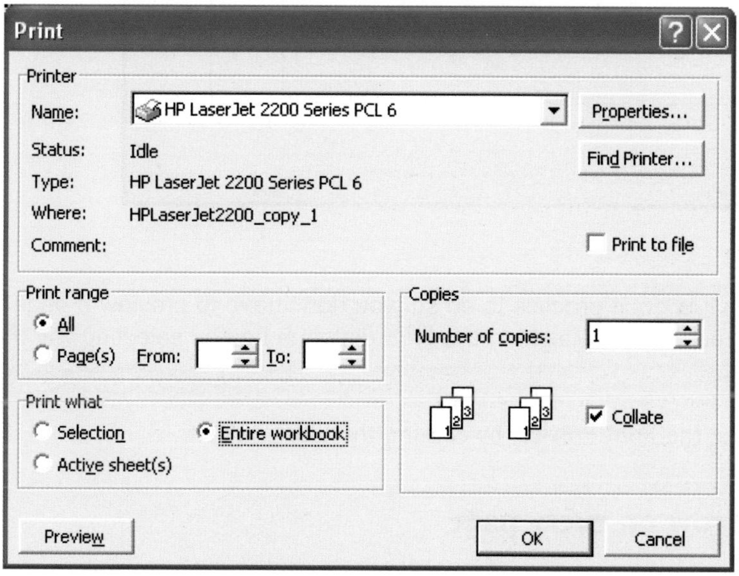

- Click the option Entire Workbook under the Print what section.

Printing row and column headings

- Make sure Sheet1 is selected, but not the chart. Select File, Page Setup from the menu.
- In the Page Setup dialogue box, click to select the Sheet tab. Click the checkbox next to Row and column headings under the Print section.
- Now click Print Preview to see what effect this has.

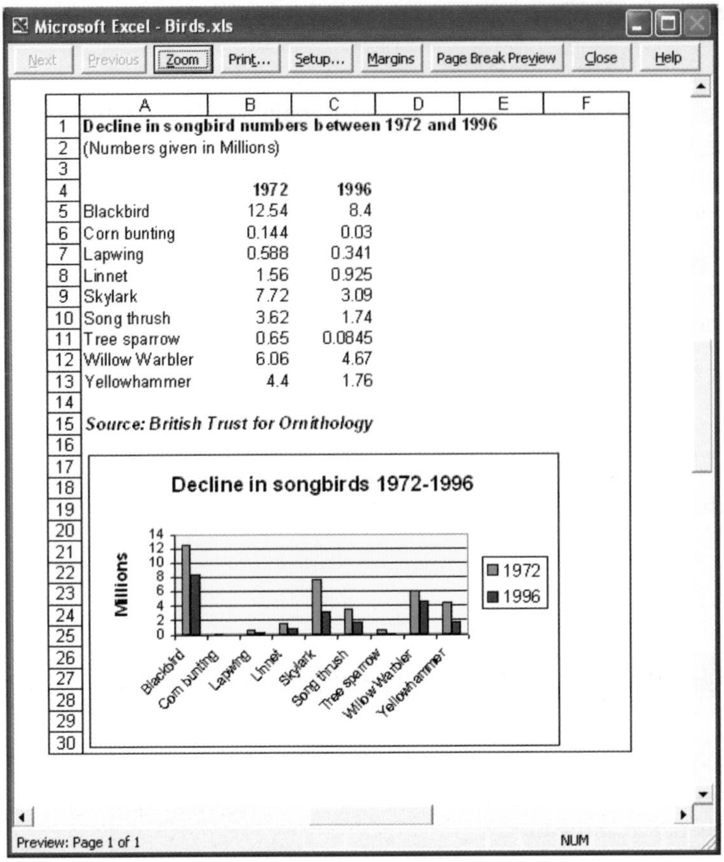

Tip:
Although it is good practice to do so, you don't have to preview a page before you print it. You can go straight to the Print dialogue box by selecting File, Print from the menu.

- Close the Print Preview by clicking the Close button.

Printing the title row on every page

If you have a very large worksheet that spans two or three pages, it is useful to have the title repeated on pages two and three. You can do this in the Page Setup dialogue box.

- First we'll set the print area to run onto more than one page. Select cell A1 and drag down to cell K80 or so.
- Select File, Print Area, Set Print Area. Click anywhere in the sheet to deselect all the cells.
- Go to Print Preview. The document is now 4 pages – 2 pages wide and 2 down. Close Print Preview.
- Go to Page Setup by selecting File, Page Setup from the menu.

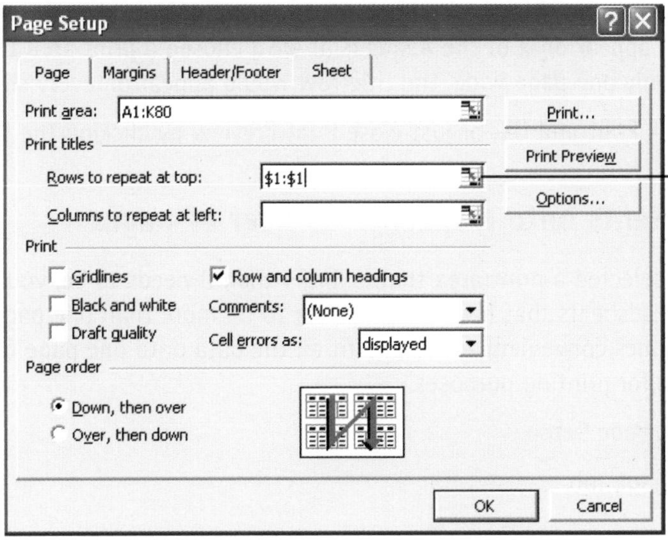

Click here to select the row

- Here you can *either*:
- type **$1:$1** to say row **1**

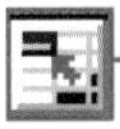

- *or* you can select the cells by clicking the icon on the right of the box. The cursor will become a small horizontal arrow, with which you should point and click row **1**.

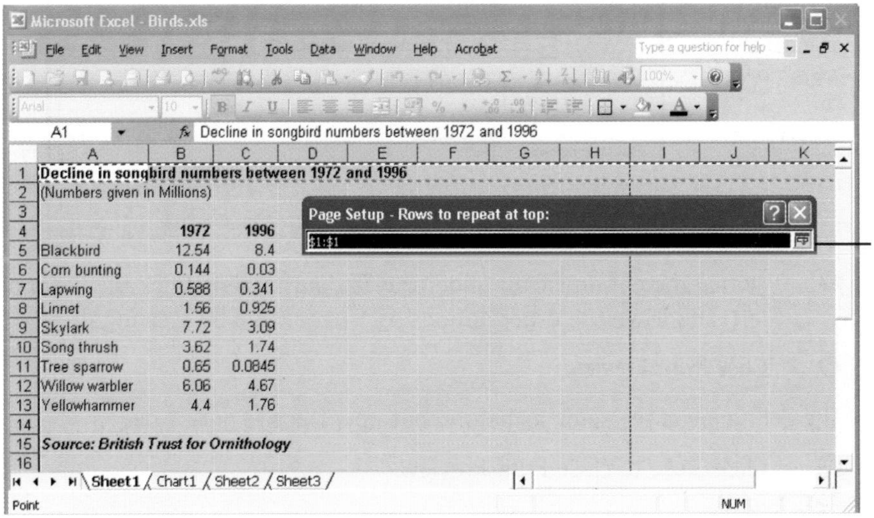

Click here once you've selected row 1

- When you have selected row **1**, click the small icon in the right of the box.
- You also have the option of repeating a column, which you do in exactly the same way as rows. Try repeating column **1**, using the same method as for repeating row **1**.
- Click **Print Preview**.

It's not very neat but the title row and column is repeated. Note that the title row and column will only appear on 2 of the 4 sheets. If we'd chosen a print area that was 4 pages long but only one page wide, the title row would appear on every sheet.

- Either click Print and OK, or just close Print Preview by clicking the Close button.

Fitting worksheet contents onto a specific number of pages

Although we've selected a print area that is larger than it needs to be, you are likely to come across spreadsheets that have enough data to fill more than one page. In this case, it is sometimes convenient to try and fit all the data onto one page or a specific number of pages for printing purposes.

- Go to File, Page Setup.
- Click the Page tab.

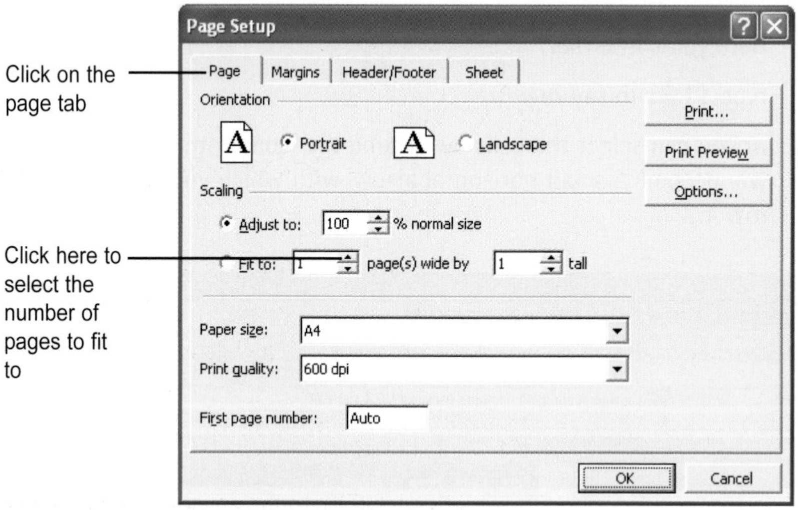

- Notice the option Fit to: under the Scaling section. Click the radio button on the left, and leave the other options as 1 page wide by 1 page tall.
- Click Print Preview.

The cell range is the same as before, but now there is only 1 page.

- Click Close to close Print Preview.

Hiding/Unhiding gridlines on printouts

Excel automatically prints without gridlines, but sometimes they can be useful.

- Click Sheet1 to select it. Select File, Page Setup from the menu.
- Click the Sheet tab at the top of the Page Setup dialogue box.

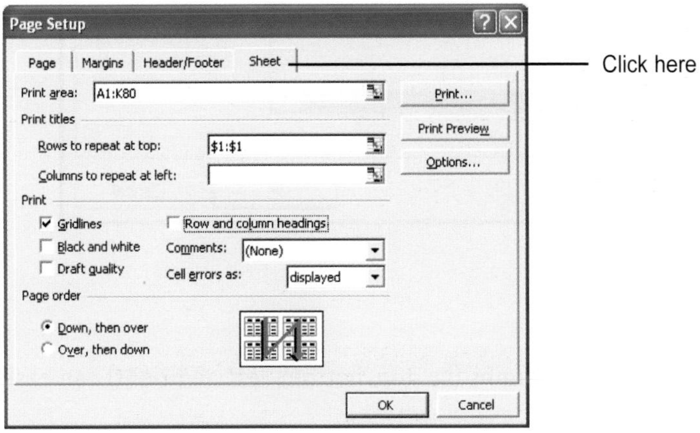

Tip:
You can also open the Page Setup dialogue box by clicking the Setup button when you're in Print Preview.

- Under the Print section, notice there is a checkbox next to Gridlines. Click this to print gridlines.
- Now go to Print Preview to see what it will look like.

Printing row and column headers

Excel will not normally print row and/or column headers, but you can choose to do so using the Page Setup dialogue box shown in the previous figure.

- Select File, Page Setup.
- Click the Sheet tab at the top of the Page Setup dialogue box and check the Row and column headings option.
- Click OK.

Paper orientation

- In the Page Setup dialogue box, click the Page tab.
- Click the toggle buttons to change the orientation from Portrait to Landscape.

Paper size

- To change the paper size, click the down-arrow on the right of the box and select the correct paper size.

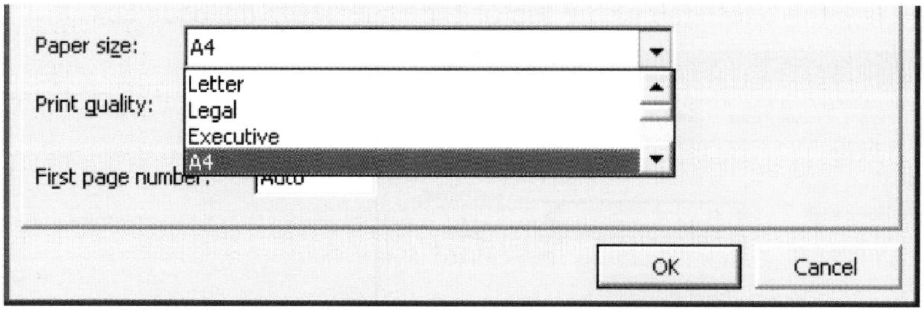

Changing the margins

The size of the worksheet margins (i.e. top, bottom, left and right) can easily be changed:

- This is also done in Page Setup. Just click the **Margins** tab and choose which margin sizes you want.

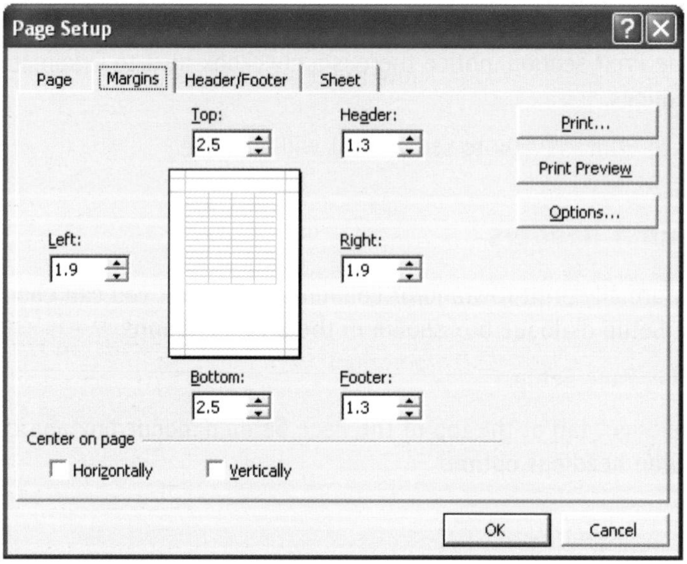

- Click **OK** to close the **Page Setup** dialogue box.

Preparation

We have looked at a number of ways to set up your worksheet before output. Print Preview is a useful tool for checking your work, but you should also check all text in a worksheet for spelling errors and make a rough check that the calculations are as you intended.

Exercise

Now you will print parts of the spreadsheets you created in previous end-of-chapter practice exercises.

1. Open the spreadsheet **Population.xls**.

2. Select the column chart only and print it.

3. Click away from the chart and print the whole worksheet.

4. Use the **Set Print Area** command to print only the figures, without the chart.

5. Close the spreadsheet.

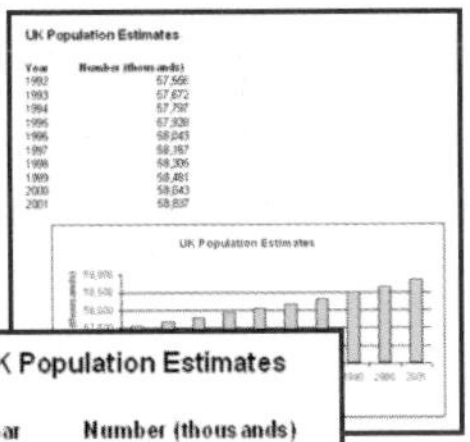

UK Population Estimates

Year	Number (thousands)
1992	57,556
1993	57,672
1994	57,797
1995	57,928
1996	58,043
1997	58,167
1998	58,305
1999	58,481
2000	58,643
2001	58,837

6. Open the spreadsheet **Birthday3.xls** and print the entire workbook.

7. Print the worksheet **Home** to show the row and column headings.

8. Close the spreadsheet.

Party Budget - at home

Item	Number	Cost(£)	Total Cost(£)
Catering	20	2.50	50.00
Magician	1	60.00	60.00
Party bag	20	1.00	20.00
Balloons	1	10.00	10.00
Cake	1	15.00	15.00
		Total	155.00
			7.75

Party Budget - Trip

Item	Number	Cost(£)	Total Cost(£)
Minibus	1	50.00	50.00
Entrance	10	10.00	100.00
Lunch	10	4.00	40.00
Drinks	10	2.00	20.00
Cake	1	15.00	15.00
	Total		225.00
	Per child		11.25

9. Open the spreadsheet **Quiz.xls**.

10. Print the worksheet in landscape orientation.

11. Print the worksheet with gridlines.

12. Close the spreadsheet.

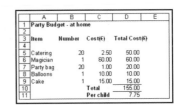

	A	B	C	D	E
1	Party Budget - at home				
2					
3	Item	Number	Cost(£)	Total Cost(£)	
4					
5	Catering	20	2.50	50.00	
6	Magician	1	60.00	60.00	
7	Party bag	20	1.00	20.00	
8	Balloons	1	10.00	10.00	
9	Cake	1	15.00	15.00	
10			Total	155.00	
11			Per child	7.75	

Quiz Night

	Round 1 History	2 TV	3 Music	4 General knowledge	5 Geography	6 Film	Joker round	Total points	Joker points	Grand Total
Team 1	18	10	15	10	19	16	1	88	18	106
Team 2	15	8	13	8	17	14	2	75	8	83
Team 3	8	10	9	12	9	11	2	59	10	69
Team 4	17	15	14	17	19	18	4	100	17	117
Team 5	12	15	10	13	10	18	4	78	13	91
Team 6	7	9	9	9	10	11	4	55	9	64
Team 7	12	14	13	15	13	16	6	83	16	99
Team 8	19	17	14	18	13	15	1	96	19	115
Team 9	12	13	16	17	12	19	6	89	19	108
Team 10	10	11	15	12	11	12	4	71	12	83
Average score	13	12	13	13	13	15			Champions	117
									Wooden spoon	64

CHAPTER 4.8 Cell Referencing

There are two different ways of referencing a particular cell in a formula.

Relative cell referencing

This is the default setting in Excel. If we take the example in the screenshot below, Excel actually remembers the formula as =the cell 3 above and one to the left. This means that when you copy the formula to a different cell, the formula will no longer say =A1.

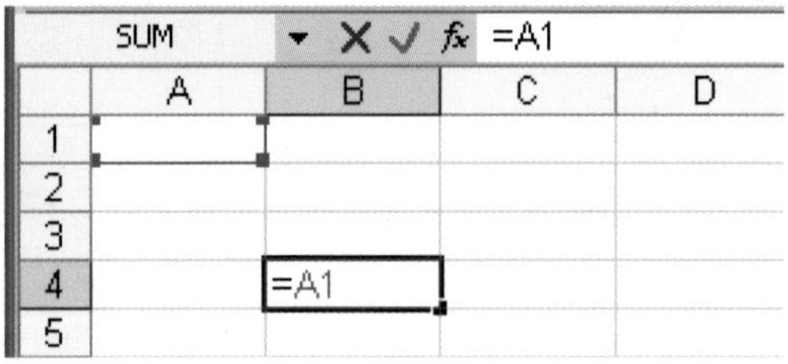

For example, if you copy cell B4 to cell C4, the formula becomes =B1, because B1 is the cell 3 above and one to the left of cell C4!

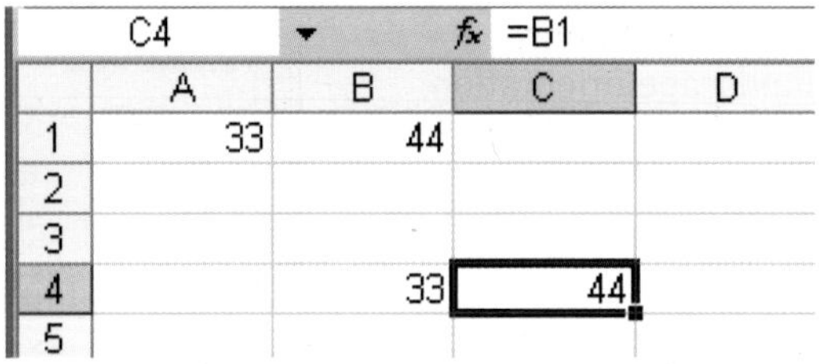

- Create a spreadsheet like the one above and have a play with copying and pasting cells and formulae.
- Close the spreadsheet when you have finished. There is no need to save it.

Absolute cell referencing

Absolute cell referencing is used when you always want to refer to the same cell. We'll work through the following project to demonstrate when to use absolute cell referencing.

Project: Car imports

- Open a new workbook. Copy the screenshot below, entering all the cell contents and copying the formatting.

	A	B	C	D	E	F
1						
2	**Current exchange rate:**	**1.55**	Euros to the pound			
3						
4						
5		**UK Price**	**Imported Price**			
6	**Car make & model**	**Price in pounds**	**Price in Euros**	**Price in Pounds**	**£Saving**	**%Saving**
7	Peugeot 206 Coupe Cabriolet	15370	20723.5			
8	VW Golf GTI	18330	24792.25			
9	Mini 16V Cooper	15465	21583.75			
10	BMW 5 Series SE	33060	44942.25			
11	VW Passat SE	17120	21692.25			
12	Alfa Romeo T Spark Selespeed Lusso	18750	24025			
13	Toyota Yaris 16V	11470	13942.25			
14						

Tip:
The text has been right-aligned so that it lines up with the numbers below. To do this just highlight the text cells and click the Align Right button on the Formatting toolbar.

First we need to enter a formula to calculate the price of the imported cars in pounds. The price will be calculated using the current exchange rate which is entered at the top of the sheet.

- Click in cell D7. Enter the formula =C7/B2. (To convert Euros to Pounds, you need to divide the Euro amount by the exchange rate). Press Enter.

We need the same formula in all the cells in that column, from D7 to D13. Let's see what happens when we copy the formula down.

- Click in cell D7. Click and drag the small handle on the bottom right of the cell down to cell D13.

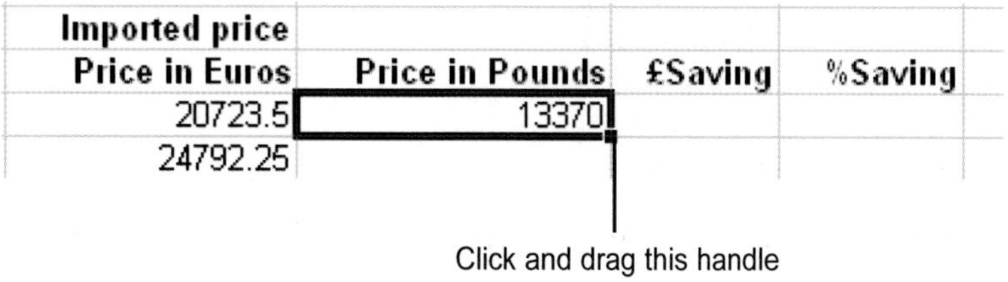

Imported price
Price in Euros
Price in Pounds
£Saving
%Saving
20723.5
13370
24792.25
Click and drag this handle

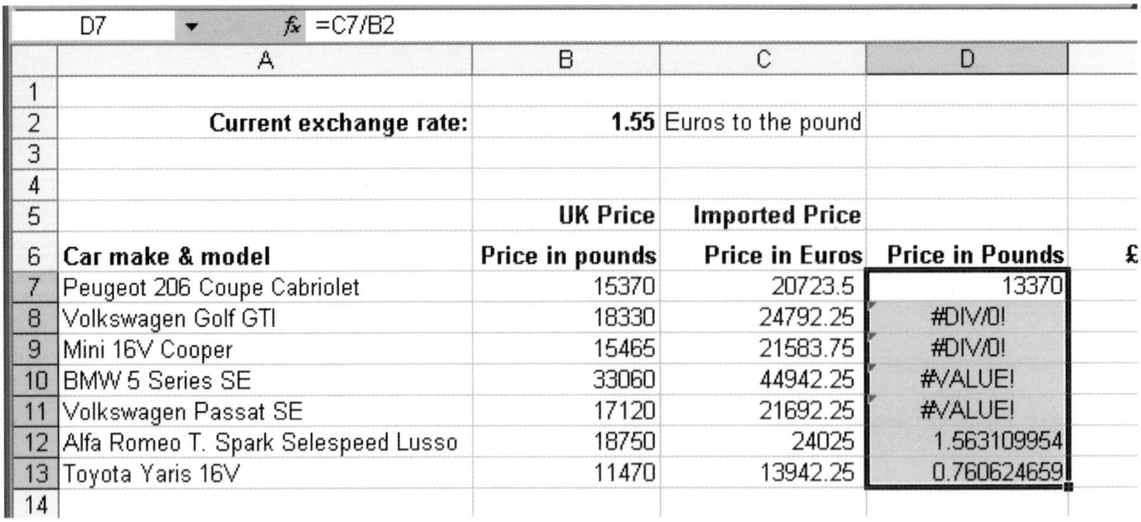

D7 =C7/B2

	A	B	C	D	
1					
2	**Current exchange rate:**	**1.55**	Euros to the pound		
3					
4					
5		**UK Price**	**Imported Price**		
6	**Car make & model**	**Price in pounds**	**Price in Euros**	**Price in Pounds**	**£**
7	Peugeot 206 Coupe Cabriolet	15370	20723.5	13370	
8	Volkswagen Golf GTI	18330	24792.25	#DIV/0!	
9	Mini 16V Cooper	15465	21583.75	#DIV/0!	
10	BMW 5 Series SE	33060	44942.25	#VALUE!	
11	Volkswagen Passat SE	17120	21692.25	#VALUE!	
12	Alfa Romeo T. Spark Selespeed Lusso	18750	24025	1.563109954	
13	Toyota Yaris 16V	11470	13942.25	0.760624659	
14					

Excel has automatically used relative cell referencing, and as you can see, it hasn't worked!

- Click cell **D8** to see what formula is there.

The Formula bar shows **=C8/B3**. What is in cell **B3**? Nothing! Take a look at the other formulae in the column. Can you see what has happened?

We should have used absolute cell referencing, as we want the formula to always refer to cell **B2** where the exchange rate is.

- Select cells **D8** to **D13** and press the **Delete** key.
- Click in cell **D7**. We need to alter the formula to make **B2** an absolute cell reference.

For absolute cell referencing, all you do is add a **$** symbol in front of the column AND row. You can put the symbol in front of the column only, but this will mean that when you copy the formula, only the column part of the formula will be kept constant. The same goes for rows. This is called **mixed cell referencing**.

- Change the formula in cell **D7** to **=C7/$B$2**.

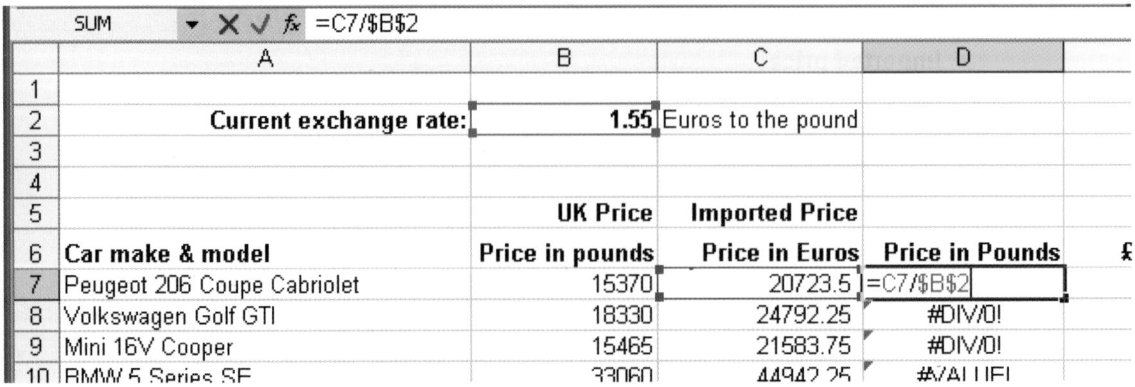

SUM =C7/$B$2

	A	B	C	D	
1					
2	**Current exchange rate:**	**1.55**	Euros to the pound		
3					
4					
5		**UK Price**	**Imported Price**		
6	**Car make & model**	**Price in pounds**	**Price in Euros**	**Price in Pounds**	**£**
7	Peugeot 206 Coupe Cabriolet	15370	20723.5	=C7/$B$2	
8	Volkswagen Golf GTI	18330	24792.25	#DIV/0!	
9	Mini 16V Cooper	15465	21583.75	#DIV/0!	
10	BMW 5 Series SE	33060	44942.25	#VALUE!	

- Now copy the formula to the other cells in the column.

D7 =C7/$B$2

	A	B	C	D	E	F
1						
2	**Current exchange rate:**	**1.55**	Euros to the pound			
3						
4						
5		**UK Price**	**Imported Price**			
6	**Car make & model**	**Price in pounds**	**Price in Euros**	**Price in Pounds**	**£Saving**	**% Saving**
7	Peugeot 206 Coupe Cabriolet	15370	20723.5	13370		
8	Volkswagen Golf GTI	18330	24792.25	15995		
9	Mini 16V Cooper	15465	21583.75	13925		
10	BMW 5 Series SE	33060	44942.25	28995		
11	Volkswagen Passat SE	17120	21692.25	13995		
12	Alfa Romeo T. Spark Selespeed Lusso	18750	24025	15500		
13	Toyota Yaris 16V	11470	13942.25	8995		
14						

That seems to have worked!

Save the worksheet as Cars by clicking the Save icon.

Entering the other formulae

- You need to enter a formula for the £Saving column. For this, use the formula:

  UK Price in Pounds – Imported Price in Pounds

- Copy the formula down the whole column. Do you need relative or absolute cell referencing for this?

Your spreadsheet should look like this – check your formulae if it doesn't!

E7 =B7-D7

	A	B	C	D	E	F
1						
2	**Current exchange rate:**	**1.55**	Euros to the pound			
3						
4						
5		**UK Price**	**Imported Price**			
6	**Car make & model**	**Price in pounds**	**Price in Euros**	**Price in Pounds**	**£Saving**	**% Saving**
7	Peugeot 206 Coupe Cabriolet	15370	20723.5	13370	2000	
8	Volkswagen Golf GTI	18330	24792.25	15995	2335	
9	Mini 16V Cooper	15465	21583.75	13925	1540	
10	BMW 5 Series SE	33060	44942.25	28995	4065	
11	Volkswagen Passat SE	17120	21692.25	13995	3125	
12	Alfa Romeo T. Spark Selespeed Lusso	18750	24025	15500	3250	
13	Toyota Yaris 16V	11470	13942.25	8995	2475	
14						

Calculating a percentage

We also need a formula for the % Saving column.

- Enter the formula for this calculation in cell F7:

  £Saving / UK Price in Pounds

It might look like the answer is 0 – this is because there are no decimal places shown.

- Use the Increase Decimal button and the Decrease Decimal button to adjust the cell to 2 decimal places.
- Copy the formula down for all the cars.

- To turn them into percentages, select cells F7 to F13 then click the Percent Style on the Formatting toolbar.

F7 fx =E7/B7

	A	B	C	D	E	F
1						
2	**Current exchange rate:**	**1.55**	Euros to the pound			
3						
4						
5		**UK Price**	**Imported Price**			
6	**Car make & model**	**Price in pounds**	**Price in Euros**	**Price in Pounds**	**£Saving**	**% Saving**
7	Peugeot 206 Coupe Cabriolet	15370	20723.5	13370	2000	13%
8	Volkswagen Golf GTI	18330	24792.25	15995	2335	13%
9	Mini 16V Cooper	15465	21583.75	13925	1540	10%
10	BMW 5 Series SE	33060	44942.25	28995	4065	12%
11	Volkswagen Passat SE	17120	21692.25	13995	3125	18%
12	Alfa Romeo T. Spark Selespeed Lusso	18750	24025	15500	3250	17%
13	Toyota Yaris 16V	11470	13942.25	8995	2475	22%
14						

- Have a play with the exchange rate. At what exchange rate does the % Saving become zero for the Mini?

The currency format

Now we'll change the format of some of the columns to give them the Currency number type.

- Select cells B7 to B13, then hold down Ctrl while selecting cells D7 to E13.
- Right-click anywhere within the selected cells to bring up the shortcut menu.
- Select Format Cells from the menu.
- Select Currency from the Category list (make sure the Number tab is selected). Set the Decimal places to 0. Excel should choose the £ symbol by default, which is fine.

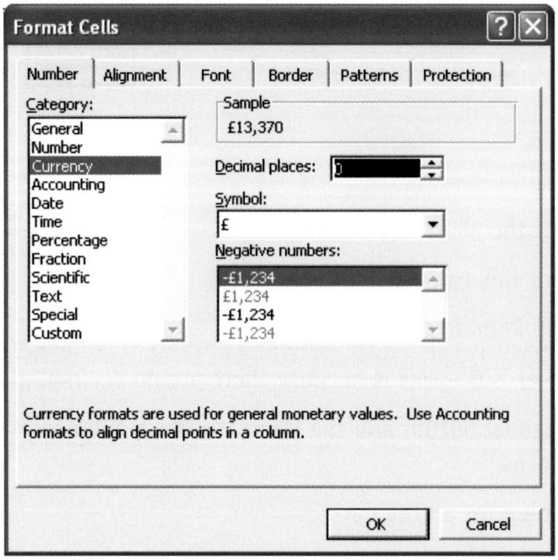

- Click OK.
- Repeat this for the Euro column. Remember to choose the Euro symbol from the Symbol list.

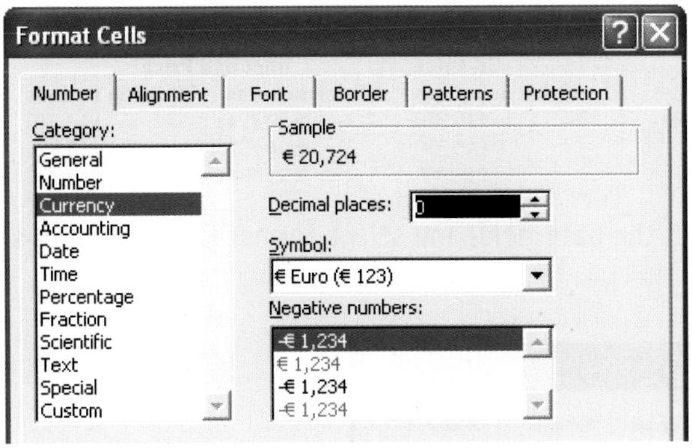

Your screen should now look like the one below:

	A	B	C	D	E	F
1						
2	**Current exchange rate:**	**1.55**	Euros to the pound			
3						
4						
5		**UK Price**	**Imported Price**			
6	**Car make & model**	**Price in pounds**	**Price in Euros**	**Price in Pounds**	**£Saving**	**%Saving**
7	Peugeot 206 Coupe Cabriolet	£15,370	€ 20,724	£13,370	£2,000	13%
8	VW Golf GTI	£18,330	€ 24,792	£15,995	£2,335	13%
9	Mini 16V Cooper	£15,465	€ 21,584	£13,925	£1,540	10%
10	BMW 5 Series SE	£33,060	€ 44,942	£28,995	£4,065	12%
11	VW Passat SE	£17,120	€ 21,692	£13,995	£3,125	18%
12	Alfa Romeo T Spark Selespeed Lusso	£18,750	€ 24,025	£15,500	£3,250	17%
13	Toyota Yaris 16V	£11,470	€ 13,942	£8,995	£2,475	22%
14						

Merge and centre cell contents

You can easily merge and centre cell contents using the button on the Formatting toolbar. This is particularly useful for titles.

- Select cells C5 and D5. Click the Merge and Center button.

That makes it a bit clearer which the imported prices are.

Adding a date field

A quick way to enter today's date is to press Ctrl-; (Ctrl and ; together) on the keyboard. Alternatively you can type a date (separated with either hyphens or slashes) into a cell and then format it.

We will add a date to show when the Current exchange rate was last updated.

- Add the text and date in cells **D2** and **E2** as shown in the next screenshot.

	A	B	C	D	E
1					
2	**Current exchange rate:**	**1.55**	Euros to the pound	**Updated:**	14/03/2003
3					
4					
5		**UK Price**	**Imported Price**		
6	**Car make & model**	**Price in pounds**	**Price in Euros**	**Price in Pounds**	**£Saving**
7	Peugeot 206 Coupe Cabriolet	£15,370	€ 20,724	£13,370	£2,000
8	VW Golf GTI	£18,330	€ 24,792	£15,995	£2,335

- Now right-click in the date field, and select **Format Cells** from the shortcut menu that appears.

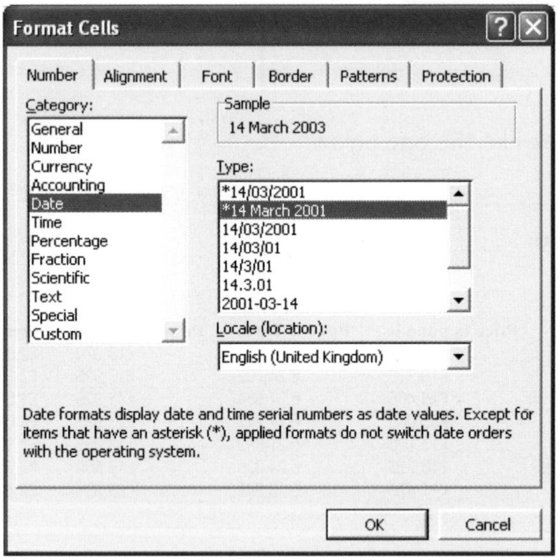

- Excel has already guessed that you want the **Date** category. Pick a date **Type** from the right-hand list. Note that although it looks like Excel has the day and month mixed up, it should get it right when you click **OK**.
- You might need to widen column **E** to display the whole date.

	A	B	C	D	E
1					
2	**Current exchange rate:**	**1.55**	Euros to the pound	**Updated:**	14 March 2003
3					
4					
5		**UK Price**	**Imported Price**		
6	**Car make & model**	**Price in pounds**	**Price in Euros**	**Price in Pounds**	**£Saving**
7	Peugeot 206 Coupe Cabriolet	£15,370	€ 20,724	£13,370	£2,000
8	VW Golf GTI	£18,330	€ 24,792	£15,995	£2,335

Wrapping cell content

Some of the car makes & models are quite long. It would look neater if the longer descriptions ran onto two lines, rather than making the column extra wide to fit them.

- Select cell A12, then right-click it. Select Format Cells from the shortcut menu that appears.
- The Format Cells dialogue box appears. Click the Alignment tab.

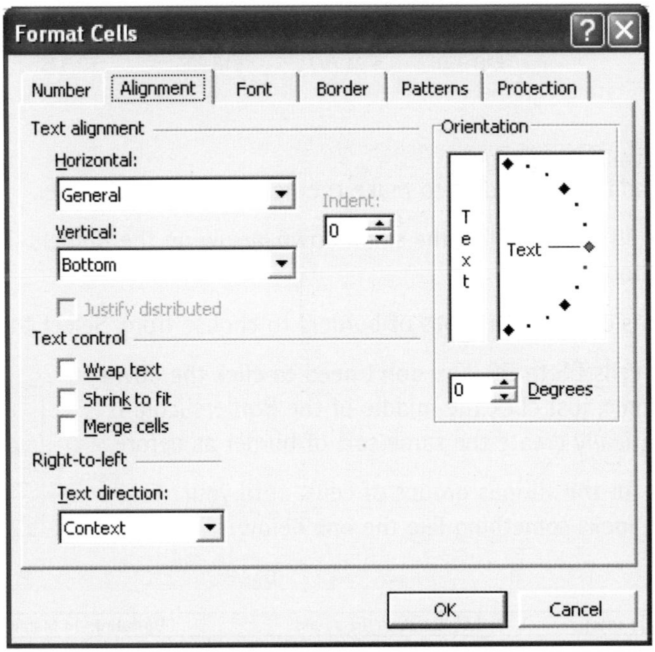

- Under the Text Control section, click the checkbox next to Wrap text. Click OK.
- Now resize column A so that it is too small to fit all the words on one line.
- Increase the height of row 12 by clicking and dragging between the row headers of row 12 and row 13.

10 BMW 5 Series SE
11 Volkswagen Passat SE
Alfa Romeo T. Spark
12 Selespeed Lusso
13 Toyota Yaris 16V

The text just fills onto the next line!

- Repeat this for some of the other cells where the Car make & model description is long.
- Now make the column headings in row 6 wrap over two lines.

- We need to move the Updated field over to the right. Select cells D2 and E2, then click and drag the border of the selection to the right.

	A	B	C	D	E	F
1						
2	**Current exchange rate:**	**1.55**	Euros to the pound		**Updated:**	14 March 2003
3						
4						
5		**UK Price**	**Imported Price**			
6	**Car make & model**	**Price in pounds**	**Price in Euros**	**Price in Pounds**	**£Saving**	**%Saving**
7	Peugeot 206 Coupe Cabriolet	£15,370	€20,724	£13,370	£2,000	13%
8	VW Golf GTI	£18,330	€24,792	£15,995	£2,335	13%

Adding borders

We'll just quickly add some borders to make the headings a little clearer.

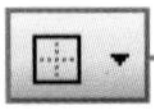

- Select cells B5 and B6. Click the small down-arrow on the Borders icon on the Formatting toolbar.
- There are lots of different types of borders to choose from. Select the one shown.

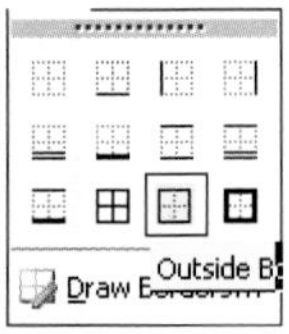

- Now select cells C5 to D6. You don't need to click the down-arrow this time, just click the middle of the Borders icon. It will automatically create the same sort of border as before.
- Repeat this for the various groups of cells, until your spreadsheet looks something like the one below:

	A	B	C	D	E	F
1						
2	**Current exchange rate:**	**1.55**	Euros to the pound		**Updated:**	14 March 2003
3						
4						
5		**UK Price**	**Imported Price**			
6	**Car make & model**	**Price in pounds**	**Price in Euros**	**Price in Pounds**	**£Saving**	**%Saving**
7	Peugeot 206 Coupe Cabriolet	£15,370	€20,724	£13,370	£2,000	13%
8	VW Golf GTI	£18,330	€24,792	£15,995	£2,335	13%
9	Mini 16V Cooper	£15,465	€21,584	£13,925	£1,540	10%
10	BMW 5 Series SE	£33,060	€44,942	£28,995	£4,065	12%
11	VW Passat SE	£17,120	€21,692	£13,995	£3,125	18%
12	Alfa Romeo T Spark Selespeed Lusso	£18,750	€24,025	£15,500	£3,250	17%
13	Toyota Yaris 16V	£11,470	€13,942	£8,995	£2,475	22%
14						

Tip:
To delete a border, just click the cell next to the border, and click the No Border option from the Borders menu.

- Finally, draw one big border around the table, using the slightly thicker border.

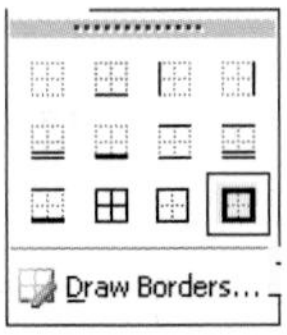

	A	B	C	D	E	F
1						
2	**Current exchange rate:**	**1.55**	Euros to the pound		**Updated:**	14 March 2003
3						
4						
5		**UK Price**	**Imported Price**			
6	**Car make & model**	**Price in pounds**	**Price in Euros**	**Price in Pounds**	**£Saving**	**%Saving**
7	Peugeot 206 Coupe Cabriolet	£15,370	€20,724	£13,370	£2,000	13%
8	VW Golf GTI	£18,330	€24,792	£15,995	£2,335	13%
9	Mini 16V Cooper	£15,465	€21,584	£13,925	£1,540	10%
10	BMW 5 Series SE	£33,060	€44,942	£28,995	£4,065	12%
11	VW Passat SE	£17,120	€21,692	£13,995	£3,125	18%
12	Alfa Romeo T Spark Selespeed Lusso	£18,750	€24,025	£15,500	£3,250	17%
13	Toyota Yaris 16V	£11,470	€13,942	£8,995	£2,475	22%
14						
15						

- Click Print Preview to see what your spreadsheet will look like when printed. You'll need to change the Page Orientation to fit it all on one page.

Tip:
You can change the Page Orientation in the Page Setup dialogue box.

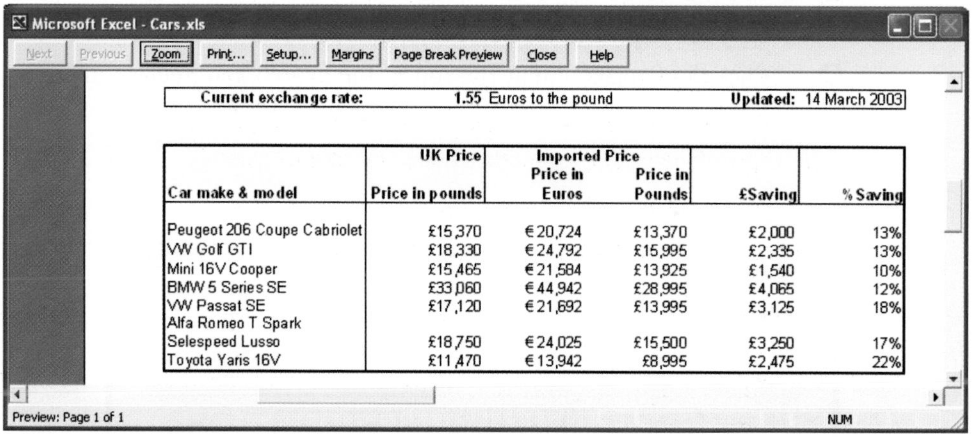

Current exchange rate: **1.55** Euros to the pound **Updated:** 14 March 2003

Car make & model	**UK Price** Price in pounds	**Imported Price** Price in Euros	Price in Pounds	**£Saving**	**% Saving**
Peugeot 206 Coupe Cabriolet	£15,370	€20,724	£13,370	£2,000	13%
VW Golf GTI	£18,330	€24,792	£15,995	£2,335	13%
Mini 16V Cooper	£15,465	€21,584	£13,925	£1,540	10%
BMW 5 Series SE	£33,060	€44,942	£28,995	£4,065	12%
VW Passat SE	£17,120	€21,692	£13,995	£3,125	18%
Alfa Romeo T Spark Selespeed Lusso	£18,750	€24,025	£15,500	£3,250	17%
Toyota Yaris 16V	£11,470	€13,942	£8,995	£2,475	22%

- Click Close to exit Print Preview.

Find and replace

There aren't many records in this spreadsheet, but in larger spreadsheets it is useful to be able to search for a particular value.

Finding a cell containing a particular word or value

- Select Edit, Find from the menu.
- Enter VW in the Find what: box.

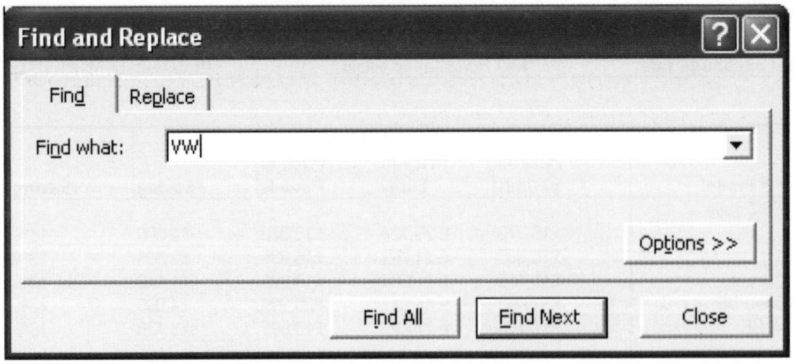

- Click **Find Next**.
- Excel makes the cell containing **VW** the active cell. Click **Find Next** again.

Excel moves to the second cell containing **VW**.

Replacing a word or value

If you have spelt a name wrongly in several different places in a spreadsheet, it is useful to set Excel to find and replace each instance of the word. For practice, we'll replace the word **VW** with **Volkswagen**.

- Click the **Replace** tab at the top of the **Search and Replace** dialogue box.

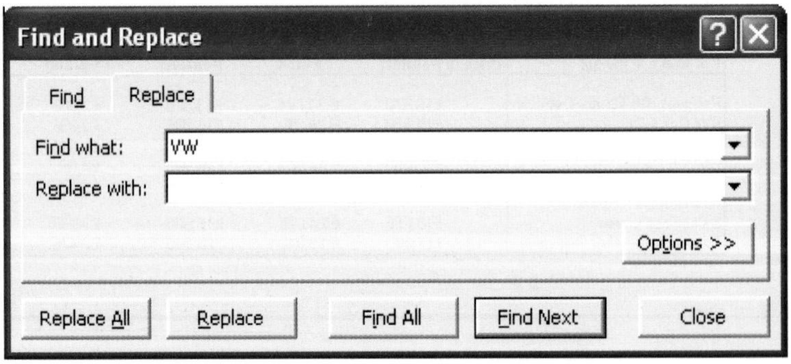

- Type **Volkswagen** in the **Replace with:** box.
- Click the **Replace All** button.

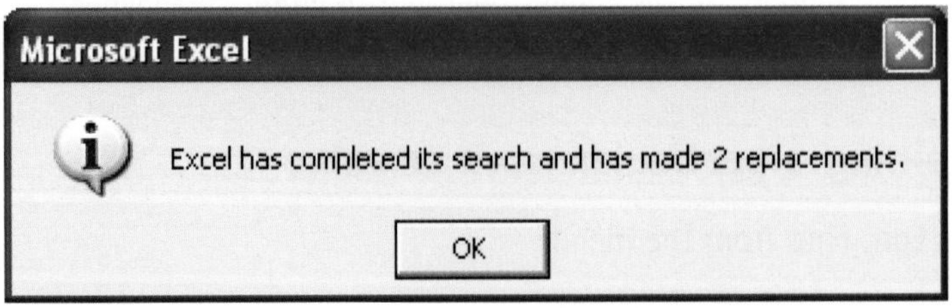

- Click **OK**. Notice that **VW** has now become **Volkswagen**. Click **Close**.

Adding Headers and Footers

Headers and footers are useful for automatically inserting information such as the current date and page numbers on larger documents.

- Select **View, Header and Footer** from the menu.

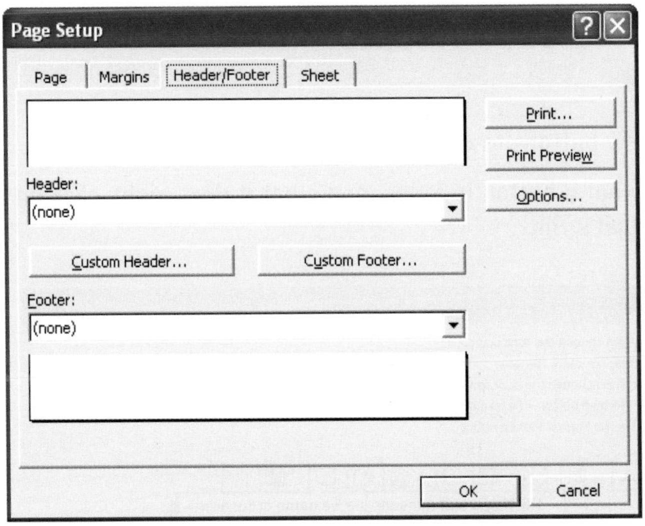

Tip:
You can also view the Header and Footer in the **Page Setup** dialogue box. Click **File, Page Setup** then click the **Header and Footer** tab.

- Click the **Custom Header** button.
- Click in the **Center Section** box and type **Car Import Savings Sheet**.

This title text should be bold, we'll do this now.

- Highlight the text you have just written, then click the **Font** button.

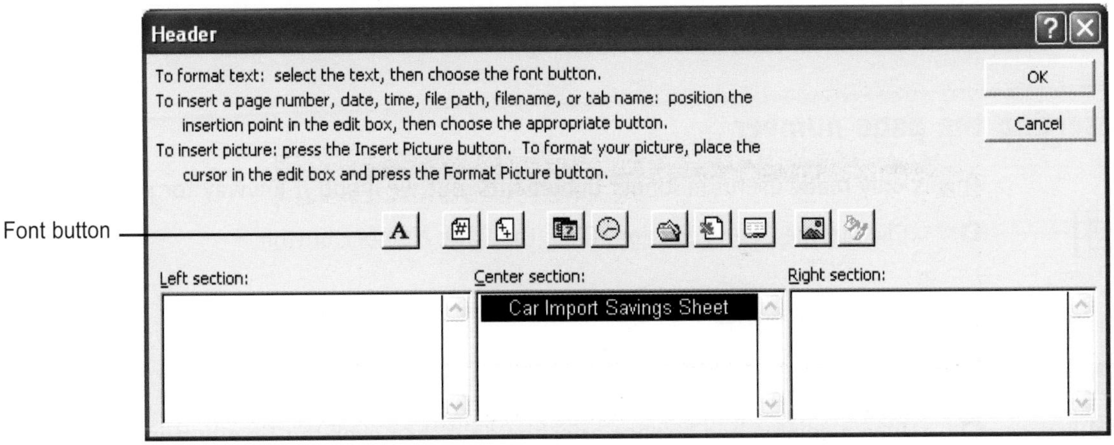

- Make the text 12 point and bold.
- Click OK. Click OK again to exit the Header dialogue box.

Now we'll insert some fields into the Footer.

- Click the Custom Footer button. You can enter text here just the same as you did in the Header. This time though we won't enter any text, we'll just insert fields using the buttons provided.

What do all buttons do?

There are quite a few buttons to choose from!

- To find out what a button is called, and what it does, right-click on a button then click What's This?.

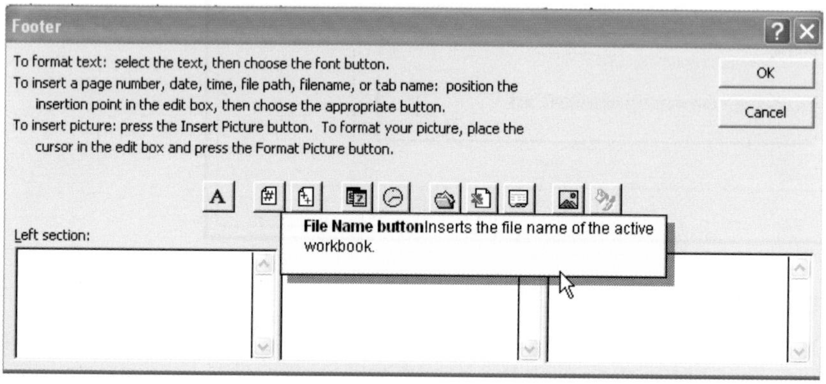

A small box pops up telling you what the button does.

Inserting the file name and worksheet name

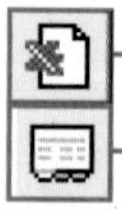

- Click somewhere in the Left section box.
- Click the File Name button.
- Type a comma and a space after the File Name expression then click the Worksheet Name button.

Inserting the page number

This is only really useful in longer documents, but we'll add it anyway for practice.

- Click in the Center Section. Click the Page Number button.

Inserting the date and time

- Click in the Right Section, then click the Date button.
- Type a comma and a space after the date then click the Time button.

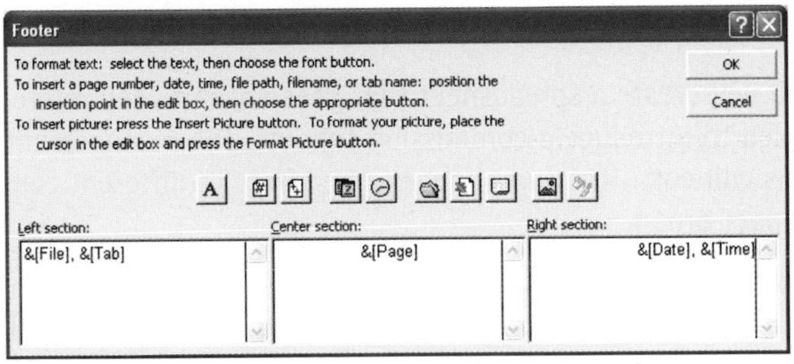

- Click OK.

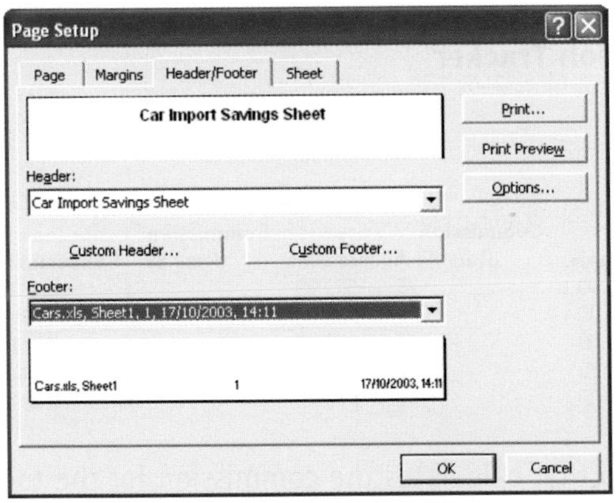

- You can see what the headers and footers will look like in the Page Setup window. Click OK when you're happy with how it looks.

- Click Print Preview to see what the sheet will look like when printed.

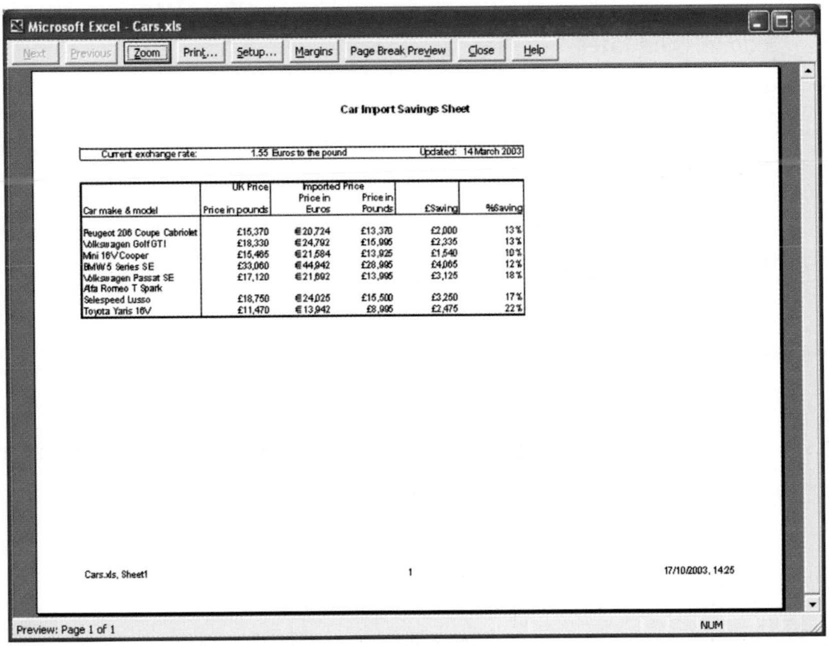

- Print the spreadsheet if you like, otherwise click the Close button.
- Save and close the spreadsheet.

Exercise

In this exercise you will create a spreadsheet that uses absolute cell referencing. A company has decided to introduce a commission scheme. The management want some idea how much this will cost. They want to see the effect of different commission levels for each product group.

1. Enter the following data into a new Excel spreadsheet and save the file as Commission.xls. Format cell A2 as a date field. Format cells C8 to H12 as currency and cells B4 to B6 as percentage. Merge and centre cells C6 to H6.

	A	B	C	D	E	F	G	H
1	**Anglebar Tools - Commission Tracker**							
2	30 May 2003							
3								
4	**Commission Rate A**	5%						
5	**Commission Rate B**	10%						
6	**Commission Rate C**	15%	**Items sold**					
7			**Tools**	**Commission (Rate A)**	**Accessories**	**Commission (Rate B)**	**Consumables**	**Commission (Rate C)**
8	Salesman 1		£ 1,300.00		£ 582.00		£ 317.00	
9	Salesman 2		£ 1,224.00		£ 280.00		£ 289.00	
10	Salesman 3		£ 1,026.00		£ 332.00		£ 297.00	
11	Salesman 4		£ 1,670.00		£ 620.00		£ 124.00	
12	Salesman 5		£ 1,488.00		£ 719.00		£ 188.00	

2. In cell D8 enter a formula that calculates the commission for the tools that salesman 1 has sold. Use the commission rate from cell B4 (absolute address) in the formula.

3. Fill the formula down to cell D12.

4. Enter a similar formula in cells F8 to F12 and H8 to H12 using the correct commission rates.

5. In cell A14 enter a label Total Commission.

6. In cell B14 enter a formula to calculate the total commission payable to all salesmen for all items sold.

7. Shade cell B14 in red and make the font colour white. Draw a thick border around the cell.

8. If the company want to reduce the total commission payment by 10% by adjusting the commission rate for consumables only, what would commission rate C have to be reduced to?

9. Insert a footer with your name and print the spreadsheet out in landscape format.

10. Save and close your work.

If...Then...Else

CHAPTER 4.9

In this chapter we'll create a spreadsheet for a Mirror shop. The shop offers cut-to-size mirrors, and they need a spreadsheet that will give an instant quote for a customer.

Project: Create a spreadsheet to produce instant quotes

The shop offers only one thickness of glass, 6mm. It offers a choice of polished, or polished and bevelled edges.

The price of the mirror is dependent on the surface area and the perimeter length.

These are the prices:

£32 per square metre of surface area

£1.70 per linear metre of perimeter for polished edges

£2.10 per linear metre of perimeter for polished and bevelled edges

- Open a new workbook, type in the text, format the text and add the borders so that your spreadsheet looks like the one below:

Book1

	A	B	C	D	E
1	Mirror, Mirror!	Cut to Size Mirrors			
2					
3					
4	Price per square metre			32	
5	Price per linear metre for polished edges			1.7	
6	Price per linear metre for polished and bevelled edges			2.1	
7					
8	Requested Mirror Size				
9	Width (m):		Type of edges (enter P or PB)		P = Polished
10	Height (m):				PB = Polished and Bevelled
11					
12	Total surface area (square metres)		Cost for surface area		
13	Total perimeter length (m)		Cost for edges		
14					
15					
16	Instant Quote:				
17					

Sheet1 / Sheet2 / Sheet3

Changing font style and size

We need to give the title and some of the other headings a bit of a makeover.

- Select cell A1. On the Formatting toolbar, select size 26 font.

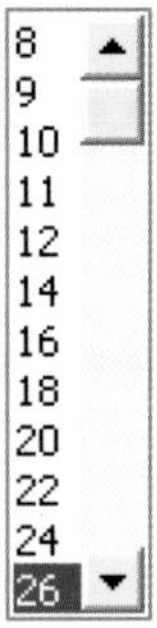

- Now change the font. Choose any font you like the look of. Make it bold also by clicking the Bold icon.

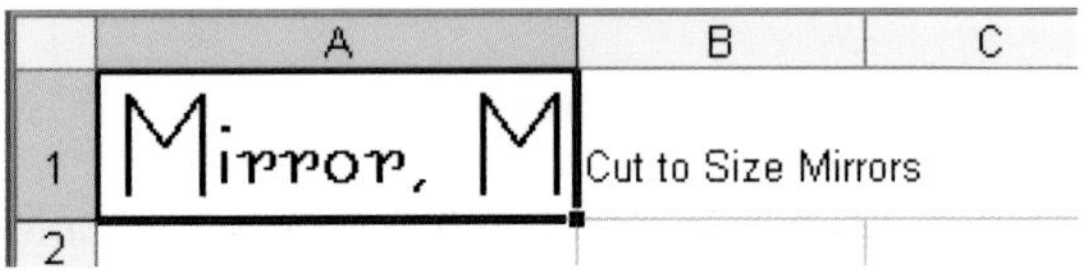

- You need to move the contents of cell B1 to cell D1. Make sure cell B1 is selected, then click and drag the black border over to cell D1.
- Change some more of the headings and formats to look like this:

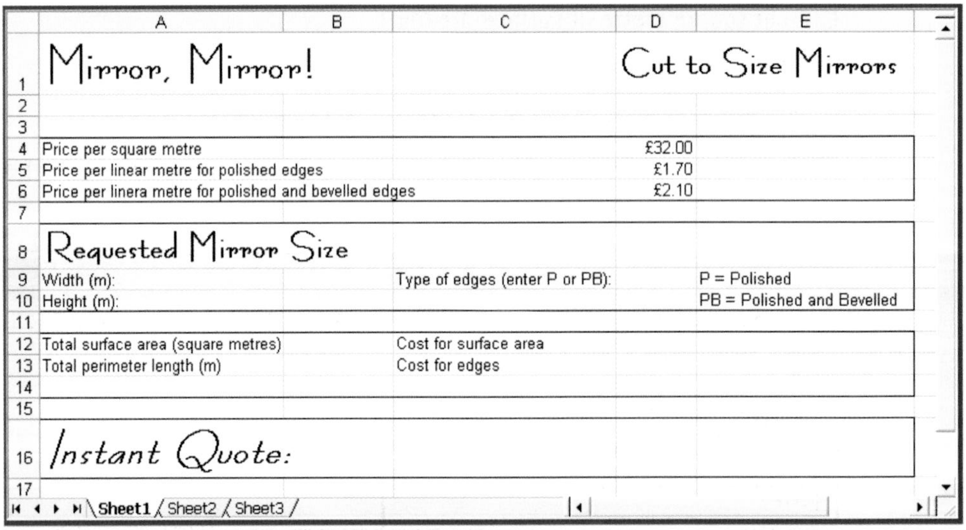

Tip:
To copy the formatting from a cell or cell range, select the cell(s) containing the formatting you want to copy. Click the Format Painter button on the Standard toolbar. Click in the cell(s) you want to format.

Adding the formulae

We'll do some more formatting in a minute. First we have to enter the formulae.

- The calculation for Total surface area is Width x Height. In cell B12, enter the formula =B9*B10.
- The calculation for Total perimeter length is 2 x (Width + Height). In cell B13, enter the formula =2*(B9+B10). You will need the brackets in the formula.
- Enter the formula for Cost for surface area. It should be =B12*D4.

- Save the workbook as Mirrors.

Now you can enter some data.

- Try out your formulae by entering the length and width of a mirror.
- Enter either P or PB where specified.

IF statements

Our calculation for the Cost for edges has to include an IF statement, so it can calculate the cost for either polished or polished and bevelled edges.

IF edges are polished THEN Cost for edges = perimeter length*D5

IF edges are bevelled THEN Cost for edges = perimeter length *D6

Breaking these statements down further:

IF cell D9 = P THEN cell D13 = B13*D5

IF cell D9 = PB THEN cell D13 = B13*D6

- Select cell D13. Click the Paste Function button to the left of the Formula bar.

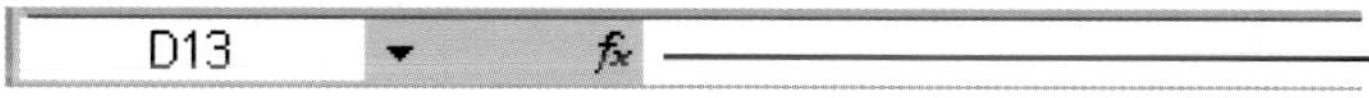

Paste Function button

- Select IF from the Select a function list. If you cannot see it in the list, change the category to Logical.

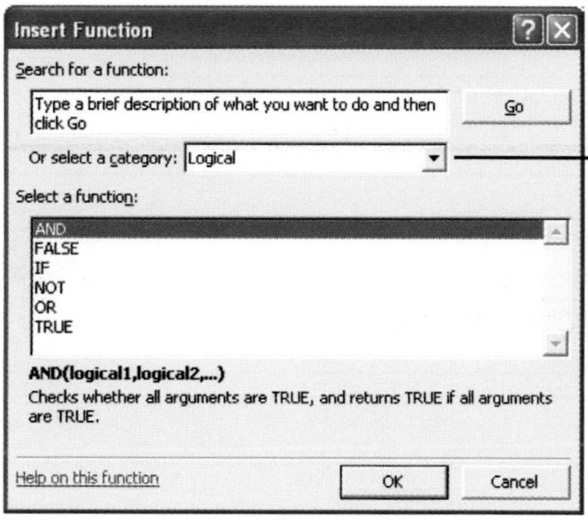

Select the Logical category

- Click **OK**.
- Enter the following formulas into the **Function Arguments** dialogue box.

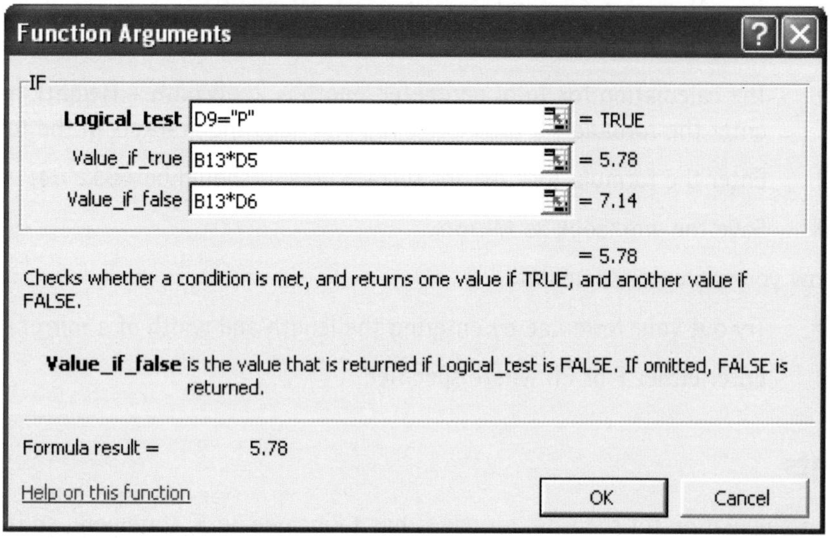

Tip:
If you're confused about how this function works, try clicking the **Help on this function** link at the bottom of the window. This gives an explanation and some more examples.

- Click **OK**.
- Format all the currency cells to show pound signs, and have **2** decimal places if you haven't done so already.
- Finally fill in the last formula for the total cost, next to the Instant **Quote heading**. It should be **=SUM(D12:D13)**.

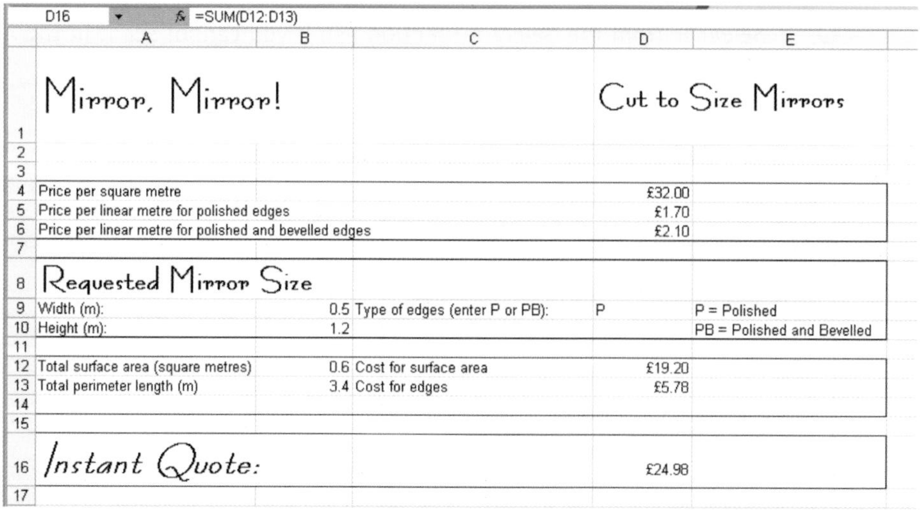

Adding some colour

It would be nice if the spreadsheet was a bit more colourful. We can do this by changing the font colour and the background fill colour.

Changing the font colour

- Select cell **A1**.

- Click the down-arrow on the **Font Color** button and select a colour.

Changing the background fill colour

- With cell **A1** still selected, click the down-arrow on the **Background Fill** button.
- Click to select a colour.

Aligning cell content

You can set where the text appears in a cell – left, right, top, bottom or centre. Use the **Align Right**, **Align Left** and **Center** buttons on the Formatting toolbar to align the cell content horizontally. You can also use the Format Cells dialogue box, which allows you to vertically align the cell contents (i.e. top, bottom or centre).

- Widen row **1** by clicking and dragging between the row selectors of row **1** and row **2**.
- Select cells **A1** and **D1**. Right-click somewhere in a selected cell.
- Select **Format, Cells** from the menu.
- Click the **Alignment** tab. Select **Centre** in the **Vertical Alignment** box.

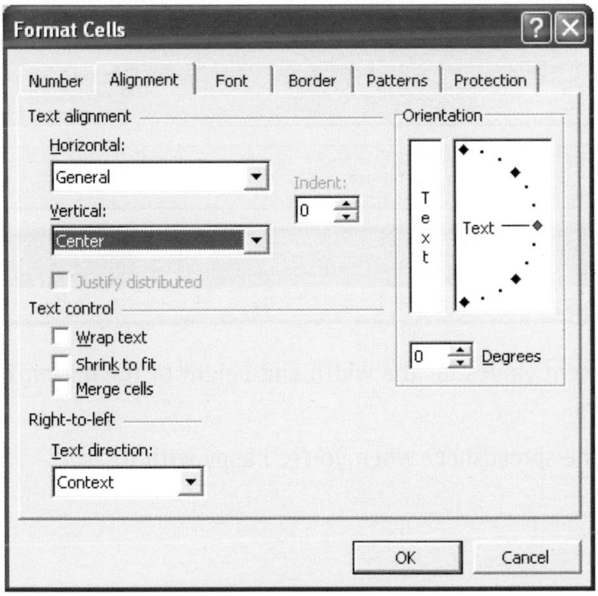

Cell content orientation

You can change the orientation of the text in the cells using the Format Cells dialogue box.

- Click and drag the red dot so that the text is slightly diagonal.

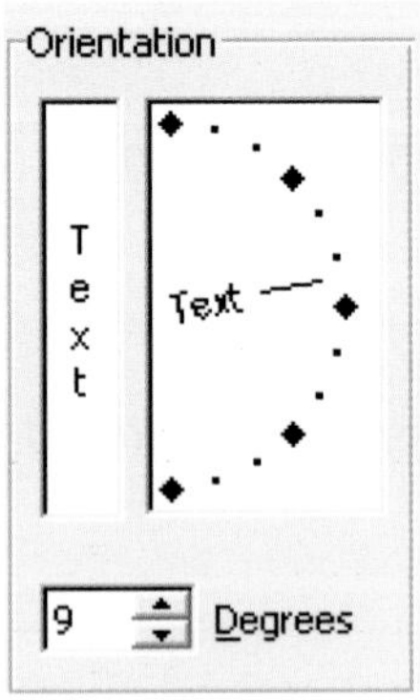

- Click OK.

Add some more colours, and play around with the formatting so that your spreadsheet looks something like the one below:

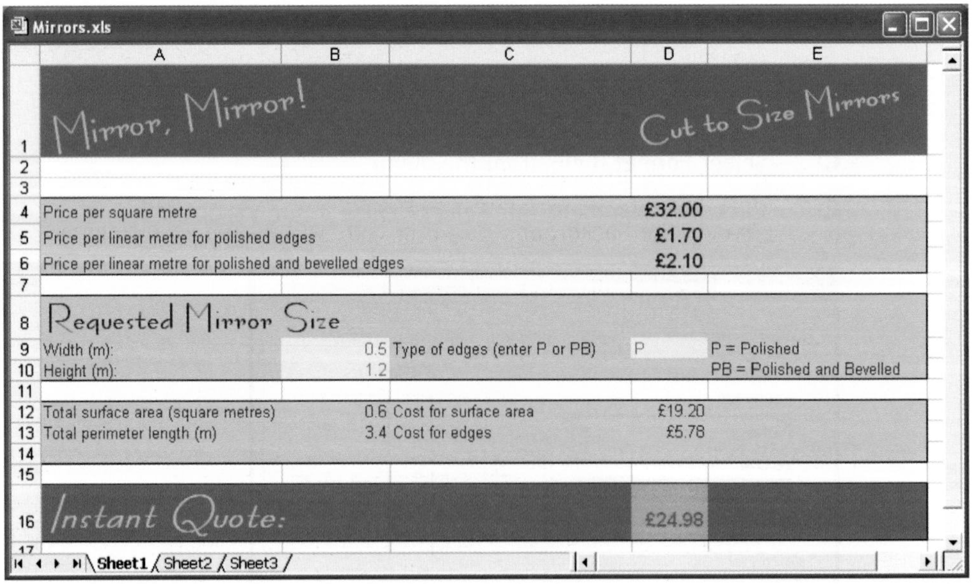

- Enter some different values for the width and height of the mirror. You can also change the prices.
- Save and close the spreadsheet when you're happy with it.

Exercise

In this exercise you will create a spreadsheet to record the times of athletes in a particular race. It will automatically indicate if the competitor has broken their personal best record.

1. Enter the following data into a new Excel spreadsheet. Format it as shown.

	A	B	C	D	E	F
1	The 2003 Ashfield Athletic Meeting					
2						
3	Event	Surname	Forename	Club	Personal Best	Result
4						
5	100mtrs	Baptist	Kyle	Hilcrest	10.99	11.01
6		Carr	Lee	Drayton	10.54	10.55
7		Coya	Paul	C&C	10.8	10.80
8		Hills	Saleem	Wilton	10.75	10.95
9		Nield	Conrad	Raylor	11.2	10.95
10		Njerba	James	Grenfer	10.94	10.87
11		Raman	Sherif	Fielden	10.8	10.99
12		Seth	Marcus	Merses	10.79	10.53
13		Williams	Odette	V&V	11.1	11.00

2. In cell G5 enter a formula that checks to see if the competitor's result is less than their current personal best. If it is, then the letters PB are inserted into the appropriate cell in column G. If it is not, then a blank space is entered into the cell.
3. Format the cells in column G to be centred, blue and bold.
4. Sort the competitors into descending order of result.
5. Change the background colour of cells B5 to F13 to a pale blue.

Your spreadsheet should look like this:

	A	B	C	D	E	F	G
1	The 2003 Ashfield Athletic Meeting						
2							
3	Event	Surname	Forename	Club	Personal Best	Result	
4							
5	100mtrs	Baptist	Kyle	Hilcrest	10.99	11.01	
6		Williams	Odette	V&V	11.1	11.00	PB
7		Raman	Sherif	Fielden	10.8	10.99	
8		Hills	Saleem	Wilton	10.75	10.95	
9		Nield	Conrad	Raylor	11.2	10.95	PB
10		Njerba	James	Grenfer	10.94	10.87	PB
11		Coya	Paul	C&C	10.8	10.80	
12		Carr	Lee	Drayton	10.54	10.55	
13		Seth	Marcus	Merses	10.79	10.53	PB

6. Save your spreadsheet as Results.xls and close your work.

Module 5

Database

In this module you will learn some of the main concepts of databases and how to use a database on a computer. You will learn how to:

- create and modify tables
- create and modify queries
- create and modify forms
- create and modify reports
- relate tables
- retrieve and manipulate information using queries
- retrieve and manipulate information using sort tools

Module 5 Table of Contents

Introduction to Databases

CHAPTER 5.1

What is Microsoft Access?

Microsoft Access is one of the most widely used database packages. Databases are used to store large amounts of information, and allow you to sort and filter the information or data to provide useful reports.

A database is based on tables of data, and each table contains many fields.

This is an example of how an art collection might look in a table of data:

Name of Painting	Artist	Gallery
Acuminatus	Mark Johnston	CCA Galleries
The North Unfolds	Neil Canning	Martin Tinney Gallery
Heat of the Day	Claire Blois	Kilmorack Gallery
Two Birches	James Hawkins	Rhue Studio

- How many rows are there in the table?
- How many columns are there in the table?

Answers:

- There are 3 columns. The column headings are the fields, so there are 3 fields in the table.
- There are 4 rows. The rows are the records, so there are 4 records in this table.

Each time the art collector purchases a new painting, he can catalogue it by adding a new record to the table.

The art collector can use the database to find out information such as:

- Whether he owns a particular painting
- Which paintings he owns by Neil Canning
- Which gallery a particular painting came from
- How many paintings he has from a particular gallery
- The artist of a particular painting

Databases are not often used for such small amounts of data, because the answers to the above questions can be easily answered just by looking at the table. However, if a gallery had thousands of paintings there would be thousands of rows, and the table would be so big it would take hours to answer the questions. This is where a database becomes very useful.

Before creating a database on the computer it is important to **plan** your database.

Planning a database

When planning a database you need to think about the answers to these questions:

- What is the purpose of the database?
- What information will you want to look up in the database?
- What data will you store in the database?

Letting Agency Database

During the course of this module you'll build up a database for a letting agency, **Hemlets Ltd**. Hemlets rents properties on behalf of private landlords in Ipswich. Hemlets needs the database to store information about the properties it manages and the landlords it deals with.

Purpose of the database

The staff at Hemlets need to be able to find out quickly and easily:

- Which properties are available to let
- How many bedrooms each property has
- Which properties are available for a particular monthly rent
- Whether a property is a flat, terraced, semi-detached or detached
- If the property is let, when the lease runs out
- Who is the landlord of a particular property
- Contact details of a particular landlord

Each property is owned by just one landlord. Each landlord may own one or more properties.

Your database should contain details on each property and each landlord. The next step is to decide which fields you need.

Based on the information given above, the table must contain the following information about each property:

- Style (flat, terraced, semi, detached)
- Bedrooms (1, 2, 3, 4, 5, or 6)
- Rent (monthly)
- Rented? (Y/N)
- Lease expiry date
- Landlord name

In addition, the following information needs to be held about each landlord:

- Title
- Initials
- Surname
- Contact number

Each of these pieces of information will be held in one field in your table.

Tip:

Remember that the fields in the table are the column headings.

A flat file database

A flat file database is a database with just one table in it. If the Hemlets database was designed as a flat file database, the table of data would look something like this:

PropertyRef	Style	Bedrooms	Rent	Rented	Lease Expiry	Landlord Title	Landlord Initials	Landlord Surname	Contact No
P1	Semi	3	800	Y	1/6/2003	Mrs	J	Welsh	01474 276499
P2	Flat	2	650	Y	5/12/2003	Mr	S	Hemmings	01474 572772
P3	Detached	4	1050	N		Mr	S	Hemmings	01474 572772
P4	Terraced	2	700	Y	15/8/2003	Mr	S	Hemmings	01474 572772
P5	Semi	3	850	N		Mr	M	Jenkins	01474 387465
etc..									

Tip:
The PropertyRef field has been added because we need one field in each record that is unique. This will be explained in more detail later.

Problems with a flat file database

It is a common problem with many flat file databases that the same data is duplicated several times. To explain why, we'll look at the example of the property table above.

Look at the different landlords who own the various properties; notice that Mr S Hemmings owns three of the properties. This means that the information for Mr Hemmings had to be entered three different times, and if he changed his telephone number, you would have to be careful to change it in all three rows of the table, for every property he owns.

This is not only a waste of time, but it can introduce a lot of errors in a database. It would be easy to make a spelling mistake when entering Mr Hemmings' details, for example entering Hennings instead of Hemmings. If Hemlets searched to see which properties were owned by Mr Hemmings, the one with the spelling mistake wouldn't be listed, and the staff at Hemlets would be none the wiser.

A relational database

The solution to these problems is to hold the data in separate tables. We need a table for the properties and a different table for the landlords. The two tables will need to be linked. A database that contains two or more linked tables is called a relational database. Before you learn how to design this sort of database you need to learn some new vocabulary.

An entity is a person or thing about which data is held. In our example there are two entities, Property and Landlord.

An attribute is a piece of information about the entity. For example the attributes belonging to the entity Landlord are Title, Initials, Surname and ContactNo.

Question: What attributes belong to the entity Property shown in the table above?

Answer: PropertyRef, Style, Bedrooms, Rent, Rented and Lease Expiry. There is also one other attribute – Landlord. (We will need to know who the property belongs to.)

Relationships

There are three different types of relationship between entities:

One-to-one e.g. Husband and wife. A husband can have one wife and a wife can have one husband.

One-to-many e.g. Football team and player. A football team has many players, but a player belongs to only one team.

Many-to-many e.g. Student and subject. A student studies many subjects and a subject is studied by many students.

Question: Which of these relationships applies to Landlord and Property in the example above?

Answer: One-to-many: A property is owned by one landlord, but a landlord can own many properties.

Entity-relationship diagrams

Each of these relationships can be shown in an Entity-Relationship (E-R) diagram, as shown below:

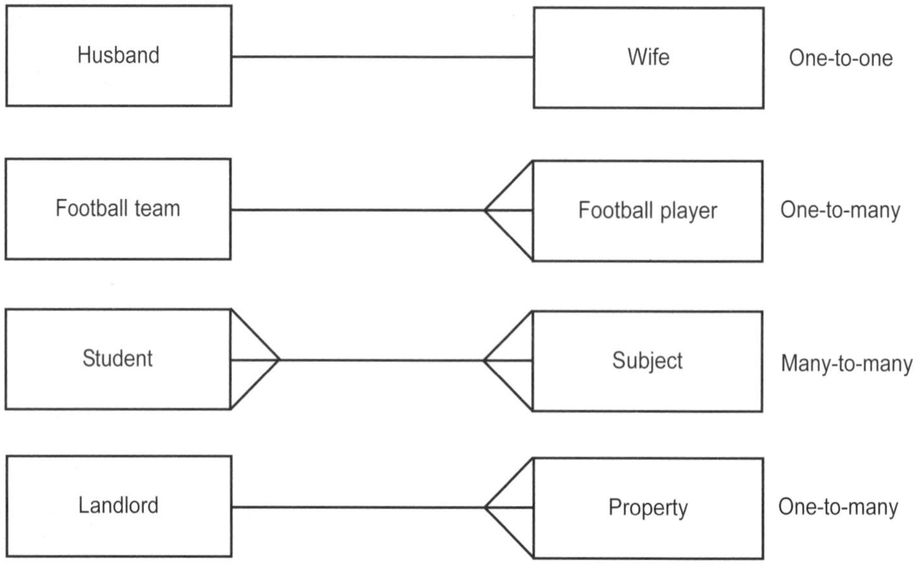

The primary key

Each entity needs its own table containing its own attributes. In addition each record in a table must have a field which uniquely identifies that record, the primary key.

We will use PropertyRef as the key field for the Property table. Each landlord will also be given a unique reference number, LandlordRef, which we can use as the key field for the Landlord table. We can't use Surname as the key field because there may be more than one landlord with the same surname.

Don't forget – although we will put the landlords' details in a separate table, we still need to know which landlord owns which property. For this, all we need to do is have an extra field in the Property table that contains the LandlordRef of the landlord who owns the property.

Now the two tables look like this:

Property table

PropertyRef	Style	Bedrooms	Rent	Rented	LeaseExpiry	LandlordRef
P1	Semi	3	800	Y	1/6/2003	L1
P2	Flat	2	650	Y	5/12/2003	L2
P3	Detached	4	1050	N		L2
P4	Terraced	2	700	Y	15/8/2003	L2
P5	Semi	3	850	N		L3
P6	Detached	5	1200	Y	25/7/2003	L4
P7	Flat	1	500	N		L5
P8	Flat	2	600	N		L5
P9	Terraced	3	750	Y	3/9/2003	L5
P10	Semi	3	900	N		L6

Landlord table

LandlordRef	Title	Initials	Surname	ContactNo
L1	Mrs	J	Welsh	01474 276499
L2	Mr	S	Hemmings	01474 572772
L3	Mr	M	Jenkins	01474 387465
L4	Mr	M	Stevenson	01474 783748
L5	Miss	L	Vacher	01474 583689
L6	Mrs	J	Hemmings	01474 856683

Question

From the two tables above, find the name of the landlord of property P7.

Answer

From the **Property** table you can see it's owned by the landlord with **LandlordRef L5**. The **Landlord** table shows that Landlord **L5** is **Miss L Vacher**.

Data types

Before you can enter these fields into your database, you need to think about what format the data will be in. Access has many different data types, which are explained in the table below:

Text	Letters, symbols and numbers, i.e. Alphanumeric data.
Number	Numbers only (no letters). Includes numbers with decimal points.
Date/Time	Dates and times.
Currency	For all monetary data. Access will insert a currency symbol before the amount (such as £ or $, etc.)
Yes/No	Used wherever the field can be one of only 2 values, Y/N, True/False, Male/Female etc.
AutoNumber	This is a unique value generated by Access for each record.

You will have to choose a data type for each field from the table given above. For example, should you hold a telephone number as a Text field or a Number field? At first you may think that a Number field would be best but in practice this is a bad idea for two reasons:

- Access will not record leading zeros in a number field. So if the telephone number is 01473874512 it will be recorded as 1473874512 which is incorrect.
- Access will not allow you to put a space, bracket or hyphen in a number field. Therefore, you should use a text field for a telephone number or you will not be able to record it as, for example, 01473 874512.

Field properties

When you enter the field names used in each table into Access, you can specify the field length for Text fields. This means that Access won't create excessively large fields when you create forms and other database objects. It can also act as a type of data validation, as Access won't let you enter anything in a field that has more characters than the specified field length.

For Date/Time fields you can specify the format of the date (e.g. dd/mm/yy or mm/dd/yy etc.).

For Currency fields you can specify the number of decimal places.

The database structure

The structure of the database can be thought of as what the table will look like without any information in (i.e. the design of the table). To describe the structure you need to know:

- How many fields the table will have (the columns in the table)
- What the field names will be (the column headings)
- What data type will be held in each field

The number of rows will change as the user enters more data, and is not part of the database structure.

It is important to know the difference between the database structure (think of the empty table) and the data held in the database (the information that you put into the table).

Questions:

For each of the following changes to the Painting database on Page 5-1, would you need to change the database structure or edit the data?

You decide to add a new field name, Price, to the database.

The painting Two Birches was actually purchased from Kilmorack Gallery.

Answers:

If you add a new field name, you are changing the database structure.

If you are changing the Two Birches record, you are only editing the data.

Naming conventions

We will use a common convention when naming tables and fields. This means putting tbl in front of the table names, and not using any spaces in any of the names. Use capital letters in the middle of a field name to make the words easier to read. Look at the table below to see examples:

tblProperty

Field Name	Data Type	Field Length/Type
PropertyRef	AutoNumber	
Style	Text	15
Bedrooms	Number	Long Integer
Rent	Currency	0 decimal places
Rented	Y/N	-
LeaseExpiry	Date/Time	-
LandlordRef	Text	4

Tip:
You can use letters, numbers, spaces and special characters like ?, &. Don't use an exclamation mark (!) or a full stop in a field name.

tblLandlord

Field Name	Data Type	Field Length/Type
LandlordRef	Text	4
Title	Text	4
Initials	Text	4
Surname	Text	20
ContactNo	Text	15

This will be the structure of the tblProperty and tblLandlord tables.

Notice that PropertyRef and LandlordRef have been underlined; this is because they are both primary keys.

In text fields, you should set the field length to be the length of the longest word you expect to be entered. We wouldn't expect a Surname to be longer than 20 letters.

Exercises

1. A library wants to keep a database to record the books borrowed by library users. Each library user has their own unique ID, and can take out up to 6 books at a time. Each book has its own unique book number. The database designer has decided that three tables will be needed, called BOOK, LIBRARY-USER and LOAN. The LOAN table will hold details of who has which books out on loan. Once a book is returned to the library, the loan record is deleted, so that there is never more than one loan record in the LOAN table for a given book.

   (a) What is the relationship between BOOK and LOAN?

   (b) What is the relationship between LIBRARY-USER and LOAN?
   Label the following entity-relationship diagram.

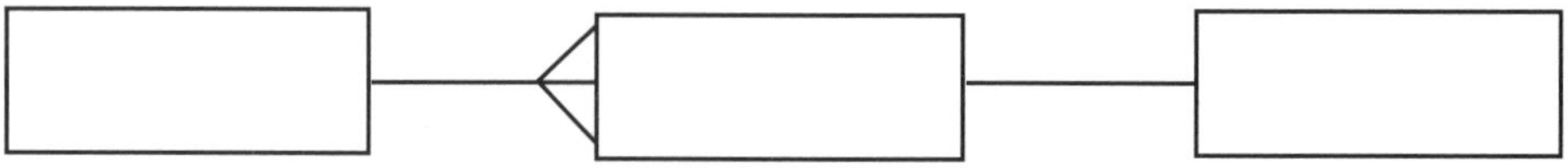

   (c) What is an attribute?

2. A school database is to be constructed to help the school keep track of who has been entered for each examination. Each student may be entered for several examinations.

   (a) Name two entities in the database. Suggest a primary key for each entity.

   (b) What is the relationship between the two entities?

3. A hospital database is to hold details of which patients and which nursing staff are assigned to each ward. Each nurse may be assigned to a single ward, but each ward may have several nurses. A patient is assigned to a single ward.

   (a) What is the relationship between WARD and PATIENT?

   (b) Name one other entity in this database.

   (c) Design the structure of each of the WARD and PATIENT tables. Show suitable field names. Show data types and field lengths for each field.

   (d) Make up three data records for each table.

4. A Sports Competition database is created showing all the competitors and events, and who entered which event. Some of the data is shown below:

COMPETITOR

CompetitorID	Surname	Firstname	Date of Birth	Sex
C1	Grand	Jane	01/04/84	F
C2	Keino	Michael	14/02/85	M
C3	Dowsett	Robert	12/04/84	M
C4	Perez	Juanita	31/07/85	F

EVENT

EventID	EventName	Men/Women
E1	Long Jump	M
E2	Long Jump	W
E3	100M	M
E4	100M	W
E5	100M Hurdles	M

Michael Keino entered Long Jump and 100M Hurdles (Men)

Robert Dowsett entered the 100M race (Men).

Jane Grand and Juanita Perez entered the 100M race (Women).

Fill in the data in table EVENT-ENTRY. (The column headings are given below):

EVENT-ENTRY

EventID	CompetitorID
...	...

CHAPTER 5.2 Creating a New Database

Over the next several chapters you will be creating and developing the Hemlets database.

Opening Access

You can open Access in one of two ways:

- *Either* double-click the Access icon on the main screen in Windows
- *Or* click the Start button at the bottom left of the screen, then click Programs, then click

Your screen will look like the one below:

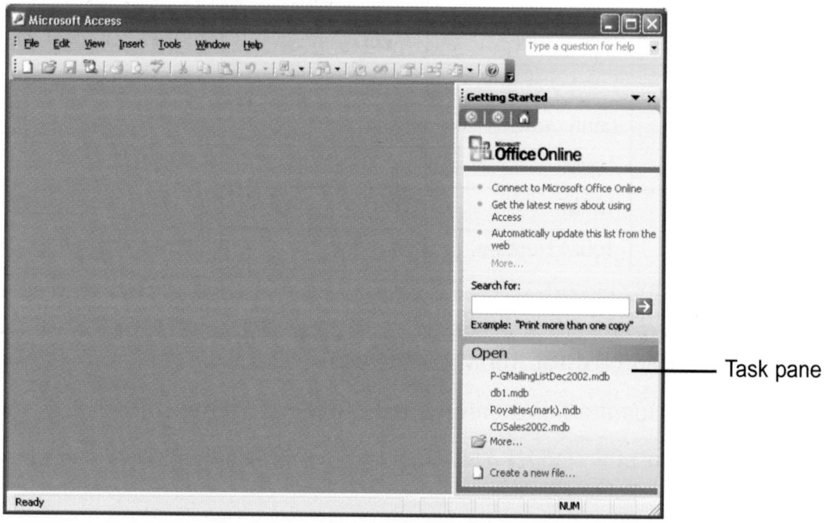

Tip:
Your screen may look different if you have a different version of Access. If so, check the Blank Access Database button and click OK.

You now have the option of either opening an existing database or creating a new one. We will create a new database from scratch.

- Click Blank Database in the Task pane.

A window opens similar to the one shown below, asking you to select a folder and a name for your new database.

- Click the Create New Folder button and create a new folder named HemletsLtd.
- In the File Name box, type the name Hemlets (no spaces).

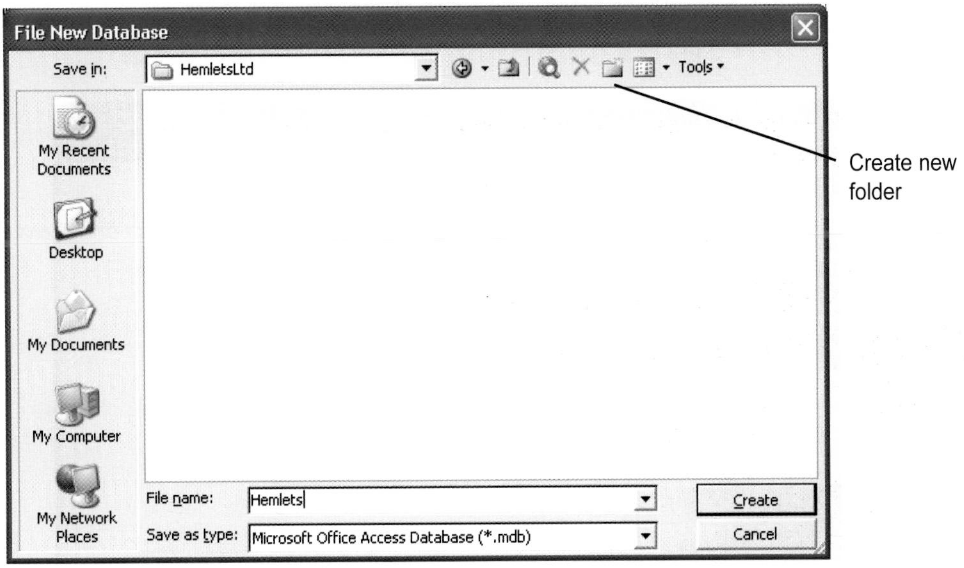

- Click the Create button. Access will automatically add the file extension .mdb.

Tip:
It is a good idea to keep each Access database in its own folder.

The database structure

The first thing you have to do is set up the database structure. As you learned in the last chapter, all data in an Access database is stored in tables. Each table has a row for each record and a column for each field. The first thing you have to do is tell Access exactly what fields you want in each record, and what data type each field is. After this has been done and the structure is saved, you can start adding data to the database.

The Database window

Access databases are made up of objects. A table is an object, and is the only object we have talked about so far. Other objects, which you will come across in this book, include Queries, Forms and Reports.

Every Access Database has a Database window. This is a sort of central menu for your database, from which you can open the objects in your database. The window has buttons (or tabs in Access 7 & 97) for each type of database object (Tables, Queries, Forms, Reports, etc.).

Tables is currently selected, and since at the moment there are no existing tables to Open or Design, only the Create options are active.

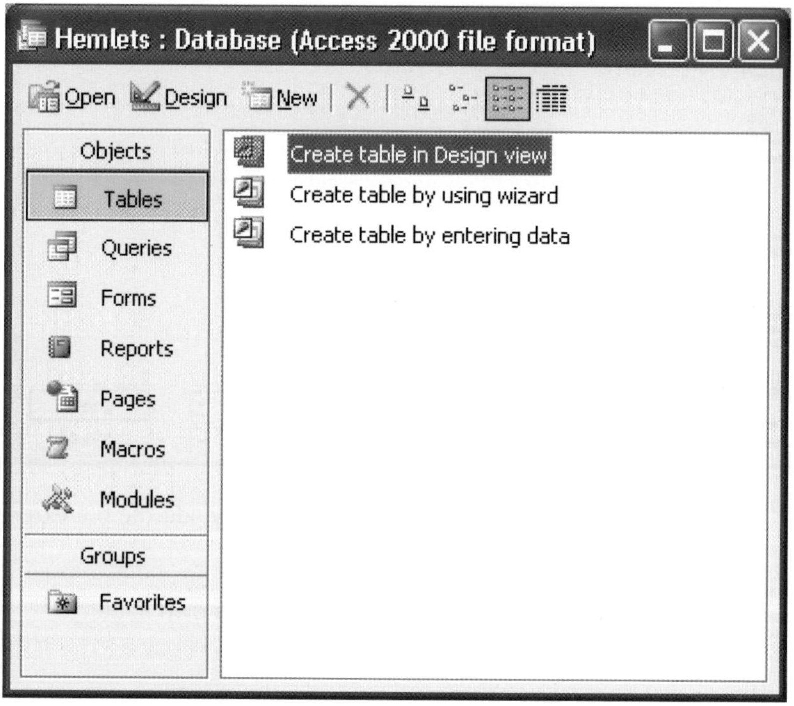

Hiding and displaying toolbars

You will learn about what individual toolbars and buttons do as they become relevant whilst you are creating your database. Here are a few tips that apply to all toolbars, which will be useful if you cannot find a particular toolbar or think that you are missing a button or two! You may find that you already know most of this – it will be pretty much the same as you have experienced in other Microsoft applications such as Word or Excel.

- You can select which toolbars are displayed on your screen. If you can't find a particular button it might be worth checking that you have the right toolbar displayed.

- Select View, Toolbars and select the toolbar you want from the list that appears.

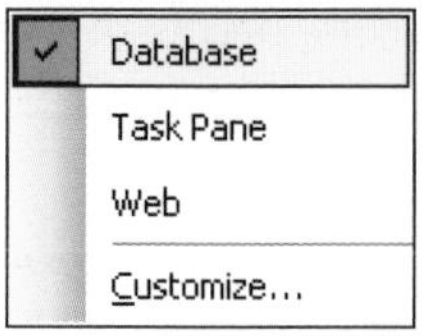

- This list will change according to what you are doing, as only a selection of toolbars will be relevant to what you are doing at any one time.
- You can hide a toolbar by selecting View, Toolbars and deselecting the toolbar.

Using the Help functions

If at any time you aren't sure how to do something in Access, you can search the Help files for instructions on your chosen subject. For example, let's search for help on creating a table.

- Select Help, Microsoft Office Access Help from the menu.

You will see the Office Assistant appear.

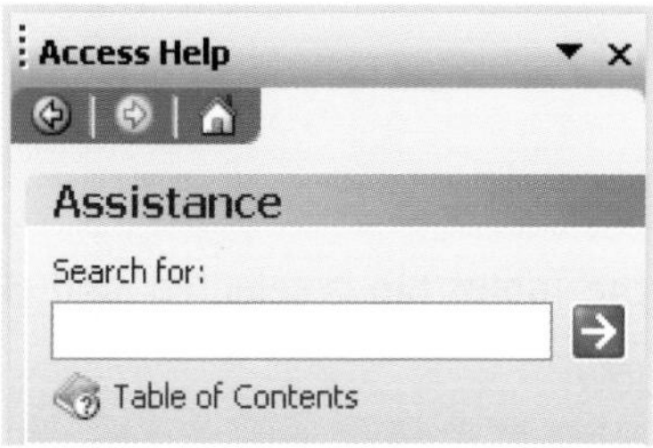

- Type create table into the Search for: box, then click the Start searching button.
- Select About creating a table (MDB) from the next pop-up box.

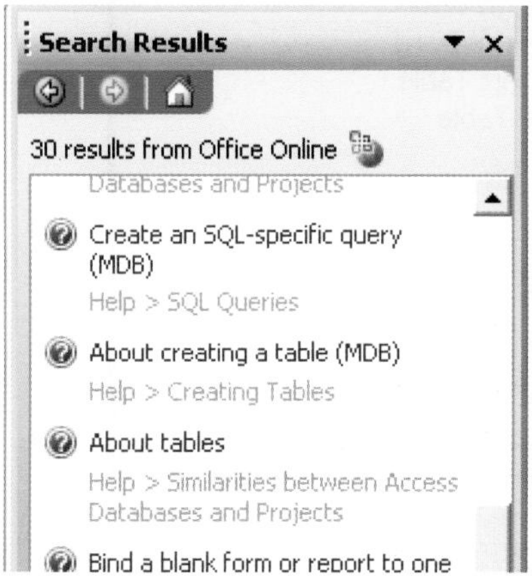

A Help window appears giving information on this topic. There's a lot of information here!

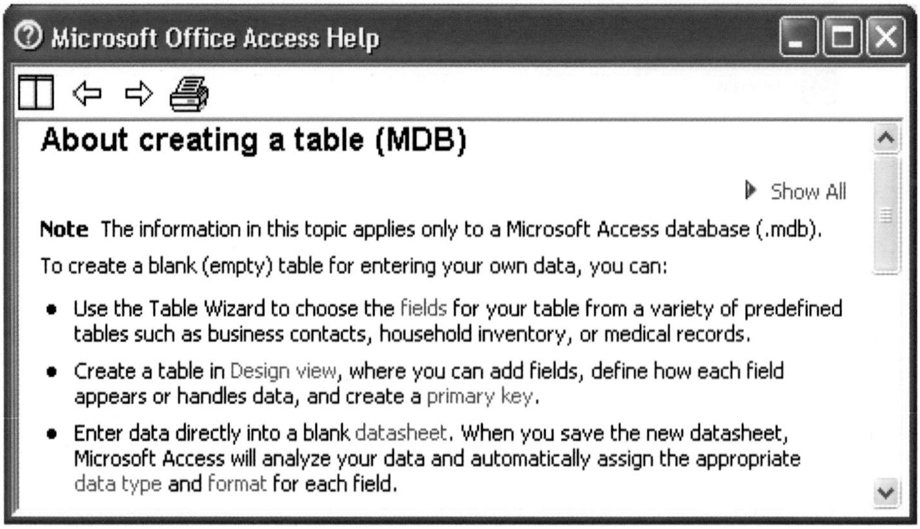

- Click the red Close button when you have finished using Help.

Tip:
Next we'll create a table using the second method mentioned - Create a table in Design view.

Creating a new table

- In the Database window make sure the Tables tab is selected, and click New.

A New Table window appears as shown below:

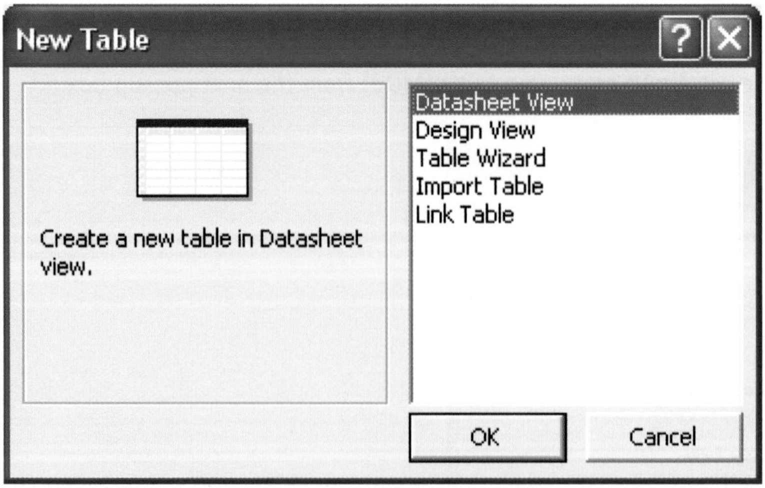

- Select Design View and click OK.

The Table Design window appears.

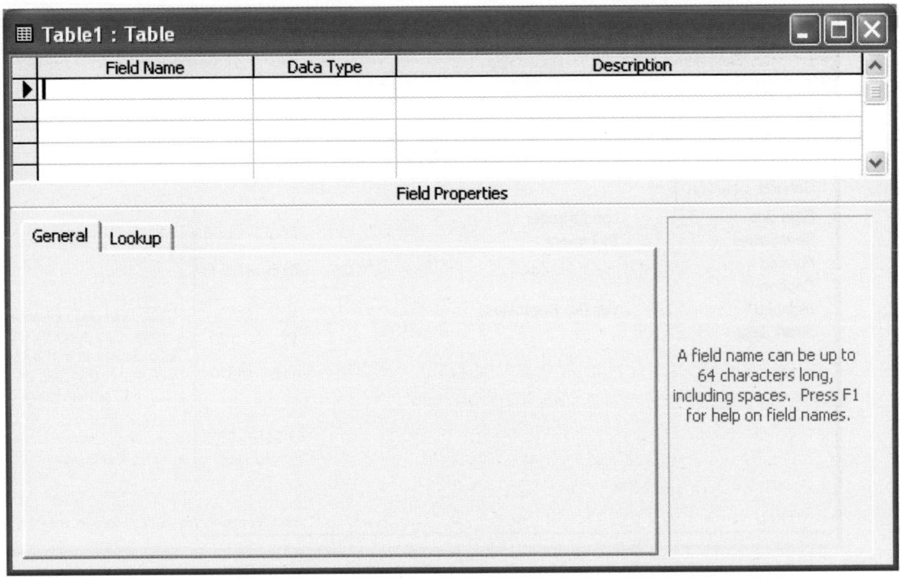

Look back at the structure of the tblProperty table on Page 5-11. All these fields need to be entered in the new table.

- Enter the first field name, PropertyRef, and tab to the Data Type column. This will automatically enter Text as the data type, but we want AutoNumber, so click the small down-arrow to the right of the field and select AutoNumber from the list.

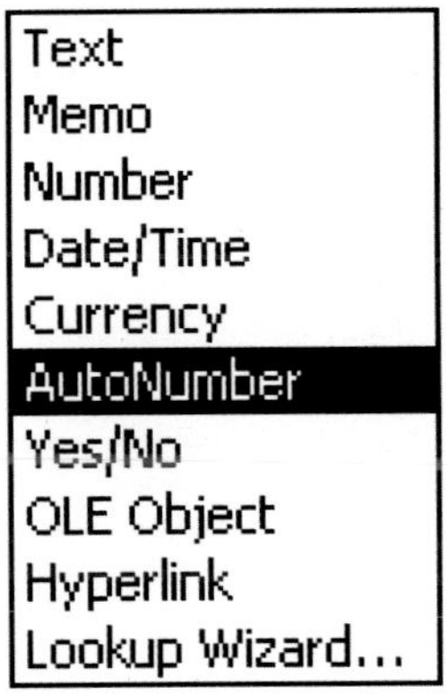

- Tab to the Description column and type This is the Key field.
- We'll leave the Field Size as Long Integer.

Defining the primary key

Every table in an Access database must have a primary key (also known as the key field). The field which you specify for the primary key must have a different value for each record. For the Property table we will set PropertyRef to be the primary key.

- With the cursor in the row for the PropertyRef, click the Primary Key icon on the toolbar. The key symbol appears in the left-hand margin next to PropertyRef.

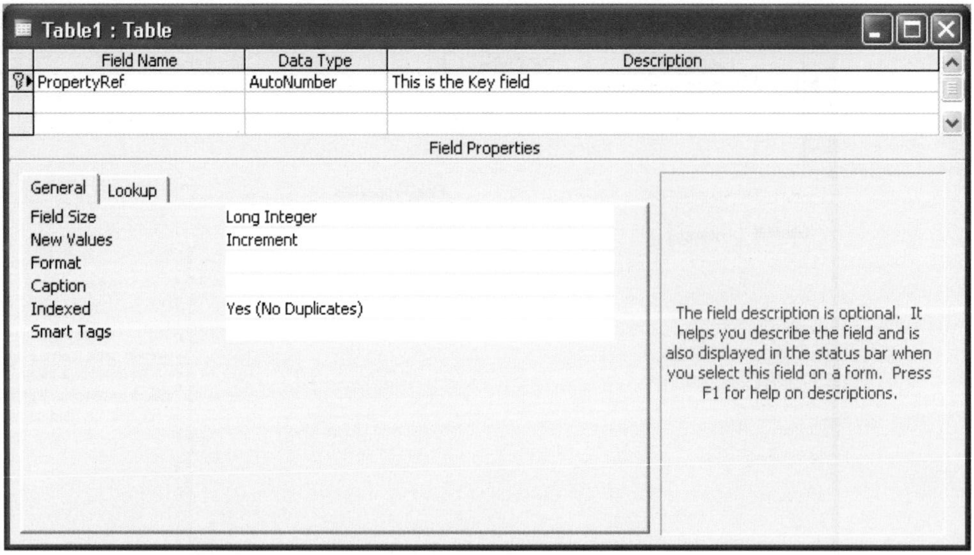

Entering other fields

Now we can enter all the other fields.

- In the next row enter the field name as **Style** and leave the data type as **Text**. Enter the **Field Size** as **15**.
- In the third row enter **Bedrooms** as the field name. Tab to the **Data Type** column and click the small down-arrow that appears. Select **Number** from the list of data types. Notice that in **Field Properties** the **Field Size** is automatically set to **Long Integer**.

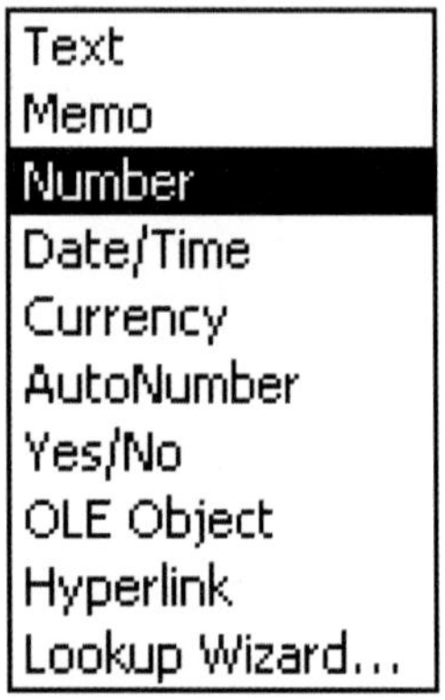

Tip:
Note that **Field Properties** always appear at the bottom of the screen.

- Enter the field name **Rent** and give it a data type **Currency**. Click below in the **Field Properties**. Notice that in **Field Properties** the **Decimal Places** is set to **Auto**. We don't want any decimal places, as the rent will always be in whole pounds. Click where it says **Auto** then click the small down-arrow on the right; click **0**.

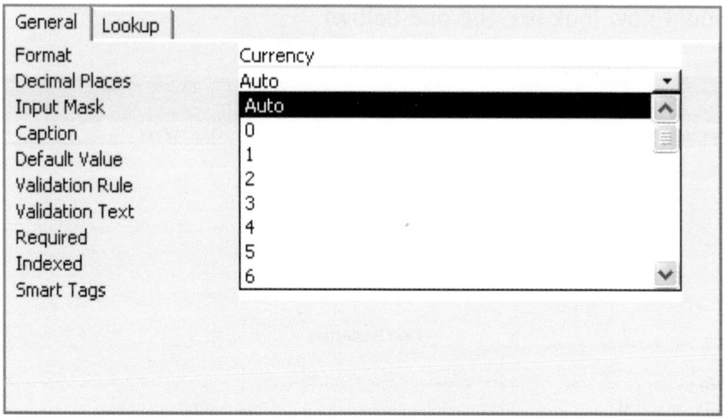

- On the next row enter the field name **Rented** and give it a data type **Yes/No**. Click below in **Field Properties** – notice that there are different types of **Yes/No** fields available – you can also choose **True/False** or **On/Off**. We will leave it as **Yes/No**.

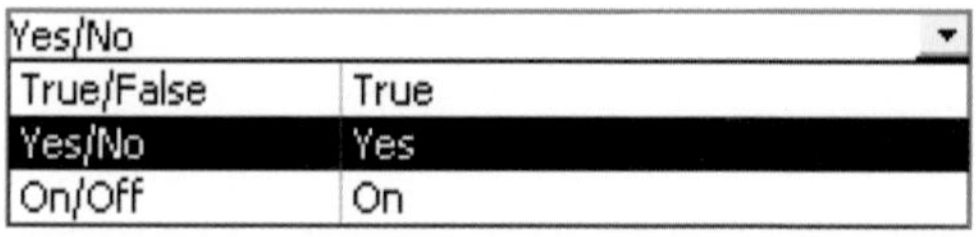

- Next, enter the field name **LeaseExpiry** (one word) and give it a data type **Date/Time**. Again, there are several formats available to choose from in **Field Properties**. Click on the down-arrow next to the **Format** row and choose **Short Date** from the list.

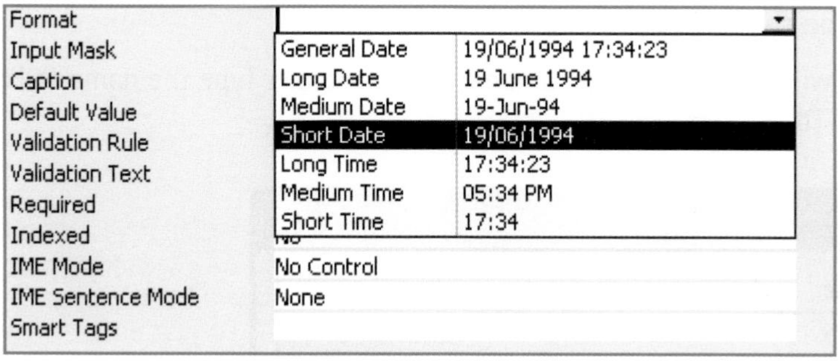

- Finally enter the field name **LandlordRef** with a data type **Text**. In **Field Properties**, set the **Field size** to **4**.

Tip:

Don't worry if you make a few mistakes - after all the fields are entered, you will learn how to move fields around, delete them or insert new fields. You can correct any mistakes at that point and it will be good practice.

Your table should now look like the one below:

Row selectors

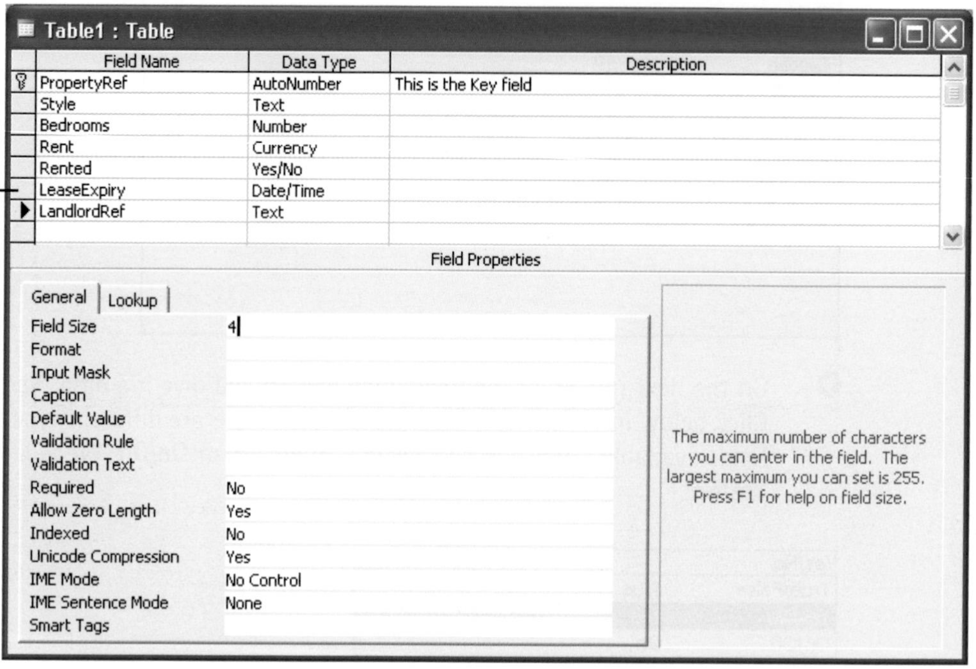

Saving the table structure

Save the table structure by clicking the Save icon or selecting File, Save from the menu bar. Don't worry if you've made some mistakes in the table structure – they can be corrected in a minute.

You will be asked to type a name for your table. Type the name tblProperty and click OK.

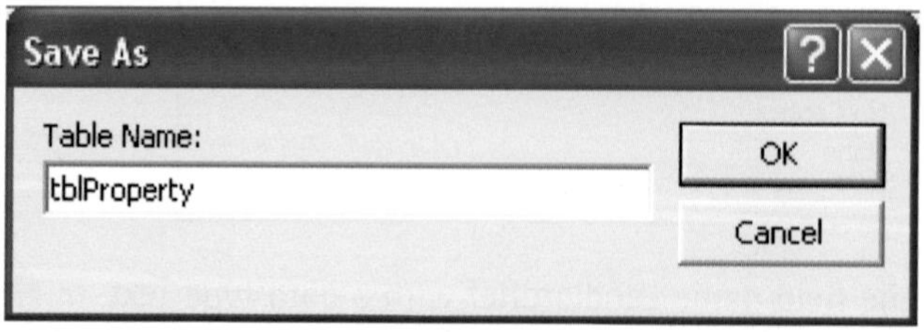

Click the Close icon in the top right-hand corner of the table to close the window. You will be returned to the Database window.

In the Database window you will see that your new table is now listed.

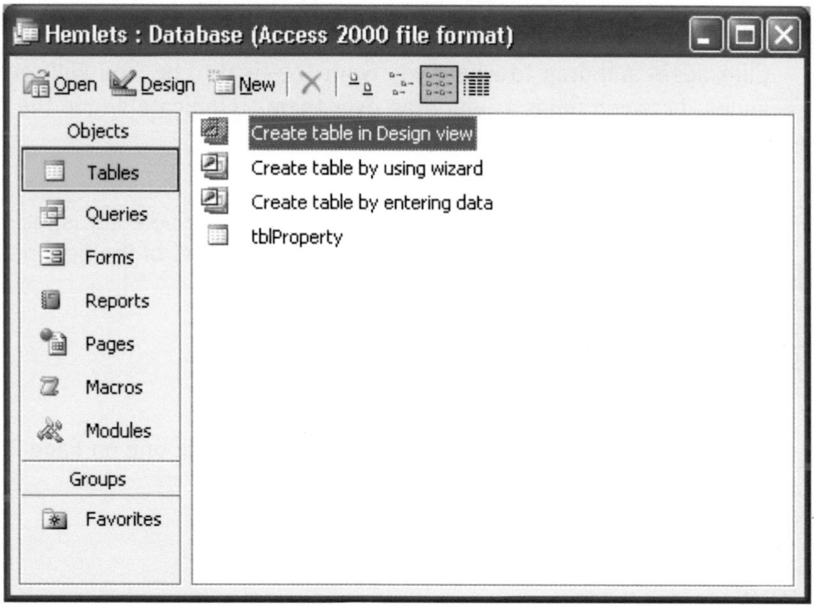

Tip:
If you have named the table wrongly, or made a spelling mistake, right-click the name in the main Database window and select Rename. Then type in the correct name. To delete a table, select it and press the Delete key on the keyboard.

Editing a table structure

- Select the table name tblProperty, click the Design View icon and you are returned to Design View.

Inserting a field

To insert a new row for a TotalRooms column just above Rent:

- Click the row selector (see the figure on Page 5-22) for Rent.

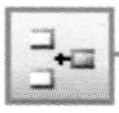

- Press the Insert key on the keyboard or click the Insert Rows icon on the toolbar.
- Enter the new field name TotalRooms, data type Number.

Deleting a field

Now, to delete the field you have just inserted:

- Select the field by clicking in its row selector.

- Press the Delete key on the keyboard or click the Delete Rows icon on the toolbar.

If you make a mistake, you can use Edit, Undo Delete from the top menu bar to restore the field.

Moving a field

- Click the row selector to the left of the field name to select the field.
- Click again and drag to where you want the field to be. You will see a line appear between fields as you drag over them to indicate where the field will be placed.

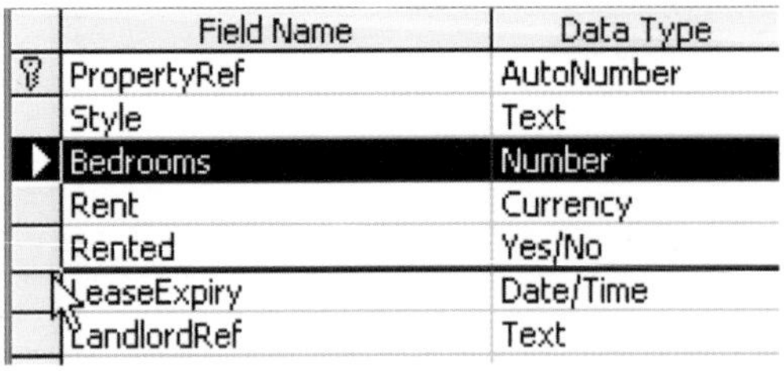

Field Name
Data Type
PropertyRef
AutoNumber
Style
Text
Bedrooms
Number
Rent
Currency
Rented
Yes/No
LeaseExpiry
Date/Time
LandlordRef
Text

Tip:
The row selector is the square to the left of the field name

- Move the fields back so that your table looks like the one on Page 5-22 when you have finished experimenting.
- Close the **tblProperty** table.

Creating the tblLandlord table

We'll do this in just the same way as the **tblProperty** table.

- From the Database window, make sure **Tables** is selected and click **New**.

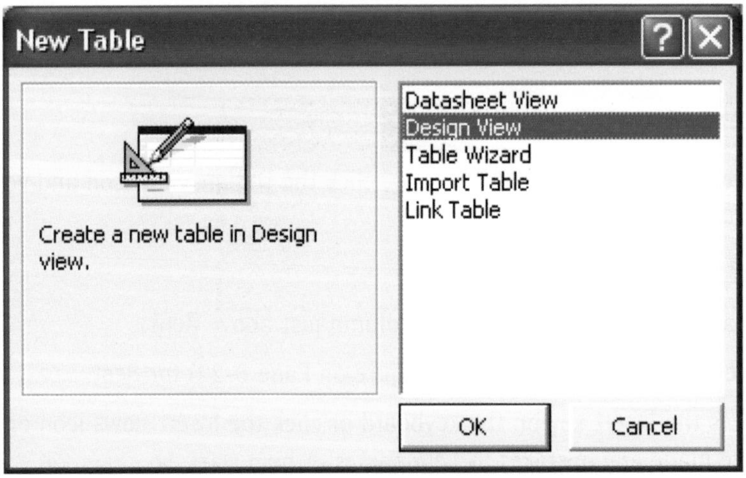

- Select **Design View** and click **OK**.
- Enter the first field name, **LandlordRef** and give it a data type **Text**. Later we will be linking the two tables using this field, and the **LandlordRef** field in the **tblProperty** table. It is very important that the two fields have the same data type and field properties or you won't be able to link the tables.
- Give **LandlordRef** a field length of **4** just as you did in the **tblProperty** table.

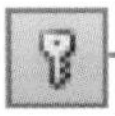

- Make **LandlordRef** the key field by making sure the cursor is in the right row and clicking the **Primary Key** icon.

- Enter the other field names, data types and field properties just as they were defined in the last chapter. Don't forget to enter the correct field lengths!

Your table should now look like the one below:

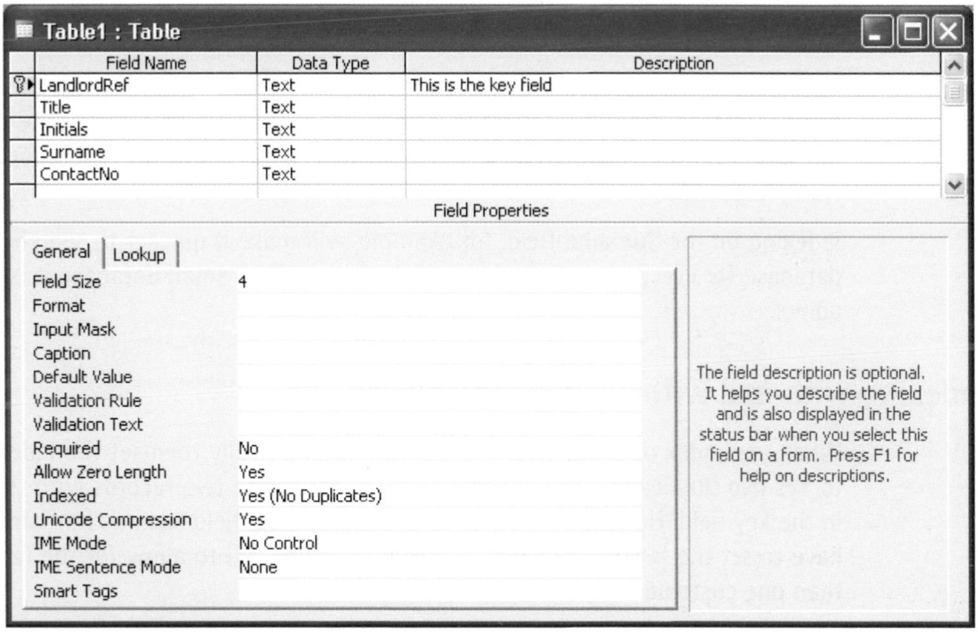

- Save the table as tblLandlord by clicking the Save icon.

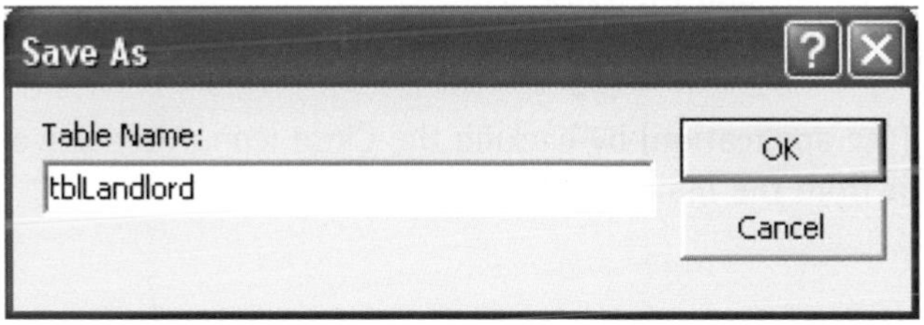

Editing field size attributes

If you have made any mistakes in field names or field sizes, you can edit them now. Remember, it is easy to make changes to the table structure BEFORE you enter any data. If you change field size attributes AFTER data has been entered, this may cause problems. For example:

- if you change the field size of the LandlordRef field in this table, it may no longer link correctly to another table.
- if you change the field size of Surname from 20 to 15, some surnames already in the database may be truncated if they are longer than 15 characters.

Indexing

When a field is defined as a primary key, it is automatically indexed by Access. For example in tblLandlord, if you click in the LandlordRef row, you will see that the Indexed property in the list of Field Properties is set to Yes (No Duplicates).

Any other field can also be indexed simply by changing its Indexed property to Yes.

Access keeps a separate Index table for each field that you index, with the record number, rather like index entries in a book. When data is entered into the table, all the indexes have to be updated as well. (This happens automatically – you don't have to worry about it!)

Indexing on the Surname field, for example, will make it quicker to search a very large database for everyone with a particular surname. On a small database it is not worth doing.

Indexing with and without duplicates allowed

When you index on a key field, Access will automatically then set the Indexed property to Yes (No Duplicates). This is because there cannot be two records with the same value in the key field. However, if you choose to index on a field such as Surname, you would have to set the Indexed property to Yes (Duplicates OK) to allow for the fact that more than one customer may have the same surname.

Closing the database application

- Close the table by clicking the Close icon.
- Close the database by clicking the Close icon in the Database window.
- Close Access (the application) by clicking the Close icon. Alternatively, you can select File, Exit from the main menu.

Exercise

This exercise is based on creating a new database table/file for an examining board. Part of the file creation is the appropriate design of the fields, including the type and size of fields.

1. Open your database application. Open a new blank database and save as ExamBoard.mdb.
2. Design a table with 3 fields using the appropriate data types and field sizes. The following fields must be created for the table: CandidateID, Surname, Initials.
3. Save the table as Candidate.
4. Save and close the database.
5. Close the database application.

Setting up Relationships

CHAPTER 5.3

In the first chapter we looked at the relationships between the tables, and drew entity-relationship diagrams to represent the relationships. Now that the tables have been created we must link them in Access.

Relationships window

- On the main toolbar, click Tools, Relationships.

The Show Table window will appear:

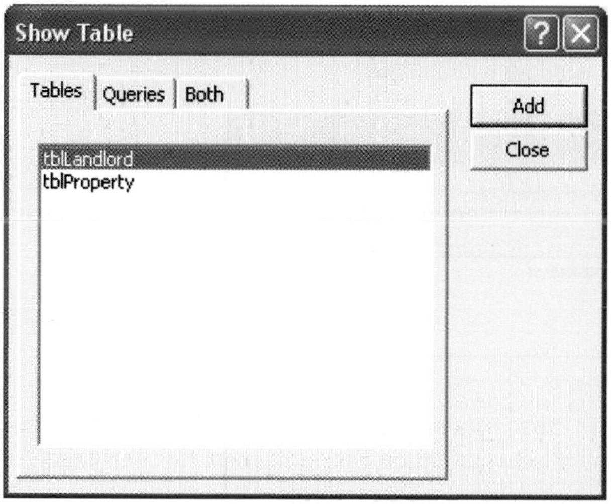

Tip:
If the Show Table window doesn't appear, just click the Show Table icon in the menu bar.

We want to form relationships between the two tables, so we want both tables to appear in the relationships window.

- Highlight each one in turn and click Add.
- Click Close.

The two tables will now appear in the relationships window as shown below.

- Click and drag the blue border at the bottom of the tblProperty table so that you can see all the field names.

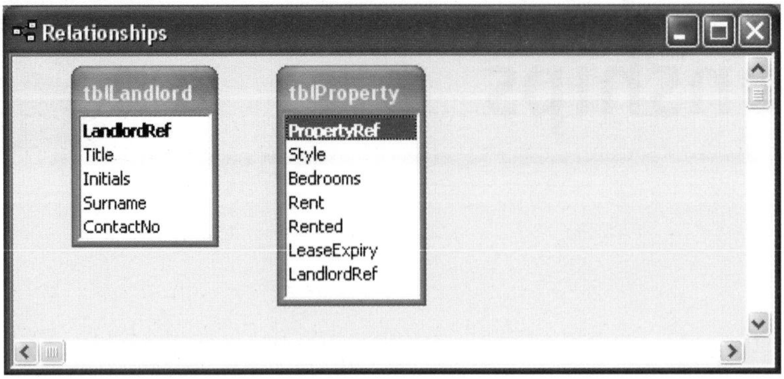

Creating a relationship

You will recall from the first chapter that we want a one-to-many relationship between tblLandlord and tblProperty.

- Click and drag the field LandlordRef from tblLandlord and drop it onto the field LandlordRef at the bottom of tblProperty. Always drag from the one side to the many side of the relationship.

The Edit Relationships window will appear:

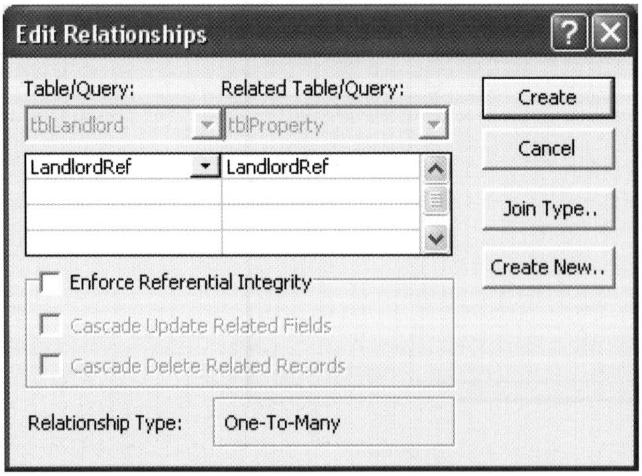

Notice that there are several options here. We'll go through what each of them means now. First here's a quick run through of which table is from which side of the relationship:

- tblLandlord is the table on the one side of the relationship.
- tblProperty is the table on the many side of the relationship.
- LandlordRef is the field which links the two tables.

Enforce Referential Integrity

You can enforce referential integrity if:

- the table on the one side of the relationship has a Primary key. In this example the table on the one side is the tblLandlord table, which does have a Primary key, LandlordRef.
- The link fields have the same data type and length. In this example the link field is LandlordRef; we have given this field the same data type Text, length 4, in both tables.

If you enforce referential integrity, the following rules apply:

- You can't enter a value into the many side of the relationship that doesn't exist in the one side. In this example, you must enter the landlord's details into tblLandlord before you can enter the properties that the landlord owns into tblProperty.
- You can't delete a record from a table in the one side of a relationship if related records exist in the many table. This means that you can't delete a landlord's details in tblLandlord if there are properties in tblProperty that the landlord owns. If you want to be able to delete a landlord and automatically delete the properties that the landlord owns at the same time you would use Cascade Delete, which is explained below.

If you choose Enforce Referential Integrity, you are given the option of Cascade Update Related Fields and Cascade Delete Related Fields.

Cascade Update Related Fields

Cascade Update means that if you change the related field (in our case the related field is LandlordRef) in the one side of the relationship, Access will automatically update related fields in the many side. This means that if you change a Landlord's LandlordRef in tblLandlord, the LandlordRef will automatically be changed in all related records in tblProperty.

Cascade Delete Related Fields

Choosing Cascade Delete means that if you delete a record from a table on the one side of a relationship, all related records on the many side will automatically be deleted. For example, if you delete a landlord in tblLandlord, all properties that the landlord owns will automatically be deleted from tblProperty.

That's a lot of information! Don't worry too much if you can't take it all in at once. If you ever need a recap you can always just type referential integrity into the Help Answer Wizard.

Creating the relationship

- First we'll try creating the relationship without enforcing referential integrity, so just click Create without checking any of the boxes.

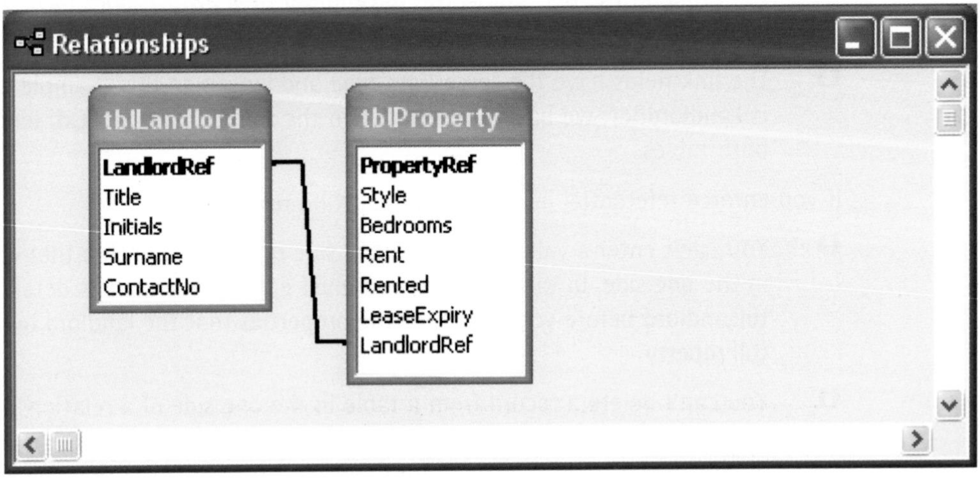

Notice that there is now a black line between the tables to represent the relationship. Because we didn't enforce referential integrity, Access has created a one-to-one relationship.

Deleting relationships

We want a one-to-many relationship with enforced referential integrity, so we will delete the relationship we just created then create a new one.

- Right-click the black line between the tables and select Delete from the shortcut menu.

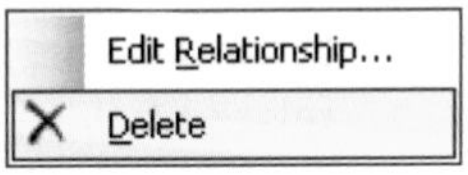

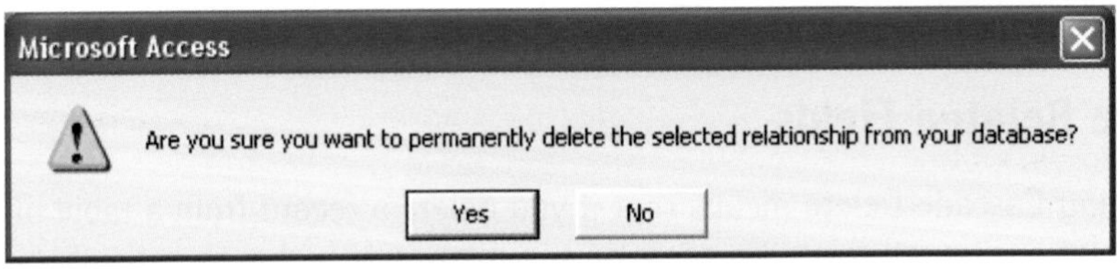

- Click Yes when asked to confirm the delete.

Now we'll create the new relationship.

- Click and drag the field LandlordRef from tblLandlord onto LandlordRef in tblProperty.

- This time, click in the box to Enforce Referential Integrity.

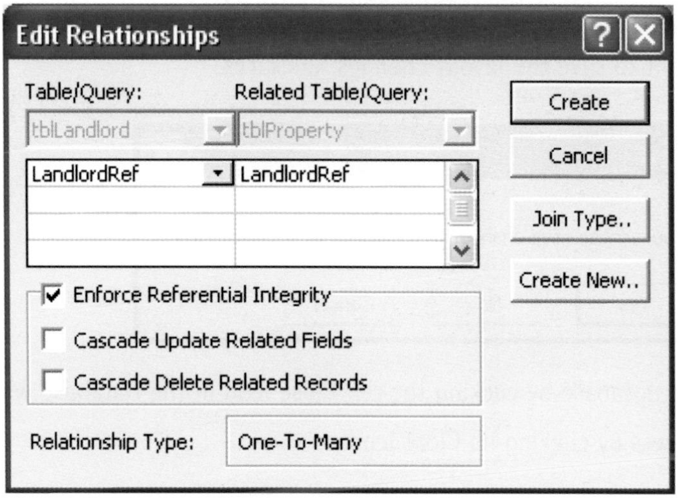

- Click Create.

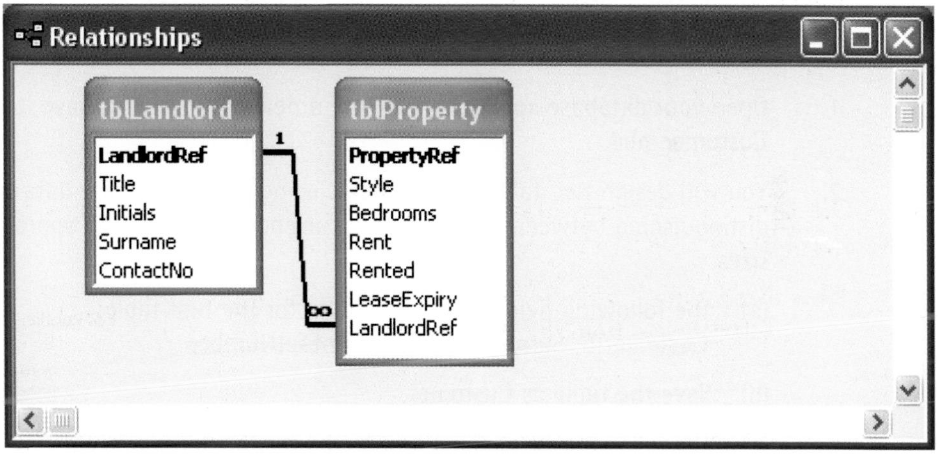

Notice that there is now a black line representing a one-to-many relationship between the two tables.

Word of warning!

When there is no data in the database it is very easy to edit the relationships. Once you have entered data, it will still be possible to edit the relationships but this is not advisable. If you change a relationship after data has been entered, Access may get confused, and you could find error messages appearing at inconvenient moments.

Saving the relationships

When you are satisfied that the relationships are correct, click the Close icon to return to the Database window. The relationships will automatically be saved, but you will be asked if you want to save the layout changes. Click Yes.

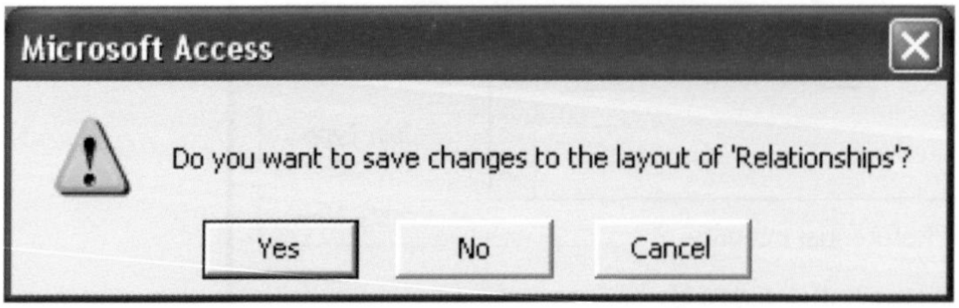

- Close the database by clicking the red Close icon in the Database window.
- Close Access by clicking its Close icon.

Exercise

In this exercise you will create a database and enter some data for a book shop. Part of the file creation is the appropriate design of the fields, including the type and size of fields.

1. Open your database application. Create a new database and save it as Customer.mbd.
2. You will design two tables with 4 fields using the appropriate data types, distinguishing between text, numeric, currency etc., and with appropriate field sizes.
   (a). The following fields must be created for the first table: CustomerID, Surname, Initials, ContactNumber.
   (b). Save the table as Customer.
   (c). The following fields must be created for the second table: OrderNumber, Date, Price, Description, CustomerID.
   (d). Save the table as Orders.
3. Relate the tables using a one-to-many relationship. The Customer table should be on the one side and the Orders table on the many.

Datasheet View

CHAPTER 5.4

Opening an existing database

- Load Access. The following window will appear.

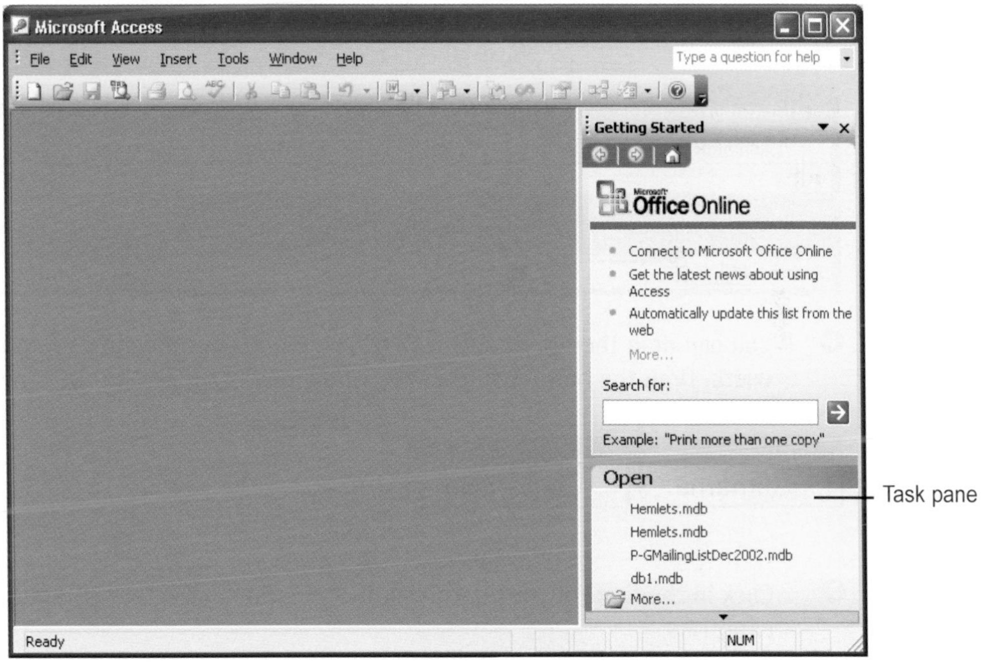

- Select Hemlets.mdb from the Task pane.

Tip:
If the right-hand pane does not appear, click File, Open from the menu bar and find the database. It should be in a folder named HemletsLtd.

The Database window will appear.

Table views

There are two view modes to choose from when making changes to your database:

- Design View is used for making changes to the database structure, for example adding a field or changing a field name. This is the view that you used in the last chapter to set up the database structure of the Hemlets database.
- Datasheet View is used for entering and editing the data held in the database. In this chapter we will be using Datasheet View to enter information about the properties and landlords into the tblProperty and tblLandlord tables.

Entering data

Because of the referential integrity rules, we will enter the data into the one side of the relationship first – i.e. the tblLandlord table.

- With tblLandlord selected, click the Open button in the Database window.

The table now appears in Datasheet view as shown below:

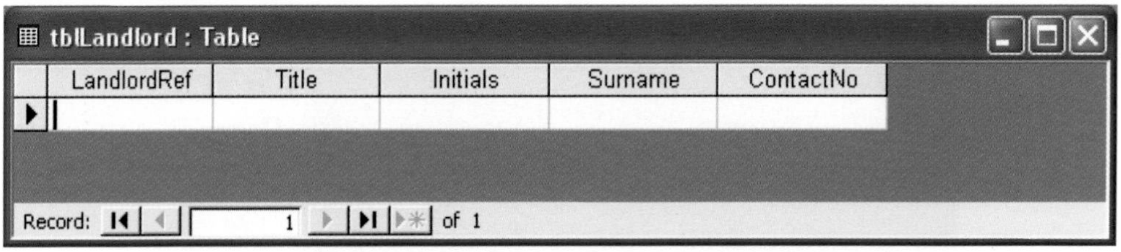

- You can drag the right border of any column header (field name) to alter its width. Drag the borders so that the whole row easily fits on the screen.

- Click in the first row of the LandlordRef column and enter L1. Tab to Title and enter Mrs.
- Tab across and enter the initial as J. Go to the Surname field and enter Welsh. Enter 01474 276499 as the ContactNo.

Your table should now look like the one below:

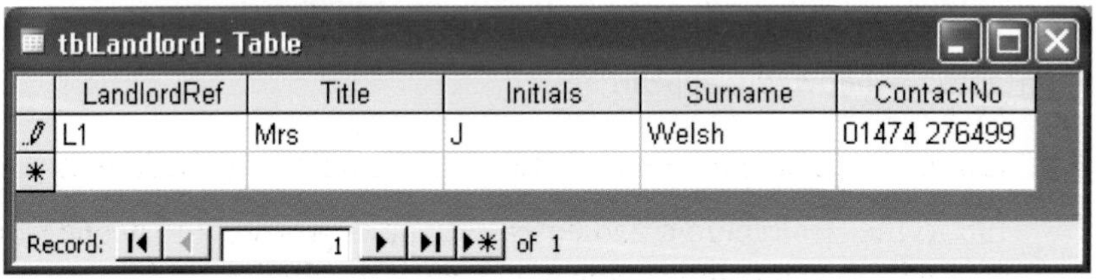

- Now enter the rest of the data as shown in the following table.

LandlordRef	Title	Initials	Surname	ContactNo
L1	Mrs	J	Welsh	01474 276499
L2	Mr	S	Hemmings	01474 572772
L3	Mr	M	Jenkins	01474 387465
L4	Mr	M	Stevenson	01474 783748
L5	Miss	L	Vacher	01474 583689
L6	Mrs	J	Hemmings	01474 856683

- When you have entered all the data, click the Close icon in the top right-hand corner of the current window. (Be careful to close just the table window, not Access.)
- If you have changed the column widths, you will be asked if you want to save the changes you made to the layout.

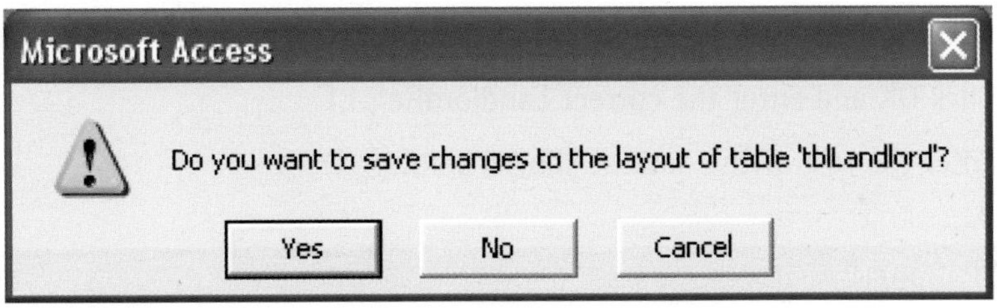

- Click Yes. You will be returned to the Database window.

Entering data for tblProperty

- From the Database window, make sure tblProperty is selected and click Open.

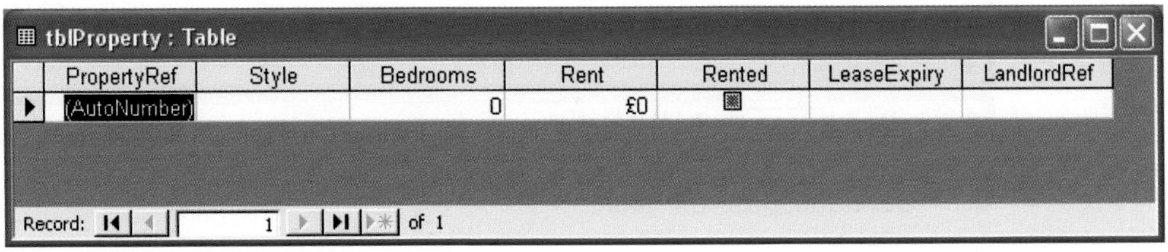

- Click in the first row of the PropertyRef column, where it says (AutoNumber). Access will automatically put a value in here, so you don't have to enter anything.
- Tab to Style and enter Semi. Enter 3 as the number of bedrooms.
- Tab to the Rent column and enter 800; don't worry if the pound sign has been deleted – it will reappear when you leave the field.

- Click in the checkbox in the Rented column to indicate a Yes.

Tip:
Pressing the Space bar in the Rented field will have the same effect as ticking the checkbox.

- In the Lease Expiry column, enter 1/6/03. Notice that when you tab out of the field Access changes it to 01/06/2003.
- Try entering L9 as the LandlordRef, and pressing the Enter key. You should get the following error message:

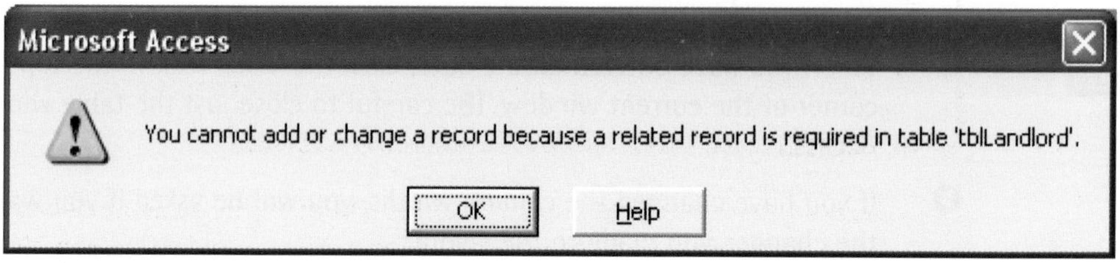

This is because there is no landlord with LandlordRef L9 entered in tblLandlord.

- Click OK and enter the correct LandlordRef, L1.
- Enter the rest of the data as shown below:

tblProperty : Table

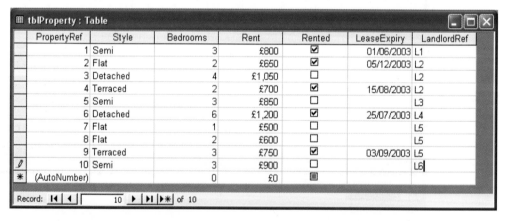

PropertyRef	Style	Bedrooms	Rent	Rented	LeaseExpiry	LandlordRef
1	Semi	3	£800	☑	01/06/2003	L1
2	Flat	2	£650	☑	05/12/2003	L2
3	Detached	4	£1,050	☐		L2
4	Terraced	2	£700	☑	15/08/2003	L2
5	Semi	3	£850	☐		L3
6	Detached	6	£1,200	☑	25/07/2003	L4
7	Flat	1	£500	☐		L5
8	Flat	2	£600	☐		L5
9	Terraced	3	£750	☑	03/09/2003	L5
10	Semi	3	£900	☐		L6
(AutoNumber)		0	£0	■		

Record: 10 of 10

- Save and close the table.

Viewing data in a table

- In the Database window, make sure that **Tables** is selected in the list of objects on the left of the window.

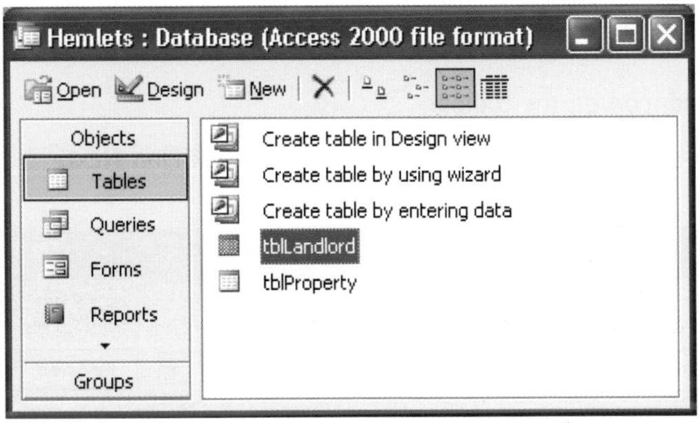

- Select **tblLandlord** and click **Open**. This will open the table in **Datasheet View**. (If you wanted to change the actual structure of the table, for example to add a new field, you would select **Design**.)

The table appears as shown below:

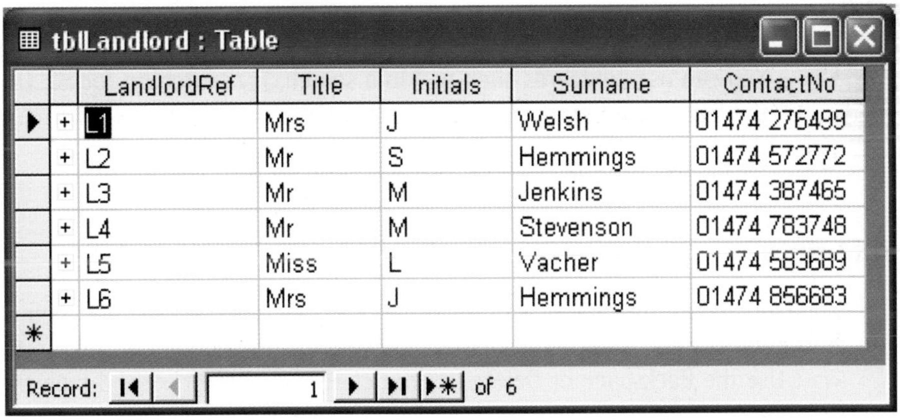
tblLandlord : Table

LandlordRef	Title	Initials	Surname	ContactNo
L1	Mrs	J	Welsh	01474 276499
L2	Mr	S	Hemmings	01474 572772
L3	Mr	M	Jenkins	01474 387465
L4	Mr	M	Stevenson	01474 783748
L5	Miss	L	Vacher	01474 583689
L6	Mrs	J	Hemmings	01474 856683

Record: 1 of 6

Using the record selectors

You can navigate to the next or previous record using the record selectors in **Datasheet View**. You can also move to the first or last record, or to a new record at the end of the database.

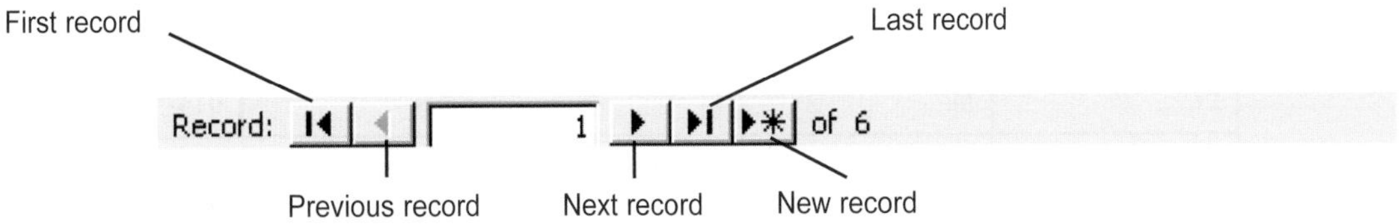

Finding a record

Sometimes you may want to search for the record for a particular landlord. Again, this is most useful on a much larger database.

- Click the mouse anywhere in the Surname column, except in Mr. Jenkins' record.

Suppose you want to find the record for Mr Jenkins.

- Click the Find icon on the toolbar.
- Type the name Jenkins in the dialogue box then click Find Next.

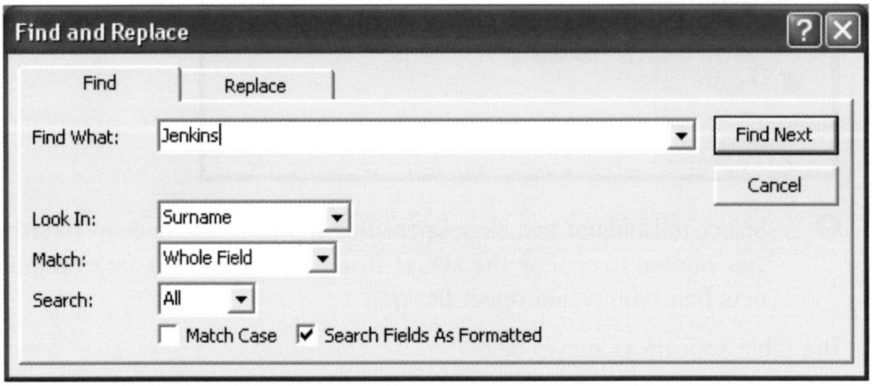

Mr Jenkins' record should now be highlighted.

- You can use wildcards such as * in a search. Try searching for H*. This will find the next record starting with H each time you click Find Next.
- Close the Find and Replace window by clicking its Close icon.

Modifying data

You can change the contents of any field (except PropertyRef which, being an Autonumber field, is set by Access) by clicking in the field and editing in the normal way. Use the Backspace or Delete key to delete unwanted text and type the corrections.

Remember you can undo changes using the Undo icon.

Adding a new record

Suppose two new landlords have registered with Hemlets, and their details have to be added to the Hemlets database. Their details are shown below:

LandlordRef	Title	Initials	Surname	ContactNo
L7	Mr	I	Iqbal	01474 733543
L8	Miss	E	Harrison	01474 898398

There are two ways to add a new record:

- *Either* click in the next blank line,
- *or* click the New Record icon on either the record selector (see the figure on the previous page) or the Table Datasheet toolbar.
- Enter Mr Iqbal's and Miss Harrison's details from the table above.

The first method is easy for such a small database, but if there were hundreds of landlords in the database you wouldn't want to scroll down to an empty row. For larger databases you would use the New Record icon.

Deleting a record

To delete Mr Iqbal's record:

- Click anywhere in Mr Iqbal's record.
- Click the Delete icon on the toolbar. You will see a message:

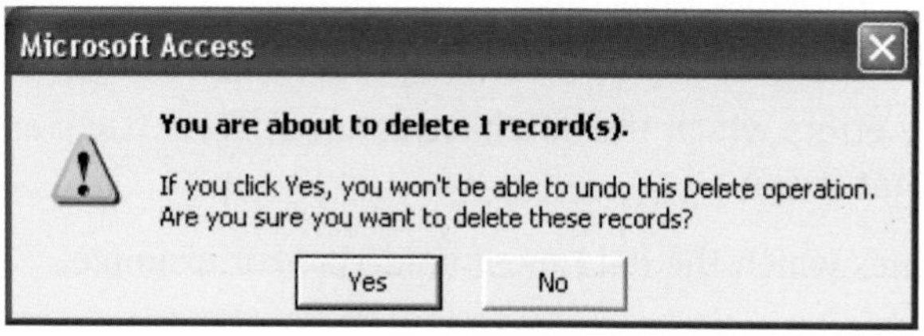

- Click Yes to delete the record.
- Save and close the table, then close the database.

Exercise

1. (a) Open the database ExamBoard.mdb created in Chapter 2.

   (b) Add the following records:

CandidateID	Surname	Initials
1	Benaud	RJ
2	Matthews	SE
3	King	AE
4	Thompson	G
5	Adams	QH
6	Matthews	D

2. (a) Open the database Customer.mdb that you created in the last chapter.

   (b) Enter 4 new customer records.

   (c) For each of these customers, enter 2 orders in the Orders table.

   (d) Save and close this database.

CHAPTER

5.5 Data Validation

Access can help to make sure that you have entered the data correctly into the database. If you make a mistake entering data, especially in very large databases, the error can be very difficult to trace. For example, if you entered **Terrace** instead of **Terraced** as the style for a property, then when you searched the database for properties where the style was entered as **Terraced**, that record wouldn't be shown.

Although there are many errors which the database cannot detect (such as a misspelt name), there are many that it can.

You can write a set of rules which the data must abide by. For example:

- The style of a property can only be **Flat**, **Terraced**, **Semi** or **Detached**.
- The number of bedrooms must be between **1** and **9**.
- The rent must be between **200** and **5000**.
- The lease expiry date must be entered as a date later than today's date. The validation rule will only be applied when the date is entered – it doesn't matter if the date becomes invalid some months after it is has been entered.

The process of checking that the data meets various 'rules' is called **validation**. The rules themselves are called **validation rules**.

Alongside each rule, you can enter some text that Access will show to the user if they enter invalid data. This is called **validation text**.

Comparison operators

There are several comparison operators that you can use, and they are listed in the table below:

Operator	Meaning	Example
<	less than	<20
<=	less than or equal to	<=20
>	greater than	>0
>=	greater than or equal to	>=0
=	equal to	=20 ="Flat" OR "Terraced"
<>	not equal to	<>"Semi"
BETWEEN	test for a range of values. Must be two comparison values (a low & high value) separated by AND operator	BETWEEN 01/12/2002 AND 25/12/2002

Entering the validation rules

- Open the Hemlets database.
- In the Database window, make sure the Tables tab is selected then click to select tblProperty.

- Click Design to open the table in Design View.

We are going to enter a validation rule for the Style field. The rule we will use is: Style can only be Flat, Terraced, Semi or Detached.

- Click in the Style field name.

Notice that two of the rows in the Field Properties at the bottom of the screen are named Validation Rule and Validation Text. This is where we will enter the rules.

- In the Field Properties click in the Validation Rule row.
- Type Flat or Terraced or Semi or Detached and press Enter. Notice when you tab out of this field that Access will add quotes.
- In the Validation Text row type The style must be Flat, Terraced, Semi or Detached.

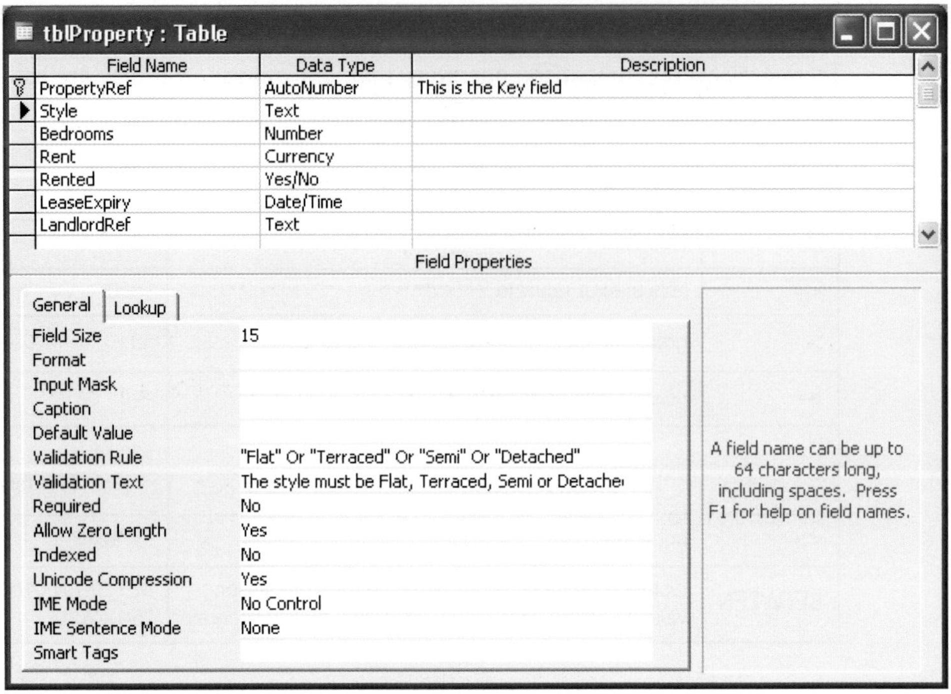

- Return to Datasheet View by clicking the Datasheet View icon.

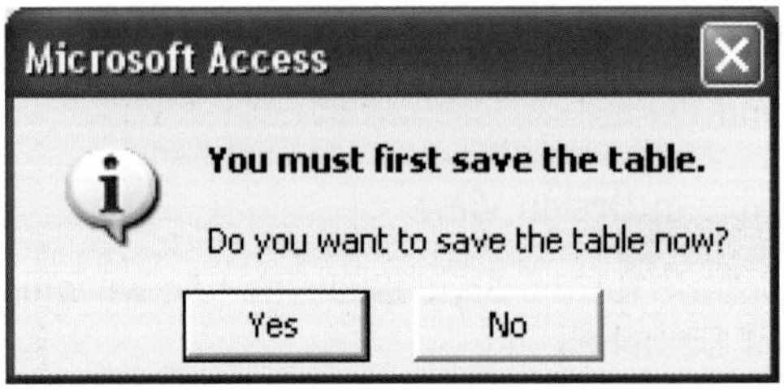

- You will be asked to save the changes you have just made. Click Yes, and Yes again to the prompt about data integrity rules.

Testing the validation rule

We will test the rule by entering a new record that does not agree with the validation rule.

Property Ref	Style	Bedrooms	Rent	Rented	Lease Expiry	Landlord Ref
(Auto Number)	Semi detached	3	775	N		L3

- Click in the empty row below the last property. The PropertyRef will be entered automatically, so tab to the Style field and type Semi detached. Press Enter.

A message will appear on the screen containing the Validation Text that you entered:

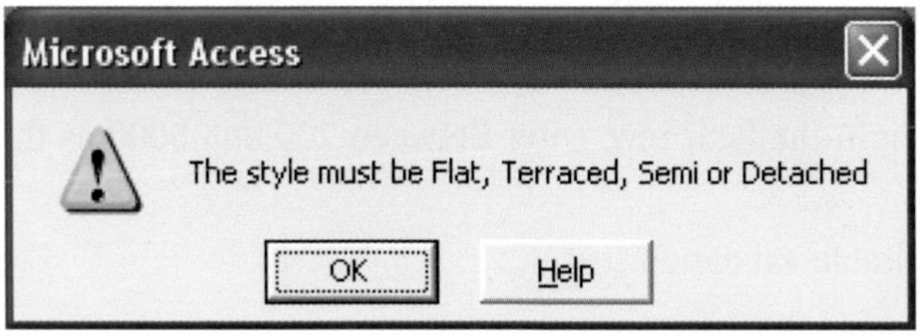

- Click OK. Re-enter the style as Semi and press Enter. Access should accept this.
- Enter the rest of the details for this property from the table above.

Tip:
Access will not allow you to exit the field until the value in that field meets the validation rule.

Setting the other validation rules

Now we'll set a validation rule for the Bedrooms field. The rule we'll use is: The number of bedrooms must be between 1 and 9.

- Return to Design View by clicking the Design View icon.
- Click in the Bedrooms field.
- Enter the Validation Rule and Validation Text as shown below:

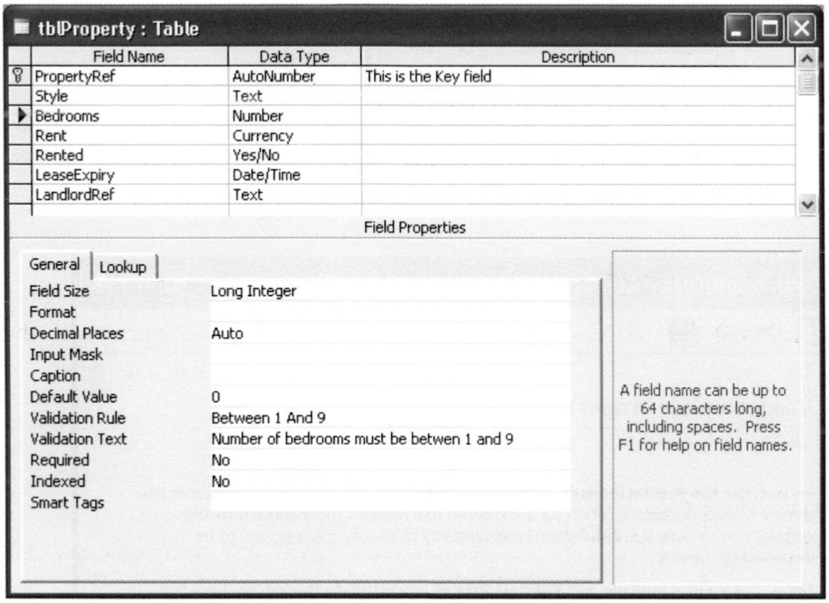

You can press F1 for help if you get stuck!

Entering a validation rule for Rent

You can enter a validation rule for a Currency field in just the same way as a Number field.

- With the cursor in the Rent row, enter Between 200 and 5000 as the validation rule.
- Enter some suitable validation text.

Entering a validation rule for a Date field

This is also quite straightforward. We want to enter the following rule: the Lease Expiry must be between 1/1/2003 and 1/1/2008.

- Make sure the cursor is in the Lease Expiry row of the tblProperty table.
- Enter the rule between #1/1/03# and #1/1/08# or null as the validation rule. Enter some suitable validation text.

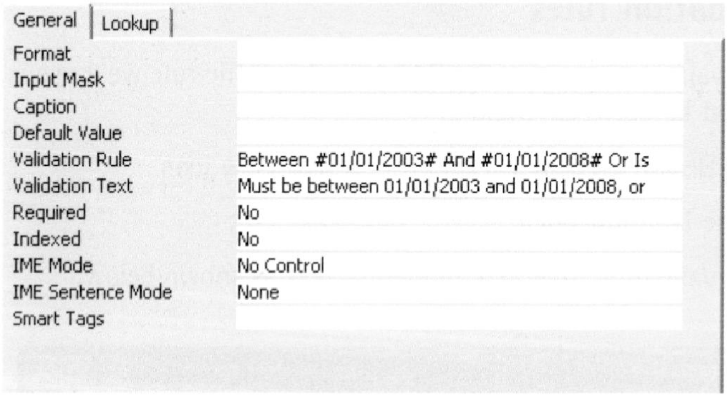

Tip:

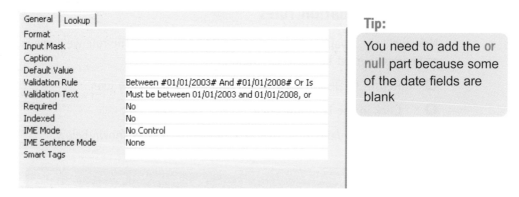

You need to add the or null part because some of the date fields are blank

When using a date in a validation rule, you must put it between # marks, so an ordinary date 1/1/03 becomes #1/1/03#. You don't need to remember all this – if you get stuck, just look up validation rule in the Help Answer Wizard, or press F1 when your cursor is in the Validation Rule row.

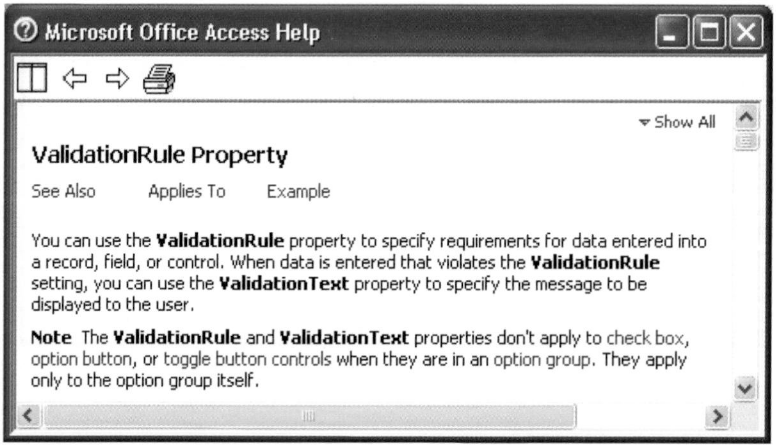

More testing!

- Return to Datasheet View by clicking the Datasheet View icon.
- Click Yes to save the changes and Yes to the prompt about data integrity rules.

In the table below are more records that have to be entered.

- Try entering invalid values for Bedrooms, Rent and Date. You should see your error messages appearing!

Tip:
Always test your validation rules by trying to enter invalid data. You can press Esc to cancel the record without saving it.

PropertyRef	Style	Bed rooms	Rent	Rented	LeaseExpiry	LandlordRef
(Auto Number)	Detached	4	950	Y	19/8/03	L8
(Auto Number)	Semi	2	750	N		L4
(Auto Number)	Terraced	2	700	Y	5/1/04	L5

- When you have entered the records with the data shown, save and close your table.
- Close Access if this is the end of a session.

Exercise

In this exercise you will validate fields.

1. Open your database application Customer.mbd.
2. In the Orders table, set a validation rule so that the date entered cannot be earlier than 2003.
3. Set another rule so that the price cannot exceed £5,000.00 and warns the user with a suitable message if this happens.
4. Enter an order record and try out invalid values.
5. Save and close the database.

CHAPTER 5.6

Sorting, Formatting and Printing

- Open Access. Open the Hemlets database.
- Double-click tblProperty to open it.
- Reduce the size of this window and drag it to one side so that you can see the database window.
- Double-click tblLandlord to open this table also.

Sorting records

Alphabetical sorts

You can perform a simple sort on one field by clicking anywhere in the column you want to sort on and clicking one of the two Sort buttons (Sort Ascending and Sort Descending) on the toolbar.

To sort the properties in the tblLandlord table by surname:

- Click in the Surname field and click the Sort Ascending icon. The records will now be sorted in ascending order of surname, as shown below:

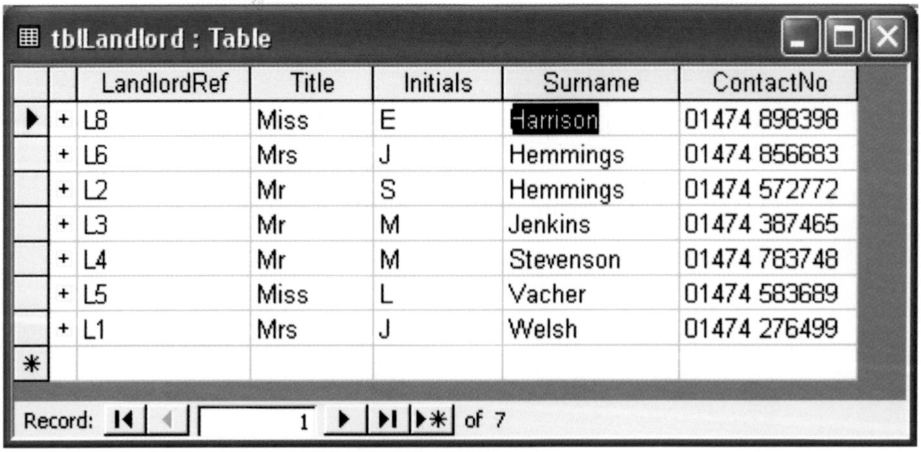

tblLandlord : Table

LandlordRef	Title	Initials	Surname	ContactNo
L8	Miss	E	Harrison	01474 898398
L6	Mrs	J	Hemmings	01474 856683
L2	Mr	S	Hemmings	01474 572772
L3	Mr	M	Jenkins	01474 387465
L4	Mr	M	Stevenson	01474 783748
L5	Miss	L	Vacher	01474 583689
L1	Mrs	J	Welsh	01474 276499

Record: 1 of 7

- Now click the Sort Descending button.

The records will be resorted in descending alphabetical order.

Numerical sorts

- Now click in the Bedrooms column of tblProperties.
- Click the Sort Descending button.

The records will be sorted in descending order of the number of bedrooms. You can try resorting them in ascending order of Rent now!

- When you have finished experimenting, close tblProperties.

Formatting and printing a datasheet

You can print a datasheet just as it is, or you can format it first by hiding unwanted columns, changing the order of the columns and changing column widths. We will practise these techniques.

- With tblLandlord open in Datasheet View, click the Print Preview icon. Your data appears as shown below:

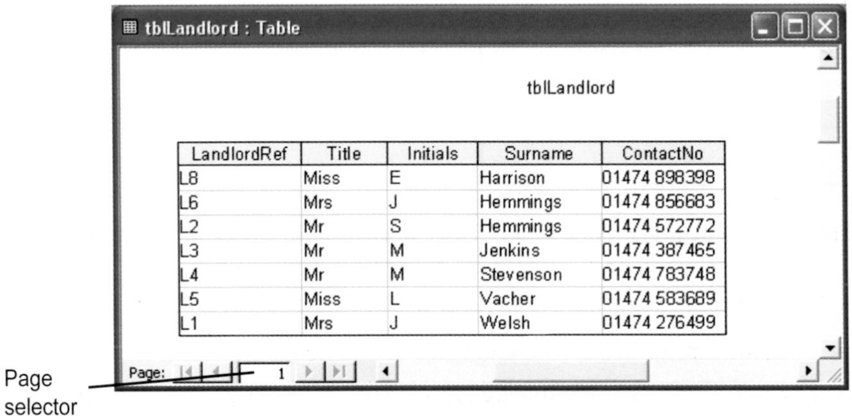

LandlordRef	Title	Initials	Surname	ContactNo
L8	Miss	E	Harrison	01474 898398
L6	Mrs	J	Hemmings	01474 856683
L2	Mr	S	Hemmings	01474 572772
L3	Mr	M	Jenkins	01474 387465
L4	Mr	M	Stevenson	01474 783748
L5	Miss	L	Vacher	01474 583689
L1	Mrs	J	Welsh	01474 276499

Tip:
If it's too small to read, click on it to enlarge it.

A large datasheet may not fit on one page in Portrait view. You would use the page selector at the bottom of the screen to view the other pages.

The Print Preview toolbar appears at the top of the screen. You can Zoom in on a page by clicking anywhere on it, or by clicking the Zoom icon.

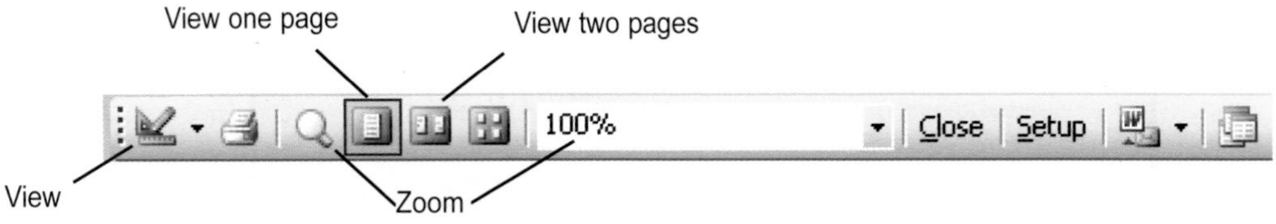

- Click Close to exit Print Preview.

Changing the Page layout

You can change the page layout to **Landscape** view.

- Select **File**, **Page Setup** from the menu.
- Click the **Page** tab in the **Page Setup** dialogue box. Click **Landscape**.
- Click **OK**.

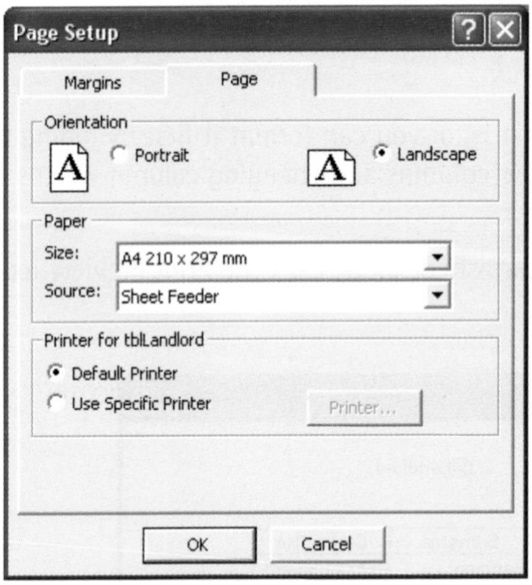

- Try another **Print Preview**. If it didn't fit on one page before, it should now.
- Select **File**, **Print** to print the datasheet.

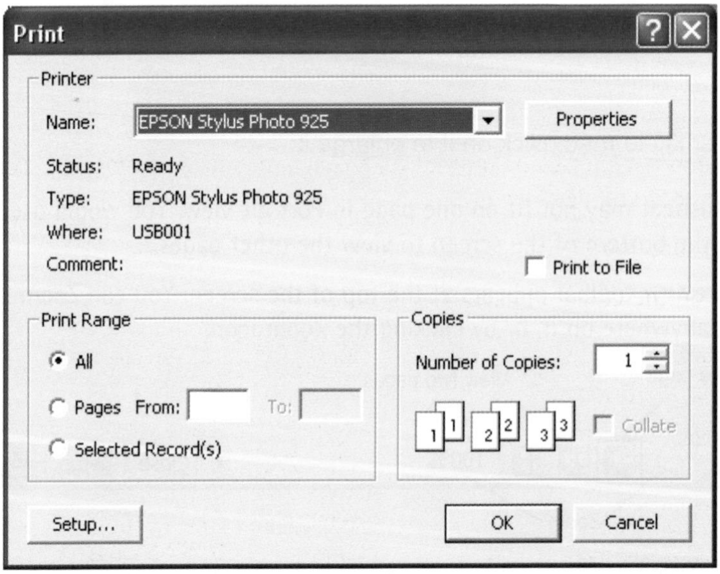

- Here you can decide which pages to print and how many copies to print. Click **OK** to print, otherwise click **Cancel**.

Printing only selected records

- With the table in **Datasheet View**, select just a few records by clicking and dragging across their row selectors.

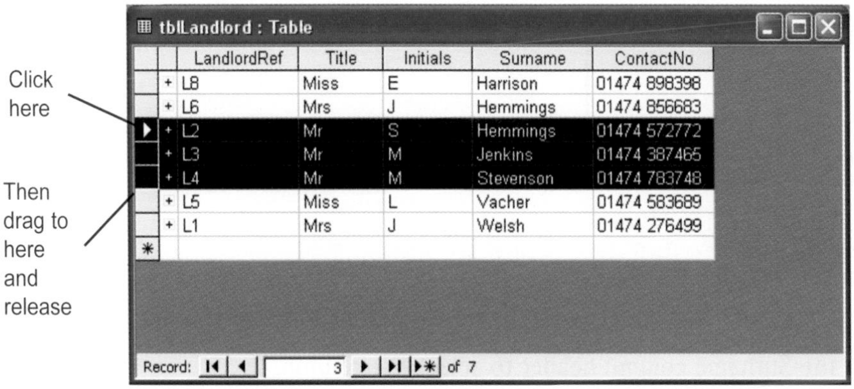
tblLandlord : Table
Click here
Then drag to here and release
LandlordRef Title Initials Surname ContactNo
L8 Miss E Harrison 01474 898398
L6 Mrs J Hemmings 01474 856683
L2 Mr S Hemmings 01474 572772
L3 Mr M Jenkins 01474 387465
L4 Mr M Stevenson 01474 783748
L5 Miss L Vacher 01474 583689
L1 Mrs J Welsh 01474 276499
Record: 3 of 7

- Select **File**, **Print** from the menu.
- Check the option **Selected Records** under the **Print Range** section.

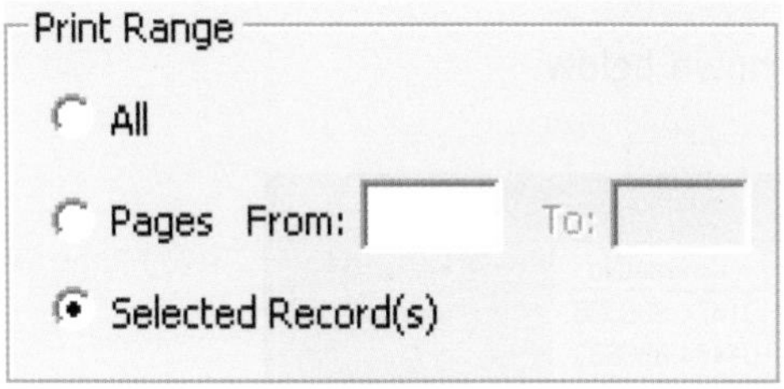

- Click **OK** to print only those records you highlighted.

Hiding and unhiding columns

Sometimes you may not want to print all the columns in the datasheet. You can hide the columns that you don't want.

- Make sure you have **tblLandlord** open in **Datasheet View**.
- Click on the column header for **LandlordRef**.

- From the menu select Format, Hide Columns. The column will be hidden.
- To unhide the column, just select Format, Unhide Columns from the menu, and tick the field you want to unhide.

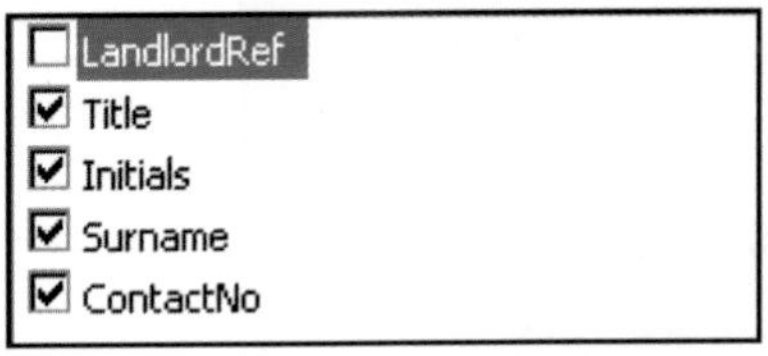

Moving columns

Suppose you want the Surname column to appear before the Title column.

- Click the Surname column header to select the column.
- Click again and hold down the mouse button, then drag the header to the left of the Title column. The table should now appear as shown below.
- Adjust the column widths by double-clicking in the column header on the border between each column.

Your table should now appear as shown below:

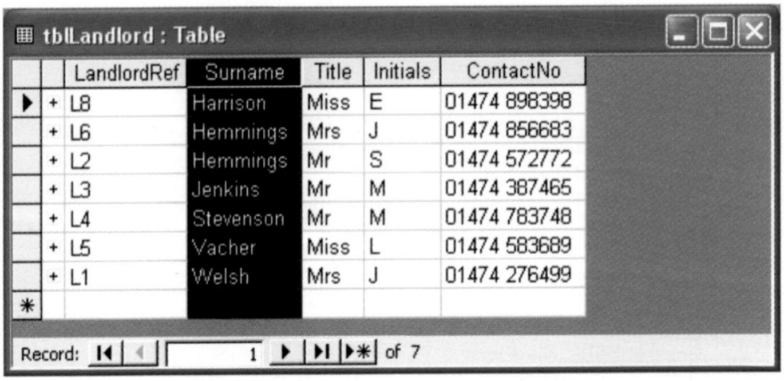
tblLandlord : Table

		LandlordRef	Surname	Title	Initials	ContactNo
▶	+	L8	Harrison	Miss	E	01474 898398
	+	L6	Hemmings	Mrs	J	01474 856683
	+	L2	Hemmings	Mr	S	01474 572772
	+	L3	Jenkins	Mr	M	01474 387465
	+	L4	Stevenson	Mr	M	01474 783748
	+	L5	Vacher	Miss	L	01474 583689
	+	L1	Welsh	Mrs	J	01474 276499
*						

Record: 1 of 7

- Click the Print Preview icon again to see what the page will look like when printed out.

- Click the Close icon and click Yes when asked if you want to save changes to the table layout.

Exercise

1. Open the ExamBoard.mbd database.
2. Print the first four records of the Candidate table with fields in the order CandidateID, Surname, Initials.
3. Print all the records with fields in the order Surname, Initials, CandidateID.
4. Close the database.

CHAPTER 5.7

Forms

User interface

You need to consider how the users interact with your computer application – how they choose what to do next, how they enter data and so on.

We will start by creating a form to allow the user to input data about landlords.

This form will be used to enter new landlords when they register with Hemlets.

Creating a new form

- Make sure the Hemlets database is open.

- In the Database window select the Forms tab.

One of the options is to use a wizard. This is usually the quickest method, and the one you normally use to create a simple form.

- Click New. Click to select Form Wizard, and select tblLandlord from the dropdown list at the bottom of the New Form window.

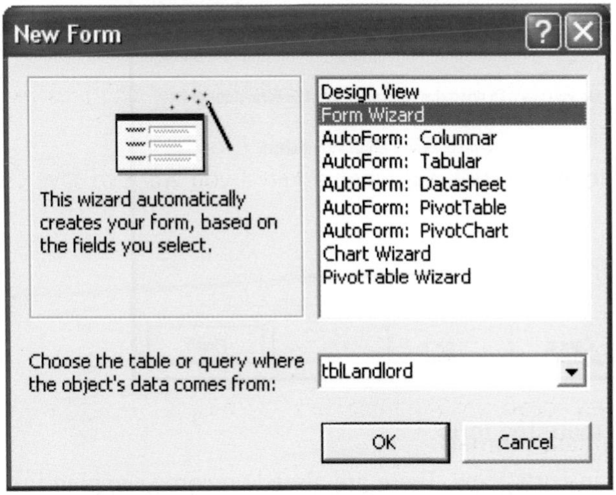

- Click OK.

- You are now asked which fields you want to appear on your form. We want all the fields, so click >>. All the fields should now appear in the right-hand pane.

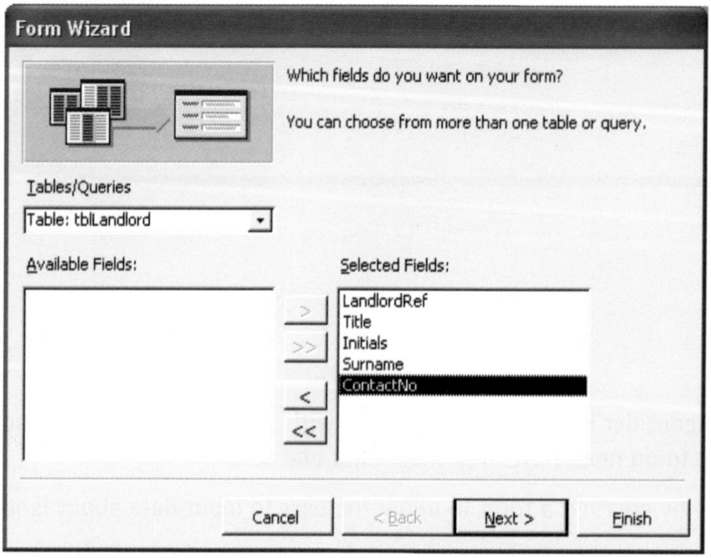

- Click Next. Leave the form layout as Columnar and click Next.
- Leave the style as Standard, click Next.
- Enter frmLandlord as the title of the form. We will change this title later, but we need to enter frmLandlord here so that Access will save the form with that name.

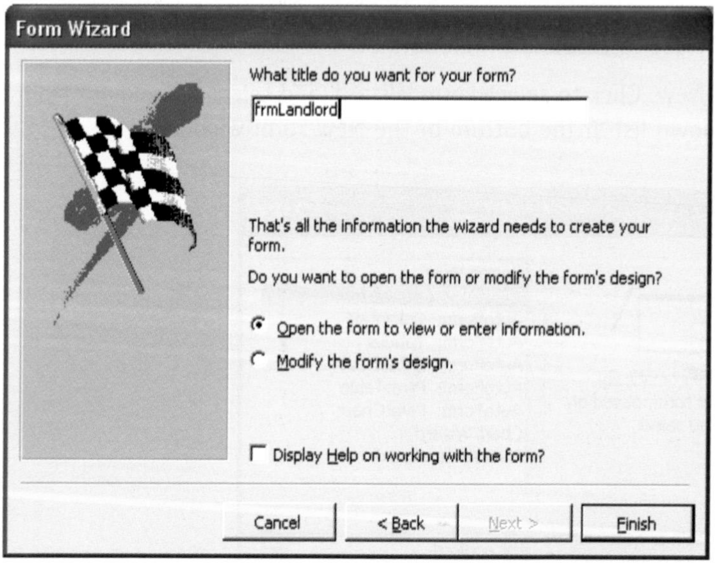

- Click Finish to create the form.
- The form opens in Form View. There are already records showing in the form – these are all the records you entered directly into the tblLandlord table.

Tip:
If the lengths of your fields look different to this it's probably because you didn't enter the correct **Field Size** for each field. You can change the **Field Size** property by opening **tblLandlord** in **Design View**; use the field sizes in the table on Page 5-12. The field sizes on the form will need to be adjusted manually now though.

Changing View mode

As with tables, you need to have the form open in **Design View** in order to modify it.

Click the **Design View** icon to view the form in **Design View**.

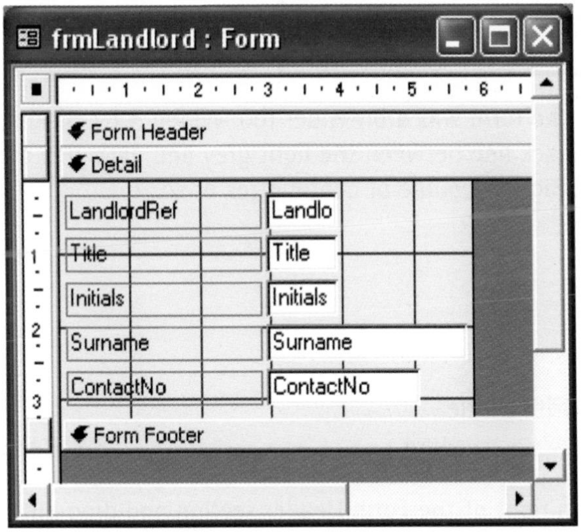

Adding text to the header

It would be nice to have a title for the form. On the form in **Design View**, notice there's a section at the top named **Form Header**. That's where we'll put the title.

First we need to expand the **Form Header** section because it currently has no space under it!

- Place the cursor on the border between the Form Header and Detail section headers. The cursor should change to a double-headed arrow, like in the next screenshot.

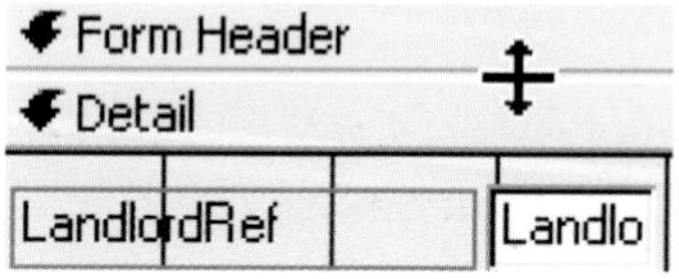

- Click and drag the border downwards a couple of centimetres or so, as shown below:

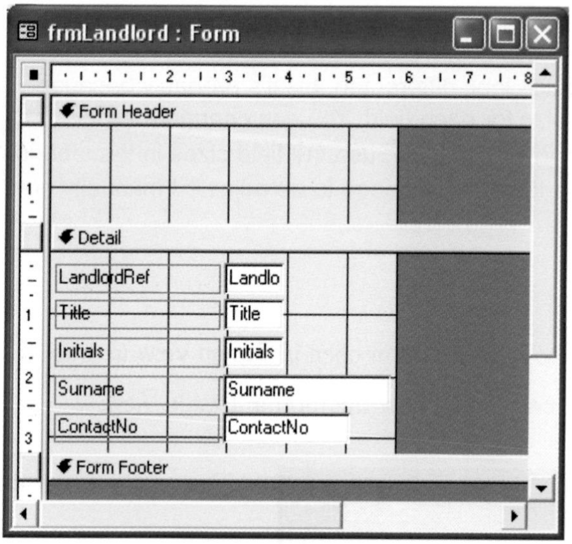

- It would be nice if the form was a bit wider too. Widen it by clicking and dragging the thin black line between the light grey and dark grey areas of the form (see below). Drag it a couple of centimetres or so.

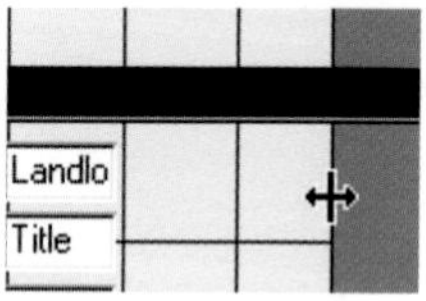

Now we've got space to write a title.

- Click the Label icon in the Toolbox.
- Now click in the top right of the Form Header section and drag out a rectangle as shown below:

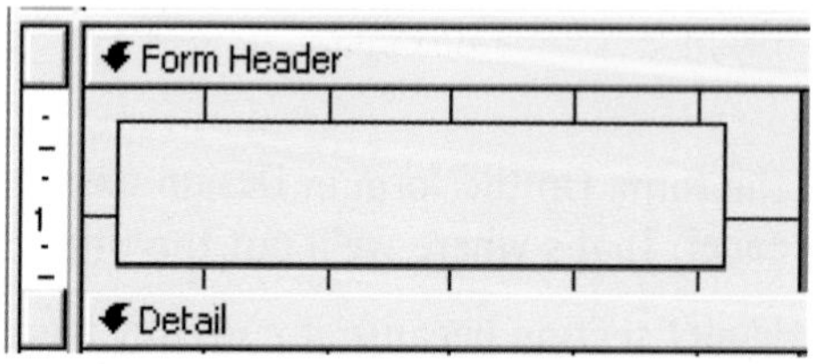

- The text cursor will be flashing in the box, so you can now type the title. Type Landlord Details Form.

The text will appear quite small and uninteresting so we need to change the size and colour of the font.

- Select the whole label box by first clicking away from the label then clicking once on it. When it is selected it should have handles around it.

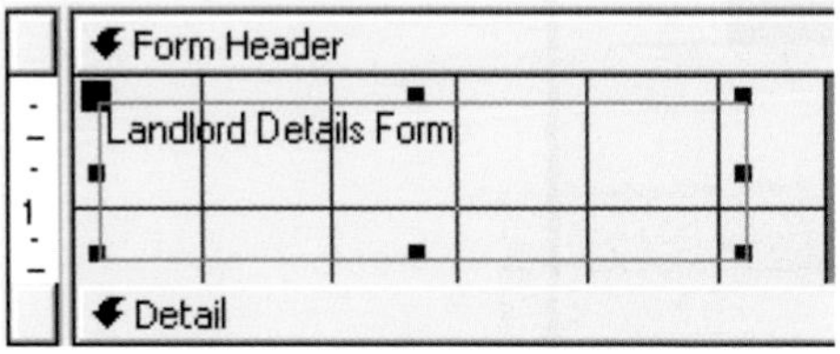

Now you can change the font size just as you would in Word or Excel – using the buttons on the Formatting toolbar.

The Formatting toolbar

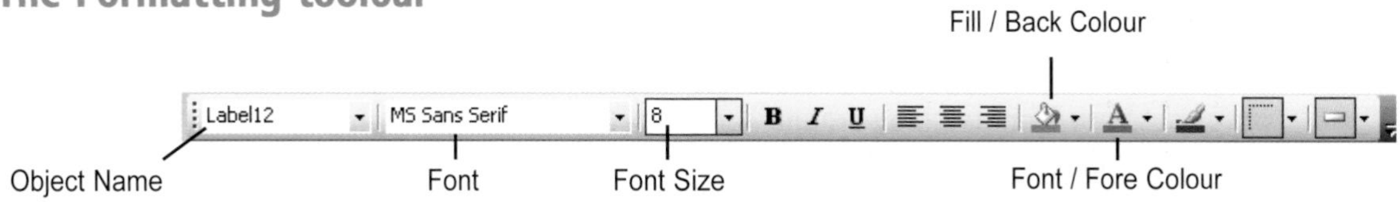

- If you cannot see the Formatting toolbar, go to View, Toolbars, then click the box next to Formatting (Form/Report).

Changing text size

- With the label selected, click the small down-arrow in the text size box. Click to select 14.

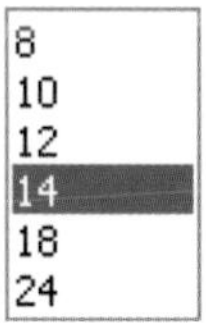

Changing text colour

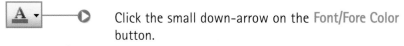

- Click the small down-arrow on the Font/Fore Color button.
- Just click to select a colour you like!
- Try changing the background colour too, using the Fill/Back Color button.
- Click and drag the handles so that the label box fills the whole Form Header.

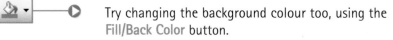

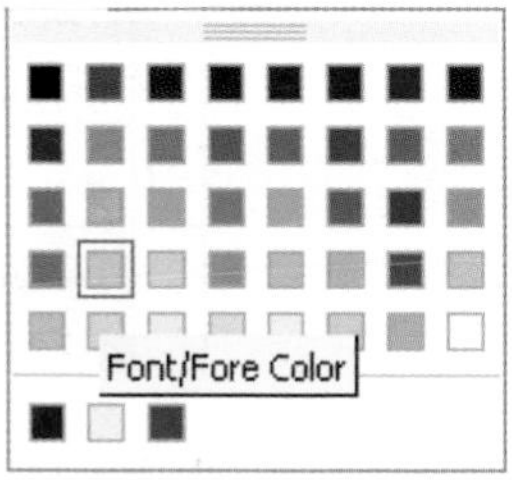

Now you can view how it will look by changing to Form View.

Click the Form View icon to return to Form View.

That looks pretty smart!

If you're not happy with your form, just return to Design View using the Design View icon and play around some more with the functions on the Formatting toolbar.

Whilst the data you enter into forms is automatically saved, you have to remember to save any changes you make to the design. Save your changes by clicking the Save icon, or by selecting File, Save from the menu.

Adding text to the footer

This is done in exactly the same way as the header, except we will use the Form Footer section instead of the Form Header.

Return to Design View.

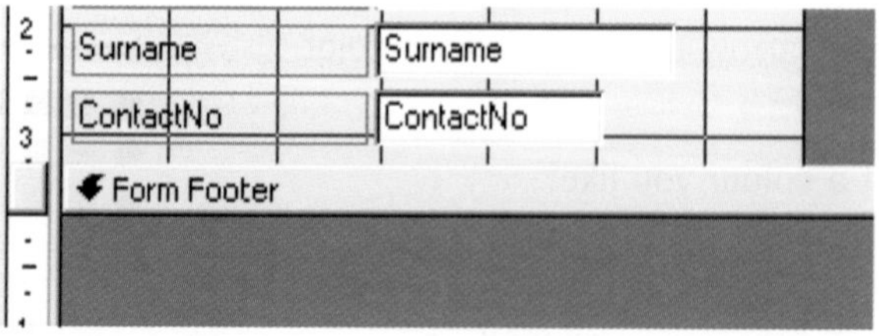

At the bottom of the form is the Form Footer section. It doesn't look like there is any room to write anything but the form will expand as soon as you put a label in the dark grey space below the Form Footer section header.

Click the Label icon in the Formatting toolbar.

Drag out a rectangle just like you did for the Form Header.

- Type the text Hemlets Database.

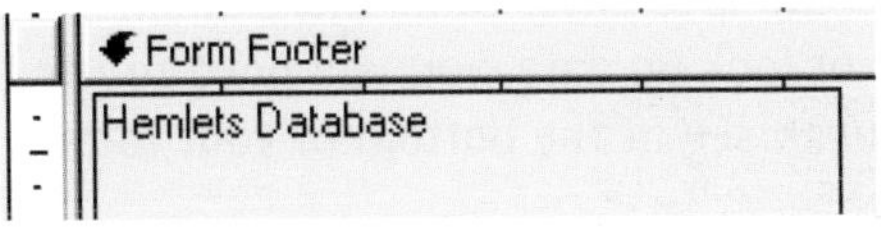

- Change the font size and colour, and the background colour until you are happy with the way it looks. You can also change the size of the label box.
- Go to Form View to see your handiwork!

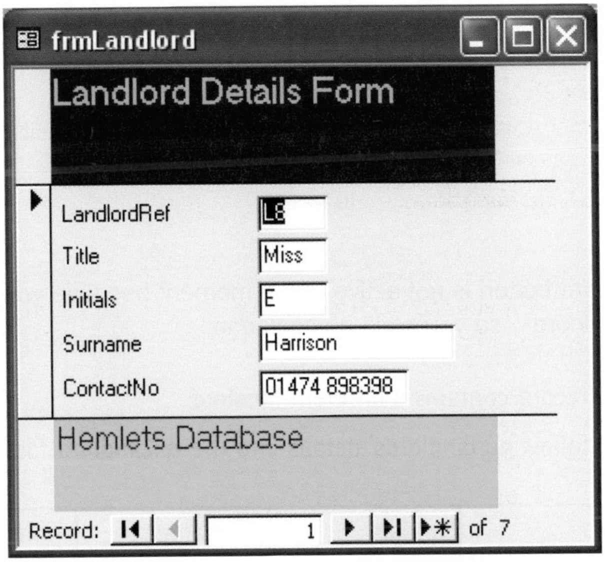

- Try resizing the form by clicking and dragging the blue border round the form. You'll see that whatever size you make the form, the footer will remain at the bottom of the window.

Closing and opening a form

- Click the Close button to close the form. If you have made changes to the design of the form since you last saved, you will be asked if you want to save the changes. Click Yes.

In the Database window, you will see the name of the form, frmLandlord, appear whenever the Forms tab is selected. If you wanted to delete the form for any reason, you could do so by clicking the form name and pressing the Delete key. Not now!

- Open the form again by double-clicking the form name.

Entering data using the form

Now we'll use the form you've just created to enter some more landlord details into the form. When using the form to enter or look up data, you will need to use the Record Selectors. These are the buttons you can see at the bottom of your form.

The Record selectors

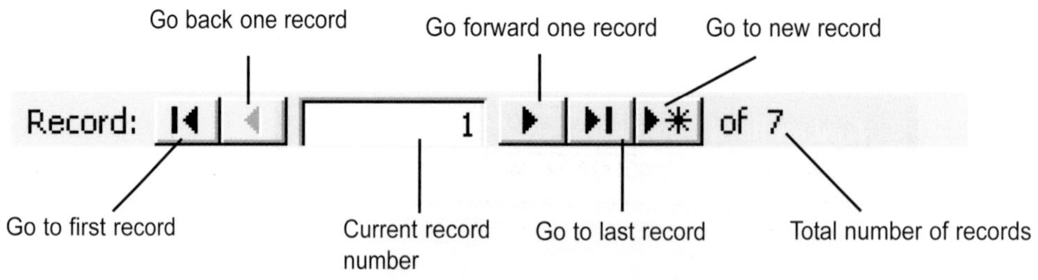

Tip:
The Go back one record button is not active at the moment because you are already on the first record – so you can't go back one.

Remember each record contains a different landlord.

We will now enter the following landlords' details into the tblLandlord form.

LandlordRef	Title	Initials	Surname	ContactNo
L9	Mr	T	Hodson	01474 243046
L10	Mr	P	Chisholm	01474 384446
L11	Miss	F	Kennedy	01474 558374

- Go to a new record using the New record button on the record selectors.
- The cursor should now be in the LandlordRef box on the new record, so type L9.
- Either click in the Title box or just press tab. Enter Mr.
- Enter the remaining details for Mr Hodson using the table above.

Your form should now look like this:

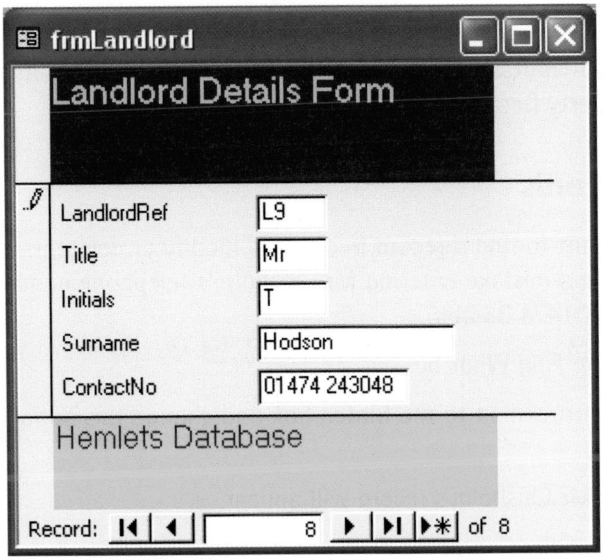

- Enter the other two landlords from the table on the previous page.

Going to specific records

You can use the record selectors to find records in a form.

- Flick through the records in the form using the **forward one** and **back one** record selectors.

- You can look up a specific record in the same way as you did in the table – using the **Find** button on the **Form View** toolbar. Alternatively, you can select **Find** from the **Edit** menu.
- With the cursor in the **Surname** field, click the **Find** button.

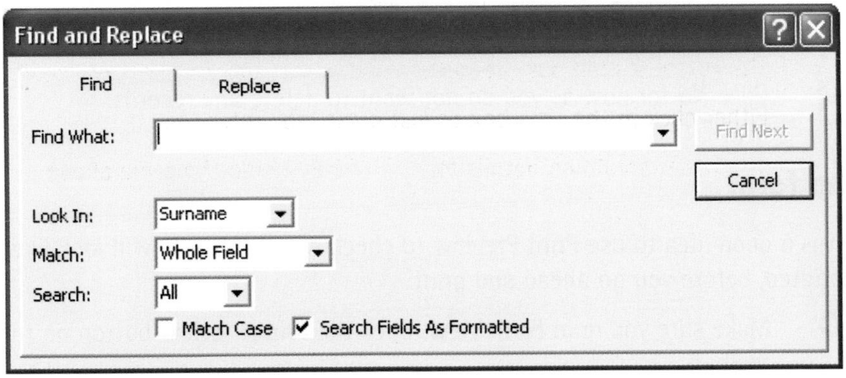

- Suppose you wanted to find the record for **Jenkins**. Type **Jenkins** into the **Find What** box.

- Click **Find Next**. It may appear as if nothing has happened, but if you now look at your form, Mr Jenkins's record will be displayed.

Note that you can search for a record with a particular number or date in a field too. Since this form does not contain any dates or numbers we will try this later in the chapter using the **Property Details** form!

Using a form to modify records

Sometimes you may want to find a record in order to modify or delete it. For example, suppose you have made a mistake entering Mr Chisholm's telephone number – it should be 01474 384464, not 01474 384446.

- Type **Chis** into the **Find What** box.
- Click the down-arrow next to the Match box and change this option to **Any Part of Field**.
- Click **Find Next**. Mr Chisholm's record will appear.
- Click at the end of the **ContactNo** field and edit the telephone number.

Using a form to delete records

You can delete the current record by clicking the **Delete Record** button when the record is displayed on the screen. You will see a message on the screen:

- Click **No** for now as you do not want to delete any records.

Printing the form

It is a good idea to use **Print Preview** to check what the form will look like when it is printed, before you go ahead and print.

- Make sure you're in **Form View**. Click the **Print Preview** button on the **Form View** toolbar.

Click the page selectors to see Page 2.

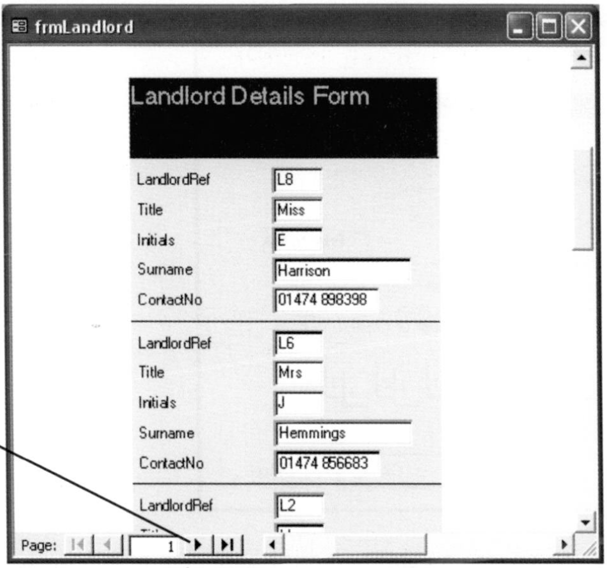

Tip:
If the form is too small to read, just click it to enlarge it

- Click Close to exit Print Preview.

Page setup

Use Page Setup to change the orientation of the paper and the paper size.

- Select File, Page Setup from the menu.

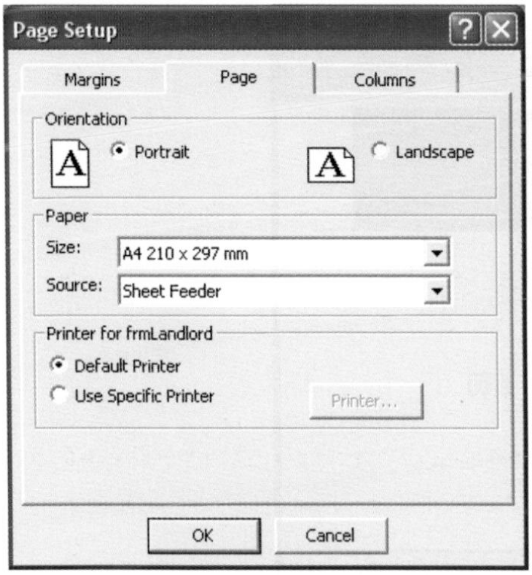

- Click the Page tab then click to select the orientation and paper size you want. Click OK.
- To print, select File, Print from the menu.

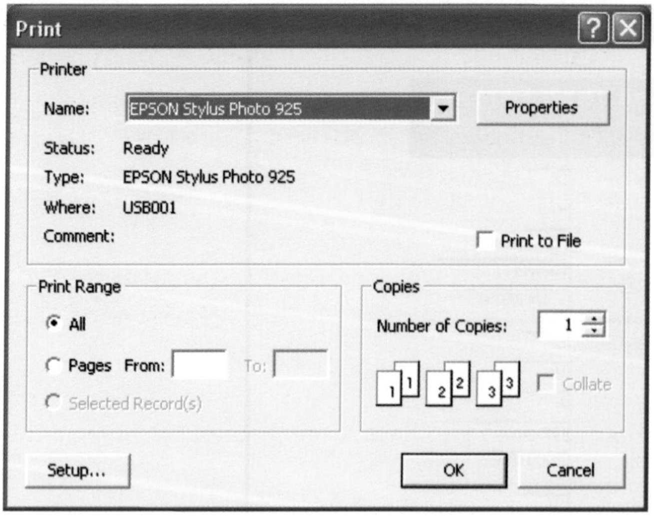

- You can enter which pages you want to print here, and also how many copies you want. If you want to print, click OK, otherwise click Cancel.
- Close your form by clicking the Close icon.
- You may be asked if you want to save changes to the design. Click Yes.

The Property form

It would be nice to have a form to enter all the property details. Using exactly the same method you used for the frmLandlord form, try and create a form for the properties. Save it as frmProperty.

When you're done, it should look something like this:

- Try using the Find button to find all the two-bedroom properties. You can click the Find Next button in the Find and Replace window to scroll through them all.
- You can also click in the LeaseExpiry field and find a record with a particular lease expiry date. Try finding the record with a lease expiry date of 05/12/2003.

Sorting data in forms

You can sort data in forms into ascending or descending numeric or alphabetical sequence. You have already practised sorting records in a table (see Chapter 5.6) and the procedure is exactly the same.

- Click in the field for Rent and click the Sort Descending button. This will sort the records in descending order of Rent. Scroll through the forms to satisfy yourself that this is so.
- Sort the records back to the original sequence by clicking in the PropertyRef field and clicking the Sort Ascending button.

That's all you need to know about forms, so now you can close your database and have a break!

- Close your database by clicking the close icon on the Database window. Close Access by clicking its Close icon.

Exercises

1. (a) Open the ExamBoard.mdb database.
   (b) Create a simple form to input data into your Candidate table.
   (c) Save the form as frmCandidate.
   (d) Enter 2 new records using the form.
   (e) Close the database.
2. (a) Open the Customer.mdb database.
   (b) Create a simple form to input data into your Customer table.
   Make all the text labels font size 14. Include a heading in a larger font on a shaded background. In the Footer section, insert the text BetterBooks Ltd.
   (c) Save the form as frmCustomer.
   (d) Enter 2 new records using the form.
   (e) Close the database.

CHAPTER

5.8 Applying Filters

Both filters and queries are used to select specific records (referred to as a subset of records) from a table of data.

In general, you would use a filter to temporarily view or edit a subset of records while you're in a table or form. Queries are slightly more complicated but also perform useful tasks that cannot be done with a filter. You'll understand more about which is most appropriate once you've had a go at them.

Using a filter in a form

We'll use a filter to select specific types of records in the frmLandlord form.

- Open the Hemlets database, then open the frmLandlord form in Form View.

Notice the filter options on the Form View toolbar.

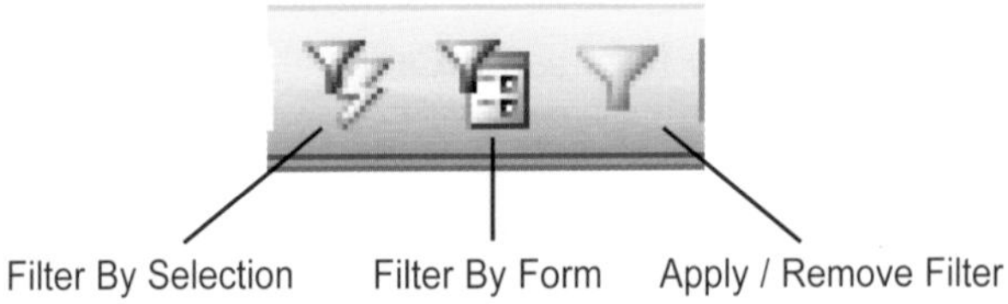

Filter by selection

With filter by selection, all you need to do is find one instance of the value you are looking for in the form.

We'll use filter by selection to select only those records where the title is Miss.

- Use the record selectors to navigate to any record where the title is Miss. Click in the Title field so that the cursor is in the same field as the Miss entry.

- Click the Filter By Selection button.

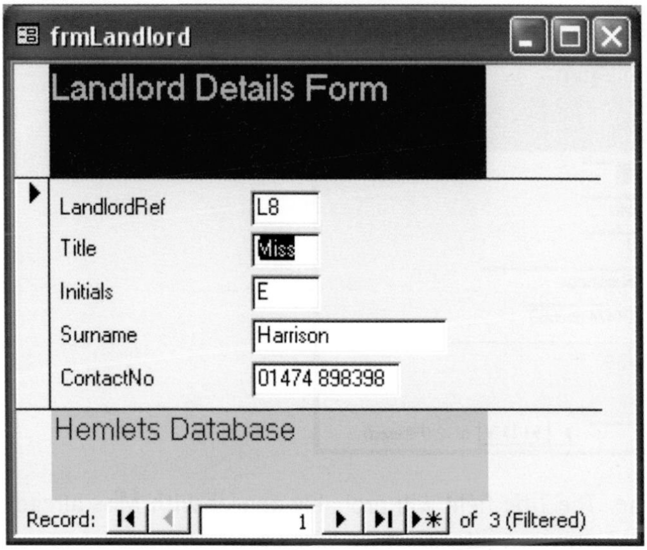

Look at the bottom of the form where the record selectors are – there are now only 3 records available to view.

- Use the record selectors to scroll through the three selected records. They should all have the title Miss.

Removing the filter

- Remove the filter by clicking the Remove Filter button (this button changes name from Apply Filter to Remove Filter depending on whether you currently have a filter applied).

The form should return to normal with all 10 records available.

- You can toggle the filter on and off by clicking the Apply Filter button again.

Filter by Form

To filter by form, you just type in the value you are looking for into a blank form. We will look for landlords with the surname Hemmings.

- Make sure that no filter is currently applied. Click the Filter By Form button.

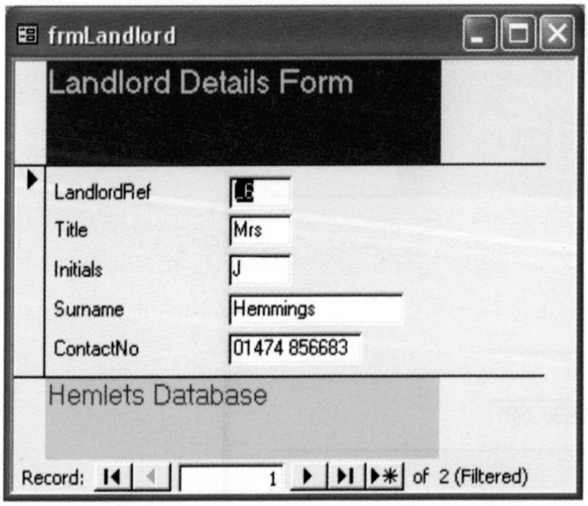

A blank form appears. The Title field will probably appear with Miss already entered simply because of the previous filter that we applied.

- Clear the query grid either by just deleting the Miss entry in the Title field or by clicking the Clear Grid icon on the toolbar.
- Click in the Surname field. Notice that an arrow appears on the right of the field. Click this.

This conveniently gives you a list of all the surnames entered in the database. You can either click a surname in the list or just type it in.

- Click Hemmings then click the Apply Filter icon.

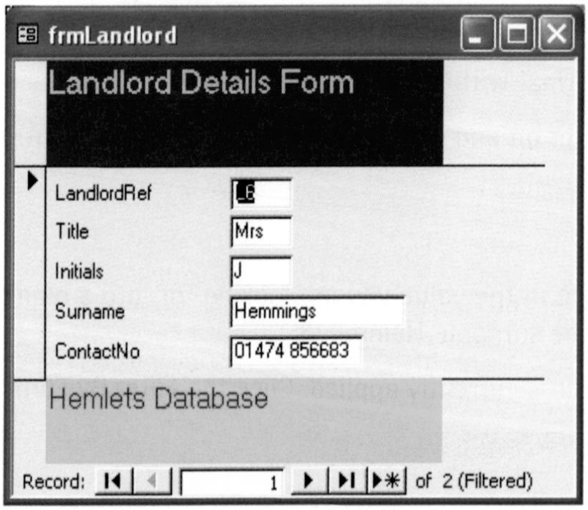

Two records have been filtered. Look at both of them to check they both have the surname Hemmings.

- Remove the filter by clicking the Remove Filter button.
- Close the frmLandlord form to return to the Database window.

Using a filter in a table

This is very similar to using a filter in a form, so we'll just run though this briefly.

- Open the tblLandlord table in Datasheet View.

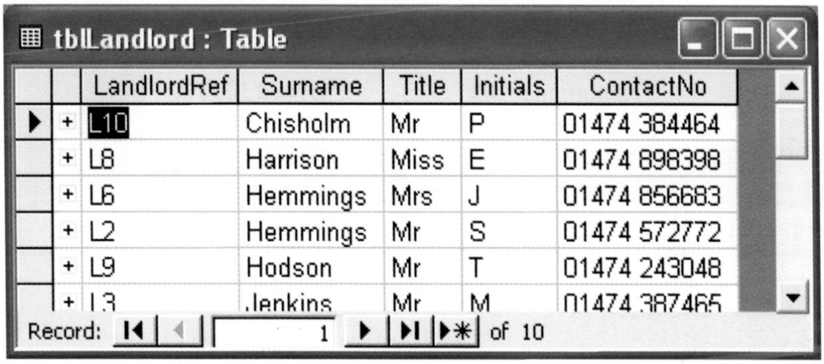

LandlordRef	Surname	Title	Initials	ContactNo
L10	Chisholm	Mr	P	01474 384464
L8	Harrison	Miss	E	01474 898398
L6	Hemmings	Mrs	J	01474 856683
L2	Hemmings	Mr	S	01474 572772
L9	Hodson	Mr	T	01474 243048
L3	Jenkins	Mr	M	01474 387465

- Place the cursor in the Title column in a record that says Miss.
- Click the Filter by Selection button.

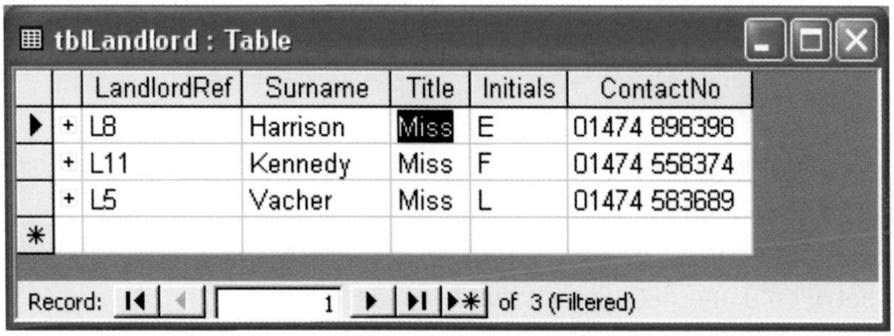

LandlordRef	Surname	Title	Initials	ContactNo
L8	Harrison	Miss	E	01474 898398
L11	Kennedy	Miss	F	01474 558374
L5	Vacher	Miss	L	01474 583689

There are three records shown with the title Miss.

- Remove the filter by clicking the Remove Filter button.
- Now click the Filter by Form button.
- Clear the grid by clicking the Clear Grid button.
- Click in the Surname field then click the arrow to show the list of surnames.

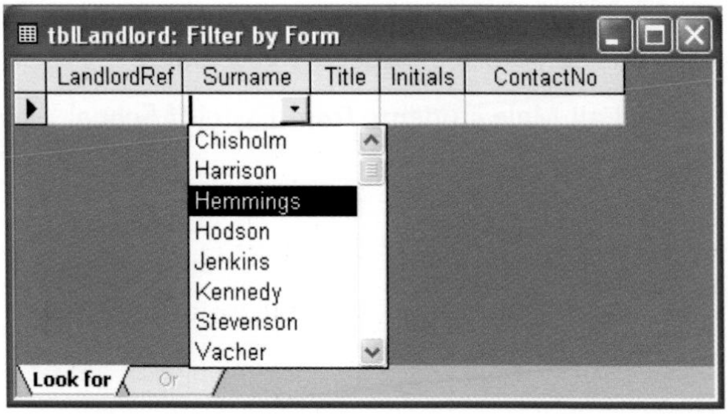

- Click Hemmings. Click the Apply Filter button.

Two records should be displayed with the surname Hemmings.

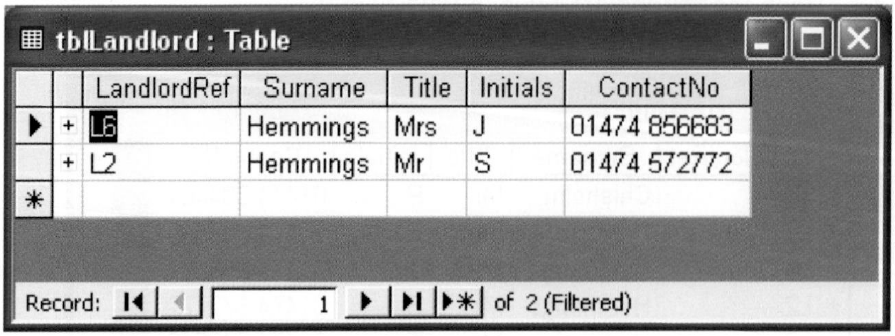
tblLandlord : Table

	LandlordRef	Surname	Title	Initials	ContactNo
▶ +	L6	Hemmings	Mrs	J	01474 856683
+	L2	Hemmings	Mr	S	01474 572772
*					

Record: 1 of 2 (Filtered)

- Remove the filter, save and close the table.

Exercise

The student database is located on the web site www.payne-gallway.co.uk/ecdl. It contains details of about 50 students applying to a college. You need to download student.mdb and save it on your own disk. Follow the instructions given on the web site to do this.

1. Open the student database.
2. Add another field named UCAS to the end of the student table. The new field is to be numeric and will hold the student's UCAS points.
3. Set a validation rule for the new field, specifying that the value entered must be between 0 and 480. Enter suitable validation text.
4. Save the table structure.
5. Create a simple form for the student table.
6. Save the form as frmStudent.
7. Write down the number of records in the database.
8. Find the record for the student whose surname is Peterson.
9. Change the name to Pedersen.
10. Filter the records to find all the students who come from Northcliff School. Write down the first names and surnames of students you found.
11. Filter the records to find all Male students from Eastcliff School. How many are there?
12. Remove the filter.
13. Save and close the database.

Making Queries

CHAPTER 5.9

One of the most useful things you can do with a database is to find all the records that satisfy a certain condition, such as "all properties that have 2 bedrooms". Queries are similar to filters, but they allow more scope for changing the format of the results. Queries are useful when you are likely to be searching the database repeatedly for the same thing, because you can easily save them. You can then run the saved query without first opening a table or form.

- Load Access and open the **Hemlets** database.

Creating a new query

We'll create a new query that finds all properties that are currently not rented. We can then add other criteria such as number of bedrooms and rent to narrow down the search for a prospective tenant.

- In the Database window, select **Queries**.

There are two options, **Create query in Design view** and **Create query by using Wizard**. We'll use the first option.

- Double-click **Create query in Design view**.

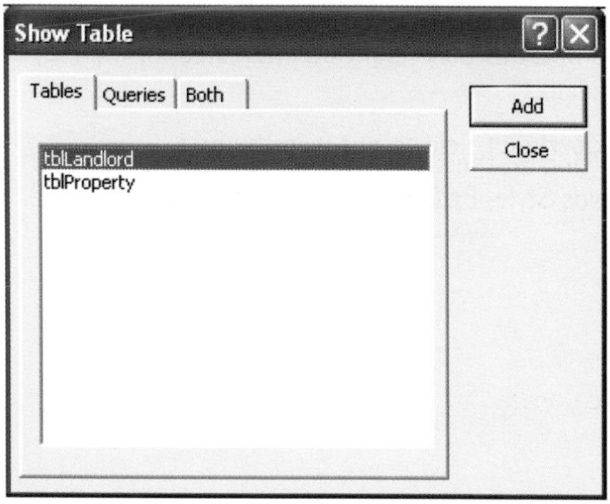

- The query will be based on the tblProperty table, so click tblProperty to select it then click Add.
- Click Close to close the Show Table window.

The empty query grid appears. Now you need to add fields from the table to the query grid.

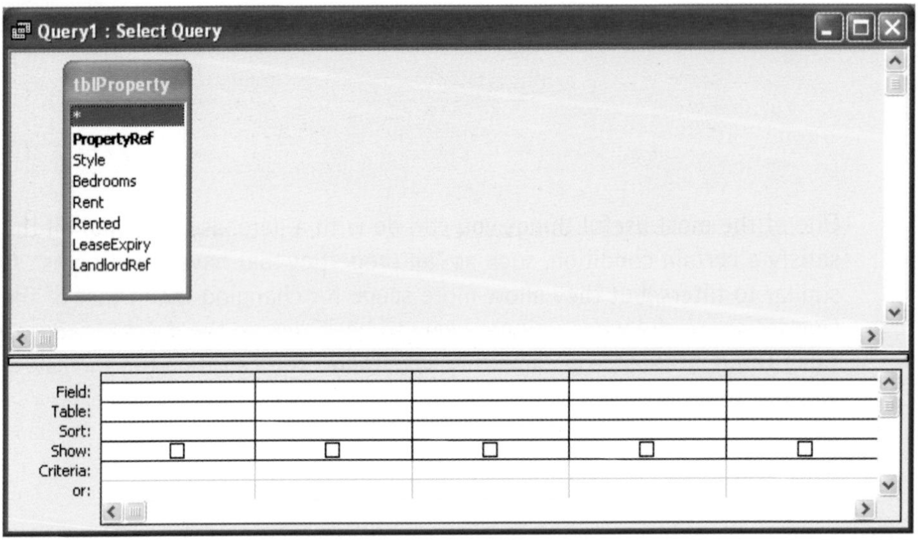

Selecting fields to appear in the query

You need to add a field to the query grid if:

- you want to specify a particular value for that field. In our case, we want to specify that the Rented field has a No value, so Rented will have to be put in the grid. We won't actually want to see this field with the results, as we already know that all records selected will not be rented.
- you want the field to appear in the results table. You need to show property details like Style, Bedrooms and Rent so that anyone looking through can make a decision on which properties they might be interested in. The PropertyRef field should also be included.
- Double-click the PropertyRef field to put it in the grid.
- Double-click the fields Style, Bedrooms, Rent and Rented.

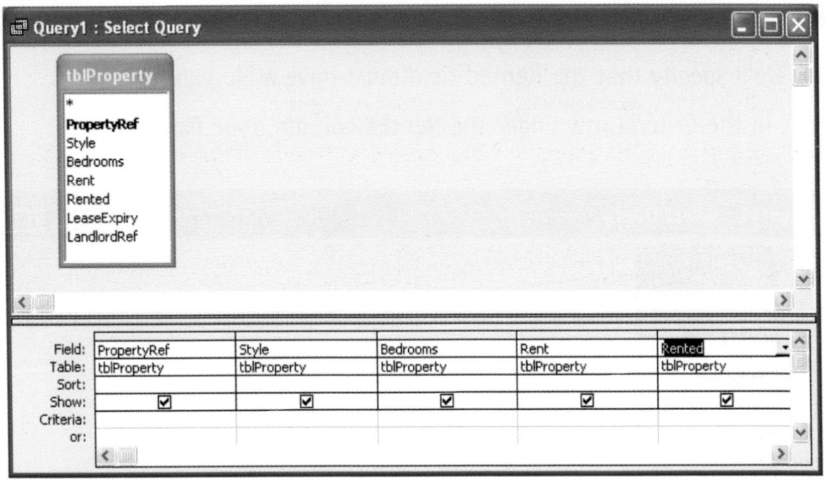

Tip:
You can click and drag a field from the table into the grid if you don't like double-clicking!

Resizing columns

You can change the width of the columns in the query grid so that you can view them all without having to scroll across. Just place the cursor between two column headers so that it changes to a double-headed arrow, then either double-click the mouse or click and drag.

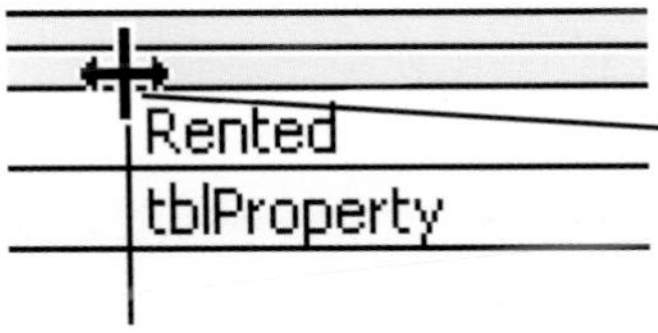

Double-headed arrow

Removing fields from the grid

- Double-click the LeaseExpiry field to add it to the query grid.
- To delete the LeaseExpiry field, click in the column header for the LeaseExpiry field then press the Delete key.

The column header

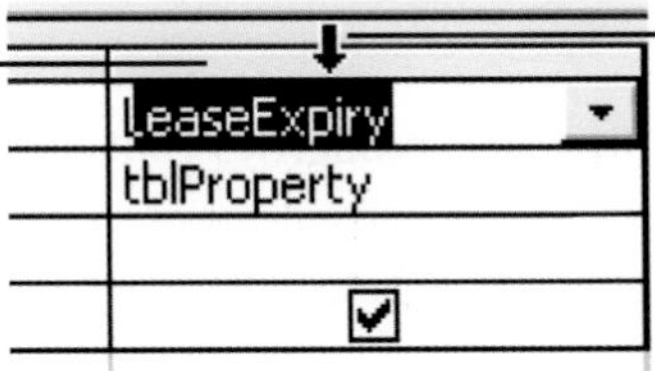

The cursor will become a small downward arrow when it is in the column header

Adding and removing criteria

Now we'll specify that the Rented field must have a No value.

- In the Criteria row under the Rented column, type No.

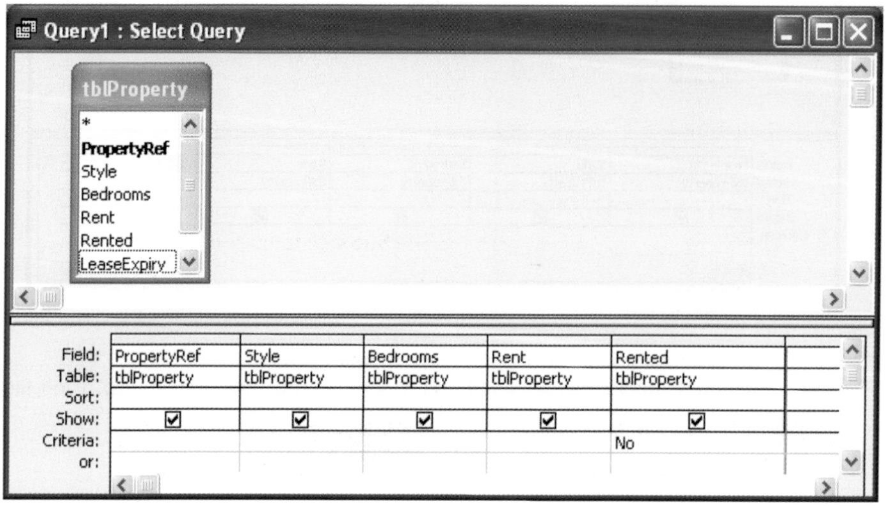

Removing criteria is just as straightforward – just double-click the criteria you want to delete then press the Backspace or Delete key.

Running the query

- Click the Run button on the Query Design toolbar.

You should get the following Results table.

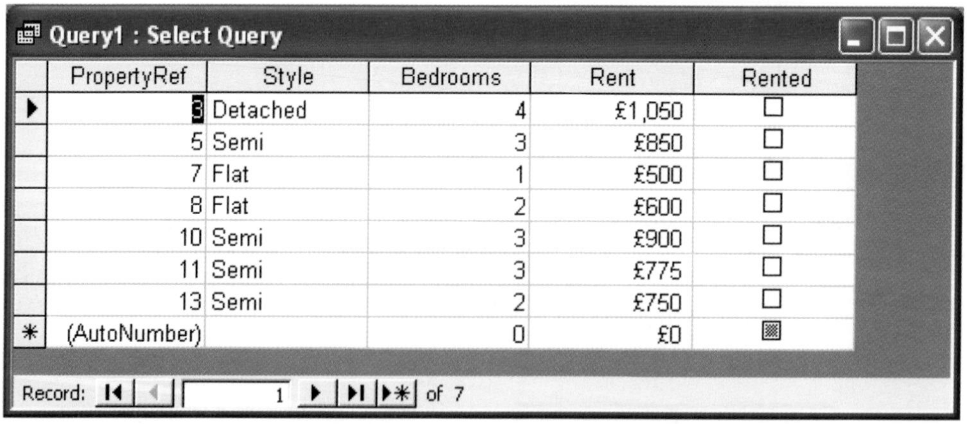

PropertyRef	Style	Bedrooms	Rent	Rented
3	Detached	4	£1,050	☐
5	Semi	3	£850	☐
7	Flat	1	£500	☐
8	Flat	2	£600	☐
10	Semi	3	£900	☐
11	Semi	3	£775	☐
13	Semi	2	£750	☐
(AutoNumber)		0	£0	

You can see that it has successfully selected only those properties that are not currently rented.

It isn't necessary to see the Rented column in the Results table because it will always be No. We'll hide this column.

Hiding and unhiding fields

We want to hide the Rented column.

- Return to Design View by clicking the Design View icon.
- Notice that above the Criteria row there is a Show row. All you need to do to hide a column is to uncheck its Show box. Click in the Show checkbox in the Rented column.

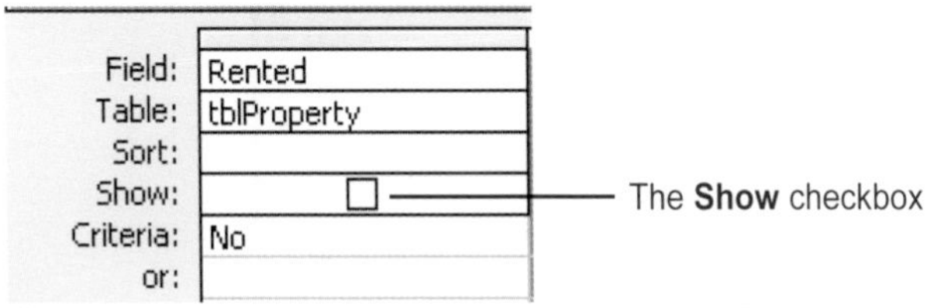

- Run the query again to see that it has worked.

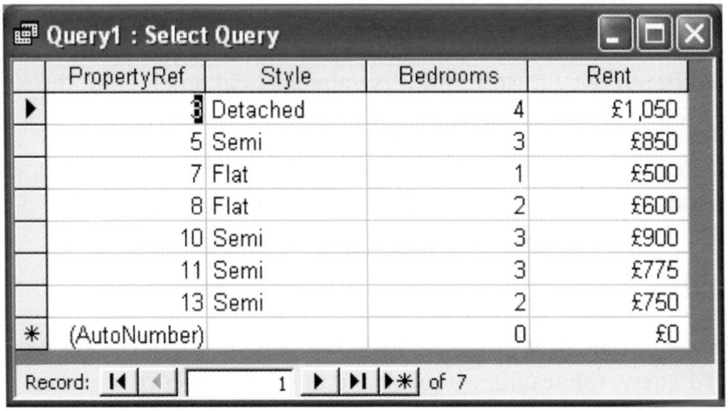

	PropertyRef	Style	Bedrooms	Rent
▶	3	Detached	4	£1,050
	5	Semi	3	£850
	7	Flat	1	£500
	8	Flat	2	£600
	10	Semi	3	£900
	11	Semi	3	£775
	13	Semi	2	£750
*	(AutoNumber)		0	£0

You can unhide fields simply by clicking the Show checkbox again so that it is checked.

Saving the query

Before you do any more, save the query. You will now be able to run this query any time simply by double-clicking its name in the Database window.

- Click the Save icon and enter qryPropertyForRent as the query name.

Sorting data in a query output

Data in a table can be sorted in ascending or descending numeric order on any numeric field such as PropertyRef, Bedrooms or Rent in the Query Results table shown above.

- Click anywhere in the Rent column.
- Click the Sort Ascending button.

Now the records appear in this order:

qryPropertyForRent : Select Query

PropertyRef	Style	Bedrooms	Rent
7	Flat	1	£500
8	Flat	2	£600
13	Semi	2	£750
11	Semi	3	£775
5	Semi	3	£850
10	Semi	3	£900
3	Detached	4	£1,050
(AutoNumber)		0	£0

Record: 1 of 7

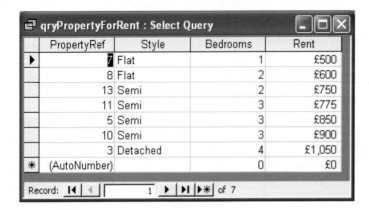

You can also sort in ascending or descending alphabetical order on a text field such as Style.

- Click in the Style column.
- Click the Sort Ascending button.
- Try a different way to sort in reverse alphabetical order. From the Records menu select Sort, Sort Descending.

Now try sorting in Descending order of Bedrooms, so that the properties with the most bedrooms appear at the top of the list.

Sorting on two fields

Sorting the query results table may be useful for a 'one-off' query but next time you run the saved query, the results will be in the original sequence.

You can specify a sort order in the actual query, so that the data will always appear in the desired sequence when you run the query. Also, you can sort on more than one field. (For example, a telephone directory is sorted on Surname and then on Initials, so that Smith J.S. appears before Smith R.A.)

In our query, it might be useful if the results were sorted by style and by number of bedrooms. When you want to sort by more than one field, Access has to prioritise which field it will sort by first. Access will sort by the left-most field first, so in this query, at the moment the Style field is left of Bedrooms, so if we sort by both it will sort by Style then Bedrooms.

- In Design View, click in the Sort row of the Style column then click the small down-arrow.

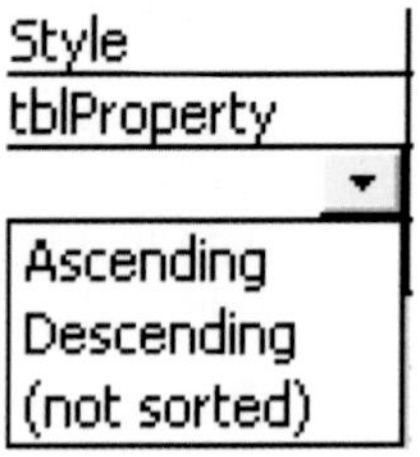

- Click Ascending so that it sorts the house styles alphabetically from A to Z. Note that if you wanted to sort house styles from Z to A (Semi before Flat), you would select Descending.
- Repeat this for the Bedrooms field. Select Ascending to sort the properties in order of least to most bedrooms.
- Run the query.

qryPropertyForRent : Select Query

	PropertyRef	Style	Bedrooms	Rent
▶	3	Detached	4	£1,050
	7	Flat	1	£500
	8	Flat	2	£600
	13	Semi	2	£750
	11	Semi	3	£775
	10	Semi	3	£900
	5	Semi	3	£850
*	(AutoNumber)		0	£0

Record: 1 of 7

That worked – but suppose you wanted to sort first by bedrooms, then house style.

Moving fields

We'll move the Bedrooms field to the left of the Style field so that Access will sort by bedrooms first.

- Return to Design View.
- Click the column header for the Bedrooms column so that the whole column is selected.
- Click and drag the column to the left of the Style field. When you are dragging, you can tell where the column will be dropped by a black line between the columns. Release the mouse when the black line is to the left of the Style field (see below).

Field:	PropertyRef	Style	Bedrooms	Rent	Rented	
Table:	tblProperty	tblProperty	tblProperty	tblProperty	tblProperty	
Sort:		Ascending	Ascending			
Show:	☑	☑	☑	☑	☐	☐
Criteria:					No	
or:						

- Run the query to see if it has worked!

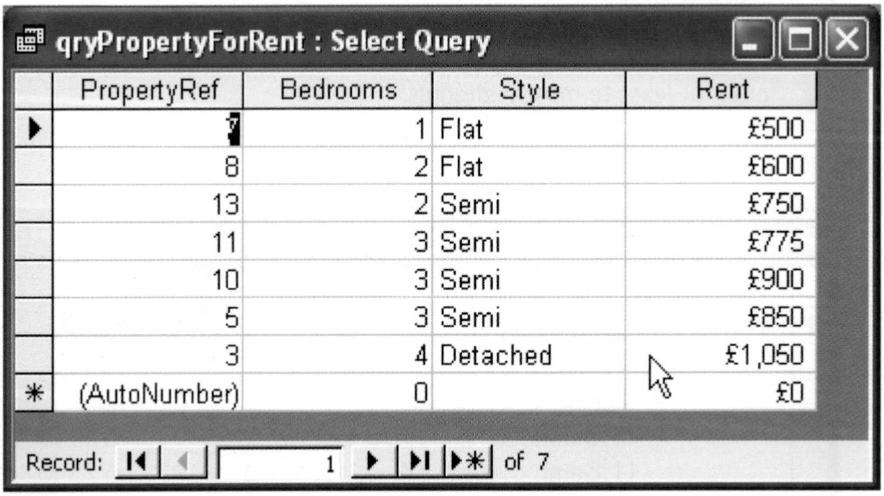

qryPropertyForRent : Select Query

PropertyRef	Bedrooms	Style	Rent
7	1	Flat	£500
8	2	Flat	£600
13	2	Semi	£750
11	3	Semi	£775
10	3	Semi	£900
5	3	Semi	£850
3	4	Detached	£1,050
(AutoNumber)	0		£0

Record: 1 of 7

Adding a second table to the query

If you wanted to see who the landlord was for each of these properties, you would have to add the tblLandlord table to the query.

- Return to Design View.

- Click the Show Table button on the Query Design toolbar.

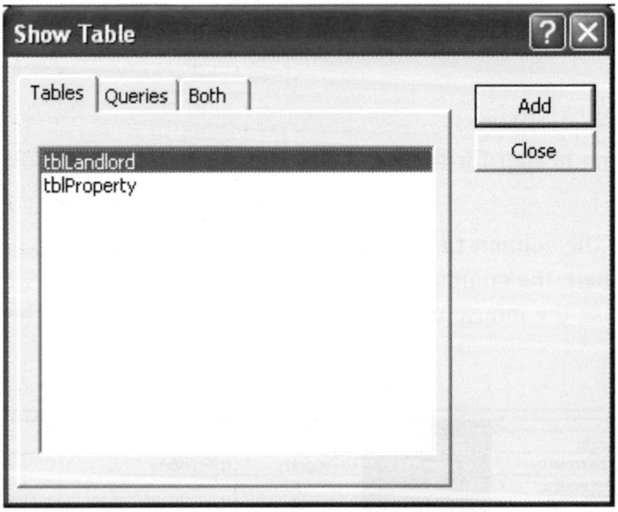

- Make sure tblLandlord is selected then click Add. Click Close.

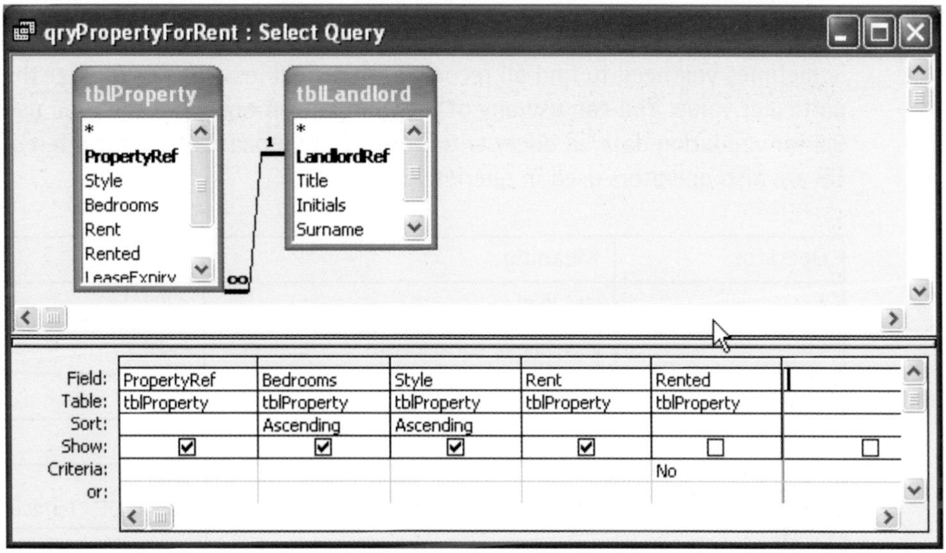

tblLandlord is added to the query. Now we want to add the fields Title, Initials and Surname from the tblLandlord table to the query grid.

- Double-click the fields Title, Initials and Surname from tblLandlord to add them.
- Run the query.

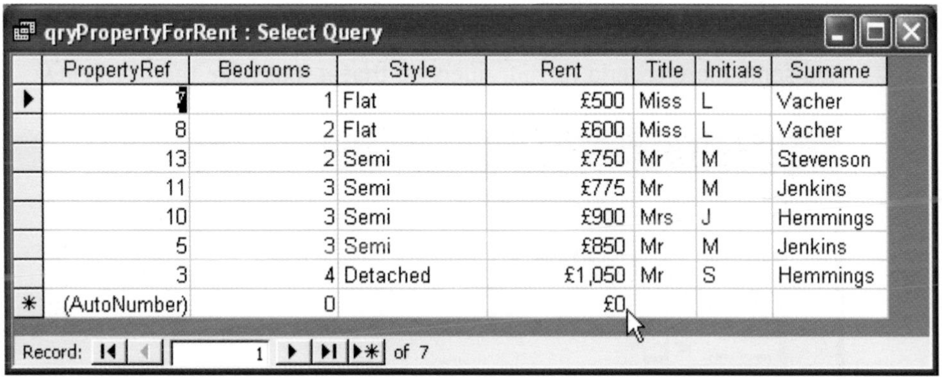
qryPropertyForRent : Select Query

PropertyRef	Bedrooms	Style	Rent	Title	Initials	Surname
7	1	Flat	£500	Miss	L	Vacher
8	2	Flat	£600	Miss	L	Vacher
13	2	Semi	£750	Mr	M	Stevenson
11	3	Semi	£775	Mr	M	Jenkins
10	3	Semi	£900	Mrs	J	Hemmings
5	3	Semi	£850	Mr	M	Jenkins
3	4	Detached	£1,050	Mr	S	Hemmings
(AutoNumber)	0		£0			

Record: 1 of 7

Now you can see who owns which property!

Tip:
If you get lots of repeated rows, just check you haven't added any of the tables more than once. Do this by using the scroll bars in the top part of the query window in Design View to search for extra tables.

Using operators

Sometimes you need to find all records with a field less than or greater than a particular value. You can use any of the **comparison operators** that you used in Chapter 5.5 for validating data, in query criteria. They are repeated here for reference. **AND** and **OR** are also operators used in queries.

Operator	Meaning	Example
<	less than	<20
<=	less than or equal to	<=20
>	greater than	>0
>=	greater than or equal to	>=0
=	equal to	=20 ="Flat" OR "Terraced"
<>	not equal to	<>"Semi"
BETWEEN	test for a range of values. Must be two comparison values (a low & high value) separated by AND operator	BETWEEN 01/12/2002 AND 25/12/2002
AND	All criteria must be satisfied	Bedrooms>1 AND Rent<800 AND Rented="No"
OR	At least one of the criteria must be satisfied	="Flat" OR "Semi"

Add some more criteria to your query so that it looks like the one below:

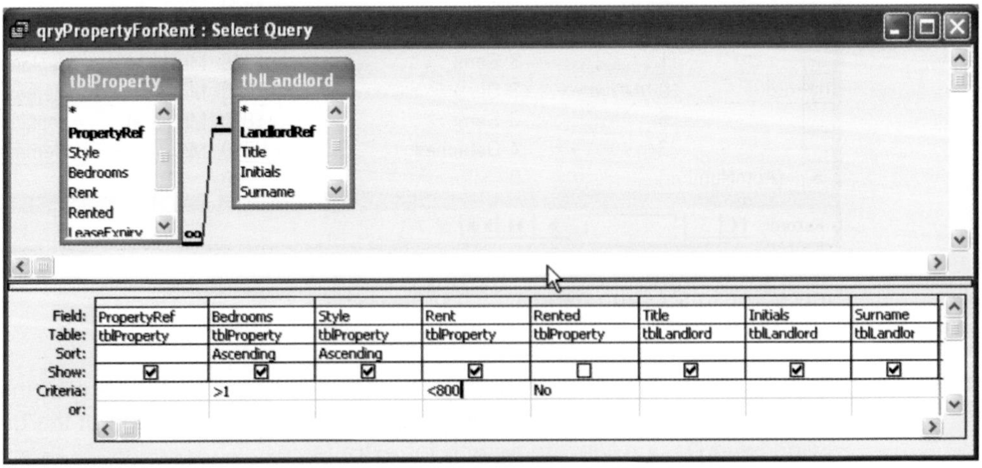

Run the query to see the effect of the criteria.

qryPropertyForRent : Select Query

	PropertyRef	Bedrooms	Style	Rent	Title	Initials	Surname
▶	3	2	Flat	£600	Miss	L	Vacher
	13	2	Semi	£750	Mr	M	Stevenson
	11	3	Semi	£775	Mr	M	Jenkins
*	(AutoNumber)	0		£0			

Record: 1 of 3

Save your query.

Notice that when you set query criteria, criteria placed on the same line ALL have to be satisfied. This is equivalent to the "AND" condition in the Operator table above.

To enter criteria to find all properties which are EITHER "Flat" OR "Semi", you could write the criteria as shown below:

PropertyRef	Bedrooms	Style	Rent	Title	In
tblProperty	tblProperty	tblProperty	tblProperty	tblLandlord	tb
	Ascending	Ascending			
☑	☑	☑	☑	☑	
		"Flat" Or "Semi"			

Alternatively, you can write the criteria one beneath the other:

PropertyRef	Bedrooms	Style	Rent	Title	In
tblProperty	tblProperty	tblProperty	tblProperty	tblLandlord	tb
	Ascending	Ascending			
☑	☑	☑	☑	☑	
		"Flat"			
		"Semi"			

You could find all properties which are EITHER 1-bedroomed OR a Flat:

PropertyRef	Bedrooms	Style	Rent	Title	In
tblProperty	tblProperty	tblProperty	tblProperty	tblLandlord	tb
	Ascending	Ascending			
☑	☑	☑	☑	☑	
		"Flat"			
	1				

This produces the following results table:

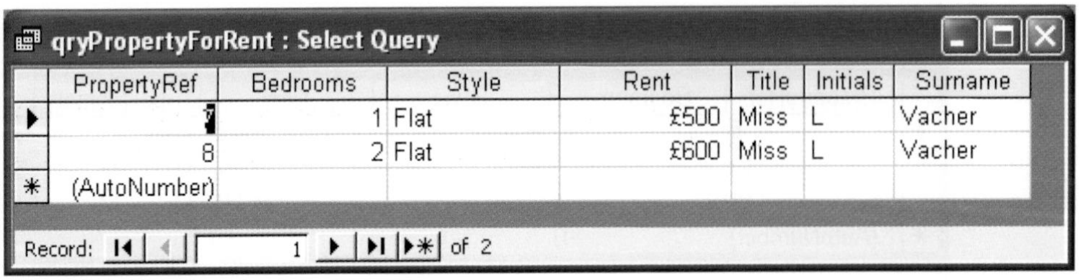

Printing a query

All the options for printing a query are very similar to those for printing a table or form.

- In Datasheet View (the Results table), click the Print Preview icon.

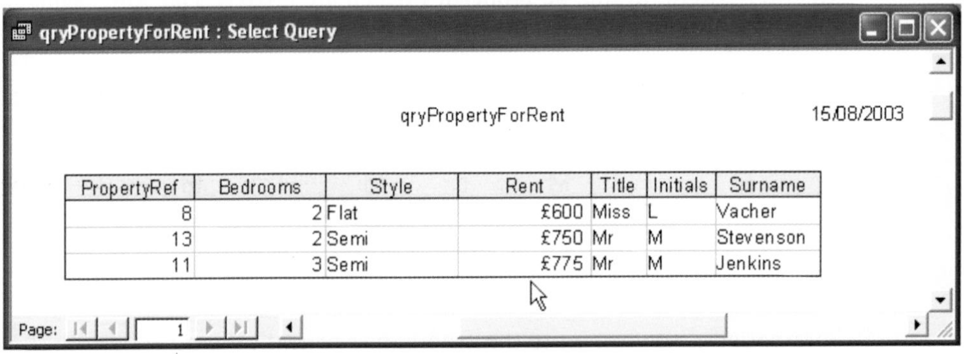

- Click Close to exit Print Preview.
- Select File, Page Setup then click the Page tab to change page orientation and paper size.
- Select File, Print to set which pages to print and the number of copies. If you want to print, click OK, otherwise click Cancel.

- Close the query by clicking the Close button.

Tip:
In the Database window, you will see your query when the Queries tab is selected. You can delete an unwanted query by selecting it and pressing the Delete key.

Exercise

1. (a) Open the student database that you downloaded from the web site www.payne-gallway.co.uk/ecdl.

   (b) Create a query to select all records of students who come from Westcliff School. Display only the fields for Surname, Forename, Sex and School.

   (c) Run the query.

   (d) Sort the records in the results table so that all the records for male students appear before all female students.

   (e) Save your query as qryWestcliff.

   (f) Print the query results.

2. (a) Create a second query to select all records of students who were born before 01/09/1986.

   (b) Sort the records into ascending order of Surname and Forename.

   (c) Save your query as qryStudentAge

   (d) Run the query.

   (e) Print out the query results on a single page in Landscape orientation.

CHAPTER 5.10 Reports

Suppose you want to present the data in a table or query in a neater way, for example with a proper title. For this you would use a Report. Reports allow you to present data in a wide variety of ways. They can be based on queries or on tables.

- Make sure the Hemlets database is open and you can see the Database window.

Reports based on tables

First we'll create a report based on the tblLandlord table which will simply list all the landlords and their contact details.

- In the Database window, click to select the Reports tab.
- Double-click Create report by using wizard.

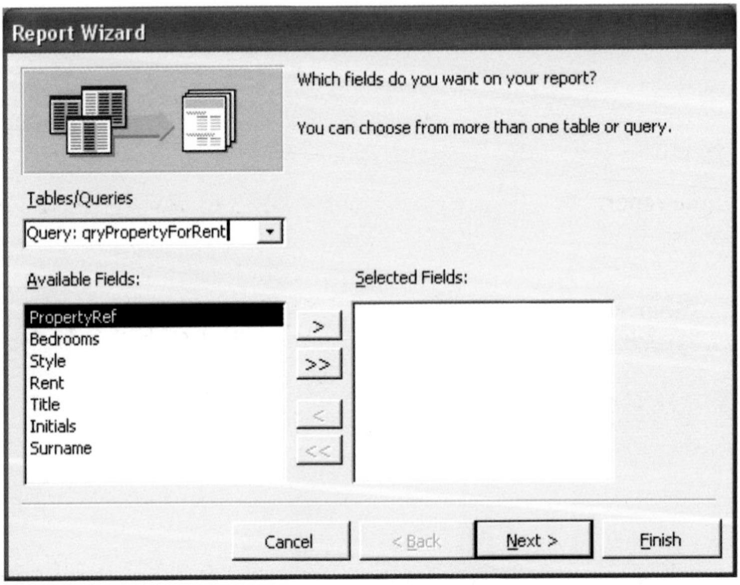

- Select tblLandlord from the Tables/Queries dropdown list.
- We want all the fields to appear in the report, so click >>. Click Next.

- You are asked about Grouping Levels. We won't need any for this report, so leave the settings as below:

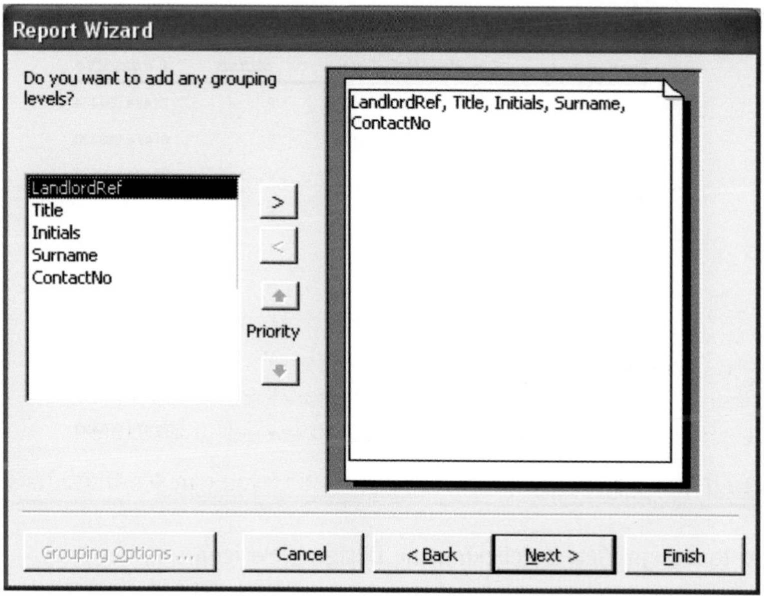

- Click Next. We can specify a sort order. It would be useful to have the landlords sorted by Surname, so select Surname from the first dropdown list and leave the button adjacent as Ascending. Click Next.

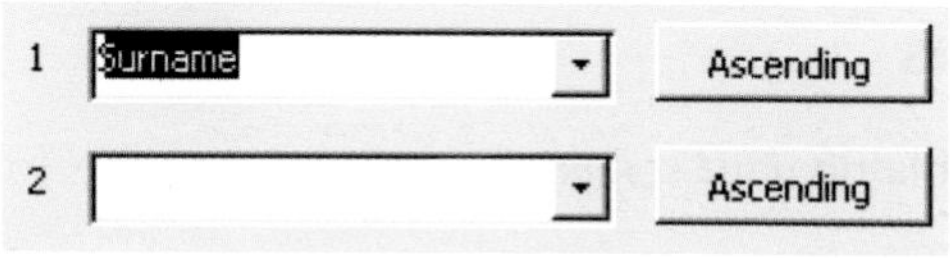

- Click Next two more times – you don't need to make changes to the presentation.
- Give the report the title rptLandlordDetails. This is what the report will then be saved as.

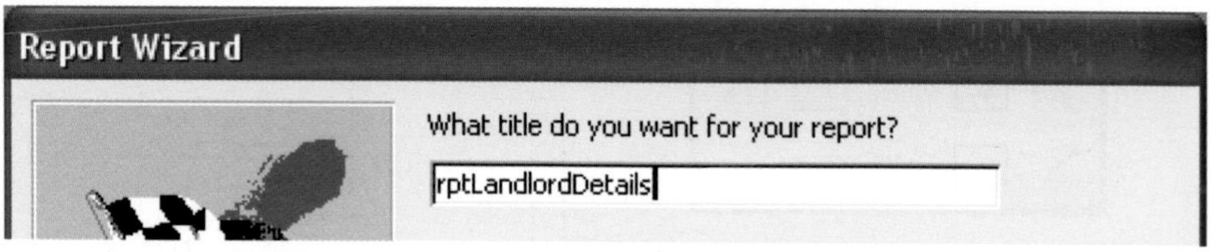

Tip:
Although Access only asks you for a title for the report, it will actually save the report with the title name.

- Click Finish to view the report.

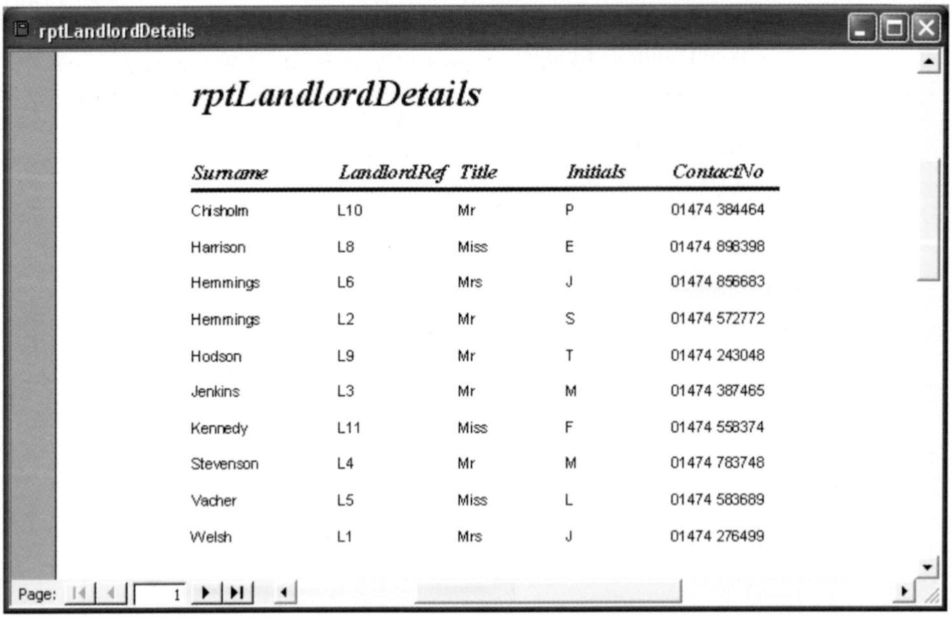
rptLandlordDetails

rptLandlordDetails

Surname	*LandlordRef*	*Title*	*Initials*	*ContactNo*
Chisholm	L10	Mr	P	01474 384464
Harrison	L8	Miss	E	01474 898398
Hemmings	L6	Mrs	J	01474 856683
Hemmings	L2	Mr	S	01474 572772
Hodson	L9	Mr	T	01474 243048
Jenkins	L3	Mr	M	01474 387465
Kennedy	L11	Miss	F	01474 558374
Stevenson	L4	Mr	M	01474 783748
Vacher	L5	Miss	L	01474 583689
Welsh	L1	Mrs	J	01474 276499

Page: 1

- Go to Design View by clicking the Design View icon.
- Now we'll change the title of the report. First click where it says rptLandlordDetails so that handles appear around the title, and then click again on the title text. Now you can delete the text and type the new title, Landlord Details.

Adding text to Headers and Footers

- The Toolbox should be visible on your screen. If it is not, click the Toolbox icon.

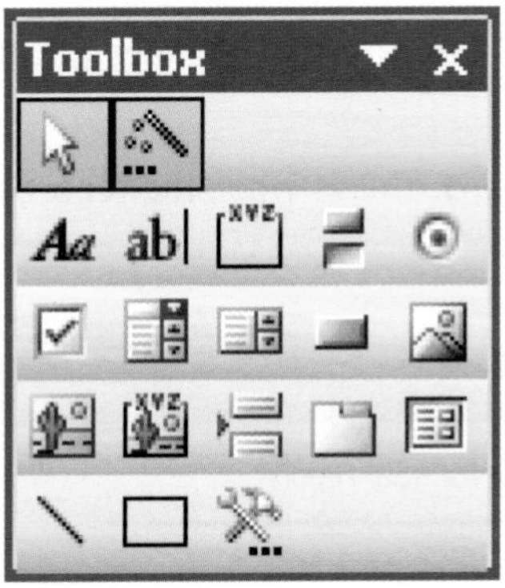

There is already some text in the Report Header – the title. We'll add another label.

- Click the Label icon, then click and drag out a rectangle to the right of the title.
- Type the text Hemlets Ltd.

Now we'll do the same with the Report Footer.

- Click the Label icon, then click and drag out a rectangle at the bottom of the report under the Report Footer. Don't worry that there's no page there yet.
- Type the text Hemlets Database.

Your report should look something like this:

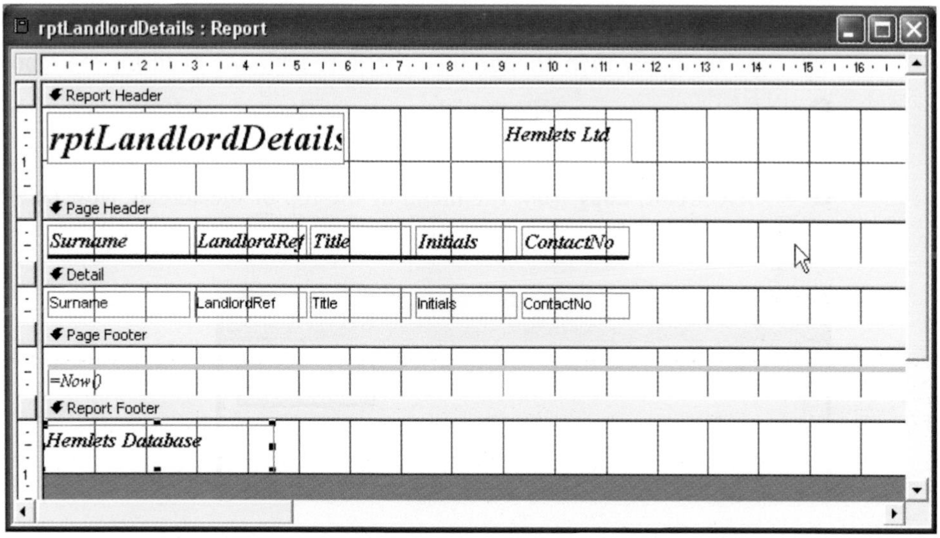

You can modify the footer text by clicking in the box and editing it.

- View the report by clicking the Print Preview icon.

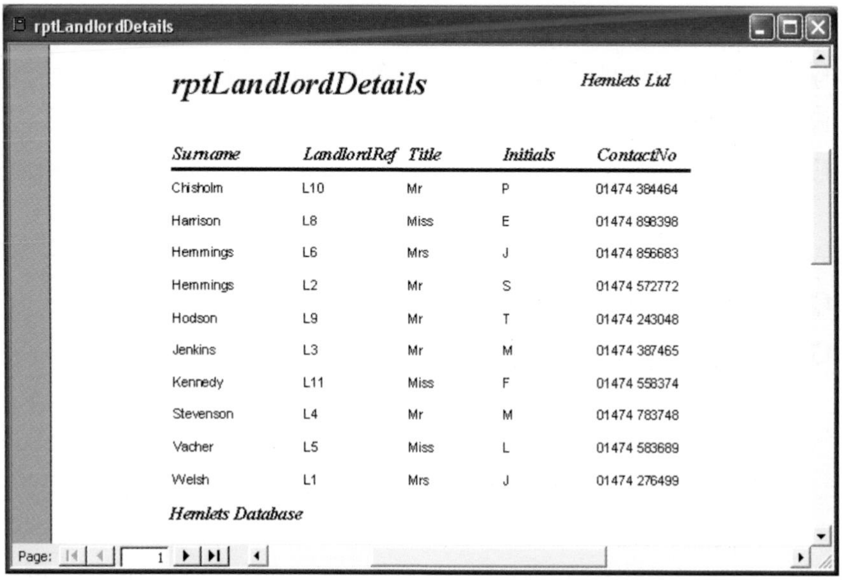

- Save and close your report.

Reports based on queries

Hemlets would like a report that lists each landlord and the properties they own that are being rented out. Hemlets will use this to calculate how much rent the landlord is earning every month.

This report will use data from both tblLandlord and tblProperty, and will use as its source a query that combines the fields from both tables.

We already have a query that contains the fields we want – the qryPropertyForRent. We will copy the query then change the criteria to what we need for the report.

- In the Database window, make sure the Queries tab is selected, then click qryPropertyForRent to select it.
- Select Edit, Copy from the menu at the top of the screen. Now select Edit, Paste from the menu.

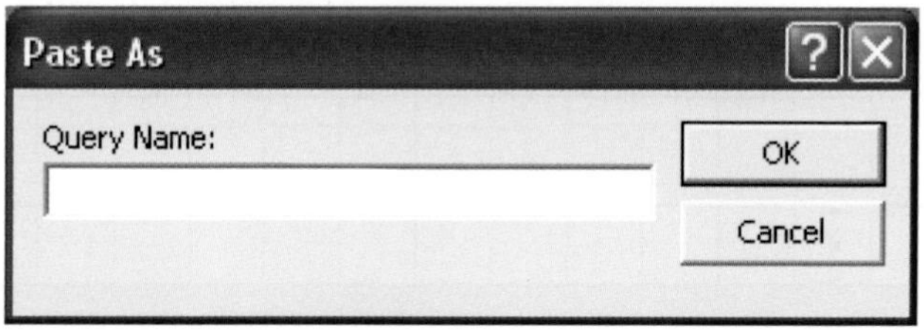

You are asked to give a name for the new query.

- Type qryLandlordIncome and click OK.

Tip:
You can copy and paste all other database objects like Tables and Forms in just the same way.

- Now open qryLandlordIncome in Design View by selecting it then clicking Design.

We'll delete all the criteria currently in the query grid.

- Delete each criterion in turn by clicking it, then using either the Delete or Backspace keys.

We also want to remove all the entries in the Sort row.

- Delete these in the same way as you did the Criteria.
- Add the criterion Yes to the Rented column. Your query should now look like the one on the next page.

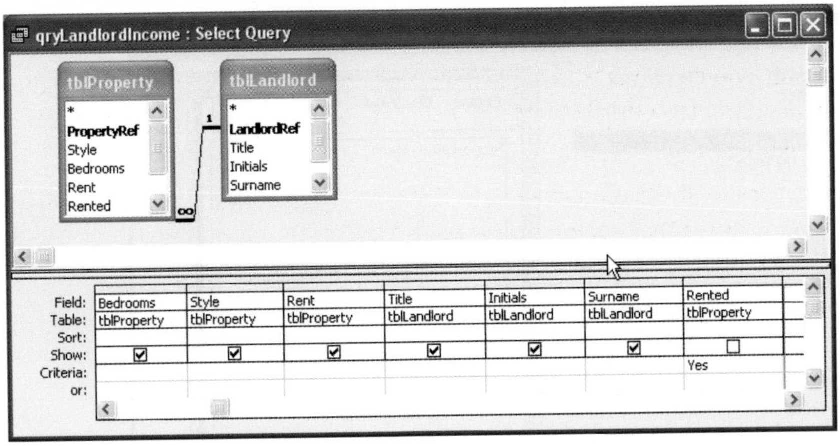

- It is a good idea to add the sorting rules in the query rather than the report. Move the Surname field to the left of the query and give it an Ascending sort. This will sort the landlords alphabetically in the query.
- Give the Rent column a Descending sort.
- Save and close the query.

Creating the report

- In the Database window, click to select the Reports tab.
- Double-click Create report by using wizard.
- Make sure qryLandlordIncome is selected in the Tables/Queries box. We want all the fields in the query except Style and Bedrooms. To include a field, just click to select it, then click >.
- Click the fields in the order shown.

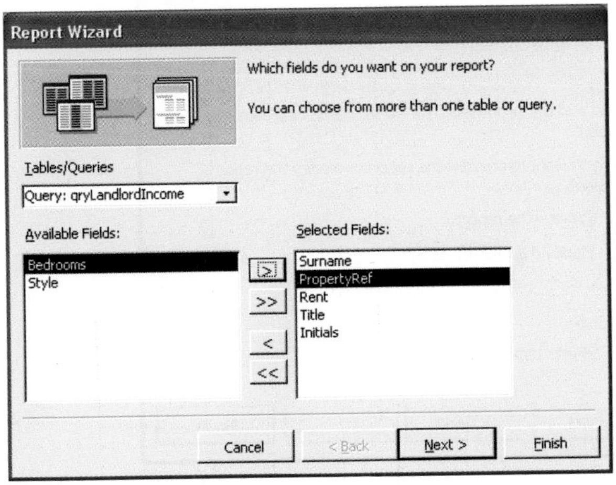

- Click Next. You are now asked how you want to view the data. We want the results grouped by Landlord, so click to select tblLandlord.

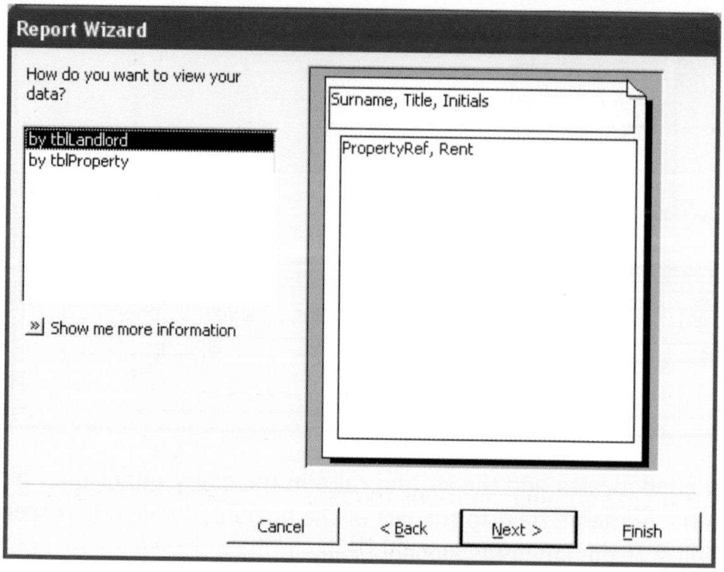

- Click Next. We don't need to add any grouping levels, as the results are already grouped by tblLandlord, so just click Next.
- You can now specify which fields you want to sort by. We've already set the sorting rules in the underlying query so we don't need to specify them again here. Click Next.
- Click Next two more times – you don't need to change any of the presentation options.
- Give the report the title rptLandlordIncome; this is what it will be saved as.

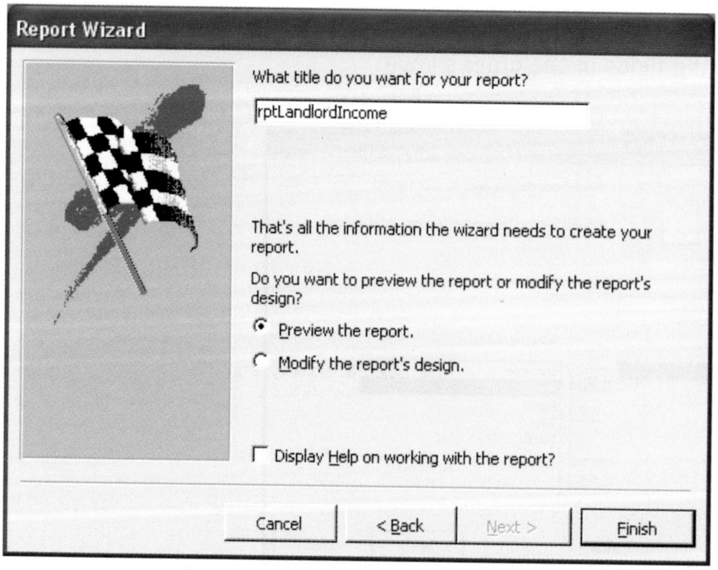

- Click Finish.

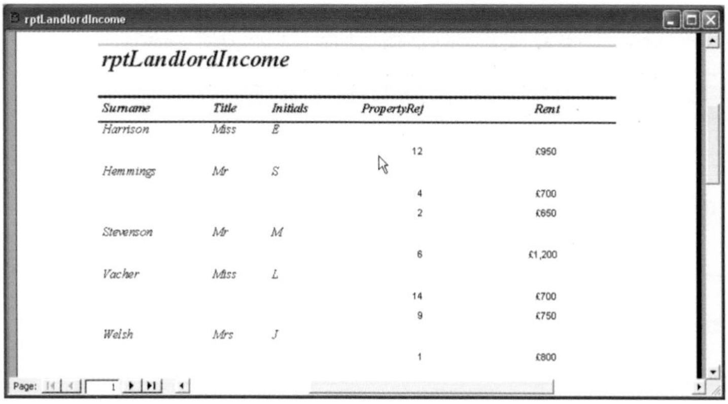

Your report will appear!

We've got a few changes and additions to make to it, which we'll do in Design View.

Change to Design View by clicking the Design View icon.

Adding a Sum field

We need the report to calculate the total income for each landlord by summing the rent for each of the properties that are rented.

To sum the rent for each landlord separately, we need to add a field to the Group Footer. Currently there is no Group Footer so we'll add it now.

Click the Sorting and Grouping button on the Report Design toolbar.

Notice that the report is sorted in Ascending order of Surname (A-Z). You could change this by clicking next to the word Ascending and selecting Descending from the dropdown menu.

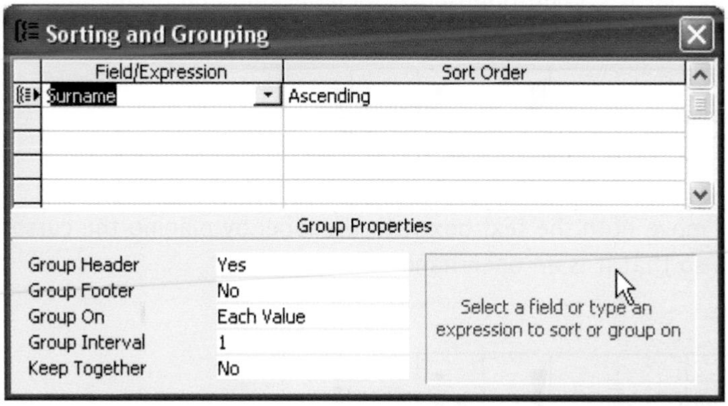

At the bottom where it says Group Footer, change the No to a Yes.

Close the Sorting and Grouping window by clicking its red Close icon.

There should now be a section on the report called Surname Footer.

Now we'll add a field. Click the Text Box button in the toolbox.

- Click once in the Surname Footer to insert the field.

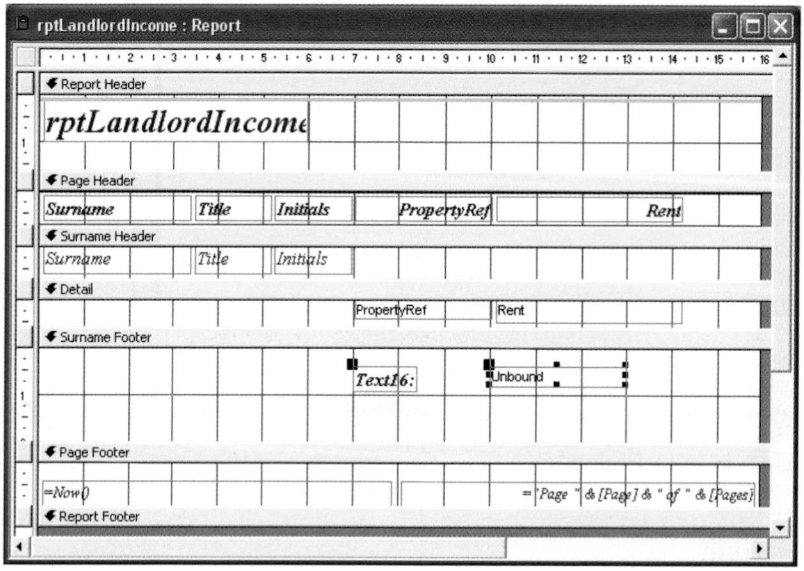

- Click where it says Unbound, and change the text to say =Sum(Rent).
- Change the label from Text16 to Total Rental Income.

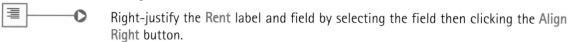

- Right-justify the Rent label and field by selecting the field then clicking the Align Right button.
- Now we'll change the title to say Landlord Income Report. Click where it says rptLandlordIncome so that handles appear around the title, then click again on the title text. Now you can delete the text and type the new title.
- You can move the fields individually by placing the cursor in the top left-hand corner so that it's a pointing finger, then clicking and dragging.

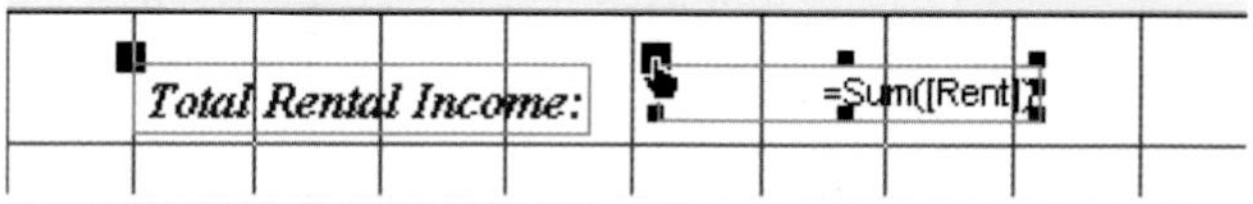

- You can move both the text box with the label by placing the cursor over the text box so that it is an open hand.

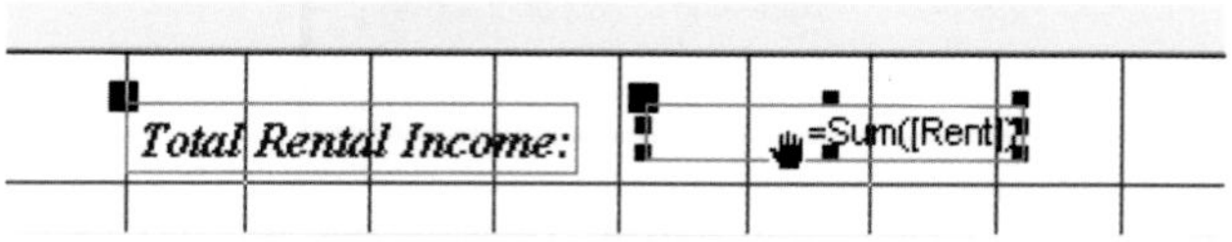

- You can make the Surname Footer bigger or smaller by clicking and dragging the grey border between sections.

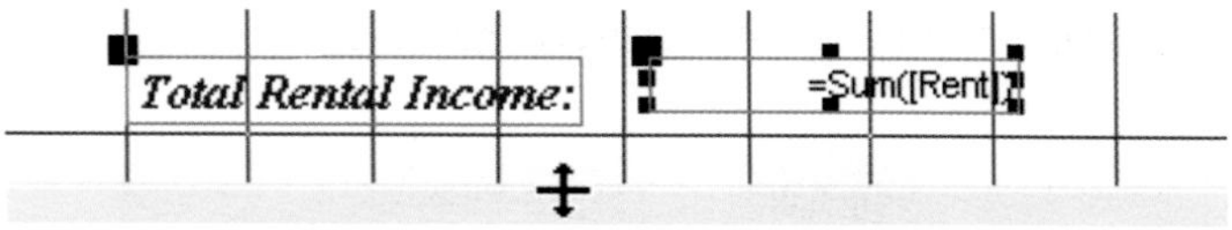

You can resize the text boxes by clicking and dragging the handles that appear when you select them.

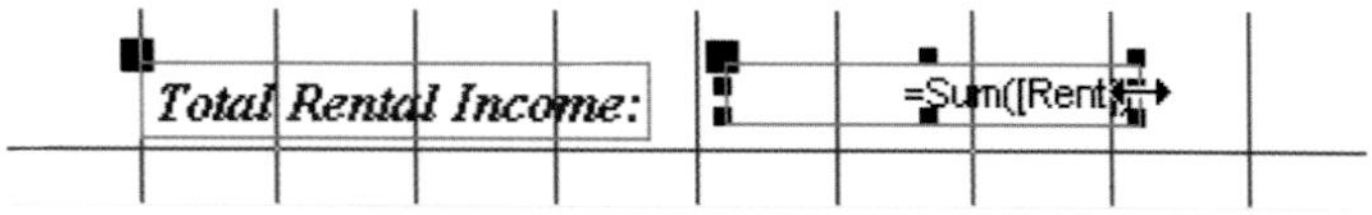

Reposition the fields to look like the report below:

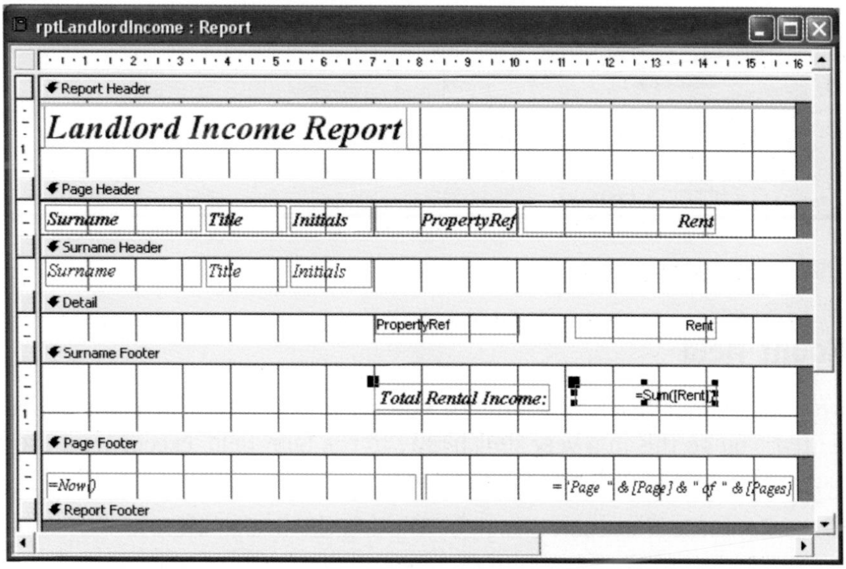

Right-click the field =Sum(Rent) and select Properties in the pop-up menu.

In the Properties box, change the Format to Currency, and Decimal Places to 0.

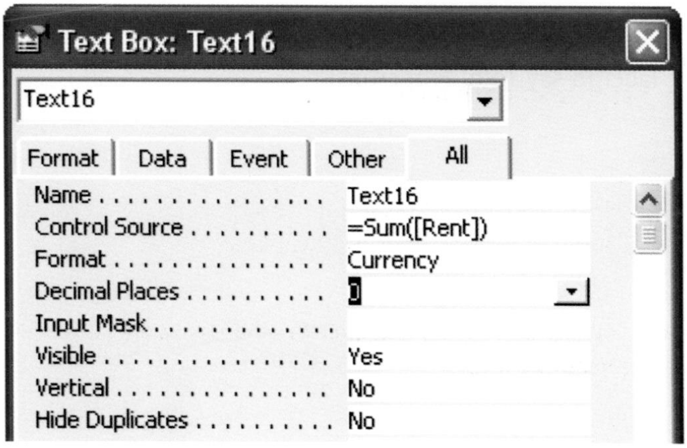

Click **Print Preview** to preview the report.

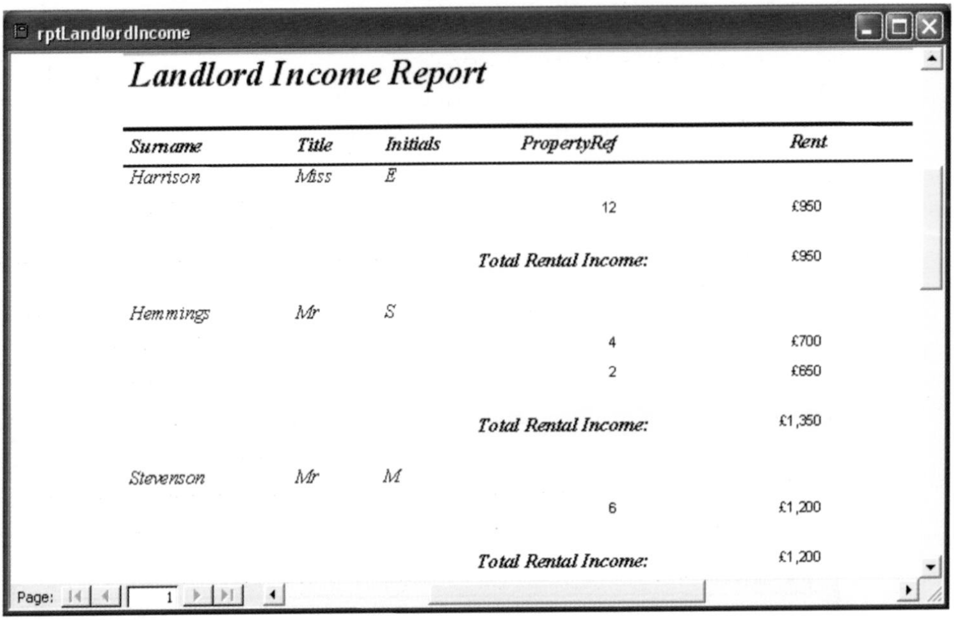

That looks pretty smart!

Adding a Count field

Now we'll add a field that totals the number of properties each landlord currently has rented. You do this in a very similar way to the **Sum** field, except we'll use the **Count** expression instead of the **Sum** expression.

- Return to the report design by clicking the **Design View** icon.
- Click on the **Sum** field you have just created. Select **Edit**, **Copy** from the menu.
- Now select **Edit**, **Paste** from the menu. The field will be copied and pasted below the original.
- All you need to do now is change the word **Sum** to the word **Count**, as shown below.
- Change the label to say **Total Properties:**.

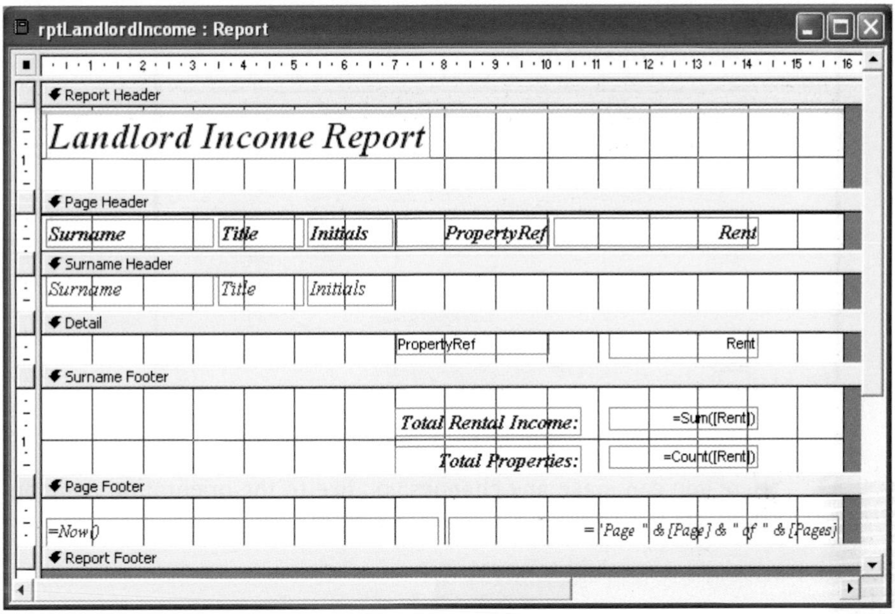

- In the Properties box, change the Format property to General Number, and Decimal Places to 0.
- Preview the report by clicking Print Preview.

Other useful expressions

So far you've used the Sum and Count expressions. Others which you can also substitute in are:

- Minimum: gives the minimum value of all values in the group. In our example, where there was more than one property it would give the value of the smallest rent.
- Maximum: like minimum, except gives the maximum rent for a particular landlord's properties.
- Average: gives the average of all values in the group. In our example where there is more than one property, it would give the average of all the rents for each landlord.

Printing a report

This is very similar to printing tables, forms and queries.

You are already familiar with the report Print Preview.

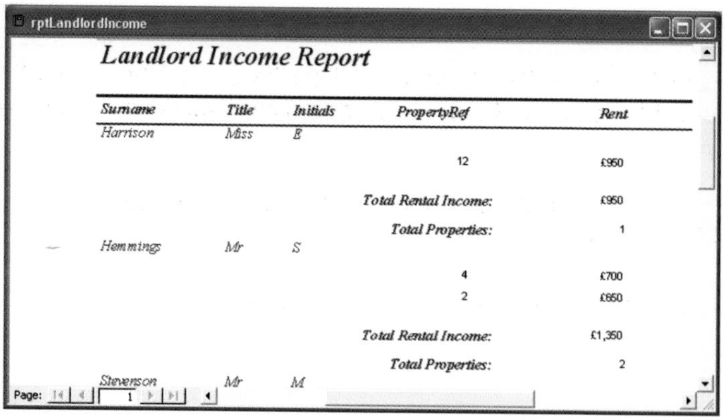

- Select File, Page Setup or click Setup on the toolbar.
- Here you can make any changes you like to the orientation and paper size. Click the Page tab to change the paper size.

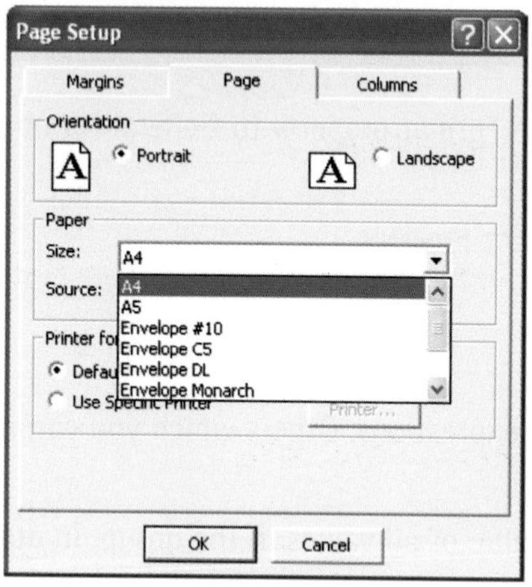

- Select File, Print from the menu.

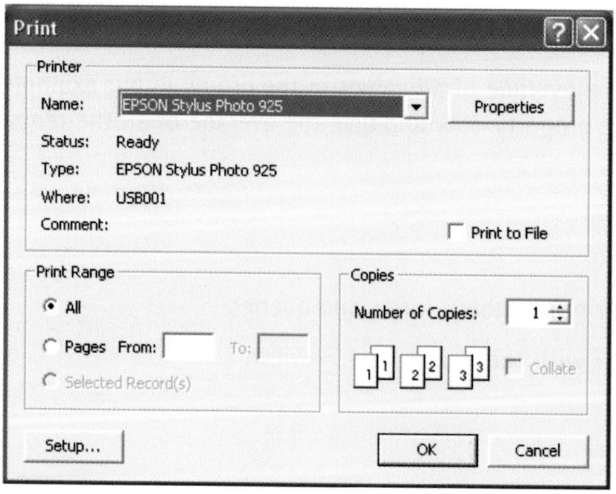

Here you can select which pages of the report to print and how many copies you want.

- Click OK to print, otherwise click Cancel.
- Save and close the report, either by clicking the Close icon or by selecting File, Close from the menu bar. Click Yes when asked if you wish to save your changes.

Tip:
You can delete an unwanted report by selecting it in the Database window and pressing the Delete key.

- Close the database. You've reached the end of the module!

Exercise

The Softball database, which you should download from the Payne-Gallway web site www.payne-gallway.co.uk/ecdl, contains information on players and teams in a Softball league. The database contains two tables, a Team table for team information such as coach name and contact number, and a Player table containing data on the players in each team, such as surname and position.

1. Open the Softball database.
2. Create a query using both tables and all fields.
3. Save the query as query1.
4. Create a report based on query1. Group the report by TeamName; sort the results by Surname.
5. Save the report as report1.
6. Add a Count field to count the players in each team.
7. Save and close the database.

Module 6

Presentation

In this module you will find out how to use presentation tools on a computer. You will learn how to:

- create a presentation using different slide layouts for display and printed distribution
- format and modify presentations
- insert images, charts and drawn objects into a presentation
- duplicate and move text, pictures, images and charts within a presentation
- duplicate and move text, pictures, images and charts between presentations
- use various slide show effects

Module 6 Table of Contents

CHAPTER 6.1

The Basics

What is Microsoft PowerPoint?

Microsoft PowerPoint is the leading graphics presentation package. You can use it to create, design and organise professional presentations quickly and easily.

Planning a presentation

To deliver an effective presentation you need to consider who your audience is, and prepare your slides to suit them.

Whoever your presentation is for, here are a few basic guidelines:

- Start with a title screen showing what the project is about.
- Don't put more than 4 or 5 bullets on each slide. People can't concentrate on too much information at once.
- Keep each point short and simple. You may want to talk around each point to explain it in further detail.
- Sound, graphics and animation can add interest, but don't overdo them!

Getting started

- Load Microsoft PowerPoint. You can do this in one of two ways:
- *Either* double-click the PowerPoint icon

- *Or* click Start at the bottom left of the screen, then click All Programs, then click

Your screen will look like the one below:

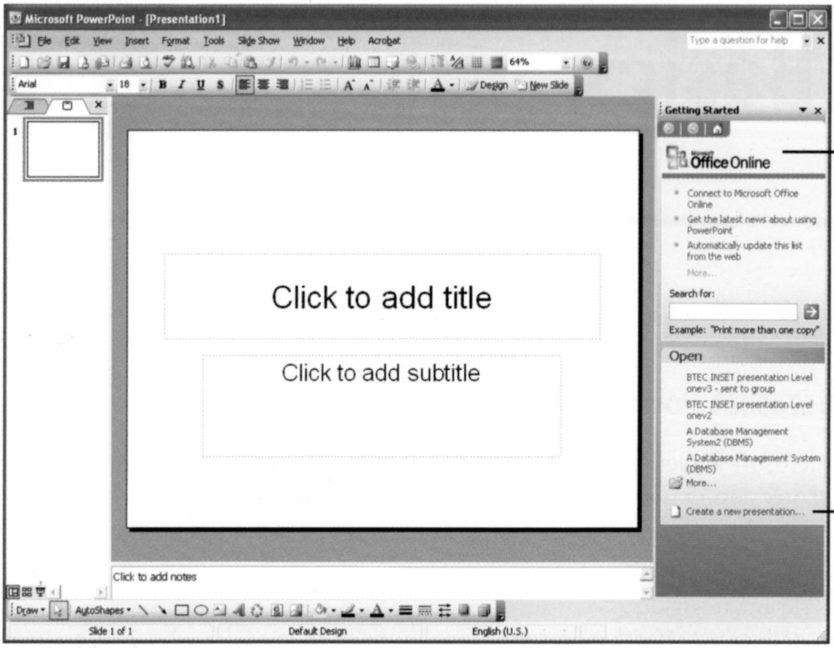

The Task pane

On the right of the screen is the Task pane. If you can't see this pane:

- Go to View, Task pane on the Main Menu bar at the top of the screen.

This pane should appear every time you open PowerPoint, and it contains a list of commonly used commands. At each stage of your presentation, PowerPoint will display different menus in this Task pane. You should find this very useful, as the contents of the menu changes according to what you are doing, so it displays the most relevant options.

If you want to see the different menus that can appear in the Task pane, or switch to a particular menu, just click the small down-arrow at the top of the Task pane, then click to select the menu that you want.

Tip:

You have probably come across the Task pane in other Office 2003 or XP applications.

Starting a blank presentation

- Click Create a new presentation in the Task pane.
- Click Blank Presentation in the New Presentation pane.

You will notice that the Task pane automatically changes to display the Slide Layout options.

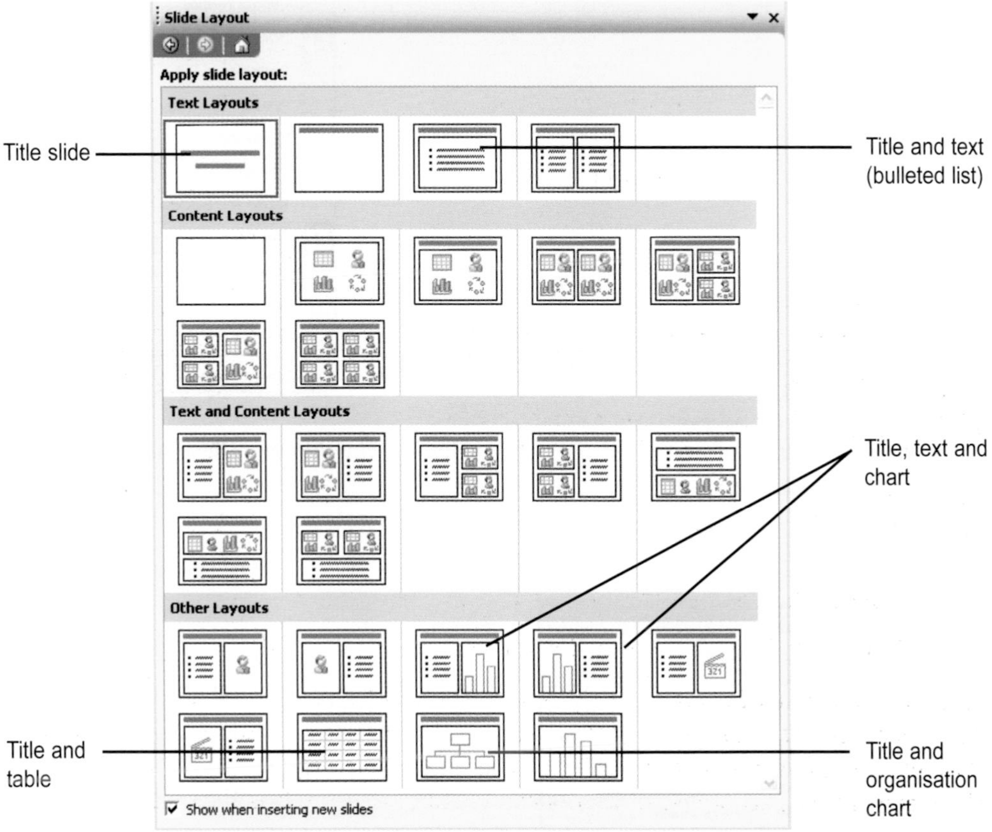

You can click on one of these options to change the layout of a slide.

PowerPoint has automatically selected the Title Slide layout, which is exactly what we want. The boxes marked out on the screen are called Placeholders. These show where you will place your text and graphics.

Toolbars

You will learn about what individual toolbars and buttons do as they become relevant whilst you are creating your presentation. The tips that follow apply to all toolbars, and will be useful if you cannot find a particular toolbar or think that you are missing a button or two! You may find that you already know most of this – it will be pretty much the same as you have experienced in other Microsoft applications such as Word or Excel.

Hiding and displaying toolbars

You can select which toolbars are displayed on your screen. If you find that you can't find a particular button it might be worth checking that you have the right toolbars displayed.

- Select View, Toolbars and select the toolbar you want from the list that appears.

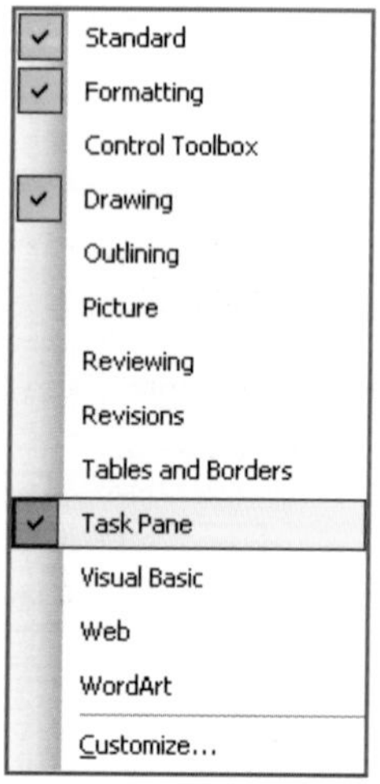

Modifying basic options

There are a number of options that users can select in PowerPoint. These are found in the Options dialogue box – let's have a look.

- Select Tools, Options from the main menu.

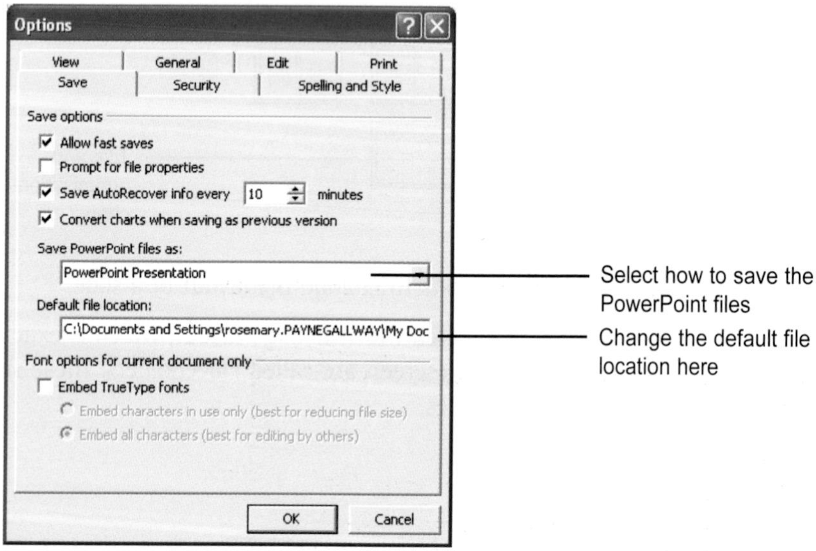

- Click the Save tab and you can select how to save PowerPoint files (i.e. as a web page or as a particular version of PowerPoint presentation) and the default location for saving your files e.g. My Documents folder.
- Click the General tab and you can change the user name (i.e. the author name listed under the file properties).

Using the Help functions

If at any time you aren't sure how to do something in PowerPoint, you can search the Help files for instructions on your chosen subject. For example, let's search for help on copying and pasting.

- Select Help, Microsoft Office PowerPoint Help from the menu.

You will see the PowerPoint Help window appear.

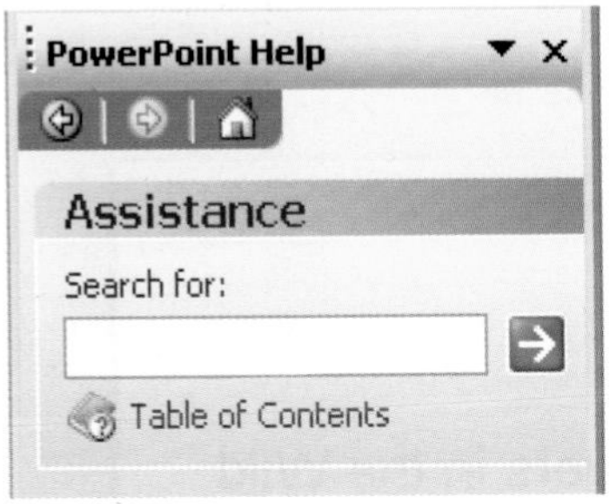

- Type copying and pasting into the Search for: box, then click the Start Searching button.
- Select Copy and paste text from the next pop-up box.

A Help window appears giving information on this topic.

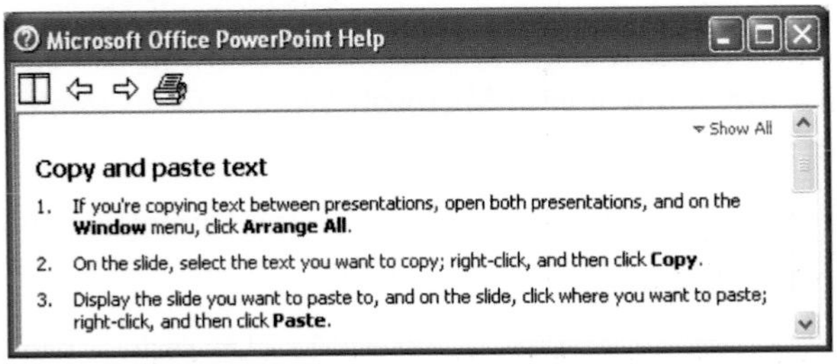

- Click the red Close icon to close the Help window.
- Click the black Close icon to close the Task pane.

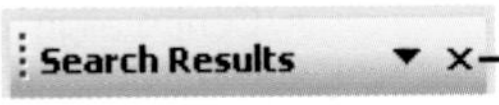

Click here to close the Task pane

Adding text to the title slide

- Click in the box marked Click to add title and type the title Conserving Tigers in the Wild.
- Now add a sub-title. Click where indicated and type Framework and Strategy for Action 2003.

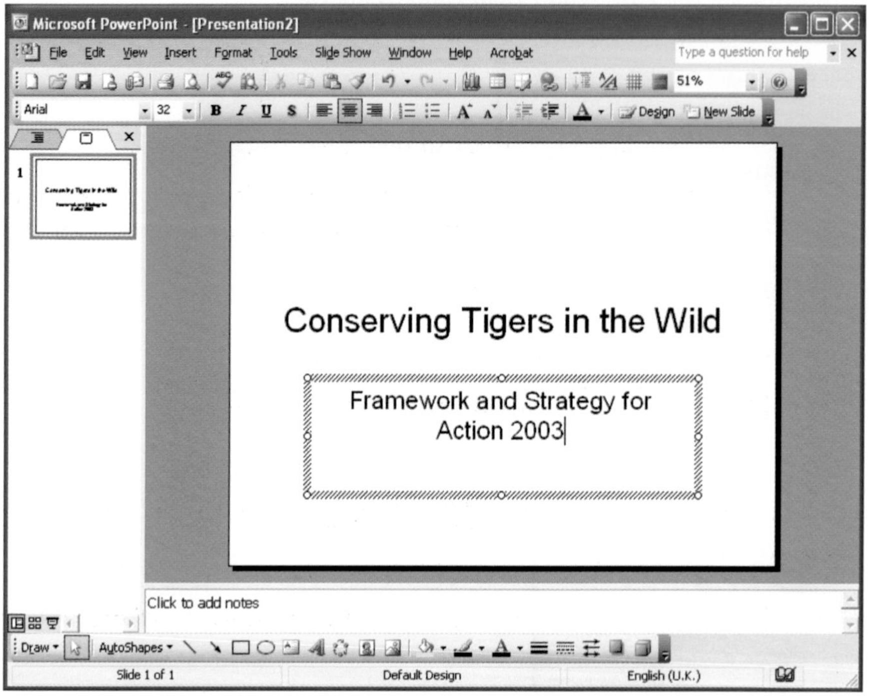

Tip:
To see what each button on the toolbar is called, just place the cursor over that button for a few seconds and the name should pop up.

Formatting and moving the text

You can click the text boxes to move them around the screen. You can also format the text in each text box just like you would in Microsoft Word – for example, change its colour, size or alignment.

Most of the commands you will need for this will be on the Formatting toolbar. Some of the most frequently used buttons are labelled below:

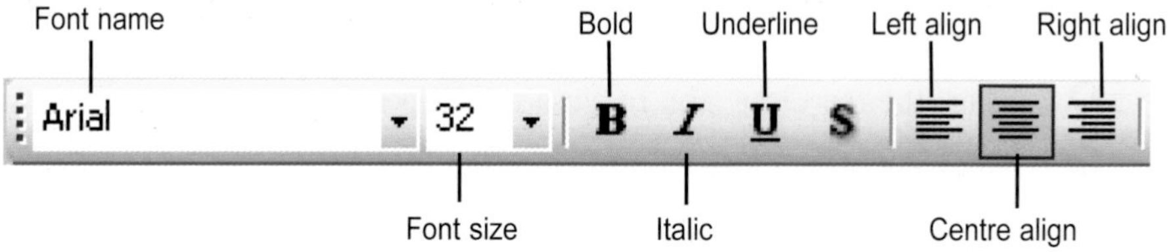

To format text you need to select the text box by clicking its border. When the border has changed from a diagonal striped box to a fuzzy one you know you can start formatting the text.

If you want to edit, add or delete text in a box, click inside the box. The border changes to diagonal stripes.

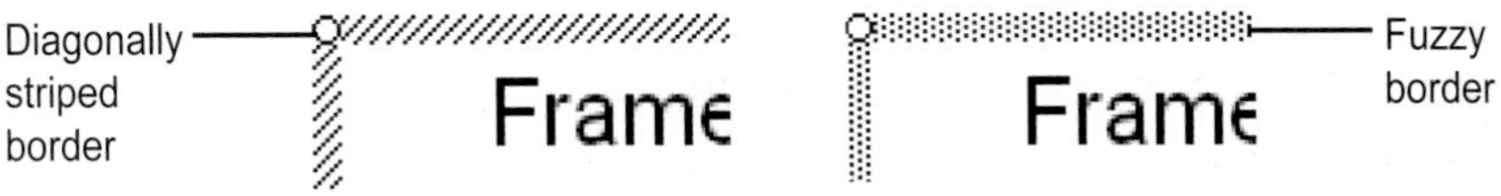

- Select the sub-title text box so that it has a fuzzy border.
- Change the font to Times New Roman by clicking the down-arrow in the Font box on the Formatting toolbar and choosing it from the list that appears.

- Make the text italic by clicking on the Italic button.

Tip:
To change the case of selected text, select Format, Change Case.

The text is already centred left and right, but not top and bottom. We will do this now:

- Make sure the text box is selected then right-click anywhere on the text.

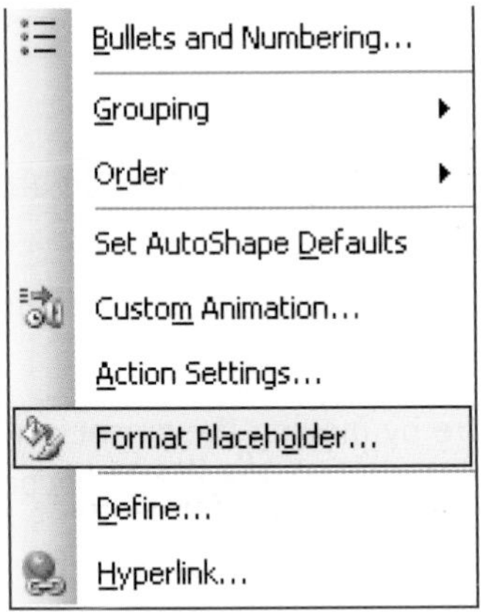

- Click to select the option Format Placeholder (this text box is actually called a Placeholder because it is part of the Slide Layout, but it is essentially the same as a text box).
- Select the Text Box tab, then select Middle from the dropdown list for Text Anchor Point.

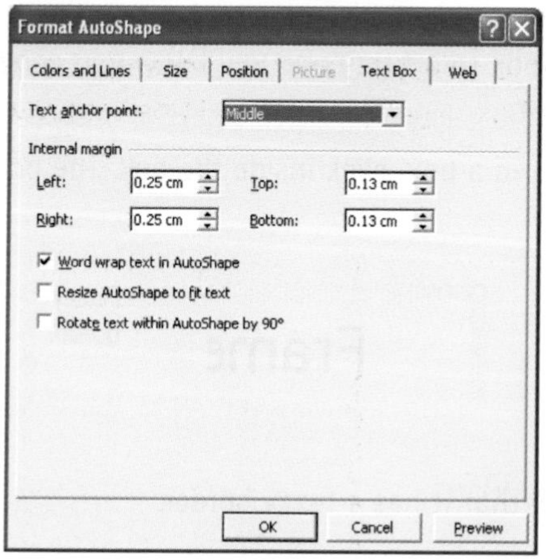

- Click OK to close the dialogue box.

The text should now be centred both ways in the text box (or placeholder).

Resizing and moving text boxes and placeholders

It would be nice if the sub-title text appeared on one line rather than two, but without making the text smaller. To do this we will alter the size of the text box using the **handles**.

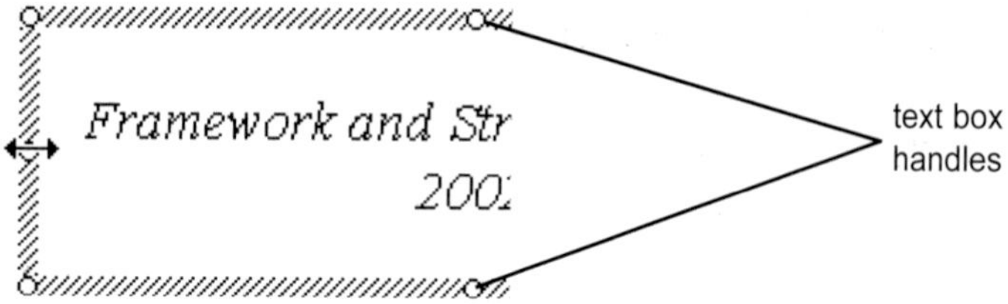

- Move the cursor over the left-hand handle so that it becomes an arrow like in the screenshot above.
- Click and drag the handle to make the text box wider. Repeat this until the text fits on one line. Don't worry that it is now a bit too far left.
- Now move the text box back to the centre by moving the cursor over the text box border somewhere where there is no handle, so the cursor becomes a cross:

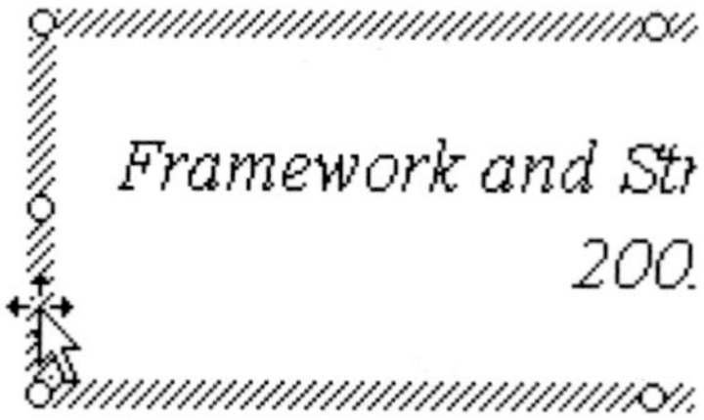

- Click and drag the box until it looks central. Click outside the text box to deselect it.

Tip:
To delete a text box, click its border to select it and then press the **Delete** key. To delete part of the contents of a text box, highlight the text to be removed and then press the **Delete** key.

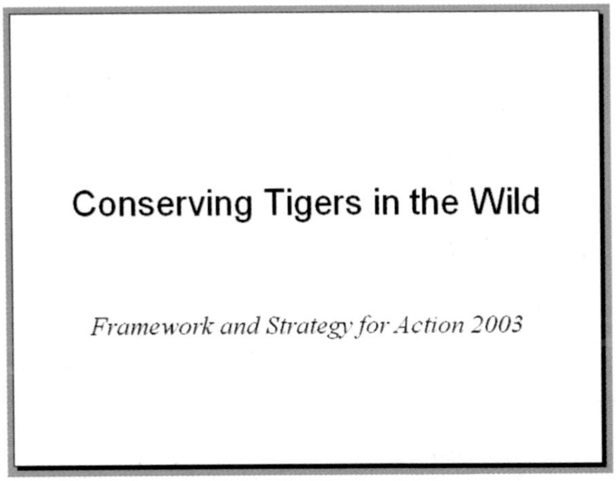

Changing the presentation view

You can alternate between various views of the presentation by clicking on the icons at the bottom of the screen (left-hand side).

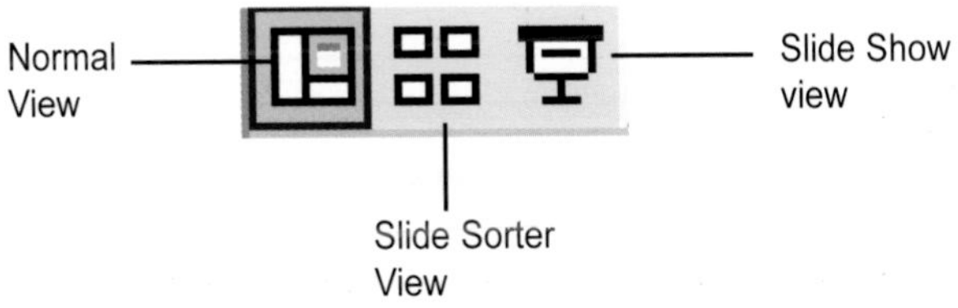

Normal View

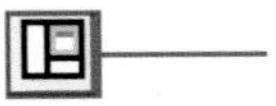

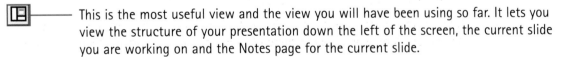

This is the most useful view and the view you will have been using so far. It lets you view the structure of your presentation down the left of the screen, the current slide you are working on and the Notes page for the current slide.

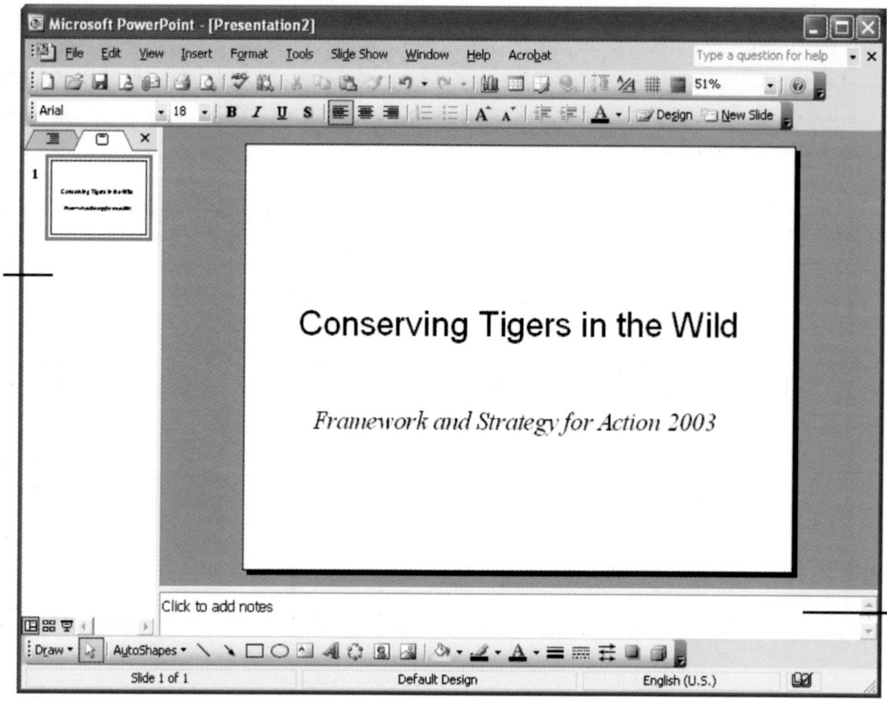

ⓘ The Outline pane has two different views – one view shows a picture of all the slides, and the other just lists the text on each slide. Click on the tabs at the top of the Outline pane to switch between the views.

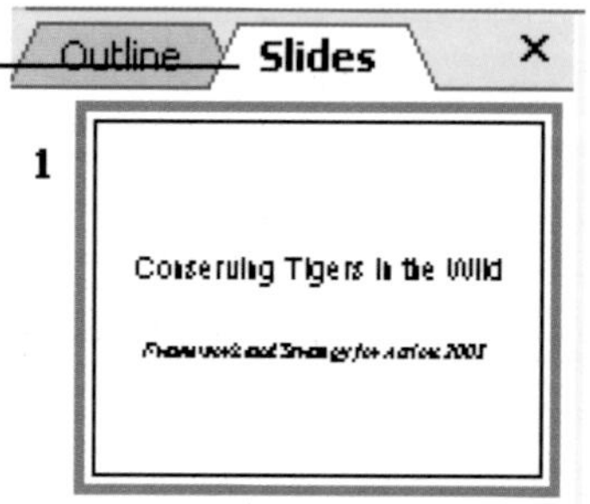

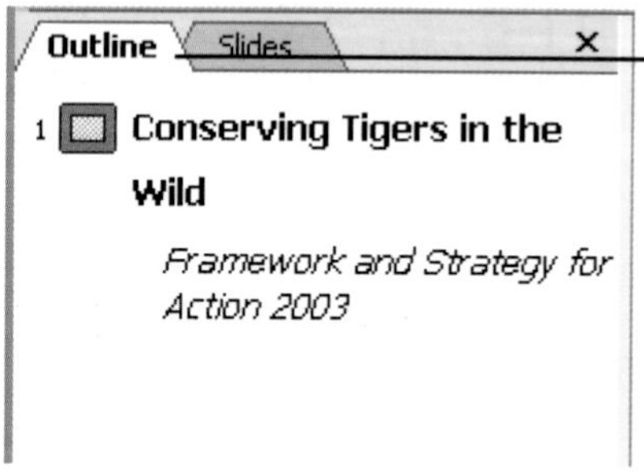

Slide Sorter View

This view helps you to organise your slides in later stages. You will use this view later when you have more than one slide. Here's a preview of what it will look like when you have more slides:

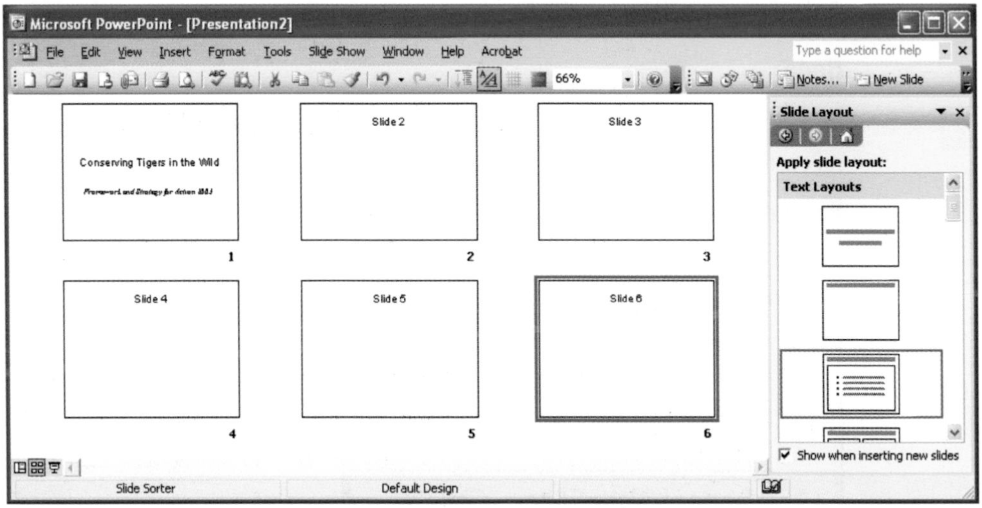

Slide Show

This is the view you use when you are actually giving your presentation.

- Click this icon to view your presentation so far.
- Exit the presentation by pressing the Esc key.

Using the Zoom tool

You can change the size of the slide in Normal View by using the Zoom tool on the Standard toolbar.

- To make the slide appear much bigger, either type 200 into the Zoom box or select 200% from the list that appears when you click the small down-arrow.
- This is much bigger than we want it for now! Most of the time you will probably just want the slide to fit into the window. To do this, click the small down-arrow on the Zoom tool, and select Fit from the list.

The Undo, Redo and Repeat commands

Undo

At any time, if you do something that you didn't mean to, or don't like, just click the **Undo** button. This will undo your most recent action; you can click it more than once to undo more than one action.

Redo

If you undo something you didn't mean to, just click the **Redo** button! If you haven't recently used the **Undo** button, the **Redo** button won't be active.

Repeat

If you want to repeat an action, for example adding a bullet point or inserting a slide, you can use the **Repeat** command. To do this select **Edit**, **Repeat** from the menu. If the action is not repeatable, the repeat command won't appear in the menu.

Saving your presentation

- Click **File** on the menu bar and select **Save**.

We'll create a new folder to save your presentation in.

- Use the arrow next to the **Save in** box to navigate to the location for your new folder.
- Create a new folder to save your presentation by clicking the **Create New Folder** button.
- Enter **Tiger Presentation** as the folder name.
- Enter **Tigers** as the **File name**.

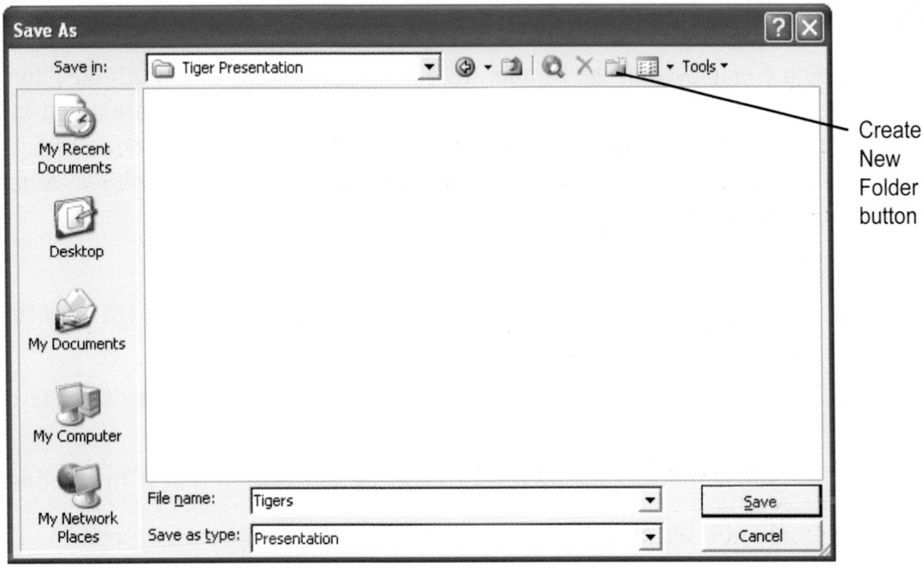

- PowerPoint will automatically save the file as a Presentation (*.ppt) file type. This is what we want for now.

- Click the Save button.

Closing the file and application

- To close your presentation select File, Close from the menu.

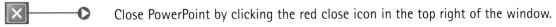

- Close PowerPoint by clicking the red close icon in the top right of the window.

Tip:
You can close files and applications by clicking the red cross at the top right of each window. When closing your presentation, be careful not to confuse the presentation Close icon with the PowerPoint application Close icon.

Exercise

You are employed in the Human Resources department of a (fictitious) company which produces and sells maps of different European countries. You are asked to create a PowerPoint presentation that can be used for the induction of new staff. This should provide information about the company and its markets. You will develop this presentation in later end of chapter exercises.

1. Load PowerPoint and enter a main heading **Mapsters UK Ltd** on a title slide. Make this heading Arial, bold size 54.
2. Enter a sub-title **Information for new company employees**. Change the font to Forte, bold, size 32.
3. Adjust the size of the text box for the sub-title so that it fits on one line.
4. Centre the sub-title vertically in the text box.
5. Create a new folder called **Presentations**.
6. Save the company presentation as **Mapsters.ppt** in your new folder.

Mapsters UK Ltd
Information for new company employees

Editing a Show

CHAPTER 6.2

In this chapter you'll add some more content to, and edit, the presentation you started in Chapter 6.1.

Opening an existing presentation

- Load PowerPoint.

You may see the Tigers.ppt presentation listed in the Task pane. Clicking this would open your presentation but for practice we will open it a different way.

- Click on the option File, Open from the main menu.

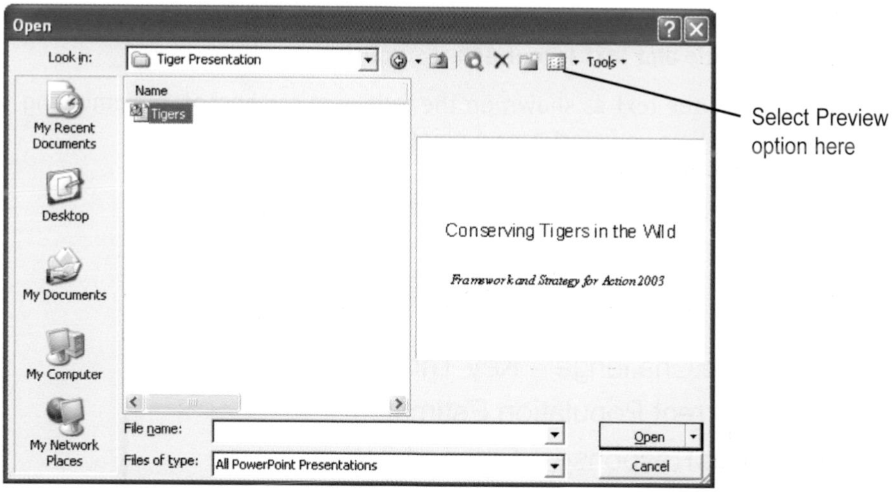

- Find the presentation by first locating the Tiger Presentation folder in the Look in: dropdown list.
- When you have found it, click to select it then click Open.

- Make sure you are in Normal View by clicking the Normal View button at the bottom of the screen.

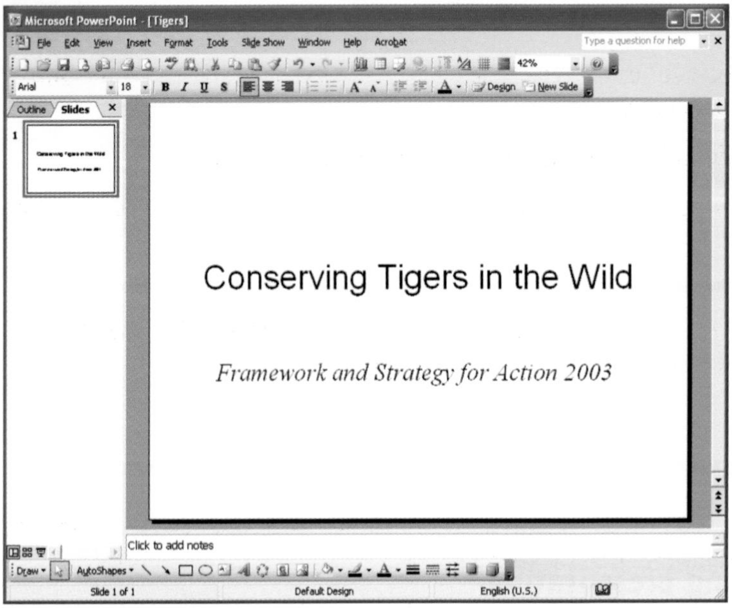

Starting a new slide

Now you can begin the second slide of the presentation.

- Click the New Slide button on the Standard toolbar.

The Slide Layout has already been selected by PowerPoint – it has guessed that we want the Title and Text layout and it's right!

- Enter the text as shown on the following screenshot, remembering to press Enter each time you start a new point.

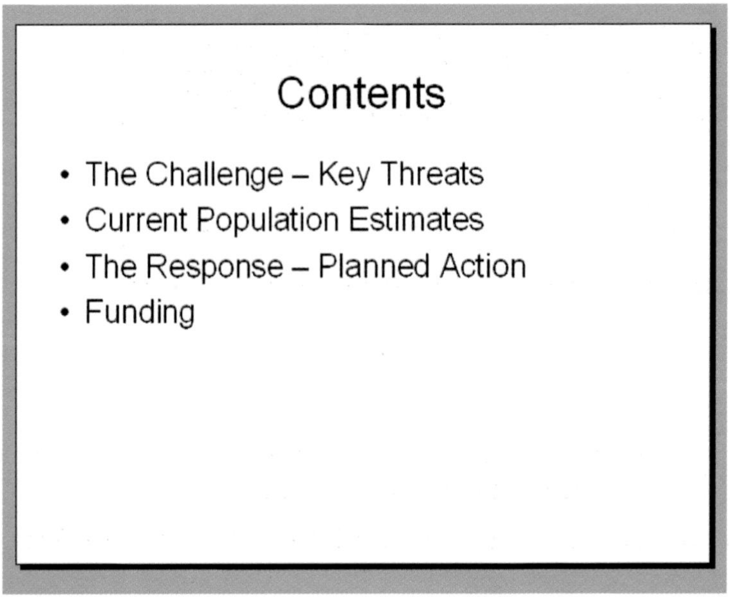

Changing text size

You can increase or decrease the size of text by using the Font Size buttons on the Formatting toolbar.

- Select all of the bulleted text on the current slide.
- Click several times on the Increase Font Size button to increase the size of the text.

Tip:
If you make the text too big, you can make it smaller either by clicking the Undo button or the Decrease Font Size button.

Changing line spacing

The text could do with being more spread out. You can increase or decrease the line spacing using the Increase and Decrease Paragraph Spacing buttons.

- With the bulleted text highlighted, click the Increase Paragraph Spacing button until the text fills the text box.

Your screen should now look something like the one below:

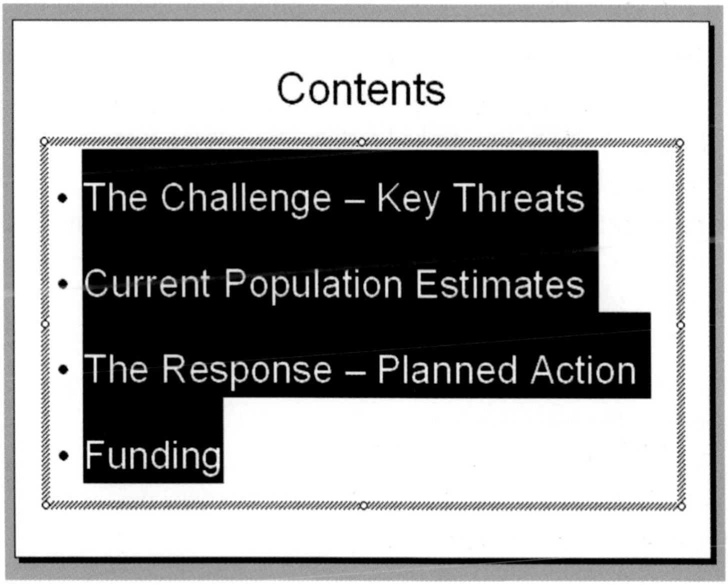
Contents
• The Challenge – Key Threats
• Current Population Estimates
• The Response – Planned Action
• Funding

Checking your spelling

- Check your spelling either by using the main menu (Tools, Spelling) or by clicking the Spelling button on the Standard toolbar.

PowerPoint will try to correct all the words it has underlined in red. These may be words that it thinks are spelt incorrectly or repeated words.

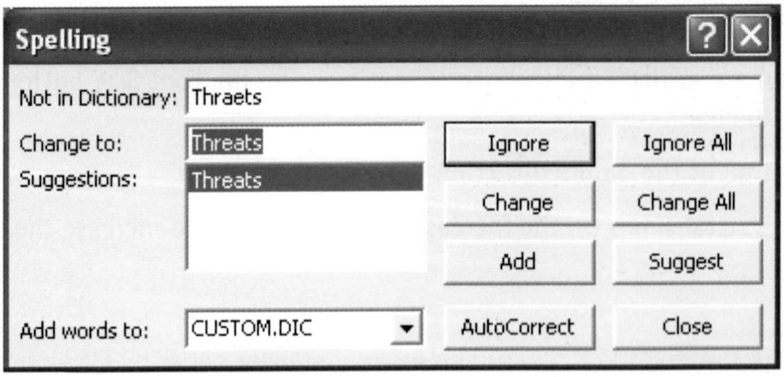

- Click on the correct spelling in the **Suggestions** box and then click **Change**. (If the correct spelling does not appear you will have to type it into the **Change to** box.)
- If the spell-check picks up a repeated word, click **Change** to delete it.
- If the spell-check picks up a word that is actually correct (e.g. a name) then click **Ignore**.
- When the spell-check is complete, click **OK**.

Adding more slides

You are going to add more slides to your presentation, this time using the **Outline** pane.

- In the **Outline** pane, make sure the **Slides** tab is selected then click on the first slide.

- Click the **New Slide** button to add a slide. PowerPoint automatically adds this slide after the first slide because the first slide was selected.
- Click the **New Slide** button **two** more times. Don't worry about the **Slide Layout** just now – we will edit that later.

Adding titles

- In the **Outline** pane, click the **Outline** tab then click the **Slide 2** icon so that slide 2 appears in the main window.
- Enter the text **The Challenge – Key Threats** either on the slide where it says to add the title, or if you just start typing while the **Slide 2** icon is selected you can type it straight into the **Outline** pane.
- Enter the other titles in the same way so that your Outline pane looks like the one on the next page.

ⓘ Try pressing the **Return** key after entering a title; PowerPoint will automatically insert a new slide. You can then easily delete the slide by clicking it in the **Outline** pane and pressing the **Delete** key.

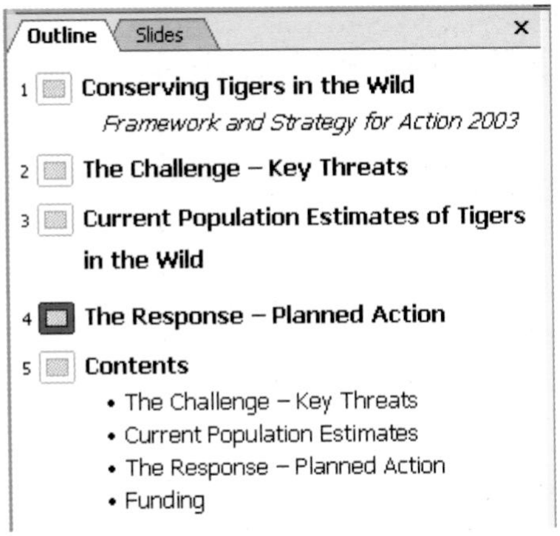
Outline
Slides
1 Conserving Tigers in the Wild
Framework and Strategy for Action 2003
2 The Challenge – Key Threats
3 Current Population Estimates of Tigers in the Wild
4 The Response – Planned Action
5 Contents
• The Challenge – Key Threats
• Current Population Estimates
• The Response – Planned Action
• Funding

Changing the order of slides

You may have noticed that since adding those extra slides, the contents slide is now at the end of the presentation – we want it to be immediately after Slide 1.

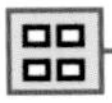

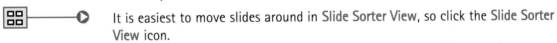

- It is easiest to move slides around in Slide Sorter View, so click the Slide Sorter View icon.
- Click on Slide 5 and hold down the mouse button. Drag the Contents slide (Slide 5) so that a grey vertical line appears after Slide 1 as shown below. Drop the slide here.

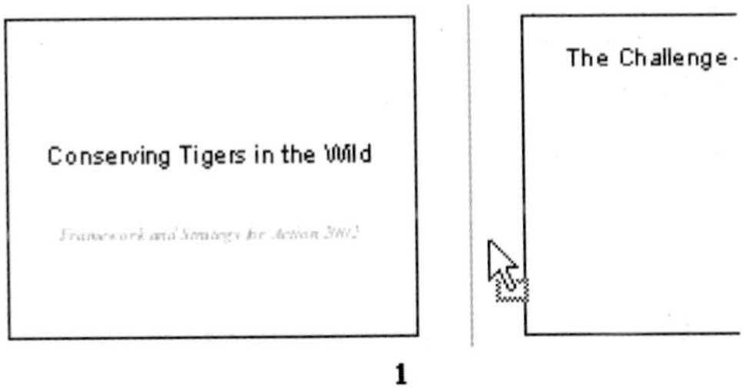
Conserving Tigers in the Wild
1
The Challenge -

Your slides should now be in the right order!

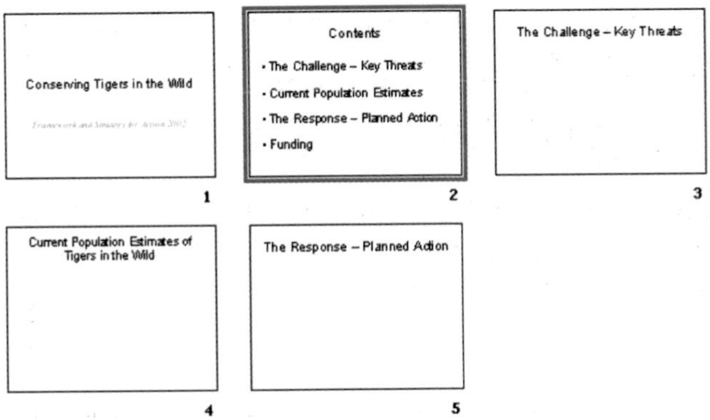
Conserving Tigers in the Wild
1
Contents
• The Challenge – Key Threats
• Current Population Estimates
• The Response – Planned Action
• Funding
2
The Challenge – Key Threats
3
Current Population Estimates of Tigers in the Wild
4
The Response – Planned Action
5

Now we'll add some more text to Slide 3.

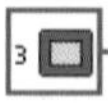

- From Slide Sorter View, double-click Slide 3. This should display Slide 3 in Normal View.
- Enter the text for the first bullet point as Poaching Driven by Illegal Wildlife Trade. Click Enter.

We want this next bullet to be indented a little. To move bullets to the right or left of the screen you use the Promote and Demote buttons on the Outlining toolbar.

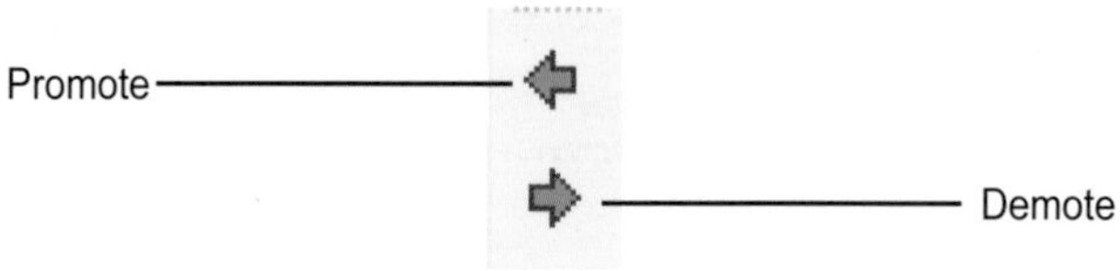

- To display the Outlining toolbar, select View, Toolbars and click on Outlining. It is normally displayed down the left of the Outline pane.

- Move the bullet to the right by clicking the Demote button.
- Enter the text Ban on International Trade of Tiger Parts. Click Enter. You will notice that the text will be a bit smaller than on the first bullet point.

The next bullet point will automatically follow the format of the previous one, which is what we want.

- Enter the text Human Pressure on Habitats as the second sub-point.

- Enter the rest of the text on the slide so that it looks like the slide below. You will have to click the Promote button to restore the bullets to the left of the slide.

The Challenge – Key Threats
• Poaching Driven by Illegal Wildlife Trade
– Ban on International Trade of Tiger Parts
– Human Pressure on Habitats
• Habitat Loss and Fragmentation
• Inadequate International Cooperation
• Funding Constraints

Customising bullets

You can change the style and colour of bullets to increase the impact of subset points.

- Highlight the text of the two demoted bullets. Select **Format**, **Bullets and Numbering** from the main menu.

A selection of commonly used bullets is shown in the **Bullets and Numbering** window.

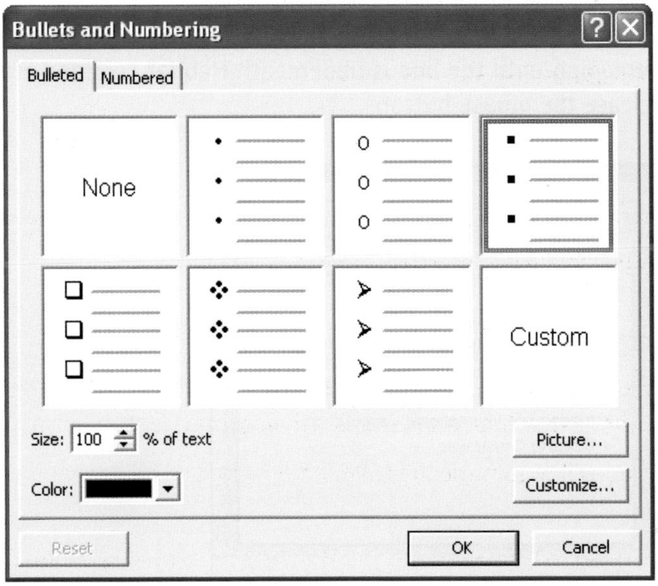

- Click to select a new shape for your bullets. Click **OK** to close the dialogue box.

Tip:
To change a bulleted list to a numbered list, highlight the bullet points and click the **Numbering** button on the Formatting toolbar. To change the style of numbering (e.g. i, ii, iii or 1), 2), 3)), select **Format**, **Bullets and Numbering** from the main menu. Click the **Numbered** tab, select a numbering style and then click **OK**.

Moving text lines around

The bullet point **Human Pressure on Habitats** should actually be under the bullet point **Habitat Loss and Fragmentation**. Move it down to its new place as follows:

Tip:
You will need to do this in Outline view in the Outline pane. To change to Outline view from Slides view, just click the **Outline** tab at the top of the Outline pane.

- Click the mouse pointer to the left of **Human Pressure on Habitats** in the **Outline** pane and you will see a four-headed arrow style pointer.

- Hold the mouse button down and drag downwards. A line will appear across the text. Keep dragging until the line is underneath **Habitat Loss and Fragmentation** and then release the mouse button.

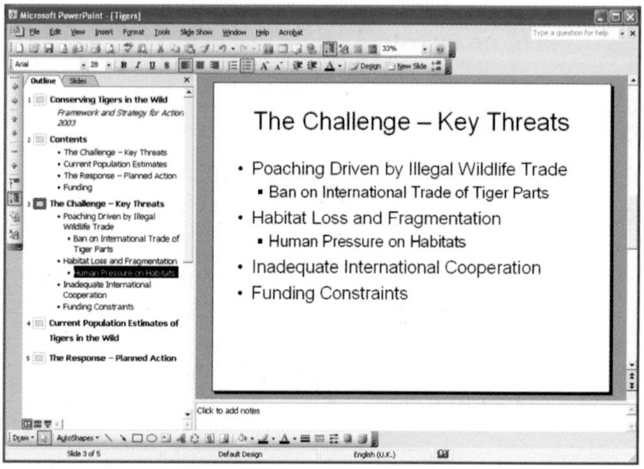

The text should have moved down the slide.

- You can move text from one slide to another in exactly the same way! Have a go at moving text from one slide to another. Just click the **Undo** button when you are done to restore the slide as shown above.

Checking your presentation

You can view your progress so far. Look at it first in **Slide Sorter** view.

- Click the **Slide Sorter View** button at the bottom of the screen.

When you click the **Slide Show** button the presentation starts at the selected slide (the one with the black border).

- Click the first slide to select it and then click the **Slide Show** button.
- Click or press the **Space bar** to move to the next slide.

Pressing the **Backspace** key goes back one slide. Remember you can exit your presentation at any time by pressing the **Esc** key.

Take a break!

- Save your presentation using the **Save** icon and then close the presentation.

Exercise

At the end of Chapter 6.1 you began producing a presentation for the induction of new employees at Mapsters UK Ltd. You will now add more slides to the presentation, edit slides and practise running the slide show.

1. Open the file Mapsters.ppt.
2. Start a new slide that has a simple title and text layout. Insert a heading Company History.
3. Change the size of the text in the bullet points to 22 and enter the following:

   Company (formally known as European Maps UK Ltd) founded in 1920 by George G Girling

   Early work concentrated on industrial and topographic wall maps for the educational market

   In 1961 production moved to tourist maps

   Mapsters series for tourists now comprises 10 maps

   Latest developments – Graphical Information Systems (GIS)
4. Increase the line spacing between the bullet points so that the text box is filled. Run the spell-checker and make any necessary corrections.
5. Add the following titles to four new slides.

   Company Organisation

   Sales by Product

   Target Markets

   Contents
6. Add the following bullet points to the last slide:
   - Company History
   - Company Organisation
   - Sales by Product
   - Target Markets

7. Move the last slide (Contents) to become the second slide.
8. Change the order of slides 5 and 6.
9. Change the order of the text on slide 2 – swap lines 3 and 4.
10. Run the slide show, then save and close your presentation.

CHAPTER

6.3 Applying Designs

Now we'll look at the overall appearance of the slides. The slides could do with brightening up a bit to increase the impact of the presentation. We'll also insert some pictures to add interest.

- Open the Tigers presentation.

Designing the Master Slide

The Master Slide is a slide that dictates the format of every other slide in your presentation. For example, if you choose a particular background colour and font for the Master Slide, this background colour and font will appear on all your slides. It's rather like a template in Word, or even the header and footer in Word – whatever you type in as the header and footer in Word appears on every page – and the same is true in PowerPoint with the Master Slide.

- View the Master Slide by selecting View, Master, Slide Master from the menu.

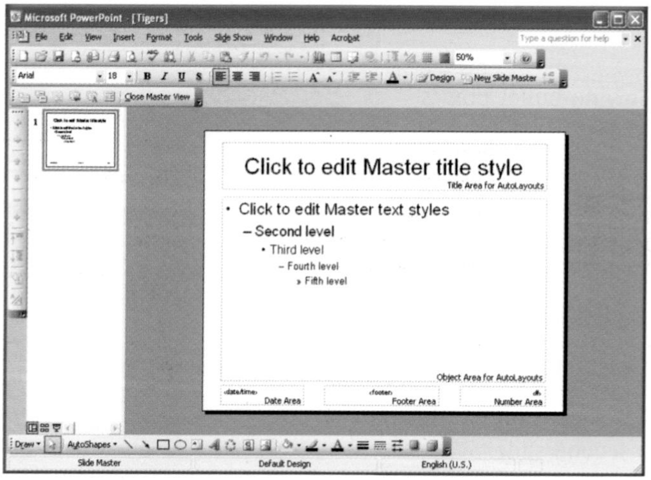

We will first put a coloured background on the slide. There are two ways to add a background design – you can either select a colour and a fill effect, or you can choose from a range of pre-designed backgrounds, or Design Templates.

Design Templates

Click the **Slide Design** button on the **Formatting** toolbar.

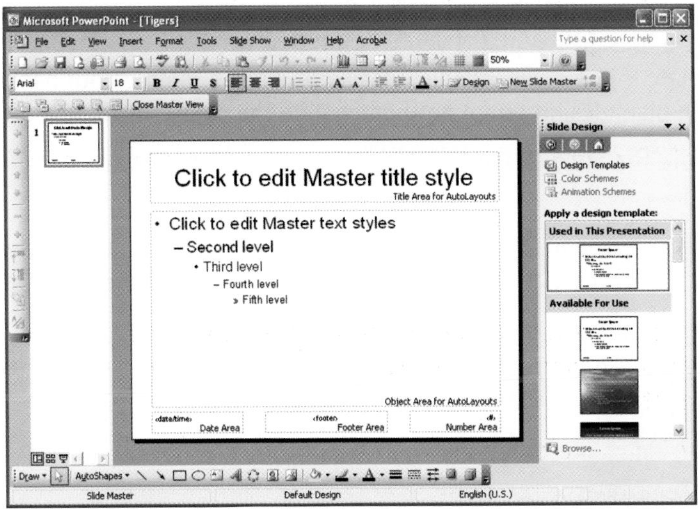

The **Slide Design** pane appears. There are options for **Design Templates**, **Colour Schemes** and **Animation Schemes**.

- Make sure the **Design Templates** option is selected. You will see a large variety of design templates available.
- Choose a design that you like, then click to select it.
- It's very easy to try a different template if you change your mind – just click a different one!

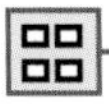

- Now view your presentation in **Slide Sorter** view by clicking the **Slide Sorter View** button.

It should look a bit more colourful now!

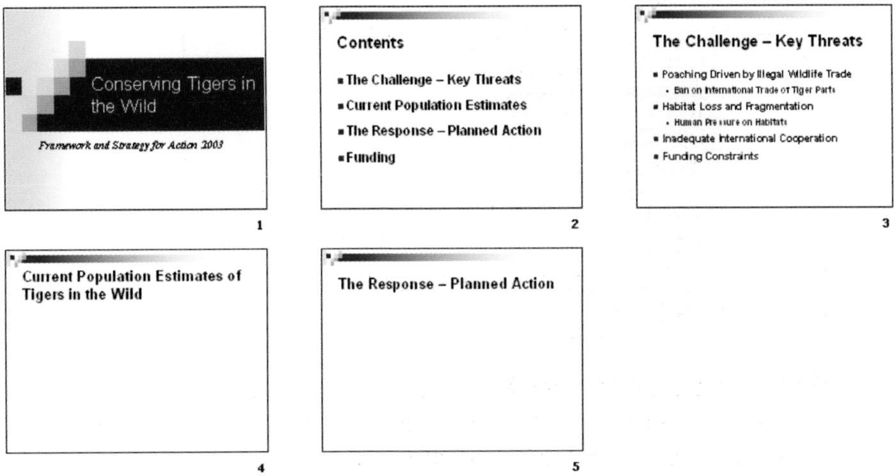

Changing the slide background colour

You can change the background colour of a slide. If the slide already has a design template selected for it, then you can change the colour of the template; if there is no template then you can just change the colour of the plain background. In fact, if you look in the list of design templates you will see that even the plain white background is a design template – just a very simple one! So to make a plain colour background, you can choose the plain design template then change the colour of the plain template.

- Make sure the Slide Design pane is visible. Change to Normal View with Slide 2 selected.
- Suppose we want to lighten the colour of the template, but keep the same pattern. Click where it says Color Schemes at the top of the Slide Design pane.

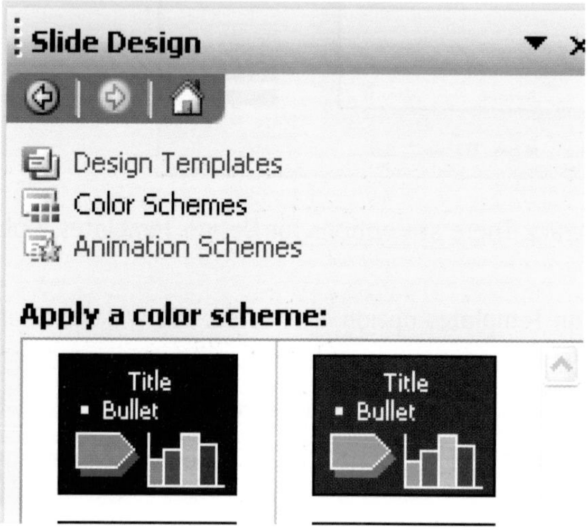

- We'll chose a dark blue background colour only for the selected slide. To apply it just to the selected slide, click the small down-arrow that appears on each scheme when you move mouse over it.

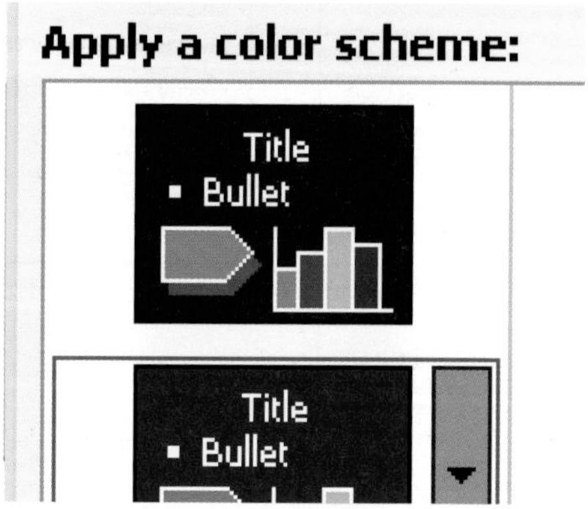

- Click to select the option Apply to Selected Slides. The current slide should change colour. If you don't like the new colour just click Undo.

- If you wanted to change the scheme for all slides, you would select the Apply to All Slides option.
- If you wanted this to be just a plain dark blue background without the pattern, you would have to change the Design Template to a plain one before choosing the colour scheme.

Plain design template

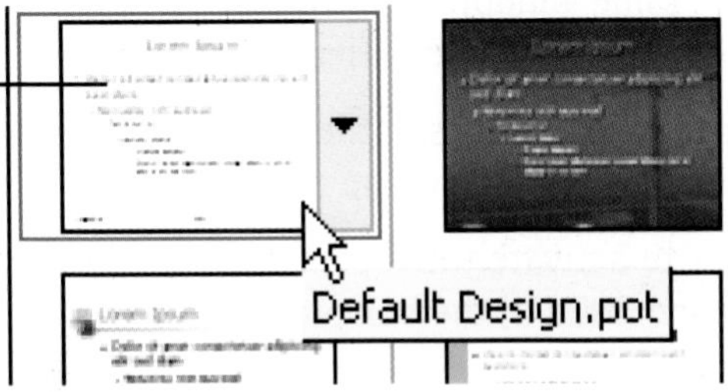

Adding page numbers

You can add page numbers to just one slide, some slides or all slides. You can also choose to have them only on the Notes pages and not on the actual slides. You can add page numbers whilst you are in Normal View or in the Slide Master.

- Select View, Header and Footer from the menu.

The Header and Footer dialogue box has options for adding a Date/Time field and Footer text as well as page numbers.

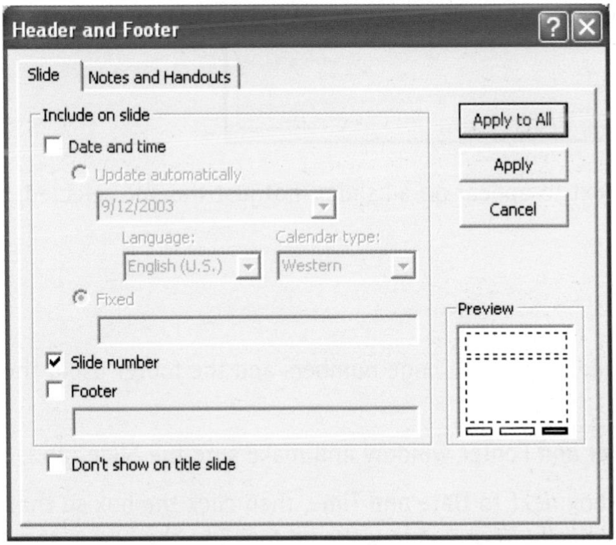

- Make sure your settings look like those in the screenshot above – with only the Slide number box checked.
- You have the option to apply these settings only to the slide that is selected, or to all of them. We want page numbers on every page, so click Apply to All.

Adding text to the header and footer

You can add text to the header and footer in just the same way as in Word and Excel. You can choose whether the footer text appears on just the selected slide, or on all slides in your presentation. We will add the text World Tiger Conservation Fund 2003 to the footer.

- To add a footer, you use the same window as for the page numbers, so open the Header and Footer window by selecting View, Header and Footer.
- We want the footer to appear on the slides, rather than the notes and handouts, so make sure the Slide tab is selected at the top of the window.
- Click in the Footer checkbox to activate the footer. You can now add the text World Tiger Conservation Fund 2003 in the box provided.

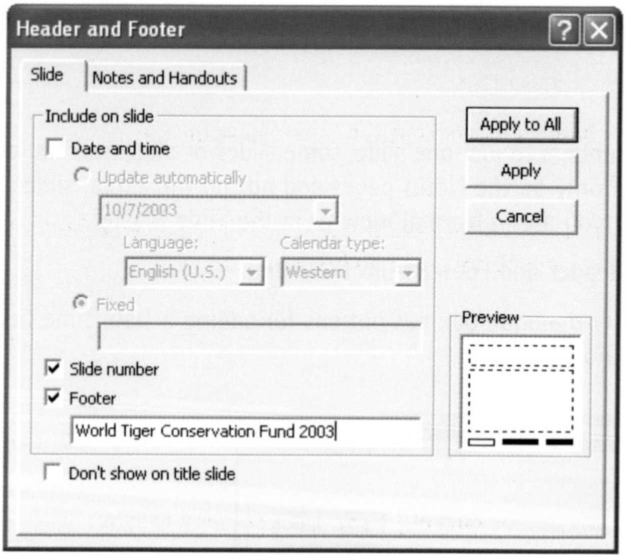

- You want the text to appear on all slides, not just the one selected, so click Apply to All.

Adding a date to slides

This is done in the same way as the page numbers and the footer using the Header and Footer window.

- Open the Header and Footer window and make sure the Slide tab is selected.
- Click the checkbox next to Date and Time, then click the box so that the date updates automatically. Your window should look like the one in the next screenshot.

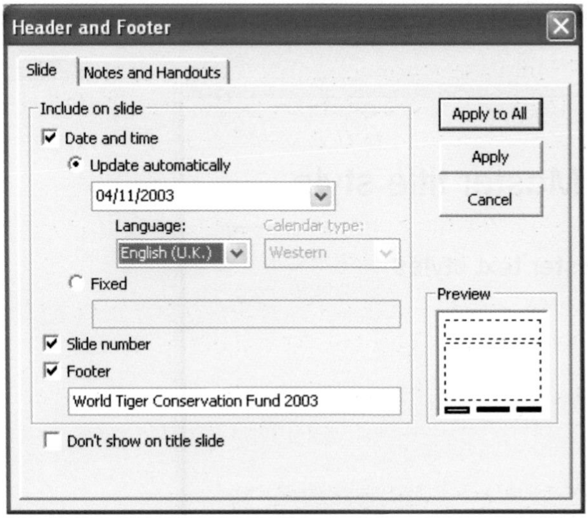

- Click the Apply to All button.

- View all these changes by clicking the Slide Show button.

Tip:
If you don't want the date to be updated automatically, uncheck the Update automatically option in the dialogue box shown above.

Repositioning the footer, date and page numbers

Notice that the footer goes onto two lines – it would look neater on one. To reposition this you use the Slide Master.

- View the Slide Master by clicking View, Master, Slide Master.

More than one master slide?

The Design Template automatically creates two Slide Masters, one for the Title slide and one for all the others.

- Click to select the master slide in the Outline pane that represents the non-title slides.

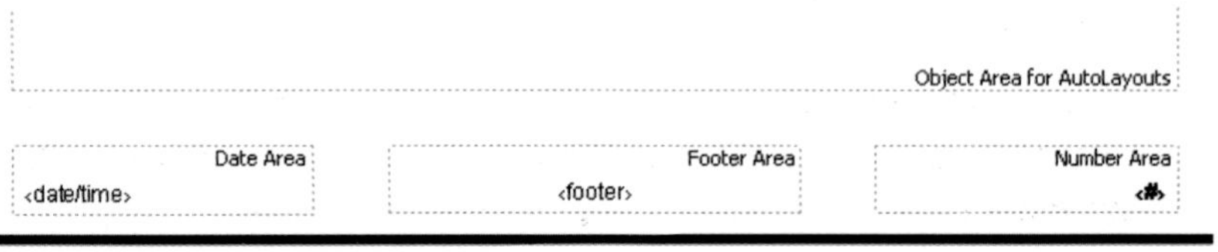

- Notice that there are marked-out areas for the Date Area, Footer Area and Number Area. To move the boundaries of each area, click in the area, then use the handles to drag the outline to where you want it.

- Adjust the areas so that your screen looks like the one below:

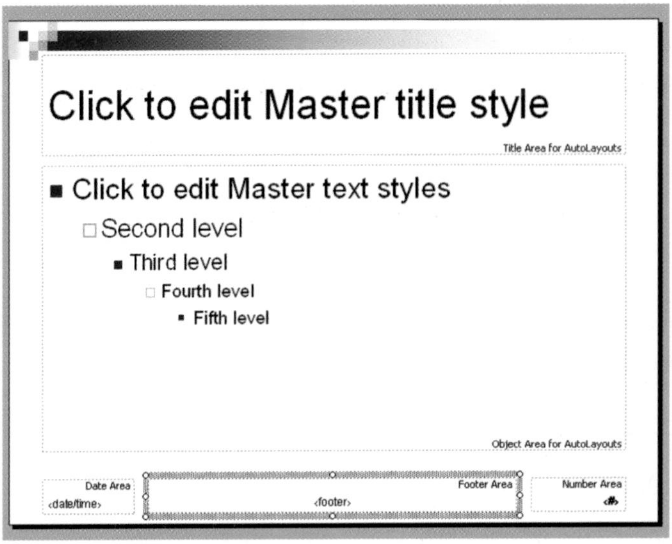

- Return to Normal View by selecting View, Normal from the menu.

Changing the layout of a slide

At any point you can change the layout of a slide, even if you have already entered text. The fourth slide Current Population Estimates of Tigers in the Wild will contain a graph, not bullet points, so the layout needs to be changed.

- Go to Slide 4 by clicking on it in the Outline pane.
- View the Slide Layout pane by selecting Format, Slide Layout from the menu.
- Click to select the Title and Chart layout from the list.

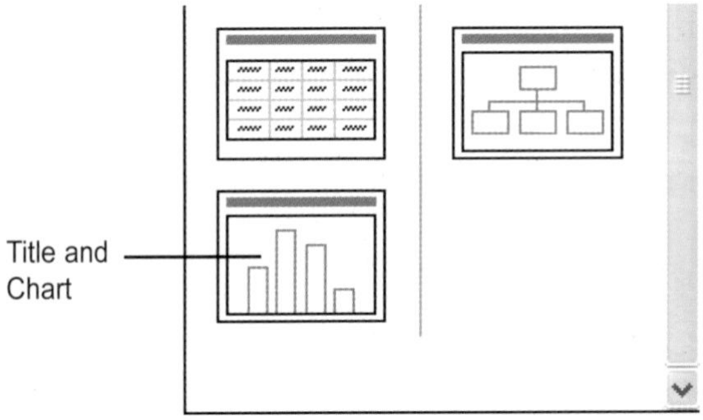

The text Double click to add chart will appear in the middle of the bottom placeholder, but we won't create the graph just yet.

Layouts that include Clip Art

The fifth slide will have a picture as well as text, so first you must change its layout.

- In the Outline pane select Slide 5.
- Make sure the Slide Layout pane is visible then select the layout named Title, Text and Clip Art.

Tip:
If you hold the cursor over a layout, the tool tip will appear with the name of that layout.

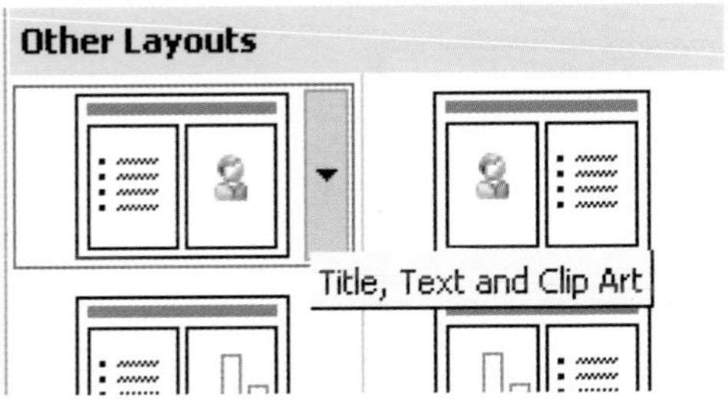

Your slide should now look like the one below:

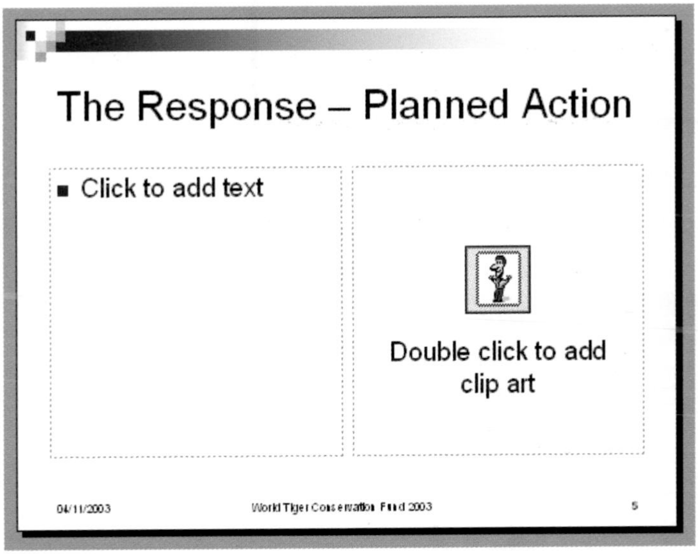

We will insert some Clip Art in the next chapter.

Tip:
If you wanted to insert an image from another file into a normal slide, you wouldn't need to change the layout. Simply select Insert, Picture, From file. Locate the image file and click Insert. To delete the image, click to select it and press the Delete key.

Creating an organisation chart

Drawing an organisation chart is very straightforward if you use the layout provided by PowerPoint. We will create a chart showing the structure of the World Tiger Conservation Fund.

- Create a new slide by clicking the New Slide button.
- View the slide in Normal View.
- If the Slide Layout pane is not visible, select Format, Slide Layout from the menu.

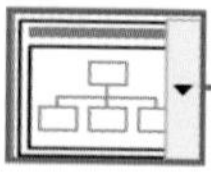

- Scroll down until you see the Title and Diagram or Organization Chart layout, then click to select it.

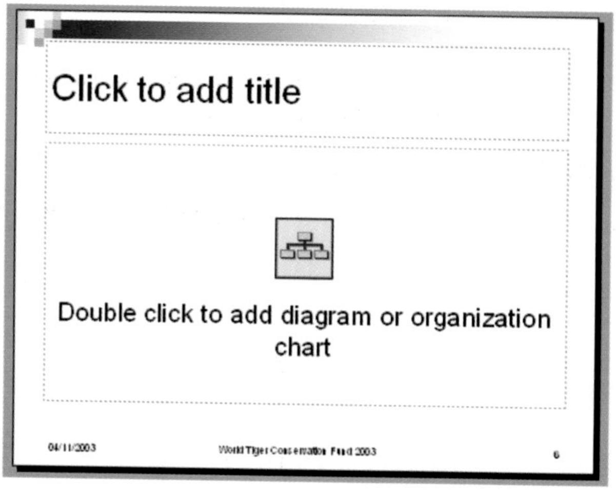

- Add the slide title The Organisation Structure and centre the text.
- Double-click where it says to create an organisation chart.

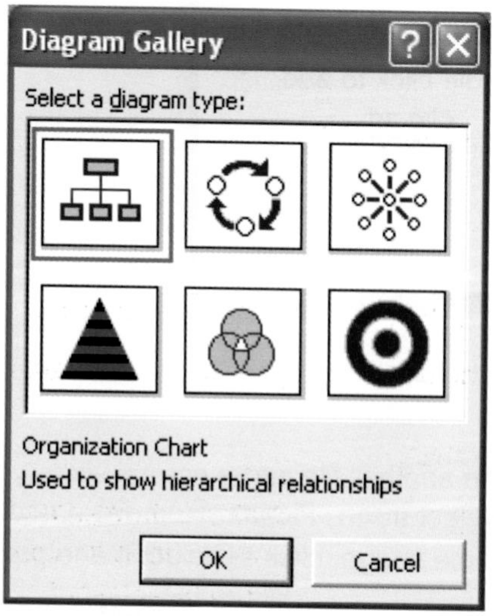

- Make sure the first option, Organization Chart is selected. Click OK.

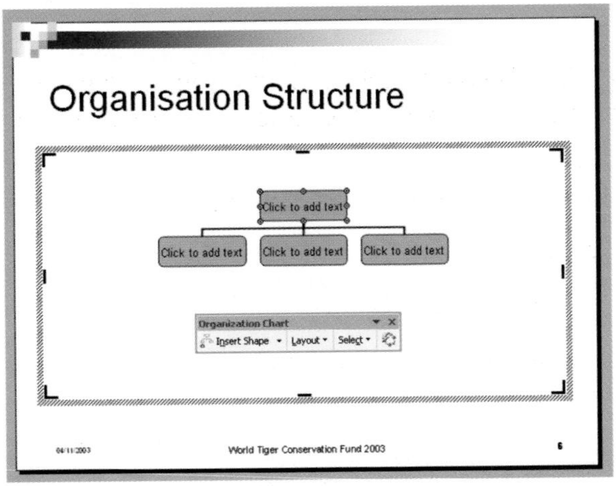

The Chief Executive Officer is Mike Stevenson and he has four Divisional Managers, Mary Wong, Omar Iqbal, Martha Kane and John Hainsworth.

- Click in the top box to add some text. Type Mike Stevenson (CEO).
- Use the same technique for the other three boxes, adding the names of the first three managers as shown in the figure below:

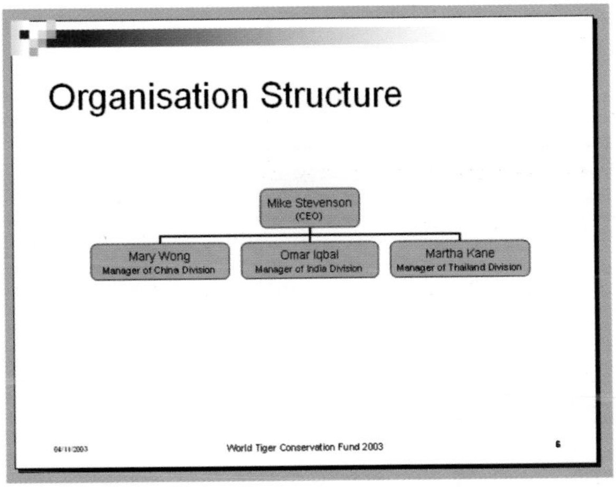

Inserting managers, co-workers and subordinates

We need to add the fourth manager as a co-worker to the other managers.

- Click on Martha Kane to select the box. The Organisation Chart toolbar will be displayed.

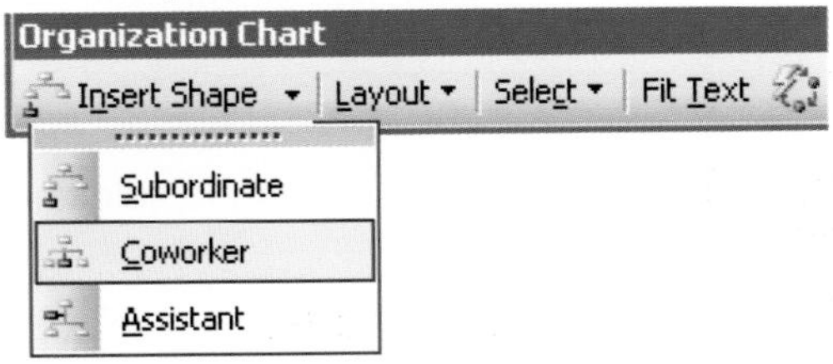

Tip:
Click the down-arrow on the Layout button to change the hierarchical layout.

Tip:
There is no option to insert a manager but all managers, except the CEO, will be either co-workers, subordinates or both.

- We need the box to be a Co-worker type, so click this option. A fourth box should appear. (Alternatively this manager could have been added as a subordinate to Mike Stevenson.)
- Enter the name John Hainsworth, Manager of Siberia Division.

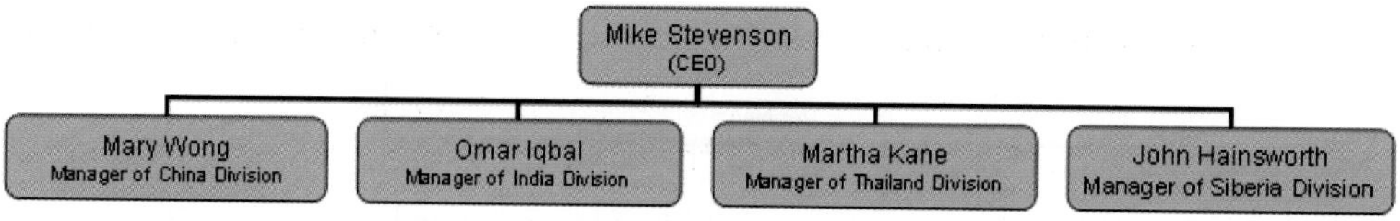

John has two subordinates, fieldworkers George Bradley and Jo Kemple.

- Click on John's box and select the Subordinate shape from the Organization Chart toolbar.
- Enter the new person's details in the box, George Bradley, Fieldworker. Repeat for Jo Kemple.

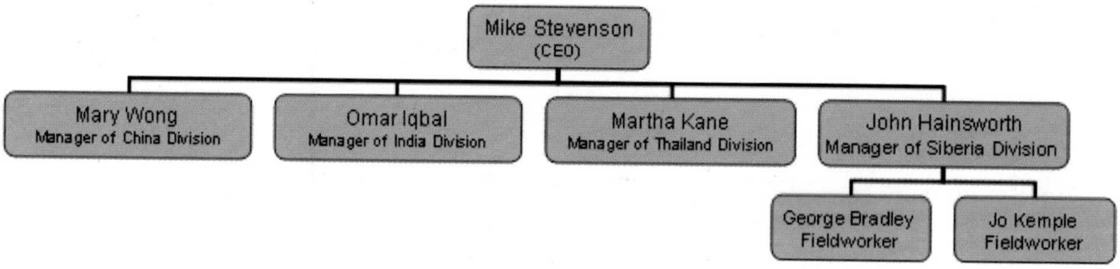

Deleting managers, co-workers and subordinates

The Thailand Division closes down, so we need to delete that manager.

- Click on Martha Kane and press the Delete key.
- Jo Kemple, one of John's subordinates and co-worker to George, is fired. Click her box and press Delete.

John Hainsworth retires and George is promoted to his position.

- Click on John Hainsworth and press the Delete key. George will automatically be promoted.

Tip:
You can delete any box except the top manager by clicking to select it and pressing the Delete key.

Exercise

In this exercise you will apply a design template to the Mapsters presentation you have been working on in the previous practice exercises. You will add footer information to slides and insert an organisation chart.

1. Open the file **Mapsters.ppt**.
2. Apply the **Watermark.pot** design template to the whole presentation.
3. Change the colour scheme to shades of yellow.
4. In the footer of all slides (except the title slide) insert the date and page numbers.
5. Change the position of the page numbers so that they are centred.
6. On slide 4 create the following organisation chart.

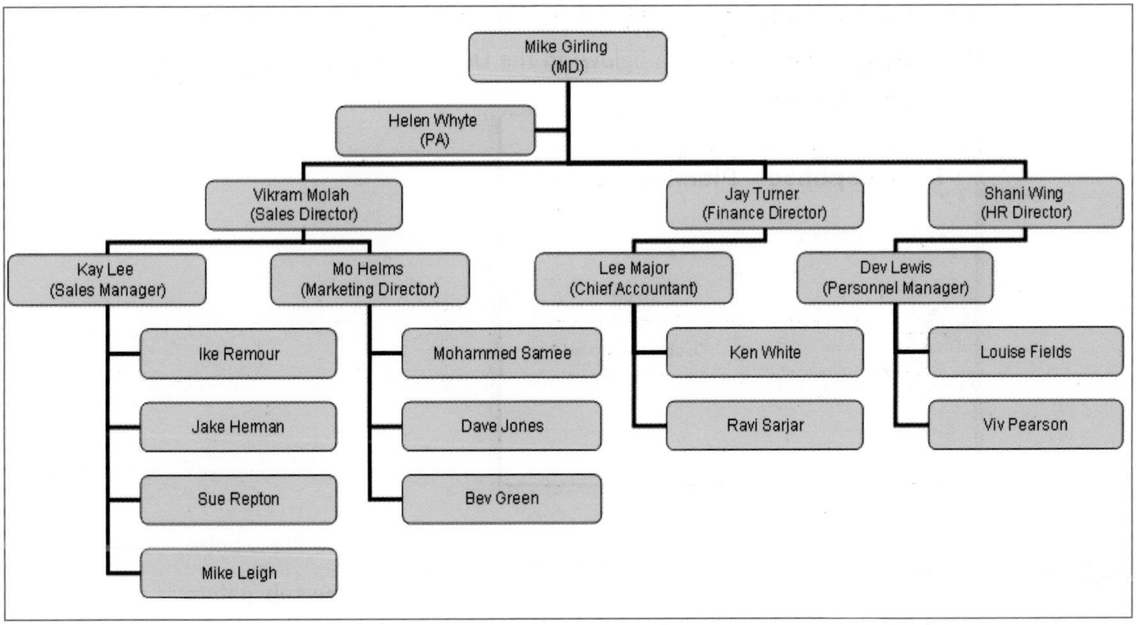

7. Save and close the presentation. You will continue working on this presentation at the end of Chapter 6.4.

CHAPTER

6.4 Adding Objects

You can add pictures, scanned photographs or cartoons to your documents. You can even put in graphs and charts.

- If it is not already on your screen, open the presentation **Tigers.ppt**.
- Click on **Slide 5** (shown below) in the **Outline** pane to display it.

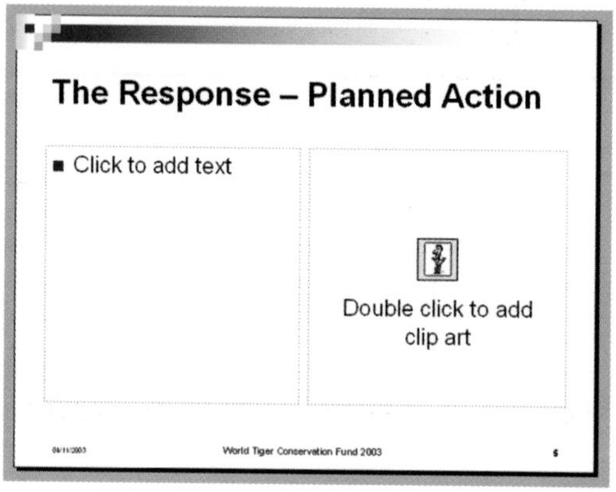

- Click where indicated to add text and type **Action at:**. Press **Enter**.

- Press the **Tab** key or click the **Demote** button. Add the sub-points as shown below:

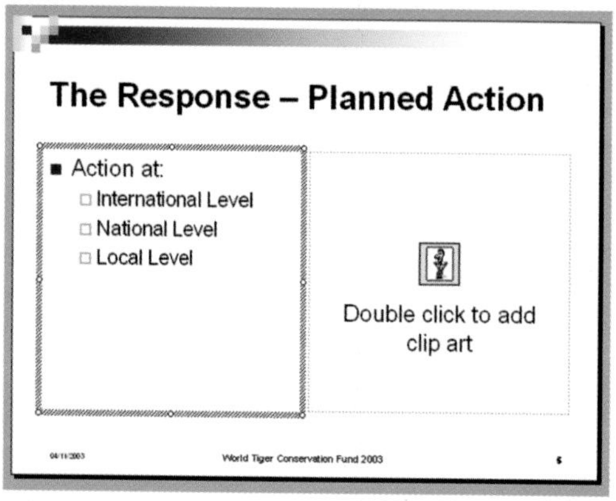

Highlight the text and click the Increase Paragraph Spacing button so that the text fills the whole box nicely.

Click the Increase Font Size button to make the text slightly larger.

Inserting a Clip Art image

You may have a CD with some Clip Art you can use. Clip Art is simply a collection of pictures and drawings that have been drawn by professional artists and collected together for other people to use. PowerPoint comes with a small collection of Clip Art.

- Double-click where shown (on the Clip Art placeholder) to add a Clip Art image.
- Search for a tiger picture by typing **tiger** into the search box and clicking the Search button.

Tip:
Don't worry if you have a different selection of Clip Art – it doesn't matter which image you use.

- Click to select a picture then click OK. The picture will now appear on the slide.

Tip:
If you change your mind and wish to delete the picture after you have inserted it, simply click to select it and press the Delete key.

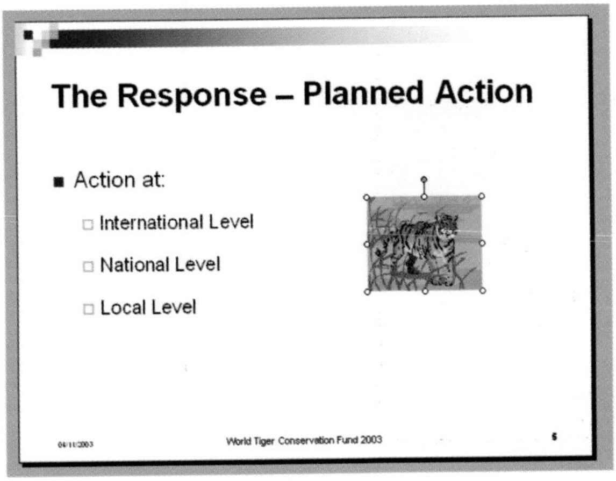

Handles

Note the little circles surrounding the graphic (picture). These are called **handles**. When the handles are visible, the graphic is **selected**.

Tip:
The Picture toolbar may appear when the graphic is selected.

- Click away from the graphic and the handles will disappear.
- Click anywhere inside the graphic and the handles will be visible again.

Changing the size of a graphic

You can make the graphic bigger or smaller without changing its proportions by dragging any of the corner handles.

- Make sure the graphic is selected so that the handles are visible.
- Move the pointer over the top left handle until it is shaped like a diagonal two-headed arrow.
- Click and hold down the left mouse button. The pointer changes to a cross-hair.
- Drag outwards. A dotted rectangle shows how big the graphic will be when you release the mouse button. When the picture is about twice as wide, release the button.

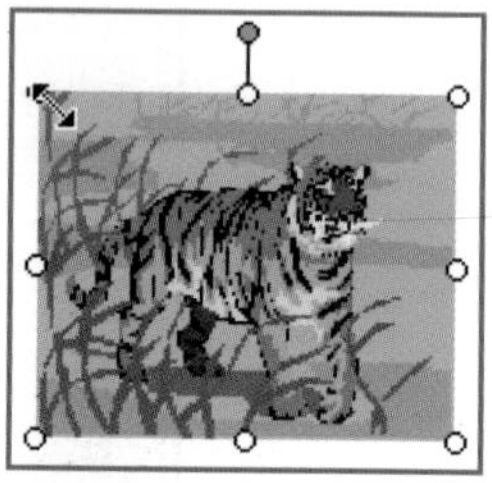

Tip:
You can also use this technique to size an image inserted from another file.

Your slide should now look like this:

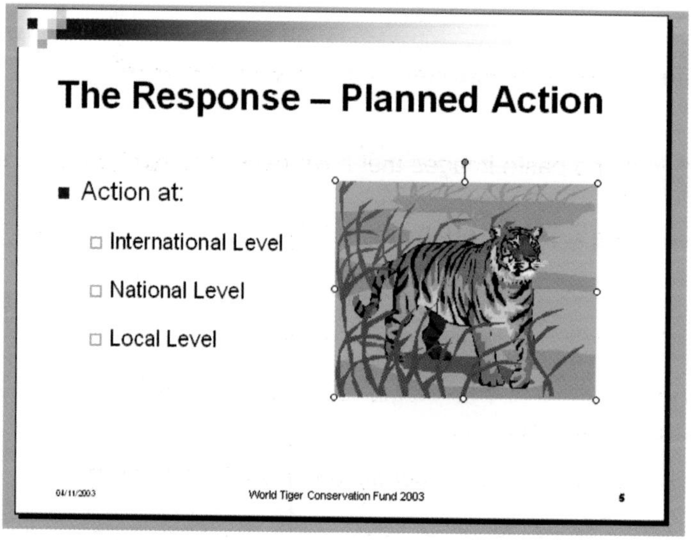

- Save your work so far.

Copying or moving an image within a presentation

Suppose you wanted this same image on the Title slide. We can copy this image across without having to insert another Clip Art image.

- Make sure Slide 5: The Response – Planned Action is selected.
- Click to select the image. Select Edit, Copy from the menu.
- You could have selected Cut instead of Copy. This would have copied the image but then deleted it. The Cut option is useful when you want to move images, text and slides from one place to another.
- Go to Slide 1. Select Edit, Paste from the menu. The image should appear on the slide in a random position.
- Move the image below the text by clicking and dragging it. Resize it so that it fits nicely.

Conserving Tigers in the Wild
Framework and Strategy for Action 2003
04/11/2003
World Tiger Conservation Fund 2003
1

Tip:
You can copy/cut and paste images that have been inserted from another file in just the same way.
Text can also be copied/cut and pasted within presentations in the same way.

Copying or moving an image between presentations

You can also copy or move text or images (Clip Art or images from other files) between open presentations in a similar way.

Suppose we want to use the same tiger picture in another presentation.

- Click File, New from the menu. Select Blank Presentation from the New Presentation pane.

- Go back to the Tigers presentation either by selecting Window, Tigers.ppt from the menu, or by clicking the Tigers.ppt button at the very bottom of your screen (in the Task bar).

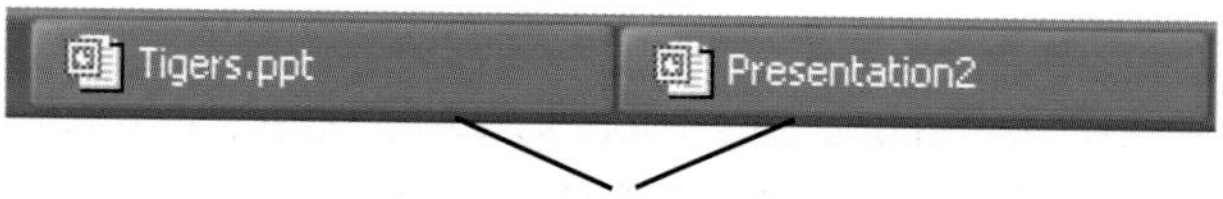

Use these buttons on the Task bar to switch between open presentations

- Click to select the image. Select Edit, Copy from the menu.
- Remember you could have selected Cut instead of Copy. This would have copied the image but then deleted it from the original presentation.
- Now go back to the new presentation by clicking on it in the Task bar.
- Select Edit, Paste from the menu. The image should appear on the slide. Move and size it appropriately.
- Save the new presentation as More Tiger Information and close it.

Inserting an image to the master slide

We will insert a tiger graphic into the Master Slide for the non-title slides. This can be done by opening the file containing the graphic then simply copying and pasting the image into the slide. You can also import it directly which is what we'll do here.

- Either find a tiger picture you like from the Internet, or download a couple of tiger pictures from the Payne-Gallway web site (www.payne-gallway.co.uk/ecdl).
- Make sure the correct Master Slide is in view.
- Select Insert, Picture, From File from the menu.

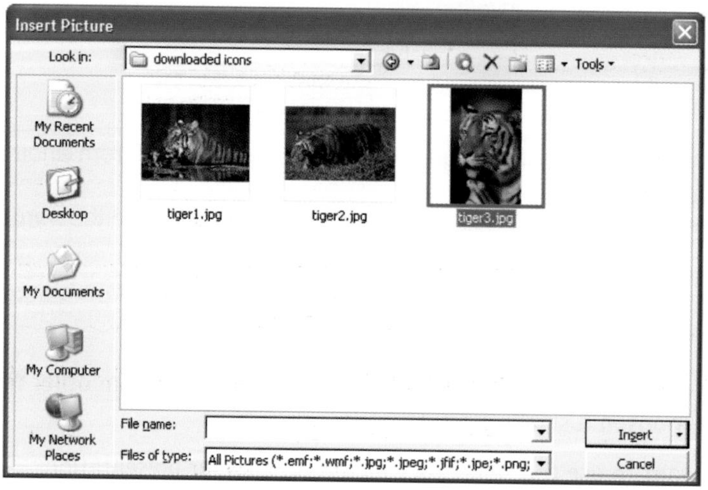

- Locate the tiger pictures that you've downloaded. Click to select one then click the Insert button.

- Now resize the graphic to be quite small, and position it in a corner.
- Add a border to the graphic by selecting it then clicking the **Line Color** button. Choose a dark colour.
- If you want to delete this image, just make sure you're in the **Master Slide** view, select the image by clicking it, then press the **Delete** key.

You could instead insert a Clip Art picture into the master slide:

- Make sure the Master Slide is displayed.
- Select **Insert, Picture, Clip Art.**
- Search for a tiger picture by typing **tiger** into the Search box and clicking the **Search** button.
- Click to select a picture and then click **OK.**

To insert a drawn object (such as a shape or a line) into the master slide use the buttons on the **Drawing** toolbar. This is covered in more detail on Pages 6-55 to 6-61.

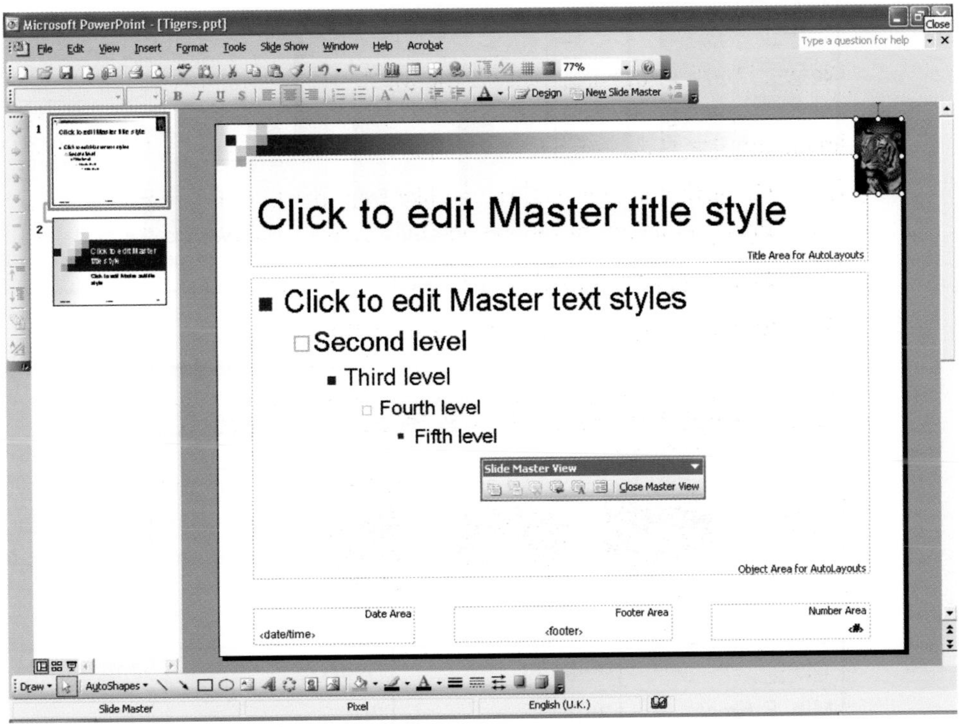

The image will now appear in the corner of all your slides – run the slide show to see!

- Select **View, Normal** to exit the slide master.

Adding a column chart

We will now add a chart to Slide 4. It will show the current population estimates of different species of tigers.

- First select Slide 4 by clicking it in the Outline pane. It should already have a Chart placeholder as we chose the Title and Chart layout in the last chapter.
- Double-click the chart placeholder on the slide.

You will then see a small spreadsheet just like you would see in Microsoft Excel. Notice that some of the icons on the Standard toolbar have changed.

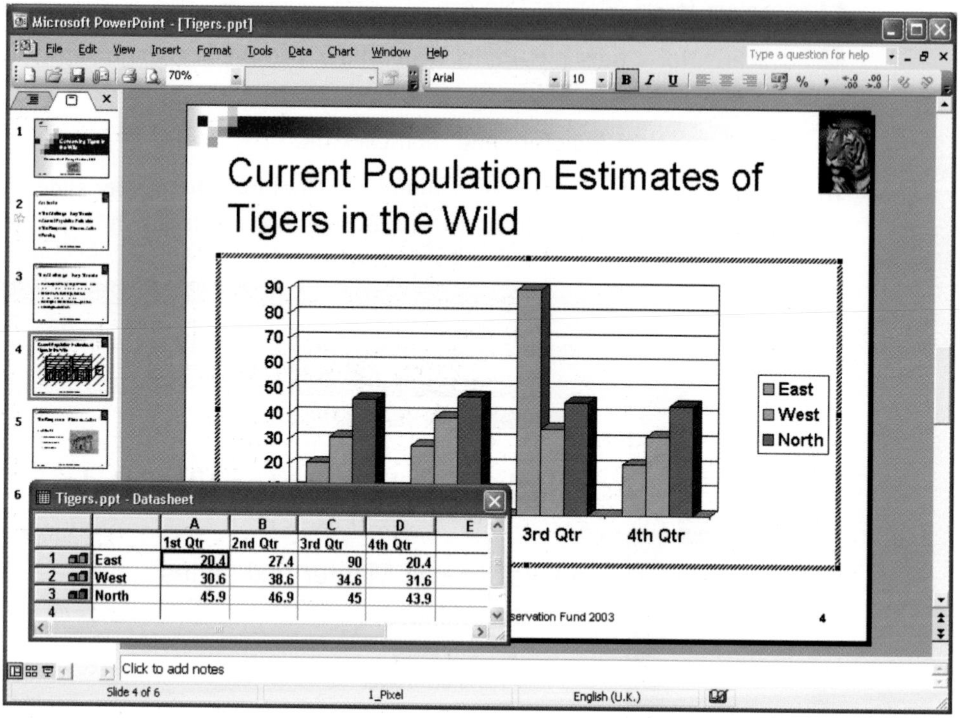

To make the chart you need to add your own information to the table. If you are asked to make a chart in the exam, you will probably be given some information in a table like the one below, and then this information will have to be put into the mini spreadsheet. We'll work through this now.

	Siberian	Amoy	Sumatran
Min. Estimate	360	20	400
Max. Estimate	406	30	500

- Click in the cell labelled East.
- Now begin typing Min. Estimate. This will replace East with Min. Estimate.
- Click in the next row and type Max. Estimate.

- Now do the same for the column headings. Click in the cell labelled 1st Qtr and type Siberian.
- Type the remaining two column headings from the table above.

We don't need the last column or the last row, so they need to be deleted.

- Click the column header D to select the whole column.
- Press the Delete key to delete all the values from these cells.
- Now click in row header 3 to select the whole row and press Delete.

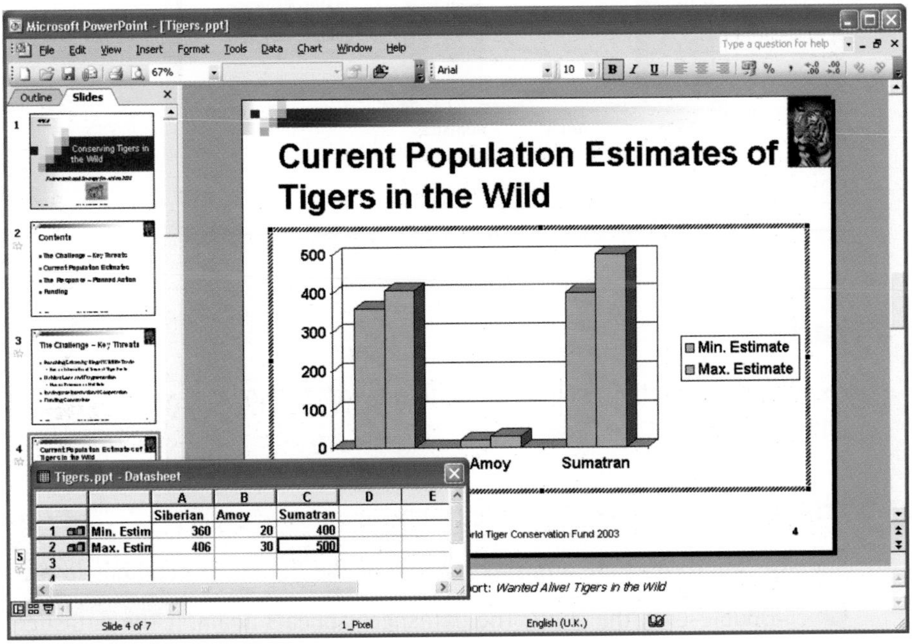

Now we need to enter the correct figures.

- Replace the figures already in the spreadsheet with the ones in the screenshot below, or from the table above.

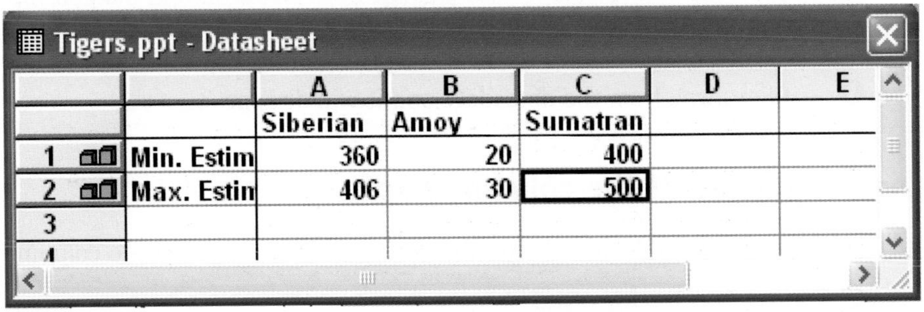

- Close the table by clicking the Close icon. Click somewhere on the slide outside the chart area to deselect it.

Your chart should now look like this:

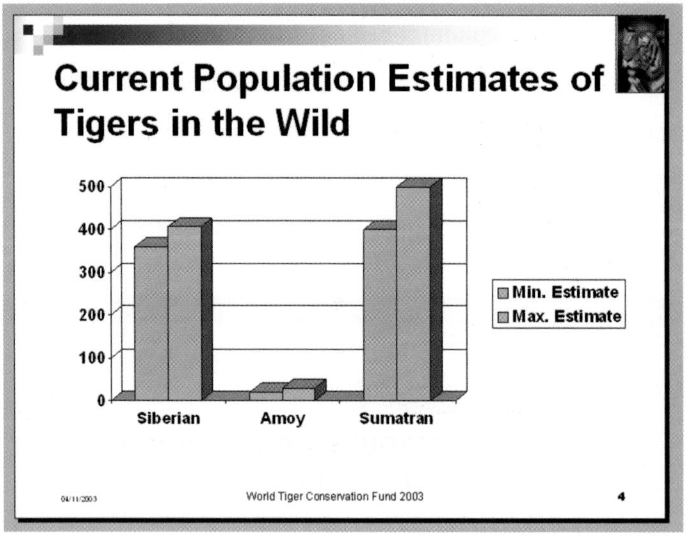

Sizing a chart

To adjust the chart size, click it and drag a corner handle inwards to make it smaller and outwards to make it larger.

Editing a chart

Suppose you have made a mistake in one of the figures or headings in the chart.

- Double-click the chart. The datasheet appears again. If the datasheet doesn't appear, just right-click on the Chart Area and select Datasheet from the menu that appears.

Tip:
The Chart Area is the dark blue area around the chart. To be sure you're in the right place, just hover the mouse pointer over that area and the Tool Tip will tell you where you are.

- Click away from the datasheet and it will disappear.

Changing the colours of the column chart

You can change both the background colour and the colour of the columns.

Changing the background

- Double-click the chart so that the datasheet appears.
- Right-click in the middle of the chart (where the Tool Tip says Walls), then select Format Walls from the menu that appears.

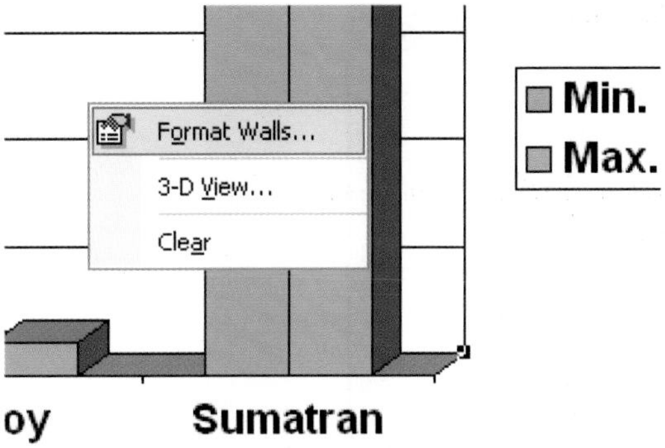

The Format Walls window appears.

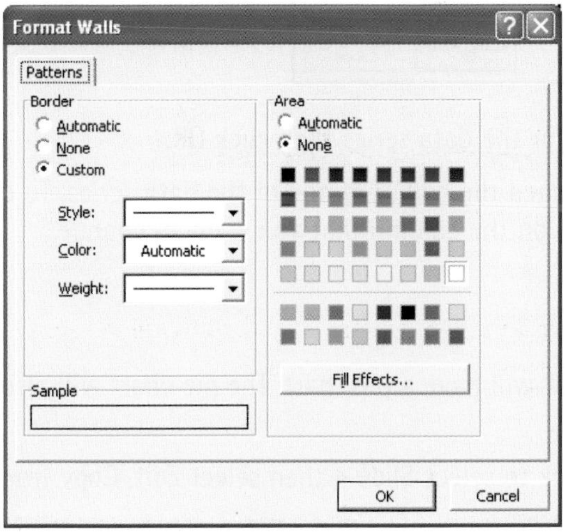

- Click one of the colours to select a background colour, or check the None box to leave the background transparent. Click OK.

Changing the column colours

- With the chart still in edit mode (with the datasheet visible), right-click on one of the columns, then select Format Data Series from the menu that appears.

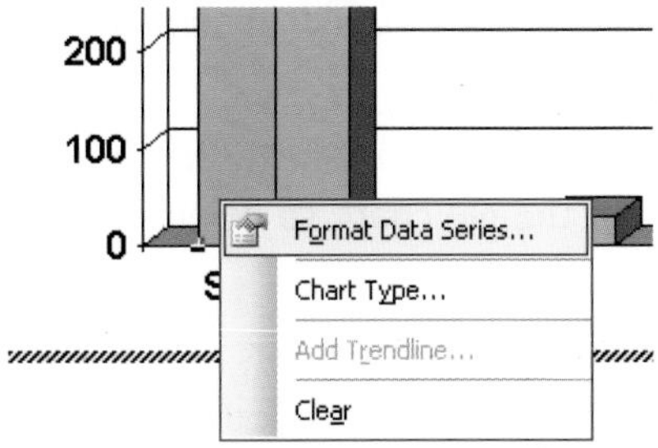

The Format Data Series window appears.

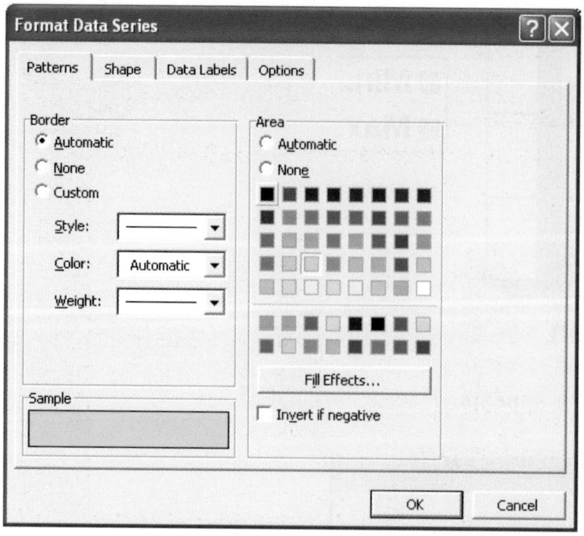

- Pick a different colour for the data series then click OK.

- This will only have changed the colour of one of the data series. To change the other colour, right-click on the column that you want to change.

Adding a pie chart

We will create a new slide that will have a pie chart. The pie chart will also be based on the tiger population estimates.

- In the Outline pane, click to select Slide 4 then select Edit, Copy from the menu.

- You could have selected Cut instead of Copy. This would have copied the slide but then deleted it. The Cut option is useful when you want to move images, text and slides from one place to another. To delete a slide, click it to select it and then press the Delete key.

Tip:

You will learn how to copy or move slides between open presentations in Chapter 6.6.

- Now select Edit, Paste from the menu. A copy of Slide 4 should appear just after Slide 4, and has become Slide 5.

- Double-click the chart on Slide 5 to show the datasheet. We only want the minimum estimates to be included in the pie chart, so delete the row named Max. Estimate.

Tip:

You can cut or copy just the chart to move or copy it to another slide or another open presentation. Click the chart and select either Edit, Cut or Copy. Move to the destination slide and select Edit, Paste.
To delete a chart, click it and press the Delete key.

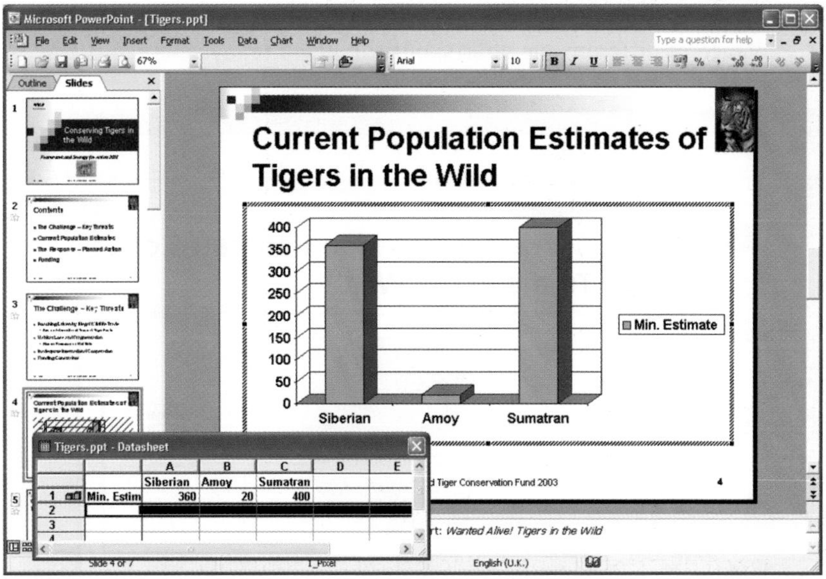

- Now we need to change the chart type. Right-click on the Chart Area (outside the actual chart, but within the chart boundary).

Tip:
If **Chart Type** isn't on your menu, you probably clicked in the wrong place. **PowerPoint** brings up different menus according to where you click.

- Select **Chart Type** from the menu that appears.

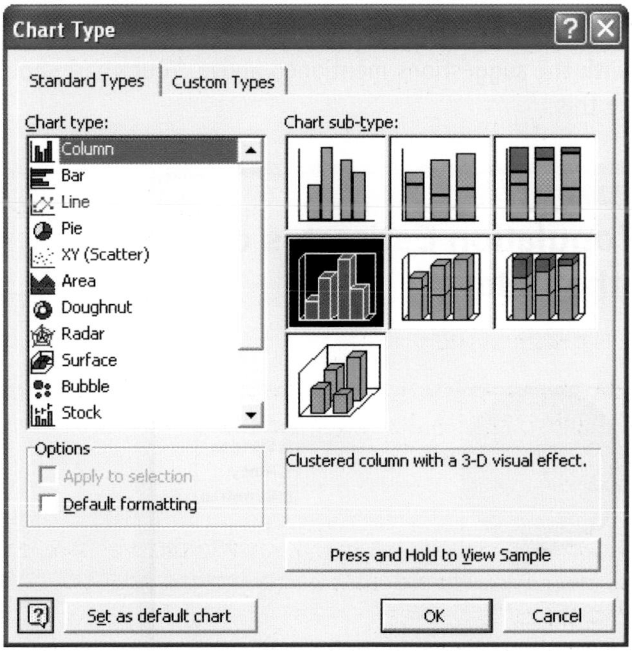

Click **Pie** in the left-hand window of the Chart Type dialogue box. You are given a choice of different pie charts, but the one already selected is fine so click **OK**.

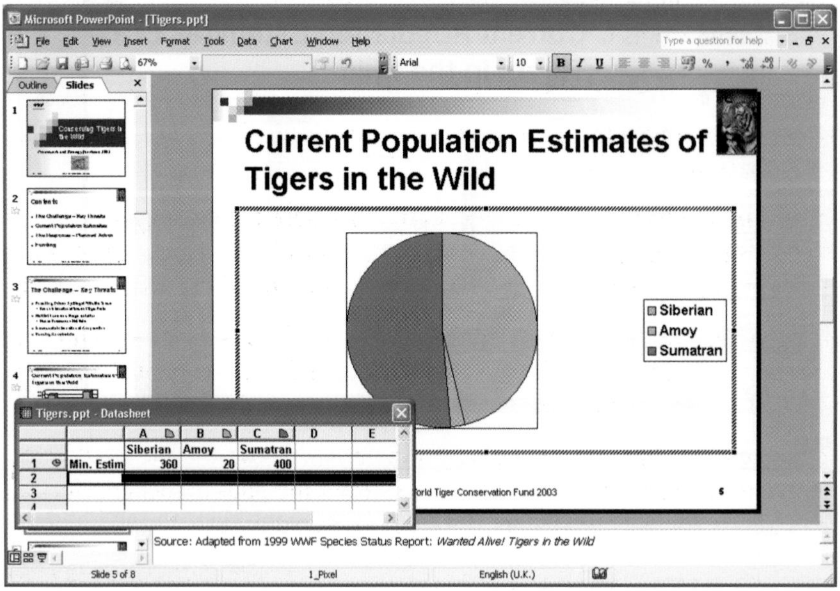

The chart is now a pie chart!

If you want to add some data labels to the pie chart, like a percentage next to each slice, right-click somewhere under the legend whilst the datasheet is in view, then select **Chart Options** and change the settings under the **Data Labels** tab. You'll need to do this whilst the chart is selected; if you can see the datasheet then the chart is selected.

Have a play with the suggestions mentioned above. Your chart should now look something like this:

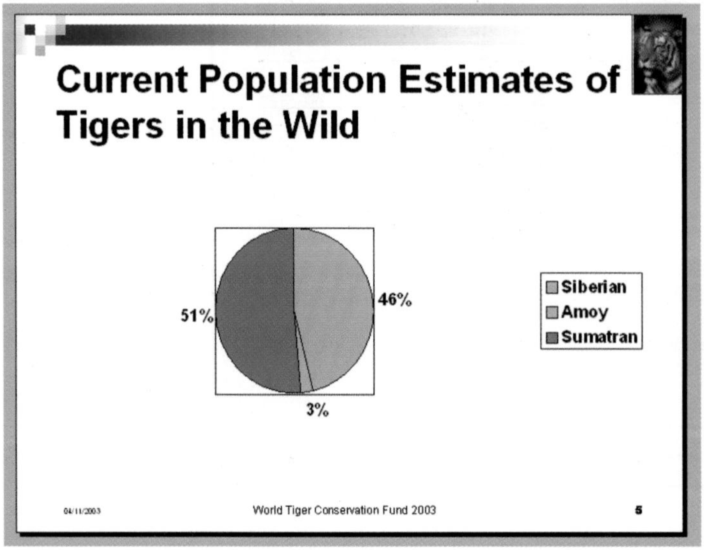

Changing chart colours

We looked earlier at how to change some of the colours in a column chart. All chart types can be formatted in a similar way. First of all take a look at some of the other chart types such as bar charts and line charts:

- Double-click the pie chart and select Chart Type from the pop-up menu.
- Select a type from the list and then click the Press and Hold to View Sample button.

To change the background of any chart, make sure the datasheet is in view, then right-click close to the chart within the background (the Plot Area). Select Format Plot Area from the pop-up menu and choose a colour from the Format Plot Area dialogue box.

You can change the colour of all columns, bars, lines or slices within a chart or you can change individual items. The technique is the same for column, bar, line and pie charts. For example in a bar chart:

To change the colour of all the bars in a data series, select the chart, click a bar once, right-click and select Format Data Series from the pop-up menu. Select a colour from the Patterns tab on the Format Data Series dialogue box.

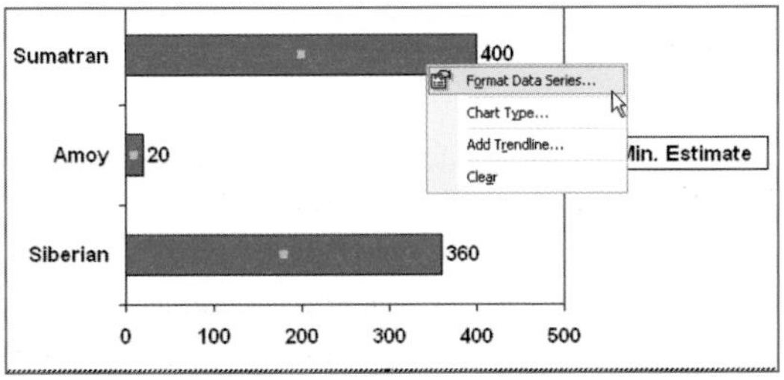

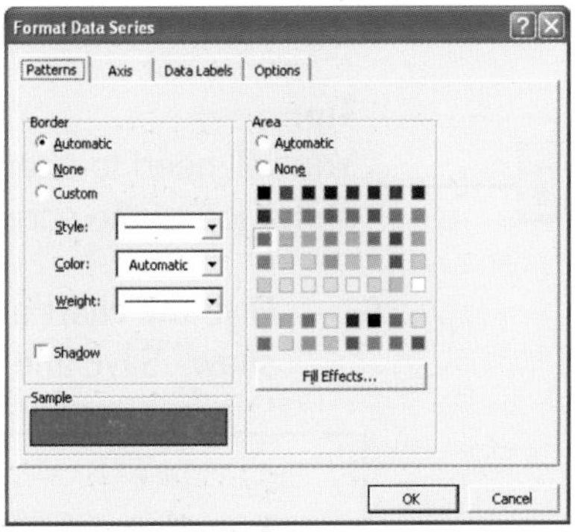

To change the colour of an individual bar, click any bar once, then click the specific bar to select it. Now right-click it and select Format Data Point. Select a colour from the Patterns tab on the Format Data Point dialogue box.

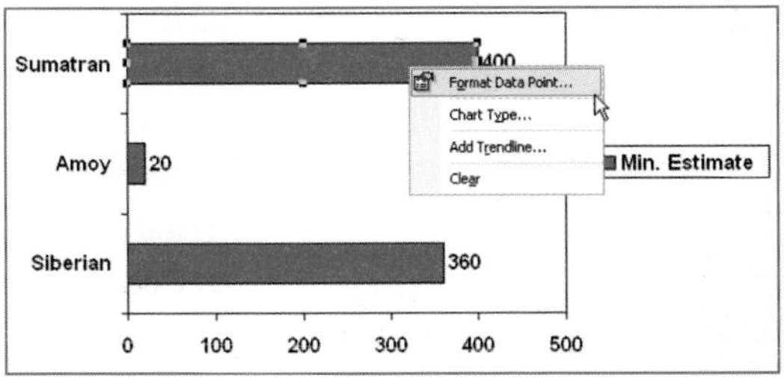

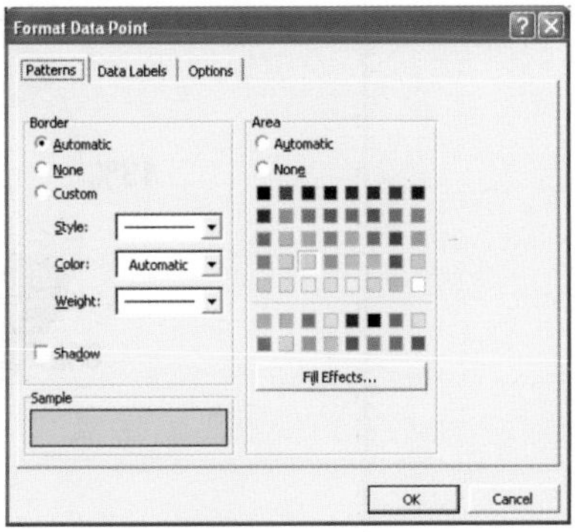

Exercise

Now you will add a graphic to the Mapsters presentation you have worked on in previous practice exercises. You will also add a chart showing the company sales by product (i.e. maps of European countries).

1. Open the file Mapsters.ppt.
2. Find a Clip Art image of a globe that would be suitable as a company logo for Mapsters Ltd.
3. Insert it on every slide except the title slide, in the top right-hand corner.
4. Size the image to fit.
5. On the Sales by Product slide insert a pie chart based on the datasheet shown opposite.

Mapsters.ppt - Datasheet

		A	B
		2002 (£k)	
1	Austria	60.9	
2	Belgium	89.4	
3	Eire	86.7	
4	France	170.4	
5	Germany	120.4	
6	Italy	130.9	
7	Portugal	86.3	
8	Spain	140.3	
9	Switzerland	98.9	
10	UK	80.6	
11			

Tip:
You will need to change the chart to By Column by clicking the icon on the toolbar at the top of the screen.

6. Give the chart a title and display the data labels as percentages. Run the slide show. Save and close the presentation.

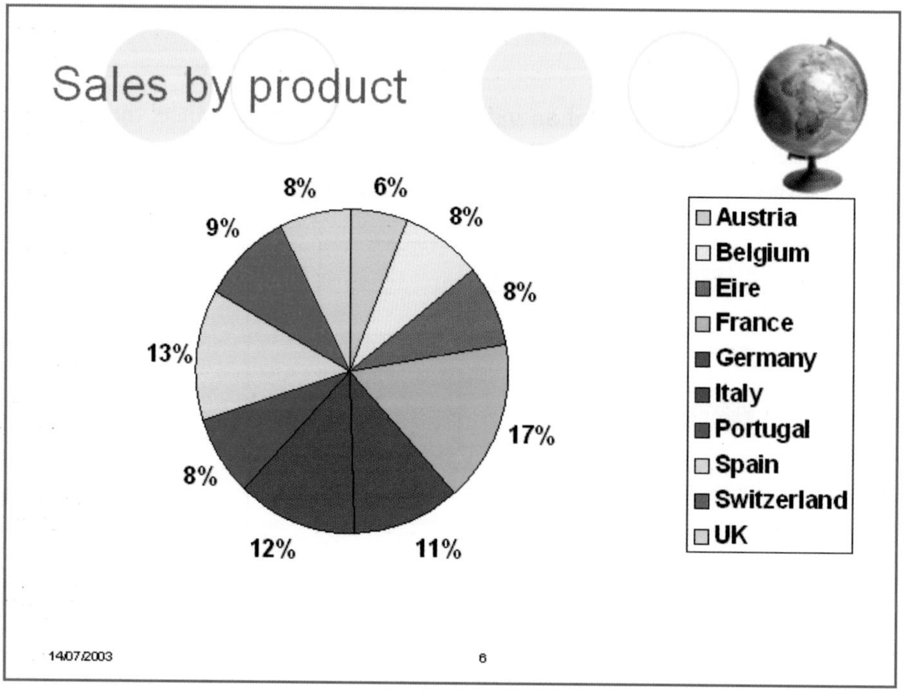

Special Effects

CHAPTER 6.5

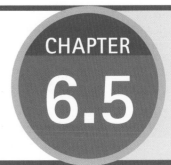

In this chapter you will be adding sounds and animation to your presentation. You can also add transition effects when each screen opens.

- Open the presentation Tigers.ppt.
- Select the Slide Sorter View and click the first slide.

Adding Slide Transitions

Transitions change the way a slide opens. You can make the next slide open like a blind or a curtain, for example.

All the commands you need to create transitions are in the Slide Transition Task pane.

- To view this pane click Slide Show, Slide Transition on the menu. Alternatively, if the Task pane is already visible, you can bring up the Slide Transition options by clicking the small down-arrow at the top of the Task pane, then clicking Slide Transition from the menu that appears.

- With the first slide selected, scroll down the list and select Split Vertical Out. This will make the first screen open like a curtain, as if it were opening in a theatre.
- You can also add a sound to this transition by simply choosing one from the Sound list.

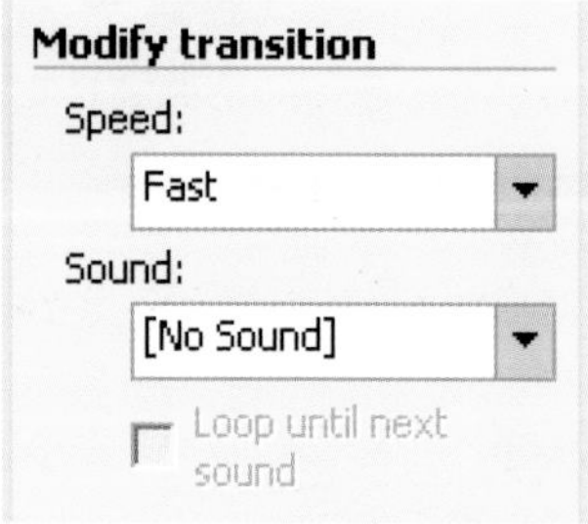

You can also change the speed at which the transition occurs. In most cases, Fast is the best. Try experimenting!

Adding transitions to multiple slides

If you wish to add a transition to all the slides, click the Apply to All button in the Slide Transition pane.

You can apply a transition to more than one slide but not all by selecting the slides first using the Ctrl key, or Shift to select a range.

To add the same transition to all the rest of the slides except Slide 7:

- In Slide Sorter View, click Slide 2 and then hold down the Shift key.
- With the Shift key still pressed, click Slide 6.
- Now choose the Cover Left transition from the Slide Transition pane.
- Now view your show to see the results!

Tip:
When you start a Slide show, it will start from the currently selected slide. If you want to start from the beginning, make sure Slide 1 is selected before clicking the Slide Show button.

Adding special effects to text

PowerPoint also allows you to add animation effects to objects such as Clip Art images, charts and bulleted lists.

In Slide Sorter View you can add animation using the Slide Design pane.

- View the Slide Design pane by clicking the small down-arrow at the top of the Task Pane, then selecting Slide Design – Animation Schemes from the list.
- At the top of the Slide Design pane, make sure Animation Schemes is selected.

- Click away from the slides to deselect them, then click Slide 2.
- Click to select an animation effect from the Slide Design pane. If you don't like it, just click another one.
- Try out your chosen effect in Slide Show view.
- Go back to Slide Sorter View and change the animation effect to Dissolve in.

Formatting text and images

Now we will create the logo of the World Tiger Conservation Fund.

Most of the tools we will need to do this are on the Drawing toolbar. This is usually located at the bottom of the screen in Normal View.

Tip:
These tools can also be used to draw objects on the master slide.

Adding a shadow to text

- Select Slide 1. Click the Text Box button on the Drawing toolbar.
- Click and drag the mouse button to draw a text box near the top of the slide.
- Enter the acronym WTCF in Arial, bold, size 24.

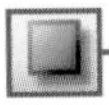

- Click the Shadow Style button on the Drawing toolbar.

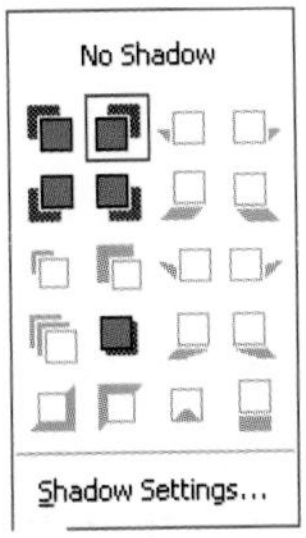

- Click to select one of the shadow options – it doesn't matter which one.

Adding lines to a slide

We'll add a horizontal line beneath the letters.

- Click the Line button on the Drawing toolbar.
- Whilst holding down the Shift key, click and hold the mouse button to drag out a horizontal line. Release the mouse button when you are happy with the line.
- The Shift key restricts the number of angles the line can take which makes it easier to draw a horizontal line. Try drawing it without!

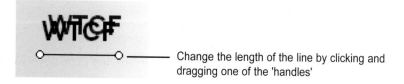

Change the length of the line by clicking and dragging one of the 'handles'

- If you want to move the line slightly higher or lower, move the mouse pointer over the line until it becomes two double-headed arrows, then click and drag.

Changing the colour of the line

- Click the line to select it. Click the small down-arrow on the Line Color button.

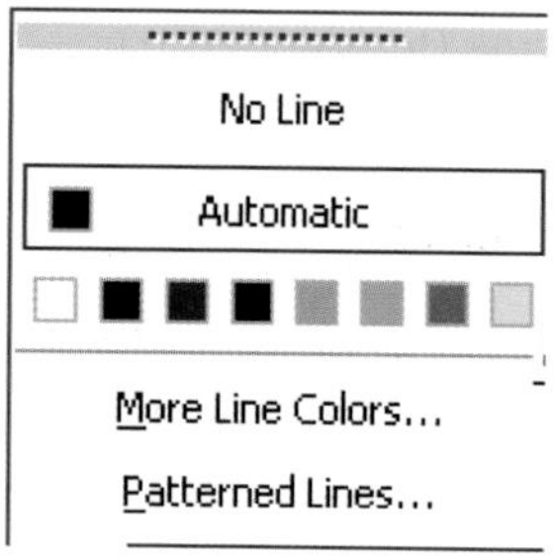

- Click to select a different colour, such as a dark blue.

Modifying the line width

Click to select the line. Click the **Line Style** button.

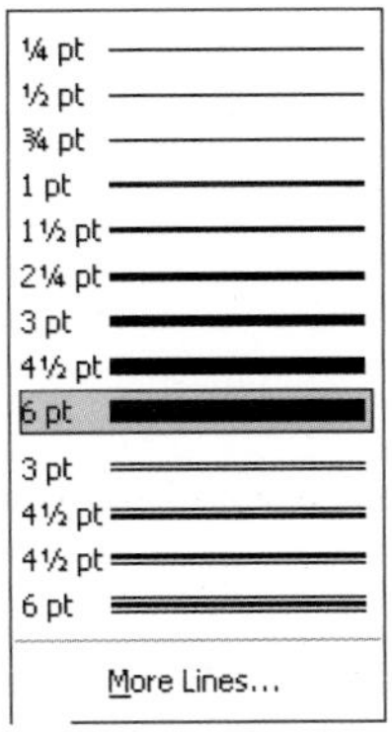

Make the line much thicker by clicking the **6pt** line.

Modifying the line style

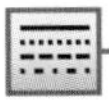

With the line selected, click the **Dash Style** button. Select one you like from the list.

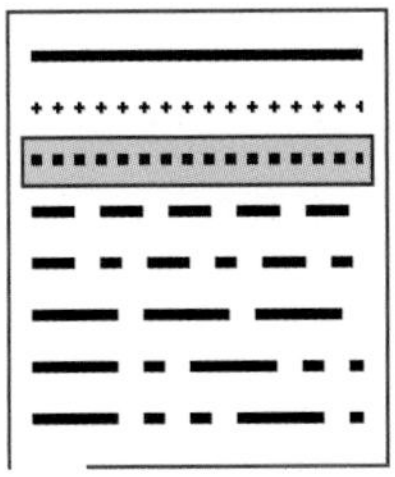

That's all we need for the logo, but let's practise using some of the other drawing tools.

Adding a free-drawn line

Click the **Autoshapes** button on the **Drawing** toolbar.

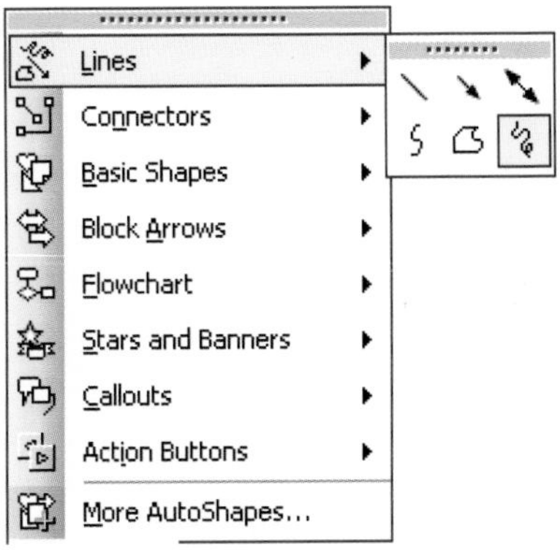

- Select Lines, then select the Scribble icon.
- Add a freehand scribble to the slide!

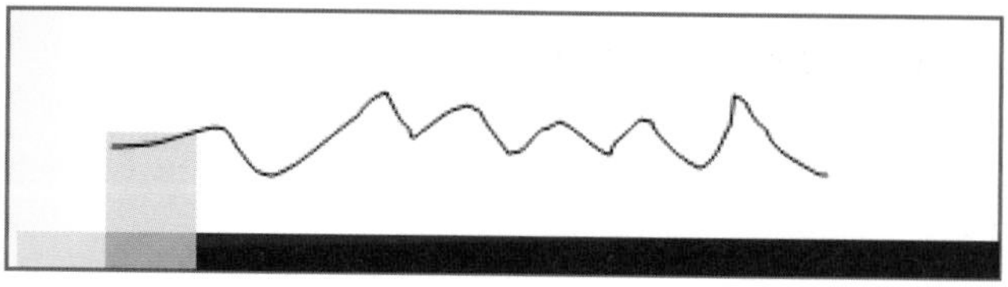

Adding an arrow

- Click the Arrow button on the Drawing toolbar.
- Click and drag out an arrow next to your freehand line, then release the mouse button.
- Format the arrow by right-clicking it, then selecting Format Autoshape from the menu that appears.

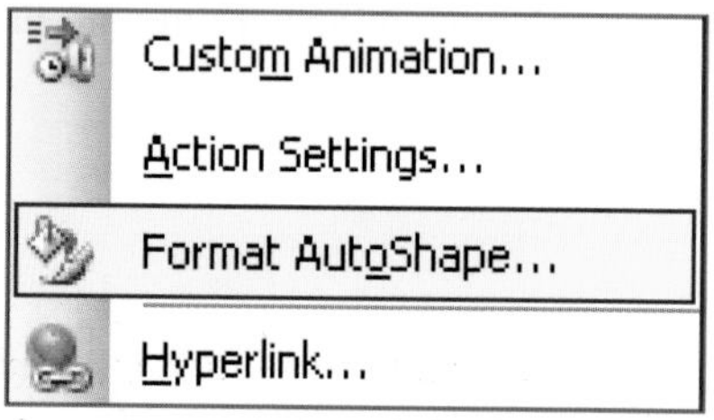

The Format Autoshape window appears:

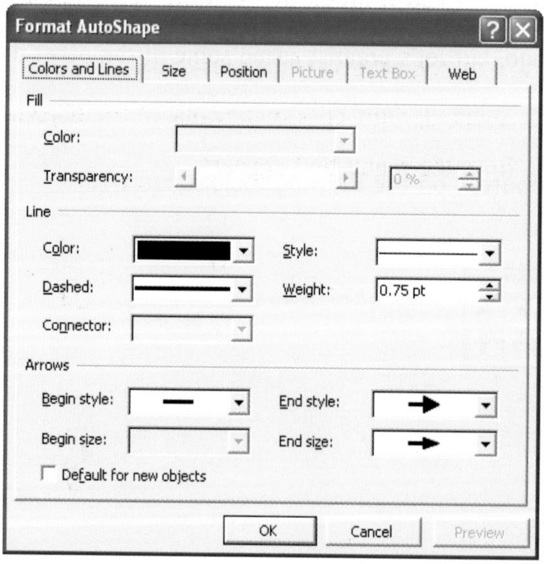

- Change the arrow beginning and end style until you are happy with it. Click OK.

Rotating or flipping an object

- Now flip the arrow you've just drawn. Make sure it is selected, then click the down-arrow on the **Draw** button on the **Drawing** toolbar.
- Select **Rotate or Flip** from the next menu.

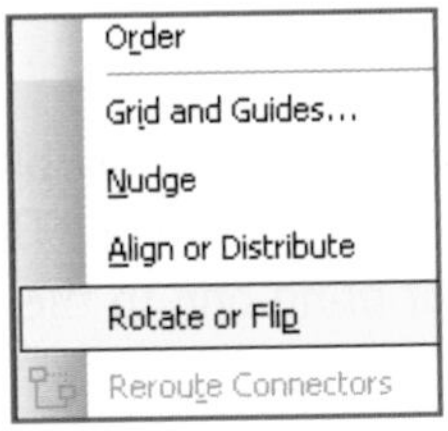

- Have a play with the different rotate and flip options!

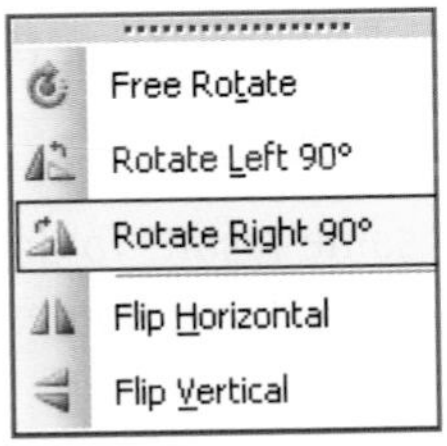

Selecting and grouping drawn objects

- You can select more than one object by clicking the first object, holding down the **Shift** key, then clicking other objects. Select the freehand line and the arrow you've just drawn.
- Grouping objects is useful if you want all the separate objects to be treated as one object. This means you only need to click once to select them all, and if you move one of the objects, all the others will be moved too.
- With both the objects selected, right-click on any one of the objects.
- Click **Grouping**, **Group** from the menu that appears.

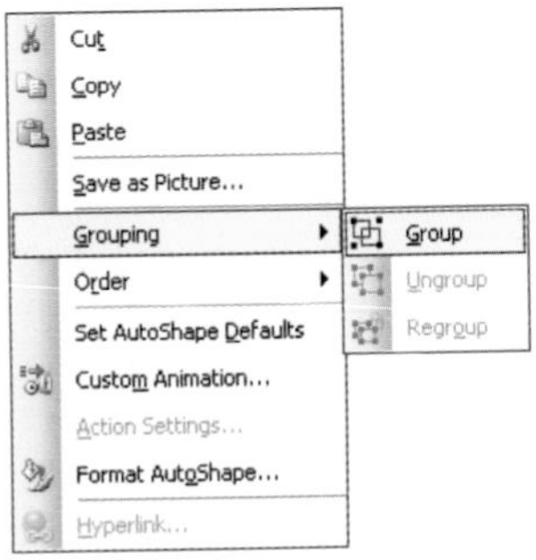

The objects are now grouped! Try selecting them and moving them around – they should move together.

Ungrouping

- To ungroup, just right-click one of the objects and select Grouping, Ungroup from the menu that appears.
- Now group the 2 lines together again.

Sending objects to the front or back

When you've got two objects overlapping, PowerPoint will automatically place the most recent object on top. If this isn't what you want, you need to change the Order of the objects, and either send one of the objects to the back, or bring one to the front.

- Drag the objects you've just drawn so that they are overlapping the text on the title page. You should see that the objects are on top of the text.

We'd like the text to be on top, so we will send the drawn objects to the back.

- Right-click one of the objects and select Order, Send to Back from the menu.

The objects will now be behind the text!

- Bringing the text to the front would have had the same result. To do this, select the text box so that it has a fuzzy border, then right-click the border and select Order, Bring to Front from the menu.

- Drag the lines away from the text and press the Delete key to remove them from the slide.

Adding shapes to a slide

As well as lines, you can add a range of shapes such as boxes and circles to a slide. You can modify these shapes in exactly the same way as lines. We'll run through this quickly by adding a rectangle at the top of the slide.

- Click the Rectangle button on the Drawing toolbar. Click and drag the mouse pointer to drag out a large rectangle like the one below:

Conserving Tigers in the Wild

Tip:
Use the Oval tool to draw ovals and circles. To draw a perfect circle or square, keep your finger on the Shift key as you drag out the shape.

Changing the fill colour

- Make sure the rectangle is selected and click the small down-arrow on the Fill Color button.
- Select a dark blue colour.
- If you didn't want any fill in the shape, you would choose No Fill instead of a colour.

Changing the border colour

- Click the Line Color button and make the border the same dark blue as the fill.

Applying a shadow to a shape

This is done exactly as for the line.

- Click the Shadow Style button then one of the shadow options.
- Now tidy up the title slide by deleting the shape you have just added: just click to select it then press the Delete key.

Moving or copying a line or shape

To move or copy a drawn object, click the object and select Edit, Cut or Copy. On the destination slide (either within the presentation or in a different, open presentation) select Edit, Paste.

Deleting a line or shape

To delete a drawn object on either a normal slide or the master slide, click the object and press the Delete key.

Aligning a line or shape on a slide

To align a drawn object on a slide, click the object and then click the Draw button on the Drawing toolbar. Click Align or Distribute and make sure the Relative to Slide option is selected. Now select how you want the shape to be aligned (e.g. left, right, centre etc.)

Tip:
Click the AutoShapes button on the Drawing toolbar to access lots more shapes such as stars, banners, triangles etc. These can be drawn, formatted and deleted in the same way as rectangles and circles.

Adding and modifying a text box

We will add a text box to Slide 5.

- With Slide 5 selected, click the Text Box button on the Drawing toolbar.
- Click and drag the mouse button to drag out a text box anywhere below the chart.

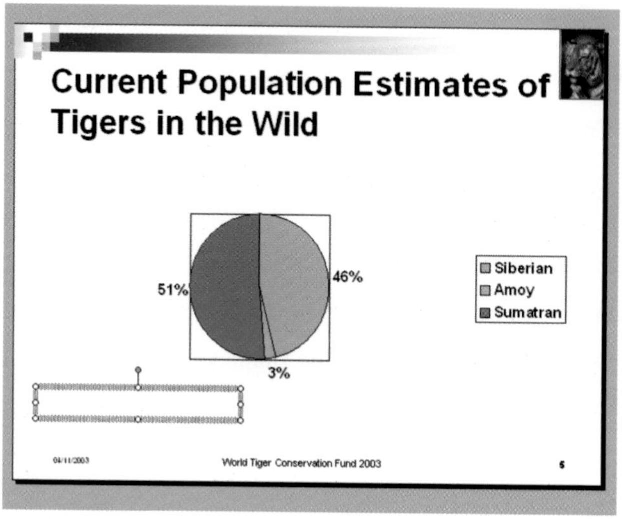

- Type the text Source: 1999 WWF Species Status Report.

Repositioning and resizing

- Click and drag the handles until the text box is positioned as shown below:

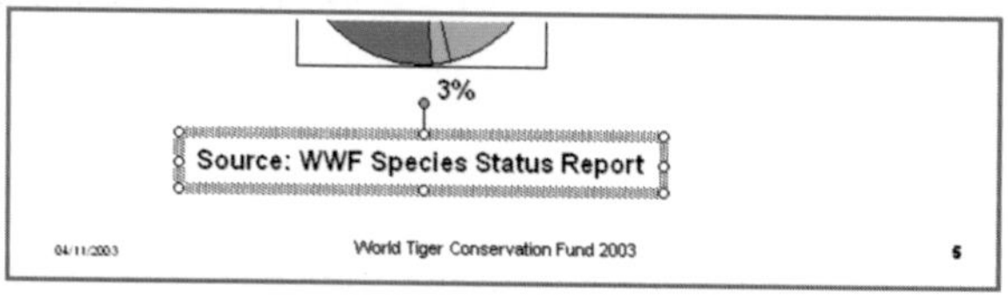

Changing the text colour

- Select the text box so that it's got a fuzzy border. Click the down-arrow on the Font Color button.

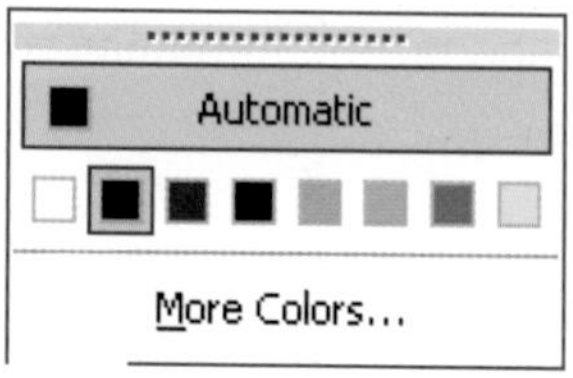

- Select a dark blue colour.

Adding a border

- Click the Line Style button. Select the 1pt line.

- You can change the colour of this line using the Line Color button.

Adding superscript and subscript text

We will add a superscript 1 to effectively footnote the Source text box.

- Add the number 1 directly after the title, without a space.

Current Population Estimates of
Tigers in the Wild1

- Highlight just the 1, then select Format, Font from the menu.
- Check the box marked Superscript.
- If you wanted to add subscript text, you would check the box marked Subscript instead.
- Click OK. The 1 should now be in Superscript.

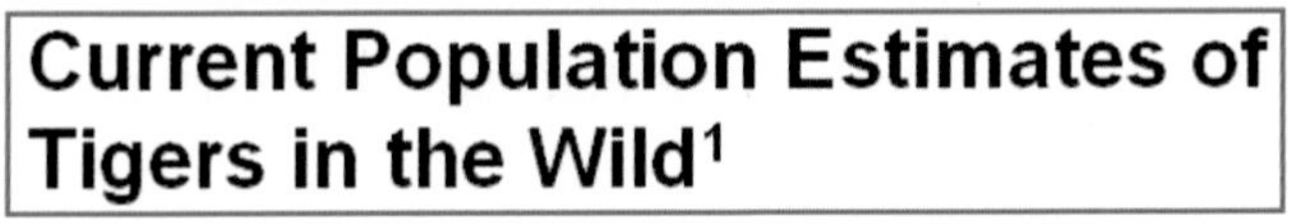
Current Population Estimates of
Tigers in the Wild[1]

- Now add a 1 before all the text in the text box. Make it superscript using the same method. It should look like this when you're done:

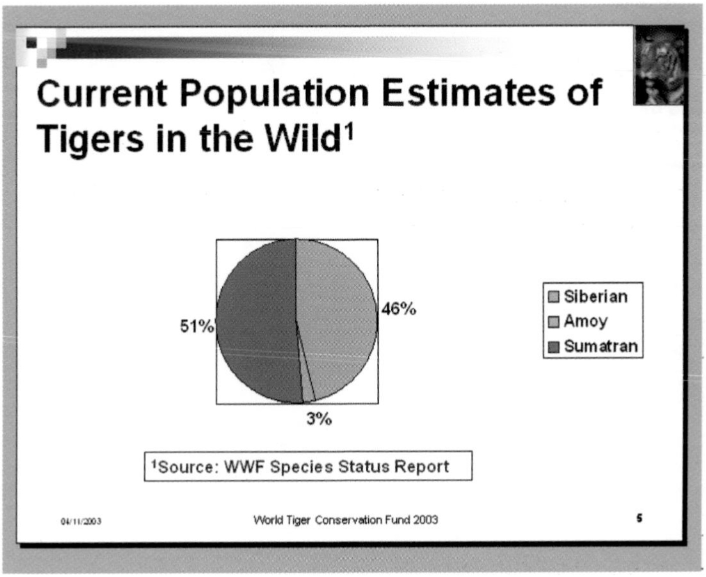

Exercise

There is just one slide left to complete on the Mapsters Ltd presentation that you have been working on at the end of each chapter. This exercise asks you to complete that slide and add slide transitions and special effects.

1. Open the file **Mapsters.ppt**.
2. On slide 5, **Target Markets**, use the Drawing toolbar to produce the following diagram:

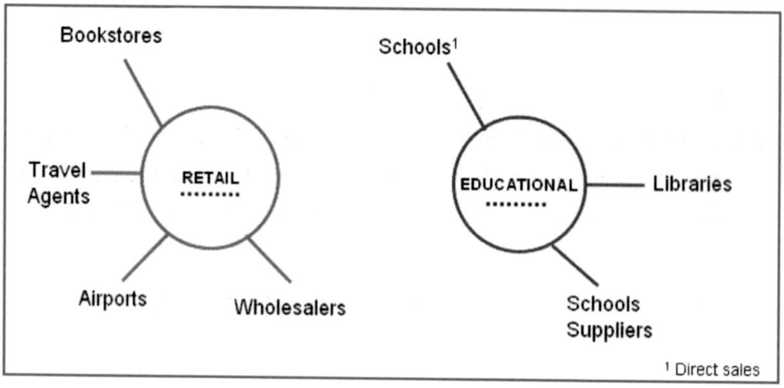

3. Add a **Blinds Horizontal** transition between all slides. Choose to advance slides on a mouse click.
4. On slides 2 and 3 insert a special effect that makes the bullet points fly in from the left at a medium speed.
5. Add a slight shadow to the headings on all pages.
6. Run the slide show and make any necessary adjustments. Save and close your work. The slides should now be looking something like this:

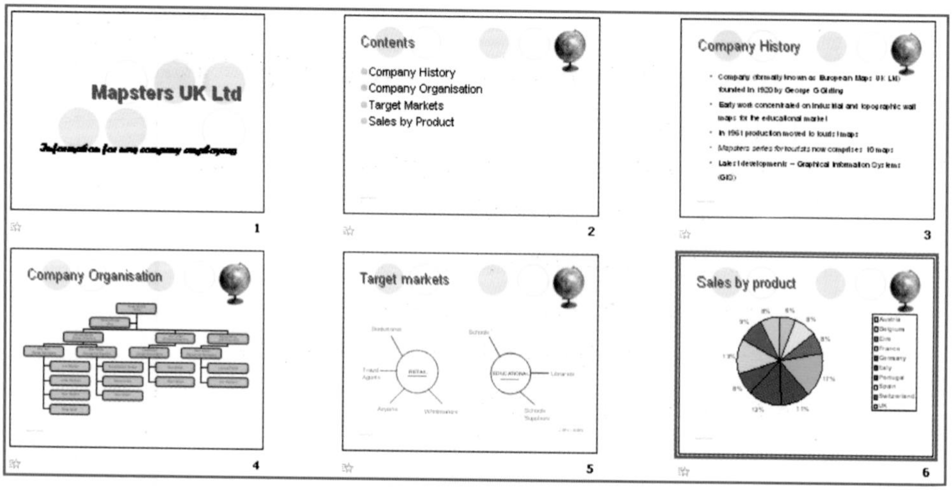

Show Time!

CHAPTER 6.6

In this chapter you'll find out how PowerPoint can help you during your presentation. Most of these features work best when you are giving the presentation on a big screen and controlling it from your computer. That's when PowerPoint presentations are most effective.

- Open the document called Tigers.ppt if it is not already open.

Starting a show on any slide

To start a show on a particular slide, all you need to do is make sure that slide is selected before clicking the Slide Show button. For example, to start a show on Slide 3:

- In the Outline pane click to select Slide 3.
- Click the Slide Show button.

The slide show should open on Slide 3: The Challenge – Key Threats.

The Challenge – Key Threats
Poaching Driven by Illegal Wildlife Trade
Ban on International Trade of Tiger Parts
Habitat Loss and Fragmentation
Human Pressure on Habitats
Inadequate International Cooperation
Funding Constraints
07/10/2003
World Tiger Conservation Fund 2003
3

Navigating your way around a presentation

Once in Slide Show mode, right-click the mouse and a small menu will appear.

To find your way around a presentation you can click the Next and Previous options on the pop-up menu. This will take you to either the next or previous step in the presentation.

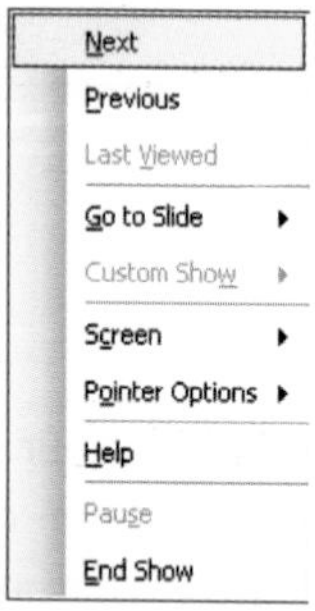

Tip:

An easier way to go to the next slide is to click the Space bar. To go back a slide press the Backspace key.

If you want to move to a particular slide, click Go to slide on the menu. This will bring up another menu in which you select By Title. Go to the Contents slide.

Hiding slides

Suppose that you don't want to show one of the slides in your presentation. We will hide Slide 5.

In Normal View, select Slide 5 by clicking it in the Outline pane.

Select Slideshow, Hide Slide from the menu.

This slide will now not appear when you run your presentation. You can see in the Outline pane if a slide is hidden because it will have the Hidden Slide icon behind the slide number.

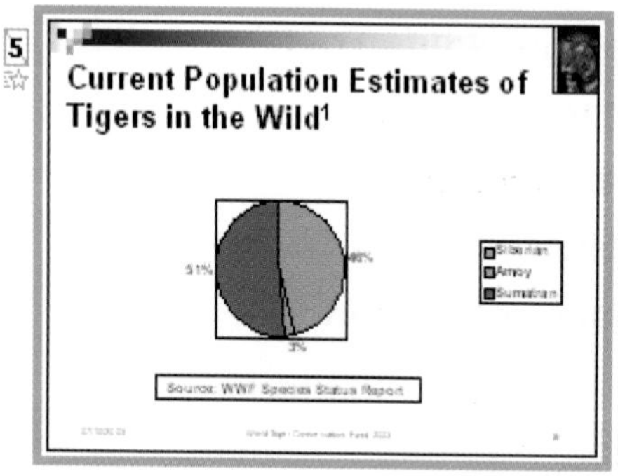

If you want to unhide the slide, follow exactly the same procedure. Just select Slide Show, Hide Slide from the menu.

Using the Notes pages

To assist you in your presentation you can make additional notes about each slide to prompt you. These notes are visible only by you, not your audience, when you print them out or view them on-screen.

- Select Slide 4: Current Population Estimates of Tigers in the Wild.

The pane below the slide is for adding notes. To make it easier to write notes, make this pane bigger by clicking and dragging the grey border above the Notes pane.

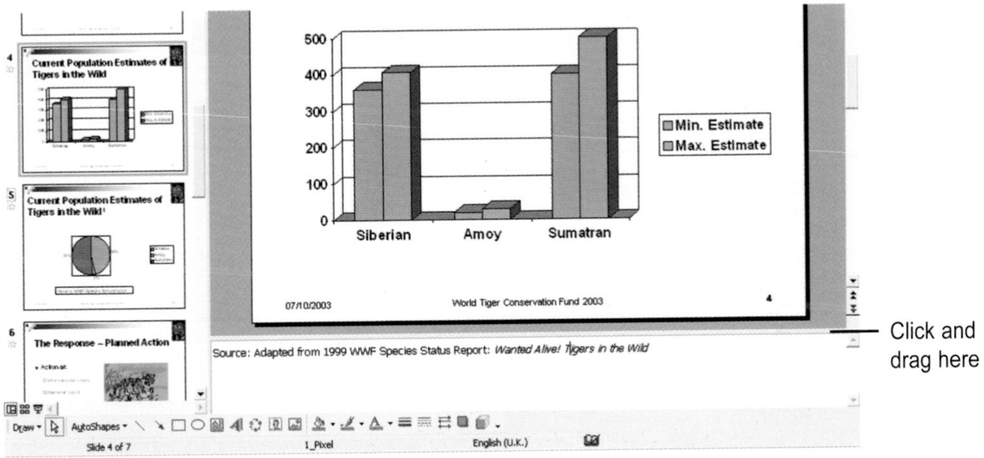

- Now you can type some notes. Type the notes from the screenshot above, or just make up your own.

Viewing your notes during a presentation

You can either view the notes on-screen if you get stuck for words in your show or else you can print out the Notes pages. We'll cover printing at the end of the chapter.

- To view the notes on-screen, right-click the mouse when you're in Slide Show mode and select Screen and then Speaker Notes. Of course you will only see notes if you are on Slide 4.

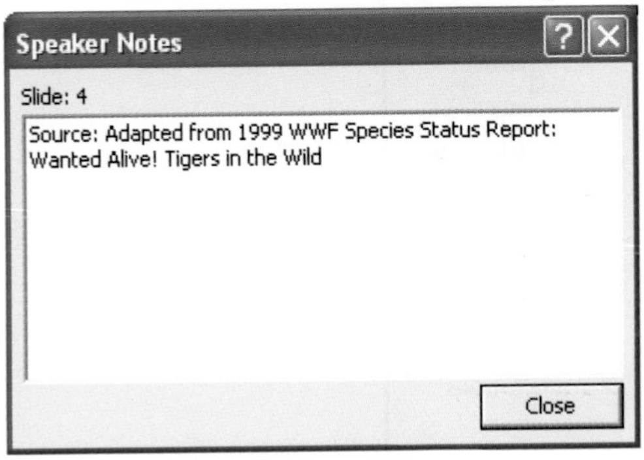

- Click Close to close the Speaker Notes window.

Slide Setup

- Select File, Page Setup from the menu.
- To change the orientation of the slides, just select either the Portrait or Landscape option under the Slides section.
- You can choose an appropriate output format using the Slides sized for: list. The options you may be asked about for ECDL are On-screen show, Overhead and 35mm Slides.

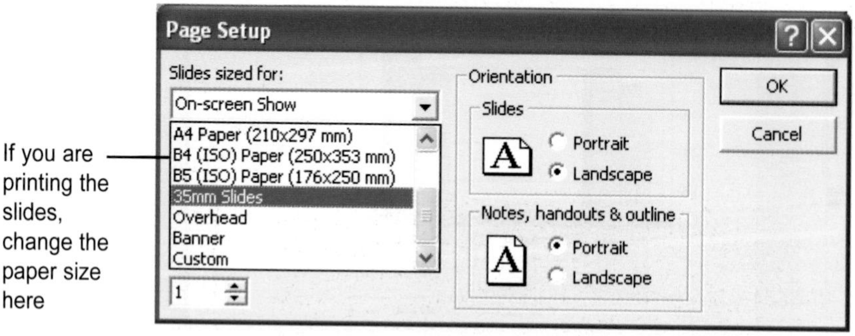

- Click OK when you are happy with the settings.

Printing

- To print anything, select File, Print from the main menu.

The following window will appear. There are quite a few different options here! Below is a list of things which you may be asked to print for ECDL, along with instructions on which options to choose for each.

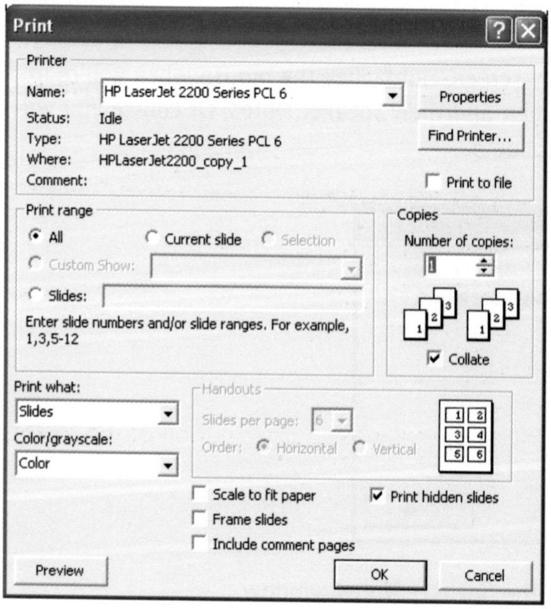

Printing slides

- To print just the slides, make sure **Slides** is selected under the **Print what:** section.
- You can change which slides are printed using the **Print Range** section.
- Set the number of copies in the **Copies** section.

- Preview the slide printouts by clicking the **Preview** button. Notice that page numbers appear on the printout because we selected them in an earlier chapter.

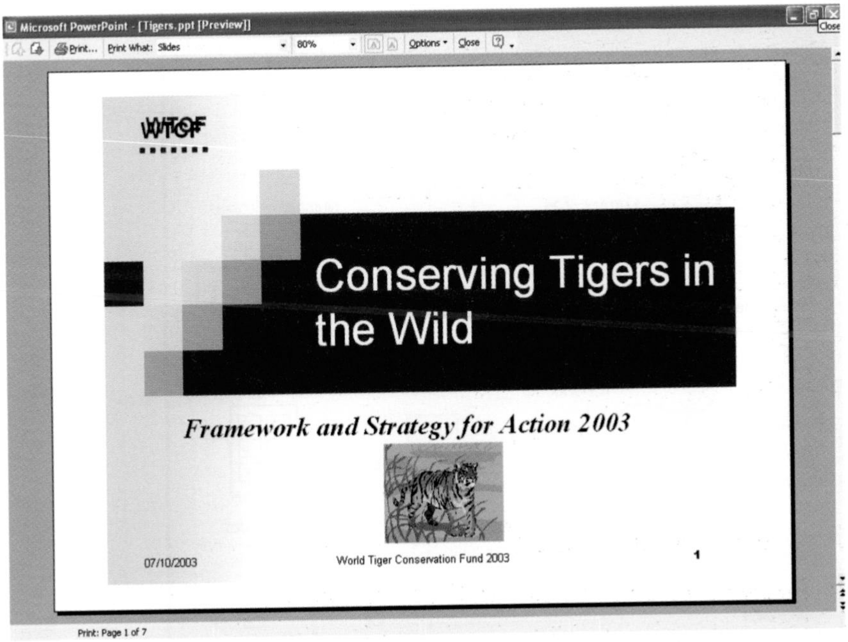

- From this screen you can also preview **Handouts, Notes pages** and **Outline View**, by selecting the different options under the **Print What:** list at the top of the screen.
- Try selecting some of these options to see the different print previews.

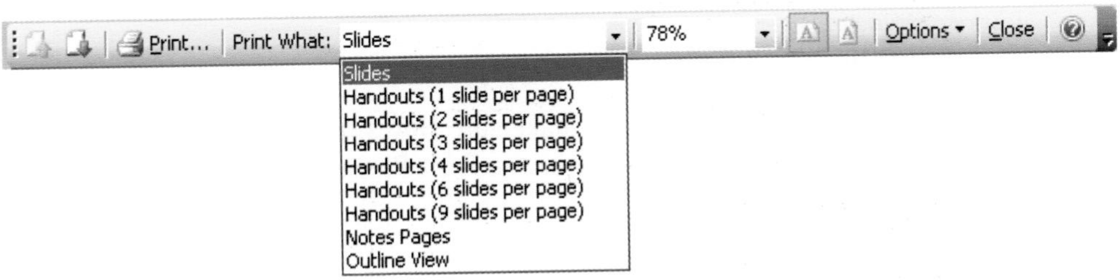

- Close the **Preview** window by clicking the **Close** button at the top of the screen.

Printing handouts

- This is very similar to printing slides. Select File, Print to bring up the Print window.
- This time from the Print what list, select Handouts.

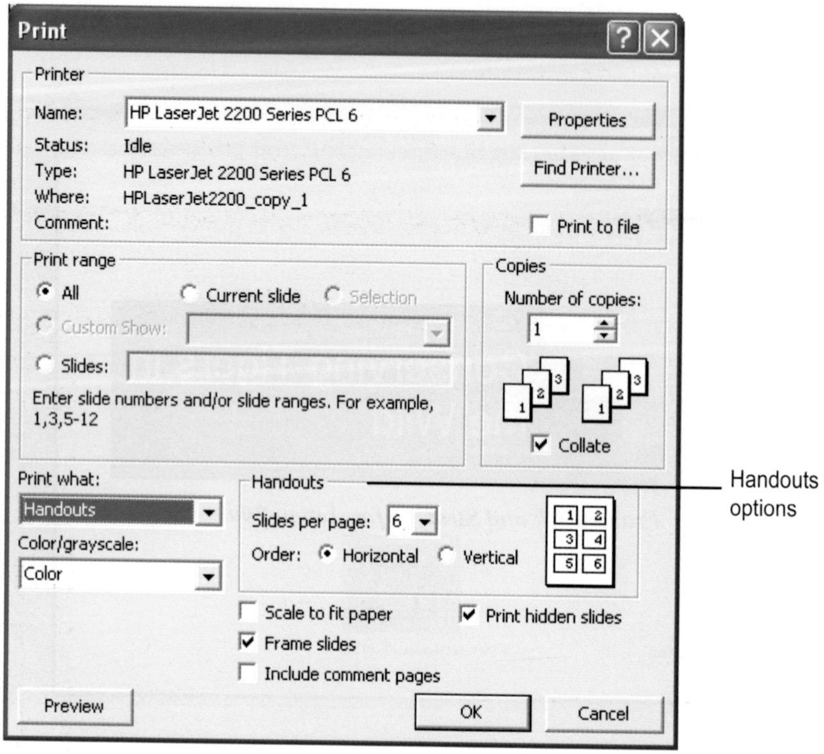

- Notice that there is a Handouts section in this window. You can choose how many slides to print on a page, and also change the order from Horizontal to Vertical. Try choosing different amounts of slide per page.
- Again, click the Preview button to see what it will look like. You can also change the number of slides on a page here using the Print what list.

Printing Notes pages

- To print the notes, just make sure Notes pages is selected in the Print what list in either the Print window or the Print Preview window.

Copying slides to a new presentation

You can copy slides between presentations. To try this out we will open a new presentation – do this whilst keeping the Tigers.ppt presentation open.

- Click File, New from the menu. Select Blank Presentation from the New Presentation pane.

We will add just a couple of slides to this presentation by copying and pasting slides from the Tigers.ppt presentation.

- Go back to the Tigers presentation either by selecting Window, Tigers.ppt from the menu, or by clicking the Tigers.ppt button at the very bottom of your screen.

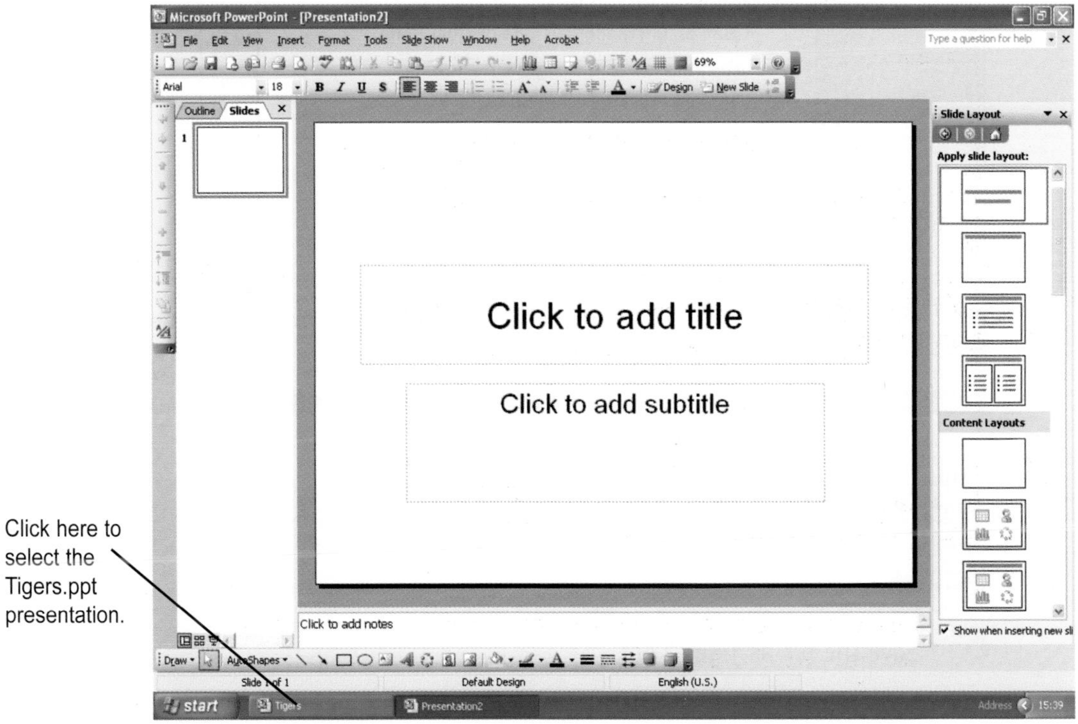

Tip:
Switch between open presentations by clicking the file names on the Task bar.

- In Slide Sorter View, select both Slide 2 and Slide 3 by clicking them whilst holding down the Ctrl key.
- Select Edit, Copy from the menu.
- Remember you could have selected Cut instead of Copy. This would have copied the slides but then deleted them from the original presentation.
- Return to the new presentation and click Slide 1. Select Edit, Paste from the menu.

The two slides will be copied to the new presentation. The background has not been copied because the slides assume the formatting of the new presentation.

If you want to keep the original formatting, click the Paste Options button, which appears under the slides you pasted, and on the button menu, click Keep Source Formatting.

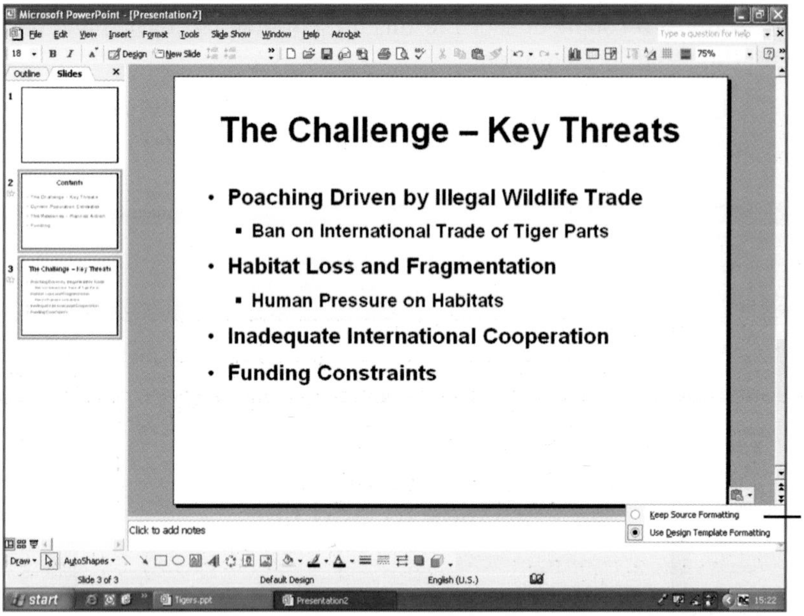

Select this option to keep the source formatting

Tip:
If the Paste Options button does not appear, select Tools, Options from the menu. In the Options dialogue box, click the Edit tab and select Show Paste Options buttons.

- Save the file as Tigers2.ppt.

Saving in different file formats

You have a choice of many file formats other than the normal .ppt format. We will save the Tigers2 file as a template.

- Go to File, Save As on the menu. Locate the Tiger Presentation folder in the Save in: box.
- Enter Tigers2 as the File Name. Below the File Name: box is the Save as type: box. There is a large selection of different file types.

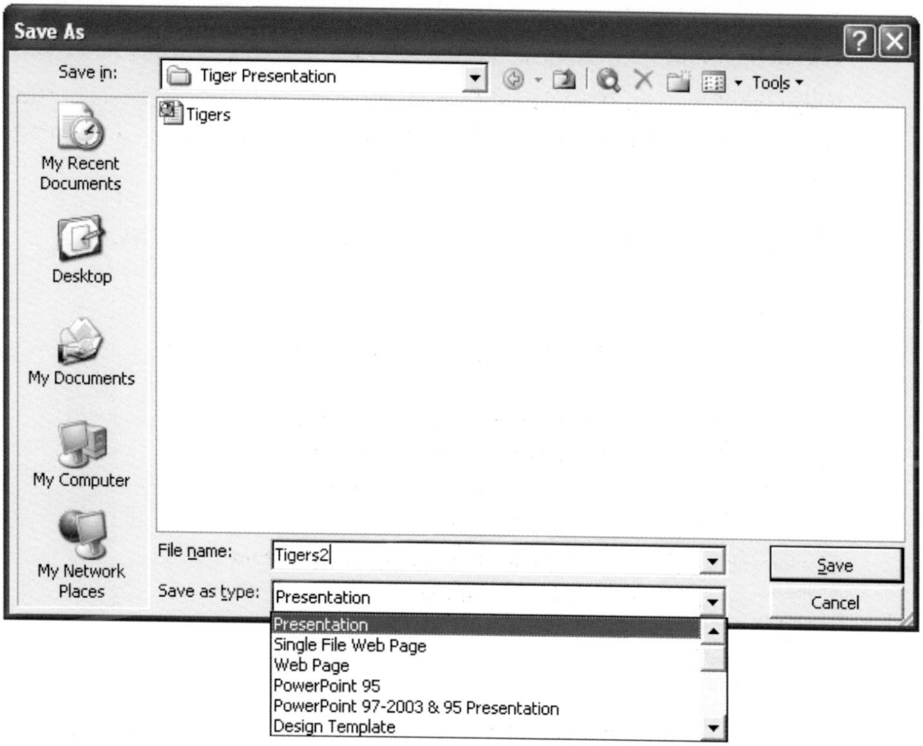

- We'll save this presentation as a **Design Template (*.pot)**. Click to select **Design Template** from the list.

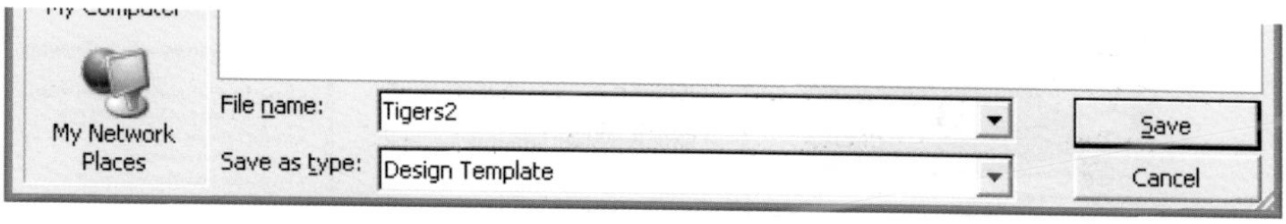

- Click the **Save** button to save the **Tigers2** presentation.
- If you wanted to post a presentation to a web site, you would save it with the **Web Page** format (*.htm, *.html).
- You can choose to save the presentation for use in a different version of PowerPoint (95, 97-2003 & 95).
- If you choose to save in Rich Text Format (*.rtf) you lose the graphical content of the presentation.
- You can choose to save a slide as a graphic (*.bmp, *.wmf or *.emf).
- You can also choose to save a slide as a graphic for use on a web page (*.jpg, *.png, *.gif or *.tif).

Tip:

To display the Help window, just select Help, Microsoft Office PowerPoint Help from the menu.

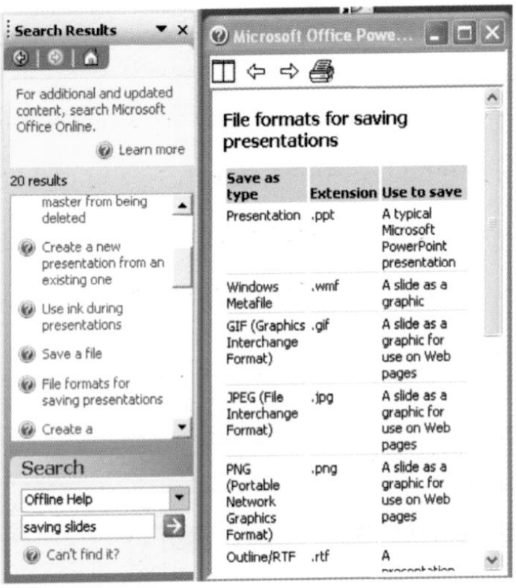

That's it!

You've now finished the presentation – yours should look something like the one below!

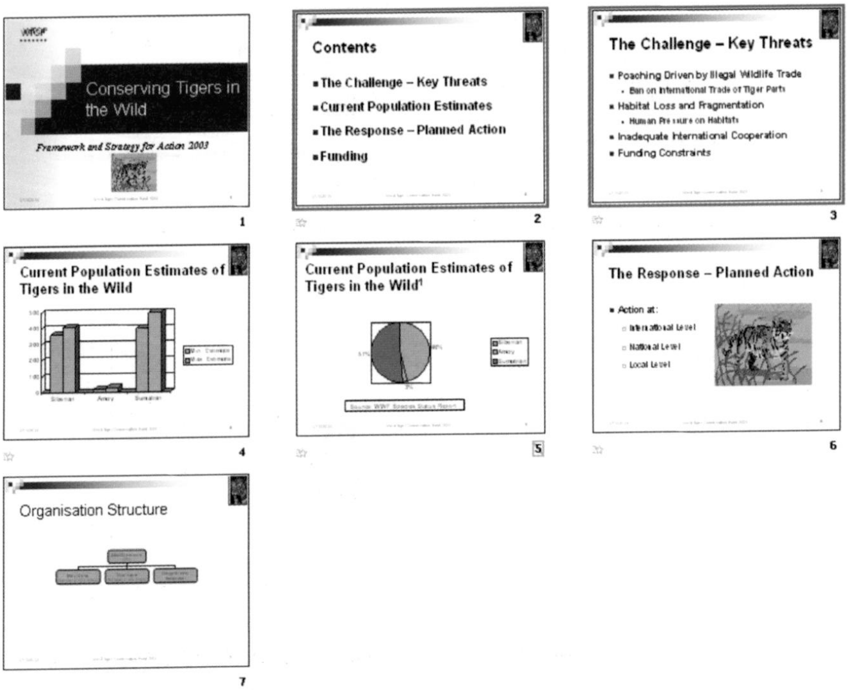

Save and close your presentation, then close PowerPoint.

Exercise

In this exercise you will practise printing the Mapsters Ltd presentation that you have produced in the previous end of chapter practice exercises.

1. Open the file **Mapsters.ppt**.
2. Check the slides in Print Preview and make any necessary adjustments.
3. Return to Normal View and add some notes in the Notes pane of each slide.
4. Run the slide show and display some of the Notes pages.
5. Print the slides on one page of A4 paper in portrait orientation.

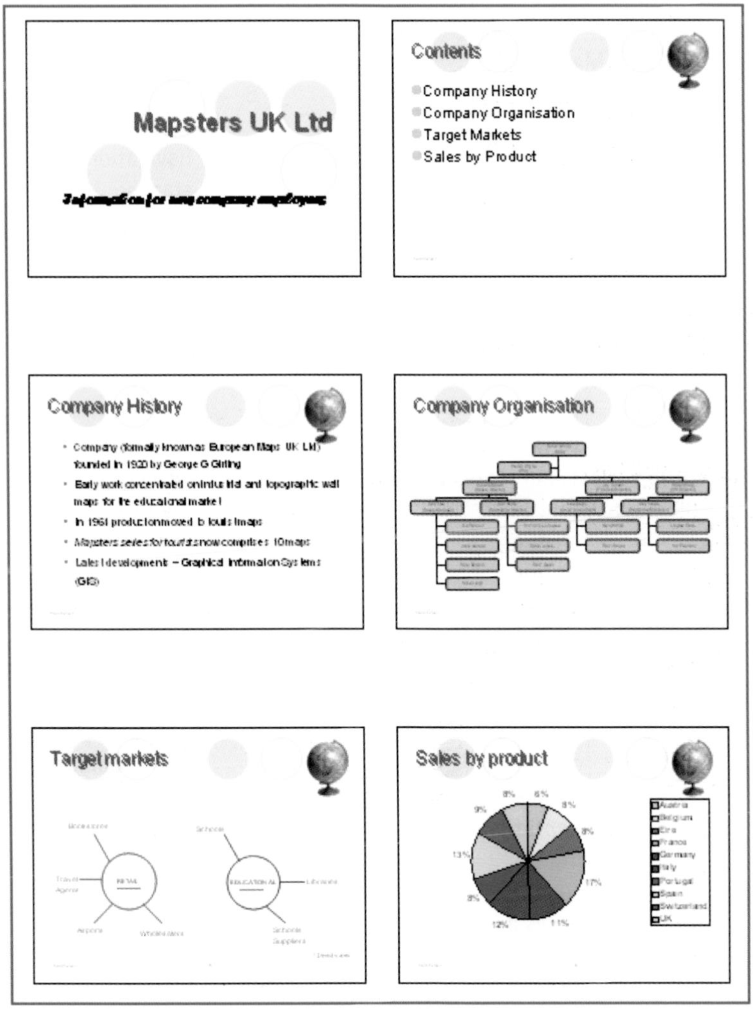

6. Now print the slides on separate pages together with the notes.
7. Save and close your work.

Module 7

Information and Communication

The module is divided in two sections. The first section, *Information*, will help you to understand some of the concepts and terms associated with using the Internet, and to appreciate the security considerations. You will be able to:

- accomplish common Web search tasks using a Web browser
- use search engine tools
- bookmark web sites
- print web pages
- navigate around and complete web-based forms.

In the second section, *Communication*, you will learn some of the concepts of electronic mail (e-mail), and gain an appreciation of some of the security considerations associated with using e-mail. You will be able to:

- use e-mail software to send and receive messages
- attach files to mail messages
- organise and manage message folders within e-mail software.

Module 7 Table of Contents

Browsing

CHAPTER 7.1

The Internet

The Internet consists of a huge number of computers connected together all over the world. While a small group of connected computers constitutes a network, the Internet is an International network of networks. Once connected, you can use the Internet to send e-mails or browse the Web.

The World Wide Web is the best-known part of the Internet. It consists of hundreds of millions of web pages stored on computers the world over, which you can access from your computer. Most large companies and organisations have a web site and so do more and more private individuals.

Web Browser software

To view web pages, you need a type of software called a browser. One of the most common browsers is Microsoft Internet Explorer which we shall use in this book.

The browser will not be able to show pages unless the computer is connected to an Internet Service Provider or ISP. ISPs include BT, AOL, Demon and thousands of others worldwide. When you connect your computer to the Internet, you connect to an ISP's computer which stores and transmits data to other ISPs and thus to other users. Your connection will either be permanent or dial-up.

To start Internet Explorer:

- *Either* double-click the icon for Internet Explorer. This is next to the Start button.
- *Or* click Start, Programs, then Internet Explorer.

- A dialogue box may ask if you want to connect: enter your username and password and click Connect.

A web page will now appear on the screen. This is probably a page that was set as a default by your ISP or computer manufacturer. In Chapter 7.3 you will find out how to change this.

Entering an address

You can go to a different page by entering another address.

- Click in the Address bar at the top of the screen. The text will be highlighted.

- Type in www.bbc.co.uk and click on the Go button or press Enter.

This should bring up the BBC web site at the opening or home page. It will look similar to the picture below, but not identical since most people and companies are continually changing their web sites.

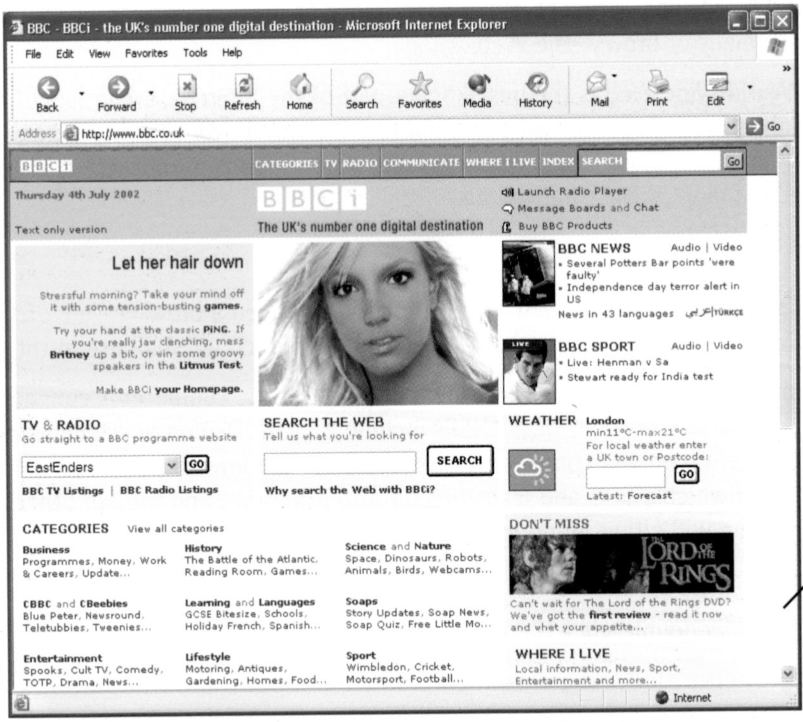

Web pages may be longer than the screen – like this one. To see the whole page, either click in the scroll bar or press the Page Down key. Ctrl-End takes you to the bottom of the page, Ctrl-Home back to the top.

Tip:

If you are looking for something on the page, choose Find (on This Page) from the Edit menu and enter the word or phrase.

Navigating the Web

Most web pages have hot links – also called hypertext links or hyperlinks – which enable you to jump to another page, or back to the top of the same page if it's quite long. When you move the mouse pointer around the screen, the shape changes from an arrow to a hand when it is over a hot area. These are usually text underlined in blue but may also be pictures.

When you click on a hot area, the browser jumps to a new page.

- Click on the History link in the middle of the page.

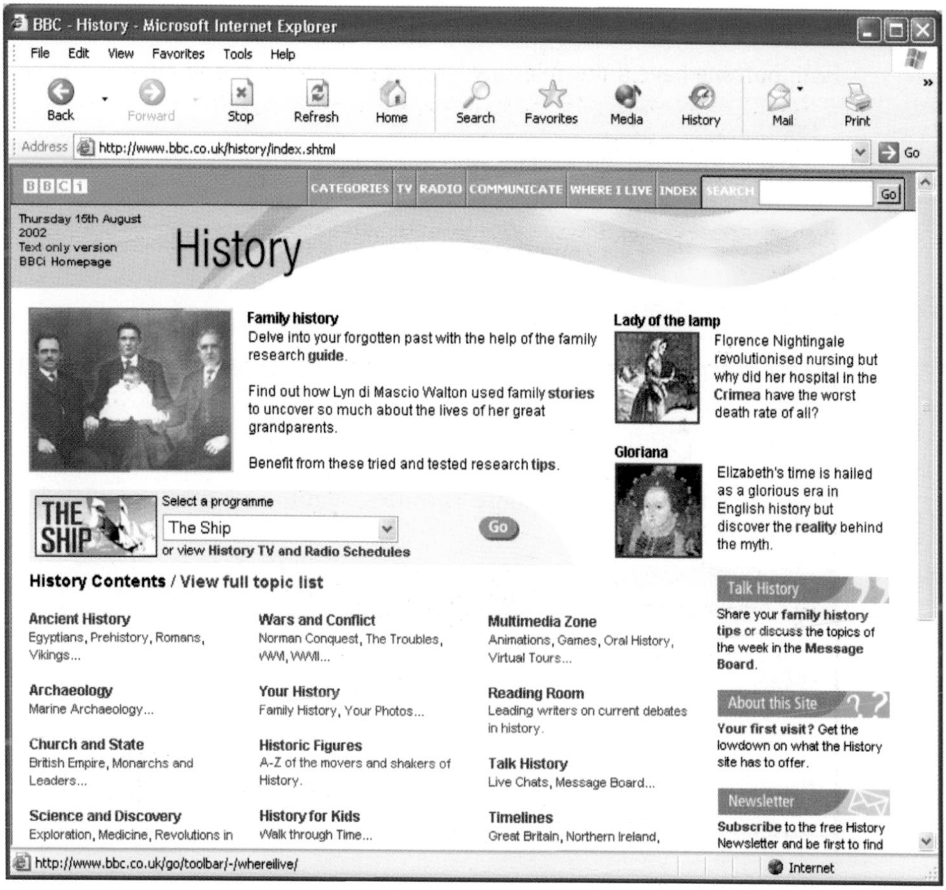

The History page lets you view the past from many different aspects, and there are numerous other links as well.

Tip:
The page may look quite different when you come to look at it but there should still be something of interest.

- Click on Timelines and see what comes up.

Returning to a previous page

To go back to the previous page:

- Click on the Back button at the left of the toolbar.
- Click Back repeatedly until you are back at the home page.

Notice that the links you have already clicked have changed colour to remind you that you've been there.

- Now try clicking the Forward button.

Notice this takes you forward through the pages you were going back through. It is greyed out unless you were going back.

Both buttons have a down-arrow – you can click on it and choose a page from the list.

Tip:
You can also use the Alt key with left or right arrow for Back and Forward. Clicking the mouse wheel also sends you Back.

Bookmarking a web page

To save having to remember how to return to a page you can bookmark it by adding it to a list of favourite sites.

- Go back to the BBC home page.
- From the menu bar choose Favorites, Add to Favorites and click OK.

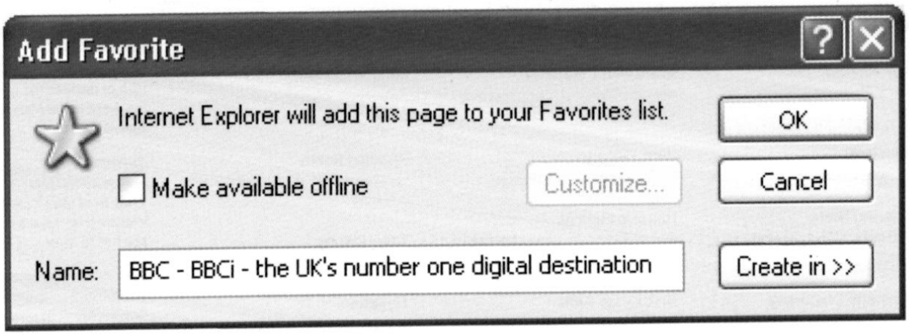

Tip:
You can also create your own folders to put entries in.

The web page address

Every web page has a unique address known as the URL – for Uniform Resource Locator. This has distinct parts separated by dots, each part having a special significance. A typical address is:

http://www.bbc.co.uk

http:// (Hypertext Transfer Protocol) is the protocol (set of rules) used by the Internet for sending and receiving data between computers. Some addresses may have https:// for a secure (protected) page with sensitive information. ftp:// (File Transfer Protocol) is another protocol which is used for transferring files.

There's no need to type in http:// as the browser adds it automatically.

www means World Wide Web and is in most but not all web page addresses.

bbc.co.uk is the domain name showing the organisation owning the site and has several parts.

co is the type of site, in this case a commercial organisation. International company domain names generally end in .com.

Some other codes are gov for government, org for non-profit organisations, ac for educational sites (edu in the USA), or sch for schools.

If the site is neither .com nor US-based there is usually a country code – uk for the UK, fr for France, de for Germany, es for Spain, it for Italy, ch for Switzerland, ie for Ireland, and so on.

There may also be the name of a file on the end of the address (after a slash) such as /index.htm. Web pages are written in a language called HTML (for Hypertext Markup Language) and each page is a file usually ending in .htm.

Here are some sample web addresses – you can probably guess who they belong to.

www.disney.com	www.cam.ac.uk	www.bmw.de
www.nationalgallery.org.uk	www.harvard.edu	www.louvre.fr
www.worldwildlife.org	www.nasa.gov	www.lastampa.it

Entering an address from the address bar

The address box in the address bar has a down-arrow at the right-hand end. If you click on this, a list opens below with the URLs of recently visited web pages.

- Click on one and notice the browser jumps to that page.

We'll now go back to the BBC home page. Instead of using the Back button, here's another way.

- Start typing the URL www.bbc.co.uk/history

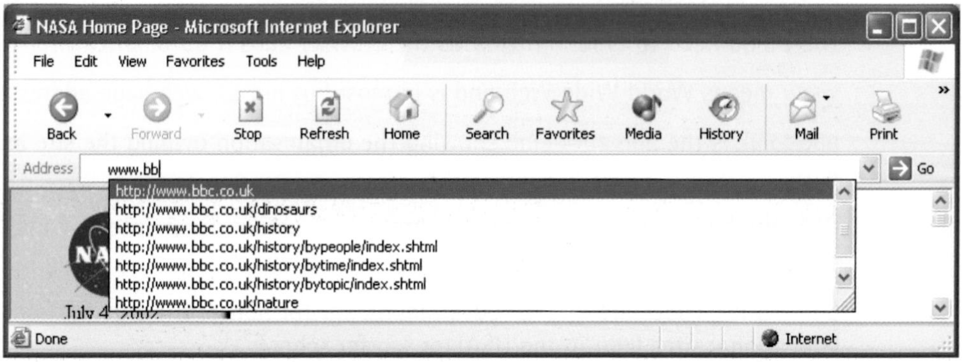

As soon as you get to www.b Internet Explorer now lists all the addresses matching what you have typed.

Tip:
If this doesn't happen, look up AutoComplete in the index.

- Select the address in the list.

Returning to a bookmarked page

For a quick way to return to the BBC home page, you could either use the Back button again or find it in Favorites where you saved it earlier.

- Click the Favorites button on the toolbar.
- Click the item in the Favorites pane on the left, to bring up that page.
- Click the Favorites button again to hide the pane.

Refreshing a web page

The browser stores the pages you browse in a file known as a cache on your hard disk. If you ask for the same page again, it is the stored page that is opened: if you are not sure whether you are looking at the latest version of the page, or you get a message that a web page cannot be displayed, click the Refresh button. This then reloads the page from the Internet, not from the cache.

Using Help functions

If you want more information on, say, how to delete pages held in cache, or assign more disk space to cache, you could do worse than look at the Help system in Internet Explorer.

- Click on the Help menu, Contents and Index.

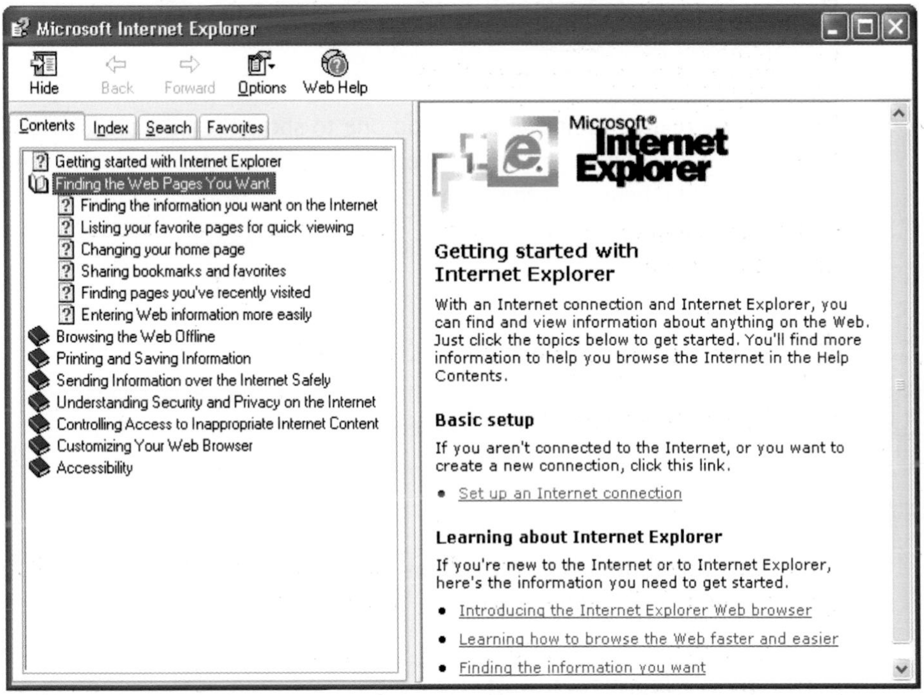

Tip:
You could press the F1 key to access Help instead.

The topics are marked by Book icons: clicking on a topic lists the items below.

- Click on an item to see the associated help information on the right.

You can also search the help index by entering a keyword.

- Click the Index tab and type cache.

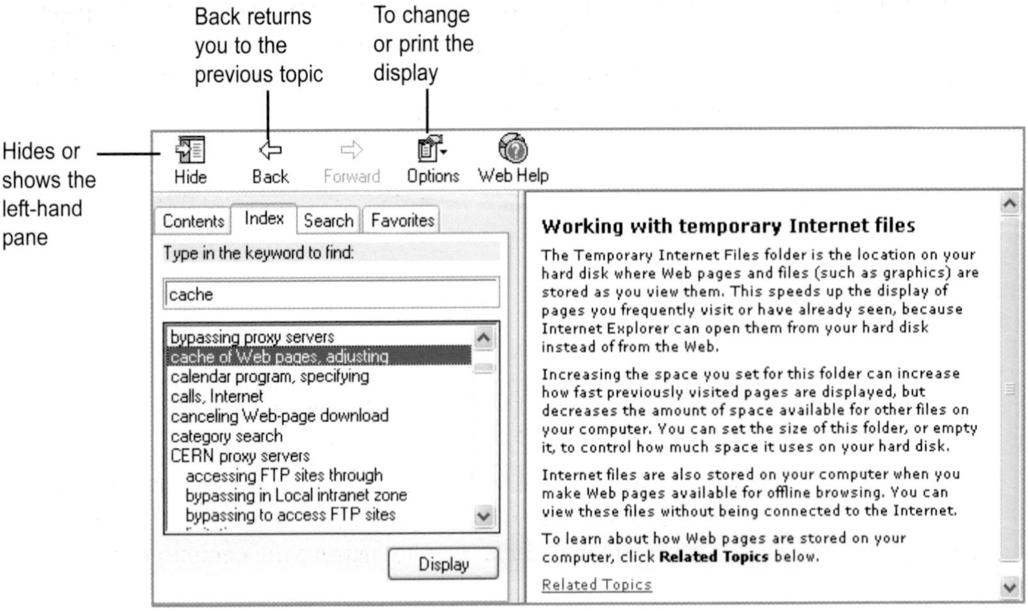

This lists the related topics; you click on one to show the help on the right. Alternatively you can enter your keyword on the Search tab. If all else fails there is also Microsoft online help from the Web Help button.

- Close the Help window when you have seen enough.

Stopping a page downloading

If a page is taking too long to open (the mouse pointer keeps showing an hour-glass), click the Stop button. This often happens if a page has a lot of pictures.

Missing page

You may find that your browser cannot find a page although you clicked on a link to it, and it displays something like this.

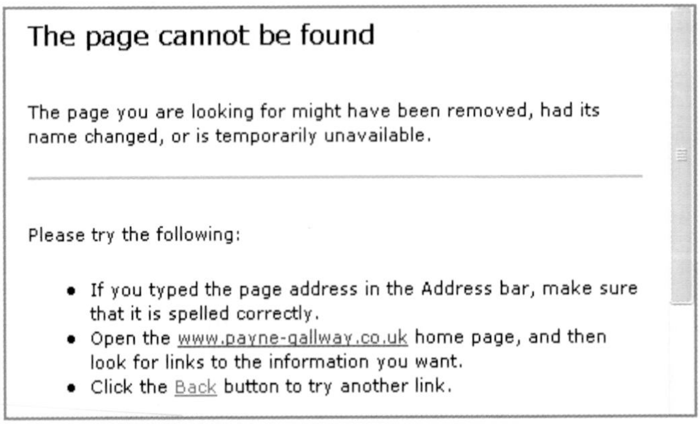
The page cannot be found
The page you are looking for might have been removed, had its name changed, or is temporarily unavailable.
Please try the following:
If you typed the page address in the Address bar, make sure that it is spelled correctly.
Open the www.payne-gallway.co.uk home page, and then look for links to the information you want.
Click the Back button to try another link.

Don't worry, this often happens! The Internet is growing so fast that many web pages have mistakes in their link addresses. This may be because the page that a link points to has been removed or had its address changed. It could also be due to a problem with the site server or because of heavy demand for that site.

Tip:
You'll see a similar message if you type an address in wrongly and the browser can't find it.

Ending an Internet session

- Close Internet Explorer by clicking the Close icon (X) at the top right of your screen, or by selecting File, Close from the menu bar.

If you have a dial-up connection you should disconnect as soon as you have finished since being on the Internet uses your phone line. Note that closing Internet Explorer does not automatically disconnect you – you have to instruct the computer to disconnect.

While you are connected, the Dial-up icon appears in the Status bar at bottom right of the screen.

- Right-click the Dial-up icon and select Disconnect.

Exercises

1. Open Internet Explorer and make sure you are connected to the Internet.
2. Enter the URL www.bbc.co.uk/music
3. Find on this page all instances of the word jazz.
4. Bookmark this page.
5. Go to the site www.multimap.com and bookmark it.
6. Enter your postcode to display a small-scale map of your home area.
7. Click the Print button to print out the map. (You may have to log in first.)
8. Disconnect from the Internet if you have a dial-up connection.
9. Close Internet Explorer.

CHAPTER 7.2 Search Engines

Using a search engine

As you can see, it's easy to spend hours browsing the Web, jumping aimlessly from page to page. Some web sites – like the BBC – have a search box to find things on that site, but to look up a particular topic anywhere on the Web you can use a search engine. There are several well-known search engines such as Google, Yahoo, AltaVista and Ask Jeeves. A search engine is software which enables you to find information on almost any conceivable topic, from holidays to university courses, best deals on electronic goods to groceries, long-lost friends to dating agencies.

- Load Internet Explorer by double-clicking the icon.
- Click in the Address box and enter the address www.google.com

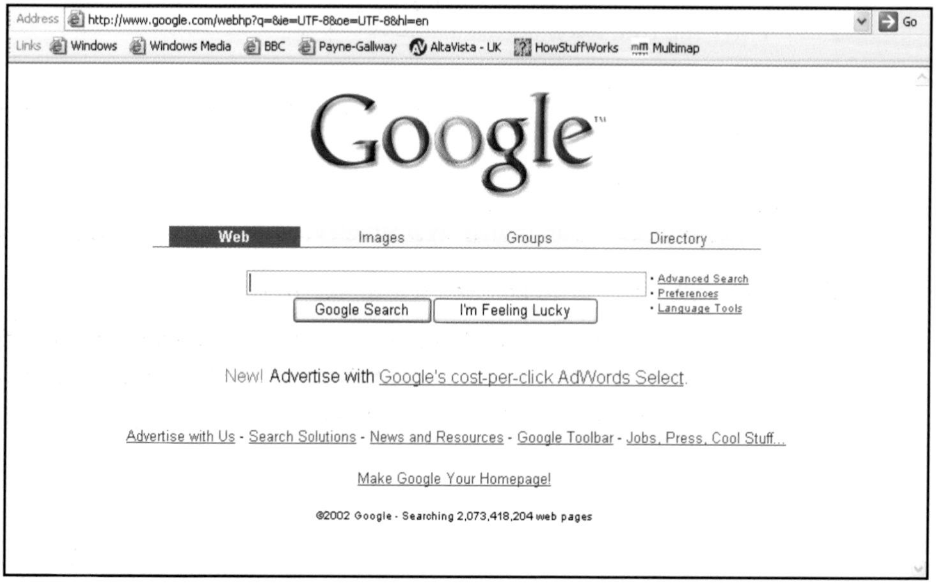

- Add it to Favorites.

Search engines usually have directories, news, local events and information but you can also search by entering a keyword.

Searching by keyword

Google allows you to type a word or phrase, and then comes back with a list of related web pages. Suppose you wanted to find the Prime Minister's official web site.

- Type 10 Downing Street into the search box and click the Google Search button.

Google comes back with a list of links to www.number-10.gov.uk of which the home page is at the top.

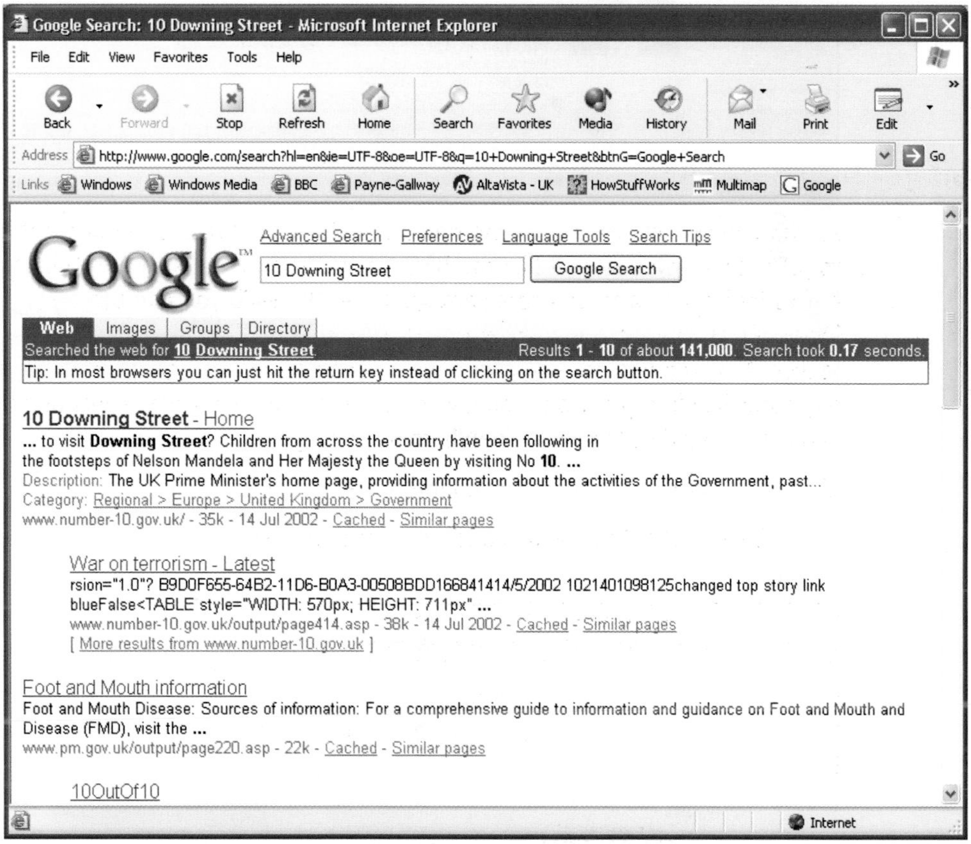

- Click the first link to admire the Number 10 site.

The Google results are consistently so relevant that they provide an alternative button I'm Feeling Lucky which takes you straight to the first result without seeing the list. In this case, this would have been all you needed!

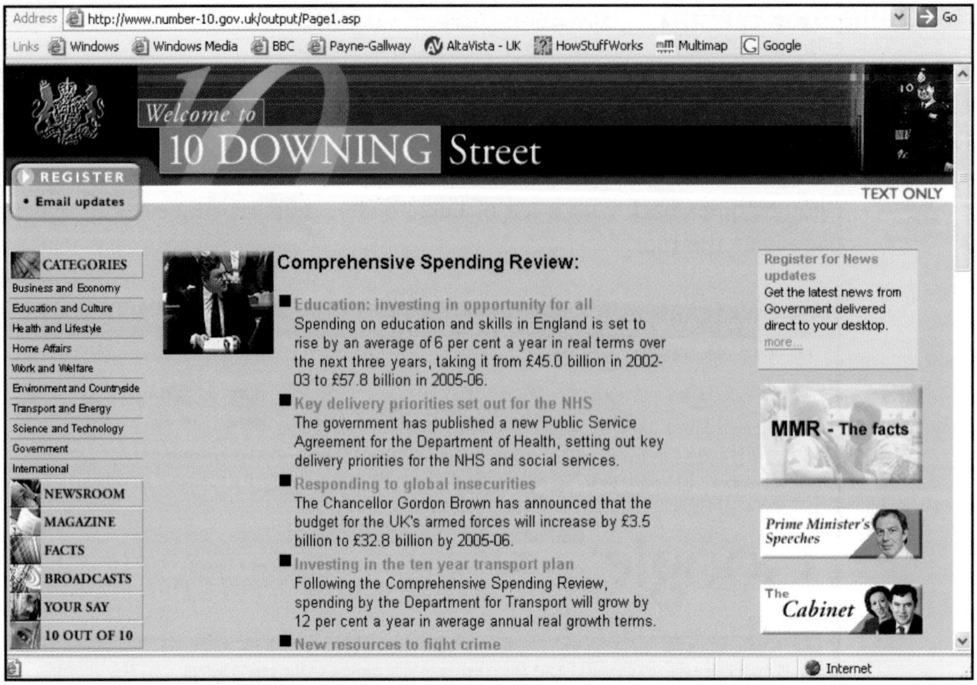

Go back to the Google home page.

Time for another search. Suppose we wanted a cooking recipe for salsa.

In the search box, enter salsa and click Google Search.

This finds a huge number of references but mostly for dance, music or cycles! Some are not in English.

We need to refine the search by including sauces and recipes and excluding music, dance and cycles.

Including and excluding pages

We can tell Google to exclude topics we don't want by adding a keyword with a minus in front. Similarly, if we are particularly interested in a topic – such as sauces and recipes – we can add keywords with a plus in front.

Try adding -music -dance -cycle +recipe and click Google Search.

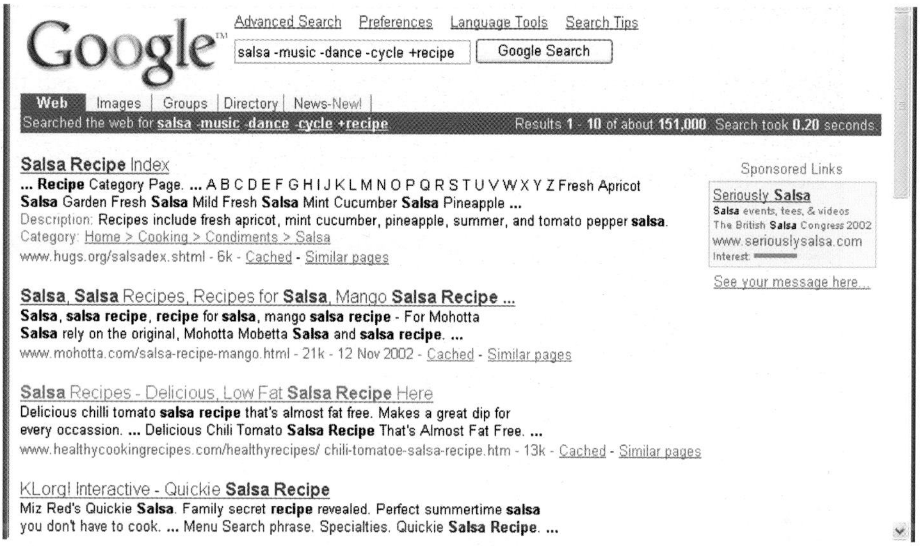

This is better, but you might be interested only in tomato, chilli or bean.

- Add +tomato OR chili OR bean to the search string.

Here the OR must be in capitals. This will narrow the results further.

Tip:

Similarly if you wanted to specify a chili bean recipe, you would put chili AND bean. You can also specify a phrase in quotes, such as "salsa recipe". For UK sites only, specify site:.uk

It is often convenient to open a web page in a new window so that you can compare pages. To do this, Shift-click on the link, or right-click and choose Open in New Window. If you want to open several web pages at a time, each in a new window, use File, New, Window.

Searching by directories

Many search engines and some other sites have information arranged by topic in categories. To see this:

- Go to the Google home page and click the Directory button.

This shows lists of categories which in turn have subcategories so that you can gradually home in on what you are looking for. If you were interested for example in scuba diving you would click on Recreation, Outdoors, Scuba Diving and then choose Underwater Photography or some other aspect.

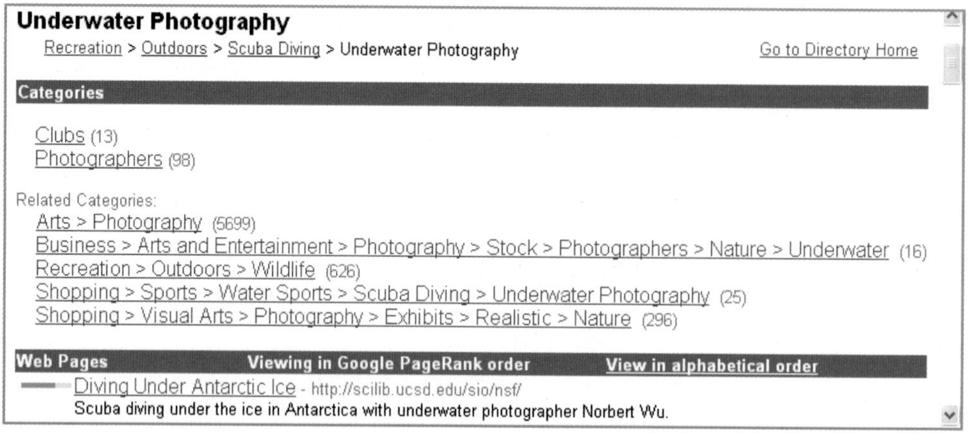

Directories, of which the best example is Open Directory Project (www.dmoz.org), are compiled by hand so the information is always relevant. Search engines on the other hand keep an index of keywords which is added to by special programs – known as spiders or crawlers – which continually search the web collecting references but these may not always be relevant.

Other search engines

There are numerous other search engines, with more appearing constantly.

For simple straightforward queries, Ask Jeeves (www.ask.co.uk) invites you to use natural language – that is, plain English.

Rather than reply instantly, Jeeves presents you with related questions (hand-compiled) using dropdown menus which will hopefully lead you to the answer, and you'll probably find other interesting things along the way.

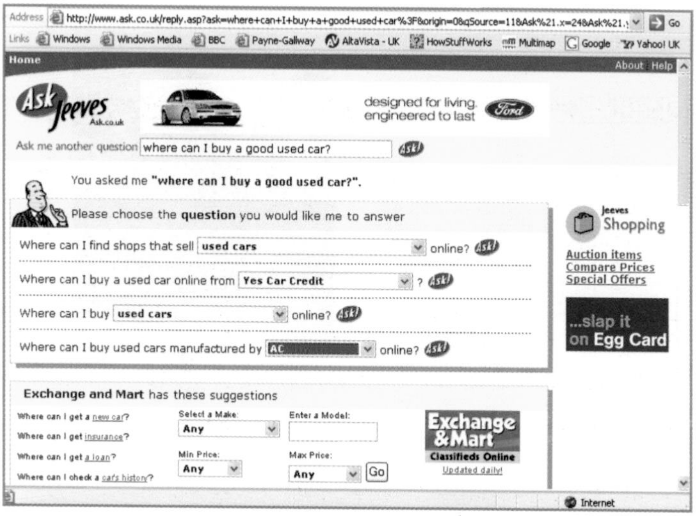

Whatever the query, whether used cars or train times, Jeeves is immediately on the case with a list of helpful suggestions.

Tip:

A few search engines – known as meta search engines – submit your keywords to several search engines at once, and pass you the results. Look at www.metor.com

Some search engines (AltaVista but not Google) allow 'wildcards' to cater for variations in words. Thus compan* will find company, companies, companion, etc.

- Look at AltaVista www.altavista.co.uk

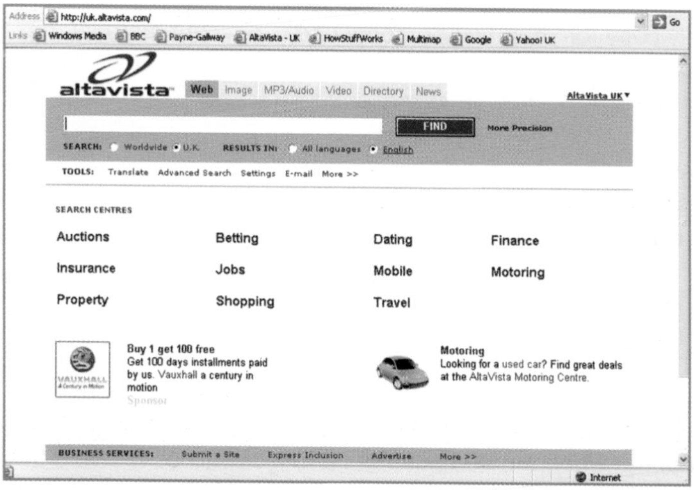

- Use AltaVista to find your dream home somewhere in the UK.

This is Powis Castle on the National Trust web site.

Duplicating text

Suppose you want to copy some of the text and graphics from this web site into a Word document.

- Make sure you have Word running and if you don't have a blank document open choose File, New.
- Go back to Internet Explorer (press Alt-Tab) or select it from the Task bar at the bottom of the screen.
- Drag to select a few lines of text (or the URL in the address bar).
- From the Edit menu, choose Copy.
- Go back to Word and from the Edit menu, choose Paste.

Note:
You may only copy for your own personal use. Copyright material may not be reproduced without permission.

Duplicating graphics

It is better to copy the graphics separately from the text.

- In Internet Explorer, right-click on the picture you want to copy and select Copy.
- Return to Word, right-click on the document and select Paste.

Tip:
The image in your document may only be a link to the web page it came from, and will disappear when the computer is no longer online. To avoid this, select the image and press Ctrl-Shift-F9.

In Word, you'll need to right-click the picture and choose Format Picture, Layout to get the picture alongside the text.

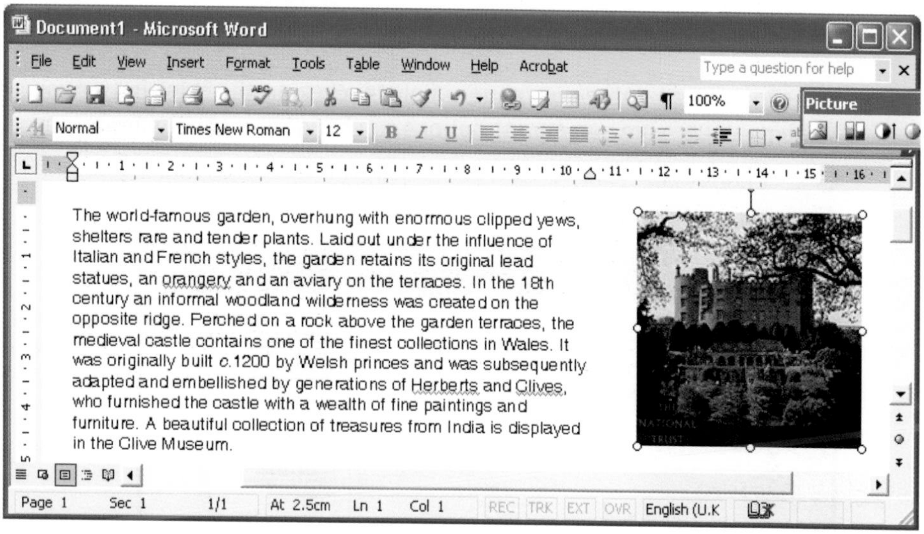

In this case, the picture was held on the clipboard. To save a web site picture as a file, right-click it, choose Save Picture As and browse to the folder you want to put it in.

In Internet Explorer 6 when you hover the mouse over an image, the Image toolbar should appear which allows you to save, print or e-mail the image.

Saving a web page

You can save a web page to look at later.

- In the browser, choose File, Save As, select a folder and type Castle as the file name. Set Web Page, htm as the file type and click OK.

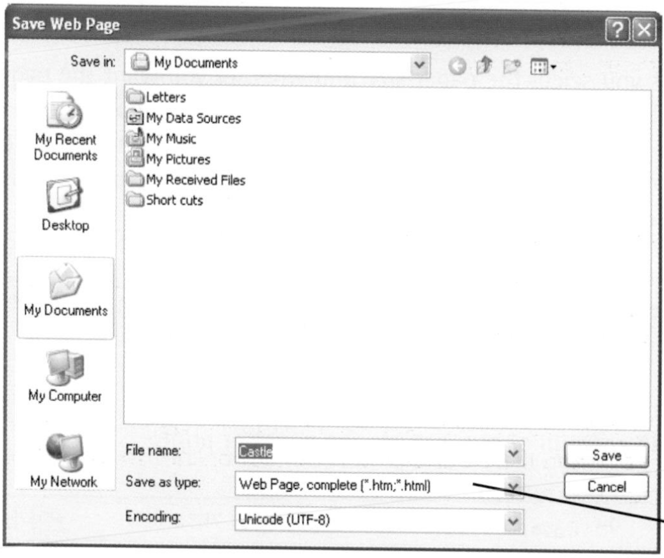

You can save it as text or html

This saves the page on your hard disk as a .htm file which can be opened later with the browser. You can also save it as text only if you don't want any graphics.

Printing a web page

You can print an entire web page simply by clicking the Print button, or by selecting File, Print. There are some print options to change the page margins and orientation.

- Choose File, Page Setup.

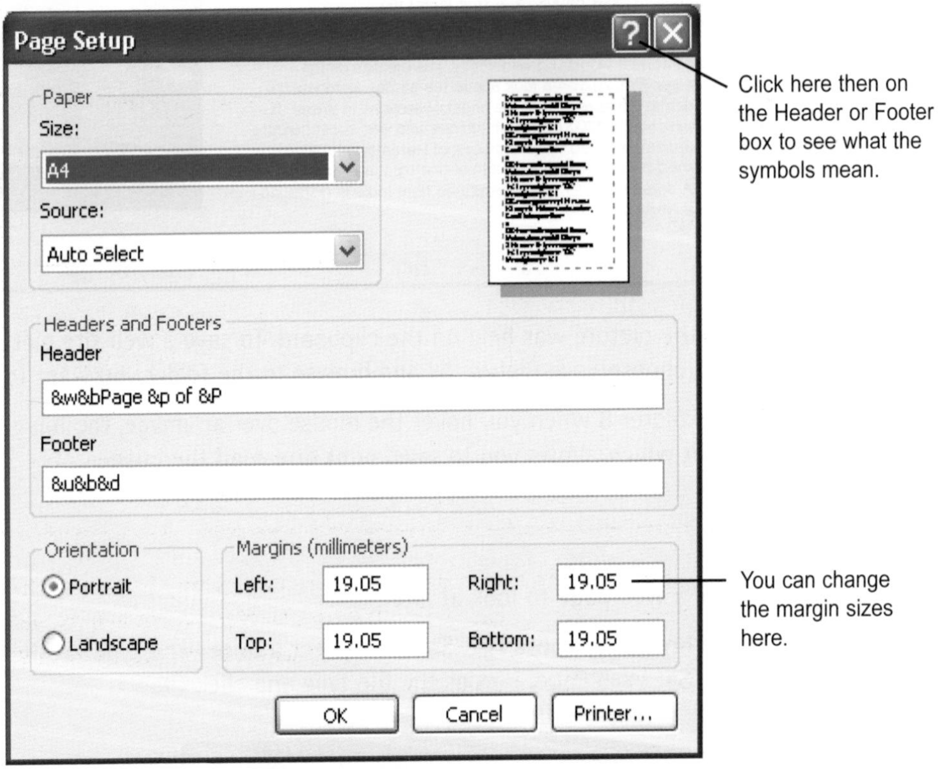

This dialogue lets you select the paper size and whether you want the page printed vertically (portrait) or horizontally (landscape), as well as the top, bottom, left and right margin sizes. The printed page will have details such as the page title, date and time at the top and bottom but you can change these and add text of your own using the symbols in the Header and Footer boxes.

Tip:

Try using context help to see what these symbols mean: click the ? button at the top right of the window, then in the Header box.

- Select File, Print Preview and preview the printed page(s). From the toolbar at the top you can zoom in or out, browse the pages or print.

- Select Print on the preview window or close it and choose File, Print.

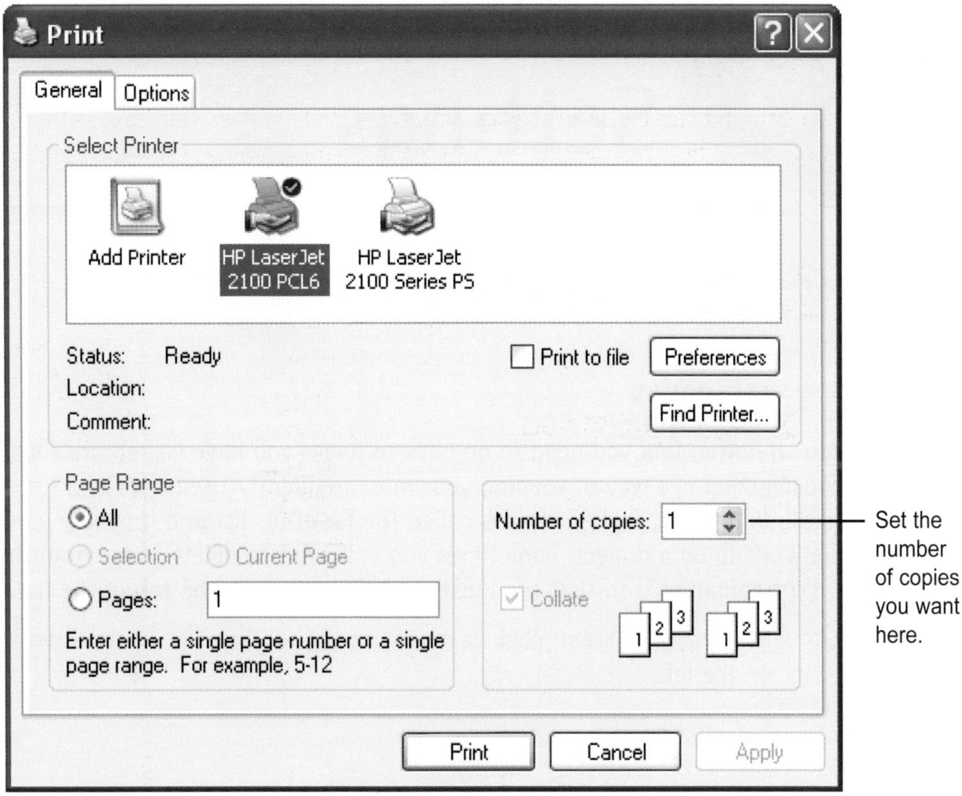

Here you can print the whole web page – which may extend to several printed pages – or particular pages, or just a part that you have selected which avoids wasting ink and paper on almost empty pages. Similarly for web pages built with frames you can print individual frames from the Options tab.

Exercises

1. Open Internet Explorer and make sure you are connected to the Internet.
2. Go to www.google.com
3. Use search keywords to list web sites about Leonardo (da Vinci).
4. Open a site in a new browser page.
5. Print out a selected area of a page containing relevant information.
6. Save the page as a .htm file.
7. Copy some text and a picture into a new Word document and save the document.
8. Close Internet Explorer.

CHAPTER 7.3 Bookmarks and Settings

Bookmarking web pages

You will often find you need to go back to pages you have visited previously and bookmarking is a way of keeping your most frequently-used sites in a list, for easy recall. In Internet Explorer this is called the Favorites list and it is very useful when you are working on a project. Sometimes you will want to delete items from the Favorites list or reorganise it so that the most used sites are near the top of the list.

- In Internet Explorer, click Favorites on the toolbar. Notice the Favorites list opens on the left.

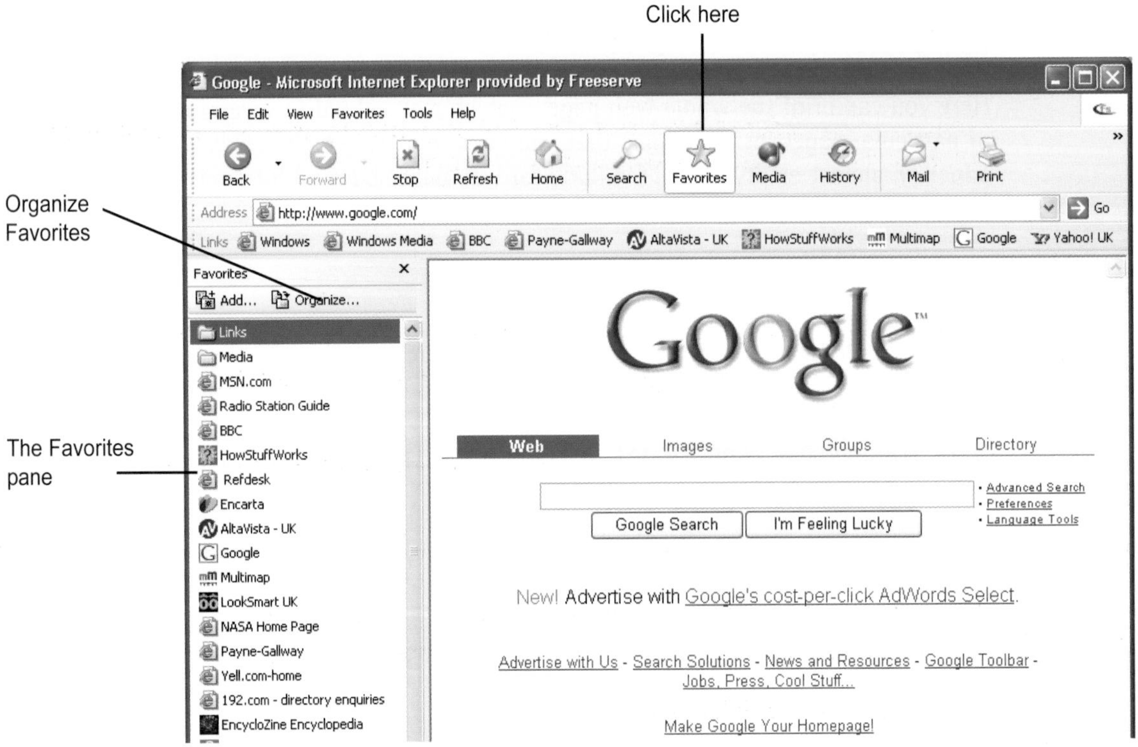

You can ignore some of the ones at the top which may be to do with your Internet provider (in this case Freeserve), and you may also have My Documents which is where Windows puts your Word files. You can now choose a web page from the list and display it.

The entries in the Favorites list appear in the order that they were added. You may want to change the order, perhaps moving the most useful ones up to the top.

- Click on Organize Favorites at the top of the Favorites pane or select Favorites, Organize Favorites.

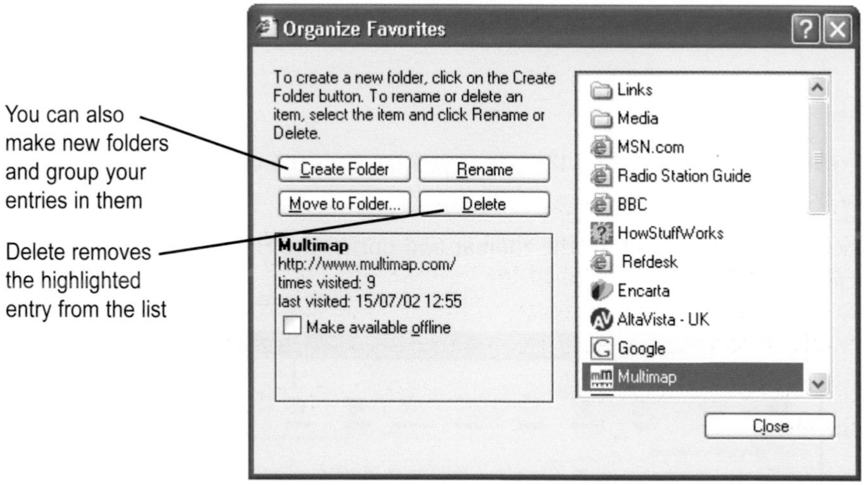

Tip:
To change the order of items in the list, just drag them up or down. To remove an unwanted entry, select it and click the Delete button.

Creating a bookmark folder

As the list builds up, it is advisable to group the entries in specific folders.

- Click the Create Folder button and type the name for your folder, for example, Reference.
- Click Close to close the window and you should now see the new folder.

Adding web pages to a bookmark folder

You can now move entries to the folder or add them to it directly.

- Select an entry in the Favorites list and click Move to Folder.
- Select the new folder and click OK.
- Close the Organize Favorites window.

To add a new web site directly to the Reference folder:

- Enter the URL for Encarta encyclopedia (http://encarta.msn.co.uk).

Tip:
Notice not all addresses have www.

- Choose Favorites, Add to Favorites then Create In, select the Reference folder and click OK.
- Hide the Favorites window by clicking the Favorites button on the toolbar to deselect it.

The History list

Internet Explorer keeps track of all the pages you have visited and when. This is kept in the History list.

- Click on the History icon in the toolbar and notice the History list pane opens on the left.

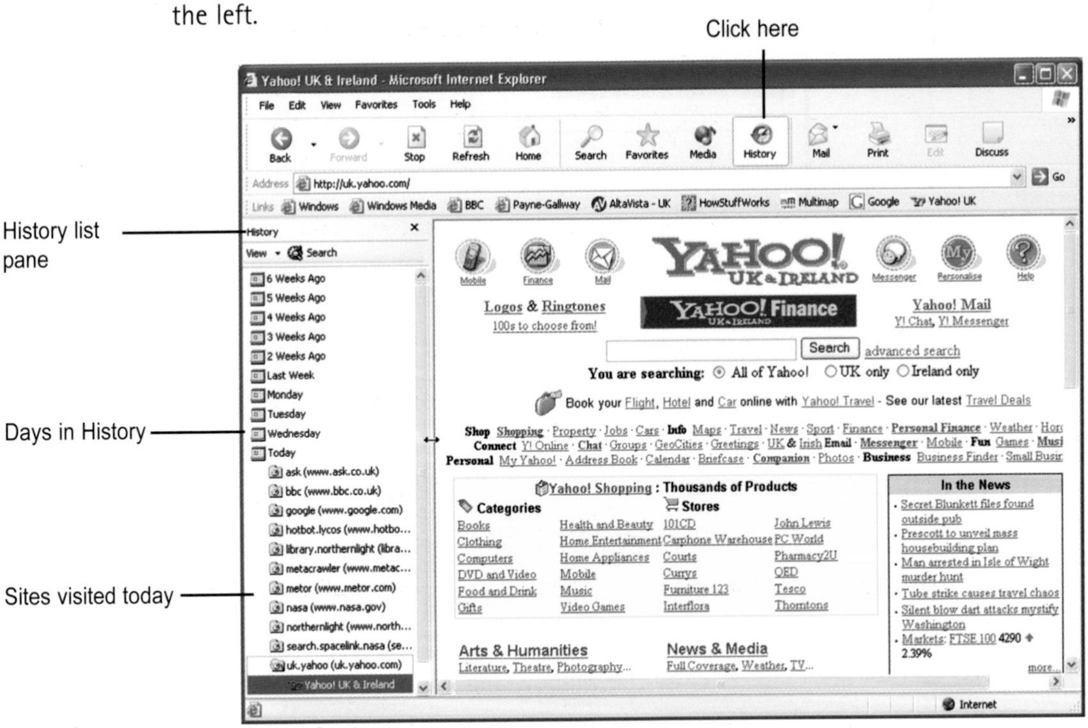

The History list lets you view the sites that you (or someone else) have visited recently. In the list, the pages visited are grouped by day. Clicking on an icon expands or contracts it, and selecting a link displays the page.

- Click on the icon for Today to expand it (if not already) and see the sites you have visited today.

As well as viewing the History list by date, you can also order it by Site or by Most Visited.

Deleting the browse history

How far back your History goes depends on how your browser is set up weeks. To delete the History list:

- From the Tools menu select Internet Options.

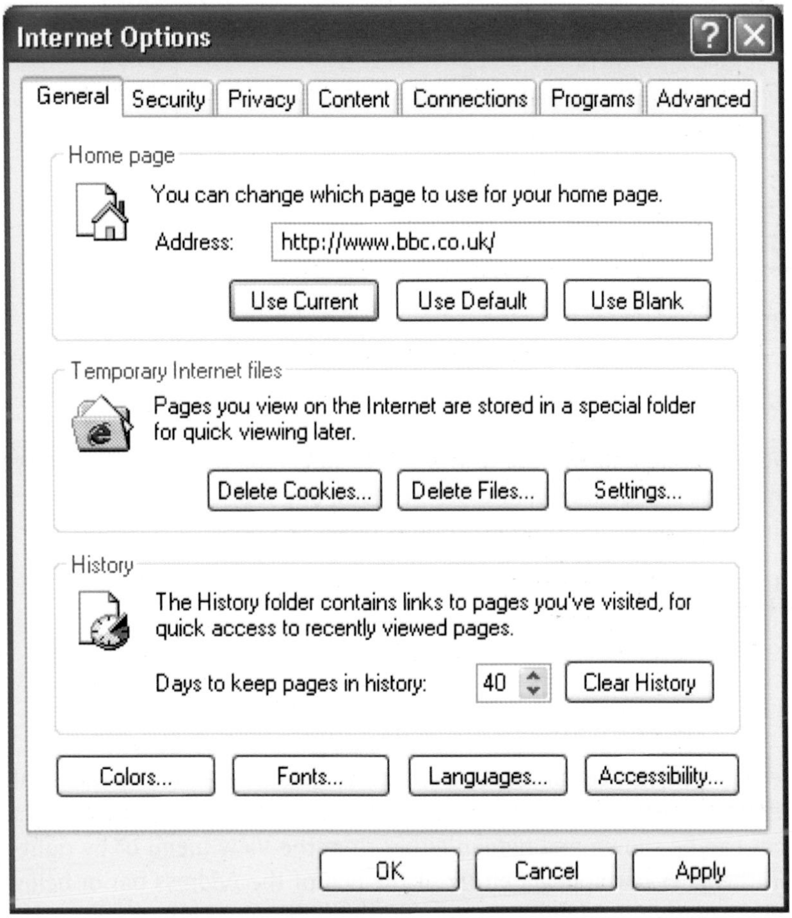

On the General tab, the Clear History button deletes all the stored history links.

Changing your start page

It is inconvenient to have Internet Explorer open with a site that is of little interest, particularly if it takes a long time to load. This can be easily changed from the General tab shown above.

- Go to the page you would like to come up, say the BBC home page.
- From the Tools menu select Internet Options.
- Click Use Current.

...ng pages without images

If you have a slow connection you can speed things up by downloading the text without the pictures on a web site. On the Internet Options Advanced tab, scroll down to Multimedia and uncheck Show Pictures.

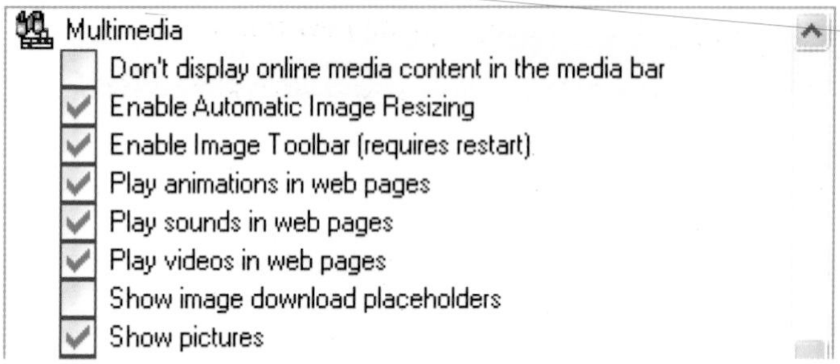

Each image position on the page is now marked by an icon.

Address box autocomplete

If, as you enter an address, the browser tries to complete the address for you instead of showing a list of matching addresses beneath, uncheck Use Inline AutoComplete in the Browsing section on the Internet Options Advanced tab.

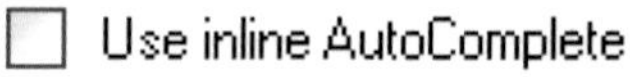

Displaying and hiding built-in toolbars

Internet Explorer has certain settings made by default – as set by Microsoft or the supplier – but these can be changed. The Standard Buttons toolbar, Address bar and Links bar can be shown and hidden either from the View menu or by right-clicking a toolbar. The Links bar appears either at the end of the Address bar or below it (if on the right, you can drag it down).

The Links bar is very versatile – you can drag an address onto it from the Address bar and drag the addresses along to rearrange them. Try it! You can delete or rename them by right-clicking and choosing from the menu.

Items on the Links bar come from the Links folder which appears in Favorites and you can add a new site directly to it. The Status bar at the bottom of the screen is also selected from the View menu.

You can make a web page as large as possible using View, Full Screen or pressing F11. This takes up the entire screen except for the toolbar icons. F11 returns you to normal mode.

Exercises

1. Open Internet Explorer and show the Favorites pane.
2. Click Organize Favorites.
3. Create a new bookmark folder called Shopping.
4. Go to www.amazon.co.uk and add it to the new folder.
5. Go to www.192.com, www.royalmail.com and www.yell.com and add them to the Links bar.
6. Close Internet Explorer.

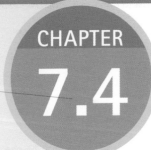

CHAPTER 7.4 Downloading Files

You can download pictures, video clips, sounds and software from the Internet. In this chapter you will learn how to find and save pictures and software.

You'll need to keep them in separate folders where they can easily be found again when you need them. If you don't know how to make a new folder, refer to Module 2.

Looking for pictures

The Internet has lots of pictures you can download. Some are copyright but many are free. Let's find something brightly coloured, say a kingfisher.

- Open Internet Explorer and connect to the Internet.
- Open the Favorites list and choose AltaVista.
- Click on Images.

You can choose several types of image from UK or worldwide. Suppose we wanted to see colour photos of birds.

- Fill in the details as shown above and click Search.

AltaVista returns a few hundred images. Many of them are are not free to copy – a popup message may warn you of this when you run the mouse pointer over them, otherwise clicking on an image will give further details.

- Find a suitable image.

11398091.jpg — Images are .jpg or .gif.

This is the number of 'picture elements' or pixels — 256x170 8 KB — This is the file size of this 'thumbnail' image

Tip:
Images from Corbis (www.corbis.com) are free to copy if they are watermarked and some are also royalty-free: check on the site. Also try www.freeimages.co.uk

- To copy the picture, right-click it and choose Save Picture As.
- Give the picture a name and save the file in the folder you created, or another suitable one.
- You can try clicking the picture to see it at a larger size.

If you don't like these, check the next Results pages. You can also enter royalty-free as a search keyword! There are also images on Google.

Tip:
Once you've saved a lot of image files, a graphic viewer program is useful to browse them. We shall see one later in this chapter.

Using a downloaded graphic

You can now open the file in a graphics package, or put it in a Word document (using Insert, Picture, From File).

Picture files on web pages are usually stored in either .jpg (pronounced jay-peg) or .gif (pronounced as in gift) format since these are compressed, giving small files which are quick to load. These files lose some quality in the compression process so are not very high resolution – a bit 'dotty' like a newspaper photograph.

Downloading sounds

AltaVista offers sounds and music in different formats. For some files, Windows may prompt you to download special software.

Warning:
Some sounds may be copyright

- Still in AltaVista, select MP3/Audio, enter a keyword and click Search.

The downloadable sounds are shown – something like this.

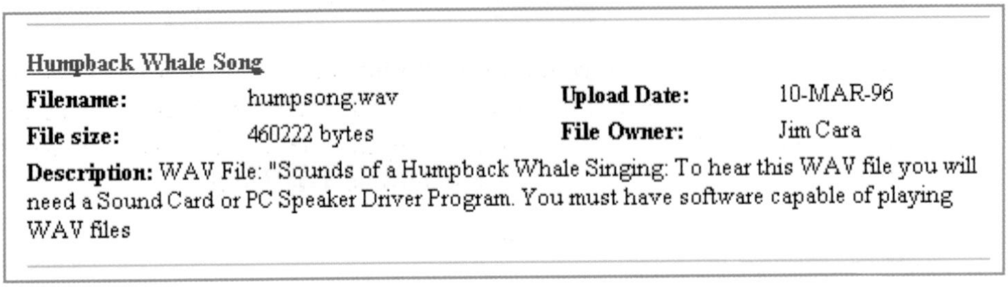

Humpback Whale Song

Filename:	humpsong.wav	**Upload Date:**	10-MAR-96
File size:	460222 bytes	**File Owner:**	Jim Cara

Description: WAV File: "Sounds of a Humpback Whale Singing: To hear this WAV file you will need a Sound Card or PC Speaker Driver Program. You must have software capable of playing WAV files

Sounds can be played using Windows Media Player. In Internet Explorer 6 you can click the Media button to open it as a pane in the Internet Explorer screen.

Tip:
You can open Media Player on its own from Start, Programs, Accessories.

- Click the Media button if you have it, then click on the sound file.

Click to play a sound again

You can copy the file by right-clicking on the icon and choosing Save Target As, which will prompt you for which folder to put it in.

Windows Media Player will play all types of sound files, including music compressed as MP3. Some links simply play a sound file without downloading it – a process known as streaming. Many sites offer this.

Downloading video clips

These are available in several formats on the Video Clips tab. You may be prompted to download special software such as RealPlayer or Quicktime. Files tend to be large and the effect can be jerky without a fast machine. Video can also be streamed.

Downloading text files

Some search engines allow you to search for specific types of file. Click the Advanced Search link in Google and try entering tiger as the keyword and .doc as the file type. This lists doc files only; click a link and specify the folder to put it in. Alternatively, go to www.payne-gallway.co.uk/ecdl and download a .doc file.

Downloading software

There's a lot of software available on the Internet and a good site is Tucows.

- In the Address box enter http://tucows.blueyonder.co.uk and click Go.

Tip:
This is a mirror site (local provider) for www.tucows.com.

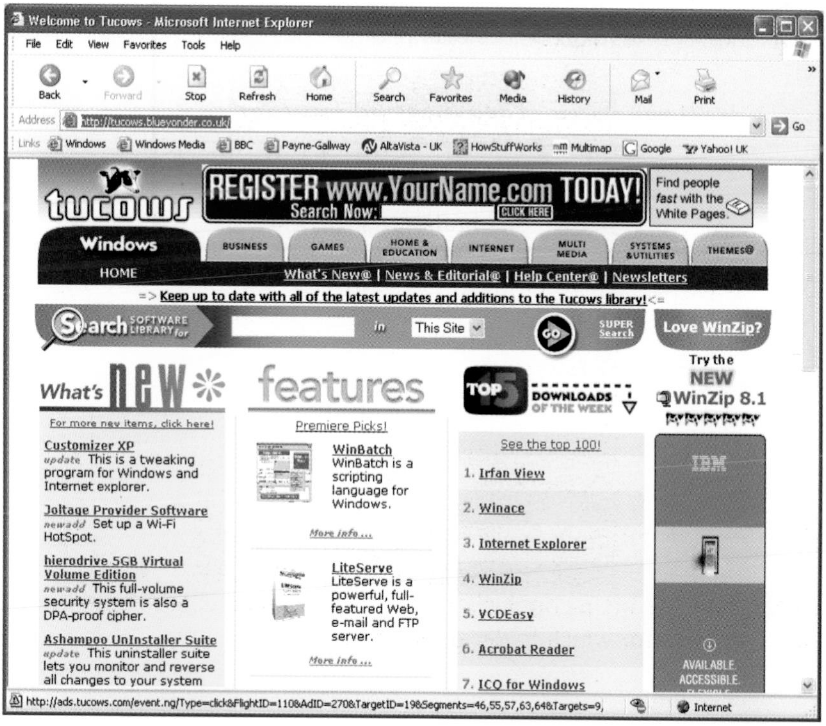

Programs are either for sale, shareware (you try before you buy), freeware or demonstrations (both free). Software for Windows is arranged by category. We are going to download some freeware – an image viewer to look at your pictures!

- First make a new folder called Download as described in Module 2.
- Click the Multimedia tab, look for Image Viewers and scroll down the list to IrfanView.

Tip:

There may be a link direct to it as shown above. If you can't find it, enter the name in the Search box.

You will see something like this. Programs have a 'cow rating'- from 1 to 5!

Irfan View 3.75
This feature-rich image viewer and converter supports many formats.
July 14th, 2002
Freeware
808.0K
Windows 95/98
Windows Me
Windows NT
Windows 2000
Windows XP

- Click the appropriate link on the right for your version of Windows.

A dialogue asks whether you want to open it or save it.

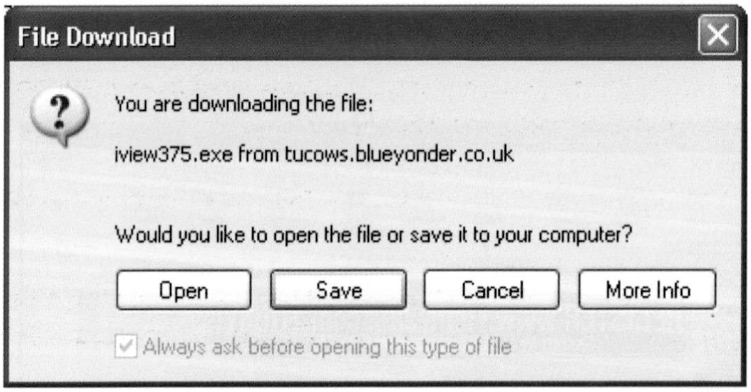

- Choose Save. In the Save As dialogue, go to your Download folder then click Save.

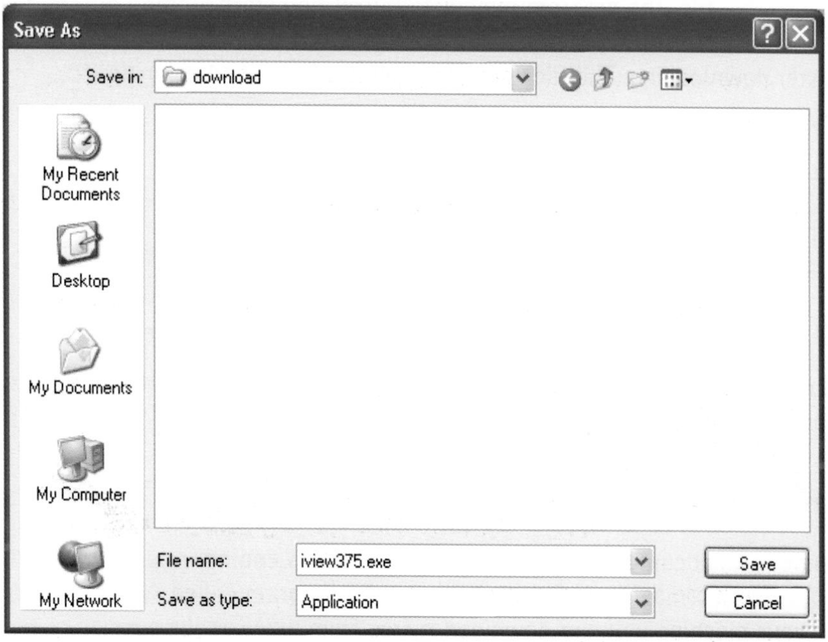

The file downloads, taking about 3 minutes with a dial-up connection.

Tip:
To see how the download is going using a modem, hold the mouse pointer over the Dial-Up icon. A status message pops up.

- Once complete, click Open Folder to show the downloaded file in your folder.

Warning:
Check the size of the file is about 800Kb; if not the download may have broken off. If nothing happens when you double-click the file, try downloading again.

The program can now be installed.

- Double-click the file in the folder and the install screen should appear.
- Without changing any settings, click Next on each screen, then Done.

The program is now installed and you can run it from the Start, Programs menu or by double-clicking the icon on the desktop.

Tip:
When downloading a large file, if the connection breaks you then have to start again. Using a download manager such as GetRight (www.getright.com) not only lets you interrupt the download but automatically resumes if the connection breaks.

Executable files

When you download a program file, it will have a name ending in .exe meaning it is an executable file. The program may install itself and start running automatically. Some .exe files are not the program file itself but a compressed or zipped version shrunk for faster downloading. The file is self-extracting. To expand or unzip it:

- Make a new folder.
- Find the file and copy it into the folder.

Tip:
Hold down the Ctrl key and drag the file to copy it.

- Double-click on the file, Browse to the target folder then Unzip.

The original and much larger file will now be in the folder. If it too is a .exe file, double-click on it to install or run the program.

Reading .pdf files

Sometimes documents you download have names ending in .pdf – for Portable Document Format. To read them, you need a program called Acrobat Reader. If it's not on your machine you can download it free from www.adobe.com

Tip:
Once Acrobat Reader is installed on your computer, you just double-click a .pdf file in Windows Explorer to open it.

Viruses

There is a risk that a file you download (or copy from a floppy disk) could be infected with a virus – a piece of computer code that can have various effects ranging from mischief to damaging your computer. Make sure you have Virus Checker software installed to catch the viruses as they arrive.

If you are on a network, it should already be protected.

Exercises

1. Open Internet Explorer.
2. Use AltaVista to download a royalty-free sound file.
3. Use Google to download a few royalty-free image files.
4. Open the IrfanView application downloaded previously and use it to display the image files.

Shopping and Security

CHAPTER 7.5

You can use the Internet for buying numerous things and it's also an invaluable consumer guide. You pay by credit card but provided that you enter the payment details on a secure site – with an address beginning https:// – it's as safe as the high street. Let's take a look.

Completing a web-based form

One of the most developed online sites is Tesco's. There's the impressive range of foodstuffs and you can order videos, books, electrical goods, home furnishings and babyware. You can arrange your personal finances (mortgage, insurance, ISAs, credit cards, loans), order currencies if you're travelling and have flowers delivered.

- Go to the site www.tesco.com

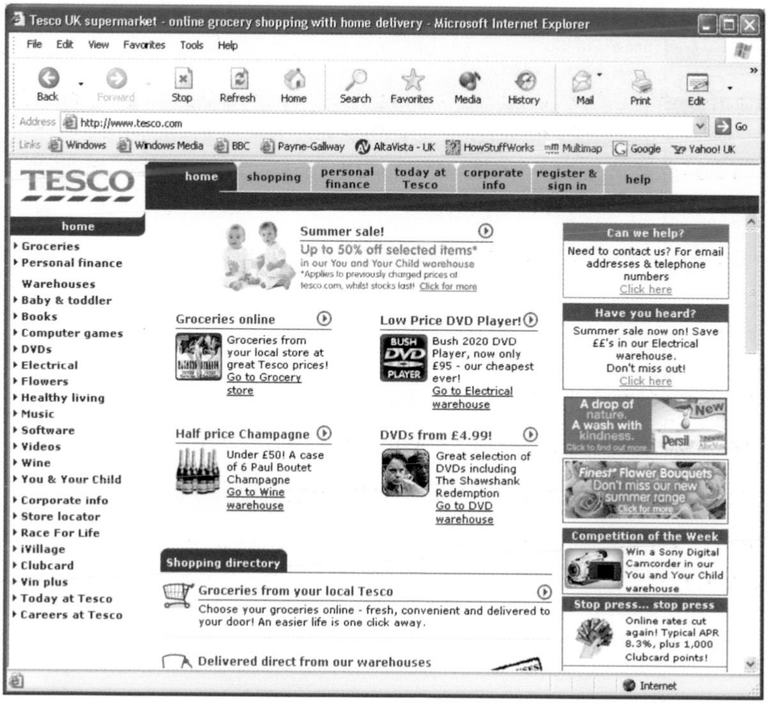

This is a protected site requiring you to register on your first visit and thereafter sign in with your username and password.

- Click on the Register & sign-in tab.

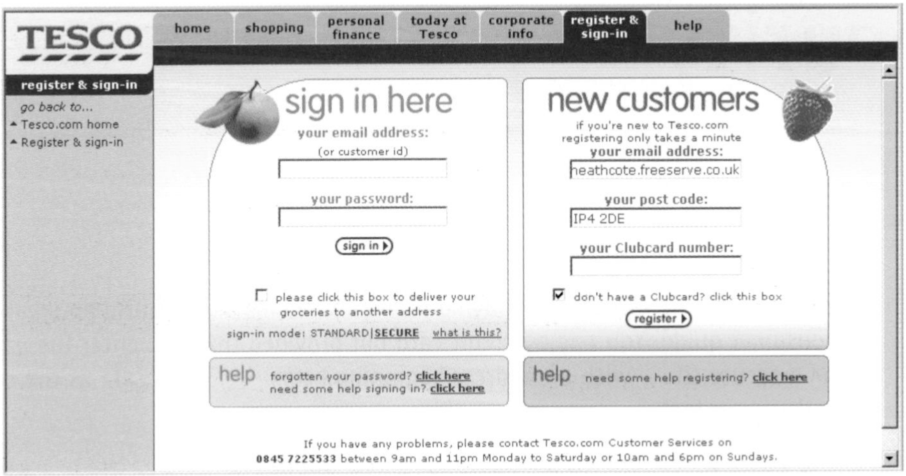

- Enter your e-mail address and post code, click register and give yourself a password.

You are immediately given a clubcard number – keep this handy with your password and proceed to the online grocery. Here you just browse the list, enter the quantities and click Add to Basket.

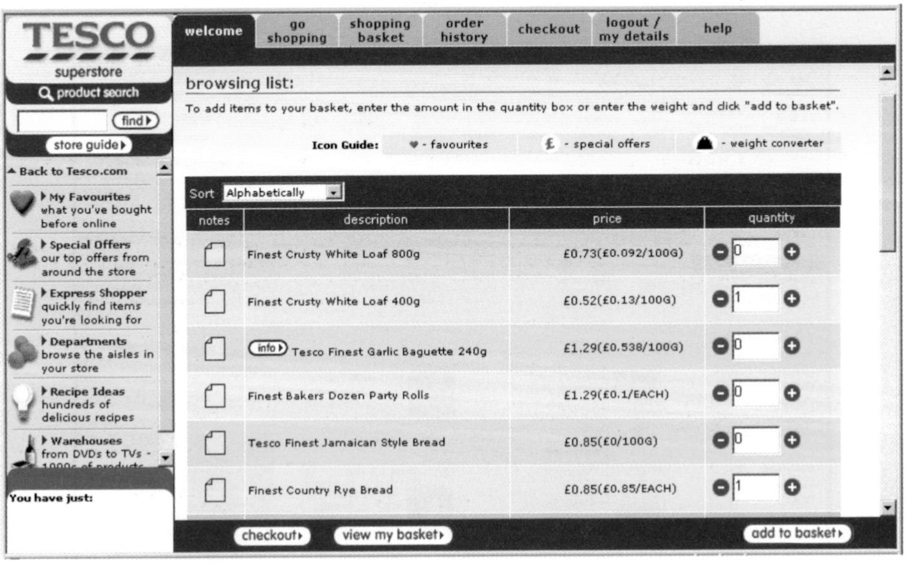

You can look at other sections from the Store Guide on the left, view your basket so far and change any quantities. This is called an interactive form, which constantly updates itself as you enter or change values.

Having chosen what you need from all sections, you now click on Checkout, and book a delivery slot.

You are now required to give away sensitive information – your credit card details – and this is done on a secure page with an address beginning https://.

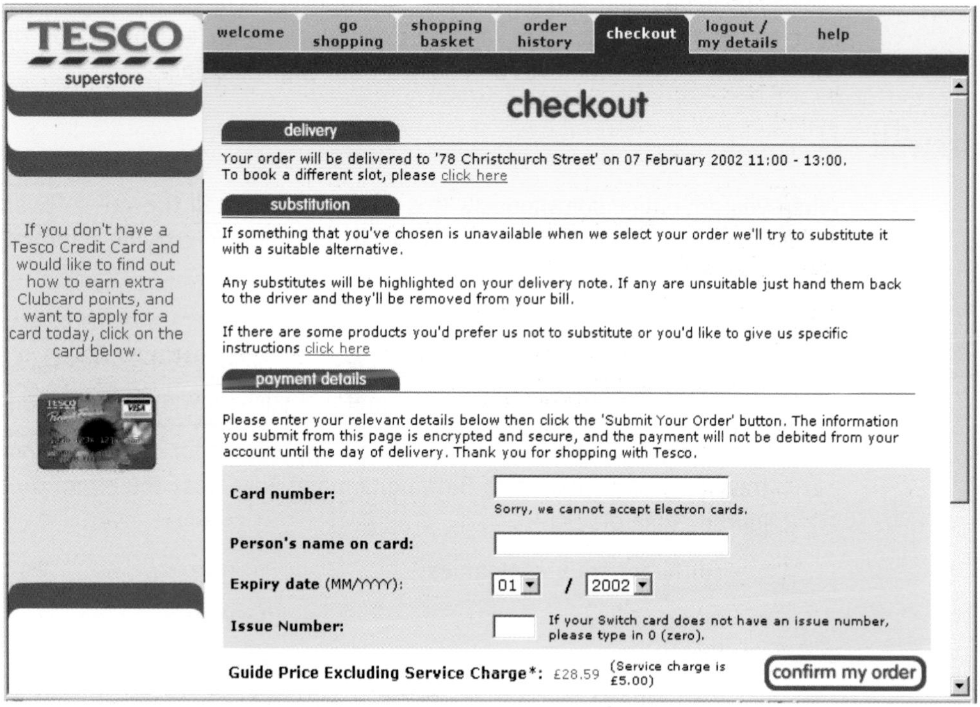

And that's all there is to it!

Security on the Web

When using a web site you are sometimes open to fraud: a site may not be who it says it is in order to obtain credit card information.

A secure page with an https:// address has a Digital Certificate (granted by a Certificate Authority) confirming that the site is secure and genuine. Information is exchanged via encrypted messages encoded using keys so that only authorised people can read it. The site sends its public key which the recipient uses together with its private key to encode the message.

Cookies

These are small files that web sites put on your computer to save your previous settings and preferences for their site and the pages you visited on it. This helps the site customise the view for your next visit, perhaps steering you to other products you might like. Cookies are usually innocent and can only send back information that you provide. Allowing a web site to create a cookie does not give that or any other site access to the rest of your computer, and only the site that created the cookie can read it. This is fine provided that sites do not share the cookie information with others who might, for example, direct specific advertisements at children. Internet Explorer accepts cookies by default but you have some control over them via the Tools, Options, Privacy pane which offers six settings ranging from 'block all' to 'accept all'. On the General pane, Delete Cookies removes all cookies from your machine.

Firewall

When you are online continuously, it is advisable to install firewall software to stop anyone hacking into your computer from the outside and copying information or making changes.

Exercises

1. Use Ask Jeeves to find a railway timetable such as www.nationalrail.co.uk
2. Use an interactive form to find some sample fares for one adult and one child travelling from Ipswich to Birmingham one way. Note the effect on the cost and journey time of:

   different train companies

   time of day

   fastest / cheapest

   number of changes

   railcard
3. Copy the times of a fastest and a cheapest journey into a Word document and save it.
4. Print out selected details.

Sending E-mail

CHAPTER 7.6

E-mail or electronic mail can be sent over the Internet to anybody who has an e-mail address. It arrives almost instantaneously anywhere in the world for the cost of a local call. The recipient picks it up when they are ready.

To use e-mail, you need both an e-mail address and a program to handle it. Both are available free.

Note:

There are two types of e-mail connection – permanent, where you are always online, or dial-up.

E-mail addresses

E-mail addresses are quite like web site addresses and made up in much the same way. The format is always:

username@domain_name

Here, username is you and domain_name is either the Internet Service Provider (ISP) who gives access to the Internet, or a web site address.

Tip:

Some ISPs you may have heard of are AOL, Demon, Virgin, CompuServe, Hotmail, Wanadoo, BTInternet, LineOne, ... and more are popping up all the time.

Sam Brown's personal address might look like any of these:

sam.brown@virgin.net

sam-brown@aol.com

sam@brownfamily.demon.co.uk

Alternatively, if you have your own registered web site name, your e-mail address can be a part of the site name – oliver@payne-gallway.co.uk for example. This has the advantage that if you switch ISPs your e-mail address remains the same.

An e-mail address has no spaces and is usually all in small letters. It MUST be entered correctly or the message will bounce – that is, come back undelivered. Every e-mail address is unique.

Using Outlook Express

The program most often used to handle e-mail is Microsoft Outlook Express which comes with Internet Explorer and that is what is used in this book.

Note:
Another type of e-mail – Web-based e-mail – does not require a special program because you access your e-mail from a web site using the browser. This means you have to be online for longer while you deal with mail but the advantage is you can check your mail from any computer anywhere that's on the Internet – particularly useful when travelling. The most popular web-based e-mail is Microsoft's Hotmail: you open an account – free – on www.hotmail.com

- Click the Outlook Express icon which is usually near the Start button, otherwise select Start, Programs, Outlook Express.

If there are other people using your computer, you may need to identify yourself by selecting File, Switch Identity and choosing your name from a list of users.

The Outlook Express window allows you to:

- compose messages
- send and receive messages
- reply to messages
- forward messages
- print messages
- keep contact names in an Address book
- file old messages in folders.

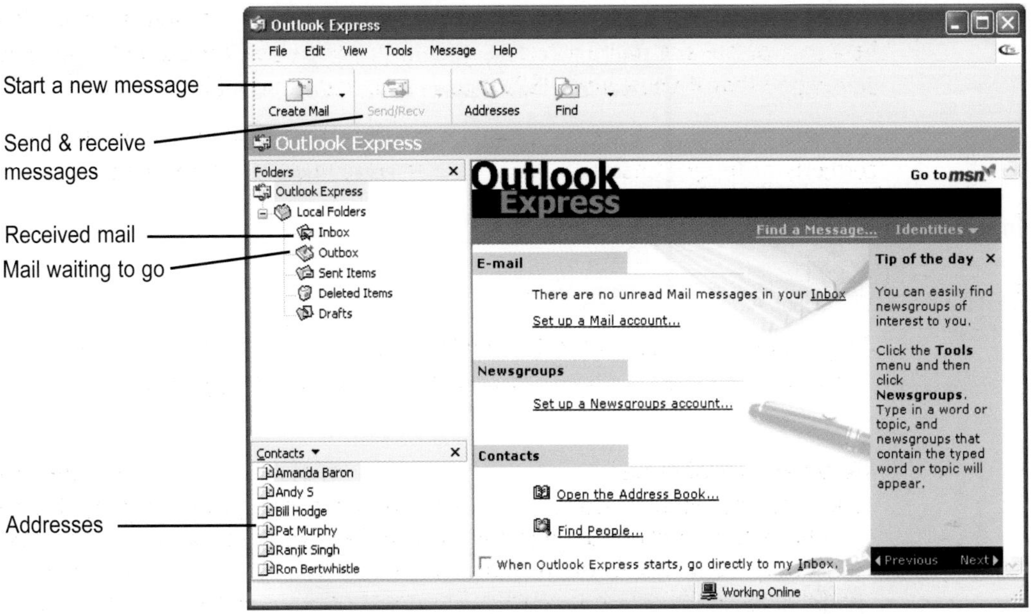

The general window layout can be altered in View, Layout allowing you to display or hide the built-in toolbars.

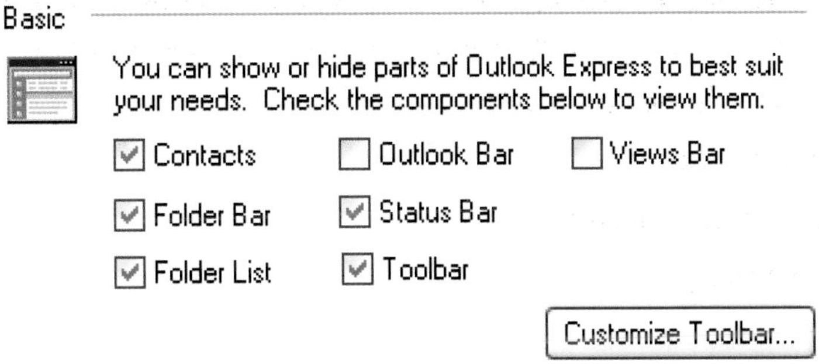

Composing an e-mail

To start a new message to someone you obviously need to know their e-mail address.

- Click on the Create Mail button on the toolbar.

The New Message window opens.

- Type the address in the To: box.
- Leave the Cc: box blank. This is used if you want to send a copy of the message to someone else.
- Type something in the Subject: box to say what the message is about.
- Type the letter in the main window (the message box).

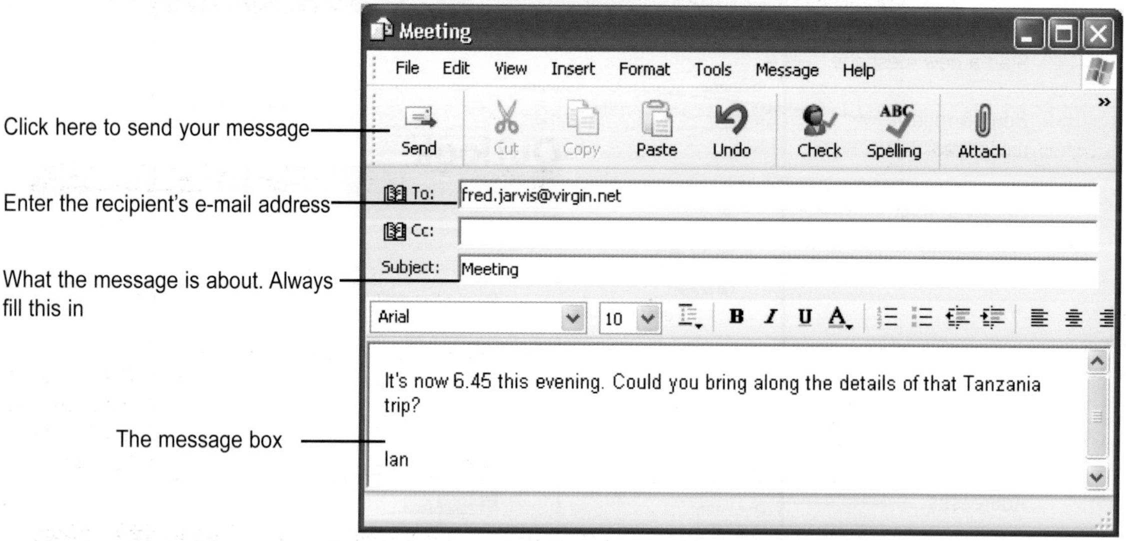

Note:
There are two sending options – sending a message immediately or putting it in the Outbox to send later. For dial-up, the Outbox is better.

- Select Tools, Options and on the Send tab uncheck Send messages immediately.

- Click the Send button on the toolbar.
- If prompted to Connect, click Cancel.

The Outbox

The New Message window closes and your message is now in the Outbox. It has not actually been sent yet. You can write messages to several people and store them in the Outbox. When you are ready, you can send them all at once – this uses only a few seconds of online time and saves on the phone bill!

You can look at the contents of the Outbox and edit a message before you send it. You can also delete a message if you change your mind about sending it.

To edit a message in the Outbox:

- Click Outbox in the Folders pane to select it.
- Double-click the message header in the Message List pane.

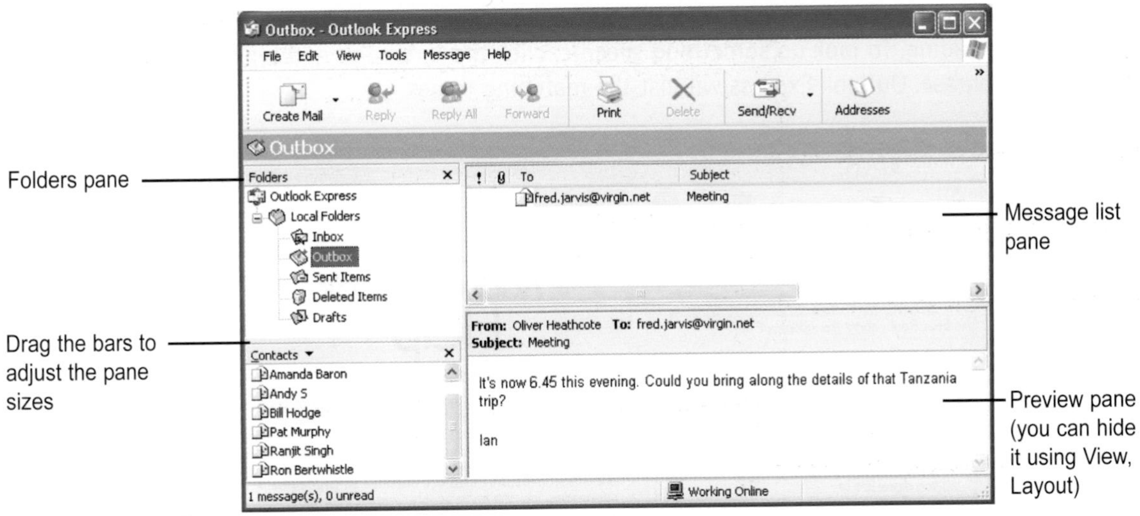

Tip:
Having an Outbox means you can write any other messages and send them all at once.

- An Edit window appears and you can edit the message.
- Click Send to put it back in the Outbox.
- If prompted to Connect, click Cancel.

Help

If you get stuck, try the Help system – choose Help, Contents & Index or just press the F1 key.

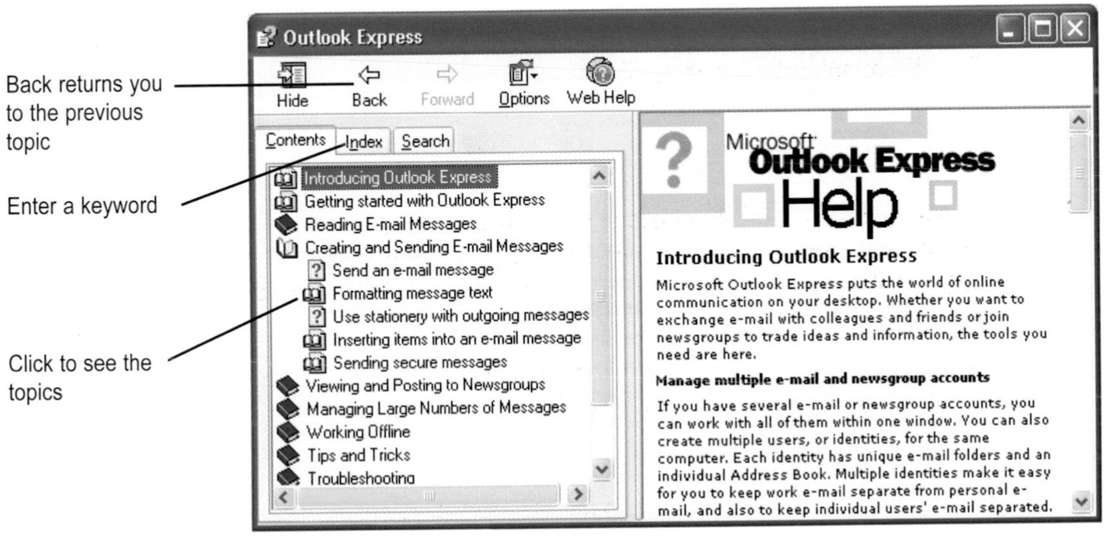

On the Contents tab, you double-click a book symbol to show the topics under the heading. To look up something specific, click the Index tab and type in the word or phrase. Outlook Express will list the matching topics.

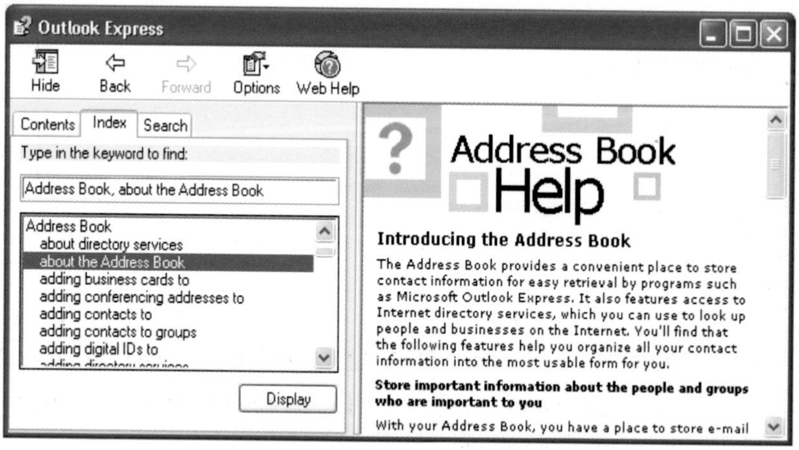

The Search tab lists the topics associated with the word you type in.

Some dialogue boxes have the ? context help button at upper right; click on it, then click on a part of the dialogue to display extra help. There is also Microsoft online help on the Help menu.

The Address Book

The Address Book is used to save the addresses of people you regularly send messages to, so that you don't have to type in their address each time.

Click on the Addresses button in the main window.

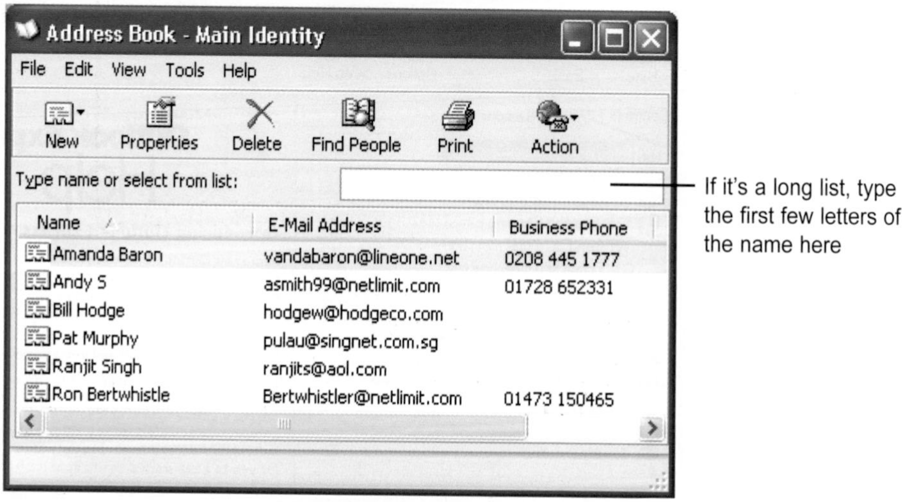

Entering a new address

The Address Book window lists any contacts who are already entered. To enter a new contact:

- Click on the New button on the toolbar and choose New Contact from the dropdown menu.

The Properties window stores the e-mail, home, and other details of each contact.

- On the Name tab, enter the First: and Last: names and Title:, with Middle: and Nickname: as well if you like.
- Click the arrow on the Display: box and choose how you want the name displayed.
- Enter an e-mail address.

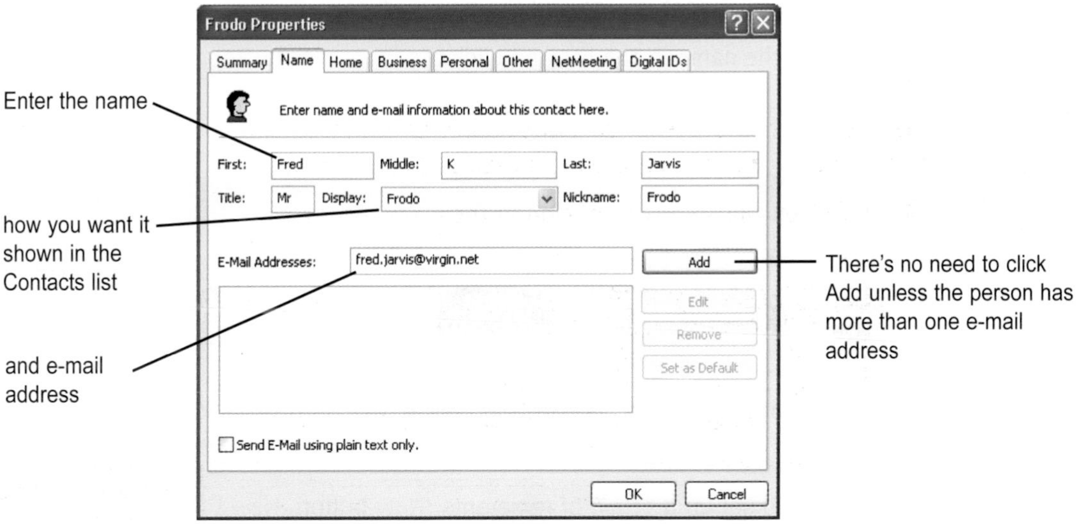

- Click OK to enter the address.

The name is now listed in the Address Book window.

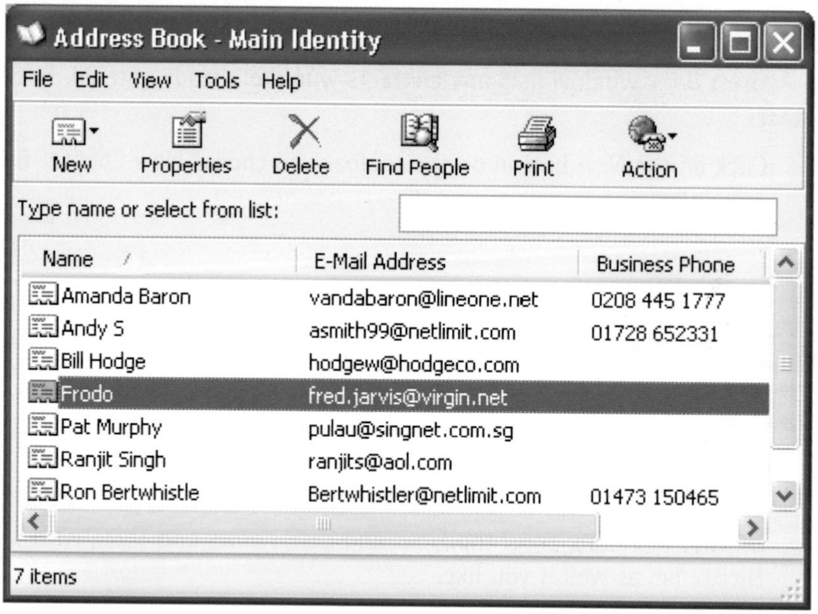

Tip:
You can remove an entry with the Delete button.

If you need to change it, say to add the home address:

- Select the name in the list and click the Properties button.
- On the Home tab, enter the details and click OK.

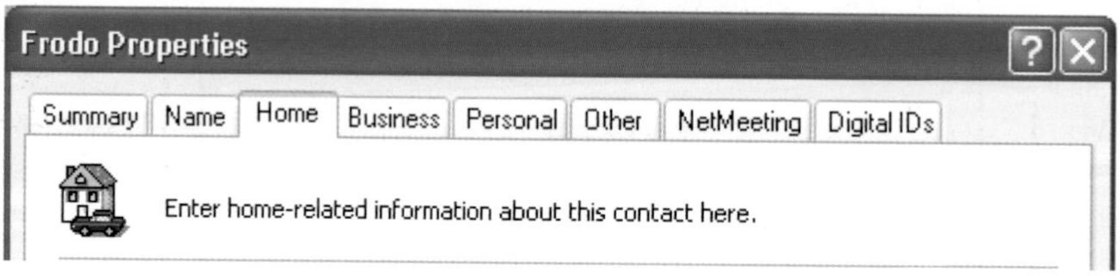

The Properties window lets you keep all sorts of details and is very useful

- Now enter two more addresses and close the address book.

Tip:
You can also set up a group of recipients (New button, New Group) and select the contacts to go into it for a group mailing. With New Folder you can start a new list.

Using the Address Book

You can now enter addresses straight from the address book when you send a message.

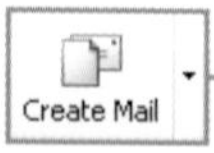

- In the Outlook Express main window, click Create Mail.
- In the New Message window, click on the icon to the left of To: (instead of in the box).

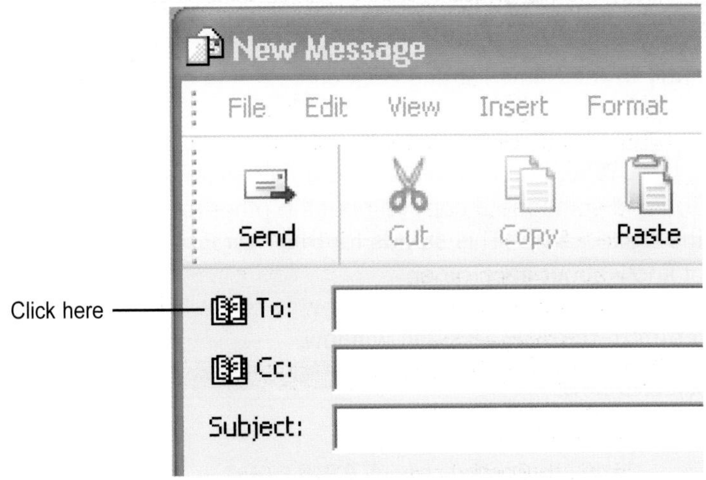

The Select Recipients window opens.

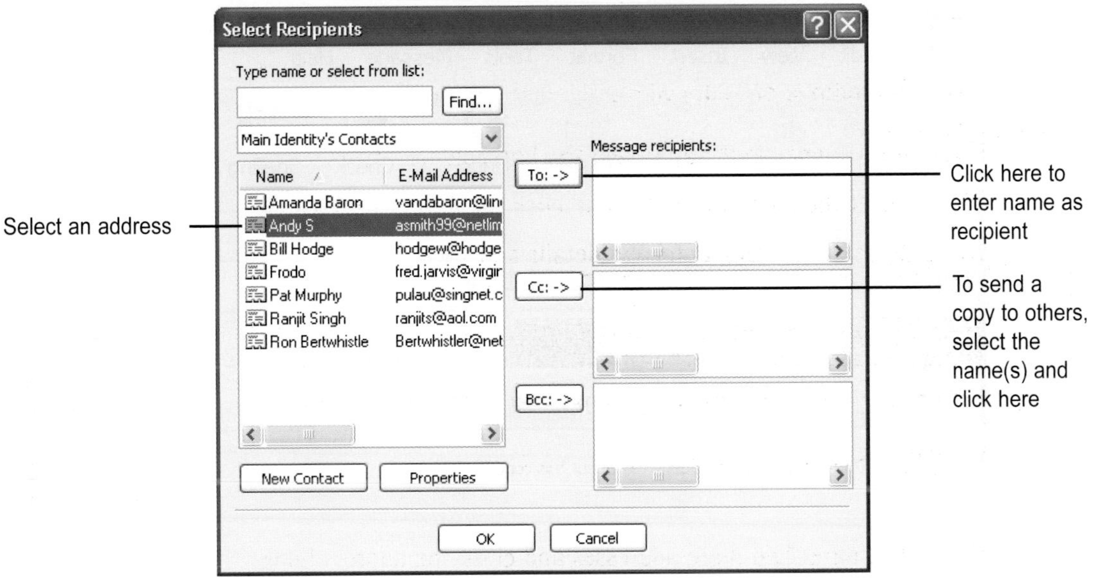

Selecting recipients

In the Select Recipients window:

- Select an entry in the Name list and click on To: -> to transfer it to the Message Recipients list.

In the same way you can send a copy of your message to someone else just to keep them posted.

- Select another entry in the Name list and click on Cc: -> to copy it over.

Note:
Cc stands for Carbon copy. When the recipients read a message, they can all see who else got it too. To send someone a copy without the other recipients knowing, enter their name in the Bcc: -> box. (This stands for Blind carbon copy.) The Bcc recipients also do not know about each other.

- Click on OK to return to the New Message window.

The recipients are all selected now.

Tip:
Bcc is not usually shown unless you select View, All Headers.

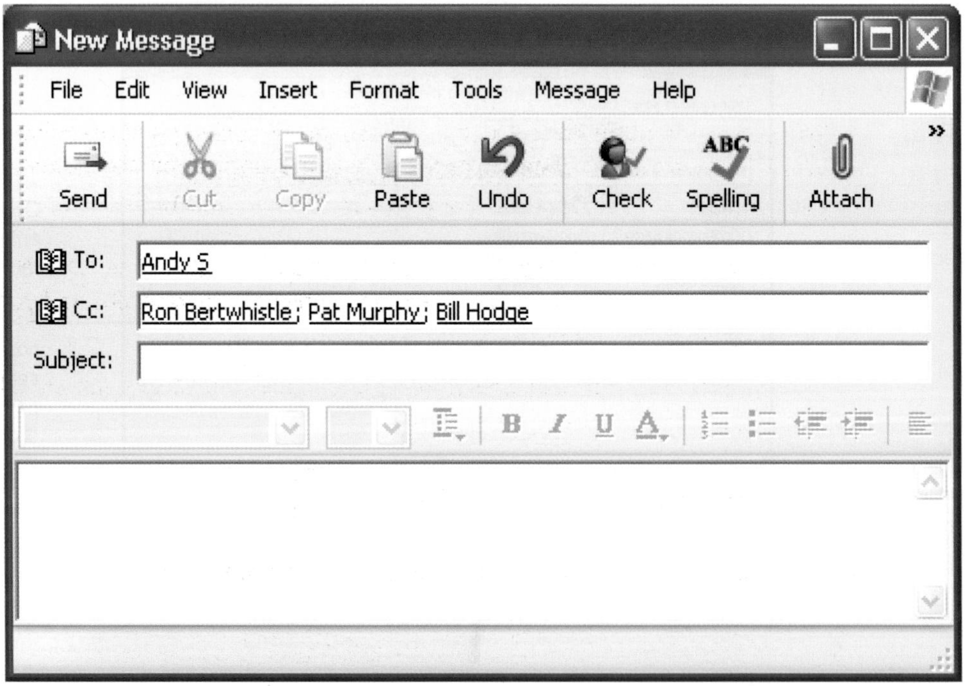

- Type in a subject line and a message.

Formatting a message

You can use the buttons on the Formatting toolbar to make text bold, underlined, etc. Notice the formatting options are grayed out until you click in the message area. As soon as you've entered the message you can try them out.

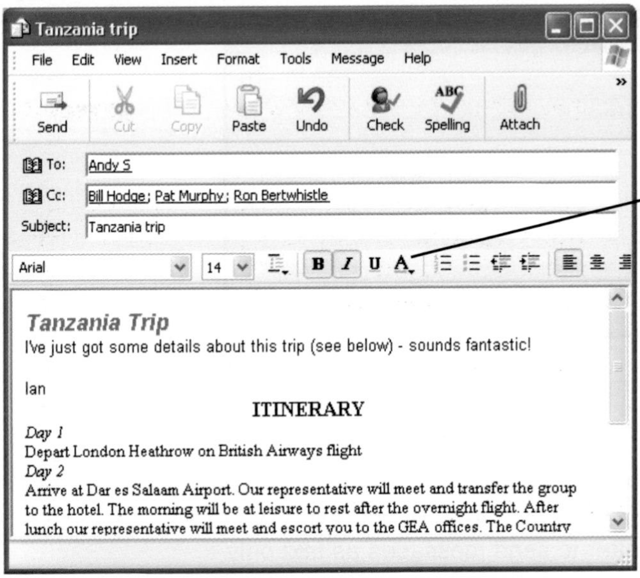

Formatting toolbar also has the usual word processing functions in addition to Cut, Copy, Paste and Undo on the main toolbar

- Type in 2 or 3 lines, then try moving, deleting, copying and pasting words.

Tip:
You can move selected text within a message by clicking and dragging, just as in Word. Text can also be copied between any messages you have open, using Cut, Copy and Paste on the Formatting toolbar or the Edit menu.

- Now try opening a Word document (such as Itinerary.doc on the web site www.payne-gallway.co.uk), select and copy some paragraphs and paste them into your e-mail message.

The spell-checking tool finds and corrects both spelling mistakes and repeated words. For example, if you had the text:

- Click the Spelling button to find the first mistake 'leabing'.

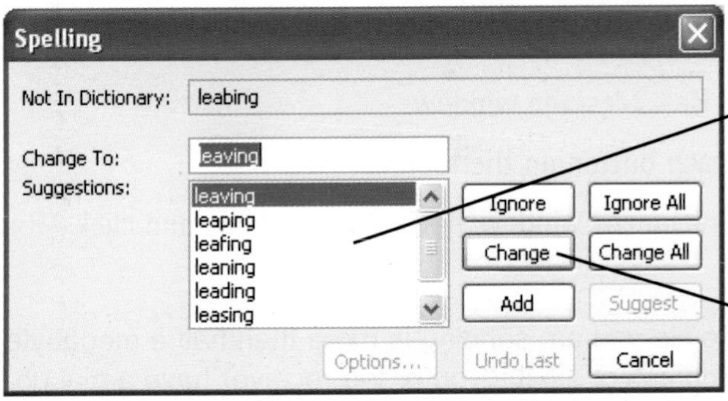

List of possible replacements

Click here to correct the word

- Click Change to replace the misspelt word with the first option and look for the next mistake.

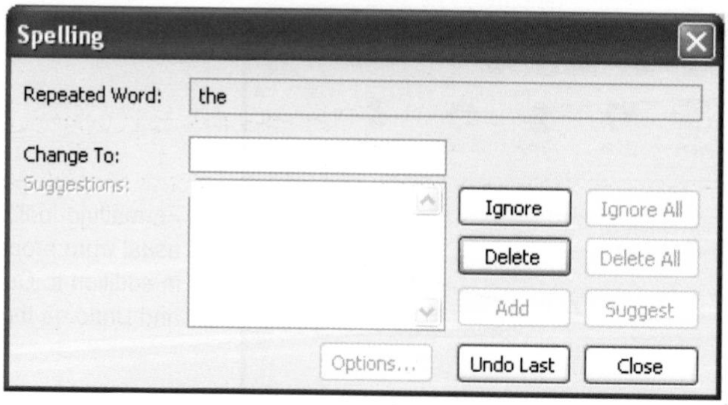

- Click Delete to remove the repeated word 'the'.

Tip:

Although you can format your message using Outlook Express, not all recipients will see the formatting if their e-mails are text only or they use some other e-mail programs. It is better to send messages as text only.

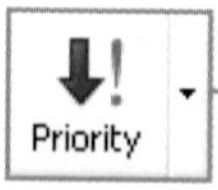

If the message is urgent you can indicate this by clicking the Priority button arrow and selecting High Priority (or Message, Set Priority, High). The message won't get there any sooner but it will stand out.

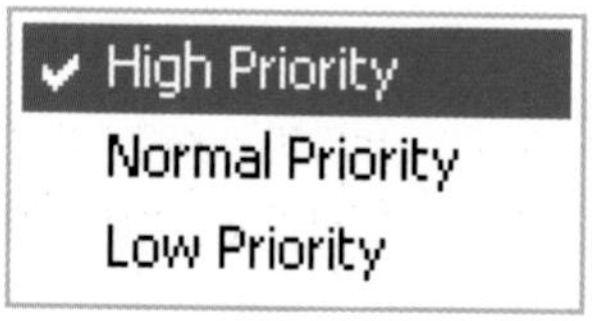

It is important that the Subject field should be accurate and the message spell-checked and not too long. This is called Network etiquette or netiquette. When the message is ready click Send to move it to the Outbox.

Attaching a file

As well as text you can also attach one or more files to a message. Each could be a word-processed document, spreadsheet, graphics file, etc.

- Create a new message and enter address, subject and some text.

To attach a file in the New Message window:

- Click on the Attach button on the toolbar.
- In the Insert Attachment window, navigate to the file and click Attach.

Tip:

If the total size of the file you are sending is more than half a megabyte (500Kb) then you should compress or zip it if you or the receiver have a dial-up connection. (It takes about 5 minutes to send 1Mb of data using a fast modem.) Compressing is described in Module 2 .

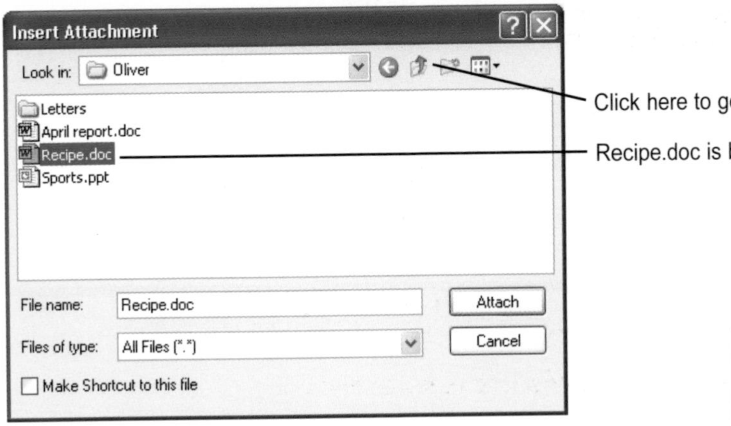

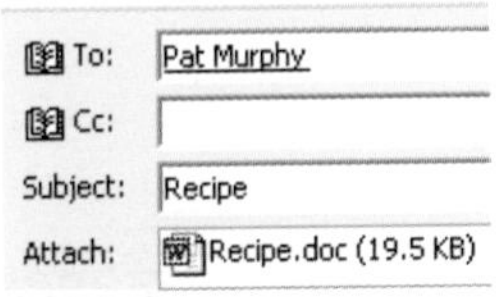

The file is now listed in the Attach box in the message header.

Tip:
If you change your mind, select the file in the Attach box and press Delete.

Your message is now complete and ready to send. When you send the message, any attached files go too.

Mailing to a distribution list

If you send regular e-mails to a large group – say a newsletter – you can make a Group in the Address book and select its members from the address list. Now you just choose the group name as one recipient.

Tip:
When sending a large mailing, each recipient may have half a page of addresses at the start of the message, which probably means having to print another page. To avoid this, send the message To yourself with the other recipients in Bcc.

Exercises

1. Look up Addressing e-mail messages in the Help system.
2. Open the Address Book and add 3 new addresses. (If you are in a class they could be other class members.)
3. Create a new mail message with one of the addresses in the To box and the others in Cc and Bcc.
4. Enter Attached file as the subject and Here's the file as the text.
5. Attach a Word .doc file to the message (preferably no bigger than 200Kb).
6. Give the message a high Priority.
7. Click Send to send the message to the Outbox. (Do not connect.)

CHAPTER 7.7

Messaging

Sending messages from the Outbox

You can send a message straight from the New Message window but it's much better to send all the messages from the Outbox so that in case of trouble they are still there.

Tip:
If anything goes wrong while sending, you could lose the message and have to type it all in again!

Click the Send/Recv button on the toolbar.

This sends all the messages in the Outbox and puts any waiting messages in the Inbox. If you have a Dial-up connection and are offline, you will be prompted to go online. In this case click Yes, then Connect at the next prompt. If the Hang Up When Finished box is checked, the Send and Receive All option disconnects you automatically at the end.

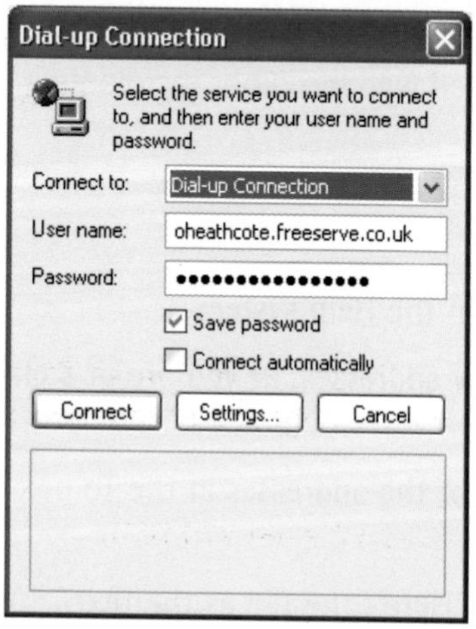

Tip:

Be sure you have disconnected after sending your messages, unless you have other work to do on the Internet. If the Dial-up icon is visible at the bottom right of your screen, right-click it and choose Disconnect.

Outlook Express now sends all messages from the Outbox, and if there are any messages waiting in your mailbox, it downloads them from the server (a computer belonging to your Internet Service Provider somewhere) to the Inbox (somewhere on your hard disk).

Outlook Express can be set to collect e-mails when you start it up although this is usually inconvenient if you have a dial-up connection. To set this, choose Tools, Options, General tab and select Send and receive messages at startup.

A message may appear telling you what is happening.

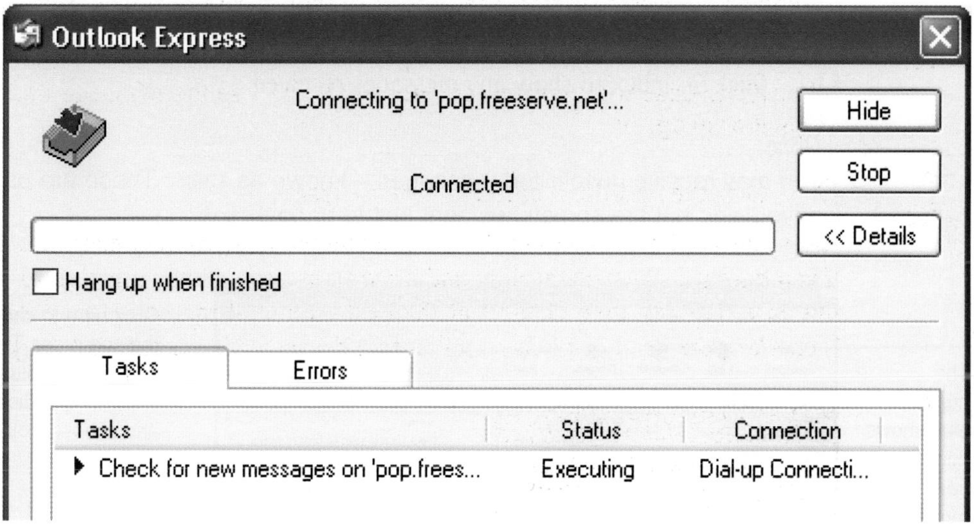

Viewing sent messages

Sometimes it is useful to be able to look up a message you sent last week or last month, to remind yourself what you said. All the messages you send are saved automatically and kept until you delete them.

- Click on Sent Items in the main window to see what you sent.

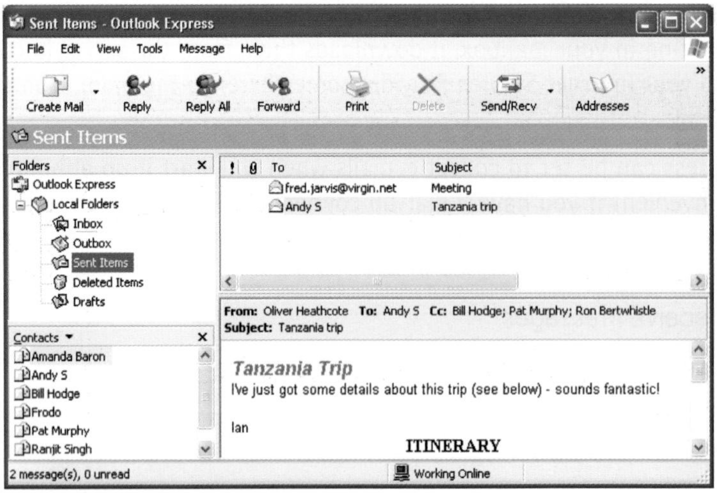

Receiving messages

- Click on Inbox to show any messages received.

Note:
You may receive unsolicited messages – known as spam. These are usually advertising but are sometimes sent just to annoy.

The number in blue shows how many new (unread) messages you have

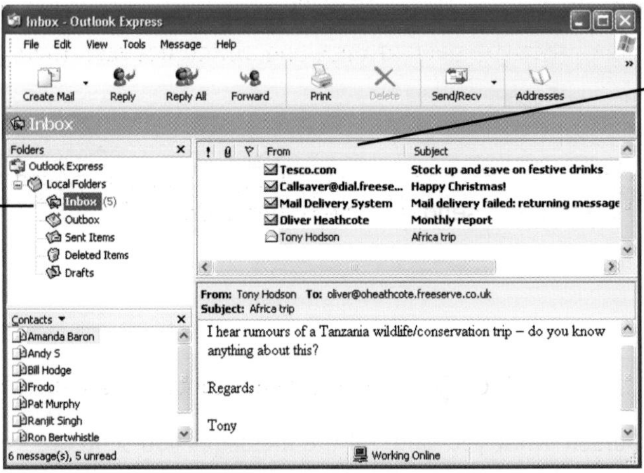

Click here to change the sort order. To change the columns shown, right-click here and choose Columns.

Unread

Read

Tip:
If you select the message title, the content is shown in the pane below.

These are shown on the right with icons indicating Read or Unread. You can sort the messages by sender, date and so on either by View, Sort By, or by clicking the column header. The message is shown in the Preview pane below but it is easier to view it in a separate window.

- Double-click on the message name in the Message List pane.

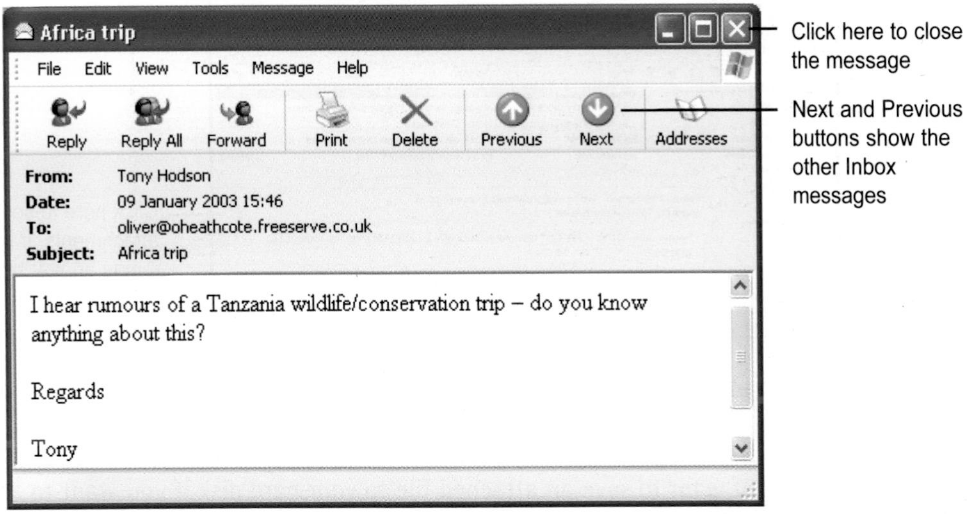

The Message View window lets you:

- read and print out the message
- type a reply
- forward it to someone else
- print a message by clicking the Print button

You can have 2 or more messages open at once and switch between them using Alt-Tab.

Tip:
If you right-click on the sender's name in this window, or on the message in the message list, you can add the sender to the Address Book.

Receiving an attachment

If you receive a file with an attachment, the message header has a paper-clip icon beside it.

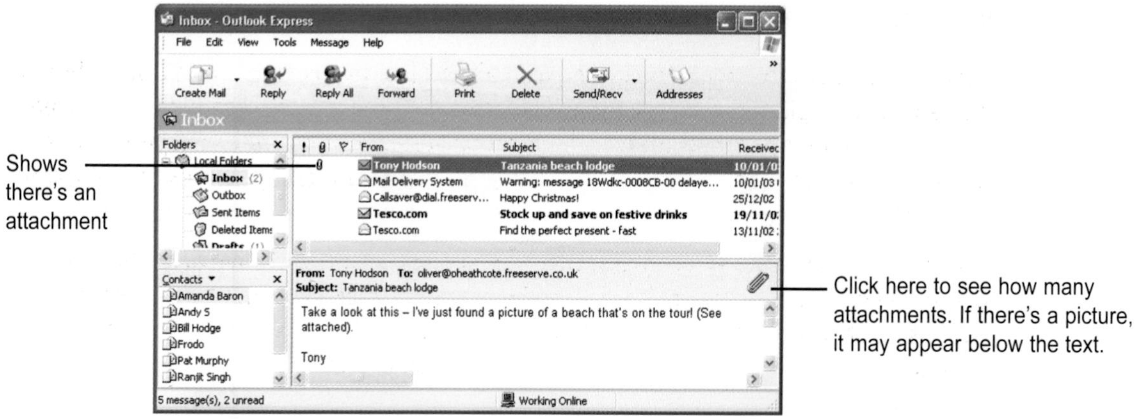

Saving an attachment

You might want to save an attached file to your hard disk if you want to keep it permanently. Otherwise, when you delete the message you'll delete the attachment too.

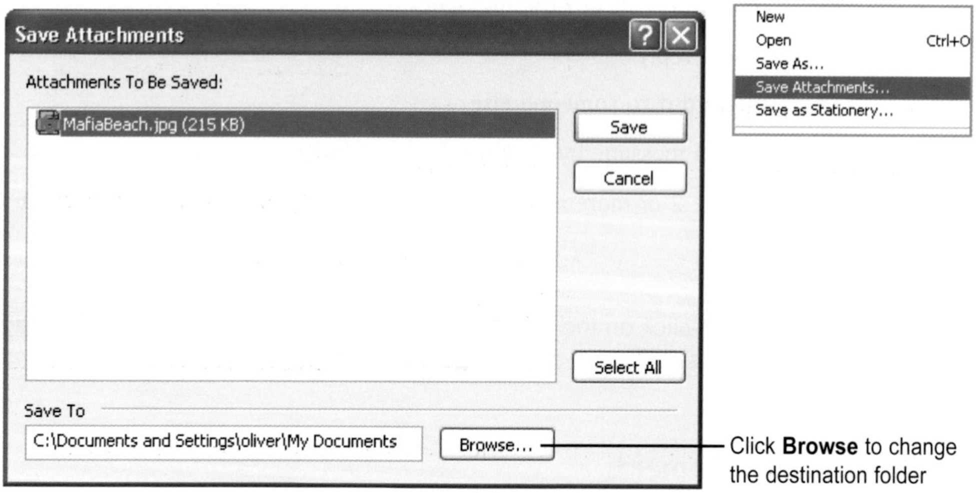

- Choose File, Save Attachments.

The default folder for saving attachments is Documents and Settings\My Documents but you can change this with the Browse button. You can open an attachment without saving it by opening the message and double-clicking on the file name in the Attach box, but first see below concerning viruses.

Virus Alert

Make sure you have an up-to-date virus checker installed. While most file types are safe, it is wise not to open files with .exe, .scr, .pif or .vbs extensions unless you are expecting them.

Opening an unrecognised mail message

There is a risk of infecting a computer with a virus just by opening a message – there's no danger from plain text but if the e-mail is in the form of a web page there may be buttons having unseen effects. You can delete a suspicious-looking message without opening it by hiding the Preview pane first (View, Layout) then right-clicking on it and choosing Delete.

If you don't trust a file attachment, save it first then scan it with the virus checker before opening it. You may not see the file extension since Windows hides them by default: in this case, in Windows Explorer choose Tools, Folder Options, View tab, uncheck Hide file extensions for known file types then click Like Current Folder.

Replying to a message

- Click on the Reply button on the toolbar.

The reply window is all set up for you to type a reply to the sender only.

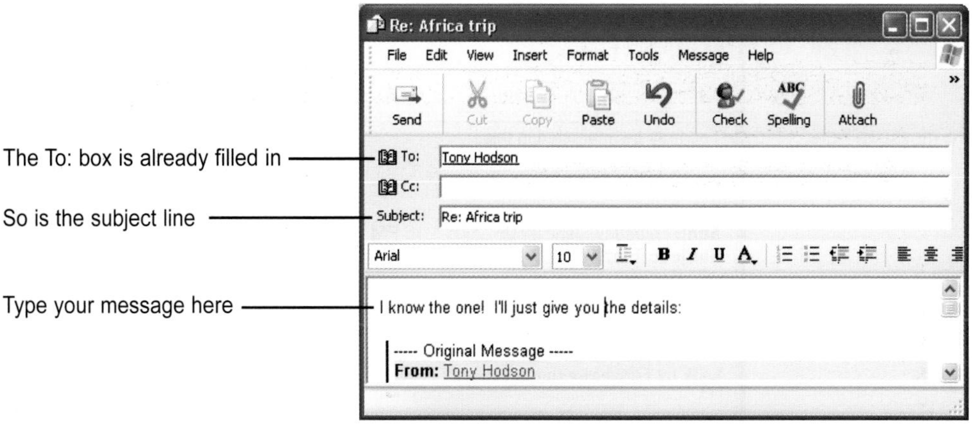

Reply All sends a reply to anyone else that that message was sent to.

- Type your message and click Send.

The reply should normally be kept brief. The original message is normally included in the reply as a reminder. If you don't want this (perhaps if the original message was very long), choose Tools, Options and on the Send tab, uncheck Include message in reply.

It should be put in the Outbox.

Tip:
We have set Outlook Express to send all messages to the Outbox.

Forwarding a message

A message sent to you might be of interest to someone else too. Try forwarding a message.

- Double-click on the message name in the Inbox to show the message view window.

- Click on the Forward button.

The forwarding window is all set up, with a subject line of Fw: [your message title]. The cursor is in the message area with the forwarding message below.

- Click To: to add the recipient's name.

Click To: to add recipients

Add your own message here

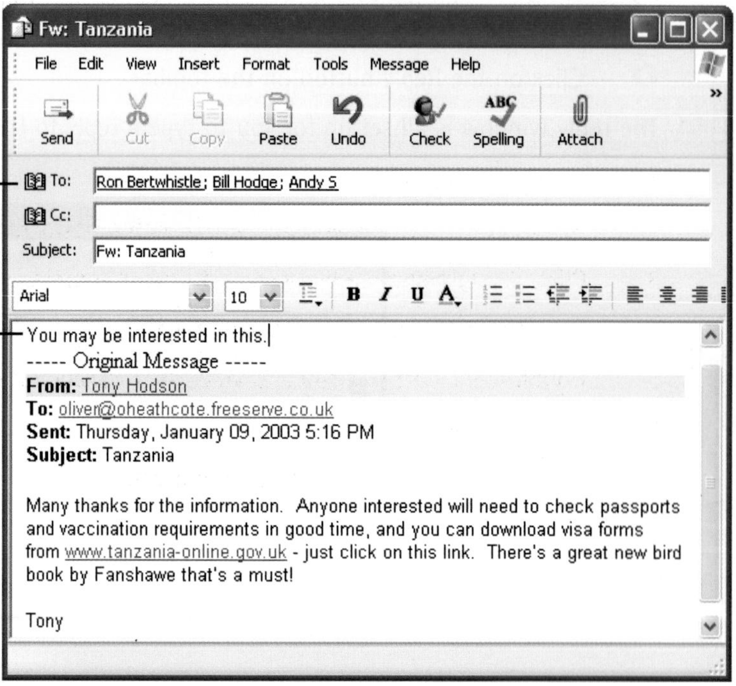

- Add your own message if you like and click Send.

Signatures

You may like to add a standard ending to some messages without having to type it all in every time. To do this, go to Tools, Options, Signature and enter the text – or even a scanned image of your signature! You then call it up in the New Message window with Insert, Signature.